# THE PAPERS OF
# WOODROW WILSON

VOLUME 9
1894-1896

SPONSORED BY THE WOODROW WILSON
FOUNDATION
AND PRINCETON UNIVERSITY

# THE PAPERS OF

# WOODROW WILSON

ARTHUR S. LINK, *EDITOR*

JOHN WELLS DAVIDSON AND DAVID W. HIRST
*ASSOCIATE EDITORS*

JOHN E. LITTLE, *ASSISTANT EDITOR*

JEAN MACLACHLAN, *CONTRIBUTING EDITOR*

M. HALSEY THOMAS, *CONSULTING EDITOR*

Volume 9 · 1894-1896

PRINCETON, NEW JERSEY
PRINCETON UNIVERSITY PRESS
1970

# INTRODUCTION

THIS ninth volume of *The Papers of Woodrow Wilson*, documenting the period from September 1894 through August 1896, reveals a man reaching the zenith of his powers as an undergraduate teacher, lecturer, and writer.

Wilson's notes for lectures in his courses on public law and the history of law at Princeton are printed herein for the first time, and in their entirety. They yield significant evidence of his advanced work in these two subjects. Other documents illustrate his increasing involvement in the life of the College of New Jersey—soon to become Princeton University—through leadership in the faculty, numerous addresses to undergraduate organizations, supervision of college athletics, and frequent speeches on the alumni circuit.

This volume also discloses a man now secure in his pre-eminence as a public speaker, much sought after in various parts of the country. For the first time he yields to the importunities of the American Society for the Extension of University Teaching and lectures under its auspices. In other lectures—on political liberty, morality, and expediency—we find Wilson's own prescriptions for a society still in the throes of a national crisis of confidence in the wake of the Pullman and railroad strikes of 1894. And in these speeches and other documents we see his reactions to events on the national and international scenes well into the presidential campaign of 1896.

The materials in this volume also richly illustrate several major events in Wilson's life during the period 1894-96. The Wilsons plan and build a home of their own on Library Place in Princeton—the only house they ever built. Wilson writes his only biography, *George Washington*, and engages in a creative collaboration with the distinguished American illustrator, Howard Pyle. He also emerges as a general interpreter of American history with his delivery of "The Course of American History" on May 16, 1895, and its publication later in that year. Another turning point is Wilson's first self-identification as a Southerner in an address to the alumni of the University of Virginia in Charlottesville on June 12, 1895. Meanwhile, and later—in early 1896—he plays an important role in a successful reform campaign against an entrenched political machine in Baltimore and participates in New Jersey politics for the first time. Finally, Wilson suffers a small stroke and makes his initial trip abroad, to Scotland and England.

Wilson returned to The Johns Hopkins University for extended lectures on administration in 1895 and 1896, and the letters between him and Ellen Axson Wilson during these periods of separation give additional insight into the continuity of their love, their family affairs, and the social life of Princeton and Baltimore.

There have been no editorial innovations in this volume. The Editors have continued to try to reproduce documents *verbatim et literatim*, insofar as it is possible to do so typographically, repairing misspelled or jumbled words and phrases only when necessary for clarity or ease of reading.

Readers are reminded that *The Papers of Woodrow Wilson* is a continuing series; that persons, institutions, and events that figure prominently in earlier volumes are not usually reidentified; and that the Index gives cross references to fullest earlier identifications. In addition, persons referred to by diminutives and nicknames are indexed under these forms.

The Editors are grateful to Mrs. Bryant Putney of Princeton University Press for copyediting and other assistance; Miss Marjorie Sirlouis and Colonel James B. Rothnie for their continued transcribing of Wilson's shorthand; and to Houghton Mifflin Company for permission to print letters from the firm's papers in Houghton Library at Harvard University.

The Editors here record with deep regret the death in Princeton on April 1, 1970, of their former colleague, Thomas Hubbard Vail Motter. Born in Philadelphia on March 7, 1901, he received the A.B. degree from Princeton University in 1922 and the Ph.D. from Yale University in 1929. After teaching at Princeton, Northwestern University, and Wellesley College, he served in the Army Engineer Corps, Middle East Command, during the Second World War. From 1944 to 1951 he was Chief of the Middle East Section of the Historical Division of the Army. He was the author, among other works, of *The Writings of Arthur Hallam* (1943) and *The Persian Corridor and Aid to Russia* (1952), and he edited Wilson's *Leaders of Men* (1952). Dr. Motter joined the Wilson Papers on July 1, 1964, and served as Consulting Editor until June 30, 1967, playing a significant role in the formation of basic policies and the editing of the first four volumes. His interest in the project continued unabated after his retirement, as did his warm personal relations with members of the staff. His lively presence will be greatly missed.

THE EDITORS

*Princeton, New Jersey*
*May 12, 1970*

# CONTENTS

# ILLUSTRATIONS

Following page 294

## TEXT ILLUSTRATIONS

# ABBREVIATIONS

| | |
|---|---|
| ALI | autograph letter initialed |
| ALS | autograph letter(s) signed |
| att(s). | attached, attachment(s) |
| EAW | Ellen Axson Wilson |
| EAWhwL | Ellen Axson Wilson handwritten letter |
| enc(s). | enclosed, enclosure(s) |
| env. | envelope |
| hw | handwriting or handwritten |
| hwLS | handwritten letter signed |
| JRW | Joseph Ruggles Wilson |
| L | letter |
| PCL | printed copy of letter |
| sh | shorthand |
| T | typed |
| TCL | typed copy of letter |
| TLS | typed letter signed |
| WW | Woodrow Wilson |
| WWhw | Woodrow Wilson handwriting or handwritten |
| WWS | Woodrow Wilson signed |
| WWsh | Woodrow Wilson shorthand |
| WWT | Woodrow Wilson typed |
| WWTLS | Woodrow Wilson typed letter signed |

## ABBREVIATIONS FOR COLLECTIONS AND LIBRARIES

Following the National Union Catalog of the
Library of Congress

| | |
|---|---|
| CtY | Yale University Library |
| DLC | Library of Congress |
| ICU | University of Chicago Library |
| MdBJ | The Johns Hopkins University Library |
| MH | Harvard University Library |
| NBuU | University of Buffalo |
| NjP | Princeton University Library |
| NN | New York Public Library |
| NNPM | Pierpont Morgan Library, New York |
| PHi | Historical Society of Pennsylvania, Philadelphia |
| RSB Coll., DLC | Ray Stannard Baker Collection of Wilsoniana, Library of Congress |
| WC, NjP | Woodrow Wilson Collection, Princeton University |
| WP, DLC | Woodrow Wilson Papers, Library of Congress |

## SYMBOLS

| | |
|---|---|
| [Jan. 26, 1895] | publication date of a published writing; also date of document when date is not part of text |
| [*May 16, 1895*] | latest composition date of a published writing |

THE PAPERS OF

WOODROW WILSON

VOLUME 9

1894-1896

# THE PAPERS OF
# WOODROW WILSON

---

## To James Shaw Campbell[1]

My dear Mr. Campbell,        Princeton, N. J.   9 September, 1894

The question you put me is a peculiarly difficult one to answer. At the University of Va. they lay especial emphasis on Va. law, of course, and I imagine that Va. law is less like that of Pa. than you would find that of N. Y., e.g., to be. At the same time, the drill given at the Univ. of Va. is exceptionally good. I should be inclined to say, on the whole, though with a good deal of diffidence, that two years at the Univ. of Va. would be of more service to you than an incomplete course at Harvard; and that (here I go beyond your question) the complete two years course at the N. Y. Law School would be better than either.

With much regard,

Most sincerely Yours,   Woodrow Wilson

ALS (WC, NjP).
  [1] Of Sewickley, Pa., who had just been graduated from Princeton. He received his LL.B. from Harvard in 1897.

## From the Minutes of the Princeton Faculty

3 P.M., Wednesday, Sep. 19th, 1894

. . . The Report of the Committee on Delinquent Students[1] was presented and approved and the cases of those students who had made application for permission to be re-examined were referred back to the Committee.

Upon recommendation of the Committee it was

Resolved, That Mr. —— of '96 for excessive conditions be required to enter the Class of '97.

Resolved, That Messrs. ——, ——, ——, ——, ——, and ——, of the Class of '97 for deficiencies and conditions be required to enter the Class of '98.

Resolved That Mr. —— of '97, who was once before required to enter a lower Class, be required for failure in three departments to leave College.

Resolved That Mr. ——, who is deficient in all subjects, be required to leave College.

Resolved That Mr. ——— formerly of '95, for failure to comply with the conditions by which he was to become a special student, be required to remain out of College.

Resolved That Mr. ———, a Special Student for deficiencies in four departments be required to leave College.

Resolved That Mr. ———, a Special Student, conditioned in various studies, be admitted under conditions to the Class of '98 to take only Freshman studies.

Resolved That Mr. ———, a Special Student, deficient in various studies, be admitted to the Class of '98 under conditions to pursue only Freshman studies. The request of Mr. ——— ('95), who had been absent from the Examination in Psychology, to be examined in that subject at home in order to be able to take a letter of dismissal to join the University of Chicago was declined. Certain students were allowed to change their electives. Requests of certain members of the Senior and Junior Classes to take Modern Languages in the lower Classes as Electives were referred to the respective Professors with power, but to report the result to the Faculty.

Students who had been allowed to pursue the study of the Modern Languages with lower Classes were allowed to continue these courses. . . .

"Minutes of the Faculty of the College of New Jersey, 1889-95," bound ledger book (University Archives, NjP).

[1] Of which Wilson had recently been appointed chairman to succeed Andrew F. West.


5 5' P.M., Friday, Sep. 21st, 1894.

. . . The Committee on Special and Delinquent Students made the following report which was approved: "That Messrs. ———, ——— and ———, be not granted further trial in Examinations; that Messrs. ———, ——— and ——— in view of certain mitigating circumstances &c. be granted another Examination on the express understanding that they remove all deficiencies on the first trial & with ten (10) days from date (Sep. 21, 1894); that Mr. ——— (Special Student) be allowed to elect studies in the Junior year as temporarily optional with the understanding that if he remove all deficiencies within a month (from 20th inst.) he be admitted to the Junior Class and if he fail he shall enter the present Sophomore Class.

——— (Sc. Sci.) was reported as having removed his conditions.

# Notes for Lectures on Public Law[1]

[c. Sept. 22, 1894-Jan. 20, 1895]

## PUBLIC LAW.

### I.

*Introduction.*

*Public as contradistinguished from Private* Law.

In order to appreciate this, *the following Analysis*:

*Private Law*:

  I. Civil, or Municipal, Law, including,

    1. The law of Personal Relationships not of contract: E.g., parent and child, guardian and ward.

    2. The law of Contracts.

    3. The law of Real and Personal Property, Wills and Successions.

    4. The law of Torts.

  II. Commercial and Maritime Law, including the greater part of the Law of Banking.

  III. International Private Law.

*Public Law*:

  I. International Law: the law of the relations of states to each other.

  II. The Law of Individual States (which may be studied either state by state or comparatively).

    1. Constitutional and Administrative Law.

    2. Criminal Law and Procedure.

    3. Civil Procedure.

    (4. Ecclesiastical Law.)

*II. Analysis*:

*Public Law*:

  1. *Constitutional Law*: which concerns the organization of the state; the powers of its several organs; their fundamental legal relations to each other; etc., etc.

  2. *Administrative Law*: which concerns chiefly the relation of the several depts. of gov't. to one another in *the detail of their business*; and the relations of gov't with individuals in the process of carrying out its own specific tasks.

  3. *Justice*: which concerns (a) *the intervention of the state* in the private affairs of individuals for the purpose of applying the law in cases of conflict,—in short, *Civil Procedure*,—; and, (b) its action in *punishing* those who commit offences, not against individuals merely, but against society itself, in the field, that is, of *Criminal Law and Procedure*.

[1] For the earlier provenance of these notes, see the Editorial Note, "Wilson's Teaching at Princeton, 1890-91," Vol. 7. They are printed here because Wilson prepared or recast most of them during the autumn semester of 1894-95. Since Wilson himself so clearly annotated these notes, the Editors have supplied bibliographical information only when references are obscure or have not been mentioned frequently in earlier volumes. This and all other footnotes by the Editors.

*Now prepared to consider the Contrasts* between these two great bodies of Law, *and, hence,*

*The Nature of Public Law*:

All law, in its untechnical aspects, *is a part of Political science*, inasmuch as it arises always out of social conditions.

*Private Law*, however, for the more [most] part concerns only *the intimate economic and natural relationships* of man with man, wh. are the products everywhere of the same processes of civilization, depending, not so much upon choice and polity, as upon *certain intrinsic and inevitable principles of order and equity.*

*Public Law*, on its part, is *the field of Polity*, where the differences between one state and another, whether in *choice, habit,* or *experience,* most evidently display themselves.

*Private Law* is, as *Thorold Rogers* says, *"a practical condition of life"*; *Public Law,* by contrast, is *a practical condition of politics.* In it, for instance, *the ideals of a race disclose themselves.* In it are to be seen the dynamic, as well as the static, forces of a nation's life

*Public Law* is *the frame-work* and *major premise* of all *social reform.*

Topics of Course.

Of the topics of the course, five will be in *the theory* of the subject, while nine will concern *the actual instrumentalities* of gov't and *the practical operation* of the State.

Theory.

1. The Actual Origins and Development of Public Law.
2. The Several Sources of Public Law.
3. The State itself as a Source of Law.
4. Sovereignty.
5. Written Constitutions.

Practice.

6. The Actual Tasks of the State.
7. The Organs of the State and its Means and Methods of action.
   I. The Head of the State.
8. II. The Actual Administration: The Ministers.
9. III. The Law-Making Body.
10. Law and Ordinance.
11. The Relationship of Administrative Acts to the laws.
12. IV. The Courts: Remedial Justice; the Constitution and Processes of the courts.
13. The Administration and the Courts.
14. Criminal Law and Procedure.

## II.

### The Actual Origins and Development of Public Law.

*The Question: What is Authority,* and what its basis? What is a *Constitution,* and what its derivation? What is *a State,* and what its genesis and right to be?

*The existence and life of States* or organic communities, essentially *the central subject of Public Law.* It is its fundamental function to explain the legal basis of the State and analyze the legal *nexus* of its functions. Hence the central position of such subjects as Sovereignty.

*Early History of Political Society.*

In order to answer this question, we must go back, so far as possible, to *the origins of communal life.*

*Materials*: *Greek, Roman,* and *Teutonic* Institutions.

*The Earliest Processes*:

The Family,⎫ *Increasing degree of inorganic character* in this
The Gens,  ⎬ series. The Tribe probably held together only
The Tribe  ⎭ until 'travelling days were o'er,' and the settled
            State had been formed.

*Authority* of the Father or Patriarch *based* primarily *upon power*; by derivative conception, *upon Religion.*

*Transition to the State,* unlike transition fr. family to gens, or from gens to tribe. It meant, not coördination (as in the earlier processes), but the subordination of the primitive units to another and greater organization.

*The primitive State rested,* not upon the tribe, nor yet upon the gens, but *upon the family,* the original crystal. The State & the Family the two persistent units. Tribe and gens survived only as religious guilds.

*The Family itself was finally subordinated*; but it was never extinguished. *In Greece* the eclipse of the Family took place at a comparatively early period. *In Rome* it came later, and was for long only partial.

*Analogous Organization of State and Family* in Primitive Society.

*Religious Conceptions* and Motives.

*Religious Symbols*: the common hearth, and the common worship.

*The King's authority and the Law's force,*—both proceed from the same sources.

*The Senate,* a council *of* family *Elders.*

*Abolition of Kingship*: Consuls and Archons. Equality of the two Consuls in Authority. Transmission of the sacrificial and priestly functions of the kings to the *Rex Sacrorum* and the *Archon Basileus. Increased weight of the Senate and Assemblies.*

*Differentiation and Contest of separating Elements* within the State *breed the Distinction between Public and Private Law.*

The first Private Law, moreover, was, not individual, but family law.

*Public Law is the result of a contest* of elements and parties within the state: the outcome of *rival forces* contending for the mastery: E.g., *The State vs. The Family.* This was most obvious in Rome, where separate family rights had the greatest persistence.

*Other Elements of the Contest* wh. produced Public Law:

(1) *The association of equally powerful tribes,* not before associated. (Ramnes, Tities, Luceres,—Albans.).

(2) *Subordination of large groups to conquering competitors,* and the creation of a master and a subject class.

(3) *Association of classes of (free) non-burgesses with the citizen class,* and their gradual aggressive entrance into

political privileges, as at both Athens and Rome. Similar classes seen dimly in the history of Teutonic peoples.

*There are also*, of course, slow *modifications* which come almost unconsciously, and *quite without struggle.*

*References*:

> *For Greek insts.*, [George W.] *Cox's* History of Greece, Vol. I., chaps. II., VI (pp. 97-105), IX., X., XII.
>
> *For Roman ints.*, *Mommsen's* History of Rome, Vol. I., Bk. I., chaps. IV. (pp. 46-49), V., VI. (pp. 93-101), XI.; Bk. II., chaps. I., II., III. (pp. 331).
>
> *For both sets*: *Wilson's* "The State," secs. 25-69 and 144-159.

*24 Sept., 1894*

### III.

*Continued.*

*The Actual Origins and Development of Public Law.*

*In Teutonic Communities*, as contrasted with Greek and Roman:
> *Not city states*, but associated rural villages; less organic, but with stronger democratic features.
> *No Senate.*
> *Law uttered (declared) by assemblies* of freemen.
> *Titular kingship*: elective chieftainship.
> *Kingship of the modern sort* created by Conquest; and developed by feudal processes totally unlike anything in Greek or Roman development.
> *The Feudal Idea of Kingship*: Ownership: hence Sovereignty.

*In England*: The *Struggle for the control of Legislation.*
> *In Rome*, the assembly assented to legislation proposed by the king, or, later, by the elective magistrate; and approved by the Senate.
> *In England*, the king (i.e. the feudal king) legislated with the assent of the Great Council.
> *Steps of the Contest*:
> 1. *Magna Carta.* (The Twelve Tables).
> 2. *Petition by the Commons.* (How the Commons came to be represented).
> 3. *Petitions must be assented to as proposed* (This the *"Lex"* inverted).
> 4. *Laws must first be Bills*: the "must" lying in the fact that the Commons all the while possess the privilege and power of supply.
> 5. *The Bill of Rights*: laws may be altered only by the act of the authority that made them.
> 6. *The Ministers*: Since all legislation must be submitted first in provisional shape (bills), and must please the Commons, the Ministers of course must observe the will and pleasure of the lower house. *Hence the present system* of ministerial responsibility.

*Analysis, Public Law in England*: A set of rules regarding the exercise of authority and the relations of individuals to the state established by precedent, and by statutes embodying precedent.

*References*: *Freeman*: "Growth of the English Constitution." "The State," 651-677.

*Chief Stages in the Constitutional History of France*:    

1. *Before the disintegration* of the old Frankish monarchy: *Grafen; Immunitätsherren. Basis of government*, in some places conquest, in others inheritance or tribal chieftainship under a feudal form.

2. *The disintegration.* The history of France begins with *the accession of the Capets.* Character and means of their kingdom.

    *English government begins with consolidation*, first under Saxon and then under Norman kings. *French government begins with disintegration*, and a feudal balance or *equilibrium* of power.

3. *Process of Integration*: and the conceptions of sovereignty resulting from it:

    *No alliance of elements* (estates) in France such as England saw, to make possible a system of individual representation; but only a representation of "estates" to the end. *The monarchy organic*: the *États Généraux episodical* only.

    *The King triumphs, therefore*, and the several estates are not fused or united, but remain separate and without national power.

    *The Process assisted by feudal conceptions* of legal relationship, *and by the precepts of* the imperialized *Roman law.*

*Result*: Relations of Individuals to the State, administratively determined. All public law issues from a single sovereign source.

*References*: *Sir Jas. Stephen*: "Lectures on the History of France" "*The State*," 358-363, 268-304.

*General Conclusion of Topic*:

*Public Law*, a study of *organic and functional development*, and of the *emergence* within the body politic, by one process or another, *of* the political and social *rights of individuals.*

*29 Sept., 1894.*

## IV.

### *The Several Sources of Public Law.*

*Enumeration*:

1. *Tradition and Custom.*
2. *Legal Interpretation.*
3. *Legislative Enactment.*
4. *Contract.*
5. *Science*: systematic analysis and discussion.

*In Detail*:

*General Remark*: these several sources *interlace.*

1. *Tradition and Custom.* Is it of any practical value to distinguish (as *Dicey* does in his "Law of the Constitution," Lecture VIII.) between the law of the constitution and the conventions of the constitution?

    *Individual, traditional rights*, issuing forth from the common, traditional law, *get into* Magna Carta, Bill of Rights, constitutions, etc., etc. "Every man's house his castle."

2. *Legal Interpretation.*

*Examples:*

In the United States, the decisions of the Supreme Court in in the bank case and in the legal tender cases.

In England, the "Proclamations Case" of 1610 (Fielden, p. 315),[2] and the constructive treason case (Fielden, pp. 3, 314). 1710 (Dr Sacheverell).[3]

*Note: Gareis denies* that this is an independent source of law, saying that it is indistinguishable from legislative enactment, inasmuch as, in the present connexion, it makes no difference whether law proceed from one or another organ of the State. It is in any case a product of Sovereignty.

3. *Legislative Enactment.*

I. *Ordinary Legislative Acts*, like

(1) *Royal decrees* with reference to some particular administrative arrangement. E.g., Prussian "Domains Chambers" or Council of State (Text book [*The State*], 448-450, 458, 459), or the French ministerial system (294).[4]

(2) *Statute.* E.g., English Septennial Bill, Reform Bills, Local Government Bills, Bill of Rights, Act of Settlement, British North America Act, 1867. (818).

II. *Extraordinary Legislative Acts*, like

(1) *Charters and Constitutions* promulgated *by* way of *grant* from the crown: the usual European method. Eg. Prussian constitution of 1851 (396); the const. of Rhode Island.

(2) *Action by some special constituent assembly or convention*, with or without subsequent submission to a vote of the people.

(3) *Action by the ordinary legislature, but under special forms and safeguards.* E.g., in amendment of constitutions: the French chambers at Versailles (318), 14 negative votes in the German imperial Bundesrath. (404).

*Basis of all*, under this head: the *self-determining sovereignty* of the State. Limitation: acceptability, workability.

4. *Contract. (Compact).*

Illustrations from our own constitutional history. Was the Constitution a compact? Certainly not in form. *Influence of the national idea. The law-making potency of opinion,* particularly in the sphere of public law.

---

[2] Henry St. Clair Feilden, *A Short Constitutional History of England* (Oxford, 1882).

[3] The Rev. Dr. Henry Sacheverell, whose impeachment by the House of Commons for preaching a high Tory sermon in 1710 led to widespread rioting and was one of the principal causes of the fall of the Whig ministry. From the context, it would appear that Wilson was referring specifically to Dammaree's Case (1710) which grew out of the riots attending Sacheverell's trial. In this case, the English laws covering treason were interpreted very broadly to cover the rioters who attacked dissenting chapels in London; that is, it was assumed by the court that an attack on one chapel was tantamount to an attack on all chapels and hence was in effect an act of war against the Queen. See David L. Keir, *The Constitutional History of Modern Britain since 1485* (8th edn., London, 1966), p. 309.

[4] Here and in other such cases Wilson is referring to sections in *The State.*

*Examples of* genuine, *unmistakable Compacts*:
*Sweden-Norway*: For Sweden a treaty, for Norway both a treaty and a legislative act (624). Special arrangements under which *Bavaria* entered the German Empire (431-434). Identical Laws of *Austria-Hungary*, 1867 (594).
*Gareis objects*: that compacts are not themselves public law, *though they may be the occasion of its creation*. In fact, they may lie either inside or outside the public law.
5. *Scientific Discussion* and Construction.
*Brings principles* perceptible only by means of systematic study and the comparison of system with system, *into recognition and conscious acceptance*. Effective, however, only so far as acceptable to the general sense or habit of the nation or community.
*Most fruitful under unwritten constitutions: Montesquieu, Burke,* (principles of individual liberty and collective privilege). *Webster, Story*, etc.

29 Sept., 1894.

## V.

### *The State Itself as a Source of Law.*

*Conceptions of the State*:
To enumerate and discuss these properly belongs to general Political Science; but it is necessary that we should briefly examine them in order to get a foundation for our present studies.
*The* "Weal State" (or "Police State").                              *Theories*
*The idea* underlying this conception, an idea, *not of organization, but of motive*. All functions are legitimate for the State whose object is the promotion of the interests of the State and of its members. This is the State with full powers of discretionary administration, the "Police State" of the German writers.
Under this conception *the administration* was *the embodiment of the judgment* and the power of the community. There lurked beneath it the delusion of *a benevolent despotism*.
*Criticism*: The idea at bottom unimpeachable: *the State is* an instrumentality for quickening in every suitable way (there has been a long history of disastrous experiment) both collective and individual development. *BUT* it provides no new or certain means of determining the common good: that is left to the discretion of an unchecked Administration. *How are we to know* that there is really an intimate organic connection between the Administration and the community as a whole: *that the Administration is in truth an organ*, and not an outside power, however benevolent in intention, holding the people in tutelage?
*The* "Law State" (*Rechtsstaat*). To this the Weal State gave way in the *development of liberal* political *thought*. It represented an effort after greater cohesion, and gave expression to a *quasi* organic conception
*Such was not the conscious purpose* of those who sought to establish this view. It was their idea to hold the "government" in restraint by the force of an outside power, to build a bulwark about popular rights, effect a balance between opposing forces.

*Its actual effect*, however, was *to bind people and Adminis-tration together* under a common system of law ("a government, not of men, but of laws"). Community and government were integrated under a common power, the power of the Law.

*Criticism*: *The life of a State cannot be summed up or exhausted in its laws.* "The laws reach but a very little way," and every govern-ment must be a government of and by men. Laws may guide, balance, define, determine; but they *do not contain life, they only reflect it.*

*This is the conception* of the State which *we have ourselves adopted*, and upon which we have constructed our written con-stitutions, together with our immense and complex body of posi-tive administrative law, with its characteristic exclusion of an administrative hierarchy (of "men") and its minute prescrip-tions of official duty and responsibility. *With us the State is* in all its parts and functions *an institute of law.*

*The* "Constitutional State." Developed in Europe under the dominat-ing influence of English example.

*The State* vs. *the Government.*

Origination of the State outside constitutional, or other posi-tive, law. *Historically, the Government has generally been the chief instrument in the development*, and even in the creation, of States. Otherwise, there has been need of a written con-stitution originating a Government.

A *Constitutional State* is a self-conscious, adult, self-regulated (democratic) State.

A *Constitutional Government* is one concerning whose powers there is a definite understanding with the Community; be-tween whose powers and the active life of the State there is a definite adjustment.

*Characteristic Elements of a Constitutional State*:

1. *A law-making body representative of the Community*, not of the Government: set to direct and control the Gov-ernment. With this body, however, the Head of the State shares the law-making power.

2. *An Administration subject to the laws*; but not neces-sarily organized, energized, and commissioned at every point by the laws.

3. *A Judiciary equipped with* a wide range of *independent powers*, and secured, by an *independent tenure*, against cor-rupt, or other improper, influences.

4. *A more or less particular and complete formulation of the rights of individual liberty*, i.e., the rights of the individual as against the Government. A pledge taken of the Gov't by the Community.

*Summary Criticism*: *Law* limits, defines, adjusts the functional life of the State; but it *creates neither the State nor the Government.* It alters no necessity of life: it only supplies *a condition.*

6 October, 1894.

## VI.

### *The State Itself as a Source of Law.* (Continued).

*We have adopted the theory of the "Constitutional State."* This involves an "organic" conception of the nature of the State.

*Every State is the historical form of the organic common life of a particular people,* some form of the organic political life being in every instance commanded by the very nature of man.

*The State is an abiding natural relationship.* It is neither a mere convenience nor a mere necessity: neither a merely voluntary association, nor a mere corporation, nor any other artificial thing, created for a special purpose; but *the eternal and natural embodiment and expression of a form of life higher than that of the individual*: that common life wh. gives leave and opportunity to individual life, makes it possible and makes it full and complete

*Whether or not a State should have this or that form of political life* must always depend upon its stage of culture, its circumstances, of age, stress, strength, and belief, of education and political consciousness.

*Elements of every State*:

A People;

A territory;

An independent and stable Organization.

*To these* elements *the organic conception adds* the following:

    1. A characteristic life and method, due in large part to,

    2. Iherited [Inherited] aptitudes and institutions, and

    3. A differentiation of functions.

    4. An identity, a personality on the part of the State as a whole, separate and distinguishable from the individual characters of its several parts.

*The State Itself a Source of Law* under this conception: speaking forth its character in institutions big and little.

*Test Cases.*

    (1) *If individuals,* however numerous, however influential, *act otherwise than under constitutional forms* or through the constituted organs of the State, their action is not, and cannot be, the action of the State itself. This true *although the whole body of voters act,* or even the regularly constituted officers of the State, acting *ultra vires. As the blood,* or the several members, are not the man, save when acting within the anatomy characteristic of man.

        *"The basis of our political systems* is the right of the people to make and to alter their Constitutions of Government. But the Constitution which at any time exists, till changed by an explicit and authentic act of the whole people, is sacredly obligatory upon all. The very idea of the power and right of the people to establish government presupposes the duty of every individual to obey the established Government. All obstructions to the execution of the Laws, all combinations and associations, under whatever possible character, with the real design to direct, control, counter-

*Marginal notes:*

"Die Idee des Staats ist das Gewissen der Verwaltung." *Stein.*

"A People organized for Law within a definite Territory." *Fricker.*

act, or awe the regular deliberation and action of the constituted authorities, are destructive of this fundamental
principle." *Washington's Farewell Address.*

(2) *In case of revolution*, the life of the State, as such, is suspended, destroyed, it may be; and then reconstituted, reborn.
*The State does not consist of its parts separated, but of its
parts united*, and alive because of their vital union. It is organic, not mechanical.

(3) *In case of a transition* from one form of government to
another, there is *sometimes slow organic modification*, sometimes revolutionary death and rebirth

*Note the law-abiding* and keen constitutional *sense of the
Romans and the English*; their careful avoidance of any break
of continuity.

E.g., Transmutation of republican into imperial institutions
by *Augustus*: English *revolution of 1688.*

*Text-book,*<br>*1126-1130.*

*Text-book,*<br>*165-9.*

*What, then, of the Law in the Middle Ages?*

Where, under the feudal system, was the organic community
whose will was the source of law?

*Perhaps the most satisfactory answer:*

*Baronies*, the feudal entities, in fact the only *organic communities. Society* was, in a fashion, resolved into its original
unit, *the Family with its dependencies*. Baronies associated
only in a very loose jural relationship.

*States emerged* from this order of things *as they developed organs* and a vital coherence of parts. No better illustration
could be desired of the essential nature of a State.

6 October, 1894.

VII.

(Used in second year course
in Administration at J. H. U.)

SOVEREIGNTY.   *Its Nature.*

*Introduction.*

*Authority there must be and always has been in every State*; Government there must always be, lawgivers and subjects, under whatever form of constitution. *There is no organization without
authority.*

*This Authority must be*, and always has been, *lodged in some definite
organ* or organs of the State. It must be determinate in character
and lodgment.

*Hence the conception* of the lodgment in every State of a supreme
authority or power in the hands of some particular person or
body of persons; and the habitual association of this idea of
vested authority with the idea of the State. *The concepts 'Sovereignty' and 'Sovereign' always go together*, as if inseparable
in thought.

FUNDAMENTAL IDEAS:

I. *Sovereignty is an active principle*, a principle of *action and origination*, and not merely of superintendence. *The will* of the Community, of the organic State as a whole, is, in the last analysis, the foundation, and in many cases the source also, of Law.

"The sovereign State can designate as its interest and raise to be a subject of law whatever interest it will, and can in the pursuit of that interest adopt what means it will,—this is Sovereignty, an essential property of the State, as the Sovereign Community." *Gareis*, 29, III.

"*Sovereignty is a power*, the power of the sovereign community, *and*, as power, *owes its existence*, not to Law, but *to Fact*." *Gareis*, 28, sec. 10.

*Sovereignty is* a thing lodged, by one process or another, with determinate organs of the State. It is *Authority equipped for command and guidance*.

*A test Case: the dogma of popular sovereignty*; that is, the 'Sovereignty' of the electoral body as a whole, under a system of universal suffrage. This, *if it be Sovereignty* at all, is *dormant* sovereignty. If the electoral body be sovereign, it is a sovereign in the anomalous position of *waiting to have matters put to him*, unable himself to suggest anything, because without organs of utterance and suggestion.

*I cannot predicate sovereignty of my physical parts, but* must ascribe it to *my Will*, notwithstanding the fact that my physical parts must assent to my purposes, and that my Will is dependent upon their submission and obedience.

*Take the case of a written constitution.* Here the powers of the government are definitely set forth and specifically lodged, and the means by which they may be differently constituted or bestowed are definitively determined. Generally the process of amendment is made to involve the assent of more than a majority of the electors. *In such a case* (unless by revolution) *even a large majority of the electors cannot change the constitution*, if they be not the prescribed majority, acting under the forms prescribed. *Are They sovereign*, then, only in their original assent to these limitations, in the constituent act? *And, after that*, who is sovereign?

II. *Sovereignty must surely*, to possess any substance or vitality, *be conceived of as* the *daily operative* principle of government; not as simply the ultimate consent of the governed.

Attributes of Sovereignty (selected from *Bluntschli's Staatslehre*, pp. 363, 364). "Theory of the State," 464, 465.[5]

(1) The sovereign power is, by its nature, *the highest in the State*.

(2) It is *subordinate to no superior* political authority.

(3) *Its authority* is *central and general*, as contradistinguished from local and partial (of a part).

*Bluntschli adds* also that it must have

---

[5] Wilson is here referring to J. K. Bluntschli, *The Theory of the State* (Oxford, 1885), a translation of *Allgemeine Statslehre*.

(4) *Unity, because the State is organic,* and unity of structural power is necessary to its welfare.

*Definition of Sovereignty: (provisional).*

Sovereignty is the organic self-determination by the State of its law and policy; and the sovereign power is the highest constituted and organized power in the State entrusted with the choice of law and policy. *The scope of Sovereignty does not necessarily include the constituent act.* That is a matter of constitution: that is, of the limitation of sovereignty (*see post*).

Recast 13 October, 1894.

## VIII.

### SOVEREIGNTY (Continued)

#### FUNDAMENTAL QUESTIONS: (Questions *of Fact*).

I. *Is Sovereignty susceptible of Limitation? Certainly* of limitation *de facto.* Susceptible *also* of limitations *de jure,* if we accept the established and recognized habit of the Community as Law. *Law* of course receives its specific sanction from the law-making power in the State; but *in fact its ultimate sanction is Obedience,* and that is a sanction outside itself: i.e., a limitation.

*If,* then, we conceive *Sovereignty* as *the* active, *originative principle* in government, and accept the habit of the community in respect of obedience as the measure of its existence and efficacy, *we relieve it of its absurd and paralyzing imprisonment in the constituent act,* and have a conception which at least squares with the ordinary operations of government in a unitary State.

"*The limit of sovereign power* depends upon the limit of habitual obedience; every command of a political superior, or (if we reject the proposition that all laws are commands) every rule of conduct which is obeyed by the bulk of a given society, is a law, provided it is coupled with a sanction appropriate to law in the state of civilization which the society has reached; and, conversely, no command or rule of conduct is a law if it does not receive the obedience of the bulk of the society." *A. L. Lowell,* "Essays on Government," p. 209.

II. *Is Sovereignty Divisible? Are sovereign powers distributable?* This is a question affecting chiefly the dual or federal State, and at present we are considering only the unitary State. In respect of the latter, it is *a question of Checks and Balances.*

*Legislative, Executive,* and *Judicial* powers may be designated as *originative, administrative,* and *interpretative.*

*Take the Courts* first. We have no instance of an independent unitary State in which the courts have the power of determining, by an authoritative interpretation of the fundamental law, the constitutionality of legislative acts. But such a power is of course conceivable. Should it exist, it *would hardly be correct,* at least under the conception of Sovereignty we have adopted, *to describe the courts as sovereign* organs. Thy [They] are, *rather, the organs thr. which the limitations of Sover-*

## P U B L I C   L A W.

## VIII.

**SOVEREIGNTY** (Continued)

**FUNDAMENTAL QUESTIONS:** (Questions of Fact).

I. **Is Sovereignty susceptible of Limitation?**
Certainly of limitation _de facto_. Susceptible
also of limitations _de jure_, if we accept the
established and recognized habit of the Community as Law. _Law_ of course receives its
specific sanction from the law-making power
in the State; but _in fact its ultimate sanction is Obedience_, and that is a sanction outside itself: i.e.,_a_ limitation.

If, then, we conceive Sovereignty as _the_ active, _originative principle_ in government, and
accept the habit of the community in respect
of obedience as the measure of its existence
and efficacy, _we relieve it of its absurd and
paralyzing imprisonment in the constituent
act_, and have a conception which at least
squares with the ordinary operations of government in a unitary State.

> "_The limit of sovereign power_ depends up-
> on the limit of habitual obedience; every
> command of a political superior, or (if we
> reject the proposition that all laws are
> commands) every rule of conduct which is o-
> beyed by the bulk of a given society, is a
> law, provided it is coupled with a sanction
> appropriate to law in the state of civiliza-
> tion which the society has reached; and,
> conversely, no command or rule of conduct
> is a law if it does not receive the obedi-
> ence of the bulk of the society". _A.L.Low-
> ell_, "Essays on Government", p. 209.

_A page of Wilson's notes for his lecture on Sovereignty,
typed on his Hammond_

*eignty are ascertained*: i.e., the established and recognized habit of the community in respect of obedience. *They declare the* principles of that higher, *constituent law* which is *set above Sovereignty*: which *expresses the limitations* upon Sovereignty operative in all States but given definite formulation only in some.

*Thomas*:
"Leading
Cases in Con-
stitutional
Law," 18-20;
11; 73."[6]

*E.g.*, Bates' Case, *Feilden*, p. 313; Case of Proclamations, do., p. 315; and Case of Prohibitions, p. 316.

*Each of these cases declares the limitations* of law or custom (i,e, the constitutional limitations) of the power of the Sovereign[.] In reality cases of constitutional interpretation by the English courts.

*See below,* "Law and Ordinance."

*As for the Executive*, it acts under the laws, and subject to them all, both constituent and ordinary. *It is an agent* of Sovereignty, but *not an originative organ*.

*The Legislature alone*, in the modern constitutional State, is the organ of origination and command (i.e., of Sovereignty); *and it is limited* (offset or balanced) only by the organic habit of the community to which it gives law.

III. *Is Sovereignty necessary to Statehood?*

*This question must be reserved* for discussion in connection with an application of theory to dual and federal States.

*References*: "The State," secs. 1209-1211, 1226-1228.

*Lowell*, A. L., "Essays on Government," "The Limits of Sovereignty."

*Dicey*, A. V., "The Law of the Constitution," Lect. III., "Comparison Between Parliament and Non-Sovereign Law-making Bodies."

Recast, 15 Oct., 1894.

IX.

Omit '96                    (Used, J. H. U. 2nd. yr. course).

SOVEREIGNTY (Continued).

*Criticism of Austin's Conception* of Sovereignty and Law.

*Austin conceived* a Sovereign very concretely, as a person or body of persons existing in an independent political society and accorded the habitual obedience of the bulk of the members of that society, while itself subject to no political superior. This person or body of persons is conceived of as exercising the full political power of the Community.

*Law he conceived* to be the explicit or implicit command of such a person or body of persons, addressed to the members of the Community, its habitual inferiors or subjects.

*It is a Question of Fact*, of course, whether there is in every independent body politic such a superior or sovereign person or body of persons: a body of persons, i.e., *exercising the full political power of the Community*.

*To answer* the question, *an historical retrospect* is necessary.

[6] Ernest Chester Thomas, *Leading Cases in Constitutional Law Briefly Stated* (2nd edn., London, 1885).

*History of the Idea, Sovereignty.*

   *The word* Sovereignty *(la souveraineté)* we find for the *first* time fully *equipped with a meaning in Bodin* ("*De la Republique*"), who drew his conception from *the existing French State* of his own time (1530-1596: Francis I. to Charles IX—and the Huguenot wars). That State had already felt the informing and centralizing power of *Louis XI.*

   *Bodin regards the Sovereign as supreme* over the laws, *but bound,* nevertheless, *(a) by contract,* and *(b) by all the private vested interests* arising under private law. He must not touch any institution, like property and the family, which was essential to the existence of society itself. *He is conditioned by the organism.*

   *He connected the idea of taxation,* also, with the idea of *property,* and denied the right of the Sovereign to tax without assent.

   *Noteworthy* that these conceptions came after the developments of the Middle Ages were complete.

*In the Middle Ages Sovereignty* was predicated of every power *from which there was no appeal.* Sovereign powers and the irresponsibility of supreme authority were associated with feudal immunities of all kinds,—at least of all the larger, ampler kinds.  <sub> </sub>*Text book,* 243.

   *The kings of France absorbed* all the greater immunities, and became, as it were, multiple sovereign: with little change of idea.  *Do.,* 268-272.

   *The Estates were left* however, and it was Bodin's idea that they *represented only property* rights,—property stripped of its old-time attribute, Sovereignty.

*History of the Thing, Sovereignty.*

   1. *Almost complete in ancient times,* in the classical states, though limited there by the sphere (both legal and religious) of the family.
   2. *Gradually the habit of obedience has been restricted,* and spheres of privilege have been blocked out outside that of Sovereignty. E.g., individual rights of opinion, occupation, etc.
   3. *Finally, higher kinds of law have been created* than those which the highest organs of the State originate and determine: i.e., constitutions.
        *The net result* is that, by one process or another, *some branches of law have come to be greater than the law-giver;* and it has come about that constitutions withhold from the highest organs of the State the full political power of the Community.

*Sovereignty and Constitution.*

   The *upshot of political history* has been that *peoples have become conscious* of their relations to the highest powers in the State, *and have sought to formulate* either in practice or in written documents *the extent and the conditions of their obedience. These formulations are our modern 'constitutions';* and the states possessing them are our modern 'constitutional' states.

   *A constitution government has always had; but* it has not until this latest age of law-making had these conscious and deliberate formulations of practice and principle which determine the whole organization and action of government.

*How could we apply Austin's definition under a written constitution?*
Must we in this case, in our search for the ultimate sovereign who is not restrained or limited, find him, or it, in *a majority,* or two-thirds, it may be, *of the qualified electors?*

*These constitute also "the bulk of the community."* Are we not, therefore, involved in a vain round of verbal distinctions without differences? Has not our analysis dissipated government into thin air?

*Reference*: Sir H. S. *Maine,* "Early History of Institutions," Lecture XII.

Recast, 15 Oct., 1894.

## X.

### SOVEREIGNTY (Concluded).

*Application of the Analysis to Dual and Federal Governments.*

*Take the German Empire and the United States* as Types:
(1) *Origins of the two* Constitutions:
*The North German States,* drawn into treaty relations with each other by the circumstances of 1866, agreed to the assembling of a National Diet, to consider a federal constitution. This Diet was composed of representatives elected under similar election laws independently passed (by agreement) by the states severally. It considered a draft constitution, amended, and adopted it. This constitution was accepted by the Allied Powers and created the North German Confederation, 1867. *The South German States* afterwards entered this Confederation by treaty, 1870-1871.

*Our own federal constitution* adopted by representative assemblies separately elected for the special purpose in the several States.

(2) *Scope of Federal Powers:*
*In Germany, until* December 20, *1873,* the usual federal powers, with the addition of a right to legislate touching obligations & notes, criminal law, and commercial law. *Since 1873,* the whole domain of civil and criminal law, including legal procedure.

*In the case of our own Gov't,—*

(3) *Amendment. In Germany,* ordinary legislative procedure, except that fourteen negative votes in the *Bundesrath* defeat.

*Secs. 404, 1043.*

*In our own Government,* two-thirds of Congress and three-fourths of the States, acting either through legislatures or special representative conventions.

(4) *Character of the Whole.*

*Secs. 403-405.*

*In Germany, Sovereignty* is held to belong to the princes of the associated German States and the Senates of the free cities, and to be representatively exercised by the *Bundesrath,* which occupies a position of special preference and initiative privilege.

*With us*, there is no such special federal organ; the federal government is a corporate whole; we have rejected the idea of sovereignty of the several States or their governments. *Even in the Senate*, not the States as Governments, but the States as elective units, are represented.

(5) *Derivation of the rights of the Member States.*

*In neither case derived*; but in both cases original and inherent. Limited by the sphere and by the superintending authority of the federal State; but not thence derived.

(6) *Scope and Nature of State Rights.*

Powers of *independent* right, not powers of duty. Powers supplying the fullest sanctions of law. Limited, as a general rule, only by the powers *actually exercised* by the federal government.

*Singular position of the German States* under the arrangements of 1873.

(7) *Relations of the Federal Government to the Member States.* In what sense their political superior?

Only in the sense of being able to set bounds to them; or, in the case of the German Empire, to occupy more and more of a specified field of law, and so draw the bounds closer and closer about the States.

*Is such a Distribution* of Sovereign Powers *Susceptible of being Squared with any Definition* of Sovereignty that will bear examination?

*Try the constitutional foundations.*

*In our own case*, the constitution first assented to when there was no (organically) single people; and afterwards adopted by the people of the several states acting se[ve]rally.

*In the German case*, approved of by a national representative body elected under similar election laws (when there was no Nation); then accepted by the governments of the several States; finally adopted (treatywise) by the governments (including the legislatures) of the several S. German states (Bavaria, Saxony, Württemberg, & Baden).

*To what Sovereignty* can we resort in attributing *the origination of the fundamental law* in these cases? To what "determinate person or body of persons"?

*Try our Definition again*: (*Sovereignty* is the organic self-determination by the State of its law and policy; and the sovereign power is the highest constituted and organized power in the State entrusted with the choice of law and policy)

*These definitions* evidently *postpone Sovereignty to the creation of the organism*: postpone life and action to birth.

*First there must be an organic State*: as there was not in this country in 1787-'88, or in Germany in 1867. *Then*, and then only, *there begins to be Sovereignty*: which is an attribute of organic political matter, not of the forces of the organizing act. The organizing, or constituent act creates a thing cabable [capable] of exercising Sovereignty and of having sovereign organs.

*After that, amendment is organic*, and upon the initiative of the sovereign organ. To exercise any other than the constituted powers, in accordance with constitutional method, is to destroy (or, at any rate, suspend) the organic life, and induce revolution:—which may produce a different organism.

*Once again* we reach *the Question*:

Here I follow Laband "Das Staatsrecht des Deutschen Reiches," I., 52-80 (2 ed.). —and Jellinek, "Gesetz und Verordnung," 201, 203.

*Is Sovereignty Necessary to Statehood?* Are the member communities of a federal State themselves States?

Yes to the latter, No to the former Question.

*Any political community whose powers are not derivative*, but original and inherent; whose political rights are *not* also *legal duties*; and *which can apply* to its commands *the full sanctions of law, is a State*, even though its sphere be limited by the presiding and sovereign powers of a State, superordinated to it, whose powers are determined, under constitutional guarantees, by itself.

*Sovereignty vs. Dominion.*

> *Sovereignty* is political action and law-giving, subject to no superior.
>
> *Dominion* is political action and law-giving, independent, indeed, in the exercise of a full freedom in the choice of means, and with unqualified power to apply the sanctions of law, but within a subordinate sphere: subordinate because limited by the sphere of a superordinated State.

*Sovereignty and Constitution* (again).

> Here again, in this complex State, with its nice adjustments of sphere and function, arises the Question: *What Relation does a Constitution bear to Sovereignty?*
>
> Does it not, in this case as in others, express *the limitations of Sovereignty*, the conditions of obedience on the part of the Community?

Omit '96

*What of the Dual State?*

Secs. 597, 602.

> *In the case of Austria-Hungary* our conclusions may be applied quite unhesitatingly. Austria and Hungary severally exercise Dominion within their respective territories. Sovereignty belongs to the Delegations and the Joint Ministries.

Secs. 628, 634.

> *More room for doubt in the case of Sweden-Norway. Apparently* Sweden and Norway retain their Sovereignty; *and yet* in foreign affairs Norway is dictated to by Sweden; and in administrative matters affecting both kingdoms there is a system of Joint Councils which seems to supply common organs of sovereign determination.
>
> *What is the character*, as regards Sovereignty, *of a mere personal union?*

*See Woodrow Wilson*, "An Old Master and Other Political Essays," essay on "Political Sovereignty."

## XI.

### WRITTEN CONSTITUTIONS.

*Documentary Public Law.*

*For us*, upon a superficial view, *the Sources* of Public Law *seem to* be reduced to *two*: *Enactment and Legal Interpretation*;—or, *at the most, three*: Enactment, Legal Interpretation, and *Scientific Discussion*.

*From one point of view*, they are reduced to *one*, viz., *Compact*.

*Noteworthy* that *our constitutions have tended to work upon our minds as definitive*, narrowing our conception of the source and origin of Public Law to a singled act of popular legislation, as we deem it; and *cutting us off*, besides, *from all the formative history* lying back of them.

*As a matter of fact*, are not our constitutions *simply codes, summing up* a great deal of previous process, and typifying much of the essential history of Law? We have had a signal advantage in *standing*, as we have done, *not at the beginning, but at the summing-up point* of a history making for individual liberty.

*It behooves American lawyers and publicists to study other constitutional law than their own*, in order to see the forces of the process by wh. their own has been generated, and the real ground and degree of its difference from other systems.

*Let us look at our historical connections*:

(1) *Our Jury System*, and therefore large part of our *"due process of law,"* dates back, at any rate in its ordered regulation, to the juries of 'recognition' and 'presentment' of the *Great Assize* and the *Assize of Clarendon*.   *1166, temp. Hen. II.*

(2) *Our constitutional statements and guarantees of individual right* are derived from *Magna Carta*, which itself sums up and repeats numerous antecedent charters of preceding reigns; from the *Petition of Right* of 1628; from the *Habeas Corpus Act* of 1679; and from the *Bill of Rights* of 1689.

(3) *Moreover*, there is in this instance *a series of judicial decisions* which define and extend these rights (e.g., *Wilkes vs. Wood*, declaring general warrants illegal), *and a great body of scientific exposition* and discussion (e.g., Coke, Blackstone, etc.).

(4) *Our organization* of Government, *conception of* its *functions, separation of* its *organs, derived from English precedent* and custom, as interpreted by scientific discussion,—especially that of *Montesquieu; as well as from colonial charter and custom.*

*Written Constitutions*, as we have them, *a summation*, therefore, of *Enactment*, both ordinary and extraordinary,

*Compact*: e.g., the tacit compact under which the Continental Congress sat.

*Legal Interpretation.*

*Custom and Tradition.*

*Scientific Discussion.*

*And these* forces are not without an abiding power to *modify and expand* the structures already put together by the art and craft of history.

*Difference between our constitutions and those of the Continent of Europe*, this:

*Ours derived from* the customs, laws, and opinions of *our own race*, with an unbroken continuity. *The continental* constitutions, on the other hand, in very many cases *attempts to adopt,* with adaptations, foreign (almost invariably English) customs, laws, and opinions.

*Much of our Public Law*, besides, lies outside our written documents (except so far as they explicitly adopt the Common Law). E.g., *Criminal Law, Civil Procedure, Administrative Law*, etc., etc.

## XII.

### TASKS OF THE STATE.

I. *The State conditions* both *the existence* and *the competence of the Individual.*

  1. *Authenticates* his *birth*, his *marriage*, his *death*, indirectly his *name* (in some States directly) by registration. *Determines age* of full legal capacity, and in some States authenticates it by administrative process.

  2. *Creates*, and after creating *equips*, all artificial persons (*corporations*).

  3. *Requires* of the individual certain *services* (of hand, knowledge, sword, and purse) *as a condition of its recognition* of his independent existence and rights.

II. *The State gives Society its means of self-knowledge*, through social, economic, and financial statistics; *and* its means *of self-management* through local subdivision and organization.

*Here* enter all the *questions as to the repression of* such movements as *the socialistic.*

III. *The State protects* Society and the Individual against *disorder* and *dangerous persons*; and also against dangers threatened by *natural forces*, such as fire, water, explosive substances, dangerous structures, deleterious processes of manufacture. *Inspection of steam vessels*, etc.

IV. *The State promotes the health* of the Individual by

  1. *Sanitation.*

  2. *Authentication of physicians*, apothecaries, etc.

  3. Establishment and maintenance of *hospitals.*

  4. Public *Slaughter Houses.*

  Etc., etc.

V. *The State stands economic guardian* to the Individual in

  *Poor relief; insurance* (pensions and other); *savings banks; forestry*, game, and fishing laws; etc., etc.

VI. *The State stands spiritual god parent in*

  *Education*, including the education of the poor, neglected, and debased classes; and in *the repression of vice* (prostitution, gaming, etc.).

VII. *The State promotes* the *economic* and other *activities* of Society by means of

  1. Establishment and policing of *public roads and waterways;*

  2. Establishment of *posts, telegraphs*, telephones, etc.

  3. Maintenance or supervision of *railways;*

  4. The *coinage* of money, and the exclusive regulation of the money standard;

  5. Regulation of *weights and measures;*

  6. Establishment of *institutions of credit;*

  7. Regulation and promotion of *horse and cattle breeding.*

  8. Maintenance of *Public Markets and warehouses.*

VIII. *The State protects, and ensures, Property* by
  1. *Administration of the estates* of minors and incapables, and the oversight of the administration of trustees in general.
  2. Regulation or facilitation of *irrigation and drainage*.
  3. *Patents.*
  4. *"Protection,"* reciprocity, free trade.
  5. Public *Insurance.*
*Reference:* Sarwey, O. von, "Allgemeines Verwaltungsrecht" in Marquardsen.

> (Taken from notes on Administration: first year lectures).[7] (29 Oct., '94)

## XIII.

> (Copied, in substance, into second year course, J. H. U., in Administration).

THE ORGANS OF STATES and THEIR MEANS OF ACTION.

*The daily life of States* is *expressed* in the action and minor choices of *Administration.*

Its *greater choices* and its means of modification are exercised *in law-making.*

Its *means of adjusting* the action of government to the life of individuals, and law to provide right, is found *in the courts.*

  *Let us begin with* its daily and most constant force: *Administration.* Necessary to *distinguish,* in respect of Administration, between *The Head of the State* and *The Actual Administration.*

I. THE HEAD OF THE STATE.

  Necessary to *distinguish* in this connection, as everywhere, between the

*Several Leading Types of States,* whose organs natuarally differ so greatly in scope and character as to need differentiation in our general statements:

*The unitary State*
*The Federal State*  ⎫
*The Dual State*     ⎬  A *brief re-discription* of these.
*The Confederacy.*   ⎭

*Several Types of Headship:*

  1. *As regards the number* of those who exercise the highest executive functions.

  The head of the state may be either *a single person,* as in the ordinary monarchy; *or two* persons, as in the case of the consuls of Rome; or *a number of persons,* like the Venetian Council of Ten, the French Directory, or the present Federal Council of Switzerland. (The list might include also, perhaps, the Spartan *Gerusia*).

  *But this* numerical criterion is, of course, *not an essential criterion* at all. An essential criterion can be found only in the relation wh. the head of the state bears to the laws.

  [7] That is, Wilson's notes for lectures on administration at The Johns Hopkins University, printed at Jan. 26, 1891, Vol. 7.

2. *As regards the relationship borne by those who exercise the highest executive functions to the laws.*

Here we have *three classes*:

(1) *Autocratic*: Where there is *an entire absence of any constitutional means of controlling* the acts of the head of the state: *Examples*: Russia, Turkey, Persia, Venice.

(2) *Constitutional*: Where there are *means of constitutional control* of the public acts of the head of the state, at the same time that there is *no personal liability* on his part to arrest or other punishment. *Examples*: England, Prussia, Bavaria, Spain, Italy.

(3) *Republican*: So far as the head of the state is concerned, a Republic may be defined, generically, as a form of government under which *the Head of the State* is made *subject to a complete subordination to the laws, and* is besides held to a *personal responsibility* for his observance of them, being subject to punishment.

*We have examples* of this form of gov't *in Rome*, where, although the consuls exercised during their term of office a quite sovereign *imperium*, their term was brief, and at its expiration they were amenable to the ordinary penalties of the law. The same was *true even of the Dictator*.

*Other Examples*: the United States, France, Switzerland.

*The typical theoretical sovereign* of the Austinian analysts is of course *the first of these*, the Autocrat.

*Such was the sovereign of the archaic family*, in a certain restricted sense (though the father was in reality as straitly subject to custom as was any other member of the family); *but such was not the sovereign of the archaic state*: He was hedged about with what were practically constitutional limitations

*Modifications in the Power of the single Monarch*, and Status of the Head of the State under Governments still in reality monarchical.

*The most archaic monarchies limited by custom* backed by the imperative sanctions of religion, and thus to all intents and purposes by positive law.

*In subsequent monarchies*, the power of the monarch limited by

(a) *physical restraints* (the danger of revolution[)];

(b) *moral restraints* (the opinion and habit of the monarch himself, shared with his subjects, and the opinion, epigram, jest of the people). *The attrition of criticism.*

*The final stage* is reached

(a) *in its first phase when the* corporate privileges of the *people* (Estates, Feudal Councils, Representatives of Taxes, etc.) *stand stiff in the way* of the monarch's will *as tough, concrete institutions*, and

(b) *in its second phase*, when the habitual ('conventional') *attitude of the representative body* towards the monarch or his ministers has *crystalized into constitutional rules*.

*All this means* simply, (a) a coming into *consciousness of power* on the part of the people; (b) an effectuation of that power in *concrete institutions*. The difference between lib-

*Comp. Gareis, "Allgemeines Staatsrecht" in Marquard- sen, I., pp. 38-40.*

erty and despotism is a difference in the kind and degree
of obedience.

*It may be stated as a generalization,* that that polity is *exceptional* (in that part of the world which knows positive law) in which *the will of the monarch is not subject to law,* constitutional and other. *The coronation oath* is typical and characteristic of the European monarchy.

*Transfer of Actual Sovereignty to* collegiate *Representative Bodies,* by a process involving

(1) *Systematic restraint,* and constraint, of the monarch, and,

(2) *An entire transfer* of law-making power to representative bodies.

*Now, therefore, the initiative* and guidance of the Head of the State is an initiative in the business of these bodies, *a guidance* exercised over them. *The Sovereignty of the monarch,* that is to say, is nowadays *mediate*: and mediate sovereignty is no sovereignty at all. The modern monarch is, consequently, *sovereign only representatively* and by reason of his participation in the determinations of the highest body of the State.

*Present Legal Status of the Head of the State*:

(1) *In the Unitary State,* his legal status is one of *participation in the origination of law* & policy; and to him belongs (always nominally and generally in a very real and substantial sense) the important prerogative of initiative.

(2) *In the Dual State,* he *occupies this position towards* the law and policy of *two states* at once: states associated by more or less close bonds of law or treaty. *He is monarch of* the two states considered as *One only in respect of foreign affairs,* in such an association as that of Sweden-Norway; *while in* such a state as Austria-Hungary, the government over which he presides is that of *a single state,* not only in the decision of questions of war and of international intercourse, but also in the administration of *a joint budget,* and in cooperation upon matters of common concern with *a Joint Committee of the Legislatures* of the two countries.

(3) *In the Federal State,* he is *either*

(A) *The executive agent of the central gov't.* in the carrying out of the laws; its representative in all dealings with other governments; and a (veto-wise) participant in the law-making function (*as in the United States*); *or*

(B) *All this, with the exception of the veto, but with the* important addition of an *initiative in legislation (as in Switzerland) or*

(C) *Member of the sovereign body* as head of a presiding member state (*as in the German Empire*).

*In all these cases* the head of the State is strictly *subject to* the laws, to *constitutional rule and procedure*; though in some cases the responsibility is direct and personal, while in others it is only through ministerial proxy.

*The Head of the State as Representative.*                    Omit '96

Representative of *the unity,* the *personality* of the State: of its *majesty* and *sovereignty.*

There is a very real sense in which the head of the State is *at least the typical source of law*, and *the action of other organs* of the State in law-making simply *a function of substitution*. Law is still in most states promulgated in the name of the Head of the State; courts act in his name; etc., etc.

*Even in the case of Switzerland* the necessity is recognized of having some single physical person act as the representative of the state in diplomatic intercourse: *the President of the Bundesrath.*

The same thing is shown in

*The Possession of the Initiative in Legislation* by the Head of the State.

*In almost all modern states*, of whatever type, the Head of the State has, through the ministers of State, an *initiative* in legislation, *as well as a wide sphere of origination*, not merely, but even of independent action in foreign affairs.

Here again the facts are significant of an original *participation* in the exercise of sovereignty, a sanction of its exercise in specific cases *by representative bodies; or a substitution* of representative bodies acting in the name of sovereignty for the historical Sovereign. Thus *justifying Gareis* in his assumption that, for the purposes of systematic discussion in public law, *the Head of the State may be spoken of as the Sovereign.* He is at any rate the formal Sovereign.

*Perhaps the Prussian constitution*, in which the sovereignty of the king is so stiffly maintained in the face of popular representation and the full theory of a constitutional régime, *is the best illustration* in point here.

*Inviolability* of the Head of the State.

*Follows of course* from the points already made. *Most modern constitutions add personal irresponsibility*: i.e., exemption from the sanctions of the law.

*English theory*, e.g., that the king can do no harm.

*Value of a single*, national *guiding Power* under representative institutions.


## XIV.

### ORGANS *of the* STATE *and* ITS MEANS OF ACTION.

#### II. *The Actual Administration.*

*The Nature of Administration.*

It is the continuous and systematic carrying out in practice of all the tasks which devolve upon the State.

*"The Administration"* is the organization effected for that purpose.

No topic in the study of government can stand by itself,—least of all, perhaps, *Administration*, which *mirrors the principles of government in operation*. It is *not a mere anatomy* of institutions. It deals directly, indeed, and principally with the structural features and the operative organs of state life; but it at every point derives its motive and significance from the essential qualities and the vital institutions of government. *"Die Idee des Staats ist das Gewissen der Verwaltung."* (*Stein*).

*The organs* of government are *nothing without the life* of government; and the organs of each State must advertise, in their peculiarities, the individual and national characteristics of the State to which they belong.

*Distinction between Legislation and Administration*:

Distinction between *will and deed*? (Stein).

Disti[n]ction between *general rules* and *the specific application* of them?

Distinction between *Independence of Will* and *Subordination of Will*: between *origination* with its wide range of choice, and *Discretion* with its narrow range of choice.

*Field of Administration*: the field of organization, of effective means for the accomplishment of effective ends. *Must answer the question*: *What is feasible*, workable, practicable?

It sees government in contact with the life of the people. *It rests its whole front along the line drawn in each State between Interference and Laissez faire.*

*Branches of Administrative Business.*

A *common, practical classification* is as follows:
1. Foreign affairs
2. Interior.
3. War.
4. Police, sometimes combined with
5. Justice.
6. Finance.
7. Education.
8. Commerce.
9. Public Works.

A *logical division* of state business among executive departments *a modern result* of long experience in very different methods of division.

*Historical Derivation of Ministers of State*:

*Originally* in every case simply substitutes or *proxies for the sovereign*. Take, for example, the five Principal Secretaries of State in England; and the original confusion of arrangements in Prussia.

*Somewhat anomalous* case of the Austrasian *Mayor of the Palace*, appointed virtually by the baronage, as a sort of associate monarch.

*Creation of Departments by Statute* vs. *Creation by Ordinance.*

*Legal relationship of the ministers to the head of the State* under the one system and under the other?

*The case of the* office of our own *Secretary of the Treasury.*

*Relationship of the Ministers to the Head of the State*, as affected by their Relationship to the Legislature.

(1) *Our own System*, by giving the heads of Departments no direct relations with the Legislature, subordinates them to the President.

*Margin notes:*

O. von Sarwey, "Allgemeines Verwaltungsrecht," in Marquardsen, II., ii., pp. 5 et seq.

Bluntschli, Statsrecht, 255.

"The State," secs. 692, 693.
"The State," secs. 448-452.

"Essays in the Const. Hist. of the U. S.," pp. 180 et seq.[8]

---

[8] Jay Caesar Guggenheimer, "The Development of the Executive Departments, 1775-1789," in John Franklin Jameson (ed.), *Essays in the Constitutional History of the United States in the Formative Period, 1775-1789* (Boston and New York, 1889), pp. 116-85.

*And yet*, because *they are creatures of statute*, they are given duties and subjected to responsibilities not of the President's determining.

*And, because of* the uniform system of *impeachment*, which affects President and Secretaries alike, they are *in a certain degree put upon an equality* with him.

Again, *upon the theory of coördination, judicial process cannot reach the executive* so long as it keeps within its constitutional sphere, and is not a mere ministerial agent of the other organs of the State.

Cooley, 107, 157.9

(2) *In England* the complete responsibility of the ministers to Parliament practically relieves them of all responsibility to their Sovereign.

(*The English courts* would probably not compel a minister to obey the executive commands of the Queen. Convention has in a degree become law.)

(3) *In France* the position of the Head of the State is still less eligible as regards controlling the action of administration, because of his *personal responsibility*, with its resulting loss of dignity and weight, combined with the responsible relation of the ministers in the Chambers.

(4) *In Switzerland* the Head of the State is itself the body of ministers.

(5) *In States like Prussia* the relation of the ministers to the Legislature, not amounting to a responsibility, but *only to a representation of the Head of the State* upon the floor of the Houses, makes them in very substantial fact subordinates of the Sovereign.

*In every case* the *Ministers* are *the Actual Administration*.

*The only question* is whether *the Head* of the State is, or is not

(a) *a vital part* of the Administration,

(b) *a governing and guiding part*.

This because of the multiplicity and range of public business.

*The Executive and the Judiciary.*

*In the widest sense* of the term, *executive includes judicial business*, inasmuch as judicial action is *but a means of executing the law*.

*In almost every country except our own*, however, there is *this fundamental* practical *difference* of function between Executive and Judiciary, that *the one* (barring the ministerial officers of the courts) is engaged exclusively in the application of *Public Law, the other* almost exclusively in the application of *Private Law*.

*In our own case*, on the contrary, and in the British colonies, this distinction is obliterated by the so-called 'constitutional' functions of the courts.

*On the continent* the distinction between Executive and Judi-

9 Thomas M. Cooley, *The General Principles of Constitutional Law in the United States* (Boston, 1880).

ciary is even more sharply preserved than with us by *the system
of Administrative Courts.*

*The Real Functions of the Administration* are *not merely ministerial*:
they are also adaptive, guiding, discretionary: and the more
play of this sort allowed, under constitutional safeguards and
responsibilities, the better for the efficiency of government.

*The European system better than our own* and the English
in respect of the freedom of the executive, *but lacking* efficient
constitutional guarantees of responsibility.

*"The laws reach but a very little way.* Constitute government
how you please, infinitely the greater part of it must depend upon
the exercise of powers, which are left at large to the prudence
and uprightness of ministers of state. Even all the use and
potency of the laws depends on them. Without them your
commonwealth is no better than a scheme upon paper; and
not a living, active, effective organization." *Burke.*[10]

*The Executive* is the *law-effectuating* branch of government.
*Unity of the Administration*: the Council of State. *Omitted from our
system* of set purpose.

(1) *The English Privy Council* and the Ministers: their legal
and their actual relations.

(2) *In France.*

(a) A *Council of Ministers* (sec. 325),

(b) a *Council of State* (sec. 353).

(3) *In Prussia, a Staatsministerium* (sec. 460).

## XV.

### LAW AND ORDINANCE.

*General Significance of the Subject*:

(1) *It creates Administration* a separate topic, a distinct science
indeed: inasmuch as it differentiates its sphere from that of
legislation, and in so doing *distinguishes its exact character.*

(2) *It furnishes the basis of constitutional government*, whose
most marked characteristics are that it

(a) *analyzes sovereignty,*

(b) *apportions function,*

(c) *fixes responsibility.*

In the language of English constitutional history, it is the
distinction between *law* and *prerogative.*

*The Prince Consort* is reported to have said on one occasion that representative institutions were on trial.

This is *true in the sense* that representative institutions
are necessarily awaiting a more perfect development of the
distinction between the spheres of law-making and administration.

*General law* must in any case rest upon general consent:
and it will be most vital when it proceeds from the general
judgment. *Administration*, however, can never have such an

---

[10] Edmund Burke, "Thoughts on the Cause of the Present Discontents," in
*The Works of the Right Honorable Edmund Burke* (5th edn., 12 vols., Boston,
1877), I, 470.

origin or foundation: and the only valid ground of objection to popular government lies on the side of administrative interference. The interference of the popular power in the field of administration can never be anything but maladroit.

*What, then, is Law* in the strict sense of the word?

*It is the will of the State* touching the civic conduct of those under its authority. It is that expression of the will of the State which has for *its object* the creation, modification, or clearer definition and development of some right or duty on the part of the citizen; *as contradistinguished from* such expressions of the will of the State as have for *their object* simply the creation of new undertakings for the State within the range of old functions, or the imposition of new or extension of old duties on the part of public servants.

Jellinek, 240-241.

*Nothing which merely adds to the items of legal activity* on the part of the State is Law; but only that which effects some change in the legal privileges or obligations of individuals. It is the delimitation of the sphere of individual action in society.

*Examples*:

(1) *Of Law*: Public authority, citizen subordination and duty, state function, individual right:—even codification, enactment of customary or case law.

(2) *Of Ordinance*: Raising a loan, selling public property; founding a university; granting temporary aid to distressed districts, or bounty to a victorious army; naturalization of foreigners; giving permission for the erection of a trust (*Jellinek*); creation of a corporation: etc., etc.

*The Characteristic of Universality*, ascribed to Law ever since Aristotle, is a usual, but *not* an *essential*, attribute. The heart test of Law lies, not in the abstract range of its application, but in its object: in what it proposes to do. Law is the characteristic act of the State: the State alone can create or modify rights and duties.

*Neither is it essential that Law should be Permanent.* It may be merely transitory, and intended to be so, if only it do for the time being the characteristic thing. And *its universality may be only potential*: it may apply to only a limited number of specified cases, and apply to these only under special conditions.

*The Provinces of Law and Ordinance often overlap.* Certain expressions of the will of the State may lie partly within the field of Law proper, partly within the field of mere governmental action.

*E.G. The Budget. Taxation*, when employed merely for the sake of revenue, has for its object the support of existing institutions. New taxes, nevertheless, *create new duties* on the part of the individual. This still more the case, of course, if taxation have for its object the direction of the economic life of the people. It then unquestionably creates new rights and obligations.

*Appropriation, on the other hand, creates neither rights nor duties*: is the merely administrative side of the Budget.

*Note, however*, the

*Imperative Character of the Budget*

(1) Because of *constitutional provisions*;

(2) Because of *statutory provisions*: so that the Legislature in voting it seems to have in reality a very narrow range of discretion, and to act a merely administrative part. Its *field of choice* lies *outside indispensable institutions* and indispensable administrative efficiency.

*Suppose no money were voted* to support the Government: how many nice questions does it not raise! Only the *purposes* of taxation is a proper question for law as distinguished from Ordinance.

*Constitutional View of the Budget* (whether under a written or an unwritten constitution.)

*Support of Institutions*:

How far imperative? How far are established institutions independent, too, of constitutional provision?

*Failure of the Budget*:

A series of causes, *bona fide, mala fide*.

Remedies.

Responsibilities.

Here arises the question, *How far has the budget-controlling body the right to command*, by means of its control of the purse, the exercise of *functions* not vested in it by the constitution? *E.g.*, in the U. S., the *treaty-making* function.

PREROGATIVE.

*Appears after the establishment of parliamentary authority* in the field of law-making. It is involved in the question, What governmental acts are beyond the control of Parliament?

*Locke's Definition*: "The power to act according to discretion, for the public good, without the prescription of the law, and sometimes even against it." "Prerogative is nothing but the power of doing public good without a rule."

*Blackstone's Definition*: "That special pre-eminence which the king hath, over and above all other persons, and out of the ordinary course of the common law, in right of his royal dignity."

*Coke's Definition*: "All powers, preëminences, and privileges which the law giveth to the crown."

*Cox defines it*, narrowly, as consisting of "all public powers which are not conferred upon the crown by statute." *Jellinek*, 22.

*Limitations*:

*Coke*: "Proclamations are of great force which are grounded on the laws of the realm."

*Blackstone*: "Proclamations are binding upon the subject, where they do not either contradict the old laws or tend to establish new ones; but only enforce the execution of such laws as are already in being, in such manner as the king shall judge necessary"; "yet the manner, time, and circumstances of putting those laws in execution must frequently be left to the discretion of the executive magistrate."

*Crucial Question*:

Is Prerogative *simply limited* by law, *or is it derived* from law?

*Gneist holds* the Prorogative is not derived from law, but only limited by it. *Coke says* "grounded on the law of the realm."

*Jellinek makes the suggestion* (in keeping with the apparent interior meaning of authoritative English writers from the first) *that in England*, which does not possess a written constitution, the legal position of the immediate organs of the State (the Sovereign and the two Houses of Parliament) *rests upon the Common Law*; and also that, out of the principle that no contribution shall be levied upon the subject without the sanction of statute, no freedom be abridged save in accordance with the law of the land, the principle has sprung "that new right and therewith new duty cannot be established by Ordinance"

*Jellinek,*
*27 ff.* *Classes of Ordinance in England:*

    (1) *Ordinances by virtue of the Prerogative*, usually taking the form of Orders in Council. Include:

        (a) *treaties* which require no legislation.

        (b) *suspensions of law*, followed by subsequent acts of indemnity. E.g., opening of the Irish ports, 1846; suspension of specie payments, 1797-1821.

        (c) *The calling, prorogation*, and *dissolution of Parliament*, together with the power to create peers.

        (d) *Nominating power*, including the Cabinet (?) and the Privy Council; county officers; etc., etc.

        (e) *Granting of Pardons.*

        (f) *Military powers*: commandershif-in-chief, etc. Note the abolition of purchase in the army by an Order in Council.

    "*The king in Council*" is *nowadays*, it is to be noted, the king in *Cabinet*; and this undoubtedly has a tendency to minimize the independent importance of the Prerogative.

    (2) *Ordinances by virtue of "empowering clauses" of statutes.* A statute may not only confer large powers of discretion, but also "by express words be operative only until annulled" or not operative until put into force by executive proclamation.

    *A case in point here* is the act of the 50th. Congress empowering the President to stop, if he should see fit, the shipment of goods through the U. S. to Canada under bond.

    (3) *It may be pertinent to add*, as a third class, the *bye-law-making powers* of local authorities, which they possess by delegation; and the power of courts to make their own rules and give to them the full sanctions of law.

*Prerogative in the United States:*

    *The President* has been *fitted out* by the Constitution *with portions* of the English royal prerogative, in his occasional power of proclamation; his powers as commander-in-chief of the army and navy of the United States; his powers of dealing with foreign governments by way of preliminary negotiation; his nominating power; and his pardoning power.

*Conclusion.*

    *The English* have manifestly mixed administrative with legislative powers in Parliament, with the result that their conception of Law is formal ("enacted by the king in Parliament") rather than essential.

*We, on the other hand,* by the adoption of the idea of checks and balances, have still further obscured the outlines of Prerogative by mixing the discretion of the Senate with the discretion of the President, alike in the exclusively administrative function of appointment and in the 'federative' functions of foreign affairs

*Ordinance is legal regulation made in subordination to Law.* Determine *who* among the representatives of the State *are subordinate to the law* and yet possess the right to issue binding commands, and you have disclosed the ordinance-making organs: *the Administration.*

## XVI.

### ORGANS *of the* STATE AND ITS MEANS OF ACTION.

### III. *The Law-Making Body.*

*Types of Legislatures:*

(1) *The Primary Assembly.* Examples of this type found in every stage of the history of law-making, whether in ancient or in modern times. Athenian and Roman assemblies, Teutonic folk moot, Swiss Landsgemeinde.

*This difference between ancient and modern* primary assemblies, that the ancient were generally associated with a Council of Elders of one pattern or another.

*Note individual initiative* in the Athenian assembly in respect of the introduction of measures, as contrasted with the exclusive *initiative of the magistrate* in Rome.

(2) *Estates.* Representative of corporate classes, conceived of as having, so to say, a vested legal individuality.

*Characteristic of the Middle Ages,* but preserved in principle in most modern houses of Lords, though often mixed in these with other principles of representation; and *in England* deprived not a little of the corporate feature by the power of *free creation of peers,* as well as by the fact that in England the *peerage* is *not of blood but of office.*

*Sec. 726.*

*The Prussian House of Lords* is a House of Classes, consisting, as it does, of princes of the blood royal nominated by the king, the heads of certain dispossessed royal houses, certain appointed noblemen, the four chief officials of the Province of Prussia, and a large number of representatives appointed upon the presentation of ecclesiastical foundations, colleges of counts and landowners, the nine universities, and forty-three cities: besides anybody else the king may see fit to nominate.

*Sec. 465*

(3) *Representative Assemblies.* Held, in germ, in the Teutonic polity from the first, but *developed on a national scale by an evolution of the Assembly of Estates.* Characteristic, therefore, of modern times only.

*Contrast between Estates General and Representative Assemblies.*
(1) *In respect of the principle* of representation *and the method of organization.*

Bluntschli, "Stats-recht," pp. 50-54.

The modern representative assembly represents *the nation as a whole.* If paid, it is paid out of the national treasury. It is responsible, in theory, to the nation as a whole.

*The Assembly of Estates,* on the contrary, was generally *not even* a *single,* united assembly: *but each estate* (and an individual or a corporation might be an independent estate) was *separately represented,* its representatives separately organized (as a separate body or house), separately paid, separately instructed, etc., etc.

(2) *In respect* of their *relations with the Head* of the State.

*In the case of the Assembly of Es[t]ates,* a relation of *barter and compact,* as if of two separate and little less than hostile powers.

*In the case of* the modern *representative assembly,* the *coöperative association* of two organs of one and the same organism.

(3) *The voting of Taxes exemplifies this.* Each estate granted taxes for itself and out of its own separate resources, in return for favours, in payment for concessions made or promised.

*Representative assemblies,* on the contrary, make up the Budget: i.e., consider the national accounts and provide for the expenses of the State out of the common resources of the whole nation.

*E.g., the Great Council in England, temp. Norman kings.*

(4) *Differentiation of Legislative and Administrative functions.* Estates tended to become confused with administrative councils. But *under the representative system,* on the other hand, a sharp line is generally run between the spheres of legislation and administration, both in theory and in practice.

*Note: The transition in England* from the system of Estates to the system of national representation.

(1) *Commons simply one Estate.*

(2) *By degrees,* the effort made to incorporate in the Commons *elements representative of all the interests* in the kingdom, in obedience to the feeling that it was the national body.

(3) *The Commons become* indeed *the national body,* and the Lords only are left to represent the principle of Estates.

*Theoretical Legal Basis of Representation* can be none other than *the conception of the State as an organic whole,* a single personality: the idea of *Law* as coincident with *the will and habit of the whole,* organically expressed.

*The representative feature one of evolution,* of political convenience, *just as every physical organ is* an expression of convenience, of functional differentiation in the presence of certain practical conditions.

*Legal Features of Rise of Modern Representative Legislature.*

Everywhere, except in England, accompanied by the *formulation of written constitutions,* which *in most of the old monarchies* had the effect of admitting *representatives of the people into partnership* with the monarch in the function of law-making.

*By inference, not* in the function of Administration. (See *ante*).

*Its Legal Status and Law-making Power.* It is the Source both of origination and of Change, whether in Public or Private Law.

(1) *In the Unitary State*, it occupies the whole field of legislation, practically without limitation.

(2) *In the Dual State*, two legislatures are associated upon a footing of equality, coöperating in matters of common concern, either with or without the assistance of associated committees ("Delegations") chosen out of their own membership.

*margin: Omit '97; Secs. 602, 633.*

(3) *In the Federal State*, the legislature represents the State as a federal whole (*Bundesstaat*) and is set above the law-making bodies of the constituent member States; yet it is restricted (functionally, organically) in the field of its operation.

*Its Relations to the Head of the State in Law-making.*

*Already shown* (in lectures on the Head of the State) to be in most States subject to the leadership, the Initiative, of the Executive in all graver matters of legislation.

This, closely connected with the fact that *the Head of the State* is associated with the legislature as *an integral part of the law-making authority*, his assent being as essential as its own. *Initiative is the obverse of Veto.*

*Initiative*, though based upon the same principle as Veto, *is more reasonable*, more efficient for the purposes of good legislation: for reasons alre[a]dy discussed in connection with the proper relations between administration and legislation.

*Various Kinds of Laws.*    *margin: Bluntschli, 123, 124.*

(1) *Constitutional*, generally issuing from the Head of the State, or originating with some extraordinary (constituent) body.

(2) *Organic*: fulfilling constitutional provisions, completing organization.

(3) *Administrative*. (Discretion; the ways; the machinery).

(4) *Financial*. (The means).

(5) *Penal and Police*. (The compulsion).

(6) *Enactments in Private Law.*

*Distinction between Imperative and Non-imperative Law*:

*Constitutional and organic* laws almost always imperative; *administrative*, in part imperative, in part directory merely; *financial and penal*, sometimes the one (laws laying taxes always imperative), sometimes the other. *Enactments in Private Law* seldom imperative.

*Examination of the Various Matters enacted by Parliament in the Form of Statutes.*

(1) *Public Statutes*. These have generally the attribute of universality of application, though even they sometimes concern mere administrative adjustments. *margin: Omit '97*

"*Le roy le veult*," the form of royal sanction.

It is a *characteristic* of general or public statutes *that they originate upon the initiative of Parliament*. This initiative is no less that of Parliament, however, because most such acts are introduced by Ministers. *Ministers introduce bills as members* of the Houses.

(2) *Private Bills, originate only in petitions*, and not upon any initiative exercised in Parliament itself. They are assented

to by the formula *"Soit fait comme il est desiré"*; and until 1615 they were never printed.

Although *the courts take cognizance of public acts as of course, private acts have to be 'proved'* in actions brought under them.

*Parliament was formerly in the habit* of passing all sorts of private bills, relieving of pains and penalties, naturalizing, granting divorces, suspending marriage prohibitions in particular cases, etc., etc.

*A petition for a private bill* may be examined by any outside party who is legally interested in its subject-matter. Such party may oppose the granting of the petition. A private bill thus contested is debated by counsel representing the parties in interest before *a committee of "Examiners of Petitions for Private Bills"* which reports its decisions to the House. The Bill is then introduced by some private member and put through the usual forms of passage like all other bills.

*It is interesting to see* the way in wh. *Blackstone* tries to give to private legislation the character of law, notwithstanding the fact that he has predicated universality of all law. He admits that an act directed against a single individual "is rather a sentence than a law," but urges that such an enactment as that offences such as a particular individual is charged with shall be considered of such and such a grade has "permanency, uniformity, and universality, and therefore is properly a rule." *The Roman idea over again.*

(3) *Money Bills.* Grants given (by the Commons: for historical, not for abstract, reasons) upon request of the Crown, the Commons not being at liberty to give more than was asked for.

*Forms and Processes of Legislation.*

(1) *Assent of several bodies.* Generally of two Houses and the Head of the State.

(2) *Publication, constructive or formal.* Thro' the publication of legislative proceedings or through formal promulgation by proclamation or by publication in some official gazette or through circular letter to local authorities.

(3) *Several "Readings."*

(4) *Machinery of consideration* within the several bodies concerned. For example, reference to committees, select or standing; etc., etc.

*How much of these forms is constitutional*: i.e., how much of them goes to the efficacy of the law? *All that is not derived merely from* the interior machinery and *self-imposed rules* of the bodies themselves.

*Difference* between this question in *the United States* and *elsewhere.* With us very much more of the process, even as to readings and reference to committees, is a matter of explicit constitutional prescription. *Even the manner in which a bill is engrossed* may come under the view of our courts.

*In all countries alike,* however, *the process of enactment* is *a question for the courts* in so far as it concerns such matters as assent and publication. *Have the necessary bodies assented? Has the law been duly promulgated* and authenticated? Under every system there is this question of constitutional formality.

*Limitations to the Validity of Laws.*

Omit '94 &
'97

*Besides the necessary forms* of adoption already discussed, *every legislature must observe* constitutionality in respect of the contents of the laws which are passed; must respect *acquired rights* which are not merely political (like the right to vote); must regard *international obligations*; must refrain from the inequitable practice of passing *retroactive laws*; and, in a federal State, must avoid all invasions of the separate rights and reserved privileges of the member states.

Bluntschli,
134 ff.

*But, in the absence of written constitutions,* and of courts having a conclusive authority in constitutional interpretation, *such limitations are simply moral,* not legal. At any rate, a legislature, when it disregards them, violates no part of law but the theory and reason of it; and it violates the theory and reason of the particular system under which it is acting only when that system recognizes individual right and international obligation.

*Inviolability of Legislators.*

*Based upon the same foundation* exactly *as the inviolability of the Head of the State.* The legislator is an integral part of the body which stands for the State in its omnipotence. The principle is deeply significant of the history of laws as respects its formal origin: *sovereignty and its dignity perching upon the head of the representative as well as upon the head of the king,* the original legislator.

*The inviolability* of the legislator *exists,* however, *only during the sessions* of the body of which he forms a part. It does not continue throughout his term of office.

## XVII.

*Relationship of Administrative Acts to the Laws.*

Omit '97

*The Question and What it Involves.*

*How far does law circumscribe, as well as effectuate,* administrative action? Are laws a ring fence, or a motive power? Is the sphere of administrative action as wide as the sphere in which it may move without actually infringing the laws; or is it only as extensive as the explicit provisions of law make it?

*Turns,* perhaps, *on the distinction between positive and conventional law*: certainly upon the distinction *between positive and inherent law*: the law which is enacted and the law which inheres in the very nature of the thing, Government,—a nature determined, as we have seen, by the historica[l] circumstances of the state's development.

*In one sense* (for one government) it is *simply the question of Prerogative,* already discussed.

Yet it is *historically wider*: the question not simply of the powers of one organ of the State, but of the powers of the whole operative part of government, aside from the process of law-making.

*Powers taken from the king have not*, in most instances, *ceased to exist, or to be administrative.* They have been bestowed elsewhere without changing their character.

*The Question must be answered separately for Each Government*, according to the characteristic development of law therein

I. *In the case of our own governments*, state and federal, we have, as before noted, attempted to realize *the theory of the "Law State."* We have even excluded from our federal law the Common Law, which all the member States of the Union possess.

Have we likewise excluded that Common Public Law which determines, historically, the nature and powers of our governmental organs? The tenour of *many decisions of the Supreme Court* of the United States would seem to indicate that we have not. That Court has habitually determined questions of privilege and competence, where distinct constitutional provision was lacking, upon *grounds of historical analogy*, upon *English precedent*, upon the *meaning of terms* in English constitutional and political usage.

II. *In the case of the English government*, it is the question, in the last analysis,

(a) *of Prerogative*, which is now defined and limited on many sides by both statutory and customary law: the so-called conventions of the Constitution; and

(b) *of the relation of the Ministers*, in their composite character as Executive, *to the Commons* in its character of authoritative censor. A question, this, not so much of positive law as of *the part each* body *shall play in suggesting* administrative action. In this country we determine these parts minutely, by statute.

III. *In the case of European governments in general*, substantially common historical considerations affect the scope and authority of administrative action. Everywhere in Europe the *"Police State" stands back of the "Constitutional State"*: administrative authority is unimpaired where there is no explicit constitutional restriction.

This is *conditioned*, of course, *upon* the *age, antecedents, and character* of each government. For example, the federal government of *the German Empire* has no historical basis or precedent save such as it derives from the constitution of the North German Confederation and its own explicit constitution, and from the brief periods of practice under these instruments.

*In the case of the historically normal government*, we may say that, *in the absence of specific legal developments to the contrary*, the presumption is in favour of the principle, that the sphere of administrative action and authority is *as wide as the sphere in which it may move without infringing the laws*, statutory or customary, either in their letter or in their reasonable inferential meaning.

*Means of Securing Legality in Administrative Action.*
  (1) *Through administrative Organization*: that is, oversight
     and control; hierarchy and subordination.
        Here it is necessary to consider the question, *what scope
     is to be given inferior officials in judging the legality of the
     acts which they are directed by their superiors to perform,*
     and in refusing obedience when they regard their instruc-
     tions illegal. Where is the line to be drawn?
        *Possibly where the French draw it*: between "authori-
     ties" and mere agents.
        And, if subordinate authorities are to have this discre-
     tion, *how are conflicts* between them and their superiors *to
     be determined? Should there be* a system of *disciplinary
     courts*, as in the continental countreis [countries]?
        *Connection of this* question *with* that of a permanent
     (*merit*) *service*: that is, officers irremovable except by judi-
     cial process.
  (2) *Through resistance by Individuals,* in challenge of (sub-
     sequent) prosecution.
  (3) *Complaint.* Provided for under foreign systems, as of
     course; but quite irregular (and offensive) under our own,—
     except indirectly, through the newspapers,—being made
     usually in person and under the influence of anger.
  (4) *Legal, that is Judicial, Determination*: adjudication.
        Accomplished through *two different methods*:
        (a) *the English-American,* under which officers who act
     illegally may be indicted for crime or sued for civil damages
     (not being regarded as officers when acting beyond their
     legal powers)
        (b) *the European, of administrative courts*: formal accusa-
     tion, trial under speedy and appropriate process, etc.
  (5) *Parliamentary Control,* effected either thr. the *"political
     responsibility"* of the Ministers, *or through* one or other of
     the following processes:
        1. *Question*;
        2. *Interpellation*;
        3. *Investigation* (usually through a special committee);
        4. *Impeachment.*
        This is *a central topic of constitutional history.*
*Here, again,* in connection with these questions, as with all others
  within the general sphere of administration, *we come upon the
  topic of the integration and organic life of government.* This
  life is summed up neither in enacted or adjudicated law nor in
  the application of it.
        *Taken from* (first year) notes on *Administration,*
        pp. 45-48.   7 Jan'y, 1895.


XVIII.

*Organs of the State: IV. The Courts.*

*The Function of Adjudication and the State's Relation to It.*
  *Adjudication has* in it *two distinct elements*:
  (1) *The Ascertainment or Exposition of the Law*;

(2) *The Application* of its ascertained principles to particular cases as they arise.

Neither of these functions can safely or reasonably be left to individuals, acting without direct commission from the State. As the State alone has power to make laws, so it alone can apply and enforce law.

*The Administration of law* must be *put in motion* either *automatically* (i.e., by a self-acting official machinery), *or upon the initiative of outside* (i.e., non-official) *parties.* Hence we have the following agencies for the administration of law:

1. *Administration,* devoted for the most part to the carrying out of Public (i.e., imperative) law. The individual no longer has the privilege of self-help.

2. *Adjudication,* devoted for the most part to the carrying out of the provisions of Private law, which is not imperative, but adjective or remedial on the initiative of the individual.

*Administration is the field of self-directed action on the part of the State*: the action of the State itself, without the initiative of private interests. In a certain sense, therefore, it is, so far as the individual is concerned, the field of tutelage as contrasted with the field of self-help. Its action may care for individual rights, but it is *objective to the individual.* It takes care of him.

*Examples*: the letter post; sanitation; industrial inspection; relief of the poor (where the individual does not even determine the fact of his own poverty); education (where the individual is denied the privilege of self-neglect).

*The Courts are the resort of suitors,* public or private. *They are not self-acting agencies* of the State.

*Difference between Courts and Ministries of Justice.*

Sec. 561, 562.     The mixed function of some of the courts *in Switzerland.*

*What is involved in the Action of the Courts.*

(1) *Determination of the facts* in individual cases *and of the law applicable* to those facts. *This is a purely logical process.* It *invol[v]es*

   (a) *The effort to establish the fact* of a certain jural relationship between the parties to the suit, subject to received rules as to evidence; and

   (b) *The effort to subsume the fact* established *under some principle* of law, statutory or customary, for the purpose of applying the sanctions (enforcing the consequences) of that principle.

   *In fact,* these two things are not so strictly separable. *The law* is *the major,* not the minor, *premiss*; and the facts must be proved with constant reference to it: else there could be no rules of *irrelevance in evidence.* The conclusion of the court is the conclusion of a *syllogism.* Given the law and the facts proved, what inference is to [be] drawn and enforced upon the parties?

(2) *Interpretation.* The law is by no means always clear either in its terms or in its specific criteria; it is by no means equally applicable to all cases that arise under it; it is subject to general principles to which the particular text under consideration may

make no reference; is constantly being subjected to modification and repeal:—is part of a complex, inter-related system, no part of which can safely be interpreted without reference to other parts. The courts must interpret each law.

1. *Grammatically*: with reference to the meaning of its language, if it be a statute, with reference to its general significance, if it be custom. *The meaning of terms depends* upon usage, and usage is a fact, making the date of a law and the historical criticism of it necessary elements in its construction. *The comma in the constitution.*

2. *Logically*, treating the plain implications of the law as if they were parts of it; reasoning away its inconsistencies; giving effect to its dominant purposes of principle. Here *both Logic and Metaphysics may enter* as aids, and even the history of thought become necessary to a full elucidation. Every law has, underlying it, a set of generally accepted philosophical principles.

3. *Systematically*, that is, with reference to *the general principles of the system* of law of which it forms a part; with reference to its own individual history as respects the repeal or modification of it; with reference to its relations to other *cognate provisions*, etc. *E.g.*, a contract to do an immoral thing or something against the policy of the law; an ex post facto application of law; etc., etc.

(3.) *Constructive Inference*, where there is no specific law which is applicable. This is the *process of analogy*, of putting laws together, for the purpose of getting some systematic suggestion as to the filling in of gaps. E.g., law of common carriers. *Conspiracy and the trades unions.*

*Differs from systematic construction* in this, that it reads a virtually new law into existence; while systematic interpretation simply brings side lights to bear on old law.

*Here courts come out upon* the field, oftentimes, of *the most general principles*: those fundamental doctrines and conceptions of the law which, if not common to all systems, at any rate seem natural inferences from the general reasoning of the particular system under administration. *Analogies drawn fr. foreign systems: e.g., the Roman.*

*Of course analogy may fail*: there may be cases wholly unprovided for; *and the court may be left without resource.*

(4.) *Equity*, (nominally confined to process). Typified in the supplying of remedies by *the Roman Praetor and the English Chancellor*. In both cases, an effort to cure the defects of a rigid system difficult to alter or to liberalize, by relaxing its formal requirements and affording substantial relief.

## XIX.

*Organs of the State: the Courts* (continued). *Omit '97 to p. 102*

*Differentiation of the Functions of Ascertainment and Application:*

*In Rome the Praetor* determined the law, in a general way by his additions to the *Edicta Perpetua*; referred each individual case to *a Judex*, accompanying the reference with general instructions; and the Judex decided both law and fact (*res* *Bluntschli, 200, 331 judicata jus facit inter partes*), with or without the assistance of expert opinion.

*Id.* 332, 333.

*Under the Teutonic system* of the Middle Ages certain Schöffen, laymen chosen from amongst the people, were associated with magistrates. *The magistrate simply presided*: questions both of law and fact were submitted to the schöffen, who expressed their own convictions under no restraints save those of conscience.

*Ency. Brit.,* "Jury."

*The English Jury.* The civil and criminal juries to be distinguished, in origin if not in function.

For argument in favour of the jury, *Bluntschli,* 328 et seq.

*The civil jury* originated in the *Recognitors* employed by the Normans in financial service, and afterwards for the ascertainment of titles (Domesday Book); afterwards,—etc. Of French origin (*taken from the Frank capitularies*), though like early Saxon usages. *A jury of witnesses.*

*The criminal jury* originally *a jury of presentment* (seen first, perhaps, in the twelve senior thegns who, according to the laws of Ethelred, are to be chosen in the county court)[.] Persons presented undergo *the ordeal* of one sort or another or resort to *compurgation.* Hence our Grand Jury.

*Compurgation* falls into disuse; *ordeal is condemned* by the Lateran Council, 1215; and *the petty jury appears. Afforcing* the jury: passes into separation of witnesses from judicial jury; etc.

*Result,* both in civil and criminal procedure, *ascertainment of law* confined to trained or at least professional judges: *ascertainment of fact* confined to lay jurors.

*The modern European system* makes the same differentiation in criminal cases, but makes none in civil. *In civil cases* the determination of all questions, of whatever nature, falls to professional judges: in most stages of adjudication to a bench of judges.

*Various Sorts of Judicial and Semi-judicial Functions*:
I. *In the field of Private Law.*
   1. *Guidance, regulation and decision of litigation,*
   2. *Authentication* and *Publication.* E.g., of wills, liens, mortgages, etc.
   3. *Authoritative Assistance* in such matters as the appointment of guardians, administrators, trustees, etc;
   4. *Arbitration,* as, for example, either in suits or in labour controversies.
II. *In the Field of Public Law,*
   1. *The prosecution* and *punishment* of *crime.*
   2. *Settlement of administrative questions,* whether between Departments of the public service, or between officers and private individuals.

*Types of Organization*:

*Superior and Inferior Courts*: original and appeal jurisdiction. One ground, the grade of cases: another, the gradation of appeal.

*Benches or single magistrates.* (See post).

*Circuit or local courts*: unity or diversity in adjudication. The
English system,–the European,–our own.

*Separate Administrative Courts* or the decision of administrative
questions in the ordinary tribunals

*Jury or no Jury.*

*Appeal. What does it cover? What is the procedure of the higher
court?*

(1) *Under almost all systems* the question is generally *a question of legal error*, whether in substantive law or in procedure: that is, either illegality or irregularity; *though in
the U. S.* an appeal is generally allowed also on the ground
of a verdict contrary to the evidence.

(2) *Procedure*, everywhere except in France, a procedure *of
revision simply. In France* the Court of Cassation proceeds,
in all cases in which appeal is allowed, to a re-[a]djudication.

*The objects of appeal* are,

(a) to give *unity and uniformity* to the law of *procedure*; and

(b) to *check the possible arbitrariness* of one tribunal by the
impartiality of another.

*Forms of Procedure.* Here the chief point of common and historical
importance is *the difference between written and oral* proceedings.

The *reasons for preferring oral* to written procedure.

*In our own Equity practice*, wherever it has retained its original forms, *all testimony is taken by written deposition; but the
arguments* of counsel are oral and public, *and the decisions* of
the judges are read in open court.

*Under the older order of things in Europe*, the arguments
of counsel, no less than the testimony and *all* other *parts of the
procedure, were in writing*, and their consideration by the judges
a *private* consideration. The judges decisions were both private
and unreasoned.

*Tenure and responsibility of Judges.*

*Historical and practical importance*, involving the questions,

(1) of *election or appointment*;

(2) of length and *security of tenure*;

(3) of *amenability to impeachment*.

*The Courts in a Unitary State.*

If *the state have a written constitution*, there will be for its courts
questions of constitutionality with respect to the laws.

If *the State have no formulated constitution*, the courts are of
course mere instruments of the sovereign body, administering
without question the laws it enacts.

*The Courts in a Subject or Colonial State.*

*Differ with the status of the State* in the matter of law-making.
*If all laws be made by the sovereign State* to which it is subject, the courts which sit within its borders are merely ministers of the sovereign State.

*If, on the contrary, it have a semi-independent legislature* of
its own, its courts will be finally authoritative except in cases
in which the constitutionality of legislation is involved: the
question, i.e., of its conformability to the laws of the sover-

State of affs.
in *Georgia*
before estab
of supreme
court.

eign State. In such cases an appeal generally lies to the courts of the Sovereign.

*The Courts in a Federal State*, or in the several Member States of a Federal Union.

It is in such a Union that *we reach the highest differentiation and development of the judicial function*, if, as in the highest forms of such a State will always be the case, the courts are given the duty of preserving the balance of legal powers between the several parts of the complex organism.

## XX.

### Criminal Law.

*Nowhere* does legal science seem *more formal* than in its Definition of Crime.

*What is Crime?*

"*An act or omission which the law punishes in the name and on behalf of the State*, whether because expressly forbidden by statute or because so injurious to the public as to require punishment on grounds of public policy; an offence punishable by law." *Century Dictionary* [(24 vols., New York, 1889-91), II, 1350].

"Crime is *that imperriling of the conditions of social life* which is determined by legislation to be averted only by punishment." *Ihering*, [Jhering], *Zweck im Recht*, 2 ed. (1884), I., 490-491.

*Its Difference from other wrongful Acts* and Breaches of Law.

It is a public wrong, and not merely a private injury. *A tort* is "an infringement or privation of the private, or civil, rights belonging to individuals considered as individuals; *crimes* are a breach of public rights and duties which affect the whole community, considered as a Community." *Blackstone*, Bk. III. chap. I., paragraph three.

But "*all* offences affect the commu[n]ity, and *all* offences affect individuals. But though all affect individuals, some are not offences against rights, and are therefore of necessity pursued by the Sovereign." Austin (Campbell's Abridgment), p. 196.

A Right is "that wh. anyone is entitled to have, or to do, or to require fr. others, within the limits prescribed by law." Kent.

("A party has a right, when another or others are bound or obliged by the law, to do or to forbear, towards or in regard to him." Id., 193.)

"Where the offence is an offence against a right, it might be pursued (in all cases) either by the injured party or by those who represent him." (E.g., in France an injured individual may appear along with the public prosecutor in a criminal trial, as [']partie civile.' Holland, 270.).[11] But, for various reasons, the prosecution for some offences is not left to the discretion of the individual, but is assumed by the Sovereign. "In this difference of procedure, and not in any distinction between the tendencies of the acts, lies the distinction between Crimes and Civil Injuries. An offence which is pursued at the discretion of the injured party or his representative is a Civil Injury. An offence which is pur-

[11] Thomas Erskine Holland, *The Elements of Jurisprudence* (5th edn., Oxford, 1890).

sued by the Sovereign or by the subordinates of the Sovereign, is a Crime."

The Derivation of the Term, which is common to all the Romance Languages, bears out this view, inasmuch as it discloses no quality. Latin, crimen; Greek, κρῖμα, a question for decision, a decision or sentence; κρίνειν, to separate, decide, judge; English discriminate, critic, etc.

It would thus seem to mean simply an accusation or charge: the thing charged, and also the decision regarding it.

Features wh. Crime has in common with all wrongful acts or Breaches of Law.

Law is the ordering of Liberty, the "external organism of human freedom." It seeks to take cognizance of and to guard certain interests, public and private, and no man may lawfully do anything to the detriment of those interests. Every breach of the fixed order of Law, every violence to the organism of freedom, must be punished.

Why distinguish private from public? Because of the confined nature of some acts, the broad and general tendency of others. Some may be measured in respect of the wrong they do, and individualized; whilst others have a poisonous quality which tends to affect the whole body politic. Their motive is more general; the act done is representative of a disposition, and may be subjected to a qualitative judgment.

Hence the prominence, in criminal law, of the question of Motive, rather than of the actual harm done to such individuals as may be affected.

Nature, Source, and Interpretation of Criminal Law.

It proceeded, historically and by way of genesis, from popular judgments,—popular moral judgments,—as to the heinousness and nature of offences. In this sense derived fr. custom.

Customary law, however, is not continuously creative of fresh principles and originative of new judgments in criminal as in private law. Neither is criminal law expanded by analogy, as civil law is. The maxim is fixed, "Nulla poena sine lege poenali" (no penalty without an e[x]press penal law); and

The Interpretation of Criminal Law is always strict, adhesive to the letter, not venturing to expand the principle or go beyond what is expressed.

In order to understand this, note

The History of Criminal Law:

All crimes were at first torts. Only by a relatively modern development has this part of public law been created. There were once no crimes, but all offences were in the nature of civil, that is, private, offences. Only by degrees did legislation pick out from private law the offences [that] were to be made public.

The lex talionis.

Example of Roman Law. Punishment, as the result of private prosecution, at private discretion, was early recognized and provided for; but the public prosecution of offences, as being aimed at the State, not till B.C. 149 (Lex Calpurnia de Repetundis, establishing a special tribunal for the trial of corrupt practices by

Austin; to whom it seems, apparently, a mere question of expediency.

See Maine, "Ancient Law," Chap. X., "The Early History of Delict and Crime."

colonial governors). This picking out of particular offences and assigning them to special tribunals or commissions (wh. were always Committees of the Assembly), continued to be the method of the growth of criminal law proper. Circ. B.C. 81, temp. Sulla, the development seems to have begun in earnest, the Leges Corneliae picking out murder, arson, forgery, and other like matters for public prosecution. This process never became complete, however, and criminal law always remained, under the Roman system, a mass of particulars but partially separated fr. private law. Reasons assigned: Growth of criminal law under a republic, as contrasted with its growth under a monarchical system of rule. The latter illustrated in England, where criminal law (the public power being definite, personal, and jealously watchful over "the king's peace" upon wh. rule depended) had a much prompter and more systematic development than in Rome. Our own criminal law derived from a monarchy.

*Compare the process by wh. the English courts grew.*

*See "Lectures on the growth of Criminal Law in Ancient Communities," by Rich. R. Cherry, LL.D., Univ. of Dublin.)*

Classifications of Crime:

1. Omissive and Commisive. Example of Omissive, silent knowledge of another's criminal intention. W. C.,[12]

   Criminal Intention and Criminal Negligence.

2. Acts criminal in themselves, and acts criminal only in their consequences. E.g., the unlicensed keeping of explosives, and the deliberate unlawful use of dynamite.

   *Causal relationship.*

   In a case of the latter sort, the causal relationship between the criminal consequence and the deliberate act must be proved.

   *Intention: preparation; Execution.*

   In a case of the latter sort, besides, both intention and the carrying out of intention must be shown. Mere preparation without execution (whatever the intention) is not criminal.

   *Dangerous acts: Damaging acts.*

   Analogous distinction between dangerous acts and those which actually or intentionally inflict damage.

3. Acts. vs. Attempts. This distinction offers a nice test for theories of punishment, to be discussed presently. The law makes a distinction, apparently on the ground that its only object is to preserve the integrity of its own order, between these two. In the one case that order has been violated; in the other it has not.

4. Police Offences. Mere breaches of order, of peace or decency or convenience.

Grades of Crime and Degrees of Criminality.

I.  The Gradation of Crime is highly artificial under all systems of law.

    French distinguish crimes, delicts (misdemeanors), contraventions (offences); Germans, Verbrechen (crimes punishable by death or by imprisonment for more than fifty years), Vergehen (crimes punishable by a briefer term of imprisonment or by a heavy fine), and uebertretungen (transgressions punishable by arrest or a fine of not more than 150 M.); English, Felonies and Misdemeanors.

    At first, Felonies were such crimes as were punishable by death, or by forfeiture of lands or goods, or both. At last they

12 Wilson's abbreviation for "wherein consider."

came to be simply offences punishable by the severer sorts of penalty. Misdemeanors are offences punishable by the lighter fines or by imprisonment for less than a year. Proposed now in England to distinguish only indictable and non-indictable offences.

II.  Degrees of Criminality.

Intention vs. Deliberation.

Limitations to responsibility in consequence of mental condition, state of duress, etc.

Principal: accessary. Accessary before, and accessary after, the fact.

It is the function of legislation to effect the sharpest possible definiteness in respect of the exact character and the exact degree, as well as the exact conditions, of criminality. Hence, also, again, the necessity for the rule of strict construction.

Time limits to Indictment. Criminal statutes of limitation generally affect only the minor sorts of offences.

Theories of Punishment.

The real nature and object of punishment can be determined only when crimes are regarded as simply one form of breach of the law. Whether a civil injury or a crime be adjudicated, the effort is, to make good the legal order. But in the case of the civil injury the primary object is, not punishment, but the rehabilitation of a private right, which has been denied or invaded; while, in the case of a Crime, the effort is, not to rehabilitate a right, but to inflict punishment for a breach of public order. There may be incidental punishment in the first case: and that is allowed to suffice. It is not deemed necessary to make punishment the chief feature there.

Criminal Law is meant to be deterrent and vindicative: it contains the fangs of Society. It attempts a qualitative, rather than a quantitative, judgment of wrong actions.

Other Theories regard punishment as

(1) Reformatory. But this object, if it enter at all, can only enter into some punishments, not into all. It excludes the death penalty, of course. It can be only subsidiary. Criminal law is merely a means wherewith to fight offences against public order.

(2) A Punishment of Motive, which should be adapted to the strength and character (e.g., personal or consciously anti-social) of the motive. Disciplinary and reformatory of motive. A variation of (1). Open to same criticism. Substantially the view of Bentham.

(3) An equivalent for the deed done: "an eye for an eye, a tooth for a tooth," a life for a life, etc., etc. Even if it were possible to carry out this view in practice, it is the crude standard of a primitive society. It leaves no essential difference between indemnification (the rehabilitation of a private right) and punishment. (See Merkel, sec. 310, Anm.)

References: Holland, pp. 269-270; 311-318.

Campbell's Austin, pp. 196-197.

Merkel, secs., 717-760.

WWT notes, with a few WWhw additions (WP, DLC).

# Notes for Lectures on the History of Law[1]

[Sept. 22–c. Dec. 1, 1894; Dec. 5, 1892-
Jan. 16, 1893; Dec. 19, 1895]

## HISTORY OF LAW.

### I.

*Introduction.*

*Relations of the course to general culture.*

*Its Relations to legal study.*
> *The legal profession* an exalted and distinguished profession in proportion as it is *a learned* profession.
> *The science of law should take precedence of the art* of law with every real lawyer, not only because it is higher and more enlightening, but also because it is fundamental to the art.

*Nature of the study*:
> *Character and variety of the phenomena* wh. we group under the general term, Law. Various forces coöperate or succeed one another in the determination of what Law shall be. *No political organism long remains simple*; and the forces wh. produce law in the youth of Society are by no means the same as those wh. produce it in stages of greater maturity and complexity.
> *Difficulty of the study in view of this variety*, a variety almost as great as that of civilization itself. *Nothing but a Grundriss possible.* An outline of more or less systematic suggestions.

*Is a History of Law possible?* It is a universal phenomenon, but has it a universal, single history?
> A history of law *just as feasible as a history of religion*, with wh., in the earlier periods of development, it is so closely associated:—more feasible, indeed, inasmuch as there is in law a *smaller element of poetic imagination.*

*Before attempting a Definition* of Law, note
> *The two-fold aspect of Law*:
> > Substantive Law } Their relation and
> > Procedure        } interaction. *Rights*
> *materialize through Process*; and the history of Law, particularly in its earlier stages, is very largely a history of process.
> *Rights*, therefore, are *disclosed and developed by experience*, and, so far as they are concerned,
> *Law may be defined* as That portion of social experience and choice with regard to the relations of individuals to each other and to society which has gained distinct and formal recognition in the shape of uniform rules backed by the authority and power of government.

*This definition*, however, *hardly covers more than the fundamental principles of Private Law.* Much of Public Law is the choice of a minority or the product of an exigency; and the social habit

---

[1] For the earlier provenance of these notes, see the Editorial Note, "Wilson's Teaching at Princeton, 1892-93," Vol. 8. They are printed here because most of them were written or recast during the autumn of 1894. [Eds.' note]

plays no part in it but that of acquiescence and accommodation. *Much of the law of procedure*, and of administration in general, *is devised rather than selected* by the power that formulates the law (enacts). Looking to such law,

*Law may be defined* as A body of rules with regard to the transactions of individuals and the action of government *originated and enforced by the sovereign power* in the State.

*Law in this latter aspect is much more easily traced* through history than social habit could be; and *all* of *law must wear something of this appearance*, for the reason that it is always through the instrumentality of definite organs of the State that law, of whatever kind, emerges into view and takes on an authoritative character.

*Topics of the Course.*

1. The Origins of Law.
2. The Origins of Procedure.
3. Roman Law: Its Character and Development.
4. The History of Law in the Middle Ages.
5. German Law: Its Sources and Characteristics.
6. French Law:      ”           ”        ”           ”

*Central Position of Roman Law,*

  (1) Because it is the only ancient system of wh. it can be said that we know its its [sic] exact character and the main features of its history.
  (2) Because it is rich, complete, systematic, and has exercised the most profound influence on the law of modern Europe.

9/22/’94.


## II.

*Origins.*

Here *the immediate object of our study* is *primitive society.*

*Primitive society* in a sense *less susceptible of analysis than modern* society, because of its unity and solidarity. Not simple,— as complex, on the contrary, as its limited materials permitted. ☞ *Note*, especially, the *mixture of religious with legal conceptions*. Ancestor worship and inheritance.

*The several Elements of a People's Life* (Savigny's analysis).

  *Language,*—Usage.

  *Constitution,*—visible authorities, powers.

  *Law* (or Jural Relationships),—Symbols.

*Our Materials:*

  1. *Language*, embodying alike symbols and their corresponding conceptions.
  2. *Belated types* of social organization, and the institutions of the stationary nations. (The Joint Family of the Hindoos, the House Communities of the southern Slavonians, the Village Communities of Russia and India).
  3. *Tradition.*
  4. *Epic and Religious Literature* (Vedas, Brehon Laws, etc.).
  5. *Very ancient Codes*, like the XII. Tables.

*General Notions*:

*Evidence of Language*

GREEK: θέμις, or θεσμός (generally in the plural form, θεσμοί)—
"*that which is right*, as appointed or ordained by heaven."
(Aryan root, DHA).

θέμιστες, either *principles* of law, or decisions, judgments,
principles (of divine origin or suggestion) *picked or
sifted* out by the magistrate.

Δίκη. *Primarily*, declarations of judgment; *in general*, abstract justice.

Νόμος. *Primarily*, use or custom; *finally*, the general term
for Law.

*Order of Ideas for the Greek*:

(1) A *divine judgment* or suggestion.

(2) *Declaration by a magistrate* as to the divine decision applicable to a particular case.

(3) *Human use or custom, added* to these.

LATIN: *Jus*. Indo-Germanic root, YU (Sanscrit, YUJ; Greek ZY;
Latin, JU). Derivatives: ζυγόν, ζεύγνυμι; jugum, jungo, conjux;
yoke. *The idea "connexion rather than constraint,"*—"*that
which is fitting,*" orderly, 'regular.'

*Lex* (*legere*, λέγειν). Primarily, to pick (Legio—picked out to
serve); secondarily, read out.

*With the Latin*, the ideas of *usage* and of *organic public will*
predominated throughout.

MOESO-GOTHIC:

*Witoth*,—"that which is *observed* or *kept*."

ANGLO-SAXON:

*Ae* (aevum, αἰέν, αἰών, aye),—*immemorial custom*.

*Asetnissa, statutes or ordinances*. Closely equivalent to the
Greek θέμιστες.

*Dom* (Aryan root, DHA, from which θέμις; and wh. signifies
to set or appoint)—judgment: *prospective*, model *judgment*.

*Domas*, the plural, very nearly equivalent to θέμις.

ENGLISH: *Law*. (Imported Danish root, lagu, laga, that wh. lies,
rests, or is fixed). *Because borrowed, generalized*, to mean
Law, in the widest sense.

*Common Law* (fr. *folc riht*) "the right common to all the
people," as distinguished from the rights of particular
classes. Analogue, jus publicum

*Right, Recht, Droit, Diritto.*

*Starting Points*. (See B. W. *Leist*: "Altarisches Jus Civile," I., 21-23).

A. *Naturalis Ratio: Religious*:

(1) *Sacrifice to the gods.*

(2) Sacrifice to *personal, family ancestors.*

(3) *To tribal ancestors*. (Fatherland).

(4) Kindness to *guests and beggars*.

*Moral*:

(5) *Purity*, physical and moral.

(6) *No rape*.

(Omit 02-3)

(7) *No personal violence*, especially murder.

(8) *No theft.*

(9) *Good faith.*

B. *Civilis Ratio*:

(a) Development of the *patriarchal* polity.

(b) *Agnatic heritas and sacra.*

(c) *Assimilation of marriage seizure to* ordinary *alienation (mancipatio).*

(d) *Prescription*, in both marriage and property relations.

22 Sept., '94

### III.

### *Origins* (continued)

*Forces of Formation*

Kinship, the *nexus*;  ⎤ Almost inextricably
Religion, the *sanction* ⎦  inter-related.

*Upon Kinship* rests *Authority*, upon *Authority*, *unity*; and Authority easily passes into the phenomena of Religion, as is shown in *ancestor worship.*

Note the invariable double function of authority and priesthood.

"Almost all the English law on the subject of the descent of Personalty, a great deal of Continental law on the same subject, and some part of our law of Realty, has for its foundation the 118th. Novel, or *Novella Constitutio*, of Justinian. This Novel is the last revision of the older Roman law of Succession after death, which was formed by the fusion of the rules of inheritance contained in the venerable Twelve Tables with the Equity of the Praetor's Edict; two streams of law profoundly influenced at their source, as no reader of M. Foustel de Coulanges can doubt, by the worship of ancestors."–*Maine*, "Early Law and Custom," 66.

*Almost irresistible tendency to fixity*, to unchangeable crystalization. The *caste nations.*

*Forces of Change.*

*Change exceptional*: Stagnation the rule.

1 *Contest*: group competition.

2 *Coalescence*, either of Tribe with Tribe, upon terms of equality, or with an aggressive non-citizen class; or association with a subjected population, originating *differences of Status*.

3 *Movement*, tribal or national, with resulting changes of environment and habit.

4 *Settlement*: The *Land* gradually substituted for Kinship, as the social nexus.

5 *Commerce.*

*See Bagehot, "Physics and Politics."*

*Change*, accordingly, *seems to have come*

(1) *In the compact city states* of classical antiquity, where there was popular attention to affairs; criticism and friction; class competition, etc.

(2) *Upon the disturbed European* stage, where there was move-

ment, the competition of groups, conquest, and the fusion of institutions.

*Stagnation*, on the contrary, was characteristic *of the oriental nations*, with their diffused rural populations subject to a single political authority; etc.

Omit '97, '98, 1900 1901 *The Germanic Village Communities*, each to a large extent a self-governing unit, stand half way in type between the two classes of states mentioned above. *The system of representation*, which seems to have characterized their polity from the first, tended to keep the state small and consciously coherent.

*There was here*, besides, that *movement* and *competition* of groups, and that *leaven of conquest*, which ensured against stagnation. The mobile *Germanic host* had no touch of oriental character about it.

*Early Codification* of the Law in the stirring, fermenting states, *before* sacerdotal authority had become fixed and unchangeable; for the purpose of making the law public and subject to deliberate alteration.

*Maine, "Ancient Law," Chapter I.* *Late codification* in the East, *after* the firm establishment of sacerdotal authority, when publication meant merely the final crystalization of the law.

*But why* was there early codification in the one case and not in the other? *Codification* was *not a cause*, but only *a symptom* of change. It showed in itself the forces which were operative, either to change or to fix institutions.

1 Oct., 1894

## IV.

### *Origins of Procedure* (or Methods of Redress).

*Procedure, in general*, and in its original, only the application of sanction (punishment). It *becomes a method of specific redress* (civil procedure) only *under later developments.*

*Comp. R. von Ihering, "Geist des römischen Rechts," I., 118-167.* *Original System of Self-Help.*

Every man asserts his own right against the wrong doer,—or, rather, every set of near kinsmen, for the family, not the individual, was the unit,—even to the extent of wreaking vindictive vengeance. *Supported by the moral approval of the community*, the acquiescence of its habit.

*Example, early Roman law*: the rights of the person wronged against *the adulterer* caught in the act; against the *nocturnal or resisting thief*, or *the insolvent debtor* (who c'd be made a bondsman, or, if indebted to several creditors, cut in pieces among them).

*Germs of Communal Interference*, seen in

*Ransom and indemnification*. Three days' offer of bondsman for redemption. Indemnification either

(1) *By private arrangement*, within bounds set by public opinion or a common precedent; or

(2) *By the intervention of a magistrate, as arbitrator*, fixing the sum of damages, wh. were in most cases, not indemnificatory merely, but exemplary as well.

*Further Regulation of Self-Help.*

   *Pignoris Capio and Destraint.*

      Confined both in Roman and in English law to a few cases of special nature.

      *In Roman law*, to

        1. *Claim of a soldier* for pay or food or forage.

        2. *Tax demands* of farmers of the revenue.

        3. *A few private demands*, such as for the price of a beast bought for sacrifice.

        4. *Damnum infectum* (?). It certainly applied in some cases to real estate.

      *In English law*, to

        1. *Trespasses by cattle.*

        2. *Taxes*, and officers' fees.

        3. *Rent.*

*Cases, all, it will be noted, of claims "not directly enforceable by the ordinary civil procedure."*

      *Under the Teutonic and Celtic systems* it was not confined to special classes of liability, but was extended quite broadly to all obligations that could be satisfied by it.

      It was, under these systems, however, *surrounded and conditioned by formulae and minute details* of procedure which materially restricted it, by rendering it *extremely hazardous.*

*Read Maine, "Early History of Institutions," 280-282.*

*Progress away from Distress.*

   *Replevin*: forthcoming or delivery bond.

   *Attachment* in certain cases; but by process of Court, and in the nature of a security simply.

   *Judgment execution.* After the courts have grown secure of their power against the defaulter in any event.

*Maine, "Early History of Institutions," Lectures IX-X.*

*Witnesses originally Guarantors*, participating in the original transaction.

   *As participants in the transaction*, they must assist in making it good. They *stand for the community.*

   *Examples:*

*The Vindex in L.A. per manus injectionem.*

      *In Roman Law*, the five witnesses of the *Mancipatio*, who must all be full Roman citizens and free from taint or disgrace of any kind,—as the *libripens* also must be. The transaction creates absolute property rights.

*Ihering, I., 140-167.*

      *Same true in the Nexus*, where the borrower becomes a judgment debtor.

      The *witnesses* in these transaction *bore*, it would seem, a *representative character*, representing the whole folk. Their number *five*, probably, as representing the *five census classes* of the Servian constitution.

      The *"testamentum in comitiis calatis"* furnishes a striking illustration of the one-time formal and solemn participation of the community itself in certain transactions. This form of *testamentum* originally *sanctioned by a Lex.*

*Comp. Maine, "Ancient Law," Chapter VI.*

   *In Anglo-Saxon Law.*

   *Proof in Court*, either

      By *"compurgators*["] (who might be produced by the litigant from amongst his own friends and kinsmen) who swore simply to their belief in the credibility of their principal; or

*By Witnesses*, who were, either *"Transaction witnesses"* (for the business of sale, gift, exchange, etc.).

"To every 'burg' let there be chosen thirty-three as witness"; "To small burgs and in every hundred, twelve, unless ye desire more." "And let every man, with their witness, buy and sell every of the chattels that he may buy or sell; . . . and let every of them give oath that he never . . . will declare anything in witness save that alone which he saw or heard: and of such sworn men let there be at every bargain two or three as witness."

*Laws of Edgar*

*"Community Witnesses,"* were produced by a party (usually in cases regarding real property or status) to testify "concerning circumstances, long-continued relations, and occurences known to them *as neighbours, or members of the community."*

*See* [Henry Adams *et al.*] "Essays in Anglo-Saxon Law," pp. 186-187.

This latter class of witnesses bears some part, as we shall see, *in the ancestry of the English Jury*

*In English Common Law, also, "compurgators";* and *"good suit"* of witnesses for debt, as late as the time of Henry II.

*Holmes,* "The Common Law," 257.

1 Oct., 1894

## V.

### Procedure (Continued).

*Beginnings of the Administration of Justice:*

(a) *Not between near kinsmen.* In such cases the father or head of the family was absolute arbiter and judge, no doubt. The *patria potestas* of the early Roman life was probably typical of Aryan organization.

(b) *Between members of different family groups*, the priestly judge or the popular court. Trial by peers. *The judge antedates the king.*

*"Ancient Law,"* 362; "Early Hist. Insts.," 252.

But, judge or tribunal, *the first function* of judgment was *mere arbitration*: and the judgment was left to be executed by the parties, not by any common functionary of the community. *E.g.*, the earlies[t] form of the Roman action was the *L.A. Sacramento.*

(c) *The king himself*, alone or with a Council of Elders,—*or a Council* of Elders alone.

*Note the king's assessors* of later times, giving expert advice.

(d) *Finally, the magistrate, or a regular process* of hearing and trial *in a popular assembly* (in the classical states).

*The King in his relation to early Civil Justice.*

*"Early Law and Custom,"* Chapter VI., p. 167 in particular.

*Conclusions drawn from the Salic Law,* "the oldest of the Teutonic codes, the oldest portrait of Germanic institutions drawn by a German."

*In the ancient classical city states* the popular courts got the better of the royal power, and the latter disappears, or, rather, is put into commission. *But in the broad-spread rural communities of the Teutonic polity*, when they were joined together under a common sovereign, the power of the latter tended to absorb the function of Justice.

(a) *Residual Justice of the King.* Hence Equity, the Roman Praetor and the English Chancellor.

(b) *The King's residual power of execution.* His officer enforces the judgments of the popular courts, either when the unsuccessful litigant has agreed beforehand to abide by its decision, or when the successful litigant appeals to the King to see justice done.

(c) *The locally elected president* of the popular court *gives place to the King's representative*, the Graf or Count or Sheriff: and this new president sees to it that all its judgments are carried out by the King's power.

(d) *Popular courts decay*, by reason of the hardships of personal service in them; and their functions fall more and more exclusively to the King's deputy.

    *Later the central feudal courts also* decay, and their "peers" give place to assessors who are experts, learned in the (Roman) law.

(e) *The King himself goes circuit* through his kingdom to adjust disputes; *and then* those expert counsellors whom he constitutes *judges go* about on a like business, and absorb jurisdiction.

    *The organization of justice* thus *grows with the development and integration of States*, and gets its present features with the completion of the process.

*Summary of Origins*:

1. *The unquestionable fact of kinship* having been the original bond of Society and the first fountain of right and obligation; *Religion* the sanction.

2. *Language, apparently, does not carry us back of the organization of the State* (unless θέμις may be the judgment of a father as well as of a King or magistrate). *Custom*, however, originally of the Family.

3. *Evidences of an earlier system of Self-help* (Distraint, compurgation, witnesses, etc.). *Limitations*: Opinion, typified by the witnesses in their representative character; minute and hazardous ceremonial; arbitration.

4. *Introduction of public*, as contradistinguished from private, *Justice*, administered by fixed tribunals (the judge ante-dating the King), *and the modifications of law thereby* resulting: first by restraint, then by control and command.

5. *The mediaeval King*, and his relation to justice. Partial *parellel* of the ancient classical *King, as Praetor*.

6 October, 1894.

## VI.

## ROMAN LAW.

*Circumstances of its Development.*
*Why did it develop* at all?

    Because of the *war of classes* in Rome, and the policy, and necessity, which made Rome mistress of a great body of subjects who were not Roman citizens. It was because of the peculiar *conglomerate make-up* given her by the circumstances of her origin; and because of her *world policy* that her law shows features and an expansion different from that of other classical city states.

*How did it develop?*

(1) *By Codification*: the Twelve Tables.

   *Cause*: Discontent of the plebeians with (a) the general secrecy and uncertainty of the law, and (b) the arbitrary power of the patricians, served by their magistrates, in the application of it.

   *A love of form*, and consequent preference for *Lex* over Custom? ([Rudolph] Sohm [*The Institutes of Roman Law*], 28).

   *Magistrate and Pontiff.* Partial co-incidence and intimate interrelationship of *'fas'* and *'jus'* in the regal period. Note the so-called *'leges regiae*,' probably "mostly the rules of the *fas* which were of interest not merely for the pontiffs but for the public, with wh. it was of importance that the latter should be acquainted, that they might know the risks they incurred from their contravention."

      *Certain Attic laws* regulating ceremonial ritual and administered by the Archon *Basieus*, were also called *'royal laws.'* Servius Tullius is said to have promulgated laws concerning contract and delict; but the *'leges Regiae*,' wh. doubtless actually date from the regal period, pretty certainly contained *only regulations of 'sacred' matters.*

   *The College of Pontiffs determined all the ceremonial* of the law: all the *formulae* relating to actions and to obligations: "*the letter* of the law, its technical application, interpretation, and utilization."

   *Remits from them determined* the *action* both of the centumviral courts (acting upon questions of Quiritarian right) and of the single *Judex* or Referee.

*Method of the Formulation* and Promulgation of the Twelve Tables.

B.C., 454 (?).

   *Ambassadors* said to have been sent to Greece and to the

*Age of Pericles*, B.C. 444-429.

Grecian settlements in the south of Italy. On their return they are said to have been accompanied by *Hermodorus of Ephesus*, to assist in the work of codification.

   *Certainly* there are *some resemblances* between some of the provisions of the Tables and certain provisions to be found in the Solonian legislation. *Other provisions* show a likeness, too,

B.C. 594.

to other legal arrangements known to have existed contemporaneously in Greece. This true, however, of *only a small part* of the Tables.

   *The two Decemviral Commissions*, B.C. 452, 451; the second of which contained three plebeians, but sat under the same patrician president as the first. These Commissions *superceded*, for the time, *all magistracies*, and, acting with unlimited power, formulated the Tables as law. After previous action of the Senate, authorizing the codification, *the Tables were submitted to the Comitia Centuriata.*

*Contents of the Tables*
>*The Jus Civile.* The larger features of the customary law, taken
>for granted. The object of the legislation simply certainty and
>equality: Certainty as to the contents of the law; equality be-
>tween classes in the application of it.
>
>>*It fixed the matters that might pinch*: the exact circum-
>>stances under which obligation accrued, the definite measures
>>of penalty and redress, etc., etc.
>
>*Thus they hinge on*
>
>>*Mancipatio, Nexum,* the four *Legis Actiones,* and *the old
>>rigours* of the *jus civile.*
>
>*Rigours of the old Family* power somewhat *relaxed. Plebeian
>gentes* recognized. *Clients* suffered to hold property. The Regu-
>lation of *self-help* fixed; etc., etc.
>
>*Examples*:
>
>>*Usucapio* (prescription) determined: movables two years, im-
>>movables, one year. (*Note* that this applied only to those
>>things,—*res mancipi,*[2]—over which quiritary rights could be
>>acquired).
>
>>*Limitation* of amount of *interest.*
>
>>*Injuria*: public slander, capital punishment; bodily mutila-
>>tion, *talio*; other injuries, a fixed fine.
>
>>*Guardianship.*
>
>>*Succession.*
>
>>*Legis Actiones,* the centre of the whole structure.    Sohm,
>>Four in number:—(1) *Sacramento,* (2) per *judicis postu-*   153-162.
>>*lationem,* (3) per *manus injectionem*; (4) per *pignoris
>>capionem.* (5) per *condictionem* subsequently added. (*Con-
>>dictio*—demanding back a particular thing, or sum)
>
>>*Quiritarian Right only* dealt with in this legislation.

*Effects of the Decemviral Legislation.*
>Although it did give certainty to the general provisions of the
>law, it *did not give certainty* to its application *to individual cases.*
>"The structure of the provisions of the Tables was not such as
>to enable the plain citizen to apply them to concrete cases, or
>know how to claim the benefit of them, without some sort of
>professional advice." (*Muirhead*).[3] *Any more than the form of
>modern statutes.* In each case, it is necessary to resort to some
>one who knows the established interpretation.
>
>'*Responsa*' *still necessary,* therefore: interpretation, in short.
>Rome was *still to wait* about a *hundred years (367?) for the Prae-
>tor* and his equity.

Re-cast, 8 Oct., 1894.

---

[2] *Res mancipi*—Land, right of way and of aqueduct, slaves, beasts of burden,
and agricultural implements(?). [WW's note]

[3] Wilson identifies this reference later in his notes. [Eds.' note]

## VII.

### Roman Law (Continued).

*The Jus Gentium and the Deliberate Development of the Jus Civile.*
*Introduction:*

A comparison
possible with
England in
every point
but the 4 [.]4
In respect
of that,
considerer
[consider]
the effects of
possible Fed-
eration.

Length and Variety of Roman History:

Extension of empire, its rule, and in the end its law. Constant choice.

Roman magisterial functions in the Provinces. Administrative necessity.

Radical changes of condition, both political and economic, in Rome itself. Economic law.

Establishment and Development of a monarchical world system. Constitutional modification.

These circumstances constituted the unique opportunity of Roman law to go out and possess the world.

Chronology of the Law:                                                      B.C

Urbs condita, ......................................................... 753
Consuls (with Republic), ........................................ 509
Secession and Tribunes, ........................................ 494
Publication of Calendar by Decemvirs, ..................... 450
Twelve Tables, ............................................... 451-450
Praetor (along with Licinian law, that one Con-
    sul must be a plebeian), ............................... 367(?)
Plebeians admitted Praetors, ................................. 337
Publication of Formulae (L.A.), ............................. 304
Plebeian Pontiffs, ............................................. 300
Tiberius Coruncanius, first plebeian Pontifex
    Maximus, gives advice and instruction to all
    comers, ...................................................... 254
Praetor peregrinis, ............................................. 242
Four Praetors ..................................................... 227
Six Praetors, ..................................................... 197

Commentaria tripertita of Aelius (who published formulae, 204, and was Consul, 198), a commentary on Tables, formulae, and juristic acts, caused the whole science of interpretation to pass from the pontiffs to the (learned) laity.

Jus Gentium enters, of necessity.

The Tables contained only jus civile, applicable only to those who enjoyed full Roman citizenship. Roman conquest extended her authority over vast subject populations who could have no part or share in this law; her commerce drew about her a great non-Roman trading population. The transactions of trade would not stay for the slow and elaborate ceremonies of the old law. Subject populations were not privileged to make use of that law. A law suitable for commerce and applicable to non-civilians became an imperative necessity. This was the Jus Gentium.

4 Here Wilson refers to "Establishment and Development of a monarchical world system." [Eds.' note]

*Distinctions*:

*Jus Civile (jus strictum)*, as opposed to *Jus honorarium*, "all such portions of Roman law as are based upon statute or custom." In the narrowest sense, *jus proprium civium Romanorum*.

*Jus Honorarium*,—law which is such by virtue of the Edict, the magistrate's use of the *imperium*. The means of introducing the

*Jus Gentium*, "That part of the private law of Rome which was essentially in accordance with the private law of other nations." It, too, was positive law, no less than the *jus civile*; and was binding upon the Roman. *Jus aequum*, as contradistinguished from *jus strictum*.

*Stages of Development*, shading off into one another, and overlapping.

*Dominance of the pontifical College*. The Pontiffs were from the first the assessors of the courts, whether of king or consul. The *sacred calendar* was in their keeping, and they alone knew the *dies fasti* and *nefasti*. The *formulas of action* were treasured up in their *oral tradition*. The early connection of law with *religion* had made them the depositaries of all knowledge of *what was permitted*.

*Praetor vs. Pontiff*: The sovereign judicial discretion of the consular magistrate (for such was in reality the rank of the Praetor) vs. the private law cult and exclusive *responsa* of the sacred college.

*The authoritative Jurisconsult*, commissioned first by Octavius, when he was Pontifex Maximus and so had authority to appoint without breach of tradition.

*The Emperor as Magistrate*

*The Emperor as Monarch. Rescripta principis* altogether supercede, after the time of Diocletion, the authoritative *responsa* of the jurists. *Responsa* and legislative process differ now only in form.

*Finally*, the *accumulating mass and variety* of the law and its sources (enactment, interpretation, commentary) make necessary, first a "*Law of Citations*," and then *a Code*.

There were several 'laws of citations'; but the most important was that of *Valentinian III*. A.D. 426.

Recast, 9 Oct., 1894.

## VIII.

### Roman Law (Continued)

*Means of Development*:

I. *The pontifical responses. Throughout the Republic* authoritative *responsa* continued to be confined to the pontiffs, notwithstanding the invading jurisdiction of the Praetors. The College "appointed one of its members every year to give 'opinions' on questions of private law."

*Their interpretations* sought to bring every thing under *the letter of the law*. They were a means of development, nevertheless, inasmuch as they sought also *a sort of 'common law equity,'* by stretching the letter (generally by means of *fictions*) to cover cases not explicitly contemplated in the *jus strictum*. An "*abstract equity immersed in matter.*"

For illustrations of the changes effected by the pontifical responsa within the first century after the XII. Tables, see Sohm, 30-38.

E. G., *In jure cessio.*

*Analogous Common Recovery* under English law (said to have been invented by the ecclesiastics to defeat the prohibitions of the statute of Mortmain). *The expectant grantee* summons the grantor into court to defend his title against his (the grantee's) claim; the tenant appears; the claimant asks and is given leave to confer with him; *the tenant does not re-appear*; and judgment goes against him by default. *The Roman lied; the Englishman abandoned the defence.*

II. *The Praetorian Edict*, by contrast, sought remedies outside the strict provisions of the *jus civile*; was *a wider processual equity*.

*Its foundation* was *the imperium* of the Praetor, who had consular power, and therefore sovereign discretion.

*Similar foundation of English Equity* in the sovereign grace and discretion of the king.

*Necessity*: the very limited application and absurd strictness of the *Legis Actiones*, notwithstanding the practice of allowing them to cover, wherever possible, what were in reality claims unknown in the old law,—e.g., damages for cutting down grape vines under the name of trees.

*Similar necessity for* the origination of *English Equity.*

(1) *Rigour and remissness of the Chancery clerks* in drawing up writs, and *illiberality of the judges (Pontifices)*

(2) *Inadequacy of common law remedies* in respect of,
*Specific relief* (the only cases of this under common law being debt, detinue, and ejectment.)
*Complex mutual accounts.*
*Collateral agreements.*
Threatened *irremediable damage* (injunction).
*Suppression of documents*, etc.

(3) *Introduction of Uses and Trusts.*

*Means of the Praetor's jurisdiction*:

*New cases*,—cases, i.e., admitting of the application of the *jus aequum*,—covered by means of *the Praetor's formulas*,—imperative sovereign instructions to the *judex*, stating the issue and the way in which it was to be adjudicated.

*The Album* (white tablet), containing,

(a) *formulae for the 'interdicts'* (administrative action by the Praetor himself, instead of by means of a *judicium*, in matters relating, chiefly, to the *public order*;

(b) *formulae for the processual agreements*;

(c) *the edicts proper*, i.e., the formulas described above.

Appointed B.C. 242

*The* Praetor peregrinus was *probably the first to adopt and develop the formulary procedure*; for in his court the L.A. applied only when both litigants possessed full *jus commercii*.

*But the real authoritative introduction* of the procedure into the body of the Roman law of course *took place* under the hands of the

*Praetor urbanus*, who also had occasion to apply remedies in cases to which the *jus strictum* did not apply. E.g., *informal sales* and loans, *negotia bonae fidei, letting and hiring*, etc.

> *Note*: *Formulas* were *admissible only where* a *judex* was appointed and *instructed de novo*; not to cases going to the centumviral court *or to cases* which did not get beyond the magistrate himself, *needing no reference*: e.g., *in jure cessio, damnum infectum*. In these latter the process was interdict.

*The formulary procedure tended* of course not only to supplement, but also *to supplant the* too inflexible and unamendable *Legis Actiones*; and really infringed upon the *jus strictum* in the most direct manner. *A sharp issue was joined*, consequently, between the *jus praetorium* of the Praetor urbanus and the *Interpretatio* of the College of Pontiffs.

There was *no* such *conflict*, of course, *between the responsa* of the pontiffs *and the* formulas of the *Praetor peregrinus*.

Recast, 9 Oct., '94

## IX.

### Roman Law (Continued)

*Legislation.*

*Legislation decided the contest* between the jus strictum and the formulary procedure, by means of the *Lex Aebutia*, B.C. 150,–after plebeians had been admitted to all the offices, after a plebeian *pontifex maximus* had offered public instruction, etc., etc.,–after the old formulae had been published, and a commentary upon them written.

*This enactment provided* that *the formulary procedure might be used by Roman citizens in the court of the praetor urbanus* instead of the legis actiones, in cases where the latter were applicable: that the formulary procedure might be used in the application of the *jus strictum*,–the very point at issue. [*Within the first milestone from the city.*]

This legislation was *afterwards supplemented by the "leges Juliae"* (probably *temp.* Augustus), *which practically set aside the legis actiones* altogether, denying them even concurrent use with the formulary procedure. [*See Sohm, 168, 169.*]

*The Edictum perpetuum* had, by Cicero's time, become *principally edictum tralaticium*. Every new provision was valid only for the year of office of its originator. But successive praetors habitually retained the formulas of their predecessors in office, while adding still others, as occasion demanded, to suit new concrete cases. The *edictum perpetuum* thus came to *resemble* a body of *case law*.

*The provincial magistrates, too*, with their praetorian powers, *had also their edicta*, of like structure, use, and import, presiding, as they did, over the development of Roman justice in the provinces.

*Codification of the Edict.*

"*Hadrian* (before the year 129 A.D.) instructed the great jurist *Salvius Julianus* definitively to revise the edicts of the *praetor urbanus* and the *praetor peregrinus, adding* at the same time to *the market regulations* (as to the liability of the vendor for faults, etc.) contained in the edict of the curule aediles. By order of the emperor, the whole was then *ratified by a senatusconsultum.* This is the *so-called Edictum Hadrianum or Julianum.* The edict issued by the *provincial* governors—praesides provinciarum—in the administration of justice (edictum provinciale) was *similarly dealt with* and finally reduced to a definite form."

*Result: not to make the Edict* binding on subjects, as *jus civile, but to make it binding upon the magistrates* themselves, who were henceforth bound to issue and observe the Edict unaltered. *The Praetors* were *deprived,* in short, *of the imperium,* and made mere ministers of the emperor. *See Sohm,* 56-58, 220.

*The Lex Cornelia* (B.C. 67) had already made it illegal for a praetor to depart from his edictum perpetuum. (*Sohm,* 51).

*For the rest, Legislation played but a subordinate part* in the development of private law during the pre-imperial period, *chiefly sanctioning* what had been otherwise brought about, adjusting the privileges of plebeian or Latin provincial, etc.

JURISPRUDENCE. Foreshadowed in the *responsa* of the pontiffs, but possible in its characteristic Roman flower only after the decline of the pontifical monopoly.

*Influence of Greek philosophy upon both jurists and judices.*

*Lay Jurists,* whose *jus respondendi supplanted* the responsive privilege of *the pontiffs* under the empire, became the authors of a scientific jurisprudence whose office it was to work, not only upon the letter of the Tables and the old procedure, but *also upon* the letter, and therefore upon the implicit equity, of the *jus honorarium or praetorium.* Its task was *to work the jus aequum into the general body of the law.*

*Such work* was, of course, *a source of equity,* hardly less than the Praetor's Edict. But there was this difference:

*The Equity of the Praetor* was remedial equity simply.

*The Equity of the Jurisprudents* went beyond formal remedy and served to develop *the intention, the bona fides* of transactions. It sought for interior principles rather than for serviceable process.

ENGLISH EQUITY *embraces both* these kinds.

*In administering uses and trusts* there was an effort on the part of the court to do what the jurisconsults sought to do, to *go behind the form* of the transaction to its conscience, its intention.

*Fraud or accident,* too, not discoverable or cognizable by the common law courts, engaged its attention. It endeavoured, besides, to restrain the assertion of *doubtful rights,* to prevent injury to *third parties,* etc. etc. *All matters* fell to it, in short, which were *too delicate and too intimate* for the dull insight and stiff methods of the common law courts.

IMPERIAL RESCRIPTA. The *official jurisprudence,* after having been lost in the general body of legal literature, continued formative in power only until about the middle of the third century,— *coming to the end* of its real vitality almost *at the same time with Caracalla's extension of Roman citizenship* to all the Roman world (A.D. 212, *Constitutio Antoniana*), which abolished all that remained of the (technical) distinction between *jus civile* and *jus gentium.*

*Ulpian and Paulus*, almost the very last of the originative jurists, were of this period.

*Note the following Periods*:

   (1) *Octavius to Diocletian* (A.D. 286). The authentic interpretations of the emperors, by means of *'decreta'* and *'rescripta'* run along with the *responsa prudentum.*

      *Instructions to officials* ('mandata') and 'edicta,' after Hadrian the only originating acts. Called, collectively, *'constitutions.'*

      *Senatusconsulta* the almost exclusive form of ordinary legislation during this period.

   (2) *Temp. Diocletian to Constantine* (284-337) the formulary procedure gives way to one wholly official, like modern pleading.

   (3) *Imperial legislation*, chiefly for the purpose of completely *accommodating jus civile and jus gentium*, and constructing a single, consistent, and sufficient body of law.

      *This*, the *period of* the *'laws of Citation,'* of which the principal was that of Valentinian III. (A.D. 426).

   (4) *Codification.* Principal and final, temp. Justinian (A.D. 527-565).

     (a) *Institutes* (a text book which had the force of law).

     (b) *Digest*, or Pandects (Citations).

     (c) *Code* (Imperial Constitutiones).

     (d) *Novels*, completing the necessary modification and expansion of the law by imperial legislation (notably in the matter of inheritance.)

Recast, 16 Oct., 1894.

Comp. *Sohm,* pp. 27-58, 76-97, 165-179.

## X.

*Roman Law* (Continued).

*Illustrative Cases of Internal Development.*

Introduction.

*The characteristic Strength and Richness of the Roman Law* lies in its great body of interpretation. "What was so entirely unique in the achievements of Roman law was, simply and solely, its masterly treatment of the casuistry of private law, a treatment which, while discovering the laws of a particular case, revealed, at the same time, both the elements of the cases, and the principles inherent in those elements, which govern all private transactions in general, and more particularly those which result in obligations,—a treatment which had solved the great problem how to reconcile a free, equitable discretion with fixed rules, the vindication of the concrete individual intention with the necessary subjection to its immutable, innate laws. It was in the writings of the Roman jurists alone that this masterpiece of Roman law had been accomplished." *Sohm*, p. 96.

*Direct the class to read* "Ancient Law," chapter IX., "The Early History of Contract"; *noting* that Maine uses the term *'nexum'* to include *mancipatio*, as the oldest form of transactions *per aes et libram*.

OBLIGATIONS.

*In this richest field* of Roman law, the responses of *the jurists generally concerned* such questions as, "The *capacity of the parties*, requisites of *consent*, consequences of *fraud, error*, and *intimidation*, effects of *conditions* and *specifications* of time," etc., etc.

*The method of amelioration and advance* was usually *the remedial procedure of the Praetors*; and the origination of these new forms of action, as well as the carrying out of the instructions of the Praetor by the Judex, were under the direct influence of the prudentes.

*Four-fold Classifications of Contracts* in Roman Law:

1. *Verbal Contract* (Sponsio, Stipulatio), to be discussed presently.

2. *Literal Contract* (*book account*). These literal contracts had the advantage of being in a sense negotiable by transcription, the debt evidenced by them being transferable by consent of parties.

   *Unlike Stipulatio*, it was not necessary that the parties should be face to face for the conclusion of a literal contract, or for its transcription.

3. *Real Contract*, performance on the part of one of the parties (e.g. delivery) constituting a (moral) obligation on the part of the other party, which the law undertook to enforce.

*Applicable* to:

Mutuum, (Loan for consumption)
Commodatum, (Loan for use). Gratuitous.
Depositum, (Bailment). Gratuitous.
Pignus. (Pledge for debt.)

} Nominate. An *'innominate'* real contract, when an obligation created by a promise performed.

4. *Consensual Contract*, an agreement without formality, or partial or one-sided performance, consisting simply in the consensus.

   *Applied to*:
   Sale,
   Partnership,
   Hire,
   Mandatum (commission).

*Besides which*, there were *quasi contracts. Not implied contracts*, but duties laid upon a person (e.g. to return goods received by mistake) where no agreement could be implied as intended, but where an obligation resulted in mere fairness and good conscience.

*For the purpose of looking into the development* of these, let us examine in some detail the *history of Mancipatio* and contract of sale. They followed lines of development very similar to one another; and, in connection with them arise all the characteristic questions of this branch of law: capacity, consent, good faith, error, conditions, etc.

MANCIPATIO.

*Was confined*, as we have seen, *to res mancipi.*

*It involved*, probably very early, *a warranty of title* on the part of the vendor. This warranty the Twelve Tables confirmed and coupled with a fixed penalty, double the price paid.

*The Tables also recognized a Nuncupatio* as a regular accompaniment of Mancipation. *"Cum nexum facet mancipiumque, uti lingua nuncupassit, ita jus esto"*—"Whatever shall by word of mouth be declared by the parties in the course of a transaction *per aes et libram* in definition of its terms shall be law as between them."

"*Cicero says* that, though by the Twelve Tables it was enough if a vendor *per aes et libram* made good his positive assurances (*uti lingua nuncupassit, ita jus esto*), *the jurists held him responsible for reticence* about burdens or defects he ought to have revealed, and liable for a *poena dupli* exactly as if he had guaranteed their non-existence."

*Mancipatio as modified by Nuncupatio.*

(1) *A genuine sale*, the price being actually paid at the transaction. (*Res mancipi*).

(2) *A fictitious sale: mancipatio sestertio nummo uno*, a mere nominal price. Thus the vendor escaped *actio auctoritatis*, —the penalty, of double the price paid (two sesterces) being practically nothing.

(3) *Mancipatio fiduciae causa* (or *fiducia*, simply). Used, e.g. for the transfer of a pledge, mortgaged, to be re-mancipated up[on] payment of the debt. Employed, of course, for a variety of other purposes, which wd. be served by formal ownership.

*The Nuncupatio evidenced the fact of a trust, but did not convey its terms.* They were contained in an informal collateral agreement. This latter was not actionable. But (reasoned the jurists) "the duty to deal with the object in good faith is actionable," being contained in the *Nuncupatio*. Hence an *actio fiduciae*.

*The plaintiff* in this action "could not call upon" the defendant "to do what he had promised in the pact, because the pact had not been 'nuncupated.' But he *could call upon him to do that which any honourable and trustworthy man could be reasonably expected to do* having regard to the circumstances of the case, the most important of which was, of course, the *pactum conventum* itself."

Recast, 16 Oct., 1894.

*The distinction between res mancipi and res nec mancipi said to have originated with the reform of Servius, as well as a regulated Mancipatio.*

*Nuncupatio.*

Comp. Sohm, 33 et seq.

Sohm, p. 36.

### XI.

*Roman Law (Concluded)*

*Illustrative Examples of Internal Development* (Cont'd).
*Contract of Sale.*        (*What of res nec mancipi?*)

> *After the Lex Aebutia* (legalizing the formulary procefure [procedure] of the Praetors and the establishment of the general action *ex stipulatu*) *Stipulation could be made a means of guarantee in case of res nec mancipi* (*habere licere*) or of *res mancipi* not mancipated; and, *by analogy* to the mancipatory warranty as regulated by the Twelve Tables, there was established a *stipulatio duplae* (which the aediles insisted on, at any rate in the sale of slaves); though the parties could by explicit agreement make it a simplum.
>
> *The Stipulatio* was *thus made to cover* every detail of *warranty.*

*Stipulatio: Its forms and Origin.*

> *Solemn form of question and answer.* "Spondesne?" "Spondeo."
> Originated about 320 B.C. (*Praetor p[e]regrinus* first appointed, 242 B.C.).
> *Three Theories of Origin:*
> "(1) That it was *the verbal remnant of the nexum,* after the business with the copper and scales had gone into disuse;
> "(2) that it was *evolved out of the oath at the altar of Hercules* and the appeal to Fides" (by which religion, instead of law, was made the sanction of engagements);
> "(3) that it was *imported from Latium,* which it had reached *from some of the Greek settlements* further south. This last view is the most probable" (Muirhead).[5] *Gaius* says that it was attributed to this last origin.
> *Development*: At first always employed to make *definite engagements,* enforceable by one of the actiones stricti juris (*per condictionem*), it was *afterwards used for indefinite* engagements, when it became actionable under the formulary procedure: *actio ex stipulatu.*

*Actio empti. Stipulatio,* with its warranties, next *becomes a presumption of law,* so that it is no longer necessary to allege a definite guarantee, but only a sale: that the thing was bought. *Warranty taken for granted* in every sale

> *At first an actio juris stricti,* therefore, in which the judge could not look beyond the letter of the engagements entered into, *it became* in the later years of the Republic an *actio bonae fidei.* In cases, e.g., where the warranties had been accidentally overlooked.
> *This is the principle:* "As the stipulatio duplae is a thing of universal observance, action on the ground of eviction will lie *ex empto* if perchance the vendor of a slave have failed to give this stipulatory guarantee, for everything that is of general custom or practice ought to be in view of the judge in a *bonae fidei judicium*" (*Ulpian*).

[5] Wilson identifies this reference at the end of this section. [Eds.' note]

*Formula in actio empti*: "Whereas the plaintiff bought from the defendant the article about which the action has arisen, whatever it shall appear that the defendant ought to give or to do for the plaintiff on considerations of good faith, in the value thereof, judge, condemn him; otherwise acquit him."

*Formula in actio ex stipulatu*: "Whereas the plaintiff got from the defendant a stipulation that certain sheep he bought from him were healthy, etc., and that he, the plaintiff, should be free to hold them (habere licere), whatever it shall appear that the defendant ought in respect of the value thereof to give or to do for the plaintiff," etc.

*Result*: "It made *a sale a purely consensual* contract in which, in virtue of the simple agreement to buy and sell, all the obligations on either side that usually attended it were held embodied without express formulation or (still less) stipulatory or literal engagement. And, in instructing the judges to decide in every case between buyer and seller suing *ex empto* or *ex vendito* on principles of good faith, it really e[m]powered them to go far beyond 'general custom and practice,' and to take cognizance of everything that in fairness and equity and common sense ought to influence their judgment, so as to enable them freely to do justice between the parties in any and every question that might directly or indirectly arise out of their relation as seller and buyer." Muirhead, Britannica, XX, 701, 2nd. column.

*Here was the open door for the* entrance of the jurists with their *"casuistry of private law."*

## XII.

*History of Roman Law in the Middle Ages.*

The Roman Law of the Middle Ages *does not rest immediately upon* the great structure of *Justinian*. The codification of Justinian (A.D. 529-534) came after the barbarian invasions,—after the so-called fall of the Western Empire (476). The history of Roman Law overlaps the beginnings of the Middle Age[s], and *the work of Tribonian (done in the East) came too late* to affect directly the first formations of the later law of Europe.

*It rested upon the earlier Codifications:*

A.D. *299 (circa), temp.* Diocletian, (284-305) *Gregorianus*, probably at the emperor's suggestion, prepared a collection of Rescripts, *plus* a few Edicts.

A.D. *365 (circa)–temp.* Valentinian I.—*Hermogenianus* compiled a similar code by way of supplement, no doubt, to the above.
*These*, though private collections, *received legislative recognition* from Theodosius and Valentinian.

A.D. *426,–temp.* Valentinian III.—*"Law of Citations."*

A.D. *429, Theodosius* appointed a commission to collate the writings of the jurists, together with the collections of Greg. and Hermog., and the edictal legislation since Constantine. *This came to nothing.*

A.D. *435, another commission*, to collect the Edicts. *Its work published, 438.* The Edicts thus collected "cover the whole field of law, private and public, civil and criminal, fiscal and municipal, military and ecclesiastical." *Subsequent Edicts* became "*Novellae constitutiones.*"

*The Barbarian Codes.*

*Nature of the Germanic Conquest.*

In Germany, of course (i.e., beyond the Rhine) kingdoms wholly Teutonic in origin and population were established. *But in Italy, France, and Spain* it was quite otherwise. There the Roman, or Romanized, populations were neither destroyed nor displaced. Although subjected, they were suffered to retain their property in part, and their law altogether. This particularly true of the cities.

*Hence the necessity for the formulation of Codes. In some instances* (e.g., that of the Burgundians) there was *a double codification*: a *code for the Teutonic portion* of the population, and *a code for the Roman portion*. A necessary definition of Rights

*Principal Barbarian Codes*, the following:

(1) *Lex Romana Burgundionum*, codified by King *Gundobad* circa 500 A.D. (The Burgundians on Rhone and Saône, 445 A.D.).

*The same king* had issued in 495 the so-called *Lex Gundobada*, a collection of ordinances of his own and his predecessors'. The *Lex Romana followed*, in the form of instructions to judges concerning criminal, private, and processual law.

It had the *same arrangement of topics* as the *Lex Gundobada.*

*Sources*: the three Roman codices (Gregorianus, Hermogenianus, Theodosianus), Pauli Sententiae, a writing of Gaius, and the text books and 'interpretations' of the schools.

*Added*, after the Frankish invasion, *to the Breviary* (below).

(2) *Lex Romana Visigothorum* (*Breviarium* Alarici), by *Alaric II.* (484-507), A.D. 506. *Goths and Romans lived under separate systems* of law *until the middle of the seventh century.*

*Sources of the "Breviary"*: (1) Enactments from the Theodosian code and subsequent Novels; (2) Gaius, Paulus, Greg., Hermog., Rescripta, and (one sentence of) Papinian's Responses. *Distinguished*, in its arrangement, *between Lex and Jus.* (Savigny, II., 46).[6] Hence our chief knowledge of Paulus.

*Superceded*, circa 650, *in Spain*, by a new *Lex Visigothorum*, which was a mixture of Roman law and Gothic custom. *Compiled by Romish priests*, and much affected by the Breviary.

*Not superceded in the south of France* until the 12th. century: when the Justinian code supplanted it.

*Published also in the north*, where it constituted the only source of Roman law for Germany and England until the 11th. century

*Visigothic Kingdom (Toulouse), 415-507; in Spain (Toledo), 507-711.*

6 Wilson identifies this reference at the end of this section. [Eds.' note]

Although used in the Frankish kingdom, however, *it never received legislative adoption or sanction there*. The Roman population there was less numerous and less separate; and Teutonic custom finally prevailed. *Hence the distinction*: "*pays du droit coutumier*" and "*pays du droit écrit.*"

(3) *Edictum Theodorici*, of the Ostrogothic kingdom in Italy (495-555,–Narses). By *Theodoric the Great* (495-526).   511-515 A.D.

Th[e]odoric *wished to be regarded as the successor of the Caesars*, and to restore the Empire at its original seats. He had no thought of destroying the Roman law, but intended, rather, to give it legislative sanction, for all classes of his subjects.

*The Edictum concerned*, especially, criminal law and procedure.

*Sources*: the three codices, Paulus, and the *Interpretatio*.

It was Roman law with the addition of some new matter. *The Lombards* for a time stamped out Roman law in upper Italy (except, perhaps, in matters of family law and inheritance), and *Lombard law remained comparatively free from Roman elements until the middle of the seventh century*. Only upon the extension of their kingdom was its influence felt. After its overthrow, their law was supplanted by the *Corpus Juris*.   568 A.D. till *Charles the Great* (774).

*Meanwhile Lombard lawyers had created a school of Jurisprudence at Pavia*, whose commentaries set the model for the later glossators of the Roman law.

*Christianity* was the *state religion* of the Empire; *the code and Novels* contained a considerable body of ecclesiastical provisions; and the maxim "*Ecclesia* (the organization, not the members severally) *vivit lege Romana*" was true almost from the first in Italy. *Hence the* peculiar Romanistic development of *Canon Law*.

*Character of the Barbarian Codes*:

*Crude and unscientific*, of course, containing very little of the characteristic riches of the Roman law. Made up, rather, of selected general statements of imperative (positive) law, adapted to the new uses in contemplation. Affected perceptibly, too, by Germanic law. Not pure Roman law by any means, even in the parts adopted.

*The best of them, that of Alaric*, with its excerpts from Gaius, Paulus, Papinian, etc.; and its *sensible Interpretatio*, directing the manner of its application.

*The Breviary became*, along with the records of Germanic law, *the basis of legal instruction in the German convent schools*.

*The law which supplanted it* in the eleventh century was, not the law books of Justinian as they were originally given forth, but as they came out of the schools of Italy (a combination of Roman, Lombard, and Canon law).

*References*: *Sohm's* Institutes, 91-97.

G. G. *Bruns* (and A. Pernice), "Geschichte und Quellen der römischen Rechts," in Holtzendorff's *Encyklopädie der Rechtswissenschaft* (ed. 1890), pp. 176-183.

*Savigny*, F. C. v., "Geschichte des römischen Rechts im Mittelalter," vol. II.

## XIII.

ROMAN LAW *in the* MIDDLE AGES.
(*Continued*)

| *Character of Germanic Law* | *Infiltration of Roman Legal Principles.* |
|---|---|
| 1. *On the side of Public Law,* framed for tribal and communal organization, and unfitted for large and ordered kingdoms, such as were constructed after migration and conquest. | A law which gave clear statement and recognition to imperial authority such as the new monarchs wished to establish for the consolidation of their kingdoms. |
| 2. *On the side of Private Law,* fully developed, but based upon a plan of communal justice and popular courts wh. was not destined to survive. E.g., declaration of law by the freemen, compurgation, etc. | A suitable systematic basis for the reconstruction of the *administration of justice* upon the inevitable decline and eventual extinction of the popular courts. This decay and substitution earlier in England & France than in Germany: with results to be discussed later. |

*The infiltration, however, was mutual*: Germanic ideas and principles penetrating the body of Roman law, as well as Roman the Germanic; though the more systematic body of principles naturally had the advantage in such a contest for influence in the courts.

STUDY OF ROMAN LAW.

*General Influences* which induced it: Not only *presence of a Romanized population*, for wh. the administration of the Roman Law was necessary, but also:

1. *The Church.* The Roman Catholic Church early effected a *conquest of the invaders.* Its law (the canon law) was deeply tinged with the maxims of the Roman jurisprudence;

    *Its constitution* sought a perpetuation (on the spiritual side) of the unity and power of the Roman Empire: was a *sort of spiritual imperialism*;

    Most important of all, *its clergy possessed the learning of the time* and were fitted for counselling in matters of organization and discipline. *Note* their great presidential influence in the framing of the (e.g., Visigothic) codes

    *Note, moreover,* the influence of the Church "in diffusing the conceptions of *free contract, individual property,* and *testamentary succession* through the regions beyond the Roman Empire which were peopled by communities held together by the primitive tie of consanguinity" of which Maine speaks. "*The Will,* the *Contract,* and the *Separate Ownership,* were indispensable to the Church as the donee of pious gifts; and they were also characteristic and essential

"*Early History of Institutions,*" Lect. IV., p. 104. With respect to contracts he is reasoning, directly, from the *Brehon* tracts.7

---

7 Commissioners for Publishing the Ancient Laws and Institutes of Ireland, *Ancient Laws of Ireland* (6 vols., Dublin, 1865-1901). [Eds.' note]

elements in the civilization amid which the Church had been reared to maturity." (*Maine*).

*The church organization was left intact by the* (christianized) *conquerors.* "*It cared for education* and dispensed *charity.* It drew into its domain the *entire control of the family relations.* It undertook, partly in its own interest, to *enforce testaments.* It was able to do all this because it had brought over from the Roman into the mediaeval world a *well-developed governmental organization.* It added to this a *complete set of courts*, with appeal to Rome." [margin: *Pol. Sci. Quarterly*, III., p. 150. Recall: "State, Statute, and Common Law."[8]]

2. *The Frankish* (and, after it, *the German*) *Empire*, with its effort to continue Roman traditions of imperial unity and power, its retinue of learned churchmen and civilians, etc., etc.

3. *The currency of the Latin language*, the speech alike of commerce, learning, and all public business: the common vehicle and repository of knowledge and the forms of business transaction.

4. *The Italian Cities*, and the special influences at work in them to induce the study of the Roman codes, leading to the establishment of the celebrated University schools of Law. [margin: *See Savigny*, "Geschichte des römischen Rechts im Mittelalter," III, 83 ff.]

   *These special influences were*, briefly, the close mixture (not mere juxtaposition) of *populations*, and the expansion of *trade. For the quick, informal, various opperations of trade* Teutonic law had made little more suitable provision than had *the old Roman jus civile*: the Roman jurisprudence supplied *the needed jus gentium.*

   *Populations*, of all the elements of the time, were mixed and united in the cities as nowhere else, by marriage, as well as by social, political, and commercial intercourse. *Every condition* demanded a systematic cultivation and development of law.

   "*In Justinian's Digest* the Italian jurists of the twelfth century found *a system of law* that was *adequate to the needs of the new commerce.* Schools of Roman law sprang up in Italy, were visited by students from all parts of Europe, and sent out masters and doctors by the hundreds. Returning to their homes, the civil doctors crowded the hereditary expounders of local usage off the judicial bench; under the fostering care of the kings and princes, there appeared a 'learned judiciary.' . . . *Thus continental Europe obtained a common commercial law in the corpus juris civilia, as it had obtained a common family law in the corpus juris canonici.*" [margin: *Pol. Sci. Quarterly*, III., pp. 151, 152.]

THE LAW SCHOOLS

   *Their establishment* began late in the eleventh century with *Bologna.* The call for the study led to a rapid multiplication of schools: *Pisa; Montpellier, Toulouse, Paris; Salamanca; Leyden* and *Utrecht.* The study taken up almost immediately *in England also*, where it was pursued until the sixteenth century.

   *This sudden spread and luxuriance* of the study is *impressive evidence of a common preparation and need* for it. Its accept-

[8] By Munroe Smith. [Eds.' note]

ance by the schools may indicate a clerical influence in some instances; but it was too general and too spontaneous to be attributable mainly to this or any other single influence.

*Priests and laymen alike* educated in these institutions and under the same influences.

*The masters of the new learning* very generally *participated in the administration* of justice and affairs in the highest tribunals and councils of their respective cities: benefiting both their own thought and the administration of the cities they served.

THE GLOSSATORS.

*Their Method*, probably *taken from* the Lombard commentators of Pavia. *Consisted* in marginal and interlinear comment, definition, interpretation, illustration: expository and textual rather than systematic. *The editing method.*

*Their material*: Roman, canonical, and Lombard law, *not the pure sources* of Roman jurisprudence.

*Chief Names*: *Irnerius*, at Bologna, in the early part of the twelfth century. Followed by a series of illustrious teachers, of whom the last of considerable importance was *Accursius* (died 1260), whose *Glossa Ordinaria* summed up the work of his predecessors, with additions and comments of his own. This was *the most authoritative* compilation of the work of the glossators. *Quod non agnoscit glossa, non agnoscit curia.* *I.e.,* (in Germany) only the glossed portions of the law were accepted as applicable and authoritative.

[XIV.]

*'Reception' of Roman Law in Europe*:

*What constitutes a 'Reception'?* Note the three European 'receptions':

*Lorenz Stein's* "Das Wesen der Receptionen und die Reception des griechischen Rechts im röm. Recht." in Grünhut,[9] I, 722 ff.

1. Of *Greek law* into the Roman.
2. Of *Roman law* into the Germanic.
3. Of *French codification* into the several national systems of Europe, and (through La.) of the American States.

*Two kinds* of Reception:

(1) *"Legislative"*: conscious, deliberate, selective, and upon lines of common development; as, e.g., in modern times, in labour reform, economic readjustment, relaxations of laws of real property, etc., etc.

(2) *"Historical"*: Through a score of channels, obvious or obscure, not only without legislation, but oftentimes in despite of it, and in the face of national prejudice and objection; through a process often centuries long; not here and there, in selected matters, but pervasively, because esteemed, by reason of its systematic and rational development, *raison écrite, ratio scripta*, the *'nature of the thing.'*

This latter is the sort of reception wh. is generally in the mind of those who use the term in this connection.

*"The historical implies* an opposition and struggle which

[9] That is, the *Zeitschrift für das privat- und öffentliche Recht der Gegenwart*, I (1874), 722-37. [Eds.' note]

is not merely formal, in legal conceptions, but rather in the great forces and factors which build up the law of a people; while the foundations of the legislative rest much more upon knowledge and a search for the useful and expedient." (p. 728). The former, therefore, a study of the forces which make law. It is a study of social forces.

I. *Example of Roman 'reception' of Greek legal principles.*

(1) *After the Punic Wars* (264-146.) (the Greek cities of Italy and Sicily having been absorbed in the Roman Empire) a sort of recognition of a likeness of institutions, and a conscious acceptance of Greek local arrangements.

(2) *In the Orient* Roman military supremacy was possible, but not Roman civilization. Necessary use of the Greek language by the Roman provincial officials. *Penetration and transfusion of Greek thought, education, sophistic training, philosophy* into Roman life, literature, advocacy, and of course jurisprudence. The Greeks looked down upon the peculiarities and antiquities of the Roman law very much as those learned in the Roman law must afterwards have looked down on Germanic custom.

[*Legislative adoption of the Lex Rhodia*]

In this second period *Rome accepted Greek views and methods* in the scientific treatment of her law. The *principle of citizenship* took the place of the family idea of state organization; and Rome accepted from Greece *the principle of free contract* in place of the restrictions of the system of family ownership and formal agreements. Greece furnished the thought, Rome the machinery.

"The *jus gentium* is the epoch of the political (as contradistinguished from the Quiritarian or gentile) private law of Rome, and the fundamental principles of *this* private law, so far as they were susceptible of development in Rome, Rome received from Greece. In *this* sense the reception of Greek law in Rome is the true *beginning of that which we call the history of European law*, the history of European society in respect of its civil law." (p. 737).

2. *What advantage had Roman Law* that it should be received into the Germanic systems? The same that Greek legal thought had had over the Roman system, *the advantage of being written, systematized reason*: the advantage of possessing a Jurisprudence of the highest kind.

3. *Reception of the French Civil Code* due to similar causes: the necessity for a rational, written, systematic reconciliation and formulation of the mixed and complex law developed in Europe in those countries where Roman law had been adapted to Germanic character and institution: *Germanized Roman law.* Same true to a great extent of the reception of the *code of Louisiana* in the United States. (*Comp. Maine*, "Village Communities and Miscellanies," "Roman Law and Legal Education," pp. 355 ff.).

7. *Period of Reception of the Roman Law* in the several countries of Europe.

It is *not possible of course to fix any definite date*: by very definition an "historical" reception could have no date. The reception of Roman Law was going forward, in more or less marked stages, during *the whole of the Middle Ages.*

1) *In the South of France* the influence of the Roman Law was powerfully operative from the first (*pays du droit écrit*); though there, as elsewhere, Frankish custom came to a hard & persistent crystalization in many things.

(2) *In the North of France* (France proper), the introduction of *Roman Law advanced*, speaking generally, *with equal steps with the centralization of the administration of justice.* Where the Crown could not effect the substitution of the general law for local custom (as was often the case) it effected the *codification of custom.* The Roman law never received formal legislative recognition in the north of France.

3) *In Italy the study* of Roman Law in the cities *increased the amount of Roman law* infused into the legal systems of the new kingdoms and principalities; *but it did not produce uniformity* because of the absence of a strong central power.

4) *In England there was a centralized system of administration of justice*, under the Normans, which was established early enough to give England an *independent jurisprudence*, and a more independent legal development than proved possible elsewhere.

5) *In Germany* the Roman law became "*Common Law*," in consequence of certain features of the development of the administration of justice,—*at the demand of litigants*, as we shall see more fully in a later lecture.

8. *Method of Reception:*—

*Reasons and opportunities* of reception already discussed: growth of central political power, and the need for a law of commercial relationships.

*The method* of reception *was Adjudication*: learning and the administration of justice in litigation. *Judgment; royal ordinance; written opinion* (that is, Jurisprudence).

*The Church* earliest supplied a common authority and a *complete set of courts*; and drew to itself *family relations*, as well as the laws of *inheritance* and, to some extent, of *contract.*

*The royal courts*, as they were developed, admitted custom, for the most part, only upon conclusive proof of its existence and of it definiteness, and *in the absence of established and definite custom* resorted to Roman Law as to a "common law."

*European* (particularly German) "*Common Law*" *vs. English Common law.* The former a foreign system accepted commonly as sup[p]lementary of native law. The latter a system of native case law, compounded of whatever elements.

9.  *The Question of Codification.*

(*See Sohm,* "Die deutsche Rechtsentwickelung und die Codifica-  *Omit '96*
tionsfrage," in Grünhut, I., 273; *Monroe Smith,* "State Statute and Common Law," Pol Sci. Quar., III., 136 ff.; *Sir H. Maine,* "Village Communities and Miscellanies," p. 355 ff.).

*Not a question of transforming unwritten into written law.* All law is now written in some form or other. *The trouble* is that there are (especially in cases like that of Germany) so many codes, so diverse from one another, so many imperative and yet different bodies of law, that the result is *"obscurity, uncertainty, and inconsistency."* This is noticeable in our own case, in the diversities of state law; How much more in the case of such national developments as that of Germany, and even that of France!

*The question* of codification is a question therefore, *of clear statement, system,* and *consistency.*

*Difference between* the question whether there should be *state codes* (the question principally debated in this country) and the question whether private law should receive a *national codification.*

5th Dec., 1892

## V [XVI].

*The Law of Germany: Its Sources and Characteristics.*   *Omit ('97) to p. 48¹⁰*

I.  *Conditions of Government under which it developed* in the several periods of German History:—   (*Comp.* "The Germanic Constitution," by *Sam'l Epes Turner*).

*These periods* may be defined roughly as follows:

(1)  *The period of the Frankish monarchy,* under the two dynasties of the Merowingians and the Carolingians. During this period there was a *veritable kingly authority* and power and a definite organization of government.   *Chas. Great, 768-814.*

(2)  The *"First Feudal Period,"* extending from the disintegration of the Frankish kingdom after its division among the heirs of Charles the Great, *to the* period of the *Interregnum.*   *843 (Verdun) to (1273) to (1509) to 1648*

(3)  The *"Second Feudal Period,"* from the *Interregnum* to the opening of the Reformation time.

(4)  *Period of the Reformation,* with its sharp contrasts of religion among the German states, and of the virtual federalization ensuing upon the Treaty of Westphalia (1648).   *Enter Roman Law*

*Then follow* the *steady decay* of imperial power and the final *inevitable dissolution* of the Empire. During this period the separate development of the several petty German states becomes more and more emphasized.

¹⁰ That is, to "Sources of the Law of Germany." [Eds.' note]

*Original Integration* (particularly in the matter of the administration of justice):—

(1) *In the Frankish period*. Under the primitive constitution of Merowingian times, the kingdom was divided into *pagi*, or *cantons, great and small*. Over the great *pagi Grafen* presided, as the king's representatives (probably the king's appointees); in each *small pagus* an *officer appointed by the Graf*. The *small district was the judicial unit*; and its court was a popular court presided over by the *Graf's* appointee. The larger district, however, had also its own judicial assembly, over which the *Graf* himself presided.

*In the Carolingian period*, there was *considerable legislation*, of a more or less systematic sort in the form of *Capitularies* (bearing a resemblance to the *English Constitutions*, of Clarendon, e.g.); and Charles the Great instituted the *system of royal commissioners*, resembling the English itinerant justices, (known as *missi dominici*) who went annually "throughout the kingdom to investigate the administration of civil, military, and ecclesiastical affairs and of the crownlands. They were empowered to hold courts, to correct abuses, and to redress grievances. The kingdom was divided into commission districts (*missatica*), and two commissioners were sent to each, of whom one was usually a bishop or abbott and the other a *Graf* or court officer." But *this good beginning* was *rendered of little account* by the subsequent processes of disintegration

(2) *In the Feudal Periods*. Here there was a *central Hofgericht*, with the usual feudal membership for the trial of each immediate subject of the crown "by his peers"; presided over at first by the *Palsgrave of the Rhine*, afterwards by an official *justitiarius curiae*. Jurisdiction over the immediate subjects of the king, over cases evoked, and over cases appealed. *In the royal domains*: royal officers, known as *Advocates*, with *Schultheissen* as their immediate subordinates (*centenarii*); these latter officers presiding over the courts intermediate in jurisdiction between those over which the Advocates themselves presided and certain village courts which were made up of *villagers under* the presidency of a *Bauermeister* chosen by them subject to the approval of the Advocate. *Judgment* was given in the principal courts by *assessors* (*Schöffen*); in the village courts by the villagers; and *executed by* the Advocate, the Schultheiss, or the Bauermeister, as the case might be.

Under this organization, the *Schöffen* were *laymen chosen from among the people*. The *magistrate simply presided*: q[u]estions involving both law and fact were submitted to the assessors; they *expressed their convictions* upon the case; and were prevented from going quite outside the law only by their own good consciences. This is the stage of that process by which the royal power begins to affect the administration of justice which Sir H. Maine discusses, at

*(margin notes)*
(1164)

Advocate.
Schultheiss.
Bauermeister.

Schöffen.

which *the king's representative presides and enforces judgment.*

There was a *similar organization in each of* the numerous *territorial lordships* into which the kingdom steadily tended to split up.

There remained for long, also, here and there, *Mark Courts*, where the old mark organization persisted and the markmen continued to govern themselves in all matters affecting their common property, etc., unabsorbed by the manor. These mark courts presided over by the *Obermärker*, whose office was either elective or hereditary. They *both rendered and executed* justice.

*Note the singular Vehmgerichte* of *Westphalia* which, resisting the tendencies of distruction of royal authority operative everywhere else, remained royal courts until the 16th. century.

*At the close of this period* we have the *Reichskammergericht* (1495), to be described under the following head.

*Dissipation of the royal power* and *local dispersal of jurisdiction*:—

1. The local dispersal of jurisdiction had begun very early, in the period of the Frankish kingdom, *by the granting of "immunities"* to ecclesiastical and lay lords and to municipalities. This, along with the process of *granting benefices*, was the method by which disintegration began.

2. *There followed upon this*, first the gradual, and then the *rapid dissipation of the crownlands* by royal grants, until at length the immediate property of the Crown was scarcely bigger than a single manor.

3. *Then,*—particularly in the times following the *Interregnum*,— came reckless and unlimited *grants of privileges de non evocando* and even *de non appellando.*

Through such deterioration of the royal power and authority, *the Hofgericht lost its hold* upon the administration of justice as a court of appeal. *The local Estates* of the several districts *kept the peace by treaty*,—by conventions of arbitration.

*Attempts at Re-integration*:—

*Establishment of a "Court of the Imperial Chamber"* (Reichskammergericht) in 1495, the first permanent royal court in Germany. It was given a regular constitution, a standing president and official membership, and a body of assessors of whom one-half were to be instructed in the law, the other half of knightly rank. *It had original jurisdiction over* those [Omit '97] holding immediately of the king; *appellate jurisdiction over* cases of the denial or miscarriage of justice in the territorial courts, and over complaints against the findings of arbitrators. It succeeded in part in organizing a system of arbitration. *But* the innumerable grants of the *privilegium de non appellendo* shut it off from jurisdiction in every quarter; and even under the oversight of the imperial Diets, which subsequently tried their hands at managing it, it steadily

declined in authority and efficiency. It was *too late to re-
integrate the Immunities.*

2. *Sources of the Law of Germany:—*
*Period of the Frankish kingdom:*—All in more or less barbaric Latin,
*The following Codes:*
*Salic* (fifth century).
*Ripuarian, Alemannic,* and *Bavarian* (reign of Theodorich, son
of Clovis, A.D. 511-535).
*Frisian, Saxon,* and *Thuringian* (framed at command of Charles
the Great, *circ.* 802).
*Formulae Marculfi* (Marculfus a Frankish monk), a body of Law
forms (*circ.* middle of 7th. century).
*Capitularies* (so called because divided into numbered para-
graphs or chapters), royal decrees, made with or without the
consent of councils. *Collected* 827, 832, (authoritatively, as
the law of Italy), and *circ.* 847.
   *Dissolution of the Frankish kingdom,* and disuse of the
   foregoing as authoritative bodies of law, tho' many of their
   principles persisted.
*Period after division* of the Frankish monarchy:—
*Royal Constitutions* of this time, generally grants of privileges,
or bodies of provisions concerning the public peace.
*The body of Law made up of*

| Customs and Conventions (*Willküren*) | becoming prescripts by authoritative sanction (*Weisthümer*), or *precedents* by judicial determination (*Urtheile*). | *Manorial Law* (*Hofrecht*) *City Law*[11] precincts (*Weichbildrecht*) *Common Law* (*Landrecht*) *Feudal Law* (*Lehnrecht*) |
|---|---|---|

*Compilations:—*
(1) In the 11th. century, a compilation of *Strassburg law*
(*Weichbildrecht*), which served as a model for many others.
(2) *In North Germany,* the "*Sachsenspiegel,*" wh. consisted of
(a) *Landrecht* ("Spigel der Saxen") and (b) *Lehnrecht;*—
both prepared early in the 13th. century by Eyke von
Repgowe (?), at the instance of Graf Hoyer v. Falkenstein.
'(a)' Continued in authority throughout the greater part
of the Middle Ages. '(b)' was superceded in the 14th. century by the *Libri Feudorum of the Lombard lawyers* (which
date in part from the beginning of the 12th. century.)
☞ The *Landrecht* of these compilations *excludes Hofrecht*
and *Weichbildrecht.*
(3) *In South Germany,* the "*Schwabenspiegel,*" (so called because assumed to be of Swabian origin), originated about
1276-1281. It was *imitated* from the "Sachsenspiegel"; but
it is free from the provincialism of the latter, "and intended
to give Landrecht and Lehnrecht wider application."
(4) *Other compilations of the same matters;* commentaries;
digests of legal processes, based upon various "mirrors";
indexes, digests, & adaptations to local use.

[11] In many cases a combination of *Hofrecht* and *Landrecht*. [WW's note]

(5) *Collections of the laws of various territories,* now separate and unified enough in administration to have developed a law of their own. E.g., an Austrian *Landrecht* (13th. cent'y) and a *Landrecht* of Upper Bavaria (1346).

(6) A *"Peinliche Halsgerichtsordnung"* of Charles V. prescribed "a uniform criminal process for all the courts in the realm having jurisdiction in criminal cases." It "had a certain vogue and served in whole, or in part, as a model for the criminal codes of the several Estates."

*The various body of law* thus sought to be brought together in some sort of systematic statement was of course *separately administered* in the several *"immunities," cities,* etc. It did not grow unified in administration by being made coherent in precept.

3. *Entrance of Roman Law:*

(*Comp. Sohm.* "Die deutsche Rechtsentwickelung und die Codificationsfrage," in Grünhut's Zeitschrift für das Privat- und Oeffentliche Recht der Gegenwart, I., pp. 245-280.).

*The period* fixed as that of the definite entrance of Roman Law in the law of Germany, the *sixteenth century.*   **Reformation.**

*This reception due* to various circumstances and influences, but *not to the poverty or imperfections of German law.* German law was both rich and full in its development,—at some points perhaps even superior to Roman Law. The *Italian Feudal Law, moreover,* was received also and yet there is no question but that Germany had quite as fully developed a system of feudal law as Italy.   **Not more highly developed.**

*It was not received,* either, *as* naturally *supplementary* to German law, *and suitable* to its development; for there were many radical *oppositions* of principle between the two systems. E.g., the *equality of persons* under the Roman system and the elaborate ranking of persons under German law; *Roman free alienation* of land and absoluteness of property and German restrictions upon alienation, communal features of ownership.   **Even inconsistent in some radical features.**

*Received because of* the *feebleness and disintegration of the judicial system* in Germany and the substitution (*without centralization*) of single judges subject to appointment for the old popular courts. (☞ See -8-, *"After the Interregnum."*)[12]   **The Cause.**

*In France and England* this substitution had taken place, along with an effective centralization, *so early as the eleventh century;* but *in Germany* it was postponed until the *thirteenth;* and was not even then accompanied by any vital or systematic control on the part of the imperial power. *The royal courts remained weak,* and lay, not at the centre, but upon the outskirts of the system of adjudication.   **But *more definitely,* in Eng., temp. *Henry II.* (1154-1189); in France, *Louis IX.,* (1226-1270).**

*Throughout the Middle Ages the popular courts remained the only vital courts in Germany;* in France, during the same period, as well as *in England,* instructed, if not learned, judges were taking the place of these courts, and *science supplanted the common conviction* as the basis of adjudication.

---

[12] Here Wilson refers to the original pagination of this section. *"After the Interregnum"* follows soon. [Eds.' note]

*In the 10th. century* a school of royal judges arose at *Pavia* for the cultivation of the practical science of the Lombard law. It was the exigetical method of this school that furnished the glossators with models. *In the 13th. century an indigenous science of law* arose in the same way in *France* and *England*. *"Das Volksgericht ist der geborene Feind der Jurisprudenz."* And when the popular courts did at length decay in Germany, as was inevitable, by reason of the weakness of the imperial courts, their disappearance accrued, not to the benefit of the native jurisprudence, but to that of the foreign jurisprudence.

*After the Interregnum*, such popular courts as remain are mere *bäuerliche Gerichte*: the administration of *justice* has everywhere become *an official function*,—the function of some deputy of the feudal lord,—a *Schultheiss*, with his *Schöffen* or assessors. But these are not learned judges. *Instead of the common conviction* of the popular courts we have the particular convictions of these remnants of the great body of freemen, the Schöffen.

*It was upon the initiative of litigants* that a foreign system of law was introduced. They were *dissatisfied with* the administration of justice in *the Schöffengerichte*: they wanted a court, a magistrate, learned in the law: the royal power supplied them with none: *they sought* therefore, *the* highest administrative officer within their reach (*Amstmann*,—sixteenth century), *who accepted a voluntary jurisdiction* and acted as arbitrator.

☞ *"The single judge must* be a learned judge, by the same necessity by which the old popular court was an unlearned court."

*"The Roman* law was *received*, not because it was the Roman, not because it was the better law, but *because it was scientific law*,"—not because of its content, but because of its form and exactitude. "Because we needed the foreign *jurisprudence*, we received the foreign law."

*The judges* were *learned in the Italian jurisprudence*, if in any; *Germans* had *studied jurisprudence in Italy* for long: it had been *taught*, indeed from their foundation *in the German universities. Theological students* had to study the Roman and canonical law as part of their regular training: for it formed the basis of the administration of the spiritual courts. "The occurrence which we call the reception of foreign law consisted entirely in this, that the jurisprudence which already ruled in the spiritual courts took possession also of the civil courts."

*What was received* was *not the Corpus Juris*, but the common law of Italy, founded upon the Roman, canon, and Lombard law. *"The Corpus Juris was terra incognita to the German jurists of the period of the reception."* "Not the Pandects, but the *usus modernus Pandectarum* of the Italian lawyers." It was *Savigny* who first carried German jurisprudence back to the pure sources of the Roman law: *and great was the confusion produced by the substitution*, on the part of the historical school, of the books of Justinian for the *Usus modernus*.

4. *New Compilations*, after the Reception; new Spiegel, combining Omit '97
   both German and Roman law.
   (1) *"Der richterliche Klagspiegel,"* ed. 1516 by Sebastian *Brandt*,
       having appeared first in the early part of the previous cen-
       tury;
   (2) *Laienspiegel*, 1509 (Ulrich Tengler with assistance from
       Brandt).
   (3) Accompanying the Roman Law, came the *Libri Feudorum*,
       supplanting all German compilations of Lehnrecht.

5. *Legislative embodiment* of the Roman Law.
   I. *Before Westphalia*, the Romanizing of German law "was pro-
      moted by several works that appeared in the sixteenth cen-
      tury, but more by legislation, and especially by *provincial and
      municipal legislation*. Several provincial *Landrechte* were pub-
      lished, embued with the principles of the civil law, notable
      among which were the *Landrechte* of Württemberg and of the
      Palsgraviate of the Rhine; the revised Bavarian *Landrecht* of
      1616; the *Landesordnungen* of Tyrol, Henneberg, and Solms;
      and the *Landesconstitutiones* of the Elector of Saxony, of
      1572."
      *Same influences* at work also in the various *"Reformations"*
      of the laws *of the imperial cities*, effected *by their jurists*:
      e.g., the Nuremberg *Reformation* of 1564 and the *Reforma-
      tions* of Frankfort, of Freiburg (i.B.), and of Hamburg.
      *Public law* was represented during this period by various
      *Wahlcapitulationen*.
   2. *After Westphalia* (1648), the *provincial Estates*, the ruling
      power hitherto, were largely *disregarded*, or, if summoned,
      were practically supplanted by *salaried councillors*.
      *Result, inter alia*:
      *Codex Maximilianus Bavaricus* (1750-1756).
      *Allgemeines Landrecht für die preussischen Staaten*
      (1794).
      *French Civil Code* (1804). "In force on the left bank
      of the Rhine, as well as in Baden in the shape of the
      Baden Landrecht of 1809)."
      *Royal Saxon Civil Code* of 1863.
      *Austrian Civil Code* of 1811.
      The *"Common Law"* (in the German sense), or the law of
      the Pandects, prevails, as supplementary law, "to this day,
      except where expressly altered by distinct local laws," in
      "Holstein with some parts of Sleswig, the Hanse towns,
      Lauenburg, Mecklenburg, part of Hither Pomerania," etc.
      (See Sohm's Institutes, p. 3).

6. *Net Result*: (*Comp. Holtzendorff*, [*Encyklopädie der Rechtswissenschaft*] p. 299 ff., §§ 28-30; and *Sohm* in *Grünhut*, I., p.
   263 ff.).
   *We must understand* of course *that neither* the German nor the
   Roman law *came out of the struggle* for supremacy *pure and
   unmodified*. There was in every case mixture, modification,

development; and the question in each case must be *What type prevailed?*

On the one hand, the German law contained jural relationships which the Roman law did not know (e.g., the *Grundlasten*); and there were, on the other hand, relationships (like that of slavery) recognized by the Roman law which could find no place or acceptance in Germany. *Sometimes*, moreover, *the developments of the two* systems had in certain particulars been *practically identical*.

*Speaking most generally*, the Roman law prevailed in the field of *procedure*, in the field of *criminal law*, in the field of *Contract* ("Obligation") and the field of *Inheritance*.

1. *The Italian law of procedure* wholly superceded the native; and with the native procedure went every right under native private law wh. depended on procedure for its recognition & realization. So went much of the native law of mortgage. "Der mittelalterliche deutsche Process hat seit dem 16 Jahrhundert keine Spur mehr hinter sich gelassen" (Sohm in Grünhut, 262).

2. *Italian criminal law* (whose *chief vehicle* of introduction was *the peinliche Halsgerichtsordnung of Charles V*,—the so-called *Carolina*) "With minor exceptions, the Italian criminal law of the sixteenth century has become the peculiar criminal law of Germany." (263).

   In its later stages of development criminal law was very profoundly affected by *speculative philosophy*, the humanitarian social philosophy of the last century particularly.

3. *The law of Obligations* (except mercantile and marine law), although a large number of contracts of a new sort have come in. E.g., contracts of *insurance*, contracts *to publish*, contracts for *annuities*, agreements respecting claims of inheritance, etc., etc.

4. *The law of Inheritance*. Except, e.g., feudal principles of succession.

*In the general field of Private Law*, however, there are *two bodies of principle*:—

I. *Roman Private Law*, which is the *Common Law* of Germany, and

II. *Deutsches Privatrecht*, the native law preserved under the legislation of the several German States.

   *The latter includes* a portion of the received law, the *Italian Lehnrecht* of the *Libri Feudorum*, which, although foreign in form, was from the *common Germanic roots*, and is commonly treated as of a piece with native German law.

   Deutsches Privatrecht *has preserved, moreover*, in general the

   *Laws of Real Property, including*

   The *distinction between movable and immovable* property,

   *Formal, public acquisition*, instead of the Roman *Traditio* (tarnsfer [transfer] of possession with the intention of transferring ownership also.).

*Mortgage by public record.*
*Reallasten* and the general principles of *Lehnrecht* as
   they affected property relationships
*"Family law"*
*Property rights of married women.*
*Guardianship.*
*Laws of association and incorporation.*
*Mining law.*
*Patent law.*

16 Jan'y, 1893

## VI [XVII].

*French Law: Its Sources and Characteristics.*

1. *Introduction*: We think of France as, above all other European
countries, the land of the 'Civil' (by which we mean the Roman)
law. *In fact* her territories have been the *home of customary law*
hardly less than those of Germany. It was by a very slow process
indeed that her law was unified. *Only at the Revolution* were the
blows struck which removed the obstacles to making it single
and simple. *Then* the *feudal burdens* on real estate were swept
away, the *principle of equality* before the law was made fundamental, the relations of *the church* to the State and *the constitution of the Judiciary* were revolutionized and the old law thereby
given a new foundation. Only then could the law be thoroughly
revised & systematized.

2. *Superficial Resemblance to the Case of Germany*:
   Here, as well as in Germany, we have a *multitude of provinces
and a multitude of local laws*, coming very slowly into definite
shape.
   *Difference*: Steady *increase of the royal domains* and growth
of the *royal power*, resulting in an increasing degree of administrative influence on the part of the Crown in even the greater
feudal dependencies, until the King's authority became virtually
complete. (See 4)

3. *The Several Parts of France*, in respect of the Development of her
Law:—
   *The French dominions in their entirety* included the following
four (4) distinct regions: (a) *Pays coutumier*; (b) *the Low
Countries* (French Flanders, a part of Dutch Flanders, Namour,
Hainault, and Luxemburg); (c) *the lands of the Empire* (Cam-
bray, Metz, Verdun, etc.); and (d) the *Pays du droit écrit*. For
our present purposes, however, we may neglect all but the first
and the last.
   *"The Roman-law Provinces"* (or *pays du droit écrit*) constituted but *about one-fourth* of the territory of France, viz. *Guy-
enne, Provence, Dauphiny, Aquitaine*, & a part of *Auvergne*
(though the latter was under the jurisdiction of the the Parliament of Paris.). These districts constituted the territorial juris-

(Comp.
S. *Amos,*
"Roman Civil
Law,"
p. 434 ff.;
and *H. Brun-
ner,* in Holt-
zendorff,
p. 320).[13]

---

[13] That is, Heinrich Brunner's article in Holtzendorff's *Encyklopädie*. Wilson
gives the title of the article later in these notes. [Eds.' note]

diction of the *Parliaments of Toulouse, Bordeaux, Grenoble, Aix,* and *Pau.*

*Their separation* in respect of their law from the rest of France was not *due* simply to the less thorough conquests by the Franks in the South. Roman law had exclusively prevailed throughout Gaul for several hundred years, in the north no less than in the south. But *in the north the disintegration of the Frankish kingdom of the Karls had gone much farther* and been much more thorough. The establishment of custom to the ousting of Roman law (*in the interest of baronial separateness* and independence of jurisdiction) took place between the ninth and the thirteenth centuries. *In the south the possession of the Roman law* continued to be allowed as a concession to the conquered, "*an inalienable constitutional privilege.*"

*Status of the Roman law* in the southern provinces: It was the ordinary law, which needed no proof. *Royal ordinances* were understood merely to supplement the Roman law and determine at most the method of its application; they *did not supercede its substantive principles. In the "customary provinces,"* on the other hand, the parts were reversed: *Roman law* was *supplementary* to the customary, filling in *lacunae.*

"*A much controverted point*": "Whether this supplementary law came in by its own inherent force, as a sort of common law, only displaced by the customs so far as they went, or operated merely by way of direction to the judge and as the best-organized expression of legal reasoning." (Amos, 438). *Probably the latter,* since Roman law got in by the *légistes,* rather than in any systematic or authoritative way whatever.

4.  *Position and Growth of the Royal Power:*

Comp. Sir Jas. Stephen, "Lectures on the History of France," Lect. IX., "The Influence of the Judicial on the Monarchical System of France."

*Division of France* into seignorial fiefs and enfranchised municipalities, with *haute, moyenne,* or *basse* "justice." In each division its own courts, the baron surrounded by his "assessors"— his immediate dependents, etc.

*A feudal constitution and court for the Royal Domain,* as well as for every other separate jurisdiction; but the feudal court could take cognizance only of feudal questions. *For other questions "Prévôts"* were appointed, therefore, *in the royal territories.*

*Increase of the Royal Domain, and of appeals* of one kind or another to the supreme authority of the king. *Missi dominici* once more appointed, therefore, who presently gave to permanent officers, under the name of "*baillis," with permanent "bailliages."* These exercised authority beyond the immediate estates of the king, *having jurisdiction in* all cases of "*haute justice*" (if such were not possessed by the particular feudatory from whose territory the appeal came); *cases where any right of the king* was drawn in question; *and cases of appeal,* leading normally to wager of battle.

*Imitation of this system* (*seneschals,* to represent the lord in his own proper court, *baillis,* and *prévôts*) by the several greater feudal lords, *resulting in a sort of uniformity* in the organization of justice throughout France, ready to the hand of royal power in later times.

*In* 1260 *Louis IX. prohibited all trial by battle* (a decree which applied, of course, only to the Royal Domain). ☞ *Result*: A more refined and thorough investigation of the final merits of every case: *its determination by some principle of law, instead of by some rude measure of mere might.* Gradual introduction, therefore, of *learned clerks* to unravel points of law, and decipher and interpret, as well as formulate, the written *depositions* which supplanted oral testimony as procedure began more and more to yield to the influence of Roman law.

*Supercession,* by natural selection, *of both the baron and his unlettered assessors* by these clerical assistants: the substitution of trained and professional magistrates for the old parliamentary courts.

*The royal baillis* (themselves tending to give way to instructed judges) steadily *more and more insist upon the maxims of the Roman law* with regard to the royal authority: extend the principle of the ordinance of 1260, *by analogy*: establish the principle of the *"declaration of residence,"* i.e. choice of jurisdiction, by suitors: etc., etc.

*Under Louis IX. royal legislation,* without consent or coöperation of any feudal assembly, began to be bold and open. E.g., the celebrated "Pragmatic Sanction" *vs.* the powers claimed by the Papacy in respect of ecclesiastical appointments and taxation by the papal see. *"One may not say,"* writes Beaumanoir, "that the king is of right the law-giver. *But* it is admitted that he may promulgate laws for the good of the realm; and it is proper to obey them, because we are bound to suppose them to result from a wisdom superior to that of other men"! Stephen, 280.

*The Parliaments:*

*At first convocations* of great feudatories, like the English Great Council, the "parliament" which came afterwards to be known as the Parliament of Paris, became, *first, a select body* of these, assisted by learned clerks, *and then the learned clerks* (by the usual process of selection of the fittest for the function) *without the select barons;*—particularly after its business became heavy, and the rule required the constant presence of the members of the tribunal in Paris. (Formerly it had been peripetetic, with the king).

*At first holding office* at the pleasure of the king, the professional members of the Parliament *gained a life tenure,* and *then a hereditary tenure,* becoming thus an exclusive class possessing one of the great functions of state.

*Baillis and Prévôts, too,* once feudal princes, were first *compelled to act by proxy, through trained clerks,* and then to transform their courts, which had once sat with the usual lay assessors (the peers of the suitors) into bodies of clerks, the assessors as well as the presidents being men trained in the law.

*Steady extension, meanwhile, of the right of appeal.* Doctrine that every separate jurisdiction "must at first have been acquired either by usurpation or by a royal grant." If by a royal grant, then the grantee had all along been merely a royal officer, a dele-

*Marginal notes:*
Lateran Council.

Beginning of 14th. century.

gate of the king's authority, and might be commanded to whatever purpose the Crown desired. (*Stephen,* 289)

*Gradual creation of other "Parliaments,"* each sovereign within
its jurisdiction, in the same sense that the Parliament of Paris
was supreme, the erection of such a body being a sign of annexation to the Crown. Their organization and their powers alike
modelled on those of the Parliament of Paris.

"*Registration*" *by the Parliaments. Lits de justice.*

5.  *The Customary Law: thirteenth to fifteenth centuries:*

1.  *Compilations:* (Borgoigne, Touraine, Anjou, Amiens, Orleans,
Champaign, Berri, Rheims, etc.)

Comp. Dr.
Heinrich
*Brunner,*
"Uberblick
über die
Geschichte
der Fran-
zösischen,
Normann-
izschen, und
Englischen
Rechts-
quellen," *in*
Holtzendorff,
305, ff.

Let *the "Coutume de Touraine-Anjou"* serve as a sample:
Its date 1246. Current also in Maine, whose customary law
was very similar to that of Touraine. *Towards the end of the
fourteenth century* there appeared *a recension* of the Cou-
toume, consisting of the text with a gloss of foreign (Roman)
law. *About 1316 another,* quite distinct, summary of the customary law of Anjou was prepared, including judicial praxis,
written in French, but entitled "*Compilatio de usibus et con-
stitutionibus Andegaviae.*["] Soon after the legal customs of
Maine, Touraine, and Poitou was prepared. Then *this Compilatio was absorbed* into another compilation of the customary law of Poitou made in the latter half of the fourteenth century, and known as the "*Livre des droiz et des
commandemens d'office de justice.*" This was *made up of*
Roman and canon law, the Établissements of Louis IX., the
Coutume de Touraine-Anjou mentioned above, judicial decisions, etc. *In 1411 an assembly (Grand Jour)* of the higher
judges, advocates, procureurs, and notables of Anjou and
Maine undertook a reformation of the Coutume. *Then followed a series* of redactions, *until 1508,* when one was made
which lasted until the Revolution.

2.  *Codes:*

1.  *The "Assises" of Jerusalem and of Antioch:* Dating from
the first establishment of Frankish kingdoms by *the
c[r]usaders* in the East. "*The Assises* of Jerusalem and
Antioch are *the product of an entirely independent jurisprudence,* wh. serves us as a picture of *old French law* and
of the form of the State in which feudalism was supreme,
and which furnishes us with retrospective inferences regarding the purely frankish empire of the time when the
pervasive influence of the kingdom and of foreign law had
not yet made themselves felt. By means of these we can
trace, in contrast with the law of the Orient, *those juristic
works which appeared in France subsequent to the middle
of the thirteenth century.* Here literary production was
dominated by *the study of foreign law* as it was carried
on in the universities of Montpellier, Paris, Orléans,
Angers, and Toulouse. French translations were made of
portions of the *Corpus juris civilis,* and the native law
began to be edited in connection with abstracts from the
foreign law[.]" *E.g.,* the "*Coutume de Vermandois*" of

Pierre de Fontaine, 1253, in which whole sections of Roman law are transcribed, even in disregard of the question of their applicability to existeng conditions. *Brunner*, 310.

These *Assises*, therefore, are *"one of the most important sources of our knowledge of national French law."*

*Documents* of the law afterwards known as the Assises of Jerusalem (which prevailed also in the kingdom of Cyprus) were *lost* with the loss of Jerusalem in 1187. *Writings embodying it*, however, *since the thirteenth century.*

There were *two feudal tribunals in Jerusalem*, the one known as the *Haute Cour*, or *Cour des Chevaliers*, and the other as the *Baisse Cour*, or *Cour des Bourgeois*.

*The law of the Haute Cour* was cast into form, for purposes of legal instruction, by *Philippe de Navarre*, particular attention being paid to the *minutiae* of procedure. This work was *soon superceded* by a much more comprehensive edition or version, the work of Philippe's contemporary, *Jean d'Ibelin*, Count of Jaffa and Askalon, embracing the *Assises and Usages of the Haute Cour* (1266). In 1369 this was *promulgated as law in Cyprus.*

*Similar compilations* were made of the rulings and usages *of the Baisse Cour*, dating from the latter half of the twelfth century.

*After* 1204 (Capture of Constantinople) these collections became *authoritative throughout the Latin empire.*

The *"Assises of Antioch"* were of like character and had a similar history.

2. *"Li Livres de Jostice et de Plet"* (Plaid), a text book in the University of Orléans, published some time not earlier than 1255. Sets forth its matter *in the order of the Pandects*: 195 of its titles, out of 342, are directly translated from the Pandects, 31 from the *Decretals* (the collected rescripts of the Popes). *Its sentences from the Roman law* are *attributed* (for purposes of popularization) *to contemporary authorities*. Especially valuable as a contribution to our knowledge of the customary law of Orleans, and of the history of the *French law of procedure.*

3. *Établissements de Saint Louis* (1272-'73), once attributed to St. Louis himself. Consists of *two Books*: I. Containing—
    (a) Certain rules for the *Prévôté* of Paris;
    (b) An Ordinance of Louis the Pious, of 1257-8, concerning the reform of *the law of evidence*; and
    (c) The *Coutume de Toulouse-Anjou* of 1246.

II. Containing the *Usages de Orleanois* of 1254.

*The whole accompanied by a gloss of Roman and canon law.* The author probably of Orléans.

It was of *wide currency and great influence*. Commentaries and glosses were written upon it; and it particularly affected the legal development of Poitou, Champaigne, Brittany, Artois, Hainault, & Flanders.

4. *Philippe de Remi, Sire de Beaumanoir*, who died in 1296,

and who had been Bailli of Clermont, Seneschal of Poitou and of Vermandois, etc., etc., wrote *an Exposition of the Customs of Clermont* (1283), which enjoyed a currency and influence in northern France *comparable to* that of the *Sachsenspiegel* in northern Germany. Beaumanoir, however, was a champion of judicial reform and concentration and of the power of the State, as the compiler of the Saxon Mirror was not.

He *knew Roman law, but knew* also *how to subordinate it* in his treatment. His chief service is his *admirable constructive method*, which was thoroughly his own, and which neither his contemporaries nor his successors improved upon. He was also *a poet and the author of romances.*

5. *Le Grand Coutumier de France*, by *Jacques d'Ableiges*, worthy of mention because very frequently reprinted between the date of its publication (1389) and 1539, as a practical handbook, so that its influence became extended and pervasive.

*Collections* were *also* made, from time to time, *of Judgments and Decisions*, notably of the Parl. of Paris.

*Influence of clerical lawyers* in all this work of compilation and recension:

"*To clerical lawyers France was indebted,*—first for compilations of the legal customs of the several greater provinces of the kingdom, . . .—secondly, for treatises explanatory of those customs, among wh. those of Beaumanoir and *De Fontaines*[14] were the most celebrated;—thirdly, for essays towards the consolidation of them all into one general code, to be called '*Consuetudines Patriae*';—and, finally, for the actual preparation of one such code, which, under the title of Établissements de Saint Louis, was promulgated by that monarch in the year 1270." (*Wrong date*).

*Stephen,*
p. 267.

*Official Redaction of Customs*: (Fifteenth and sixteenth centuries).

*Reasons*: 1. *The irregular entrance of Roman* law, thr. legislation and doctrine; 2. The *shifting* and indeterminate *relations of the elements thus received* to local law; 3. The *shifting* and indeterminate *relations of local law to the general law* of France, which had been taking shape since the thirteenth century; 4. The *obsolescence of* much local *customary law.*

*After sporadic attempts* at official codification in various provinces (e.g., Anjou, Poitou, and Berri) *Charles VII.* issued an Ordinance (1453) ordering that "*coutumiers practiciens*" and the "*gens de chacun état*" should everywhere reduce the customs and usages of their several provinces to writing and submit them to the proper Parliament for examination and approval. *The work* thus enjoined was *spasmodically carried forward here and there* for more than a hundred

---

[14] "Coutume de Vermandois," 1253. [WW's note]

years; but it was *not completed until* the latter half of the sixteenth century.

*Method*: *In each province a special commission* was appointed, by the king or the local lord. This commission called together *the notables of the province* or parliamentary jurisdiction, together with *those learned in the law*, and submitted to them its proposals for codification. Their approval was known as a "Homologation." *If there was no opposition*, the commission at once promulgated the code. *Objections* led to reasoned decisions or judgments by the commission, against which an appeal lay to the appropriate Parliament. *Finally*, in either case, the "homologated" code was sanctioned by the king.

*Contents*: Not an *exhaustive* exposition of the whole law of the province. "*The common law*, partly Roman and partly Germanic in its origin," was in each instance *presupposed*, and *only* the *distinctly local or provincial* features of the *law* were *codified*. Unlike the compilations and codes of the thirteenth and fourteenth centuries, accordingly, these gave very *little attention to procedure*. Along with the provincial laws, moreover, went promulgations of the peculiar *laws of particular bailliages, seigneuries*, and *villes*.

*Result*: "Der Beginn der Fixierung der *Coutumes* bezeichnet zugleich den Stillstand in der Geschichte des coutumiären Rechts. Die Fortbildung des Rechts geschieht seit dem sechzehnten Jahrhunderts vorzugsweise durch die königlichen Ordonnanzen, von denen die wichtigeren mit Zustimmung der *États généraux* erlassen zu werden pflegten." *Brunner*, 321.

*Tendencies thenceforth* (i.e., from the middle of the fifteenth century): 1. Towards the *final crystalization of customs*; 2. *Unification of law by* means of royal *ordinances*; 3. *Scientific formulation* of the law by Jurisprudence.

6. *Jurisprudence in France*: The French universities did little for the development of French law proper. The *collecting* and editing of decrees, decisions, and the rules and forms of pleading *fell to practical lawyers*: such collections being made for the several parliamentary jurisdictions. The *official redaction* of customs produced a plentiful literature of commentary, *first* of a practical nature (and here the principal name is that of *Du Moulin*, who died 1566); *and then* of a richer and more liberal character: and here the representative name is that of *Antoine Loisel* (died 1617), "who in his celebrated *Institutes coutumières* set forth the general principles of French law in short sentences in the form of legal maxims." *Eusèbe Laurière* afterwards wrote a commentary upon this work which greatly enhanced its value. Together they constitute "an indispensable means for the study of French legal history." When, *in 1672*, the *first chair of French law* was established, in the University of Paris, *Loisel's book* furnished *the text* for recitation and lecture.

The *names of Laurière, Savary*, and *Pothier* bring us down to the present century. Laurière took a chief part in the development of the scientific treatment of the *customary* law; *Savary* in the development of *commercial law*. *Pothier* (died, 1772) *Professor in the University of Orléans*, was *the greatest of the French jurists*. His principal works were, a *Commentary on the Customary Law of Orléans*, "the most excellent elucidation that ever French custom received," and a *Traité des Obligations*. After this came *a series of essays* on questions of private law, *which showed how the oppositions between Roman and French law might be reconciled or overcome*, and wh. served as the most fruitful matter for the Napoleonic codification. *Pothier* stands *unrivalled in method*, whether for *clearness* or *comprehensiveness*, among the great jurists of France; and his influence has been of the most profound sort.

7.  *Royal Legislation, from the Time of Louis XIV.*

Before Louis XIV royal legislation was without consistent plan. *Until that time* it was concerned principally with the unification and simplification of *Procedure*. From the time of Louis XIV uniformity in the principles of the law began to be insisted on.

*Method and Object*: After procuring a report of all old and new Ordinances relative to the subject, "to compare them with the views transmitted from the Provinces," and out of the whole form a *body "of clear, precise, and certain laws*, which shall dissipate all the obscurity of those which went before."

*Louis XIV.,*
*1643-1715.*

In 1667 appeared the *Ordonnance civile*, a general code of civil *procedure*; 1670 an *Ordonnance criminelle*, regulating both the principles and the procedure of the criminal law; 1673, *Ordonnance du commerce* ("Code Savary"); 1681, *Ordonnance de la marine*; 1695, laws governing the *ecclesiastical jurisdiction*.

*In the next reign D'Aguesseau*, the Chancellor, effected a codification of a portion of private law also: E.g., *1731, an ordonnance governing deeds of gift*; 1735, *an ordonnance concerning wills*; 1747, *an ordonnance regulating "Substitution"* (the creation of a series of partial estates, passing from one holder to another by the original terms of title). *This last* piece of legislation was so advanced in its principles that it *subsequently went almost unchanged into the Code Napoléon.*

*Louis XVI.* instituted sundry reforms in the spirit and *under the* influence and inspiration *of the philosophy of the Law of Nature*, presages of the Revolution and its characteristic work of legal reform.

8.  *Final Codification, (directed to be undertaken by the Constitution of 1791).*

*Comp. "Die*
*neueren*
*Privat-*
*rechts-Kodi-*
*fikationen,"*
*by Dr. I. F.*
*Behrend in*
*Holtzendorff*
*pp. 399, 400.*

*A Commission appointed by the Convention* reported a draft, through its chairman, *Cambacérès*, 1793, but it was rejected because not radical enough!

The legislation which established the Consulate renewed the project; and Napoleon undertook it. *Four men* were entrusted with the drafting of the work: *Tronchet, Portalis, Bigot de Préameneu*, and *Maleville*. By dividing the work among them they *finished it in four months*. Then followed consideration and approval by the *Court of Appeals* and the *Cassation Court*, and finally by the *Council of State*, in whose debates Napoleon himself took an active part. Then followed consideration (without debate) and approval by the *Corps Legislatif.*

The Code Civil, 1804:—

*Three Books*:

I. *Persons* (Personal and family right)

II. *Property*, and the several sorts of Proprietorship (Things, ownership, personal and praedial servitudes).

III. *The several means of acquiring property*, (Inheritance, transfers *inter vivos*, testaments, obligations, security, prescription).

*Superceded all other law*, whether Roman, customary, statutory, or by decree. The *Coutume de Paris* forms to a large extent the basis of the customary law of this Code. *The Code is unrivalled for precision, logic, transparency, sharpness and brevity of provision.*

"The Code Napoléon . . . *owes much* of its intrinsic worth to the exact and learned treatment of legal subjects *to which the labours of Pothier* gave so great an impulse." *Its distinguishing feature* is, "that it incorporates as regards inheritance, family relations, and marriage law, *the customary laws of France* with the jurisprudence of Rome; whilst *the laws of Rome*, in respect to Obligations, the rights of Property, rules of Procedure and Servitudes have been accepted as a model." (*See* "Modern Roman Law," by F. J. *Tomkins and* F. D. *Jencken*, p. 7.)

Other Codes: Code de Procédure Civile, 1 Jan'y, 1807; Code de Commerce, 1 Jan'y, 1808; Code d' instruction Criminelle, 1808; Code pénal, 1810.

Inheritance Family—Marriage —

Obligations—Property—Procedure—Servitudes.

Dec. 19, 1895.

WWT notes with a few WWhw and WWsh additions (WP, DLC).

## From the Minutes of the Princeton Faculty

4 5′ P.M., Wednesday, Sep. 26, 1894

. . . The report of the Committee on Special and Delinquents was presented & approved as follows: Resolved That Mr. —— of '96 be made a Special Student until his deficiencies in Soph. Mathematics are removed.

Resolved That return postals of the type used in Feb'y last be sent by the Registrar to all students having Conditions; and that failure to return these postals on time be reported to the Committee on Delinquent Students.

Resolved, That in view of the fact that Messrs. ——, ——, and ——, understood that they would be allowed a chance to re-enter their Classes this fall, provided they tutored in the summer, they be allowed to take their Examinations on the understanding that they remove all deficiencies at the first trial.

A number of Candidates were reported as Special Students who will be admitted upon presentation of Certificates of recommendation or dismissal and their names will be enrolled in Roll hereafter, &c

Resolved That Messrs. —— and —— of the Class of '97 be admitted as Special Students. . . .

The Dean reported from the Committee on Dicipline that Mr. ——, who had been recommended to the Board of Trustees for expulsion for his participation in hazing last year but upon whose care [case] the Board had not taken formal action, had applied for such a letter as would allow him to enter Columbia College. The Dean was authorized to write a letter stating the facts in the case. . . .

The Dean also reported cases of disorder by certain graduates of the College, members of the Class of 1894, whereupon the following action was taken; Whereas on the night of Saturday, Sep. 22nd, some members of the Class of 1894 visited certain rooms, destroying College property as well as property of students occupying the rooms,

Resolved That the Faculty refer the case to the Trustees Committee on Grounds and Buildings with the recommendation that as soon as possible they authorize the Curator of Grounds & Buildings to have warrants issued for the arrest of such persons.

Resolved, That the Clerk be directed to furnish the Curator of Grounds and Buildings with an attested copy of this resolution. . . .[1]

[1] There are brief WWhw notes dated Sept. 24, 1894, relating to this incident in the body of notes described in n. 1 to the extract from the Princeton Faculty Minutes, Sept. 23, 1891, Vol. 7.


## To Lucretia Shaw Woodbridge Perkins[1]

My dear Miss Perkins,          Princeton, N. J.   1 October, 1894

It will give me sincere pleasure to lecture at the Parker Memorial, as you so kindly suggest, and to take the topic you name, "Political Liberty, Expediency, and Morality in the Democratic State." It would be *possible*, too, for me to accept Wednesday, Nov. 14th as the date; but it would not be convenient,—on account of other engagements,—and, if Wednesday, Dec. 19th,—or any other Wednesday in Nov. or Dec., for that matter,—would suit you just as well, I should much prefer it.[2]

As for the honorarium, there is doubtless some sum, over and above expenses, that you expect to pay the other lecturers you name, and I will be quite content with that.

Thanking you very much for your cordial letter,
    With much regard,
                    Very sincerely Yours,   Woodrow Wilson

ALS (in possession of Mrs. Frank W. Nevins and Fanny Norris).

1 Prominent in the civic affairs of Concord, Mass., she had invited Wilson to speak in Boston under the auspices of the Benevolent Fraternity of Churches.
2 For a report of Wilson's address, see the news report printed at Dec. 20, 1894.


## A News Item

[Oct. 1, 1894]

GRADUATE ADVISORY COMMITTEE.

A joint meeting of the Graduate Advisory Committee[1] was held in the Osborne Club House at noon Saturday.

There were present of the Advisory Committee Messrs. Tracy Harris, H. G. Duffield, Allen, Wilson and C. C. Cuyler, also head coach, Mr. J. B. Fine;[2] of the Executive Committee, Trenchard, Millbank, Bissell, Elliott, James, Huntington and Turner.[3] Tracy Harris was elected chairman in place of C. C. Cuyler, resigned. T. J. Perkins, University Treasurer,[4] made his report and submitted an estimate of the expenses for the coming year. C. H. Bissell, baseball treasurer for the past year, submitted his report, which shows a balance on hand of $2,879.89. T. S. Huntington, treasurer of the Track Association for last year, also made a report, after which the meeting adjourned.

Printed in the *Daily Princetonian*, Oct. 1, 1894.
1 The University Athletic Association, which had general responsibility for and supervision over all athletics at Princeton, was governed by a Graduate Advisory Committee and an Executive Committee of undergraduates elected by the various undergraduate athletic associations.
2 Tracy Hyde Harris, '86; Henry Green Duffield, '81, Assistant Treasurer of the College of New Jersey; Frederick Warner Allen, '94; Cornelius Cuyler Cuyler, '79; and John Burchard Fine, '82.
3 Thomas Gawthrop Trenchard, '95; Albert Goodsell Milbank, '96; Clarence Hamlin Bissell, '95; James Johnston Elliott, '96; Darwin Rush James, Jr., '95; Theodore Sollace Huntington, '95; and Edward Bates Turner, '96.
4 Thomas Jefferson Perkins, '94, treasurer of the University Athletic Association.


## From John Bell Henneman[1]

Dear Professor Wilson,          Knoxville, October 1st, 1894.

I hope it is not too late to thank you for your cordial letter of last spring,[2] also for the material assistance which the General Catalogue lent me in some private work.

I take the liberty of sending you the enclosed programme of our Irving Club.[3] You will see by referring to the date of October first, that I have just been "talking about" you—in fact, have read a paper which gave me great pleasure in preparing, and to which, I can assure you, the club listened with all the attention that either the subject or the writer could wish. As I do not feel that it would be exactly right to talk about anybody behind one's back, I now confess this sin of commission, and trust that the liberty will be condoned.[4]

I suppose you will let me thank you for the article in the September *Forum*.[5] As an interested student in both subjects—the records of our literature and the history of our institutions—I could read it with peculiar sympathy.

[Walter] Page of *The Forum* wishes an article on the South Carolina social revolution—for it is little else—and I have been trying the last few days to supply one. It is my native State, and I have been watching its history for years with marked interest. I am not yet quite satisfied with some of my points, however—as it is not always easy to get the exact proof for positive convictions. For instance, there are some interesting points in the evolution of the Middle Class in South Carolina. In the up-country, even before the War, conditions somewhat favored the existence of what might more nearly be called a middle class. Then, by the post-bellum division of large into small holdings, consequent upon the change in the nature of labor, this process gradually moved southwards until a new "class" was differentiated. But, ready material is so scanty, I cannot be quite sure I have *all* the elements in my induction. However, perhaps I am seeking too much. Yet, I see *others* so often misled by following false clues. But pardon my troubling *you*.

You will allow me to extend the warmest wishes in the work you are doing, and with renewed thanks for your kindness, I remain          Sincerely yours,    John B. Henneman.

ALS (WP, DLC) with WWhw notation on env.: "Ans. 10 Oct., 1894." Enc.: printed program of the Irving Club entitled *Topics*.
[1] At this time, Professor of English and German at the University of Tennessee; later Professor of English, Dean of the College of Arts and Sciences, and editor of the *Sewanee Review* at the University of the South.
[2] It is missing.
[3] Presumably a literary club at the University of Tennessee. The university's catalogues for this period do not mention it.
[4] Henneman's paper, published as "The Work of a Southern Scholar," *Sewanee Review*, III (Feb. 1895), 172-88, was the first extensive biographical essay on Wilson. It is printed at Feb. 1, 1895.
[5] "University Training and Citizenship," printed at June 20, 1894, Vol. 8.


## A News Item

[Oct. 4, 1894]

MASS MEETING OF ENTERING STUDENTS.

There was a meeting last evening at 6.45, in the Old Chapel, for the purpose of impressing upon the new men the advantages obtained by joining Hall.[1] R. H. Carter, '95, called the meeting to order and introduced the speakers, who were Professor [Andrew F.] West, Prof. Wilson, Prentice, '92,[2] and W. D. Ward, '95. Prof. West showed the important part Hall played in college life, its advantages for a profession or a political career. Prof. Wilson followed with remarks upon the superiority shown in after life by a man who has received a Hall training over one who has not. The remarks of the other speakers were to the same effect. Mr. Carter closed the meeting with the announcement that there would be two initiations, one on Friday, Oct. 12, and the other two weeks after the mid year examination, and, as the pamphlet of information states, "each man will be required to pay the sum of $5 to the joint committee when he makes his application for membership. He will be credited with this amount when he pays his initiation."

Printed in the *Daily Princetonian*, Oct. 4, 1894.
[1] The American Whig and Cliosophic Societies.
[2] William Kelly Prentice, born New York City, Oct. 28, 1872. A.B., College of New Jersey, 1892; A.M., same institution, 1895. Studied at the Princeton Theological Seminary, 1893-94; the University of Marburg, 1894; and the University of Halle, 1897-1900. Ph.D., the University of Halle, 1900. Taught at the Lawrenceville School, 1892-93. Spent his entire teaching career afterward at Princeton as Instructor in Greek, 1894-97; Assistant Professor of Greek, 1900-1905; Professor of Greek, 1905-38; and Ewing Professor of Greek Languages and Literature, 1938-40. Author of several books and many articles on the classics. Served on The Inquiry, December 1917 to August 1918; captain, United States Army, Office of the Chief of Staff, October 1918 to January 1919. Died Dec. 13, 1964.

## Newspaper Report of an Address

[Oct. 9, 1894]

MONDAY NIGHT CLUB.

At the last meeting of the Monday Night Club,[1] Prof. Woodrow Wilson spoke on "Edmund Burke, the Man and his Times."[2] In his remarks he said: "Burke was a mouthpiece for English politics, and England may well forgive Ireland for all the trouble she has given if by so doing she might gain a few such men as Burke. Burke's words, though framed for the circumstances of the time, emerge to-day with vigor unabated. As a University man he learned much, but not from his masters. He took education into his own hands, seeking books for what they could give him in thought. In Cicero he found a master and model. Both his 'Vindication of Natural Society' and 'Philosophical Inquiry Into Ideas of Sublime and Beautiful' are apprentice work, and as philosophy have not worn well. He turned from philosophy to public affairs, which afterward became his absorbing passion. In his generation his tone must have seemed disproportioned to the part he played. His opinions were almost immediately transferred into conviction, and his generalizations, never derived from abstract premises, were always devoted to practical ends. In his Parliamentary career his associates felt that they were dealing with a man of broad outlook, and a philosophy of politics was visible in all his work. An intense party man, passionate in the extreme, he wrote calm papers in excited times. First and last a master of principle, he expended the full strength of his powers on the political questions attendant on the French Revolution. Burke should be remembered for two things, his effort preceding the War for American Independence and his administrative reform in the home government. He was the apostle of the great English doctrine of expediency of the higher sort."

Printed in the *Daily Princetonian*, Oct. 9, 1894.
   [1] Established by the Class of 1894, this organization, whose members consisted entirely of seniors, met weekly for discussion of philosophical, scientific, and literary subjects.
   [2] For the provenance of this lecture, see the Editorial Note, "Wilson's First Lecture on Burke," Vol. 8.


## From the Minutes of the Princeton Faculty

4 5′ P.M., Wednesday, Oct. 10th, 1894.
   . . . Resolved. That the functions of existing Committee on Special and Delinquent Students be divided and assigned to two Committees; that is to say that the entire charge of the Academic Special Students delinquent or otherwise be assigned to one Committee and the charge of the Delinquent Students of the four Academic Classes be assigned to another Committee. . . .[1]

   [1] After this division, Wilson became chairman of the new Committee on Special Students, and Samuel Ross Winans, chairman of the Committee on Examinations and Standing.


## A News Item

[Oct. 18, 1894]
### MEETING OF THE SOUTHERN CLUB.

There was a meeting of the Southern Club last evening, in the English room,[1] at 7.15. J. W. Garrett '95, the president of the club, called the meeting to order and introduced Prof. Woodrow Wilson, who spoke of the Southern spirit which existed in the college and its influence on college life. J. M. Scott '98, of Kentucky, was elected a member of the executive committae [committee], after which the meeting adjourned.

Printed in the *Daily Princetonian*, Oct. 18, 1894.
¹ Of Dickinson Hall.

## An Announcement

[Oct. 25, 1894]

### COLLATERAL READING IN PUBLIC LAW.

Prof. Woodrow Wilson announces the following collateral reading for the course in Public Law:

Freeman: "Growth of the English Constitution."

Sir Jas. Stephen: "Lectures on the History of France."

Bluntschli: "Theory of the State," (portion on sovereignty.)

A. L. Lowell: "Essays on Government," essay on sovereignty.

Maine: "Early History of Institutions," lecture XII.

Dicey: "The Law of the Constitution," lecture III.

Austin: "Jurisprudence," chapter VI.

Gareis: "Allgemeines Staatsrecht," in Holtzendorff[']s "Encyklopädie der Rechtswissenschaft."

Bluntschli: "Staatsrecht."

Laband: "Das Staatsrecht des deutschen Reiches," chapter II.

Jellinek: "Gesetz und Verordnung."

"The State," sections 25-69, 144-149, 165-169, 221-254, 268-335, 358-437, 515-558, 594-603, 624-635, 651-747; and chapters XI-XV, inclusive.

Printed in the *Daily Princetonian*, Oct. 25, 1894.

## A Newspaper Report of an Address

[Oct. 30, 1894]

### LECTURE BEFORE SOCIOLOGICAL INSTITUTE.

A meeting of the Sociological Institute[1] was held Friday evening [October 26], at the Seminary. Dr. Purves,[2] the president, introduced Prof. Woodrow Wilson, who spoke on "The Ethics of the State." In the course of his remarks he said: There is nothing accidental in the present prominence of sociological research. Modern science has given rise to it. Through the inventions of science, men have been drawn into cities, and have formed a congestion of population, which has brought the social problem upon us. Our great tendency to-day is sentimentalism—scattering sympathy broadcast, without understanding the causes or needs of the evil. This has hindered the remedy and often increased the evil. Few understand the true nature of the state. "A state is a people organized by law, within a definite territory." Its fundamental element is *law*. Law is made, not for a distinct class, but for the whole people. It must be broad in its conceptions. It embraces two elements: first, it is a body of principles, general and well defined; second, it is an active force, for whatever a whole community accepts is necessarily a ruling element. Progress includes everything that advances civilization. It is both material and immaterial. The special function of law is to affect progress immaterially—that is, to produce equipoise in the state. The factors of progress are struggles, religion, education and law. But this latter can be instrumental to progress only where it represents the true feelings of the masses. The social reformer must ever keep this in mind. He must study the organism and nature of society and never propose as laws those which do not represent the universal sentiments. He who violates this principle commits social immorality, for he transgresses the law of progress.[3]

Printed in the *Daily Princetonian*, Oct. 30, 1894.
[1] This organization, sponsored by Princeton Theological Seminary, was concerned with the practical application of the principles of Christianity to existing social conditions. Biweekly meetings, open to students of both the Seminary and the College, were addressed by members of the two faculties and by outside speakers.
[2] The Rev. Dr. George Tybout Purves, Professor of New Testament Literature and Exegesis, Princeton Theological Seminary.
[3] There is a WWhw outline of this address, entitled *"The State and Progress"* and dated "Princeton Seminary 26 Oct., '94," in WP, DLC.

## To Robert Bridges

My dear Bobby,                    Princeton, N. J.    16 Nov., 1894
    I will come with pleasure. I did not know that you had moved. Neither did I know when your vacation was to occur, and I called on you while you were away—had no card with me to leave. I have been, and am still, intensely busy: but I will come to Billy's dinner,[1]—and it will double the pleasure that I am to stay with you.
        As ever,        Affectionately Yours,   Woodrow Wilson

ALS (WC, NjP).
[1] William Burhans Isham, Jr., who in 1884 had begun the practice of giving annual dinners for members of the Class of 1879 at his home in New York. See Alexander J. Kerr, "The Isham Dinners," *Fifty Years of the Class of 'Seventy-Nine, Princeton* (Princeton, N. J., 1931), pp. 199-206.

## To Walter Hines Page

My dear Mr. Page,      Princeton, New Jersey, 5 December, 1894.
    I very cheerfully reply to your question as to my estimate of the present influence of the *Forum*.[1]
    I believe I never contributed to it before the reduction was made in its price; but I have been little less than astonished at

the number of persons I seem to have reached in the papers I have written for it within the last two years. Nothing I ever wrote, I am sure, ever attracted the attention of so large a number of persons as did my "Calendar of Great Americans."[2] If I wished popular notice and wide currency, I should certainly write for the *Forum*.

Moreover, I have recently heard the *Forum* warmly commended in all sorts of quarters; and a very general opinion expressed that it has of late been steadily improving in tone and quality: becoming more solid as it becomes more popular.

It gives me real pleasure to say these things, as I may, with the utmost heartiness.

Most sincerely Yours,   Woodrow Wilson

WWTLS (W. H. Page Papers, MH).
  [1] Page's letter is missing. At this time, Page was attempting to wrest financial control of the New York *Forum* away from its businessmen founders by interesting prominent intellectuals in investing in the magazine. This attempt was soon to fail. See WW to W. H. Page, July 4, 1895, n. 1.
  [2] Printed at Sept. 15, 1893, Vol. 8.


## To Frederick Jackson Turner

My dear Turner,      Princeton, New Jersey, 10 December, 1894.

It seems an [a] very long time since we exchanged letters: what's more, it *is* a very long time,—much too long.[1]

Have you not known for a great while what was coming: that I was going to ask you to read my *MSS.*[2] and deal most faithfully with me in the criticism of it?

But not yet. There's no whole, unit piece of it yet; and the evil day is still some little way off for you. I now simply warn you that it is coming: and beseech you, as you are an honest man and a true friend, to get ready to decline (kindly but firmly) if you wish or think best. I should lose a great deal; but I am not small enough to be hurt.

I can report progress. I am about half through with the portion I shall devote to the period from the settlement to the year of grace 1755; and I expect to have reached the latter date by next Commencement. It goes slowly, for I've fallen in love with "the sources"; but the labour is a most pleasant pain.

The only business object of this note is to ask you if it is possible for me to obtain a copy of that map that I saw in your study:[3] a photograph (was it not?) of a clay model of the continent. I have hunted high and low in these parts for the like, and cannot find anything half so satisfactory. Of course I have that very small reproduction on your university extension syllabus;[4] but that's too small. Is there someone from whom I could procure a large[5]

WWTL (F. J. Turner Papers, MH).
[1] For their last correspondence, see F. J. Turner to WW, Dec. 20, 1893, Vol. 8.
[2] Of his "Short History of the United States," about which see the Editorial Note, "Wilson's 'Short History of the United States,'" Vol. 8.
[3] Either when Wilson visited the Turners in late December 1892 or in late July 1893. See WW to C. K. Adams, Dec. 23, 1892, n. 1, and WW to EAW, July 29, 1893, n. 1, both in Vol. 8.
[4] See F. J. Turner to WW, July 16, 1893, n. 4, Vol. 8.
[5] The remainder of this letter is missing.

## A Memorandum

[c. Dec. 18, 1894]

Expediency is the first, second, and the last criterion of the excellence either of constitutional provision or of statute: and that nation, and that only, is capable of self-government which is capable of sufficient self-restraint to do nothing but that which is expedient. This is political wisdom, political balance, political self-direction.

WWhw memorandum (WP, DLC).

## Notes for a Public Lecture[1]

[Dec. 18, 1894]
*Liberty, Expediency, Morality in the Democratic State.*

*"In the democratic State?"* What is a Democratic State?
*One in which the people rule?* No: that is impossible. No one can be said to rule who has not the initiative; and *the People have not the Initiative.*
A *State in which the people are a condition of all rule*, and government is deliberately a[d]justed to their consent. A State in which the People have (not quite a veto) but an Objection.
*Choice* is *a function of the Few*: *Protest*, and *dictation of terms* of *coöperation, the function of the Many.*
*The Democratic State provides regular machinery for this latter function. Other forms* of Government provide *only irregular*, most perilously irregular, means of exercising this function.
LIBERTY, is *not* "scientific anarchy," *as little government as possible*: *but simply the best all-round adjustment.* "Scientific anarchy," if you will but analyse it, is the product of a reaction, *not against institutions, but against tutelage*: against the system under which their [there] was no regular adjustment between government and the general assent, but a few persons determined the rights and cooperation of all.

[1] Based in large part upon the notes entitled "Political Liberty, Political Expediency, and Political Morality in the Democratic State," printed at July 2, 1894, Vol. 8.

*Liberty is found only where there is the best order*, the least friction. The *machine* runs free with perfect adjustment; *the skein* is free that is without tangle; *the man* is free whose powers are without impediment to their best development.

Bondage of the *kite and sailing vessel*, held fast by external force. Freedom of the *steamer*, having an originative force in its own bowels. Yet the kite and the sailing vessel may also sail *"free" if they be perfectly adjusted to the force which controls them*, and so use it for the flight or passage they are essaying.

POLITICAL LIBERTY, *also an adjustment*.

*A reasonable accommodation between individual right and public power*. A properly adjusted balance between the forces of individual character and public convenience.

RUSKIN.

"How false the conception, how frantic the pursuit of that phantom which men call Liberty. . . . There is no such thing in the universe. There can never be. The stars have it not; the earth has it not; the sea has it not; and we men have the mockery and semblance of it only for our heaviest punishment.

"The enthusiast would reply that by Liberty he meant *the Law of Liberty*. Then why use the single and misunderstood word? If by liberty you mean chastisement of the passions, discipline of the intellect, subjection of the will; if you mean the fear of inflicting, the shame of committing, a wrong; if you mean respect for all who are in authority, and consideration for all who are in dependence; veneration for the good, mercy to the evil, sympathy with the weak; if you mean watchfulness over all thoughts, temperance in all pleasures, perseverance in all toils; if you mean, in a word, that *Service* which is defined in the liturgy of the English church to be perfect Freedom, why do you name this by the same word by which the luxurious mean license, and the reckless mean change; by which the rogue means rapine, and the fool, equality; by which the proud mean anarchy, and the malignant mean violence? Call it by any name rather than this, but its best and truest is, *Obedience*.

"Obedience is, indeed, founded on a kind of freedom, else it would become mere subjugation, but that freedom is only granted that obedience may be more perfect; and thus, while a measure of license is necessary to exhibit the individual energies of things, *the fairness and pleasantness and perfection of them all consist in their Restraint*. Compare *a river* that has burst its banks with one that is bound by them, and *the clouds that are scattered* over the face of the whole heaven with those that are marshalled into ranks and orders by its winds. So that though restraint, utter and unrelaxing, can never be comely, this is not because it is in itself an evil, but only because, when too great, it o[ver]powers *the nature of the thing restrained*, and so counteracts the other laws of which that nature is itself composed. And *the balance wherein consists the fairness of creation* is between the laws of life and being in the things governed and the laws of general sway to which they are subjected; and the suspension or infringement of either kind of law, or, literally, disorder, is equivalent to, and synonymous with, disease; while *the increase of both honour and beauty* is *habitually on the side of restraint* (or the action of superior law) rather than of character (or the action of inherent law). *The noblest word* in the catalogue of social virtue is *'Loyalty,'* and *the sweetest* which men have learned in the pastures of the wilderness is *'Fold.'*

"Nor is this all; but we may observe, that *exactly in proportion to the majesty of things in the scale of being,* is the completeness of their obedience to the laws that are set over them. *Gravitation* is less quietly, less instantly obeyed by a grain of dust than it is by the sun and the moon; and the ocean falls and flows under the influences which the lake and river do not recognize. So also in estimating the dignity of any action or occupation of men, there is perhaps no better test than the question *'are its laws strait?'* For their severity will probably be commensurate with the greatness of the numbers whose labour it concentrates or whose interest it concerns."[2]

*In confirmation,*

> *Note our instinctive homage* to the equable and elevated in character, demeanour, utterance,—not the quick shot, but the steady crack shot. Note *the impotency of irregular force*: the absence of dignity from an accident.
>
> We rightly conceive *the highest freedom* to consist in *self-government, self-direction,* a *self-originated rectitude* and adjustment to moral forces, a *self-sustained order.*

*Constitutions of Liberty* vs. *Constitutions of Government.*

> *The Differences*
> (1) *In Age,* the deliberate recognition and formulation of Liberty being comparatively modern.
> (2) *In Character: Organization vs. Restraint* of Government. Negative statement, accordingly, of the items of privilege. *Bills of Rights* are *meant,* not to keep the hands of Government off, but *only to prevent irregular and arbitrary* (unadjusted) *exertions of power* or authority.
> (3) *In Source.*
> (4) *In distinctness and sharpness of definition.* The Restraints need much more explicit statement than the organization, which may be merely habitual.

*Historical contradiction of Socialism,* which seeks to give preference to organization.

*A "constitutional Government"* one in which authority is restrained by *a distinct recognition of Liberty*: of an adjustment and balance between the freedom of the individual and the authority of the Government.

*POLITICAL EXPEDIENCY.* Whose field is *the field of statesmanship.*

*The Law of Progress* in Society is the law of Modification. This is the law that furnishes the standard of political Expediency.

---

2 John Ruskin, *Seven Lamps of Architecture,* Chap. 7, Sects. 1-3. This quotation was a favorite of Wilson's. He copied the first two paragraphs in his Confidential Journal on Dec. 29, 1889 (printed at that date in Vol. 6, pp. 463-64), and had recourse to the passage regarding "that Service which is defined in the liturgy of the English church to be perfect Freedom" elsewhere in his writings.

*Modification in the modern democratic State* means the adjustment and *accommodation of the general opinion and purpose to changing social or political conditions:—Law following after* and resulting from such changes, like a *chemical precipitation.*

*The GENERAL OPINION*, in this conception of progress, means the organic opinion, *the efficient opinion*, formed by the concert and prevalence of commanding minds,—not of commanding numbers, merely. The movement, *not* of *commanding, but* of *persuaded numbers.*

*REVOLUTION can never be expedient*, though it *may* sometimes *be* necessary in the sense of being *inevitable, as death is.* Then there is death and re-birth; destruction and reconstruction. But *Revolution destroys the atmosphere of opinion and purpose which holds institutions to their form and equilibrium,*—as the physical atmosphere holds man's frame together.

*What is EXPEDIENT SPEECH? Not that which* creates distemper and *overheats*, overmasters the judgment: but that which *points out the best means of accommodation*, and of Progress by means of Accommodation.

*POLITICAL MORALITY.* Has *no other standard than that of Expediency*, as just expounded. *The individual Ethic* is absolute; but *the social ethic* is utilitarian.

*"Sin is the transgression of the law"*: the law, that is, of political progress.

*MORALITY* is *the science of RELATIONSHIPS*, of the best adjustments, on the one hand, of man to God, and, on the other hand, of man to his fellow men.

*It is immoral*, therefore, *to act* as if *regardless of* these *relationships.*

*Progressive morality* is an *improvement* of these *relationships*, from step to step, not breaking the law of progress, which is Modification. It is always conservative, never radical or revolutionary. It is tender of conditions, regardful of points of view.

*LAW OF ENDEAVOUR. To create and illuminate social movement. The law of Instruction*, of illumination, whether by speech or action. *Leadership is necessary* in order to make in the political system an effective role for enlightening speech. *Speech must be rendered sure of a hearing*, irrespective of party.

*EFFECTIVE SPEECH comes from a true vision of affairs*, such as will appeal to those who know and have their eyes always open, as well as to those who simply feel and have their hearts open. When what is seen with such vision is *put with the imaginative and illuminative words of insight, and with a feeling for human nature as it is* (not as it may become) and a sagacious appreciation of the existing situation: then it carries: *carries reform and creates morality.*

> *"Slight those who say*, amidst their sickly healths,
> Thou livest by rule. What doth not so but man?
> Houses are built by rule and Commonwealths.
> Entice the trusty sun, if that you can,
> From his ecliptic line; beckon the sky.
> Who lives by rule then, keeps good company.

*"Who keeps no guard upon himself* is slack,
And rots to nothing at the next great thaw;
Man is a shop of rules: a well-truss'd pack
Whose every parcel underwrites a law.
Lose not thyself, nor give thy humours way;
God gave them to thee under lock and key."
                                *George Herbert.*[3]

18 December, 1894.
for delivery before the "Benevolent
Fraternity of Churches," at Boston,
19 December, 1894.

WWT MS. (WP, DLC).
[3] George Herbert, "The Church Porch," from *The Temple.*

## A Newspaper Report of a Public Lecture

[Dec. 20, 1894]

### LIBERTY AND GOVERNMENT.

Prof. Woodrow Wilson of Princeton University delivered an address last night in Parker Memorial Hall on "Political Liberty, Political Expediency, Political Morality, in a Democratic State." He spoke as follows:

You will notice that the last part of this title is "in a democratic state." You will ask me what I mean by a democratic state. I suppose that is not a term which goes without definition. I suppose that it would not be easy for every one in this audience to say exactly what he or she meant when using the term "a democratic state."

You say that the very meaning of the word discloses the meaning of the thing. It is a state in which the people rule. Well, now, is it a state in which the people rule? Have you ever known a state in which the people ruled? Is it not impossible that the people should rule?

You know that in order to rule it is necessary that there should be initiative and choice. Do the people take the initiative and exercise the choice?

I was debating this question the other evening in New York with some gentlemen, and they said: "Why, of course, the people take the initiative and exercise the choice. Look at this tremendous upheaval we have had."[1] "Yes," I said, "I have followed that, but do you think it is taking the initiative to smell a smell? Is it taking the initiative to perceive that there are hideous things in

[1] The recent overthrow of Tammany in New York, the culmination of the crusade begun in 1892 by the Rev. Dr. Charles Henry Parkhurst.

the conduct of the business of a great corporation? Is seeing taking an initiative? Is crying out when you see it the initiative?"

Is it not true that the person or persons who created the awful sight are those who took the initiative in this matter—that those who made the smell created the occasion for the nostrils of the people to perceive or smell? Is it not taking the initiative to perceive that something is wrong and to utter a great and overwhelming protest against wrong? For what comes after the protest?

What are you going to do about it? Change the men in office? Certainly. But you have changed them before. Have reforms? Certainly, have reform. But who is going to suggest the reform as a whole? You know that that is impossible.

People like suggestion after it is made. But yes and no are words of consent, assent or dissent, and they are not taking the initiative. I say it is impossible that people should take the initiative as a whole. I say without fear of contradiction that they never have taken the initiative on any occasion whatever. It is just as impossible, as Lord Macaulay said, as to conduct a military campaign by means of a debating society.

You cannot initiate, begin, originate things where everybody is talking. You must let some one person go out with a committee and bring in propositions to be acted upon. You must let some one take the initiative and see what the people will do.

Well, if a democratic state is not a state in which the people rule, what is it? Why, it is a state of people conditioned to rule in. Ah, you will say, in every state the people are in condition to rule. But is it not true that if you have a despotism and are a despot, you must look to it what you do, or you will have a revolution on your hands?

The people do the ruling. I doubt whether despots themselves have an impression that they do anything that they please. It is true, they may select a few prominent individuals and take their heads off, and deprive them of their property, and do other things arbitrarily. But there has never been a despot who dared touch the very bonds which held the very community together, because the very moment he broke these bonds he knew there would be anarchy, desperation and revolution.

So I believe that every despot is more or less conscious, as he is more or less wise, that his rule is conditioned by the people.

But there is this difference between the Democratic state and any other state that in the former the way in which they condition the ruling is made regular and habitual, whereas in every other state it is irregular and without the consistency of habit. The democratic nation is one in which the ruling is deliberately adjusted to the assent of the people; in which the lead is deliberately conditioned by the following in which the leaders go, always with their eyes over their shoulders seeing if the body of the people are following, not daring to tread any untrodden road along which the people will not follow them, not daring to take any initiative step without previous consultation or without some definite indication of what is to be said and done by the great body of the commonwealth in respect of the thing to be proposed.

So that a democratic nation does not differ from other nations in the mere fact that people condition the ruling, but in this fact that there are deliberate means; that there is a regular machinery provided whereby the assent of the people is ascertained from time to time. But it is not initiative. It is assent. It is not proposal. It is consent.

And so you will find that initiative choice is always the gumption [function] of the few, and consent is always the function of the many.

Not only that, but choice is always the function of a particular sort of few—that particular sort of few that can catch the common thought, which can perceive the movements of the common atmosphere, which can see, as it were, instinctively, what direction is to be the safe direction of leadership; whereas consent amounts to this: It is making the promise of co-operation. I propose to do such and such things. I cannot do them by myself. Will you join me? Yes, upon such and such understandings.

All of that is regularly provided for in a democratic nation. Now it is that sort of nation we speak of this evening when we speak of liberty, expediency and morality.

In such a state what is liberty? There is no word which brings, I suppose, such mischances as the word liberty. There is no word which has so intoxicated men. There is no word upon which such words have been spoken, about which such deeds of horror and such deeds of cowardice have been done as the word liberty.

I take leave to say that liberty is not synonymous with what we call scientific anarchy. By scientific anarchy we mean anarchy where there is no disorder. Ordinary anarchy means where everybody does what he pleases, following his passions.

Scientific anarchy is a state in which everybody is following his virtues. We are to have scientific anarchy in heaven, because we are told there is to be no rule there—that is, no constraint—because we shall all desire the good and follow it.

If every man desired good and were wise enough to follow his knowledge, there would be no need for government and restraint, and that would be scientific anarchy. The brakes would be removed because there was no hill; the restraint would be taken away because there was no danger.

Now, liberty is not such a conception, for you observe that in the present state of human nature we are not all actively following our virtues.

As human nature exists at present, we are a great many of us following our passions, and following them very diligently. We say we are following scientific law, namely, the law of self interest. Nobody has ever studied this law. If he has, he has observed that self interest is a pasison [passion]—that a man's desire to promote his own interests is something that will inevitably lead, unless checked by very many virtues, to his trampling other men under his feet and crowding the men to the wall.

You have only to look around you to the men who are following that passion without regard to humanity. That is as dangerous for a man to follow as his lusts, because it is irregular.

I judge of my interest because of my understanding. My understanding may not be strong. Then I have the opinion of a man whose understanding I shall not be willing to follow or accept. There are some men of whom the quip is justly made, as against a fellow not noted for virtue and understanding, and to whose head somebody referred by saying that it was not a head, but something the Almighty put there to keep him from ravelling out. (Laughter.) That is true of a great many.

We don't want to follow that sort of understanding. Therefore as human nature is at present, we must adjust some sort of government to the needs of society, and see to it that we secure order. How is the common judgment any better than the single man's judgment.

There you go back to the old trouble suggested by Carlyle— how, out of a multitude, to make a body that shall be wise—how, out of an infinite number of ignorant persons, to create a body that shall have knowledge. This looks a difficult problem.

But the advantage of having a single individual controlled by the majority is this: You see a man come to words with his neighbor and then come to blows. It is not your quarrel. You look on and are cool, you say. These men are acting outrageously, and you interpose and stop them, if you can. Why? Is it because you would not quarrel with your neighbor in such circumstances? No, but because while you are cool and keep your head, they are excited and loose [lose] their heads.

Now, that is exactly where society controls the individual. The individual is moved by his passions hidden from the mass, and the mass keep their heads. It is like what occurs at a football game. The players sometimes lose their heads and the umpire sometimes loses his head, but the spectators keep cool, and they see what things are being done, and if it were possible they would stop them.

Thus, what the mass does for the individual is done not because it is wiser, but because it is not excited, while the individual is excited. If the passion of the individual swept through the whole body of individuals, the whole body could not control the individual; but by a merciful providence it strikes only a few of us at a time, and the rest, not being passionately engaged, can act as umpires.

Though the judge on the bench may sometimes do an act of outrage or cowardice, he judges justly of another man's act, because it is not his affair, and he does not feel the passion that moves the other.

Now, I say it is impossible that we should call liberty scientific anarchy, every man following his best judgment on the supposition that every man will. I believe that it is very clear how liberty came to be struggled for as it has been. The revolt in respect of the history of liberty is not against institutions. It is not against government. It is not against control.

It is against a particular set of institutions, a particular sort of government and control, and I think I can tell you very clearly what sort of control we have kicked against and resisted. It is the sort where the few individuals picked out the course for the large numbers, without ever consulting the large numbers. What we have been angry with in the past has been, not institutions, but tutelage. We did not want to be tied to the apron strings of a class, submissive to the dictates of hereditary monarchs, because we did not want to take the chances of hereditary monarchs. We did not want to support the closeted group of men who always stay closeted and never know what the general interest is.

There have been governments conducted with the very best consciences which, nevertheless, were the worst governments. What man is to be trusted to see the whole nation, and in his own closet to perceive what the interests of all classes demand? How are you going to know that unless you consult all classes?

It is not that we have resisted government, but that we have resisted little coteries and groups of men of privileged classes, who have come to regard themselves as being a state, whereas we would like them to know that the state contains us as well.

Now, if not anarchy, if not relief from government, if not escape from institutions, what is liberty? Why, it is simply the best all round adjustment.

I think I can illustrate that. Physiologists tell us that by the pressure of the atmospheric air—for we have the air outside of us as well as inside of us—whatever comeliness of person we possess is preserved. Remove the atmosphere and that comeliness will disappear. It is dependent upon a restraint.

Not only so, but they are inventing new cures for all sorts of diseases by putting particular parts of the body under new restraint, putting men in a corner and firing a stream of hot water at them with a 60 pound pressure and bringing the organs into order by a sudden halt called to their irregularity. This is a means of bringing back readjustment by a pressure from outside.

So that order consists in this nice sort of equilibrium. Let us illustrate in this way: We will say that a skein of yarn is free when it is without tangles. We say that a man is free when he can come to the best development of his powers. Suppose that you could not count on the co-operation of other men, and that there was a situation which should realize even scientific anarchy —that is to say, a state where every man was following his virtues.

Suppose such a situation, and you would suppose a situation in which you would be enslaved and not free. For this reason. If I cannot count on you for even a temporary degree of co-operation, see what I shall have to do. I may have tomorrow to make my own hat and coat, to kill my own food and do everything for myself. Thus we should not be free from human restraints, but subject to an absolute slavery of nature.

Do you suppose that if we were to disassociate ourselves we should continue to have the civilization we have? We have that by reason of infinite co-operation, and the moment you stop that you make it necessary for every man to carry the whole of this civilization on his shoulders, if he wishes to continue it.

If we were to say, every one of us, that we would go away and look out for ourselves, we should not have any spiritual life. What is one of the claims of the workman to which we all take off our hats? He says, you keep him at the bench all day, and then at night he has only time to go to bed or to go on a spree. Now, just so far as you tie a man like that you deprive him of everything of his intellectual life and leave him very little of his animal life except what he puts into his food. You reduce him in the scale of being just so much nearer to the scale of the beast.

Now, whatever a man demands in order that he may be a man is that he may be released from his physical tasks enough that he may have a little time to think, so that we may release that part of him which we denominate the spiritual part, and not depend on that part which he shares with the animal creation, his physical part.

Now, all of that advantage he gets at the price of co-operation. It is the product of civilization. If we had all of us to do these tasks ourselves that are done by civilization, I should say, let us reduce ourselves to a simpler scale and not do them. It is not worth the whistle. If we cannot get leisure we cannot be men. If we cannot get time to use our souls we cannot save our souls. If we cannot get time to use our minds we cannot have any minds.

The price of civilization will be universal death and torpidity. Now, if that is not to be the product of civilization, I do not see any use in having civilization at all. Now, all that you get by co-operation, for without co-operation there could not be leisure.

You say a kite sails free, yet the kite is held tighter than anything I know of. You say a steamer runs free because she has the moving force in her own bowels, and is independent of nature. Is she? Is not this steamer just as much a servant and co-operator as is the sailing vessel? It is only a different set of machines, but the principle is the same.

Just so far have I my physical freedom, just so long as I obey the laws of nature. If I indulge in some vice, nature calls a halt, and if I follow some pursuit too closely, nature says, "You are not obeying me," and if I continue to disobey there is no obviating the consequences.

If a man violates the laws he is going to Dante's Inferno, because unquestionably we can go to hell before we die if we make our minds up to do so, for in Dante's Inferno, you know there were men who were still living, and I suppose every man knows that he can make such a character for himself that he would find hell a relief from it. I am at liberty, I suppose, to dash my arm against this wall, but suppose I did, nature would take it away from me. I keep it on condition that I will not make an insane use of it, that I will not thrust it in the jaw of nature and have it bitten off.

Nature makes all our joists whole, and so I will take it for granted that nature is minding her own business, and so it is adjustment which gives freedom itself—perfect adjustment.

Let me use another illustration, which appeals to every one in this country—that is the "manifest destiny" of this country upon this continent: That matter has been a puzzle to all foreign writers. They say, "Your continent is big," and they laugh at the idea that therefore the country must be great. They say, "We don't have so big a continent, but we have a great country. What has the size of a country to do with it?"

Ah, but doesn't it? Didn't it take a nation that knew how to put shoulder to shoulder to achieve what we have achieved? Look what we did. We came here, landed, and found certain clearings which the Indians made for us, and we took possession of them. And we branched out, but while we were exploring we kept to those cleared lands pretty close.

We presently came to great mountains, which we had not known anything about. We first supposed that we would have a free passage to go to Asia and see all the things that Marco Polo dreamed of if we could but pass certain mountains of which we knew. But we found mountain after mountain that would not yield an inch, that would not come under our mastery unless we mastered it, and so we marched across this continent until the last census informed us that there was no longer any frontier.

Now, I say, that is something to feel, if not proud of, strength in. We have known how to be masters, and if there had been even scientific anarchy we would not have even stayed upon the little strip. So we have gotten everything for the price of cooperation.

Now, I have been dwelling upon liberty, scientific and everything else. But political liberty is not of a different kind. It comes from the best adjustment of the rights of the individual to the powers of the government, and the freest government is that where that adjustment has been best worked out.

You know some of the difficulties some of the European governments are getting. It is because they simply copied England. England worked out her constitution in a very interesting way and on some interesting occasions—at Runnymede and in the revolution of 1688. I take it that the reason that we have written constitutions on this continent is because there was already the experience. Every bit of it is old to us.

That is what is the matter with some of the continental nations —they have accepted England's conclusions en bloc. It took generations of experience to know how to use that machine, and shall our young people use that machine and not ruin it or ruin themselves? Our freedom consisted in the oldness of our ideas embodied in the constitution—working out upon a new field and in a new direction the old principles to which we have been habituated.

So the whole matter is a matter of experience and adjustment. We have it all summed up in the reply of the Englishman who said it was so absurd to call "bread" "pain." "Well," said a friend, "isn't it equally absurd to call it 'bread'?" "Oh, but [it] is 'bread,' you know." (Laughter.)

And I think we feel that way with reference to all our institutions. We feel that if we can reply: "I never heard of anything so absurd in my life," it must be absurd. Well, most of us have lived long enough to know that there are some things we formerly believed that we have no more faith in, and we do not longer feel that because we never heard of a thing it must be impracticable.

Yes. I feel that it is the strength of our institutions to feel that way. "I never heard of doing such a thing"—that is to say, we won't try a bridge until we know it will bear us, until generations have gone over that bridge and we know whither it leads. We don't want to go where we have to be pioneers.

Now, I am going to read an extract from Ruskin on this subject: "How false the conception," he cries: "how frantic the pursuit of that phantom which men call liberty. . . . There is no such thing in the universe. There can never be. The stars have it not, the earth has it not, the sea has it not, and we men have the mockery and semblance of it only for our heaviest punishment."

The enthusiast would reply that by liberty he meant the law of liberty. Then why use the single and misunderstood word? If by liberty you mean chastisement of the passions, discipline of the intellect, subjection of the will; if you mean the fear of inflicting, the shame of committing a wrong; if you mean respect for all who are in authority, and consideration for all who are in dependence; veneration for the good, mercy to the evil, sympathy with the weak; if you mean watchfulness over all thoughts, temperance in all pleasures, perseverance in all toils; if you mean, in a word, that service which is defined in the liturgy of the English church to be perfect freedom, why do you name this by the same word by which the luxurious mean license, and the reckless mean change; by which the rogue means rapine, and the fool equality; by which the proud mean anarchy, and the malignant mean violence? Call it by any name rather than this, but its best and truest is obedience.

Obedience is, indeed, founded on a kind of freedom, else it would become mere subjugation, but that freedom is only granted that obedience may be more perfect; and thus, while a measure of license is necessary to exhibit the individual energies of things, the fairness and pleasantness and perfection of them all consists in their restraint.

Compare a river that has burst its banks with one that is bound by them, and the clouds that are scattered over the face of the whole heaven with those that are marshalled into ranks and orders by its winds. Restraint, utter and unrelaxing, can never be comely. This is not because it is in itself an evil, but only because, when too great, it overpowers the nature of the thing restrained, and so counteracts the other laws of which that nature is itself composed. And the balance, wherein consists the fairness of creation, is between the laws of life and being in the things governed, and the laws of general sway to which they are subjected: and the suspension or infringement of either kind of law, or literally, disorder, is equivalent to and synonymous with, disease; while the increase of both honor and beauty is habitually on the side of restraint, or the action of superior law, rather than of character, or the action of inherent law. The noblest word in the catalogue of social virtue is "loyalty," and the sweetest which men have learned in the pastures of the wilderness is "fold."

Nor is this all; but we must observe that exactly in proportion to the majesty of things in the scale of being is the completeness of their obedience to the laws that are set over them. Gravitation is less quietly, less instantly obeyed by a grain of dust than it is by the sun and moon; and the ocean falls and flows under influences which the lake and river do not recognize.

So, also, in estimating the dignity of any action or occupation of men, there is perhaps no better test than the question, "are its laws straight?" For their severity will probably be commensurate with the greatness of the numbers whose labor it concentrates or whose interest it concerns.

Now, I believe that is a perfect expression of the matter which I have been trying to illustrate. See what a homage we pay to everything that is regular, equable, and elevated in character, in demeanor, utterance, to everything that is elevated in sentiment and conduct. See, how we respect a man in whose actions we have confidence. We like a "character" or two among us, a man who does not do what may be expected; it lends variety, but if everybody did the same thing it would make chaos.

We do not respect the "character," so much as we tolerate him and are pleased by it whimsically, because it amuses us and gives piquancy which it would not have if life were all on a dead level.

How absurd an accident is. We see a man slip and we laugh, without first asking if he is hurt. Men do not habitually make their progress in that fashion. We watch a dignified man cross the room and admire him and say, "What dignity and elevation of character, what excellence of deportment." It is making the most of life without friction.

Now, I ask you to look with me for a few moments at the history of the institutions in respect to this matter. Look at the difference of the constitution of liberty and the constitution of government among us. For we have a constitution of both. We have a constitution of government in which we say so and so shall be. Then we have another part that we call our bill of rights, wherein we say no man shall be deprived of life, liberty, etc., without due process of law. Those are our items of liberty.

There is great difference in the age of constitutions of liberty and constitutions of government. Constitution of government has always been. There has never been government without a constitution. It is true that only in very recent times that has been written down. But liberty has not so long had a constitution. Liberty has only had a constitution, I should say, since Runnymede, since Magna Charta, since the nobles and commons of England parleyed with King John, when Magna Charta was drawn up. You will notice that Magna Charta is negatively cast.

It does not say "Men shall be free." It says they shall not be restrained except under certain circumstances. It is manifestly taken for granted that they are free. Men are free under every government. That is, they have all the impulses, but they cannot always count upon being able to do as they desire.

The source of the constitution of liberty is different from the source of the constitution of government. It comes from the distinct formation in the minds of the body of the people of an idea of their relations to the government.

No government was ever liberal enough to promulgate a constitution of liberty. They have never been granted, they have been demanded. Th[e]y have been extracted from government. Children never could get their liberty from parents, but when they have grown up they secure liberty. So a nation that was in childhood has never gotten its liberty, even when it has been offered by agitators and given it.

It is necessary that the source of liberty should be outside of government—not offered by it. You are necessarily bound to leave for government a margin of discretion; you must make its terms inexact. But the terms of the constitution of liberty are very exact.

I believe there never was an age in which there was a greater uneasiness, but look at the infinite number of phases it assumes. How many men want the same thing? If you could get people into one great convention and have them resolve, who would frame the common resolution? There is no one who knows all of the things which all of those people would all agree to. It is an age of uneasiness rather than an age of purpose, and the only thing in which purpose begins to show itself definitely is upon the wrong side, if I may be allowed to use that word. Socialism itself, unimpeachable in its motives, does not put its motives in the most prominent place, but its purposes.

I believe the machinery of government is the result of purpose, and not purpose the result of machinery, and that it would not make a picayune's difference how we were organized if we did not have the same purposes after we were organized.

I never knew of the way of doing things saving anybody. The act may save, but not the way of doing it. Take the matter of the initiative and the referendum. You say, we cannot elect representatives any more who can be trusted to represent us.

Suppose we don't trust the representatives to make laws, but suppose we look at Switzerland, and do as they do do [sic] there—take the initiative. A certain percentage of voters sign a petition for a certain measure, and it will be necessary for the Legislature to submit it to the people for their vote. We have not the discretion to choose men, yet we have the discretion to choose measures.

I believe it is infinitely harder to choose measures than men, properly. Instinctively, from the beginning of the world, we have been choosing those whom we would trust, but the hardest thing has been to properly choose measures. Now, we want to change our machinery, because it has broken down. Go on and have a revolution, and you will be centuries backward when it is ended.

Revolutions always put things back, and sensible reforms are postponed. Out of that may be considered the law of political expediency, whose field is the field of statesmanship. The law of progress in society is the law of modification. This is the law that furnishes the standard of political expediency. Modification in the modern democratic state means the adjustment and accommodation of the general opinion and purpose to changing social or political conditions.

The general opinion, in this conception of progress, means the organic opinion, the efficient opinion, formed by the concert and prevalence of commanding minds—not of commanding numbers merely. Revolution can never be expedient, though it may sometimes be necessary in the sense of being inevitable, as death is inevitable.

Slight those who say, amidst their sickly healths,
 Thou livest by rule. What doth not so but man?
Houses are built by rule and commonwealths.
 Entice the trusty sun, if that you can,
From his ecliptic line; beckon the sky.
Who lives by rule, then, keeps good company.

Who keeps no guard upon himself is slack,
 And rots to nothing at the next great thaw;
Man is a shop of rules: a well-truss'd pack
 Whose every parcel underwrites a law.
Lose not yourself, nor give thy humors way;
God gave them to thee under lock and key.

At the close of his address Prof. Wilson answered a number of questions which were put to him by persons in the audience.

Printed in the *Boston Herald*, Dec. 20, 1894; some editorial headings omitted.


## From Frederick Jackson Turner

Dear Wilson:        Madison Dec. 24, 1894

I have delayed answer to your letter because I was out of town for several days at the time of its arrival, and came back with a severe cold which I am still nursing, while looking over 150 examination books!

Your intimation regarding your MSS has many temptations in it for me. I would gladly know what you think of many problems that I have been working on in that same period. Indeed this makes the difficulty in the way of my reading your work. I am likely to publish at least monographs in the same field myself before your book is in print, and I know that our point of view has so much in common that I could not help absorbing into my own work many of your ideas. It is with real regret that I come to this conclusion,—but it seems to be a choice between enjoying your book before others, and abandoning my own publication. I suppose I ought to begin to write.

I have been rereading your Division and Reunion. It is a wonderful little book—at once a contribution to knowledge and an example of the wedding of a good literary form to historical writing. There is a vitality,—a flesh and blood form—to the book that I like very much. Your full history will be *the* American history of our time, I believe. Did I ever tell you how much I enjoyed your Calendar of Great Americans? I tried the same kind of a test on Franklin once, in a review of Hale's Franklin in France, I, in the *Dial*—coming to the conclusion that he was the first typical great American,—great as America was great.[1]

With this I send you an old photograph of my map.[2] I hope you can use it. The exaggeration of the vertical scale conveys false impressions, especially for the Cordilleran region, but on the whole the map is the most suggestive for historical use of any relief map I have used—except that great one, built on the curve of the sphere by Howells,[3] I think, of Washington—and for photographic use, mine is quite as serviceable perhaps.

The most history I ever found in any map, however, I found in the contour maps of the US Geolog. Survey—nine sheets, without any names, or political boundaries on the map—giving lakes, rivers, and contour lines only. It is a revelation. The same thing is published with county and state boundaries, names of towns, rivers &c. But this destroys its value as showing the part played by physiographic conditions. Address Mr Gannett,[4] U. S. Topographer, U. S. Geological Survey, Washington, D. C. It is not for sale.

Mrs Turner and I send Christmas greetings to your wife and yourself.              Cordially yours   Frederick J. Turner

What call has Dr E. B. Andrews to write an Am. History?[5]

ALS (WP, DLC) with WWhw notation on env.: "Ans. 27 Dec. '94."

1 F. J. Turner, "Franklin in France" [a review of Edward E. Hale and Edward E. Hale, Jr., *Franklin in France*, Vol. I (Boston, 1887)], Chicago *Dial*, VIII (May 1887), 7-10.

2 This enclosure is missing.

3 Edwin Eugene Howell.

4 Henry Gannett, Chief Geographer of the United States Geological Survey.

5 In the missing portion of Wilson's letter to Turner of December 10, Wilson had perhaps referred to the publication by Elisha Benjamin Andrews, President of Brown University, of his *History of the United States* (2 vols., New York, 1894).

## To Frederick Jackson Turner

My dear Turner,        Princeton, New Jersey, 27 December, 1894.

I appreciate most heartily your letter of the 24th., and wish to thank you for it very warmly. Of course you are right to decline to read my MSS.; I am only a bit ashamed of myself that I did not, in my self-absorption, appreciate the objection before it was urged, and refrain from asking the favour. I am very sorely disappointed: that I must admit; for I have been counting from the first upon your counsel and judgment in many points. But your reasons carry their own sufficient weight, and I am satisfied. Perhaps you will not feel the same objection to looking over the proofs, some years hence, when the publication is imminent; but

I am not going to ask you to pledge yourself to that now, so long beforehand. A great many things may happen before, say, 1898.

It was very kind of you to send the photograph of your map. It will be of real service to me. I have written to Mr. Gannett to try for a set of the sheets of the Geological survey, and hope I shall succeed in obtaining them. They are just what I want, as you describe them.

I devoutly pray my History may be what you expect; and it heartens me greatly that you expect such good things of it. But, oh, it goes hard! If what makes hard writing makes easy reading, it ought to go with a most excellent relish on the palates of my readers. The little Epoch, which you so generously praise, was child's play compared with it,—at any rate compared with this effort to weave the colonial story together into a single consistent narrative. I pray it may grow easier or it will kill me. And yet it would be a most pleasant death. The ardour of the struggle is inspiriting. There is pleasure in the very pain,—as when one bites on an aching tooth!

I am sorry to hear of your cold in combination with the 150 examination books. I know what that means; and hope you will not have to stand it long.

I know what call E. Benj. Andrews had to write our history. He wrote it for some company (an insurance company, I believe) to use as a premium; but the company failed and Andrews worked the premium off on the Scribners!

Give my very warm regards to [Charles Homer] Haskins. Mrs. Wilson joins me very heartily in all the greetings of the season to you both.     Faithfully Yours,   Woodrow Wilson

WWTLS (F. J. Turner Papers, MH).


## From Albert Shaw

My Dear Wilson:                         New York.  January 5, 1895.

I have asked the Century Company to send you a copy of my forthcoming book on Municipal Government in Great Britain.[1] I should be more than a little elated if your conscience would permit you to say that you think it is a half-way good piece of work. I have no very good opinion of it myself. After you look it over would you be willing to venture an opinion as to the extent to which it would be useful as collateral reading in connection with college or university lecture courses?

With best wishes for the new year,
                         Sincerely yours,   Albert Shaw.

TLS (WP, DLC).
¹ Albert Shaw, *Municipal Government in Great Britain* (New York, 1895).

## A News Item

[Jan. 11, 1895]

Sunday, Jan. 13. . . .
5 p.m. Services in Marquand Chapel [will be] conducted by Prof. Woodrow Wilson.

Printed in the *Daily Princetonian*, Jan. 11, 1895.

## Notes for a Chapel Talk

SUNDAY afternoon, January 13, 1895.

Read *Isaiah*, XI., 1-9.
  *Job*, XXVIII., 20-28.
*"The fear of the Lord, that is wisdom; and to depart from evil is understanding."*
*Quite reverses our own judgment.* We should say, "The fear of the Lord, that is *mysticism*; and to depart from evil is *prudence*."
*Shall we fear what we neither see nor can understand?*
We stand uncovered only in the presence of the demonstrable: fear only ignorance, because it is bondage.
  *To go with your eyes open*, that is wisdom; *and to seek* diligently *for knowledge* is understanding.
*But the Wisdom here meant* = *insight*, perception, a knowledge of spiritual values: true *appreciation* of men and situations.
  *understanding* = wit to take the deeper meaning of the universe of men and affairs.
*For the Christian, to fear* = to heed with reverence.
  *What will that lead us to?*
    *The plan of salvation*, which comes by belief, acceptance, and saves, not by conduct, but by *regeneration*, by becoming of the blood of Christ.
  *To know Christ, that is wisdom; and to accept him, understanding.*

WWT MS. (WP, DLC).

## Two Letters from Edward Southwick Child¹

Child & de Goll, Architects.
My dear Sir,          New York.    January 14, 1895
  In another enclosure is sent the perspective of your house.²
I have deviated more widely from your sketches and instructions than I generally do, and will go over in detail these points
  1—The position of the steps are altered and placed with abutments in front of the front door. That long stretch of wall look[s] bare as it was drawn first.

2 Have put heavy windowheads over each of the triple windows in Parlor and Library. This is necessary to support the flat arch in the stone work.

3 Have made an arched window into hall[.] Think the two arches give an appearance of strength and support to the overhanging gable.

4—Have indicated a rough stone bracket support to seats and to second story overhang[.] A section through wall would be thus[.][3] There will be no weight on these—the idea is to give an appearance of strength.

5. Instead of 3 oriels on second story two are shown. The English[4] did put oriels on projected gables, but I think projections on projections are not good. There is no rule about this, however, and there are precedents in both ways.

6 The window effect in the projection and in the gable is different from your sketches[.] There is no definite reason for this either except—that as I drew it first—it seemed that six triple windows were too many on a flat front.

Our estimate from data given us, on this house would make the cost without heating or mantels $7400.

The design has been much admired and Mrs Wilson deserves compliments for having laid out elevations in such proportions.

We should be very glad to give you any further information in our power. We have a tracing of the perspective, and I return herewith, your plans.

Yours very Truly,   E. S. Child.

The elevations in pencil I have at home but will send them.

ALS (WP, DLC).
    [1] A New York architect, born 1859, died 1918; author of *Colonial Houses for Modern Homes* . . . (New York, 1903). At this time a partner of Guyon de Goll.
    [2] This letter is the first evidence in the documents of the Wilsons' definite plans to build a house of their own. They had bought a lot, approximately 120 feet by 195 feet, adjacent to the McGill property that they were renting on Steadman Street (renamed Library Place in January 1896) for $3,000 from Colonel and Mrs. Samuel Witham Stockton on October 29, 1894, with a mortgage of $2,000. Mercer County (N. J.) Deed Book 200, pp. 500-502; S. W. Stockton to WW, April 1, 1895, printed as an Enclosure with J. Davidson to WW, May 28, 1895. The Wilsons had undoubtedly begun to plan for their new home during the autumn of 1894, for Wilson wrote to Ellen on January 27, 1895, about the plans which had brightened Ellen's "dear face for so many months past." Wilson sold a forty-five foot frontage along the northern side of the lot to Willard Humphreys for $1,350 on November 23, 1897. Mercer County (N. J.) Deed Book 219, pp. 315-16.
    [3] At this point Child sketched a stone bracket support.
    [4] The Wilsons had planned a half-timbered house.

My dear Professor Wilson:          New York. Jany 16, 1895.

Your favor of the 15th January, with enclosure as stated check for $15.00 for sketch is thankfully received. I am very glad to hear that the sketch pleases you as I was quite anxious it should do.

I will be at this office on Saturday next, the 19th inst, as you request, and will be at leisure to give full attention to you. I see no reason why we cannot slightly modify the cost of the house, and it may even be that we have estimated higher than it can be built for in Princeton.          Yours truly,   E. S. Child

TLS (WP, DLC).


## To Child & de Goll, Architects

Dear Sirs:          New York. Jany, 19, 1895.

You may get up for me the working plans, details and specifications for a house from the sketch made by you, and from my instructions. These are to be submitted to me in pencil for such modifications as I may desire, and then are to be finished and delivered to me. If I desire to have you superintend the construction of the house it is to be a matter of future agreement. It is understood that you are to use your best endeavors to bring the house within the cost of $7.000, not including heating or mantels.

For the drawing of the plans I am to pay you $150.00 on delivery of the completed plans, and upon this amount I am to have credit of $15.00 paid for the sketch.          Woodrow Wilson

Accepted
Child & de Goll

WWTLS with hw endorsement (WP, DLC).


## To Ellen Axson Wilson

My own darling,      906 McCulloh St., Baltimore, 24 Jany, '95

It's hard to tell which is the most painful letter to write, the first one, the last one, or any one of those between the first and the last. It's all one pain: the varieties do not differ greatly in intensity. Yet it's a sweet pain, isn't it, love; growing, as it does, out of the deepest, most satisfying affection that ever man and woman had for each other! Was there ever such *happiness* as ours? And this pain is but the evidence of that happiness.

A flood of recollections has been pouring in upon me ever since I got here last night,[1] sweetheart: for I have been put once more in my old, my *first* room,—third story back at 909[2] (my address, by the way, is *not* 908, but 906) where my old life and my old anxieties were lived out, till I went south to be happy with you; where part of "Congressional Government" was written; where you and I lodged the year[3] the children were here with us: the room to wh. so many times, now, I have been brought back, as if it were a sort of centre. It reminds me of so many hopes, fears, achievements, disappointments that it is, for me, almost like the studio round which life circled for the Laird, Taffy, and Little Billee,—without the tragedy.[4] You may be sure that all the *tender* memories of the old place centre about you. I feel both younger (as if reminded of the days when I was making my start, and so made aware how much the same fellow I am,—with all the old sensibilities alive—alive sometimes like the nerve of a tooth!) and older in this room: the memories have *lengthened* so, so much change has come: I seem myself to have become in so many ways another fellow,—more confident, steady, serene, though not less susceptible to all sorts of influences wh. experience might have been expected to render me indifferent to: enjoying in a certain degree a sense of power,—as if I had gotten some way upon the road I used so to burn to travel, and yet fairly restless and impatient with ambition, as of old—a boy and yet a man—carrying about with me the marks and records of all the turns and experiences in my life of which this room reminds me! I talk as if I have seen the world, boxed the compass in the vicissitudes of my life, don't I! Well, I *have*,—*inside* of me; quiet and even and uneventful as the outside *fortunes* of my life have been. Oh, love, love, what a passion it has all bred in my heart for you, my delightful lover, my perfect wife. I love you and long for you more than I dare say!

I am quite well and *tame*.        Your own    Woodrow

Wont you let [Winthrop M.] Daniels know my *correct* address— and Robinson,[5] who is to send the visiting cards.

Kisses uncounted for the chicks, love for Ed. & Geo.[6]

Your    W.

ALS (WC, NjP).

[1] To begin his annual lectures on administration at the Johns Hopkins. The notes that he used in 1895 are printed at Feb. 1, 1892, Vol. 7.

[2] The address of Mary Jane Ashton's boardinghouse when Wilson had lived there as a graduate student. The number had been changed to 906.

[3] That is, 1891 or 1893.

[4] Three of the principal characters of George Du Maurier's novel *Trilby* (London and New York, 1894).

[5] C. S. and H. L. Robinson, printers, 30 Nassau St., Princeton.

[6] Edward Axson and George Howe III.

# From Ellen Axson Wilson

My own darling,          Princeton, N. J.   Jan. 24/95

Just one day—twenty-four hours—has passed since I saw your cab turn the corner and was left lamenting! Oh how lonely it is! But I *won't* dwell on that!—not in words and if possible not in thought. It isn't good for the health!

I have been going steadily from one place of business to another ever since you left,—am too wise to stop and brood over your absence *yet*.

As soon as you left I went, after bathing the children, to the Hibbens,[1] had a very interesting time, and gained some valuable points.[2] Then I went to the Ricketts.[3] They asked me to tea and I accepted, coming home first to see about the family. Had a very pleasant time:—met the younger brother[4] who is quite agreeable. I came home early, half past eight, and wrote to Mr. Child.

This morning after lessons were over—at 12.30—I went out with the "petition,"[5] got the signatures of Mrs. Brown,[6] Dr. Purves & Mr. Brenton Green,[7] then carried it to the Paxtons[8] for them to get the rest. One of the Paxton girls came with it a moment ago to say her father said he and Dr. Purves had no right to sign after all because it read "property *owners*" only. Of course we didn't want to omit such influential names though, and besides Dr. Purves had already signed, so we decided to insert "and residents."

We are all pretty well—that is Jessie and I are *quite* well. Nellie is just the same and Margaret has renewed her cold a little. She is quite hoarse today but seems well otherwise. It is bitterly cold but bright. How eagerly I am waiting for tomorrow & my letter! I hope you had a pleasant journey & are *quite* well and happy. Oh how I love you, dear,—how constantly and intensely my heart yearns over you!—how entirely I am

Your own    Eileen.

ALS (WC, NjP).

[1] The John Grier Hibbens. Hibben was born in Peoria, Ill., April 19, 1861. A.B., College of New Jersey, 1882; A.M., 1885; Ph.D., 1893. Studied at the University of Berlin, 1882-83, and at Princeton Theological Seminary, 1883-86. Ordained to the Presbyterian ministry in 1887, he was pastor of the Falling Springs Presbyterian Church, Chambersburg, Pa., 1887-91. Married Jenny Davidson on Nov. 8, 1887. Spent his entire academic career at Princeton as Instructor in Logic, 1891-92; Instructor in Logic and Psychology, 1892-94; Assistant Professor of Logic, 1894-97; Stuart Professor of Logic, 1897-1912; Stuart Professor of Philosophy and President, 1912-32. Author of numerous works in philosophy and recipient of many honorary degrees. Died May 16, 1933.

[2] The Hibbens had just completed a half-timbered house at 50 Washington St. on the lot which Mrs. Hibben had purchased from the Wilsons in 1893. See JRW to WW, May 11, 1891, n. 2, Vol. 7.

³ Eliza (Mrs. Palmer Chamberlaine) Ricketts and her daughter, Henrietta, who lived at 80 Stockton St.
⁴ Louis Davidson Ricketts, State Geologist of Wyoming.
⁵ For the extension of Steadman Street northward.
⁶ Susan Dod (Mrs. David) Brown, of 65 Stockton St.
⁷ The Rev. Dr. William Brenton Greene, Jr., Stuart Professor of the Relations of Philosophy and Science to the Christian Religion, Princeton Theological Seminary, of 60 Stockton St.
⁸ The Rev. Dr. and Mrs. William Miller Paxton of 20 Steadman St.

## To Ellen Axson Wilson

My own darling,                    Baltimore, 25 January, 1895

Your first letter has just come: I have just been enjoying it, with a great pain at my heart. Oh, how unspeakably sweet it is to be loved so *by you*. If I dared, I would try to tell you what feelings it stirs in me, sitting lonely here in this haunted room. But I dare not yet. Instead, I will follow your wise example and tell you what I've been doing this long time past,—dear me *how* long it seems (and certainly you did a great deal in it, you efficient, businesslike little girl!).

The night I arrived I sat here in my room and read "Trilby" till I was fairly aquiver with the strange emotions which the book begets,—fairly hypnotised and went to bed in a dream,—just the narcotic I wanted, to deaden my own sadness, by enjoying another's! Yesterday morning I made my official calls on Dr. [H. B.] Adams and Mr. [D. C.] Gilman (the latter bade me to dine with him next Sunday at 2 o'clock), and went through the new quarters of the Department.[1] Then I went down street and bought some ink,—wrote to you,—and went to lunch (Miss A's dinner is at six now). When I went to lunch I found a letter from father, saying he was certainly coming here about Feb'y 1st., and enclosing $2,000![2] I immediately sat down to acknowledge the money and send him my notes for the amount.[3] Then I wrote to Cuyler that we would need $7,000 on the 1st. of April;[4] prepared my lecture (a resumé of what I lectured about last year); delivered my lecture to about the usual number of men, who gave me perhaps more than the usual attention,—the new men, as always, looking at the fluent, humourous lecturer with a sort of puzzled surprise which was very diverting; went down to the Post Office and sent the $2,000 by registered letter to the Princeton Bank (where it is no doubt by this time safely deposited) and "Trilby" back to the Library; and was ready for dinner!

After dinner I went to the Peabody Library, to kill time till eight; and then I crossed the street and sat with Mrs. Bird[5] till ten,—saw her brother, Mr. Thos. Baxter, and his wife, the

boy Edgeworth,[6] who has a little down on his lip and is getting
the first touches of the man on his face, with promise of singular
good looks, of a distinguished type, compounded of genius &
high breeding, Mrs. Smith[7] charmingly arrayed for a ball, her
husband and Mr. 'Tom.' Gresham,[8] arrayed to accompany her.
That was as full a day as yours! Don't you marvel at your dilatory,
inefficient husband? I did not overcome my loneliness, of course,
or conquer my sadness—nothing will do that but your embrace;
but I did not think about the forlornness: was much too busy
to mope. Perhaps, at the same pace, I can get something done
here! Oh, how passionately, how yearningly, how delightedly, how
intolerably I love you. I am altogether

Your own   Woodrow

ALS (WC, NjP).
  [1] The Departments of History, Politics, and Economics had moved to a spacious suite of seven rooms on the third floor of the newly completed McCoy
Hall, described in WW to EAW, Feb. 21, 1895, n. 3.
  [2] JRW's letter is missing. The money, as Wilson implies later in this letter,
was to be spent in constructing their new home.
  [3] About these notes, see WW to EAW, Feb. 2, 1895.
  [4] See C. C. Cuyler to WW, Jan. 26, 1895, printed as an Enclosure with WW
to EAW, Jan. 27, 1895. Cuyler's involvement is further explained in WW to EAW,
Feb. 2, 1895.
  [5] Wilson's old friend, Sarah Baxter (Mrs. William Edgeworth) Bird.
  [6] Mrs. Bird's grandson, Edgeworth Smith.
  [7] Mrs. Bird's daughter, Saida Bird (Mrs. Victor) Smith.
  [8] Thomas Baxter Gresham.


## From Ellen Axson Wilson

My own darling,                      Princeton, N.J. Jan. 25/95
  I havn't had a free moment all day for writing you; so my letter
will I fear not reach you when you expect it. There has been a
stream of visitors all the afternoon and Nellie too was unwell
and in constant need of 'Mamma,' so I have been somewhat torn
both ways, & could not even think of writing. Nellie was quite
sick last night with fever, &c. (temp. up to 103°.) I had quite
an exciting night,—(or *half* night rather, for she slept well the
second half) she had two terrible nightmares. Luckily Margaret,
instead of joining in, according to her old habit waked up in complete posession of her senses and waited on me quite nicely.
Nellie has had no return of the fever today. She slept almost constantly until 1 P.M. and then waked up apparently feeling almost
as well as ever. Margaret's hoarseness has almost passed off too.
  Mr. Daniels and his sister[1] called this afternoon. He said he
had written to you at 108;—so if the letter has not turned up
you will know where to find it. I sent word to the printer too. I

have just had to answer another letter of Mr. Child asking more questions; & I find that I am so "dead tired" & sleepy that I shan't try to answer now that *dear* letter, but simply thank you for it & say that with all my heart I *love* you, my own Woodrow.

Your little wife    Eileen.

ALS (WC, NjP).
¹ Edith Daniels, a student at Evelyn College in Princeton.

## To Ellen Axson Wilson

My own darling,                                    Balto., 26 January, 1895

No letter from you yet to-day: something, no doubt, delayed your writing. It does not make me anxious,—and nothing just now could add to my longing for you, my loneliness without you. It's an elevating sort of wretchedness: by thinking of you and what my condition is without you, I am made to think so much the more seriously of what I am with you, and of what I ought to be because of you,—what I owe it to you to be: and that's good for me. It's the best possible guide to ambition,—as you are the best possible stimulous to ambition. Ah, my dear, clear eyed, understanding little wife, how it *speeds* all the processes of my mind and heart to have you always with me! That's as much as I can say yet, at this stage of the sorrow.

The dollar bill I enclose is to cover the express charges on some books that will be sent from here: the bound volumes of Johns Hopkins studies exchanged (for a consideration) for the unbound volumes I brought down in my trunk.

The second lecture went off about as well as usual, thank you.

I have seen a good many of our friends, the Machens¹ amongst the rest, and they are all looking unusually well. I have *not* yet called on Miss [Edith] Duer and Mrs. [Harry Fielding] Reid, you will be relieved to learn,—but only because my visiting cards have not come yet,—bad luck to that blundering Robinson and his confederate, the Philadelphia printer, whatever his name is!

I am about to start out (execrable weather notwithstanding) to find a room near at hand, if possible, for father. I tremble a little, for him, at the prospect of having him in this slow, provincial town. There is nothing here that I can think of to keep him interested for more than a day or two: and he will soon tire of the social duties that await him. But he's resolved to come; and that's an end on't. He will enjoy it for a while, I hope; and he'll be great company for me.

I am doing a little work on the *Immortalia*,² in the way of a very leisurely examination of some of the sources, which are to be found here but not in Princeton. I may get full enough of matter in the process to write a few pages,—but that's not part of my *plan*. I mean simply to keep the subject matter in mind, and letter [let] it *simmer* without coming to a hard boil. I'll write only if I can't help it.

Try to have as good a time as possible, darling. Have a ladies' luncheon or a tea or two; invite the few you like best to the house frequently upon one pretext or another,—be gay and social! Wont you[?]  I love you, darling,—ah, how I love you,—with what a deep fervour and devotion. I am wholly,—desperately,

Your own   Woodrow

ALS (WC, NjP).
1 Mr. and Mrs. Arthur Webster Machen.
2 His projected "Philosophy of Politics." For background, see the Editorial Note, "Wilson's First Treatise on Democratic Government," Vol. 5, pp. 54-58.

# An Outline of and Memoranda for "The Philosophy of Politics"

[c. Jan. 26, 1895]
Woodrow Wilson

    I. The Democratic State
       (a) Its History
       (b) Its Nature
       (c) Its Structure
       (d) Its Ends and Functions.
   II. Political Progress
  III. Political Prejudice
  IV. Political Expediency
   V. Political Morality
  VI. Practical Politics.

*Political Sin* is the transgression of the law of political progress (rightly understood)[.] The act which is politically sinful in one generation, consequently, is not so in another generation; for the law of political progress, though in one sense always the same, does not utter the same particular commands from generation to generation. It is unchangeable only in being uniform.

*Parallel*: The Laws of Ethics, as developed independently of Revelation.

Democracy = mutual responsibility—sometimes mistaken for a basis for socialism. Political democracy is one thing, *economic* democracy another. Not that the State is not the same thing and subject to the same rules in one activity as in another: but mutual responsibility comprehends every man's bearing his own burden, as so must helping others to their duty—to such individual manliness and strength as makes—when man is added to man to make a people—a nation's vitality and greatness. I am responsible for not allowing my brother the best discipline by which to develop his manliness and individuality: and active state regulation of the economic life of the individual ends nowhere *in principle*.

WWhw in notebook (WP, DLC) with WWhw inscription on cover: "VII Notes."

## Random Notes for "The Philosophy of Politics"

[c. Jan. 26, 1895]

*Introduction*, Part I. *Mem.*

The world is full of hope. The dreams of Socialism, the visions —even the distempered visions—of democratic privilege, the uneasy movements of labour for its betterment and elevation, the compulsion of ideals of every kind, mark a world alive with hope and quick with the energy of great motives and inspirations. But the hope is without moderation, the purpose without practical programs, the energy without guidance. The most helpful service to lead those waiting for fulfillment of visions would be an illustration out of the history of the laws of social growth and political revolution, and an exposition of the statesmanship of progress, the philosophy of associated movement and action of men as states. That is the purpose of these pages.

If we had by heart the experiences of pre-historic politicians, if we could see Athenian affairs as Pericles saw them, if we had not lost clear-headed Aristotle's analysis of the constitutions of the Greek cities, if we could read Cicero without glasses, if things now piece-meal and obscure were pieced and plain—we might frame a few infallible political rules which would make state-craft easy. But unhappily the world forgets with fatal facility. We have to go to books to find out what our grandfathers thought and did; and only the studious amongst our grandchildren will know what we ourselves were like.

Experience by proxy is not half so good or half so much respected as personal experience. We heed what we ourselves remember or what our grandfathers can relate: this, rather than the records of history, we *realize*. A man who lives amongst us, has had long life, prominent experience, and retains a strong memory of events can give the most eminent of historians odds in a game of influence on present thought and action. The past seems dead. What interest there is in the conversation of the garrulous old lady who heard the reply to Hayne [blank]

"The end of Political Science is the supreme good; and Political Science is concerned with nothing so much as with producing a certain character in the citizens, or, in other words, with making them good, and capable of performing noble actions." *Aristotle*: Nichomachean Ethics (Welldon's trans.), p. 22.

Education in self-government. The higher education should be made an ally of the state—Note University of Berlin and Wm v. Humboldt and Stein. The influence of the capital upon the Univ. and of the Univ. upon the capital. A body of able and disinterested critics at the very doors of the govt. They can see the small, the technical, things which the nation could never see: but there must be certain gross features which the nation should see, and of which the nation should be the only competent critic. There is an education possible in politics if ministers be in a position of well-defined, quickly-operative responsibility. Univ. critics may throw much light, derivable no-other-whence, upon methods; but the nation must decide policy. The Univ. can be the eyes of the nation in finding out the personal and particular features of administration, but there must be a personality in affairs large enough for the whole country to see and understand.

Why do men of action crave "strong," concentrated govt. to govt. by discussion? Because of its readiness and efficiency. But is it not possible to have this too in govt. by discussion? In every efficient govt. the *few* must originate, but in a govt. by discussion the many criticize; and in a *free* govt. the criticism of the many is *authoritative*. It is the *authority* of the criticism which distinguishes free from despotic govt. Russia at one extreme; Germany in a middle, half-and-half place; Eng. at the other extreme. Cong. Govt. is all criticism and no *rule*. The many both originate and criticise: whereas they are fit for the one function, but not for the other.

*What is responsibility*?—as illustrated by the *sort* of light thrown upon the actions of executive officers and upon the actions of bodies of legislators. What illustrations from history?

Take municipal government as depicted by Mr. Rose (on the city govt. of Baltimore, Hist. Sem. Nov. 15, 1884).[1] The theory of the restraining power of the *legislative* body by the executive—especially in view of the common power of confirming appointments conferred upon such bodies. By-the-way, this power in the case of the Senate possibly represents what was taken to be the principle of the Eng. Const. at that date as regarded the influence of the Commons over the choice of ministers(?) The mayor's appointments (in Balto.) controlled by the council: as the President's appointments came near being controlled, and *could* be controlled, by the Senate.

The true limitation to universal suffrage is limitation of *direct* control. The people should not govern; they should elect the governors: and these governors should be elected for periods long enough to give time for policies not too heedful of transient breezes of public opinion. The power of the people ought to be the power of *criticism* and of choice upon *broad* questions.

WWhw and WWsh memoranda in notebook described at Aug. 28, 1892, Vol. 8.
1 John Carter Rose, lawyer, associate editor of the Baltimore *Sun*, and statistical critic for the New York *Nation*, whose paper was summarized in the Minutes of the Seminary of Historical and Political Science of The Johns Hopkins University, November 14, 1884.


## From Ellen Axson Wilson

My own darling,        Princeton, N.J.  Sat. Jan 26 [1895]

It is after two now so I must write a hurried little note only for the 2.30 collection—since if I wait till tonight it may as well go unwritten.

Nellie had a fine night and seems well today,—as do the others also. The two older ones were out a long time yesterday, & I am relieved that M's cold is not worse in consequence. Once when I went out to see what they were about Margaret was sliding on the ice and informed me that she was "practicing falling down without crying"! At the same time Jessie was racing up and down the sidewalk being, as she said, a runner in the Olympian games. She told me with great excitement how many "other boys" were running too & how she beat every time.

What wonderful energy you are displaying, to be sure! It quite takes my breath away to think of that days work. It is also exciting to think of such real progress being made towards beginning the house. You will not have to wait until your return—will you?— to raise Col. Stockton's mortgage & stop that interest from growing.

Mr. Child says he hopes to get down on Monday with the plans.

Tell Mr. Gilman he will now have to "hustle" if he ever wants you in Balt.!

And now no more 'till tomorrow dearest. With a heart full to aching with love for my darling I am ever

Your own    Eileen.

ALS (WC, NjP).


## To Ellen Axson Wilson, with Enclosure

My own darling,                              Balto., 27 January, 1895

I feel as if I were thrusting a knife into you, to enclose this letter of Cuyler's; but of course you must know at once. I have written to Cuyler that my "mistake" as to the rate of interest makes it impossible for me to borrow at all, in all likelihood; but that I will take a few days to think it over. You see how it stands. $7000 at 5½% is $385. For one of the thousands borrowed from father we pay 5% ($50), for the other 6% ($60). This makes the total interest $495; and we shall certainly need all that money, over and above the price of the lot. Subtract $70, the interest on our Ohio mortgage,[1] and the annual balance against us would be $425. Add taxes and insurance, and I see not a cent left with which to make provision for the principal. It would not even be *honest* to count in such a matter on what I *might* make. We must reckon only on what I do actually earn as things go now.

Oh, I don't know how I am to stand this. If ever my heart came near breaking it was this morning as I read Cuyler's letter, on the street cars returning from the Post Office,—not on my own account, God knows, but on yours! I could hardly keep from sobbing, from sobbing your name, as I rode along, chilled through and through as if steel had been run through me. It is only by force of will that I write this letter to you, blasting all your hopes —[(]oh, my darling!)—cutting you off from all the plans wh. have brightened your dear face for so many months past. My heart rebels and trembles so that I can hardly see or think. May not my love break the force of the blow a little, my poor, poor darling? God grant you some comfort. The only relief I have had has been derived from thought of him and submission to his Providence. It must be for the best. God grant we may see it soon, before this blackening of the future cuts us too near the quick.

Let Mr. Child go on, of course, dear—he must now; and we shall have the plans complete and payed for, to wait what Providence shall bring. I know that your judgment will confirm mine —that we must simply give our plan of building up altogether for the present—till we sell the other lot.[2] Let us scrape together money enough to pay for this lot; sell the other for $4,000, if we can; and then borrow $4000 or $5000 in the open market, and say good-bye to these friends with whom we make so many mistakes. To play with this other scheme, under which we must borrow $9,000 at an average of 5½%, and trust to uncertainties for the future, is to play with fire and subject ourselves to an anxiety that would be killing. Oh, my darling, my darling, how shall I comfort you for this! My poor, my sweet, my precious little darling! Ah, and when, I wonder, will this terrible knawing pain at my heart cease. I am fairly shaken by it when I think of you,— and I think of you all the time.

I wrote Cuyler a temperate, dignified letter such as I think you would approve. Write to me at once, please, pet, as soon as you have had time to think this cruel business over; and let's break off the negotiations in New York as soon as may be. The "few days" I told Cuyler I should take were to write you in, not to think. There's no use thinking of $9000 at 5½%, alas! T'would be folly.

I dare not say more,

Your devoted, distracted   Woodrow

P.S. I am calmer now, pet. I've been to the right source. We must be wise and patient, and all will turn out for the best. Rashness or impatience would undo us.        Your own   W.

ALS (WC, NjP).

[1] There are no records concerning this investment in Ohio, which they had probably made through the Dickinson Trust Company of Richmond, Ind., about which see WW to EAW, Jan. 30, 1895, n. 1.

[2] That is, the balance of their original lot on Washington Street, about which see JRW to WW, May 11, 1891, n. 2, Vol. 7.

E N C L O S U R E

## From Cornelius Cuyler Cuyler

My dear Wilson,                           New York. 26 Jan 1895

I have your favor of Jan 24th and have had a consultation with [Moses Taylor] Pyne in relation to your proposition.

You are mistaken as to the rate of interest at which a loan can be had and I know you are too good a business man and fellow, as well, to ask Pyne to do anything except in a business way. The best rate at which you can borrow is 5½%. This is what the Princeton Inn pays on a comparatively small mortgage upon a valuable piece of property.

Accordingly my understanding is that Pyne will be ready to advance you $7000. @ 5½ under the ordinary business conditions which he as a lawyer will advise you of.

I am very glad to have been the intermediary in this matter and know you will be glad to learn that same is practically closed, so far at least as I am concerned.

I have advised Pyne that you will need the $7000. by April 1st and with kind regards, I remain,

Yours faithfully,   C C Cuyler

ALS (WP, DLC).


## From Ellen Axson Wilson

My own darling,                     Princeton, N.J.  Jan. 27/95

It is Sunday evening. The children are at last safely asleep, after a long and funny discussion as to the various things they mean to do "in life." (You will be grieved to hear, by the way, that they all propose to go to college!) Since leaving them I have been loafing a bit by a cosy little fire, at my old tricks,—house-planning! It had suddenly occured to me that there was one serious defect in our plan—the servants piazza is only twelve feet,—less than the width of a room from ours! Imagine the result on summer evenings when both are occupied,—the interest they would take in our conversation and the pleasure we would derive from theirs! Luckily I think the defect can be very easily remedied just by "scooping out" their little porch from the *corner* of the house; and putting the closet with its little window where the door was before. I have just worked it out, and it seems to make a more convenient and roomy laundry than the other arrangement; though the whole laundry extension is really two feet shorter than by the other plan. Of course I shall ask Mr. Child as to its effect on the exterior though.

Nellie had another bad "half-night"—this time it was a severe pain at her stomach; there has been no return of it today however, nor of the fever either. She has seemed very bright indeed. Fortunately she does not cough much and I am able to spare her the cough medicine. The rest of us are quite well. It is very cold and bright. Margaret and Jessie went to church with me & were rather bored with the cold and wind. We had a superb sermon from Dr. Purves,—one of the best I ever heard from him.[1]

I suppose you heard our friend—Mr. Babcock.[2] I hope you had a pleasant time at the Gilmans after. I had as pleasant a day as I *could* have, darling, without you for I had a long peaceful time after dinner in which I needed not to do anything or say anything but merely to watch the fire-light and think of *you*!

"How sweet it is, . . .
With half-shut eyes ever to seem,
Falling asleep in a half-dream!" . . .
"To lend our hearts and spirits wholly
To the influence of mild-minded melancholy
To muse & brood and live again in memory!"[3]

Though indeed the only 'melancholy' in the dream was that which arose from a sense of your absence. Sweet, altogether sweet, and "dear is the memory of our wedded lives"—to quote again from the same poem. I had intended to *write* to you after dinner but I couldn't,—I was too busy thinking of you. Now don't ask *what* I was thinking all that time. I shan't—because I *can't*,—tell you. To translate such moods into words is impossible,—to attempt it even quite breaks for me its delicate charm. But knowing as you do all the depth and breadth and fullness of my love for you and my faith in you the main tenour of my dreams may well be left to your imagination. Ah Woodrow my love, my joy, my pride, I wonder if you do know, after all,—if you *can* know half the love that is felt for you by

Your little wife   Eileen.

ALS (WC, NjP).
    [1] Dr. Purves preached at the evening service at the Second Presbyterian Church.
    [2] The Rev. Dr. Maltbie Davenport Babcock, pastor of the Brown Memorial Presbyterian Church in Baltimore.
    [3] From Alfred Lord Tennyson, "The Lotos-Eaters."

## To Ellen Axson Wilson

My own darling,                    Baltimore, 28 January, 1895
    If ever there was a black day in my calendar, yesterday was that day. I kept busy enough, heaven knows, to escape thought. My letters to you and Cuyler were written during church time— my mind was in too great a whirl to do anything till they were written. When they were finished I went all the way to the P.O. to mail them. At two o'clock I went to Mr. Gilman's to dinner, and stayed until after four, talking as busily as possible. From there, I went immediately to Charlie Mitchell's and stayed till six. After supper I went to church; waited after the service to speak to Mr. and Mrs. Babcock; came home (after finding Hiram Woods out on my way back) and went post haste to bed.
    But my dreams were as troublesome as my day. And, oh, what a day! Never, I believe, have I been so driven and beaten by a passion of grief. My darling's plans for a life time! My poor, poor

darling! It almost maddened me to think what you would suffer when my letter and its enclosure reached you. Even now, as I write, you are opening them, have read them: I have just been on my knees praying for you. Somehow disappointments come almost without pain to me. I've never been sanguine. Things hoped for have never been real enough to me to build upon with confidence. Since I married my only dread has been lest disappointments should touch you to the quick. I know you, how staunch and brave you are. I've not feared for a moment that this cruel blow would be more than you could and would bear like the splendid, brave woman you are. But it has shaken me almost beyond endurance to think what the pain would be that was sure to strike to your heart, spite of all your courage and sweet acquiescence. I looked about almost desperately for some way of escape. Why not take the money, even at 5½%, now we are so deep in, and make what struggle we might to carry and then remove the burden of debt? But I knew at once why we dared not do that. All my plans and all my energies would have to be bent to money-making: the worry would, maybe, kill me, and I would wound you that way irreparably. There's nothing I would not do, including slaving it for money into the grave, to save you even a disappointment! That I know since yesterday, if I never knew it before. May God help me to find the right way to serve and keep you! But I know what a debt so much beyond our certain, and even our probable, resources would mean. It's not giving up my plans. I could give up the History, and P.o.P. ["Philosophy of Politics"] too, tomorrow, without a pang, to give you that house, that home, that sweet nest you want. But that's not it. Writing and lecturing for money, striving every year to make an uncertain budget a certain one, would kill me, perhaps before the job was finished, and (unfortunately for such a scheme) you love me, and that would not be serving you.

And so this old room has seen another turn in my life! Perhaps the greatest turn of all. Some day, no doubt, this cruel disappointment will fall into its just proportions and seem a small thing after all, and for the best (for we do not know what God has in store for us). But its significance will never be diminished in one respect. These hours of agonizing love have shown me one more depth of my feeling for you. I am happy, even now, to think that there has not been in it all a moment's thought for myself. Every thought, every pang, has been for you,—and once more I know how I love you—that it is not a selfish love,—that I would die for

you, and be, oh, so happy that I could. The whole world seems
full of you: there's nothing else *in it* that seems worth living for.
My Eileen! God keep you and comfort you! and make a better,
wiser man, for your sake, of        Your own    Woodrow

ALS (WC, NjP).


## A Memorandum[1]

[Jan. 28, 1895]

Col. Marshall:[2] *Notes of conversation*, after dinner, Jan'y 28,
1895 (Mrs. Machen's)

Was present (as chief of staff) at Lee's surrender. Grant
crossed the room and handed to Lee a pencilled statement of the
terms of surrender, the officers horses to be given up. Lee called
his attention to the fact that most of the horses were owned by
their riders. Grant immediately changed the terms to read
"public" horses.

Said that Grant urged Lee to see Mr. Lincoln and talk over with
him the policy to be pursued towards the s. states, saying that
he believed that they could agree: that the reasonable people of
the South would accept what Lee thought best, the reasonable
people of the North what Mr. Lincoln approved. Lee declined,
on the ground that he was still under the instructions of his gov't.
Grant accepted the reason as sufficient and declared his purpose
to advise Lincoln himself.

WWhw MS. (WP, DLC).
  [1] For the origin of this memorandum, see WW to EAW, Jan. 30, 1895.
  [2] Charles Marshall. See Frederick Maurice (ed.), *An Aide-De-Camp of Lee:
Being the Papers of Colonel Charles Marshall* . . . (Boston, 1927).


## Two Letters from Ellen Axson Wilson

Princeton, N. J. Jan. 28/95

Ah my darling, it seems to me I could *literally fly* in my eagerness and impatience to be with you *now*—at this moment—to reassure you as to my feelings in this matter of the house and so
comfort you; for how plainly it appears in every word of your
dear, heart-breakingly sweet letter that all your thought, all your
distress *is* for *me*. I have been such a little goose over the house
—so absorbed in plans about it—that no wonder you thought that
disappointment in regard to it would "cut me to the quick" and
that perhaps I would show neither sense nor self-posession when
it came to the decisive point. But I *gladly* agree with you that the
only thing to be done is to give it up, and I am as far as possible

from having to "force myself" to say it. Let me whisper a secret, —I am rather relieved to have it over with! I believe it is providential; for ever since it became apparent that it must cost $9000 instead of $7000 before we fairly got into it I have been tormented with misgivings and it was only the desire to profit while we could by Mr. Pyne's good offer (!) that prevented my proposing that we back out. The misgivings, as you must divine, were wholly regarding the effect of the undertaking upon you. I could not but fear that the debt and the responsibility would burden and harrass your spirit, that your precious time might be frittered away in attempts to relieve the strain by extra earnings. I feel my spirits rising by leaps at the thought that now we are not to incur such risks, and if I could only send this letter to you through a pneumatic tube so as not to suffer from the thought that for twenty-four hours more you will be agonizing over *my* disappointment I should be perfectly happy. It is too bad about the hundred and fifty to Mr. Child—is it not? But perhaps we may use them some day yet;—or perhaps we may sell them—the plans— to Mr. Harper.[1] I fancy he would like that sort of house.

And now my darling you must believe that from the bottom of my heart I mean every word I say,—that I am *perfectly happy* with you in *any* house,—that no disappointment can hurt for more than a few moments as long as I have *you*, my joy, my pride, my life! How do I know but that we were indeed making a "mistake" —though not the one of Mr. Cuylers invention,—a mistake that might have gone far to prevent your achieving the work for which God meant you,—and *I* should have been responsible! the very thought makes me tremble. Woodrow darling *you* are all the world to your little wife                     Eileen.

It seems to me that my eyes are so opened now that I no longer *want* to borrow more than $5000 even at 4%. In fact wouldn't do it.

[1] George McLean Harper, who was engaged to Belle Dunton Westcott. They were married on May 9, 1895.

My darling,          Princeton, N. J. [c. Jan. 28, 1895]
A-pro-pos of the letter from Mr. Wylly which I enclose,[1]—don't you think you had best consult Mr. Tom Gresham or Tom Baxter about the prospects of the Southwestern R. R. & if they think best order Mr. Wylly not to sell at present but merely to keep you advised. Of course there is now no absolute necessity for selling at once. We would only save some $40.00 of annual interest to

father by so doing. On general principles it would seem rather unwise to sell in such very dull times unless we must.

In great haste—I am going to a tea at the Sam Stocktons given to Mrs. Reid.[2]                    Yours devotedly   Eileen.

While you are about it please ask those people what they know about "Central"[3] and "Eagle and Phoenix"[4] too.

By the way I see the Hilton sale[5] is to be over in three or four days now. People tell me I ought to go to town for bargains *before* the first of Feb. anyhow, because then *all* their "sales" are stopped & they begin to take stock & prepare for spring. So if it doesn't make *any* difference perhaps you had better send me a check to be drawn from the $2000 so that I may go to town this week.

ALS (WC, NjP).
    [1] The enclosure is missing.
    [2] The bride of Legh Wilber Reid. The Reids were tenants of the Samuel Witham Stocktons at 48 Mercer St.
    [3] The Central Railroad of Georgia.
    [4] Cotton mills in Columbus, Ga., in which Ellen owned some stock.
    [5] Hilton, Hughes and Co., the New York department store, afterwards Wanamaker's.

## A Final Examination

January 29, 1895.

### HISTORY OF LAW.

1. What were the forces of formation in the early history of law? Give Leist's Aryan starting points. What were the forces of change?

2. Discuss the *Jus Gentium*: (1) its origin, (3) [(2)] the means of development, (3) its significance and general office in the development of Roman Law.

3. Contrast Germanic law with Roman law at the time of the Teutonic invasions.

4. Why was Roman law studied in feudal Europe? Why was it "received" in Germany; how, when?

5. Why was Roman law "received" to almost the same extent in Germany and France despite the radical differences in their development?

6. Which parts of German law are of Teutonic origin, which parts of Roman origin? Explain this difference of derivation in the several cases.

7. What are the principal names in the history of French

Jurisprudence? For what particular contribution does each stand?

8. By what processes was French customary law codified? With which portions of the law did royal legislation deal before the Napoleonic codification?

9. Which portions of French law remain largely Roman in origin? Why should these parts have felt the Roman influence more than the others?

10. Reproduce the main ideas of Maine's chapter on The Law of Nature and Equity.

11. Give a synopsis of Maine's sketch of The Early History of Contract.

"I pledge my honor as a gentleman that, during this examination, I have neither given nor received assistance."

Printed examination (WP, DLC).


## To Ellen Axson Wilson

My own Eileen,                          Balto., 29 January, 1895

Never, surely, did any man have such a wife, such a lover as I have,—so sweet, so spirited, so brave, so wise. I *knew*, darling, as I said yesterday, how bravely, how like a perfect woman, you would come out of the disappointment: what I feared was its first quick cut to your heart, the first great pain, the woful upsetting of all cherished plans. You are the wisest, most Christian little woman I ever knew; but you are *so sanguine*:—so sanguine that it frightens my timid mind to see how confidently you can hope,—and I have no means of knowing how a sanguine person would be affected at the first shock of being ruthlessly snatched back at the very threshold of realising everything that had been hoped for. It did not do me any harm to agonize over your disappointment: it has left me with a sweeter consciousness than ever of how I love you: and there was not a thought in it all that it would not make you glad to know,—no shadow of a doubt what you would do. My agony was for what you would *suffer*. Yesterday, about the middle of the day, my spirits began to rise. I seemed to feel the struggle was over,—seemed to feel the sweet serenity and patience and love that breathe in this blessed letter that has given me life again. Was ever such a letter written before, I wonder. There's enough love in it to keep a man's heart full for a life time. I've been on my knees again, since beginning this letter, to relieve my heart of its great burden of thanksgiving.

We are closer together than ever now, darling, incredible as that may seem, and my heart seems almost about to break with the excessive joy it gets from loving you. How can I give you any idea of my love, my burning admiration, my absolute devotion to you, my Eileen, my queen. It seems to me as if my life *consists* in loving you

Of course we will complete the plans in detail, darling, just as if nothing had happened; and we will not sell them, to Harper or anybody else, but use them when we can,—no doubt before very long,—as soon as the other lot is sold. Meanwhile, we'll have the sketch framed and possess our souls in patience.

Oh, Eileen, how sweet it is to love you, how wonderful and blessed to be loved by you,—with such a love as you alone could give. My love for you is so persistently a romantic love, so naturally, so inevitably! I walk in such an ecstasy to be your lover. Never so long as we live can I be anything else. Should we grow very old together, I am sure that to the last I shall desire you as a young man desires his bride. The years can make no difference: I shall always be just as I am now,

Your lover, your passionate lover,   Your own   Woodrow

ALS (WC, NjP).


## From Ellen Axson Wilson

My own darling,                    Princeton, N. J.  Jan. 29/95

What with the school[1] and Mr. Child's visit and the Employment Society[2] I havn't had a moment for writing today. Thought I would certainly have plenty of time tonight but Nellie had one of her worst nightmares and has coughed so much and been so restless ever since that I have not dared leave her side. Indeed she is still coughing and I ought to be there now,—so you see as it is half past ten already my letter must go unwritten. But I comfort myself with the thought that at any rate the one of yesterday has reached you and that therefore your trouble about the house is a thing of the past. My *darling* my Woodrow!—how I shall treasure these letters about it in spite of the pain of them. I am *quite* sure there was never anyone so unutterably sweet & noble and unselfish as you,—and oh *how* I love you!

Your own   Eileen.

ALS (WC, NjP).
[1] Mrs. Wilson was teaching her daughters at home.
[2] A women's charity organization in Princeton.

## To Ellen Axson Wilson

My own darling,           Balto., 30 January, 1895

You don't say what sum you want for shopping, but I enclose a check for forty dollars ($40.). I hope it will be enough and that it will reach you in time,—though Friday *is* the 1st. February. Wont you open the safe, dear, (79-22, 3rd. time,—90, 2nd. time), get the mortgage bond Dickinson[1] speaks of from amongst the papers in the little drawer within, cut off the coupons for March & September, 1895, and send them on to him, in a registered letter? They ought to be sent at once, as he requests. Address as on the card.

I will write to Wylly to hold the South Western stock till further instructions are sent him. I will see Mr. Gresham and ask him what he advises. Mr. Baxter has gone home to Georgia.

I am afraid we shall have to leave the mortgage on the lot till the 1st. April, dear, and pay interest both to Mr. Stockton and to father: for there is Child's bill, $290 for insurance, and the rent to pay, in the meanwhile (in all $565), besides 'running' expenses, and we must keep some money in bank. Perhaps Col. Stockton would let us pay him part, say $1500, at once, but I don't know. I'll write to-day and ask him. When you get the coupons out of the safe, sweetheart, note the date of our deed for the lot, so that I may calculate the interest I owe him. We'll get straightened out in time!

What a singular letter this is,—or, rather, what a singular bundle of notes,—from Mr. Barnett.[2] It touches me very deeply that he should take such an interest in helping me to the right points of view. Some of his notes are trite enough, but others are very curious and suggestive and my [may] help me to some very interesting matter.

I suppose I shall have to accept this Washington invitation.[3] Alas! I wish I had a decent excuse to urge!

I dined Monday night with Mr. & Mrs. Machen and a very interesting company, amongst the rest Miss Edith Duer, whom I took out to dinner, and 'Col.' Marshall, a grandson of the great Chief Justice, Gen Lee's chief of staff (present at the surrender— at everything!), one of the leading lawyers of this delightfully provincial town,—altogether a very notable and attractive figure. You can imagine with what an ear of appropriation I listened to some of the experiences he related. Mr. and Mrs. Edgeworth Smith (no, Victor Smith) were there, a young Hopkins professor and his wife, and a young lady to whom I was not introduced! The guests of honour were Mr. & Mrs. Columbus Shriver[4] (You met Mrs. Shriver at Miss Garrett's[5] gallery ). I was placed between Mrs. S. and Miss Duer. If I had only received your Monday letter then, I could have been very jolly indeed. I talked about you as much as I dared—told Mrs. Shriver I expected to be a lover all my life, and Miss D. that I should have been nothing without you,—and so relieved my heart as well as I might of its burden of love,—going as near as decent to telling everybody that I was

Your own   Woodrow

ALS (WC, NjP).

[1] Samuel Dickinson, president of the Dickinson Trust Company of Richmond, Ind., who had invested some of the Wilsons' money in mortgages.

[2] Samuel Barnett to WW, c. Jan. 26, 1895, TL (WP, DLC). Wilson had corresponded with Barnett, an old friend of Washington, Ga., about his "Short History of the United States."

[3] To speak at the annual banquet of the Princeton Alumni Association of the District of Columbia and Southern States on February 12, 1895. See the news report printed at Feb. 13, 1895.

[4] Christopher Columbus and Cora Payne Shriver, who lived at 1319 North Calvert St. in Baltimore. Shriver was president of the Metropolitan Savings Bank.

[5] Mary Elizabeth Garrett, daughter of John W. Garrett, former president of the Baltimore and Ohio Railroad. Founder of the Bryn Mawr School for Girls in Baltimore and a benefactress of the Johns Hopkins, Miss Garrett lived at 101 West Monument St.


## From Ellen Axson Wilson

My own darling,                    Princeton, N. J.   Jan. 30/95

I have been again forced to postpone writing until night,—think I had better give up trying to do it in the day altogether. This time the difficulty was, among other things, a long visit,—some two hours,—from Mrs. [Bliss] Perry who came to see if I could help her out with her plans. The artist had made them very charming, but too large and expensive and with a great deal of waste space. I think I was able to be of material assistance to her. Her exteriors are really lovely; he has given her three to choose from, and it is rather an embarrassment of riches. Their man is certainly an artist. They are to have quite a help in the matter of building; his father wants to give them five thousand, they to pay him interest on it as long as he lives.

By the way, they were only preliminary pencil drawings that Mr. Child brought. I told him merely that we had decided not to build "this spring,"—that there was therefore no haste about going on with his work and that I would keep the drawings until you came and we could consult over them. So you need not pay him, nor communicate with him at all, until your return.

Your letter that should have come tomorrow has arrived tonight! That is making good time. Was glad to hear that you had been to such an interesting dinner. How I wish dearest, that you could have been entirely at ease in your mind! I hope you will see a lot of Miss Duer and of all the other interesting people, of whom there certainly do seem to be more there than in Princeton. I am hoping much for you from the change; trust it will both rest and stimulate you as much as it did last year. "All the same" dearest, I am very, very happy to [be] able to check off the first week! Oh how much I want you! and yet how close I feel to you in spite of the absence,—closer than ever as you say in your precious letter of this morning. Were there ever such letters as *yours* & did ever *woman* before have such a lover as has

Your own    Eileen

ALS (WC, NjP).


## To Ellen Axson Wilson

My own darling,                    Balto., 31 January, 1895
    I am so distressed to hear of dear little Nellie's having so many bad nights! It makes me anxious about her, and it makes me fear, besides, that so many broken nights mean severe fatigue and strain for you. *Please* take care of yourself, my precious one, and find time for rest—*make* time for rest—in the day. Do you not think that you had better get from the doctor a tonic for our baby, or try cod liver oil,—or something? It will not do to let her be a little sick too long. And are *you* perfectly well, my Eileen? Your health and strength are more precious to me, almost, than I dare admit to myself. It seems to me as if all my hopes and plans and aspirations were centred in you,—and would be gone like a dream without you. Do you know, my matchless little wife, that there is not another woman in the United States,—not another woman out of the old legends,—who could have taken the disappointment about the house as you did. It was the finest possible test of character, and you bore it so easily, so splendidly, so triumphantly, that I could almost worship you,—as the most gloriously sweet and love-deserving woman that ever lived. Well as I knew you, implicitly as I believed in you and trusted you and expected all things of you, this has come to me like a new revelation; and has plunged me into delights and prides of love such as even your accepted lover—accepted these twelve years—had not known in their fulness before. I am not unselfish, my sweet love; you use the wrong word, being misled by appearances. I am simply *absorbed*,—absorbed in you. Any excellence you may think you see in me is simply a reflection of you. Oh how I love

you, my beautiful Eileen,—beautiful through and through,—from the sweet surface of your dear face and exquisite body to the centre of your heart—beautiful in feature and bearing, I sometimes think, *because* beautiful in thought and motive. It's an education,—oh, how sweet an education,—to live with you, to love you, to serve you. I only wish I were more worthy! But, I'll break my heart at this pace! I can't stand very much of it yet,—I can't stand abandonment to it till I get you once more in my arms. Oh, Eileen, for one kiss, one long look into your eyes!

A package of examination papers came yesterday,[1]—and last night I plunged into the realities of things by beginning to read them. Well, at any rate, it affords engrossing occupation, even if it does not bring sweet oblivion. I got the latter last Saturday night by reading Weyman's "Under the Red Robe."[2] I sat down to it at 7:30 and finished it at 12:10, knowing little else in the meantime. Such are some of the dissipations of

Your own   Woodrow

Love always to the precious girlies and to the boys

ALS (WC, NjP).
[1] In his course in the history of law. The examination is printed at Jan. 29, 1895.
[2] Stanley John Weyman, *Under the Red Robe* (London and New York, 1894).

## From Ellen Axson Wilson

My own darling,                    Princeton, N. J.  Jan. 31/95

I have just successfully opened the safe and gotten the coupon which I will send this afternoon. (You didn't mean me to send the Sept. one too, did you? You seem to say so, but Mr. D calls only for the March one.)

The date of the deed to Mr. Stockton is Oct. 29, 94.

The money is of course much more than I need for shopping. Will do however for expenses until your return I hope, as I still have the ten.

I shall go to New York tomorrow if the weather keeps bright. Nellie seems much better of her cold again now, and the others quite well. One of Jessie's front teeth was so loose that I had to pull it out last night, much to my grief. But the disfigurement won't last long as the new one is already in sight. She of course goes with me to be fitted with the cloaks, as Margaret had the other trip.

I saw what Mr. Barnett's letter was but did not have time to read it. Am sorry too about the Washington dinner. I don't see why you must accept when others from Princeton are to be there. If you *must* go there though I should at least positively decline the Philadelphia one,[1]—I suppose of course they will try to get you as usual. Excuse haste,—am hurrying to catch the 2.30 mail. I love you, my own Woodrow, more than words can tell—I am in every heart throb,                    Your own     Eileen.

ALS (WC, NjP).
  [1] She was referring to an invitation to address the Princeton Alumni Association of Philadelphia and Vicinity, which Wilson declined if, indeed, he received it.


## From the Minutes of the Johns Hopkins Seminary
## of Historical and Political Science

Bluntschli Library, February 1, 1895.

The meeting of the Historical Seminary was called to order by Professor Adams at 8 p.m. . . .

The principal paper of the evening was by Mr. Samuel R. Hendren[1] on "The Indians of Virginia." Mr. Hendren stated that his plan was to treat in detail (1) the habits; (2) the domestic economy; (3) agriculture; (4) military affairs; (5) political affairs; (6) religion among these Indians; and (7) Indian survivals. He presented to the Seminary selections from his preface and chapters I. & II. The thesis is based almost entirely upon a study of the original authorities, each of which was briefly characterized. Our materials are rather meager and unsatisfactory because very little attention was paid to the Indians by the early settlers of Virginia.

The most characteristic branch of the Virginian Indians is that inhabiting the eastern portion of the State. Of the forty-three tribes which were located there, thirty, according to John Smith, were united in the confederacy of Powhatan. This confederacy is fully as deserving of attention as that of the Iroquois. Each tribe had its chief, while the emperor presided over the common council. But the federation was chiefly due to the personality of Powhatan. The economic connections with interior tribes were extensive.

In the discussion following Mr. Hendren's paper, Professor Woodrow Wilson stated that such studies are merely of curious interest since the institutions of the Indians did not directly affect our own—they only exerted a restraining effect. A study of confederation, however, is always valuable from a comparative point of view. Professor Adams emphasized the general historical interest of the subject as an aid in the study of primitive man. A picture of Indian life at that time is highly desirable. The literary form of a thesis is very important. . . .

Frank R. Rutter,   Secretary.

Typed entry, bound ledger book (MdBJ).
  [1] Samuel Rivers Hendren, who received his Ph.D. in history from the Johns Hopkins in 1895. His thesis was published under the title *Government and Religion of the Virginia Indians*, Johns Hopkins University Studies in Historical and Political Science, XIII (Baltimore, 1895), 543-96.


## To Ellen Axson Wilson

My own darling,                    Baltimore, 1 February, 1895

Yes, I *did* mean to send the September coupon on to Dickinson. I thought his request read to that effect, and I did the same last year. But if I did not read the card aright, of course follow its directions.

I am having as quiet a time as it is conceivable a fellow should have: writing letters and reading in the forenoon; shaving, lecturing, and walking in the afternoon; going through examination papers in the evening,—quite like a staid old gentleman. I have all the roving, Bohemian impulses the wildest young colt could have. There are a thousand and one things I long to do,—did my purse and my conscience allow: there are scores of ways in which I long to be amused, innocent, questionable, undoubtedly wrong: a city tempts me as much now as it did years ago,—more now than it did then. On the whole, therefore, it is safest to sit in my room and read examinations, and grow old after my kind,—the sedate and respectable college professor.

I wonder what other wife there is in the world, herself pure and innocent and wholesome-minded, to whom her husband could make such disclosures of himself as I dare make of myself to you! I wonder that you trust me out of your sight! I marvel that you love me and believe in me. If I had no conscience, and no fear, and could do it, not grossly, but like an epicure, I would lead the most irregular of lives. As it is, I sit in my room and grind, like a monk doing penance; think of the lovely, matchless little woman in my sweet home, deeming me everything that I am not; and feel that the most poetically just thing I could do would be, to go hang myself. Then I go to bed, and sleep as comfortably as if I were the purest minded, most guileless young fellow in the world. 'Tis a rum world, my masters! I suppose I ought to be satisfied if I get through it without doing anything scandalous!

Dear father writes that he expects to leave Columbia next Monday evening and reach Baltimore the next morning. I have secured a room for him near at hand, #925 McCulloh St. I only hope he will not be dissatisfied and will find something, somebody to enjoy. This dear provincial town is not like New York; and my fear is, that he will be hankering very soon after the latter. Take it all in all, I think Mrs. Grannis[1] is about as undesirable a companion as one could find in the ranks of chaste women,—as demoralizing as anyone could well be to one's manliness and self-respect.

I am to take tea (I believe it is) with the Babcocks to-morrow (Saturday) evening; and, on Sunday, dinner with Mrs. Bird, tea with the Emmott's.[2] In what a frame of mind I shall go to bed after that! A better frame, maybe, than I sometimes go to bed with after an evening alone.

With full heart and a love which this letter only proves,

Your own   Woodrow

ALS (WP, DLC).
[1] Elizabeth Bartlett Grannis, the subject of much correspondence in earlier volumes.
[2] Professor and Mrs. George Henry Emmott. Emmott was Professor of Roman Law and Comparative Jurisprudence at the Johns Hopkins.

## From Ellen Axson Wilson

My own darling,                      Princeton, N. J.   Feb. 1/95

Just a line tonight to report our safe return from New York, after a very successful day. I am, as usual on such occasions, quite tired, so wasted the first of the evening looking over the "Century." Then just as I was about to write, young Turner[1] called & made a long visit. So now it is after ten & I *must* go to bed!

Nellie is better, the rest quite well.

As ever with all my heart and soul

Your own   Eileen.

ALS (WC, NjP).
[1] Probably Edward Bates Turner, '96.

# A Biographical and Literary Study of Wilson

[c. Feb. 1, 1895]

### THE WORK OF A SOUTHERN SCHOLAR.[1]

Among the races who have left the deepest impress of their individuality on the American character is the Scotch-Irish. In their settlements they did not enter the Chesapeake or the Massachusetts Bay or the mouth of the Hudson River; it was along the waters of the Delaware Bay and River that they made their homes. The northern part of Delaware, southeastern Pennsylvania, and western and central New Jersey received the earliest and largest portion of this emigration. From the banks of the Delaware River as centre they spread, chiefly West and South, through southern Pennsylvania; some went across the Potomac up the Shenandoah Valley into the highlands of Virginia and thence to the Carolinas: some from these States crossed the Alleghanies into Kentucky and Tennessee and on to the Southwest; others passed directly from the original home to western Pennsylvania, to Ohio, and thence afterward further beyond. Their faith was in the main Presbyterian. They were keenly alive to the best educational interests, the necessity of a classical education and the study of the Holy Scriptures in the original. Wherever they went they established schools. The pastor of a congregation was also teacher. He assembled the youth around him for instruction, and, in turn, often made preachers of them. This was the beginning of the "log colleges" in Pennsylvania: even of the University of Pennsylvania and Delaware College in part; of Princeton, near the centre of the original settlements and always the leading, as it was the first, Scotch-Irish institution; furthermore, of Dickinson, Jefferson, and Washington Colleges in Pennsylvania, of Washington and Lee and Hampden-Sidney in Virginia; of the State University and Davidson College in North Carolina; of Washington, Greenville, Tusculum, Blount, Maryville, and Cumberland Colleges in Tennessee; of Transylvania and Centre in Kentucky, and of the University of Ohio and Miami in the Northwest. The strenuous logical mind and rugged strength of character, that was often carried to extremes of austerity and sternness through the practical application of Calvin-

---

1 "Congressional Government, A Study in American Politics"; by Woodrow Wilson. Boston: Houghton, Mifflin & Co., 1893. "The State: Elements of Historical and Practical Politics"; by Woodrow Wilson. Boston: D. C. Heath & Co., 1890. "Epochs of American History: Division and Reunion, 1829-1889"; by Woodrow Wilson. New York and London: Longmans, Green & Co., 1893. "An Old Master, and Other Political Essays"; by Woodrow Wilson. New York: Charles Scribner's Sons, 1893. [Author's note]

ism to matters of daily life, and intensified by inherited traits and education, became almost race characteristics. Great theologians, who were at the same time great teachers and forcible speakers, were the especial product of this training. Nor did they eschew politics. From the settlement of this stock in the Carolinas sprang Andrew Jackson as well as his great opponents on nullification, Calhoun and McDuffie. John C. Calhoun, indeed, stands as the highest exemplar of this race in extreme logical vigor and relentlessness of philosophic speculation addressed to political methods and not to theology. To the present writer it is more than a fancy, it is a conviction, that these racial characteristics can be traced in the subject of this paper, Mr. Woodrow Wilson, whose Scotch-Irish ancestry bequeathed to him much of the logical reasoning power and of other marked characteristics of this sturdy race. It is therefore worth while first to glance at the career of his father, who is still living.

Joseph Ruggles Wilson was born in Steubenville, Ohio, in 1825, and was a son of the Hon. James Wilson, a prominent Whig politician, member of the Legislature, judge, editor, and proprietor of a paper which was in those days of great power in all that western country, the *Steubenville Herald*. James Wilson was born in County Down and his wife, Anne Adams, in Londonderry. The son went to Jefferson College, in Canonsburgh, Pa., and was graduated in 1844, at 19 years of age. Jefferson College, like its sister, Washington College, with which it has been associated since 1865, is remarkable for the number of preachers it has turned out—a general characteristic of Scotch-Irish institutions. From a total of 1,950 names in the general catalogue of 1889, 940, or nearly fifty per cent., have become ministers, 428 lawyers, 208 physicians. All other classes number 374. Trained in this atmosphere, the young man very naturally directed his attention to theology. He studied one year at the Western Theological Seminary, in Pittsburg, and two years at the Princeton Seminary. He was licensed to preach in 1848 by the Presbytery of his native place, Steubenville, and his ordination was solemnized in 1849 by the Presbytery of Ohio. Two weeks before, like many another ministerial candidate, he was married. His wife was Miss Jessie Woodrow, daughter of the Rev. Dr. Thomas Woodrow, a Scotch Presbyterian minister who seems to have come over with his family from England to America. A son of Dr. Thomas Woodrow was later also a student at Jefferson College and became the well-known Dr. James Woodrow, of the Presbyterian Theological Seminary, in Columbia, South Carolina, who was tried for his opinions regarding the Creation. Dr. Wood-row is now President of the South Carolina College in Columbia.

After his marriage and ordination, Joseph R. Wilson spent the first two years of his ministry as pastor of a small church in Pennsylvania at Chartiers, and then accepted the professorship of natural science in Hampden-Sidney College, Virginia. This call removed him to the South in 1851, and so determined his future field of labor. The college was the leading institution in southside Virginia, founded by a liberal minded and patriotic people in 1775, just before the outbreak of the Revolution, and, after William and Mary, the oldest college in Virginia and there-fore in the South. The President at this time was Dr. Lewis W. Green, an eloquent Kentuckian, who had been professor in the Theological Seminary at Pittsburg, and probably had known young Wilson there. Under Dr. Green's administration the college was in most flourishing condition, having about one hundred and fifty students at each session—men of high character and stand-ing, as proved by their later lives. Ex-Governor McKinney, of Virginia, the present President of Hampden-Sidney, other mem-bers of the Board of Trustees, and several prominent ministers of the Presbyterian Church, were students in Prof. Wilson's classes, and all report the warmest expressions of opinion of him at that time both as a teacher and as a man. Of course, "natural science," as taught in our colleges in the early fifties, was a popular expository subject with simple apparatus rather than a series of practical and exhaustive investigations of knowledge. The chair which the young professor was filling at Hampden-Sidney was the same the noted scientist, John William Draper, had held; and the curious apparatus with which Draper was said to have taken the first sun-picture in America was still there. So rapid has been the progress of photography in America, both as an art and as a science! Dr. Green afterwards removed to his native State, where he was successively President of Transylvania University and of Centre College, but he is best known, perhaps, to the generation of to-day as the father of the wife of Vice-President Stevenson, who was a student at Centre College. Be-sides his family, he seems to have taken with him to Kentucky the germs of a second edition of the "Anaconda" Club, as the housekeepers at Hampden-Sidney had named a well-known lit-erary association, in existence from time immemorial, from the notoriously voracious appetites of the members which were as ex-haustless as their discussions.

It was not, however, under these happy conditions at Hampden-Sidney that Woodrow Wilson was born, but in Staunton, Virginia, whither his father, after a four years professorship, had gone as pastor of the First Presbyterian Church in 1855. Here the father remained two years, the son being born meanwhile in the year 1856. He was named Thomas Woodrow, after his mother's father, and on the pages of the catalogue of the University of Virginia as late as 1881 the name was still "Thomas Woodrow Wilson," but it was simplified soon after.

The boyhood and early manhood of Woodrow Wilson was spent in different spots, for ministers and the families of ministers know what it is to remove from charge to charge, and from old associations to new. In many respects this change of scene and influences was doubtless an advantage. In 1857 the father accepted a call to Augusta, Georgia, and remained there all through the war, and, indeed, until 1870. Then for four years (1870-'74) Dr. Joseph R. Wilson was professor in the Theological Seminary at Columbia, where his brother-in-law, Dr. Woodrow, had been located since 1861. Woodrow Wilson was, therefore, in South Carolina from his fifteenth to his nineteenth year. About this time he must have gone as a raw student to Davidson College, North Carolina, the Presbyterian institution for both Carolinas. Probably enough, he had received in his early years close instruction under his father's immediate guidance. He seems to have entered later upon college life than most students, and there can be little doubt that this is one of the chief reasons for the maturity of powers recognized in his undergraduate years, entirely apart from his undoubted natural gifts and inherited traits. However, it was not everyone who was able to discern promise of distinction in the fresh inexperienced student. One of his former professors at Davidson was once heard to remark informally: "Well, I never supposed that that young fellow would ever do anything worth talking about." In 1874 his father removed to Wilmington, North Carolina, to become the pastor of the Presbyterian Church, and remained in that city for the next eleven years. In 1885 he went to Clarksville, Tennessee, as professor in the Theological Seminary, but has since given up that position.

Wilmington and North Carolina were the places of registry of Woodrow Wilson while a student at both Princeton and the University of Virginia, for he soon left Davidson to attend the oldest and greatest Presbyterian college in the United States at Princeton. Here he graduated in the class of 1879 with the degree of A.B. Despite its ultra-conservatism in college circles, Princeton has always been distinguished for encouraging the literary spirit among its students. In the literary training he received, both in the literary society halls and through the medium of the college magazine, the *Nassau Literary*, the powers of the young student had full opportunity to mature and ripen.

The autumn following upon graduation found him a student of law at the University of Virginia, the great Southern school of the day. The law department of this institution has been directed since 1845 by one mind, Mr. John B. Minor, as professor of common and statute law. Wilson was in his law classes for a session and a half, and the teacher's influence upon his work is unmistakable. Any one familiar with Mr. Minor's textbooks on the law, with the precision which marks them and the logical summaries and detailed index prefaces with which they are provided, will detect similar qualities in the work of his brilliant pupil. For instance, prefixed to his volume on "The State" are thirty-six pages of outline indicating the table of contents and presenting to the eye the relations each part bears to the other.

Reference to these incidents and impressions of college and youth needs no excuse. It is in these that one finds the incidents that go towards making the scholar and the future man. Already he had won distinction as an essayist in his last college year, for while the first literary medal was awarded to an essay on "John Randolph of Roanoke," two other pieces were signallized with equal commendation, either of the two taking second place without distinction, and both from the same hand, that of Mr. Woodrow Wilson. They were two articles on the English statesmen, "John Bright" and "William Ewart Gladstone." The authors had been unknown except to a few personal friends. It came out that the writer of the article on Randolph was Mr. [William Cabell] Bruce, whose boyhood had been spent in the immediate neighborhood of Randolph's home, and who was able to amass and incorporate fresh traditions about this most eccentric of characters. One is happy to record that both these gentlemen are fulfilling in their respective spheres the high promises set for them.

Particular attention has been called to these seemingly unimportant incidents of college life for a special purpose. It must be remembered that at this time Mr. Wilson was a comparatively mature young man of twenty-four. In the author of the essays on John Bright and Gladstone there is clearly foreshadowed the future writer of "Congressional Government," the earliest, the most striking and most popular of his books. The essays on

Bright and Gladstone appeared in the *Virginia University Magazine* in 1880. The volume on "Congressional Government" was published four years later, 1884-5. There is the same hearty admiration of English forms of government, inherited, possibly, in part from his name-sake, his maternal grandfather, to be found in the earlier productions as in the latter. There are the germs of the same belief that the English system of responsible government by a ministry, which may be called upon by a vote of lack of confidence to resign, is superior to the irresponsible and impersonal government by congressional committees; that the Speaker of the American House has too absolute a power over legislation in forming the complexion of these committees; that a brilliant man, however capable, unless placed upon a particular committee, can find little or no opportunity to display his powers and influence legislation for the State; that, through the trend of events, the lower house of our Congress is but a body to ratify or reject or slightly modify committee work, but not to legislate in the largest sense. This is the burden of his later analysis in "Congressional Government." The same note was struck clearly while he was a student of law at the University of Virginia. Indeed, it was struck even earlier, and it has been sounded more than once afterwards. For in the summer of Mr. Wilson's graduation from Princeton (1879) there appeared an article in the August number of *The International Review*, entitled "Cabinet Government in the United States," by the new alumnus. It contains the essence of this idea of responsible government by a cabinet who could have a voice on the floor of the House and direct and shape legislation. Mr. Wilson has been the especial champion before the public of this idea which Mr. Gamaliel Bradford, in the New York *Nation*, took hold of and emphasized so vigorously.

Woodrow Wilson returned to the University of Virginia to complete the law course of two years, but he left before the session ended without taking his degree in law. Singularly enough, some of the men with whom he most closely affiliated as students have in their later career displayed somewhat similar interests in literary and historical pursuits. Contemporary associates in his own Greek letter society were Drs. [Richard Heath] Dabney and [Charles William] Kent, professors of history and English literature respectively in the University of Virginia, and Professor [William Peterfield] Trent, of the chair of English and History in the University of the South.

Perhaps from the fact that he had spent so much of his early

life in Georgia, and because Atlanta was then regarded as a
rapidly growing city with a fine future—"the Gate City of the
South"—upon leaving the University young Wilson entered upon
the practice of law in Atlanta. It is said he did not make a success
of it; but apparently, for no other reason than that he soon left
a beginner's struggling practice for the more congenial pursuit
of the student in the history of institutions, a predilection already
clearly manifest in his early work. No doubt, too, his preferences
and habits of mind fitted him far more for a consulting lawyer
than for a shrewd successful jury pleader. It was, beyond question, innate interest and the force of an unerring instinct of his
peculiar fitness that led him to take the step he now decided
upon.

The Johns Hopkins University had opened its doors in the centennial year, 1876. Its methods of work proved[2] revolutionary in
all our American institutions. It forced Harvard, and Yale, and
Columbia, and Cornell, and Michigan, and Pennsylvania, to
stress and develop their post-graduate courses, and leave the
undergraduates to instructors, or to whom it pleased Providence.
It created the atmosphere that later rendered possible institutions
like Clark and Chicago and Stanford Universities. In 1882, the
year after young Wilson left the University of Virginia, Professor
Herbert B. Adams began his courses in history at Johns Hopkins,
and opened his Historical Seminary. A year or two later the
Bluntschli library was brought over from Europe for the young
university, to serve as a nucleus for larger gatherings in the
field of political science. The great fact to be marked is that the
history of American institutions was now studied virtually for the
first time in our own country in a systematic and scientific manner. Numbers of bright young men from all parts of the country
flocked to Baltimore to take the advantages offered. Young Wilson, alert to every intellectual stimulus, and primarily a student
of organism and life and the evolutions of institutions and government, closed his law office, proceeded to Baltimore, and
entered Professor Adams' classes. He drew plentifully from the
inspiration that filled the university. Perhaps, its most important
work and that producing the richest results, has been just along
these lines in dealing with our home material and studying home
conditions and home institutions. Of all the young doctors in the
School of History and Political Science that Johns Hopkins has
turned out, who have reflected full credit upon their *alma mater*,
perhaps the best known are Albert Shaw, editor of the *Review*

---

[2] The line "the centennial year, 1876. Its methods of work proved" was
printed out of place in the original. [Eds.' note]

*of Reviews*, Professor Jameson, of Brown, and Woodrow Wilson. The latter was already a Fellow in History at the Johns Hopkins in 1884, the year of his work on "Congressional Government." Before receiving his Doctor's degree, he was elected in 1885 Associate, and a year later, Associate Professor in History and Economics in Bryn Mawr College, near Philadelphia. This was the newly opened school under the control of the Friends, for giving opportunities of advanced work to women, and was the only institution for the higher education of women which followed in its methods the German university instead of the English and American college. In almost every point it was modeled after the Johns Hopkins University for men, likewise the first instance of German university ideals transferred to American soil. Bryn Mawr was supplied in its teaching force, in a large measure, by graduates from Johns Hopkins. The new Professor had here free opportunity for mapping out and working up advanced and special courses which should prove the basis of future work. His volume on "Congressional Government," as stated, had already appeared. He was formerly [formally] invested with the title Ph.D., by the Johns Hopkins in 1886, and was so much appreciated by that university, that he was placed on its regular staff of lecturers. A year later, 1877 [1887], the Baptist institution for North Carolina [Wake Forest College], awarded him the honorary degree, LL.D. After three years at Bryn Mawr he accepted, in 1888, a call as Professor of History and Economics, to the Wesleyan University, Middletown, Connecticut, the oldest Methodist college in the United States. In the meantime he had married Miss Axson, of Rome, Georgia, the daughter and granddaughter of Presbyterian divines. To his wife is dedicated his next volume on "The State," published in 1890.

Mr. Wilson remained in Connecticut two years, adding fresh laurels as a scholar and teacher to those he had already won. At the end of that time, his *alma mater*, the College of New Jersey, in Princeton, called him back to herself as Professor of Jurisprudence and Political Economy. His immediate predecessor had been a Connecticut scholar, Professor Alexander Johnston. It was an honor to succeed a man who had made a splendid name for himself in such short time by his concise utterances and clear expositions in the department of American History and Polity, both in Lalor's Political Encyclopædia, in the Encyclopædia Britannica, and in his own widely studied "American Politics," but who had, unfortunaticly [unfortunately], been cut off in the midst of his great promise. Nor could the mantle have fallen upon worthier shoulders. Indeed, for grasp of fundamental ideas, and the recognition of threads of organic law running throughout all history, in short, as a philosophic historian, Mr. Wilson seems his superior. In grace and neatness of finish, Professor Johnston will best bear the comparison.

The positions Mr. Wilson now holds are these: he is Professor of Jurisprudence and Political Economy at Princeton; he is Lecturer of Constitutional Law in the New York Law School, New York City; and he is Lecturer in the Science of Administration (giving twenty-six lectures annually) in the Johns Hopkins University in Baltimore. He thus reaches and influences a wide circle of hearers. His readers are still more numerous, as he is a frequent contributor to current periodicals. He is especially a favorite in the pages of the *Atlantic Monthly* and the *Forum*. A partial list of his most important earlier magazine articles is given in the publications of the American Historical Society for the year 1892.[3] The topics all show the trend of his writing and thought: they are upon problems and questions in political and governmental science.[4] It is the reproduction of some of these with added material that constitutes his recent volume, "An Old Master, and Other Political Essays." The "Old Master" is Adam Smith.

Two articles in the past year which appeared in the *Forum* deserve passing notice. The one in the February number discussed "A Calendar of Americans" and what constituted true Americanism. The author found this quality in Franklin, and in a different way in the real Washington, but not in Hamilton, nor in Madison, nor yet in Jefferson. But it was present in John Marshall and in Daniel Webster, though not in the great provincials, John Adams and Calhoun. He observes it in Andrew Jackson, clearly accentuated as a genuine product of the soil, while not of the most refined type. It was also in Henry Clay, and still more in Abraham Lincoln, a man, who, like Jackson, had sprung from the people, but was in every quality nearer the universal

3 *Annual Report of the American Historical Association for the Year 1892* (Washington, 1893), pp. 299-300. [Eds.' note]
4 "Cabinet Government in the United States," *The International Review*. August, 1879. "Committee or Cabinet Government," *The Overland Monthly*. January, 1884. "Responsible Government Under the Constitution," *Atlantic Monthly*. April, 1886. "On the Study of Politics," *The New Princeton Review*. March, 1887. "The Study of Administration," *Political Science Quarterly*. June, 1887. "An Old Master," *The New Princeton Review*. September, 1888. "Bryce's American Commonwealth," *Political Science Quarterly*. March, 1889. "The Character of Democracy in the United States," *Atlantic Monthly*. November, 1889. "The English Constitution" (four parts), *The Chautauquan*. October, 1890, to January, 1891. "The Author Himself," *Atlantic Monthly*. September, 1891. [Author's note]

popular heart. So, too, true Americanism was in Grant, and also in Lee. All were different, but all were genuine American types.

In the September *Forum* Mr. Wilson writes the first of a series of articles on the American ideal in education which the *Forum* has undertaken to publish. These articles are to set forth the consensus of opinion of men educated under different scholastic systems, as to the truest educational ideals and the best means of attaining these. Mr. Wilson believes that only two things are absolutely essential in the education of the American citizen. For it is to American citizenship he would have him educated as the ideal. All other studies he thinks may be left as elective according to the various inclinations and predelictions of different men; but, to be prepare[d] for the duties of a citizen, the college course should give an acquaintance through all four years with the great works and highest thoughts of the masters of the language, and at least for the last two years the student should study his own institutions. Let him comprehend and appreciate the government under which he lives and by which he is protected; let him understand and be filled with the thought and inspiration of his own literature.

Two of his late volumes remain still to be noticed. In 1890 appeared "The State, Elements of Historical and Practical Politics." It was evidently the result of classroom lectures, and is a very complete gathering together and condensing of material not otherwise accessible. It is a study of corporative politics following throughout the historical method. For an introductory course in the study of politics there is no better book. It shows many of the chara[c]teristics of the author; it is a concise, methodical summary, and clear exposition of the government of the Greek cities, of Rome, of the Teutonic feudal ages, of Germany, France, Switzerland, Austria-Hungary, Norway-Sweden, England, and the United States. The only Teutonic country of importance omitted, singularly enough, is the Netherlands. These several expositions of specific instances of laws and government are preceded by introductory chapters on the probable origin of government and its probable early development. Historic government in Europe begins with the patriarchal State of Homer as depicted in the Iliad and Odyssey, and the evolution is carried from that point down to the forms of the present day. The concluding chapters constitute a concise discussion of the principles underlying the nature, form, functions and ends of government and law. One of the most valuable features—and it is a characteristic sign of modern educational methods—is the excellent bibliography and full list of authorities cited. The limitations of a book of this nature can readily be seen; necessarily, in special cases, many details must be omitted within the limits of a volume of less than 700 pages. The enclyclopædiac nature of the work is in obvious imitation of German models. In fact, it is based in large part upon such a general compilation under the editorship of a German scholar, all of which is distinctly avowed in the preface. It is a book consequently, where not the brilliant, so much as the solid, qualities of the author, best shine forth; a clear, concise exposition of facts and principles over which each one of us may at some time have puzzled. It is just what it was intended to be, a useful compendium for students of government and of corporative law.

It remains to say a few words of his volume on "American History." It is really his only work in the province of pure history as contrasted with the study of government and institutions, where Mr. Wilson's peculiar strength has thus far been recognized.

Two series of volumes on periods in American history have been lately published, the one by Longman's, Green & Company, and the other by the Scribner's, the latter of which is not yet complete. Professor Albert Bushnell Hart is the editor of the former. It is a series of three small volumes treating consecutively of the development and history of the United States. The first volume, on the Colonial Period, was handed over to Mr. Reuben Goldthwaites [Gold Thwaites], the efficient Secretary of the Wisconsin Historical Society. The second volume on the formation of the Government, bringing the history down to 1829, was treated by Professor Hart himself. The last division, the period from 1829 to 1889, the thirty years before the outbreak of the War and the thirty years since, was written by Woodrow Wilson.

One is hardly wrong in making the assertion that this book, however small and concise and modest, is unique. This is simply to say that it reflects the peculiar influences and training and position of Mr. Wilson among American scholars. That he can find audiences wherever he lectures is proof of his popularity. That he has had the special training he has undergone and has risen, step by step, in his profession until he has achieved the position he occupies, is proof of his scholarship. That he is at Princeton is, perhaps, again fortunate—Princeton, in New Jersey, half way in the Middle States, between the extremes of the New England school of politics and history on the one hand, and the Virginian and Carolinian on the other. This fact is demonstrable, also, in the work of other professors of History at Princeton. It came out in Alexander Johnston, even though his Connecticut leaning was at times obvious. It is most apparent in the recent volume on "The French War and the Revolution," by Professor William M. Sloane, who is writing the *Century's* life of Napoleon. It is a relief to read in the work of these catholic minded scholars that not South Carolina alone, not Virginia alone, not New York alone, nor Pennsylvania alone, not Massachusetts and New England alone, founded this great union of States, but that each and all, and particularly every race element in it, performed its share in preparing the secure foundations for the structure.

But Mr. Wilson's attitude is still further unique. He is perhaps the only man endowed with his natural qualities and habits of mind and fortunate in the rigid scientific nature of his training, who holds an undisputed position in scholarship and letters, and has had his wide opportunities of personal acquaintance with different sections of country and different peoples. He was born by an accident, we may say, in Virginia. He lived in the South as a boy during the War. He grew up under the actual presence of Southern reconstruction. He was educated at a college north of Mason & Dixon's line with markedly conservative tendencies. He was a law student at an institution where the flower of Southern youth of his age are wont to go—an institution which had represented in its walls the ripest and richest fruit of every State and section and thought of the South. His leading instructor here was a large-minded, high-souled, Virginian gentleman, who always maintained to his classes that secession was unconstitutional and never justifiable, and that the Madisonian exposition of the Constitution was the golden mean. He was later a student in a university situated in the heart of the nation as between North and South, and only forty miles from the capital of the common country. Here his guide was a liberal New England scholar, an investigator who was fresh from the training and the inspiration of the German universities. Finally, he has been teaching now for ten years in three different representative institutions in the Middle and New England States.

From all these varied sources, Woodward Wilson has drunk and drawn inspiration and help. Possessing, as a natural gift, soberness of thought and clearness and precision of judgment, bringing a fresh, clear mind to a vexed subject, acquainted with the peoples of both North and South personally and professionally through his life and relations, he was able to write a book, modest in its proportions, yet of singular breadth and scope in its grasp. In such a work, proceeding from such a source, the Southern question for the first time could be treated with sympathetic understanding. His predecessor, Alexander Johnston, had honestly endeavored to do justice to every section as far as was consistent with his views of truth, but sometimes failed from unconscious ignorance of the real points of view. Mr. Wilson knew them, understood them, and yet was never afraid to speak out and criticise them. It is in this that his position among the scientific writers of American history is absolutely unique.

His volume bears the distinc[t]ive title: "Division and Reunion, 1829-1889." It differs, naturally, from Professor Hart's book, which immediately preceded it. The main difference, in spirit and temper, may be stated in a nutshell. Professor Hart tends to accept the present view of the Constitution, now in the logic of events universally adopted, as necessarily the correct view in 1789 or 1829, or in any other decade. Mr. Wilson is the truer evolutionist in his methods. He accepts the fact that there were distinct and very diverse views in 1799. He perceives the fact that men conscientiously differed in their interpretation of the instrument that they were voting in common to ratify. He then allows one idea to develop, tracing it in every step it takes. Finally, he shows how, by the accession of new territory, the creation of new States, the accentuation of new needs, the development of new life, one idea and conception had gained an ascendancy and validity in 1859 that it did not possess in 1789, while a whole section, owing to the peculiar conditions of life, still maintained, as they had persistently maintained in every decade, the same old views of 1789. It was as clear and certain in the evolution of ideas and facts as anything in history that the one had to contend with the other for its existence. Nor was it less certain in the same evolution that the views of the majority must prevail.

It is a striking booklet. It deals systematically, even tenderly, with views that the unerring logic of events, as the author recognizes, had committed to self-destruction. It is in this insight, this inborn clearness of vision and appreciation of facts, apart from the working out of theories in our government, that Mr. Wilson's characteristic qualities are best seen. Again, if there is any one distinctive quality of his temper with which one could fittest image forth the spirit of his work, it is found in the word "Americanism." Mr. Wilson is one of our truest "American" writers and scholars.

He is still young, under forty. His first book was published in

1885, and he has been before the public for ten years. He is reaching a constantly widening circle. The conditions of his life are known, and this honest, rigid, unswerving, fearless pursuit of truth is recognized. What he writes is reckoned as a factor, even by those who deny his premises and reject his conclusions. Doubtless, he feels himself that he has but begun his life-work in the field of American history and government. Attention has been called both to his life and to his work in these pages, as much through belief in his promise as from recognition of his achievement.            "X." [John Bell Henneman]

Printed in the *Sewanee Review*, III (Feb. 1895), 172-88.


## To Ellen Axson Wilson, with Enclosure

My own darling,                                    Balto., 2 February, 1895

I have answered the enclosed letter, and I have also written to Pyne. To both I said the same thing, taking it for granted that I had your approval. I said that, finding we must go a good deal deeper into debt than we at first supposed ($2,000 of father's at average of 5½% = $110; $7,000 at 4½% = $315; total; $425; minus $70, $355), we had decided not to build or borrow at all for the present. Of course I did not go into detail with them: I only thanked them, smoothed things over, and closed the business in the best way I could. Are *you* satisfied, dear, with my declining this offer? Oh, how hard it is to have to decide these matters, affecting your happiness so directly as they do, without consultation with you! It stands this way, darling, in my mind. We could take care of the interest plus taxes and insurance easily enough; but could we accumulate so big a principal without a great deal of wretched anxiety? If you are satisfied with this reasoning, only one more thing remains to be said: and that is with reference to Cuyler and Pyne. It was a cruel blunder of Cuyler's to mislead us so; but I believe it was an entirely innocent one, arising out of the utter inability of a man in his position to understand the necessity for nice calculation on the part of people situated as we are; and I don't believe Pyne knew anything beyond the fact that we wanted to borrow on less than the usual security. Generosity was out of the question; for of course he would not have ventured to offer us pecuniary favours. In short, the whole matter must pass from our minds without leaving so much as a vestage of hard feeling.

Heigh-ho! the thing tells on my spirits in spite of me! I can't tell whether it's my part of the disappointment striking in, or the dull pain at my heart because of you. When I think of all the sweet light that shone in your eyes at thought of that house, of all your charming enthusiasm about it, of all said and done, to the enlistment of your whole nature, the disappointment seems more than I can bear. My spirits go from me utterly; I cannot rally them. Even your submission, your unutterably sweet acceptance of the cruel facts, causes me a sort of maddening grief: such sweet suffering as yours seems more pathetic than I can endure. The sheer love it excites in me is a sort of exquisite pain. This whole affair is a *love* affair with me, Eileen! I want the house as *your* house,—your frame-work and possession,—your setting, my jewel: and I will work for it unremittingly from this time out. The history itself may be made to pay for it! I know what you will say, my lovely pet; but I also know what my love for you demands. I have found out to the bottom what it means to be

Your own   Woodrow

ALS (WC, NjP).

ENCLOSURE

## From Cornelius Cuyler Cuyler

My Dear Wilson:                                    New York.  31 Jany 1895
    Replying to yours of Jan. 29th I now beg to advise you that Pyne has decided to extend the loan to you on the basis of 4½%. On consultation with him I found that his understanding of the matter was not precisely correct and he desired me to assure you that the rate is entirely satisfactory to himself on the 4½% basis. He candidly told me yesterday that this money which he expects to loan you is from Bonds being paid off at the present time and which have been bearing interest @ 4½%. Accordingly you will see that he is not offering you any assistance in the way of concession as regards the rate as he is simply retiring one first class security and getting another at same rate.
    I sincerely trust that you will now allow no possible doubt to arise in your mind as to the entire propriety of your accepting this money @ 4½% as I can assure you I have treated this matter with Pyne as a strictly business affair and am in no way responsible for his reducing the rate from 5½% to 4½%, his decision being reached on the ground that as the securities being paid off had borne 4½% the loan to you offered a good exchange.
    Accordingly my advice to you is to close the matter by writing him at once and accepting the loan @ 4½% as my sincere hope is that you may soon have a home in which you may live to end

your days in Princeton for we could never spare you from the
old town.                          Yours sincerely   C C Cuyler

ALS (WP, DLC).

## From Ellen Axson Wilson

My own darling,                    Princeton, N. J. Jan. [Feb.] 2/95
   I have been in a rush with "jobs" of one sort an[d] another today
& am now scribbling in great haste to catch the 2.30 mail.
   Nellie is much better, but I am going to begin the cod-liver
oil today,—have always intended to as soon as I could leave off
the powders. *They were* a tonic the doctor said last winter; and
it was not safe to omit them as long as there was danger of fever.
She has slept quite well for several nights now. I am *quite* well,
and so are the others.
   I am sorry you are having such a dull stupid time, darling,
do go [to] the theatre now frequently! Later your invitations will
probably pile in so that you won't have much time for it. And
then Father will be there too. *Don't* say you can't afford it! Do
it for your health. Think what a plodding life you lead here the
rest of the year and how much you need a little variety. And
why don't you go to see your friends more? Are you still waiting
for those wretched cards?
   The children's cloaks have come and are very pretty and becoming. They were $7.50 each,—enormously reduced of course—
a great bargain. But my *greatest* bargain, was a dress for each of
them of the finest material & beautifully made for $3.50 each,
reduced from $12.00 each. You couldn't *begin* to get the material
for the former price. It means that I shall have *no* dresses either
to buy or to make for them next winter. Yet I am dubious about
the purchase simply because I fear we are not in a condition at
this juncture to afford bargains! I also had to get a whole set, 8
pairs, of flannel drawers for them,—always expensive articles. I
had hoped to make their old ones last through this their third
winter, but they have dropped to pieces on them, so that they
were most insufficiently protected from the cold. But alas! the
total sum of these "bargains" & immediate *necessaries* combined,
with two car fares &c. &c. was even more than the $40.00 so that
I am almost out of money again; for I have to pay Lizzie and the
chicken man now. At any rate the spring shopping is almost all
done & next winters too,—which ought to be some comfort!
   With *dearest*, truest love I am now and always,
                          Your own    Eileen.

ALS (WC, NjP).

## To Ellen Axson Wilson

My own darling,                    Baltimore, 3 February, 1895
   I went to the Babcock's last night, to a meal which they called supper, but which, as usual in such cases, was a sort of a cross between dinner and supper: very delightful in every dish, but very anomalous. The Gilmans and the Griffins[1] were invited to meet me! Was not that nice for them! I have felt a little sad lately, and so was not in a very lively humour. Stories went round the board, but I told none at all! Nevertheless I had a good time, and enjoyed myself,—or, rather, the others,—most genuinely. No one could very well help enjoying such people as the Babcock's,—and I have begun to find out this time that Mrs. Gilman is one of the wittiest and most interesting woman one can meet anywhere. I had a talk with her last night which was really delightful; the most interesting of the evening. The Babcocks are certainly in every way genuine and charming. It's wholesome, as well as stimulating, to be with them.
   To-day I take dinner with Mrs. Bird and tea with the Emmotts.
   My visiting cards came some days ago, and I mean to begin my calls this week. My lectures, it seems, have been mentioned from day to day in the papers, and so most of my acquaintances know that I am in town, and will be wondering why I do not call.
   I enclose a check, my darling, for fifty-four dollars ($54). Annie's[2] wages are due to-day (the 3rd.), and Maggie's[3] will be due on the 9th. There will be a balance of twenty-five dollars ($25). Don't fail to let me know when that *begins* to run low. I am so glad, my sweet little provident wife, that you were so successful in finding the bargins you did. You are always wise in these things; and I don't think the bill need embarrass us at all.
   You need not be afraid, sweetheart, that I will not go to the theatre. I've been twice already—before the first of February. But the plays, so far, have been so poor that it was hardly amusing. I've confined myself to the orthodox and respectable,—and I am likely to continue to do so, now that father is to be here to look after me! No doubt my morals are safe enough from this on,—so far as going where I ought not to go is concerned! I'd be a much more comfortable fellow, no doubt, were I only dull and phlegmatic and without ideas, like—Emmott, say,—to say nothing of your comfort in me!
   Well, sweetheart, this week will take me almost half way to the end of my course—12 lectures will have been delivered before Sunday comes again! I think of you, it seems to me, more and more every day,—more and more earnestly, yearningly,—with a

more and more intolerable longing. My life somehow hangs upon
you, Eileen. You preside so subtly over every movement of it,—
you are so strangely sweet, and masterful, conquering in your
sweetness,—have so complete a dominion over

Your own   Woodrow

ALS (WC, NjP).
<sup></sup>[1] Professor and Mrs. Edward Herrick Griffin. Griffin was Professor of the
History of Philosophy and Dean of the College Faculty of the Johns Hopkins.
[2] A servant whose last name is unknown.
[3] Maggie Foley of 238 Nassau St.


## From Ellen Axson Wilson

My own darling,                        Princeton, N.J.  Feb. 3/95
  I have just been forced to answer a letter of Mr. Child's which
demanded a prompt reply and the necessary explanations &c.
have taken a large part of my evening. I seem fated to write to
you, dearest, only when I am either very hurried or very tired,—
and equally stupid in either case! I havn't even had time to enter
upon the subject of Mr. Child's visit and what came of it, because
I knew it was a matter which would require several pages! I
rather dreaded his coming of course because I didn't quite know
what to say;—there seems to me a certain indelicacy in telling
anyone the *whole* truth about this business, the Pyne part of it! I
havn't breathed a word of it even to the boys. But as it turned
out Mr. Child himself solved the difficulty as to what I should
say simply by *raising his estimate!* He was very vague, he had,
of course, not made detailed estimates, but he talked about
$10000 (!)—(to be sure for every thing complete even to gas
fixtures.) I almost laughed in his face; it seemed as though the
whole business had gotten so completely in the region of farce.
Of course Messrs. Cuyler et al can now be truthfully relegated
to the background, since $10,000 is a *quite* sufficient and *neces-
sary* reason for sounding a retreat even had we the money at 4%.
I merely told him then that we would almost certainly have to
postpone building; and the next day I wrote him more fully,—
partly because I couldn't help hoping that, since he had,—unin-
tentionally—misled us, it might turn out that we would not have
to pay all of the $150.00 but might pay for these pencil drawings
as for so many sketches & let the matter end there. Indeed he is
very nice and I believe would be willing to do that if we told
him plainly that we wished it. It would be *so* absurd to have
plans &c. prepared which we can *never* use. But of course I
didn't dare go that far without consulting you. I merely told him

that I was much perplexed about it all but that two things were clear, we would not try to build this spring and we could not build a ten thousand dollar house. The only alternatives were to build a very cheap house of wood or to postpone building altogether until we could afford something nearer what we wished. I preferred the latter alternative. But in either case what was to be done about the drawings &c. for this house? He replied very pleasantly indeed,—though he didn't say what was to be done about the drawings! He was sorry he had said anything about $10,000, it might be a great deal less; what I had best do was to send back the drawings & let him make a detailed estimate,— then if it proved too much we could either postpone building, build of wood, or build "shallower"! So there the matter stands. *Do* you think we must have the drawings completed? If so we must certainly have them made of a fashion that will not be impossible under *any* circumstances—it cannot be *these* plans. Perhaps we could "sop shallower" in more senses than one! I merely asked him tonight not to go on with the drawings in any form until your return.

And now I will have to say, good-night, darling, because it is quite late. I don't want to at all though, this seems such a wretched excuse for a letter. Pardon it and believe that I love you in very truth more than words can tell. Always & altogether
Your own   Eileen.

ALS (WC, NjP).

## A Final Examination

February 4, 1895

### PUBLIC LAW.

1. What is the theory of the "Law State"? What criticism may be made of it? How does it differ from the theory of the "Constitutional State"?

2. What is the real historical nature of the State? What are the several necessary elements of a State? In what sense and by what processes may the State itself become a source of law?

3. What are the fundamental ideas underlying the conceptions of Sovereignty? What are the several essential attributes of Sovereignty? Where, in a federal State, is Sovereignty resident?

4. What are the actual tasks of the State in every modern society?

5. What is the difference between a "constitutional" and a

"republican" form of government in respect of the position occupied by the Head of the State?

6. What are the relations of the ministers to the Head of the State in the United States; in England; in France; in Switzerland; in Prussia?

7. Is the function of the Administration merely ministerial, merely the execution of the laws?

8. Compare and contrast Initiative and Veto.

9. State carefully the several means of securing legality in administrative action.

10. What effect did the Revolution have upon administrative organization in France? What was the nature of the administrative reconstruction effected by Napoleon? What is the present character of French administrative organization?

11. What is the composition and what are the functions of the German *Bundesrath*? How is the imperial administration organized?

"I pledge my honor as a gentleman that, during this examination, I have neither given nor received assistance."

Printed examination (WP, DLC).


## To Ellen Axson Wilson

My own darling,                              Balto., 4 February, 1895

I had a very good time yesterday. Poor Mrs. Bird, who was looking better than I ever saw her look before when I called just after my arrival in Baltimore, had been suffering from neuralgia all the week and was rendered almost pathetic by it; but she was without pain yesterday and seemed really to enjoy having me with her: so that I enjoyed my*self* and staid till after five o'clock.

Then I came to my room and spent half an hour steadying my nerves for the evening at the Emmotts! I expected it to be an ordeal, so correct and dull are the good people. But Fortune was kind to me. Dr. [Henry] Wood, of the German department of the University, and his wife were invited also. I knew Dr. Wood slightly and had heard several things that made me wish to know him better: and certainly he rewards the knowing. A better talker, of the sound, substantial sort, I never heard: human, withal, humourous, many-sided, Catholic: a man and a scholar every inch of him! Mrs. Wood, a sweet, bright woman, speaking a quaint sweet English,—pure, idiomatic, yet not born with her: carefully conceived, deliberately uttered. Dr. Wood is a Massachusetts man who has been educated, mellowed, oriented by the world (of Europe and America); but Mrs. Wood is a German: she reminds me of Mrs. E. J. James[1] with a certain added touch of refinement and elegance, as if bred in a less bourgeois atmosphere. She pleased me immensely; but her husband delighted me, and seemed to string my mind to its right tone again: so that this morning I feel more like myself again.

You need not worry about the necessity of writing to me in the evening, my love. Your evening letters, if put in the box the same night, come post-marked '8 A.M.' and reach me at 5 o'clock the same afternoon. There is no reason, therefore, why you should rush yourself to catch the 2:30 collection. We are not so very far apart, in time, after all, thank God!

Yesterday was communion Sunday at the Brown Memorial. Dr. Babcock did not preach at all: there was only a most simple, affecting service, which touched and soothed, and helped me very much. The example might well be followed elsewhere.

I love you, my Eileen, my darling. It's been a little difficult to tell you so, of late. I've loved you too much to risk my self-control in speaking of it,—too pathetically, with too strong a passion of pity and sympathy. Sometimes I write about my love for you out of sheer self-indulgence: but I ought to be in thoroughly good form before attempting it. Else it leaves me, after the letter is written, all a-tremble with violent emotion, and I can settle down to nothing but reveries. How exquisite a pleasure it is to *have* you, my darling, how exquisite a pain to be without you! With all my heart,                    Your own    Woodrow

ALS (WC, NjP).
  [1] Anna Lange James, wife of Professor Edmund Janes James of the University of Pennsylvania, who, like Mrs. Wood, was a native of Germany.


## From Ellen Axson Wilson

My own darling,                              Princeton, N. J.  Feb. 4/95
   Of course you were *exactly* right to answer Cuyler's letter as you did! Right for *many* reasons,—for *every* reason. And when you receive my last night's letter you will find that you were even more right than you supposed. Now if we could only escape paying the $150.00, and if you will only cease being "sad" over it I will have *no* regrets in the matter.

Please, my darling, believe me when I say that I have never had a *moment's* "suffering" to endure on the subject, except what came at first from the consciousness that you were torturing yourself and I could not *immediately* reassure you, but must wait on the slow mails. My strongest,—almost my *only* feeling,—apart

from that,—was one of relief that we were now to escape the
risks about which my heart so misgave me. And you may imagine
how completely that feeling has overpowered all others since
Mr. Child's visit. How could there be *room* in my heart for silly
regret and disappointment when there was such a blessed escape
from imminent danger to you to be thankful for? Won't you believe me *entirely*, dear, and, so to speak, come out finally from
under the shadow of this house? You will break my heart if
you continue to grieve about it, and especially if you talk, or
think, of "working for it unremittingly." For of course *I* am responsible for all this distress of yours;—the house building scheme
was altogether mine from the first. So you see, sir, if you don't
want to have me consumed by bitter remorse you will *have* to
recover your spirits and forget all about this;—to find some cure
for that "dull pain"! Oh if you were only *here*! You could *see* then
in a moment—for when could I ever conceal anything from you?
—that I am *not* nerving myself to "suffer and be strong" (!),—that
I am not in the least a heroine, but am really and *absolutely* light
hearted about it. It amuses me to plan and scheme, but my heart
is never so set on the carrying out of my plans as you suppose.
I have too much to be *really* happy about to care overmuch about
trifles;—in short I have *you*!

I fear this scrawl is almost unintelligible the children are
talking to me so much & I am in such haste, for Mrs. Dewitt[1]
has again sent her tickets and I am going to the concert.

With a heart full—full of love for my Woodrow—my treasure—
I am ever                                His own    Eileen.

ALS (WC, NjP).
   [1] Elinor De Witt, wife of the Rev. Dr. John De Witt, Professor of Church
History at Princeton Theological Seminary, who had given Ellen tickets to a
concert by the Kneisel String Quartet in the Old Chapel on the afternoon of
February 4. This was the fourth concert of the first series presented in Prince-
ton by that famous Boston ensemble. They were to present a series of concerts in
Princeton every academic year until 1917, when the Quartet disbanded. See
Suzanne Wever, "The Kneisel Quartet at Princeton: The First Concerts Spon-
sored by the Ladies' Music Committee," *Princeton University Library Chronicle*,
XIV (Summer 1953), 183-93.


## To Ellen Axson Wilson

My own darling,                          Baltimore, 5 February, 1895
   I am so sorry that the trouble and embarrassment of dealing
with Mr. Child under the present circumstances should have
fallen upon you. You are perfectly right: we cannot explain the
situation to *any*body. We must simply say that the cost arrested
us: that we could not prudently raise the necessary money for

such a house as we needed, and so have given the plan up. But I think that we must let Mr. Child complete the plans and the estimates, exactly as if nothing had happened. That is our contract with him, and I should feel uneasy at changing it in any respect. I don't see any reason for postponement, either. Why not let him go ahead with the thing at once? Though we may never be able to use the plans as they stand, in all respects, they may serve as a standard,—from which to work *down*, if necessary, or shallower. No modification made in the dark, upon the 'ifs' of the future, would be wise,—and we can afford to pay the money now as easily as later. My judgment is, that you should send the pencil plans to Mr. Child, instruct him once more to regard economy at every stroke of his pen, and complete what he has begun as carefully as he can. Makeshifts are out of the question now. To pay him for what he has already done would be to pay him for nothing complete and certain,—a waste of money. To change the plan would be foolish now,—for we have no other ideas or purposes yet. To go on and finish what we have begun, it seems to me, is the only wise,—and the least wasteful,—thing.

Of course I *know* that you are telling the literal truth, my precious one, in what you say about your thoughts and feelings in this whole business: you are incapable of anything else, and the comfort to me is infinite,—the wonder and sweetness of it all. Being of a tragical spirit, it affects me as a poem full of nobility and a great music affects me. It fills my eyes with tears. My sadness is not grief: it comes from a deep sense of beauty,— of the great and tender forces that are in the world,—in *my* world,—from the sense of humbleness, the sense of personal unworthiness, wh. always comes upon me with such thoughts. It is not a weight, but an exaltation, to be in such a mood, my love. I hope it makes me a better man. Besides, the *comfort* of such love and constancy of spirit and courage as yours is no less than infinite. I am not unhappy. If I could only be with you I could be in spirits such as you would love to see. Don't think that I have the blues, my pet. I have not. I am in my usual Baltimore frame of mind,—neither sad nor gay, now: but equable, ready to be amused, able to work without worry, always and in every thought

Your own   Woodrow

Long, long kisses for the chicks; love to the boys. Father comes this morning.

ALS (WC, NjP).

# From Ellen Axson Wilson

My own darling,          Princeton, N. J. Tuesday [Feb. 5, 1895]
     I am delighted indeed that you are having a good time again,—
seeing pleasant people and feeling brighter. How much happier
it make[s] *me* feel too; therefore, dearest, for *my* sake you must
not spend any more evenings brooding alone but when you can't
enjoy *yourself* go out and enjoy someone or something else.
     But though I am extremely well in spirits, as above mentioned,
I am a bit miserable in body, the combined effect of the Employment Society and "the first day." I only need a night's sleep to
"set me up," a remedy to which I shall very promptly betake
myself. In the meantime I shan't try to write a *letter*—if I did it
would be stupid past endurance,—would only *try* your love instead of gratifying it. Are you having this frightful weather there?
It is said to have been at zero last night and even colder now,—
there is such a cutting wind. I was afraid to face it today under
the circumstances, so had Guin[n][1] to take me to Witherspoon St.
and bring me back.
     By the way, Mr. [Allan] Marquand's mother is dead[2]—it was
the grip running into pneumonia.
     I have had a letter from Helen [Bones]. It seems she *is* intend-
ing to come to Evelyn [College] in the spring on a visit; so of
course I must invite her too. In that case had I not best invite
Ellen[3] for the same time? It would save me such a *world* of time
& *bother* to have them together. Ellen is old enough now,—
eighteen this month. It is almost certain however that the invitation would be a mere form, that they could not afford to send
her after this hard winter.
     I had a lovely time at the concert yesterday; there were de-
licious solos on both violin & cello. I had the offer of *four* tickets
for it. The Dewitts took Mrs. Purves & Mr. Frothingham.[4] I took
*Mr.* Ricketts, at his mother's request, declined Mrs. Purves' &
gave Mr. F's to George [Howe]. I love you, *love* you,—dear,—can
you guess how much?          Your little wife     Eileen.

ALS (WC, NjP).
     [1] William Guinn of 10 Charlton St., who ran a hack service.
     [2] Elizabeth Allen (Mrs. Henry Gurdon) Marquand, who died at her home in
New York on February 3, 1895.
     [3] Ellen Axson, daughter of Randolph Axson of Savannah.
     [4] Arthur Lincoln Frothingham, Sr.

## To Ellen Axson Wilson

My own darling,                    Balto., 6 February, 1895

First for two items of business. Will you not do my check book (which you will find in the top drawer of the left hand tier in my desk) up in stout paper and send it to me by mail? I have endorsed the Houghton and Mifflin check, which I enclose. If you want the money, draw it; if not, let Ed. deposit it for me in the bank.

Dear father arrived yesterday morning and is already settled in a cheerful and very comfortable front room just a few doors away, No. 925, in the house of a nice, plain, old fashioned Virginian lady who seems to know what nice people from her part of the world want to eat. I hope he will like the place, and not go on to New York. After my lecture in the afternoon, he joined me at the University and we went around and called on Mrs. Machen, whom father has known and been fond of almost all her life. We would have gone out in the evening, either to call on Mrs. Bird or to see some play, had not the weather been so bitterly, so terribly cold. I never felt such weather here: they have seldom had such; and I feel cheated at not getting the comfort I had a right to expect from being further south. But it is *clear* as well as cold: there is tonic in the air for those who can stand it. I feel perfectly well, and have nothing to complain of except that I am not comfortable out of doors. I wish I could believe that your rooms were as warm and comfortable as this one. I should not know from anything I feel within doors that it was such a winter without. Beg Ed., my love, to watch the furnace—carefully,—*very* carefully,—and everything connected with it. This is the time when hot pipes and red fires mean danger to houses, unless every precaution is taken. He can't be too watchful and careful.

I am *so* glad, my Eileen, that you again have had an opportunity to attend the Kneisel concert. If Mrs. De Witt keeps this up, I shall become very fond of her indeed. I'm debtor to any one who gives my darling pleasure: and I am specially glad that you have found music that gives you so much pleasure. It is very interesting and significant that it is only the *best* music, rendered by real artists on the most sensitive and responsive instruments, that attracts you. It is only such music that is the real thing: and it is like you to pick it out. If there is one thing more characteristic of you than another, it is, that you respond only to what is best— most refined and most artistic, whether in one art or another. You are tuned only to the fine harmonies. That's the reason that

so many things that are coarse and too broadly masculine in me
bring a look into your eyes, an air into your manner, that rebukes
and sobers me like the cool and shaded air of a temple. And yet
your genius for loving permits me to be
Your own    Woodrow

ALS (WC, NjP).

## From Ellen Axson Wilson

My own darling,          Princeton, N. J.  Wed. [Feb. 6, 1895]
Before anything else, let me ask if Mr. Norris' letter reached
you?[1] I was under the impression that it came *after* I forwarded
the last budget. But I cannot find it; so *must* be mistaken. Will
take no chances however, but say that it was an urgent invitation
to you,—and me,—to stay with them when you go to Washington
to lecture.[2] His address I have in my note-book. 1751 N. St. Washington. His first name—one of them at least—is *Thaddeus.*

I cannot agree with you, dear, that it would be well to have
*these* plans finished;—plans clearly beyond our means even after
the lot is sold. But I rather anticipated that you would decide
we were in honour bound to have *some* plans drawn, and have
already been bringing my powerful intellect to bear on the question!—with very happy results I think. I told Mr. Child in my last
letter that I had just made a rough sketch of a "shallower" house,
as he suggested, and would send him the plan when I had worked
out my ideas. I enclose you his answer to that. I will now send
the plans to you *first*; please return them as soon as convenient
and I will forward to Mr. Child—I really havn't time to make
two copies. (By the way, why not forward yourself to Mr. Child—
62 New St.?)

The exterior of the house in front will be exactly as first
drawn—to avoid unnecessary angles in the stone work the lower
bay afterwards added to the library will be omitted. Besides that
we save the back stairs, the elaborate staircase window, and the
cemented terrace. The overhang is also omitted at the back.
Seven ft. is subtracted from the depth of the house, but instead
the laundry extension is, as it were[,] extended across the whole
end—which seems something like robbing Peter to pay Paul, yet
the saving on the ground floor is 165 ft. (I *had* hoped to make it
212 but this is the best I could do.) By the way, before these
questions of expense arose Mr. Child reported his Englishman
as saying that the house would be much prettier and more "in
style" if it were "longer and less deep." I like this plan quite as

well as the old,—in some respects better. You see it has a nice little trunk-room, and *inside* passage to the piazza and a direct way from the kitchen to the front door. The steps and door from the kitchen to the landing will do quite well instead of a back stairway; and you know I never wanted the parlour. The piazza is necessarily smaller, which will further diminish the stone-work. I only hope nothing is radically wrong about the staircase! I will enclose the old plans for you to compare.

But it [is] 25 mi. past two!!

With dearest love & devotion          Your own    Eileen.

ALS (WC, NjP). Encs. missing.
    [1] This letter is missing.
    [2] Wilson had accepted an invitation to give two lectures at Columbian University (now George Washington University). Reports of the lectures are printed at Feb. 21 and 22, 1895.

## To Ellen Axson Wilson

My own darling,                          Balto., 7 February, 1895
    I will send your plans direct to New York this morning. I like them very much indeed. You are of course wise in the decisions you have made, and my judgment goes with you entirely. I don't see why, *if* we sold the other lot for $4,000, we *could* not build a ten thousand dollar house; for we should then have $5,000 of our own, and could borrow the other $5,000 even at 6% ($300). But of course it is much wiser and more reasonable for people in our circumstances to build a small cottage: and these new plans of yours are certainly ingenious and admirable. I haven't a word of criticism. I shall send them to Mr. Child without comment, telling him to look to you for instruction. Hurrah for my fertile little planner! I not only cannot better these plans— I never could have originated them. Bless you, my dear little sensible girl!
    Yes, Mr. Norris's note came in your last budget but one, and I have answered it. I am to stay in Washington just long enough for each lecture, and so can't "make use" of anybody's house: but the invitation is none the less gratifying, and I answered it in as warm terms of cordiality as I knew how to use.
    Father and I went out on a spree together last night, in spite of the keen and bitter cold,—went to see "The Black Crook,"[1]—a really magnificent spectacle,—and how pure and innocent beside some of the modern plays to which everybody goes! Everybody goes to see the Black Crook now, for that matter. One has fash-

ionable company nowadays in almost any place of amusement.

To-night, the Princeton dinner here! I've been invited, but the invitation said nothing about a speech. The morning's paper supplies the omission. It announces that Prof. Wilson will be one of the speakers.[2] Dr. Patton is to be present. I am at my wit's end what to say. I can think of several stories, but of nothing that they might be made to illustrate!

Ah, my darling, how the days lengthen that keep me away from you! My calendar pad for to-day has this note upon it: eleven lectures delivered, fourteen yet to come: the half-way point not yet reached, the crest of the hill from which I can see my way sloping towards home, and the climb seems most labourious where the top is so near at hand! After this week I shall seem to have my face turned towards all I love and long for; and, though I cannot quicken the lagging pace, the distance will none the less obviously decrease from day to day. You need not trouble yourself, my sweet one, about my state of mind. My spirits have settled to their usual level once more, and I am all right. My present burden is examination papers![3]

*Please*, love, take the most guarded care of yourself, this terrible weather, remembering what you are to your little ones, and to                    Your own   Woodrow

ALS (WC, NjP).
    [1] This was a touring revival, which played at Harris's Academy of Music in Baltimore from February 4 through February 9, 1895, of one of the most popular stage extravaganzas of nineteenth-century America. Based on a melodrama by Charles M. Barras, *The Black Crook* created a sensation when it opened at Niblo's Garden in New York on September 12, 1866. The plot was flimsy, and the prime attraction was a chorus line of one hundred girls clad in costumes considered very daring for that day. The play is now considered to be the direct ancestor of the modern musical comedy as well as of burlesque. See Howard Taubman, *The Making of the American Theatre* (New York, 1967), pp. 105-106, 141; and Glenn Hughes, *A History of the American Theatre, 1700-1950* (New York, 1951), pp. 199-200, 308.
    The Baltimore *Sun*, Feb. 5, 1895, commenting on the current revival, noted that the play had been "coming to Baltimore nearly every year" and that "the delightful old spectacle was just as fresh and just as entertaining last night . . . as if it were not the first of all such plays in which graceful ballets, beautiful scenery and bewildering transformation scenes form the chief, it not the only, charm."
    [2] "The Princeton Alumni Association of Maryland will hold its tenth annual dinner and meeting tonight at the Lyceum Theatre Parlors, in this city. . . . The speakers will be President Patton, Professor Wilson [et al.] . . . ." Baltimore *Sun*, Feb. 7, 1895.
    [3] Wilson was probably still reading the final exams in his course in the history of law. In addition, he had just received the final examination papers in his course in public law. The exam for the latter is printed at Feb. 4, 1895.

## From Ellen Axson Wilson

My own darling,        Princeton, N. J.  Thursday [Feb. 7, 1895]

I am sorry you too are suffering from the terrible weather,— was hoping you would escape the worst of it by being so far south. It has been below zero here for three days now. The house of course feels like a barn, but we can keep the nursery warm, and I manage to thaw out at intervals by sitting over the register as much as possible. If I could keep my hands warm I would do bravely, but they remain so stiff and numb that it is rather painful to try to write or sew. But I see we are promised warmer weather after today. Fortunately the children have not caught fresh cold because of it. Nellie is looking better & coughs very little now: she is taking the cod-liver oil. The others are quite well.

Am glad Father has arrived & hope you will enjoy each other. I had supposed he would take his meals with you at Miss Ashton's,—wouldn't he enjoy the young men there? What class of boarders are at his house? Are there any interesting men at Miss A's this year? You have said nothing about them. I have feared she was getting her crowd too big and promiscuous. What is going on at the University? Is your general department in the same amorphous condition as heretofore—no better equipped? Have they any good public lecturers this year? Has anything come of their scheme for selling their country place[1] and so increasing their resources? By the way, speaking of schemes, don't forget that you were to strike for better pay there!

But Ed is waiting to mail which makes me feel so hurried that I don't know what I am saying! Love to dear Father and a heart full to brimming over with love for my own darling from—

His own    Eileen.

ALS (WC, NjP).

[1] Johns Hopkins had included his country estate "Clifton," located well beyond the Baltimore city limits, in his original bequest for the founding of The Johns Hopkins University. Although the first Board of Trustees hoped eventually to locate the main campus at "Clifton," considerations of economy and convenience of location near the libraries of downtown Baltimore led the trustees to place the original campus near the center of the city. Financial stringencies of the late 1880's made it impossible to consider a move to "Clifton" at that time. Meanwhile, portions of the estate had been condemned and purchased for a city reservoir and a belt line of the Baltimore and Ohio Railroad. In 1895, by a "friendly condemnation suit," the City of Baltimore took over the rest of the estate for a public park, paying the University $710,000 for some 250 acres of land. The University did not find the site for its permanent campus until 1902, when the "Homewood" estate was presented to it. See John C. French, *A History of the University Founded by Johns Hopkins* (Baltimore, 1946), pp. 57-60, 119-30, 463, and *Twentieth Annual Report of the President of the Johns Hopkins University* (Baltimore, 1895), pp. 9-10.

## Notes for a Talk to the Maryland Alumni

Balto. 1895 [Feb. 7, 1895]

Dr. P[atton] in the part by wh. he was cast by nature: I, at home, among 'the boys.'

Reflecting (after M. Montaigne) upon the *character* of the college, as contrasted with its *reputation*. ("Oh, yes, the celebrated wag.") Princeton's proper character, a great common school for citizens Princeton's reputation: (1) a school for candidates for the ministry (2) A training place for athletes (3) A group of technical schools, in that sense a university.

Guard the proper character: keep out the microbes of the scientific conception of books and the past.

As for foot-ball: paternal legislation? Prevention? Cure? (Flees and lice). Character: sportsmanlike character the only cure. That produced by atmosphere: by the common school of virtue.

WWhw MS. (WP, DLC).

## A News Report of a Meeting of the Maryland Alumni

[Feb. 8, 1895]

### THEY HONOR PRINCETON

Carmina Princetonia—songs of old Nassau—rang in the Lyceum Parlors last night, when the Princeton Alumni Association of Maryland gathered for its tenth annual banquet. . . .

President Patton's was the first toast, "Princeton." He remarked that it had been a cold day, but that it would have to be a very cold day when he would remain away from a reunion of the Maryland alumni. He wished these reunions were held about once a month. "I wouldn't like to go back to Princeton," he continued, "and tell some of the stories of old college days that I have heard here tonight. They interested us, but I fear their moral effect. An elevated plane of morality exists at Princeton now, more elevated, possibly, than in the past, and I don't want to prejudice the good cause.

"I don't know of any institution where advanced research on the part of its students stands so high as at that university of whose president I have had the honor to be the guest—the Johns Hopkins. While I may hope that Princeton may reach an equally high place in the future, it is my belief her mission lies along the line of giving young men their bachelor's degree in the best possible way. That must be old Nassau's great work."

Attorney-General John P. Poe[1] responded to "Alma Mater" and Congressman Barnes Compton[2] to "Princeton in the Fifties." Other addresses were made by President Gilman on "The Johns

Hopkins University"; Mr. Leroy Gresham,[3] on "Princeton Under Dr. McCosh"; Prof. Wodrow Wilson, on "Athletics"; Dr. B. C. Steiner,[4] on "Yale," and Mr. Leigh Bonsal,[5] on "Harvard.". . .

Printed in the Baltimore *Sun*, Feb. 8, 1895; one editorial heading omitted.

[1] John Prentiss Poe, '54, Attorney General of Maryland.
[2] Barnes Compton, '51, former congressman from Maryland.
[3] LeRoy Gresham, '92, a student at the University of Maryland Law School.
[4] Bernard Christian Steiner, Yale, '88, Librarian of the Enoch Pratt Free Library in Baltimore.
[5] Harvard '84, a lawyer in Baltimore.

## To Ellen Axson Wilson

My own darling,                    Balto., 8 February, 1895

How it troubles me to think of your probable serious discomfort in that cold house this bitter, bitter winter. If I were only there to help take care of you! Ah, my lovely one, be very, very careful of yourself!

We had something not unlike the blizzard of 1888 here last night, and I had to make my way through it (the street cars being blocked) to the Princeton dinner, and back again after midnight! I received no damage from it at all, so you need not be in the least anxious about the consequences: the attendance at the dinner was not sensibly diminished by the storm; we had a very jolly time; and my speech, made about midnight, went off as well as I could have desired. I came last on the list of speakers, but everybody seemed more than willing that I should speak,—as long as I might wish to. When I had finished I was warmly congratulated on all sides, and Bob. Henderson, who was present, said "You were never in better form, old fellow." So much for your delectation, my little lover. Dr. Patton made an excellent speech, adroit, persuasive, and quite thoroughly won the company, I think. It was pleasant,—and a bit surprising,—to see how enthusiastically he was received. It was not at all surprising to see him so attentively listened to while he spoke. What he said was all of it well worth hearing.

Ah, what a sweet delight it is, Eileen, to be able to report any sort of success to you, and know that it will make you happy out of mere love for me. Nothing so fills me with exalted sensations as the thought,—so wonderful, and yet so assured,—that you love me. The sweet proofs I have of that love cling about me like a perpetual blessing and make a monotonous life, which would much of it seem intolerable, so full of poetry and a sweet pervasive romance, that its flavour of sweetness and its zest never fail. I can live with all my powers at their best strength so long as you love me, my Eileen: shall keep the desire and the zeal for work which now make the days all too short. You are my inspiration, your love is my tonic. I love you so intensely that there is a constant excitement in being with you and enjoying you: I admire you so intensely that there is a constant and conscious stimulus to be worthy of you, to do and be the best I can: and so it comes about that you are my *motive force*; the excitant, and, as it were, the *cause* of all my powers!

Eileen, my precious one, my sweet wife, my queen and mistress of my whole heart, I am yours: your lover, your worshipper, your knight and servant, your liegeman and husband—the happiest, most fortunate, most inspired and strengthened man in the wide world, because                    Your own   Woodrow

ALS (WC, NjP).


## From Ellen Axson Wilson

My own darling,              Princeton, N. J.   Friday [Feb. 8, 1895]

It seems idle to write today as the letter certainly can not go through to you on account of the blizzard. Oh how I miss yours! If I were not so perished with cold I would write you a long letter, anyhow, so as to try and bring you nearer in feeling. But I will send this line, in any event, to take its chances and tell you as soon as it can that all goes as well with us as could be expected under the circumstances. Of course we are having endless trouble with frozen pipes, &c., but none have burst so far. The children keep quite well and happy in spite of all,—which is certainly the greatest of blessings. Nellie coughs a little but is *much* better.

How I hope my darling keeps well and comfortable. And oh how I long to see him! It ought to make me happier to think that the time will soon be half gone, but I believe the thought only makes things worse, for I feel as though you had been gone a *year* already—it follows that there is still a year of absence before us! But I *must* posess my soul in patience. Love to Father, and love beyond all words for my own Woodrow.

Your little wife,   Eileen.

ALS (WC, NjP).


## To Ellen Axson Wilson

My own darling,              Balto., 9 February, 1895

You say nothing of the way in which this terrible weather has affected *you*, and the omission makes me uneasy: do you, too, keep well in spite of it all? Surely, *surely*, darling, you have been keeping a fire all day in the parlour, to sit by and sew! If you have not, it is extraordinary. You speak of "thawing out" over the *register*. *Surely*, darling, you have not relied upon that! Ah, me! what a trial it is to be here helpless and miserable, leaving you to take care of your*self*, and knowing that you will not take *thought* for yourself. I don't know what to think of it all. It is, I suppose, the stubborn, unreasonable side of your otherwise lovely unselfishness. But it may some day cost those who love you and depend on you very dear—terribly dear. Forgive me, my Eileen, if I am blaming you unjustly and without foundation; my heart is upon such a stretch of anxiety about you all the time that any additional alarm startles me quite out of my self-possession. Surely you do keep a fire all the while in the parlour!

There is *no* news about the University at all. The Department is in exactly the same condition: there is no talk, that I have heard, about the money or the use to be made of it, should the city purchase the Hopkins suburban place, nor of any changes to be effected in the Department; and I have hesitated to ask any very pointed questions. I may get an opportunity, however.

No, there are no public lectures at all booked for this season of the year here: everything is just about as dull as can be. I'm none the less happy. Attending lectures is as poor a pastime as delivering them. The best thing I have to record about myself is "twelve lectures delivered: thirteen to come." I shall have reached the crest of the hill when I reach the middle of my next lecture!

Dr. Patton was kept here over yesterday by a sick headache, and I went last night to dine with him, at Mr. Gilman's, where he is staying. I did most of the talking, and so there is nothing to record about the evening.

What with the cold and the absence of anything in particular to do, I am afraid dear father is having a pretty rum time of it here; but it is just as bad everywhere else, and so he grins and bears it.

I am quite well. My room is most of the time perfectly snug and warm, and so I have nothing to complain of except the miseries common to us all,—of frozen pipes in bath-rooms, walks to and fro in freezing winds, and the rest. If warmer weather is indeed at hand, we can forget all this, and I shall be happy, if only my darling comes off unhurt. What a pain it is to love as I love you, know you are in peril, and be unable to move a finger for your assistance! It's enough to try the constancy of any man's nature—it's just as much as can be endured by

Your own   Woodrow

ALS (WC, NjP).

# From Ellen Axson Wilson

My own darling,                    Princeton, N. J.  Feb. 9/95

I had a great disappointment just now;—the whistle of the post-man was again heard in the land. Imagine how I rushed for the mail—and then my disgust when I received only an invitation to an *Ivy reception*![1] It is hard to think or write of anything but the weather,—never did I pass such a week,—first 48 hours of that frightful cold, then 48 more of the *same* cold and in addition that furious monster of a blizzard howling constantly at doors & windows. The snow was blown into the hall-way 4 ft. under the closed and bolted door. The bathroom & pantry pipes are all frozen, & have been for days. Mr. Margerum[2] is at work now trying to thaw them out,—we having exhausted our resources. He will have to tear up the floor of the bath-room;—says the case is very bad, but not at all our fault; that it is due to the hot-box of the furnace not being made right; that he told Dr. Magill[3] it wasn't. But he says everyone else in town is frozen up too.

The furnace coal is going at the most alarming rate and apparently to *no* purpose, for the house is like a barn—or a vault; —and that is a combination of grievances which would tempt Job himself to use "langwidges." That is a feeble metaphor after all, for that good man seems to have been as famous for his forcible speech as for his alleged patience. His fort was certainly not silent endurance. But, speaking of *our* troubles,—though the end is not yet, I hope it is in sight; it is six degrees warmer & though the wind is still very high it is not quite a gale.

I rather think that if the Hopkins should make you an offer just at this juncture I should hail the event with great glee. All this has inspired me,—doubtless *temporarily*—with a fine disgust for country life. Or rather for *village* life, which seems to offer all the discomforts and privations of the *real* country with none of its advantages;—as for instance *cheap* living, sitting under ones own haystack, and driving about with ones own old plough-horse! But enough of grumbling. I still have the *great* cause of thankfulness that the children remain well. I too am pretty well;—better than I have been for some days,—have some aches & pains, neuralgic I suppose, but nothing in the least serious.

With a heart full of love for you, dear, and a longing for you so great that I don't *dare* talk about it today I am
                    Always and altogether,   Your own   Eileen.

ALS (WC, NjP).
  [1] The Ivy Club on Prospect Avenue, the first of the undergraduate eating clubs at Princeton to have a permanent building.
  [2] John H. Margerum, plumber, of 32 Mercer St.
  [3] Dr. John Dale McGill of Jersey City, owner of the house.

## To Ellen Axson Wilson

My own darling                    Balto., 10 February, 1895

I am almost too sick with anxiety to write to-day. These two letters I brought from the Post Office this morning,—written Friday and Saturday,—for all they tell me so little of what you have really suffered, give me knowledge enough of it to bring into my heart a pain almost beyond endurance. I know that your 'period' coincided with this awful season of storm and piercing cold, and I fear I know not what as a consequence. I shall not soon forget *this* visit to Baltimore: I believe it must have left almost a *visible* scar upon my heart: first that cutting sharp off of a plan that was to make you happy, make you queen of your own house, and now this bitter suffering of my dear ones from cold,—from want of proper shelter and warmth,—with possible illness as a consequence! I dare not think about it. I can only pray God, who has been so merciful to us all our life together, to succour my darling and her little ones, and keep them. *I* have not suffered, within doors, desperate as the rigour of the weather was here: but any physical pain would be easy and pleasant to bear compared with this tearing at my heart that torments me all day! Darling, will you not write me, in detail, how you have been affected; will you not promise me to consult the doctor about every pain you do not understand and know to be harmless? You *must*, Eileen, if you wish me to endure this strain and do my work here without such hurt as will bring me back to you older, and without elasticity for the tasks that await me at home.

Ah, my pet, it's a serious matter to love as I love you: with such an absorption that my life seems literally to ebb and flow with yours, my spirits to move with every incident or chance that affects you. It's even a serious *intellectual* matter to have to write letters to you, because of the nature and intensity of my love and of my desire to express it. The intense and yearning effort I have made day by day, on my successive visits here, to find words into which to put my thoughts about you has done more, I venture to say, to unlock, as if by force, the closer and deeper parts of my heart, and more to coin, as it were, my blood itself into phrases, than anything but great love could have done. *Some-times*, in striking about for the right chords I have struck for an instant the authentic tones of my heart,—so that you must surely have heard them. I have felt that I was labouring for you: that I owed you the keen pain of such words of search and revelation. If I have struck any note that lay at the centre of my heart in such a way that you could really hear what, and of what kind, my love is, I am more than repaid. I would do anything to make plain my love for you: I would die to show myself

Your own   Woodrow

ALS (WC, NjP).

## From Ellen Axson Wilson

My own darling,                    Princeton, N. J.  Feb. 10/95

I know you will be glad to hear that things are looking up with us considerably today. It is some ten degrees warmer and the wind has somewhat abated. I did not try to go out and have really been comfortable sitting by the register. I am feeling quite well again; and the children are still well. Also the pipes are still unfrozen. We keep, by Mr. Marjerums advice, the two small oil stoves burning in the bathroom all the time. The trouble it seems is with the pipes that let in cold air to the furnace; they are not boxed, as they should be, and the water pipes run near them. He says the trouble must repeat itself whenever the weather is cold enough. He was working here almost the whole day,—until after dark.

We have at least had something good to eat through it. A box of chickens from Rome [Ga.] came in just ahead of the blizzard very unexpectedly,—by way of filling the old order I suppose. They are as nice as birds.

Mrs. Perry came all the way down to see me yesterday afternoon—walking too;—wasn't it good in her? She wanted to see how I was bearing the cold and lonliness combined. Miss Ricketts also came in yesterday but not for purposes of cheering me up, for she was in the depth of despair herself, poor girl; both her brothers[1] had started west just before the blizzard & were doubtless delayed, she had no idea where.

But a letter from *you* which came late yesterday afternoon of course has made more difference to me than anything else. Oh how glad I was to get it—and oh how desperately I want its writer! You need not expect a love-letter from me today, dear, if it *is* Sunday!—I don't dare. The ache at my heart is too overmastering, and I am too painfully conscious that you are all the world to

Your own   Eileen.

ALS (WC, NjP).
[1] Louis Davidson Ricketts, mentioned earlier, and Thomas Getty Ricketts, M.D.

## To Ellen Axson Wilson

My own darling,            Balto., 11 February, 1895

Yesterday morning father and I went to hear Dr. Murkland;[1] the church was full of old friends of father's, of course, being a southern congregation, and, after the service, he was fairly surrounded and beset by cordial people. He was taken off to dinner by a lady you do not know, who used to live near us in Augusta, and I went to dine with Mr. Babcock,—being admitted, as he said, to the standing of a croney. I did not stay more than a few minutes after dinner, you may be sure, but I had a good time while I stayed. I, once more, as before at that house, enjoyed *him*, not myself: for I had in my heart all the while a picture of my loved ones shivering and distressed that it almost put me beside myself to think of. How I have trembled with the cold myself since I have felt it *for you*! Ah me! God grant the time may go quickly here, so that I may be free again, and not enthralled as I am in my anxiety and helplessness! Two weeks from Friday, my Eileen, and I shall be at home again, *with you*! Let's remind ourselves how short the time is: how *soon* we shall be in each other's arms again! That's the only way to endure this separation, this suspension of full life. How idle it is to say that we are separated only in body: that our spirits are never parted! Their close and constant *communion* is broken. We go different ways during the day: we are intent upon different objects: there are a score of thoughts we cannot share every day: there are deep longings wh. must go unsatisfied unless we can keep together hand in hand and have the *same* life in detail from hour to hour, looking in each other's eyes and reassured of sympathy every moment by the loved tones of each other's voices. Letters are a blessed device, but they are not uttered and answered upon the instant and in the same mood. They are but a momentary respite. After all, lovers ought to be *together* all the while: 'tis evidently the law of love and of nature: the law of friendship, endearment, communion! Well, darling, it will soon be so. You will be in my arms very soon now—and I shall not know how to let you go—shall not know the way to the station except upon compulsion!

Have you met Mrs. Ashley?[2] Daniels writes me that she is visiting Mrs. [James Mark] Baldwin: and he speaks of her with warm appreciation—warm for him. Of course you must have been invited to meet her. I hope she has cheered you by being interesting and attractive. Don't stay at home. Amuse yourself *some* way, *any* way, rather than be miserable in solitude.

This afternoon at 4:25 (long before you get this epistle) I shall be *half through* my course of lectures—and shall be hastening homeward: with a light heart, if you have escaped hurt,—with a speed I would increase if I could,—in every throb of my heart,

Your own   Woodrow

ALS (WC, NjP).
[1] The Rev. Dr. William Urwick Murkland, pastor of the Franklin Street Presbyterian Church, Baltimore.
[2] Probably Annie Hill (Mrs. William James) Ashley, wife of the first incumbent of the chair of economic history at Harvard University.

## From Ellen Axson Wilson

My own darling,                    Princeton, N. J.  Feb. 11/95

I feel sadly repentant for having grumbled so in my Saturday's letter, now that I find it has caused such a panic on your part;—and I might have *known* it would have that effect too! I should have put a better face on it all. Now the opportunity for heroism is past, for all is well again; the wind has died down and the weather is bright and decidely pleasant. The children are actually out now at 12.30 P.M. They are *quite* well, except of course that Nellie still coughs a little; and I too am *perfectly* well. My aches and pains had nothing whatever to do with the "period"; *it* was *quite* normal in every respect and without pain. The aches, such of them as were not in the head & face and distinctly neuralgic, were in the back between my shoulder-blades, doubtless due to draughts and cold. They are *entirely* gone. I think I have done finely, for I have escaped taking one of my heavy colds,—only had a little sore-throat. I am as *well* as ever now & when I get out again, as I shall just after lunch while the sun is bright, I shall also feel as *bright* as ever.

Isn't it terrible about Florida—the trees gone as well as the fruit! They are probably ruined for years to come. I have been very wicked to complain when I have had so little to bear compared with others.

Two of your letters came this morning,—am so thankful that you are well & have been comfortable indoors. You seem to me to be having a stupid time this year though. I trust it will be "more gay" in the latter half; it generally is.

Speaking of lectures, isn't it a bore that I must miss another of Mr. Perry's lectures? He delivers one tomorrow to the Tourist Club[1] on Hawthorne, and as before I must be at the Employment Society.

We have had a great excitement over a freshman who was missing for two nights. He & a friend started to skate to Trenton.

The friend broke through and came home soaked, but he *would* go on alone. Then he didn't return and the canal was searched all the way to Trenton;—and in the midst of the excitement the boy himself came back on the train from Phila.!² What do you think ought to be done to him?

I enclose another letter from that mysterious cousin in Cleveland;³ but now with father at your side you are equal to the situation! Give my dear love to father.

I write in great haste[,] do excuse.

I love you—*love* you, dear, with all my soul, I am altogether

Your own    Eileen

ALS (WC, NjP).
¹ Apparently an ephemeral literary club, which is unknown to the Editors.
² This episode went unnoticed in the local press.
³ The enclosure is missing, and the cousin remains mysterious.

## To Ellen Axson Wilson

My own darling,                    Baltimore, 12 February, 1895

These last letters from home, telling of the return of comfort once more to my dear ones, have lifted a load off my heart. No indeed, my dear little girl, don't say you ought to have "put a better face" on things, to save me anxiety! You *could* not do that. You are bound by more promises than you could count to keep nothing back from me. And of course I knew what weather you were having—what a house you were living in—what things you *must* be suffering. It was a great deal kinder to give me specific details than to leave the whole situation to an anxious man's imagination.

No, I am *not* having such a very stupid time as you suppose. I am keeping closer within doors than usual, working off, among other things, this pile of examination papers (I am nearing the end of that job, by the way, and shall come home a free man!); and I have not expatiated on what I was doing, simply because I had not a heart at leisure for that: but, barring anxieties, I've had as good a time as usual, and enough amusement to make a return to steady writing at home very palateable;—if that were all I might expect to return to there.

I called on Miss Duer, but she was excused, and I must try again. Yesterday afternoon I made my first call on Mrs. [Harry Fielding] Reid. They have had a great deal of illness in their house of late: both she and her mother have been quite ill; her mother is by no means well yet,—and I hesitated to call till I could be reasonably sure of being welcome. My welcome was as cordial as I could have desired, and I found her as fascinating as ever, though she looks a shade paler and older—like herself only when her face is thoroughly alight with interest.

To-night I am due in Washington. It may not be possible for me to write at my usual time to-morrow morning; so don't feel uneasy if my next letter is a little belated. Dr. Patton is not to be there: I don't know whether [William M.] Sloane is to be or not. It's possible I may have to make the 'official' speech. I hope not! It's such a bore to be important.

Thirteen lectures delivered, only twelve to come, darling! By the time this reaches you the score will be, fourteen-eleven! I have reached and passed the crest of the hill, and am on the slope that gets its light from where my sweet home lies! I am marching straight for you, with a light heart again and a cheery step. I *feel* as if I were going home, and it seems to alter the whole prospect, make the lectures easier, even the examinations papers less tedious! Ah, what a difference it makes whether I am going *from* you or towards you. My life seems to run a *strong* course only when it runs towards you—my queen, my haven!

Your own   Woodrow

ALS (WC, NjP).


## From Ellen Axson Wilson

My own darling,        Princeton, N. J.  Tuesday [Feb. 12, 1895]

Mr. Harper and Miss Westcott made a long call this morning on me and the children. We all enjoyed it very much, though it gave us a set-back as regards the lessons, which were hardly finished before one. After lunch comes the employment society so I am in something of a rush, you see. By the way they were both delighted with our house, inside and out. Mr. Harper was *wild* over it—said it was perfectly ideal. So I am sure we *can* turn it over to them and get back our $150.00. Isn't that good? Good for two reasons, for I should really like to see that house materialize. It seems as though somebody ought to build it.

No, I had not heard of Mrs. Ashley. The lecture this afternoon is at the Baldwins;[1] if I could go would probably see her there. By the way, please send me by the next mail a few of your cards. The Sloanes give a huge reception on Thursday afternoon, when I shall need them. The "young Brenton Greens"[2] also give a large evening reception on the 19th to which I must send both our cards.

We are still quite well and the weather is pleasant. Best of all your dear letters are coming regularly again. Ah how I love every word of every one of them, how I love *you* for them as for everything! You do indeed, love, strike the authentic tones of your heart so that I have heard them. If I could but tell you how my heart has responded to those tones! But I long in vain for that power of expression. Not the most intense and yearning effort suffices for it with me. I too have felt the "keen pain" of attempting it, but it has always been futile pain with me. So futile indeed that I have thought I should perhaps never attempt it, lest I should find myself actually looking forward to the hour for writing you with dread and distress. And precious as are each of these letters of yours to me, darling, I beg that neither will you make *too* great an effort to write them. Remember that letters have at least one advantage over the spoken word; they are not gone in the uttering: each of your love-letters is a precious *posession* to which I can & *do* return over and over again. For the daily fare I am content with the simplest, easiest record of what you do & how you fare; for such a record never fails to breathe unconsciously and without pain or effort the love and confidence that is so sweet to me. I know, I *do* know how you love me, dear, and to know it is a joy so deep & perfect that my heart can hardly bear it. Yet that heart can and does hold even such and so great a love for you, my Woodrow, my husband, my lover! Now and forever

Your own     Eileen.

ALS (WC, NjP).
<sup>1</sup> That is, Perry's lecture on Hawthorne to the Tourist Club.
<sup>2</sup> Prof. and Mrs. William Brenton Greene, Jr.

## A Report of a Meeting of the Washington Alumni

[Feb. 13, 1895]

### FEEDING THE TIGERS

Of all college dinners that mark the winter season in Washington none are more enjoyable and interesting than the annual banquet of the Princeton Alumni Association. Last evening the members of the association gathered around the board at Wormley's, and until after midnight sang and spoke the praises of the old college that nestles so picturesquely under the elms of the old Jersey village.

It was a notable gathering of men, for it numbered many who had made their mark in the different pursuits of life and who enjoy the opportunity of getting together once a year to live over the old days and to tell what each one owes to the influence of that famous old institution of learning. There were a number of guests of honor from the college and from the representatives of other colleges of the land. Among those who came from a distance to be present at the dinner were two members of the faculty and a graduate, who, although still a young man, has already made a name for himself and reflected credit upon his alma mater by the position he has taken in the literary life of the country.

Prof. William M. Sloane, who holds the chair of history at Princeton, is perhaps better known now throughout the country as the author of the life of Napoleon which is running in the Century Magazine. Prof. Woodrow Wilson was also present. He fills the chair of jurisprudence at the college, and, although himself a recent graduate, has already made a name for himself as a political economist and as the author of several works on government. Mr. Robert Bridges, who came from New York as one of the guests, is one of the editors of Scribner's Magazine, and is also well known for his contributions to Life over the signature of "Broch [Droch]." . . .

The banquet room was beautifully decorated with palms and flowers and behind a great mass of green in the bay window was concealed a guitar and mandolin club, which rendered appropriate selections during the evening. Every time they played a college song the boys around the table joined in with lusty voices, and made the hall ring with Old Nassau or the triangle song[1] and others that are closely connected with four years of life under the old Princeton elms. The table was arranged in the form of the letter T, with President McCammon[2] at the center of the upper table and the guests of honor about him. . . . Down the center of the table ran broad streamers of orange and black, and at short distances were great baskets of pink and white roses surrounded with maidenhair fern. At each plate was a copy of the menu, one of the handsomest ever seen at such a dinner in this city. It was in the shape of a cannon, a reproduction of the old cannon from the battlefield of Princeton, which now stands nose down and half buried in the center of the campus, the focal point of all the life of the college. The menu was tied with orange and black ribbons and opened like a book, with pages containing the list of officers, the list of members and guests, the musical program of the evening and the menu proper.

After the dinner had been disposed of as college boys can, it came the time of speeches usual to such an occasion, and Mr. McCammon acted as toastmaster. Since the last dinner of the association Dr. McCosh, the venerable ex-president of the college, has passed away, and his death came with a feeling of personal loss to every Princeton man all over the land. Scarcely a speech was made last evening that was not replete with references to the dear old man, as each one knew him, and many stories of his quaint originality and never-ending good nature were told. . . .

In introducing Prof. Sloane to speak to the toast of "Princeton," Mr. McCammon referred to his eminent work as a scholar, and especially to his recent exhaustive life of Napoleon, which is attracting so much attention. In beginning, Prof. Sloane paid a high tribute to Dr. McCosh and spoke of the inspiration which he had always been to the college faculty and students alike. Dr. McCosh's mantle, he said, had fallen on no weak shoulders, and the work as begun will go on uninterruptedly and successfully under Dr. Patton. After the battle of Austerlitz, Prof. Sloane said, Napoleon had medals struck off which contained the simple but appropriate inscription: "I was there—Austerlitz—I was there." So it may be said of every man who has been a student at the college of New Jersey it means something simply to say that he has been there, for to a certain extent his position in the intellectual life of the world is assured. He made an earnest plea for the teachers of the land, and for the profession of teaching, claiming that it was not nearly as dignified a profession nor as well rewarded as it deserved to be. Speaking of athletics, Prof. Sloane said that, in his opinion, their influence was for the best, giving all the men in a great university a common bond of feeling and bringing out the best in each. Yet at the same time, foot ball, for instance, should not be allowed to get the best of a college. The college should get the best of foot ball.

Prof. Woodrow Wilson spoke to the toast, The scholar in political literature. His was an unusually bright and witty talk, but at the same time was full of good, hard, common sense when he came to speak of the college he loved so well. He referred at some length to the other two great universities of learning, Harvard and Yale, and to the characteristics that make each distinctive. The influence of esthetics and of beautiful living is all powerful at Harvard. At New Haven the spirit of success prevails and the Yale man is remarkable for his abilities to "get there" every time. The characteristic of the Princeton man, which makes him noteworthy anywhere is his spirit of intense loyalty to his college, his class and to his society.

Princeton, he continued, has had several different reputations. It was supposed to be a place where ministers were made. It had been called the home of athletics, but its true sphere now was that of a university. He would define Princeton as a true school of citizenship. The trouble with foot ball, he said, was that we had not yet found out how to translate true gentlemanliness into the game. He thought that Princeton was all right in this line, but was obliged to say that some of the teams with which the team had played were lacking in this respect.[3]

Mr. Robert Bridges, '79, spoke to the toast of Princeton in the editorial chair. . . .

Printed in the Washington *Evening Star*, Feb. 13, 1895; some editorial headings omitted.

[1] "Old Nassau," the Princeton Alma Mater, composed in 1859, with music by Karl Langlotz and lyrics by Harlan Page Peck, '62. The "Triangle Song" was another old Princeton college song with lyrics by Henry van Dyke, '73. It had no relationship to the later Triangle Club.

[2] Joseph Kay McCammon, '65, president of the Washington Alumni.

[3] There is a WWhw outline of this speech in WP, DLC.

## To Ellen Axson Wilson

My own darling,                                   Balto., 13 February, 1895

Surely you don't mean that you wish to dispose of our house plans entirely to "the Harpers"; that you have given up the hope that we shall be able to use them ourselves; or, that, if we should build, you would be content to make entirely new and different plans. I have my doubts about their being willing to use the plans and let us use them too,—so that we should have duplicate houses. If they were willing to assent to that, and let us, too, use the plans, we could not, of course, ask them to pay more than half the price ($75.00) anyhow. Besides, I have little twinges of doubt about whether that would be quite fair and generous to Mr. Child. I have by no means abandoned the hope that we may build, before very long, and build *this house*, which I already love. I don't *know* that I should object to letting the Harpers build one just like it; but I am by no means willing to give it up. Surely, darling, if we are going to build *some* time, this $150.00 for the plans, so far from being sunk or thrown away, is in a sense saved. The cost is, so far, *distributed*; there will be just so much less to pay and provide for when the actual work begins to be done. I don't grudge the sum at all; and I *hope* you will think better of this, and not dispose of the plans. That would disconcert me not a little!

The Washington dinner was in no way remarkable, but was very enjoyable. Sloane was there and will tell you about it. My speech was received quite as well as I could wish. Bridges, too, was there. Both he and Sloane made capital speeches. I took a midnight train back, and got to bed here about a quarter past one o'clock: so that I am feeling rather "rocky" this morning.

But I don't want to talk about the dinner: it doesn't interest me just at this moment. My heart is just now full of the precious love making of this dear letter of Tuesday that lies here before me. *Why* do you say, darling, that you can't express your love? You *do* express it, exquisitely. The little love sentences that you crowd in at the end of your letters are like so much music, they ring so clear and true: and this precious letter in which you let the delightful strains run on for two pages has smitten me with a delight that will not soon be forgotten. Every syllable of love you utter, every word of endearment you use, be it never so incidental, seems to me the sweetest thing ever uttered: and now that you have ventured to write a love *letter*, it seems to me I cannot be unhappy,—however impatient I may grow,—again. Oh, Eileen, my matchless little wife, if you only knew what *words* of love from you mean to me, you'd understand my present ecstasy. To *know* from your own lips after what sort you think of me: to be received and cherished as

Your own   Woodrow

Have you forgotten the check book, sweet?

ALS (WC, NjP).


## From Ellen Axson Wilson

My own darling,     Princeton, N. J.  Wednesday [Feb. 13, 1895]

I went to the lecture after all and it was *delightful*,—one of the best lectures I ever heard! I wish you could read it. Am so glad I was naughty and went. I went to the society, but the ladies "invited me away" and as there seemed to be "plenty left" I *yielded* and withdrew,—after rather hypocritically urging Mrs. Wright[1] to go. She is a new 'sales-lady' who has appeared at my counter,—(Mr. Marsh's[2] daughter). After getting through with the children at 12.30 I went out with *that petition*, just returned by the Paxtons, to Mr. Sam Stockton's,—hoped to find him at home by going at one, but missed him, so don't know when I will see the petition again.

So now I have but a few minutes to write between lunch and mail-time. We are all well. The children are happy at being able to be out again. They have been having an imaginary school in which they were teaching a large number of children what Jessie calls "strongery,"—viz to leap[,] to box, to wrestle, &c. Margaret says she is teaching them to be Amazons,—Jessie says she has killed *all the Austrians*! She has a long tale as to how she accomplished it. She says she wasn't the General or the Captain, she was the *hero*! After the battle she made a great "oration" to the Swiss. It takes some-what the form of a *saga* and is chanted with much action. She says after she finished the Swiss were so surprised to find that it was "only a little girl standing there *speeching.*" But it is 25 minutes past! Love to father and a heart full for your dear, *dear* self from     Your own    Eileen.

ALS (WC, NjP).
  1 She is unknown to the Editors.
  2 Crowell Marsh, of Marsh & Burke, druggists of 30 Nassau St.


## To Ellen Axson Wilson

My own darling,                    Balto., 14 February, 1895
    This is St. Valentine's Day. I wish I could find some sweet and perfect way to tell you such secrets as should be told by lovers at such a season! Somehow I feel as if my love for you *were* a secret, so little of it have I been able to tell. There are so few means! I can't talk very much, within the bounds of taste, to other people about my passion for you:—and there are deep sentences of the story that are too sacred for any ear but yours. And yet I can't tell it *all* to *you*! When I look into your dear face or hold you in my arms, or have any sort of close and intimate speech with you, my love overmasters my powers of expression. I am then too excited by my love and your sweet presence to be able to give *deliberate* utterance to anything. I can only exclaim. I believe I've come nearer to putting my love into words in my letters than I ever came when speaking with you face to face. But in my letters there is no tone of voice or shading of emphasis. I cannot kiss you, to show how passionately every word is meant, or tell you with any gesture how tenderly I feel every phrase I utter when I speak of you. After all, sweetheart, it is best to be in each other's arms and have no need to say anything, isn't it? There are many things I *dare* not say in my letters, because I know, from past experience, how they bring a blush to your face and force from you a gentle protest. When you are in my arms there is no need to say them. Ah, my little wife, how hard it is, loving you as I do, to love you as delicately and nobly as you demand and deserve. You are so bewitching a little person that a fellow can't *always* keep his self-possession with you. You seem made, not only to be an intellectual man's close confidante, companion, counsellor, but also *Love's Playmate*, led on to all the

sweet abandonments and utter intimacies of love,—as if you had
been made for nothing else; and *I*—well I need not tell you *now*
what *I* am. All I can urge is, that my love for you is the pure
poetry of its kind: a love that elevates and refines in the same
proportion that it excites and inspires me,—and that in all things
I am                                    Your own   Woodrow

ALS (WC, NjP).


## From Ellen Axson Wilson

My own darling,        Princeton, N. J.   Thursday [Feb. 14, 1895]
    I am *so* ashamed of myself,—I did forget the check book en-
tirely! It must have been because I was so demoralized by the
cold about that time. I fear it has put you to serious inconvenience; pray excuse me. It goes this afternoon.
    No, I did not mean to share our house with the Harpers. Am
sure they would not want a duplicate any more than we. But
the chance for ever building seems so extremely small that I
thought perhaps we had better recover our $150.00,—if possible
sell the new lot too and so get out of debt and retrieve all my
mistakes as quickly as possible. However the Harpers are not
thinking of building immediately, and nobody wants the lot, so
there is nothing to decide at present. They have the lowest of the
three lots on the hill yonder,[1] the [John Howell] Westcotts in the
middle[,] so the Perrys have the one they were so anxious for.
The Richardson[2] house is begun.
    Mr. Humphrey Ward lectures tonight.[3] I intended to go with
Ed, but don't know whether I shall feel like leaving Nellie. She
has renewed her cold somewhat, coughs a good deal again and is
quite oppressed with it in her head;—had a restless night. It is
quite discouraging; as usual I am racked in my mind as to
whether she ought to be out or not. The weather is lovely, but
there is the snow on the ground. I have kept her in today.
    I am so glad, dear, that the Washington trip was pleasant and
successful,—and glad too that it is over. I hope this is the end
of after dinner speaking for *this* winter. I find I have forgotten
the dates of the other Washington lectures; when are they? You
ought to let father go down with you and hear them. To think
he has never heard you speak yet. But for that matter neither
have I heard you *speak*, exactly; I have heard you read two of
your written lectures. Don't you feel sorry for me?
    I have heard from Stockton—yesterday,—still pleased with Har-
vard and getting on well,[4]—though he has bad days and that

"was one of them"!—a short and rather unsatisfactory letter after all this time.

I still must insist, dear, that I can't express my love! I feel the love and I see the words—and they don't *match*! It is just as impossible for me to say what I think of you or "after what sort" I think of you as it would have been for me to paint Michel Angelo's "Adam." You will have to take it on faith; only believe that I love you just as much as you would wish me to, and in every way you could wish,—tenderly, passionately, devotedly,— that I am altogether          Your own    Eileen.

ALS (WC, NjP).
    [1] At the western end of Mercer Street in what was then called Mercer Heights.
    [2] Ernest Cushing Richardson, Librarian of the College of New Jersey.
    [3] Ward delivered the first Spencer Trask lecture of the academic year on February 14. His subject was Sir Joshua Reynolds.
    [4] Stockton Axson's letter is missing. He must have been auditing lectures at Harvard, as he was not listed as a student in the Harvard catalogue for 1894-95.


## To Ellen Axson Wilson

My own darling,          Balto., 15 February, 1895

I have not changed to this smaller paper of choice. It is some I got for notes: I've run out of the other; and have not been 'down town' for a week.

The check book is here. The delay made no difference, except to our creditors.

I actually finished the last of the examination papers last night, and mailed my report to the Registrar! Isn't that jolly? Now I have time for much more interesting jobs.

What is there in this letter of yesterday that disturbs me? There is something. Were you 'blue' when you wrote it? It would seem so from one or two sentences in it. You speak of giving up our house plans entirely to the Harpers, of selling the new lot, and so retrieving *your mistakes*! My darling was not herself when she wrote that sentence, and somehow my heart aches when I read it. Was it that Nellie had renewed her cold, or was there some private heart-ache that made my sweetheart write so? And then this pathetic little matter of fact disclaimer of any power to express her love for her lover, who reads her words as he reads her eyes, with an instant and instinctive recognition of their meaning! Ah, my Eileen,—*don't*! Don't be an innocent! The only thing about your writing that shows that you are a novice is the way you talk about it. You "feel the love and see the words and they don't *match*"? Who said they could? For whom did they *ever* consent to match? The delight in reading them comes, not from the fact that you are doing an impossible thing, but from the fact that you are making the *effort* to put your love into words, and that, before the phrases have been long accumulating, you have *some*how succeeded—*no* one knows *how*,—but apparently because a score of approximations may *together* make up the full picture. Mind you, darling, I am not urging you, as I used to, to write deliberate love letters. I've seen how selfish and cruel it is to tease you that way. I am now only insisting that the proof that you *can* write them is found in the fact that you *do* write them,—exquisitely when you will. Try or not, as you please, nature will sometimes force you to it, or surprise you into it: and then I know something about you that you, apparently, do not know: my senses and tastes are all given a full delight, and my heart becomes too full to say anything but that I am

Your own   Woodrow

ALS (WC, NjP).


## From Ellen Axson Wilson

My own darling                    Princeton, N. J.  Feb. 15/95
    Your letter was in spite of me crowded out entirely this morning. But though I waited until evening expressly to secure more *time* I don't know that I have bettered myself; since it is half past nine now. I havn't been free to write before and now I am almost too sleepy to know what I am saying!
    Nellie seems to have thrown off this cold beautifully, it is apparently quite gone. She slept finely last night.
    I went to the [Ward] lecture after all, and found it "pretty po." Nothing new, and the old facts presented without any charm or freshness or skill of any sort. Still the facts themselves were sufficiently interesting—to me, at least. I seem to have been less bored than most of the audience, judging from the comments I have heard. As for the *boys* they left in a solid *procession*; and to make matters still more interesting there went forward just outside, through the whole lecture[,] the most savage of *dog-fights*! I never heard such unearthly yells and howls as proceeded from that "under dog."
    After chapel this morning Dr. Patton jumped all over the boys,—as they expressed it,—for their conduct last night.[1] Mr. Humphrey Ward will probably remember his visit to Princeton! Not only were all these things against him but it seems Mrs. [Legh W.] Reid was very saucy to him at the reception yesterday,—

told him he was "extremely rude" &c. &c. It seems that he is
excessively superior and—in short—*British* in his manners. But so
far from resenting her remarks he appeared to become completely fascinated by her! I forgot to say that the lecture was on
"Sir Joshua Reynolds," and he showed a few of his pictures on
the screen; that was interesting of course but still more comical
because of their gigantic size,—twenty times larger than life at
least—Brobdinagian babies. I wish Sir Joshua could have seen
them. How it would make him "gasp and stare."

Why should we import such lecturers when we can do so much
better at home? There is Mr. Perry—not to come *still* nearer home,
—what a contrast to this man! *His* lecture was really fine,—graceful and delicately beautiful in form,—vital in thought. It was *true*
criticism of the most serious, penetrating illuminating sort.

Speaking of speeches, Mr. Sloane says your Washington speech
was "*the* effort of your life"—that is was "magnificent!" Let me
congratulate you—as heartily as he did *me*. But I must close at
once or I shan't get this mailed tonight.

With a heart *full* of love and a score of kisses in return for that
sweet little Valentine letter I am          Your own    Eileen

ALS (WC, NjP).
    ¹ In its news report of Ward's lecture, the *Daily Princetonian*, February
15, 1895, did not mention these disturbances or Patton's rebuke. However, an
editorial in this same issue accused students of the Princeton Theological
Seminary of leading the mass exodus from the lecture, although it did admit
obliquely that college students were involved by remarking, "For the benefit
of the underclassmen who followed the example of Seminary men, we would
say that this is not Princeton etiquette." A group of "Princeton Alumni of the
Seminary" wrote a letter to the *Daily Princetonian*, which was published in the
issue of February 18, indignantly denying that the seminarians had been
principally responsible for the walkout. In an editorial in this issue, the editors
insisted on the accuracy of their charge and added that their purpose was to
bring about a general reform of student conduct at public lectures.


## To Ellen Axson Wilson

My own darling,                    Baltimore, 16 February, 1895
    My only letter this morning shall be these lines:

> It fell to me when lots were drawn
> What way men should their faiths proclaim
> And speak unto their fellow men
> Upon the things of life and fate,
> That I should use, not golden words
> Nor those that ring along the line
> Like strings atuned to music
> And the mellow cadences of song:

There fell to me, unwrought and rough,
Such speech as every man must use
In street and market, when he hails
His friend, or speaks in simple wise
Of how he fares upon life's way.
Not words that search along the chords
Of life, and find the secret
And the solemn mysteries of love.

Rude tools, plain words, untempered, dull,
That must be wrought upon and forced
Ere they will serve to cut and shape
And set, like jewels in a crown,
The thoughts men wear in honour's name
Upon their foreheads, for a sign
That they were born to worship
And make solemn festival to God.

And yet the lot that brought me these
Brought with them little heart or ease
To use such tools, and left me still
With heart and ear and thought and will
That waited still and longed to hear,
Or make, or compass, if I might,
Some song endued with magic
And the noble melodies of love.

Long was I thus, without a clue
Why I should wish to sing and do
What poets can with word and line,
When sing they with an ease divine
Of thoughts that spring like life and light
Into the eye, and kindle there
As if suffused with heaven,
Bright with sweetest phantasies of hope.

How could I know till thou dids't come
Into the path were I did stray
Like one who would—he knew not what,
And caught my heart at sweet surprise,—
How should I know till thou dids't come
What melody I waited for,
Or power fit to free me
From the troubled helplessness I knew?

You were the song I waited for.
I found in you the vision sweet,
The grace, the strain of noble sounds,
The form, the mien, the mind, the heart,
That I had lacked and thought to find
Within some spring within my mind,—
Like one awaked from dreaming
To the blessed confidence of sight.

The lot dealt kindly when it gave
But homely speech and common phrase,
To set me, first, with steadfast foot,
To follow toil and find my strength.
For you it kept the choiser things
That make men glad and make them free,—
As if endowed with insight
And a conquering constancy in faith.

Then, when the world had given me strength,
And showed me where my tasks should lie,
You came, with largess, like a queen,
And gave me what had been withheld
What time good Fate first sent me forth
And bade me use what tools she gave,—
Like one inspired by pity
And the divine passion of sweet love.

And so by you my heart was loosed,
Was freed from bondage, and the fear
Of what is coarse and dull and dread.
You brought me life, you gave me speech,
And made me kin unto the men
Whose speech is song, whose vision clear
As any angel deeming
Of the deepest mysteries of life.

Shall I not tell what you have wrought,
What you have done to make me free?
Shall I not sing my song aloud,
That thou hast taught me by thy love?
I am thine own, thy instrument;
Thou playest upon me as thou wilt,—
As one by love transmitting
All the lovely beauty of thy soul.

                              Your own    Woodrow

ALS (WC, NjP).

## From Ellen Axson Wilson

My own darling,                     Princeton, N. J. Feb 16/95
   I enclose the letters, &c. received today.¹ Mr. Weston neglected
to enclose the "card" of which he speaks. As usual your mail
seemed to fall off to nothing as soon as you left.
   I believe I *was* a bit blue when I wrote that letter; there was
certainly no reason for it except Nellie's apparent relapse,—and
I suppose the sense of lonliness "striking in" a little deeper than
usual. I am all right again now. So too is Nellie. They all seem
well and as happy as possible—barring the usual disputes. Yesterday I heard Nellie saying with intense earnestness "Margaret,
I *will* have my little Europe,—my own little Europe. Papa gave
it to me!" So you see your little keep-sakes are properly treasured.
By the way Jessie has decided that she is *Homer*, or rather "the
other man of the same name." She says she lived when Homer
did and she and he made up the poems together. You know
how busy they keep me trying to define words; now they are
constantly setting me a still harder task, viz. to sit in judgment
on the relative "greatness" of every character they ever heard of
real or imaginary. Who is the greatest, Shakspere or Homer,
Milton or Dante, Themistocles or Miltiades, Zeus or Odin, Aes-
chylus or Sophocles, Epaminondas or Washington? I think that
last "parallel" as coming from them quite interesting for I had
never said a word to associate the two names in their minds.
   But I am extremely busy today & *must* cut this short. Love
to Father and to your dear, *dear* self. Oh for the "great heart
word" that would let me tell you all that you are to
                                 Your own   Eileen.

ALS (WC, NjP).
¹ All these enclosures are missing.


## To Ellen Axson Wilson

My own darling,             Baltimore, 17 February, 1895
   In the ardour of my recent effusions, I have neglected to answer some of your questions, and to chronicle my simple doings
here. My lectures in Washington are set for the 20th and 21st,—
next Wednesday and Thursday,—at 4:15 in the afternoon. I have
made arrangements here to deliver my Hopkins lectures of those
dates in the mornings of the days named.
   I have not had any engagements since the examination papers
were finished,—and there are no plays in town worth seeing,—

so that I have been very quiet for the last two or three days. On Wednesday evening I dined with the Greene's[1] (the Greenes are the people who are in the place the [Caleb T.] Winchesters ought to have had). The other invited guests were Prof. Elliott[2] of the University, and Miss Schroeder and Miss Wood,[3] both of the Bryn Mawr School here. Greene is a stick! I overheard him say, speaking of [James Russell] Lowell's comparative failure and indifference as a teacher, "After all, he probably did as much good as if he had been a mere pedagogue"! Those were his exact words, his "wery lenguadges." Miss Schroeder,—a German,—proved vivacious and charming,—Miss Wood intelligent and interesting. Elliott and I came off together, and joined in unmeasured condemnation of the Bryn Mawr [College] methods,—which, it seems, are continued as abominably as ever. The[y] have just turned adrift another man,—a young fellow with wife and children who gave up a permanent place at Sewanee to go there. His name is Page.[4] Elliott says it's just the same way at the Bryn Mawr School, under the Thomas-Garrett reign.[5] Heaven grant they may soon be thoroughly exposed and brought to their knees to escape ruin: unless, indeed, ruin itself would be the juster doom!

Oh, yes, there was another engagement. Last night Father and I went to dine with Hiram Woods—Mitchell and Miss [Elizabeth] Hall, Mrs. Woods' sister, being the other guests. Father expanded into a very happy vein, and the evening went off most agreeably. When we reached the house we found that "the baby ["] (*aetat*, 3½)[6] had just fallen and, it was supposed, *broken her arm*. A closer examination, however, discovered that it was no fracture, and our minds were at ease for the evening.

We go presently to Mrs. Bird's to dine, and I must come to a sudden close, not to be caught.

I love you as          Your own    Woodrow

ALS (WC, NjP).

[1] Professor and Mrs. Herbert Eveleth Greene. Greene was Collegiate Professor of English at the Johns Hopkins.

[2] A. Marshall Elliott, Professor of Romance Languages at the Hopkins.

[3] Ida Wood, Ph.D. in English from Bryn Mawr College, who was Secretary of the Bryn Mawr School in Baltimore, and Olga Schroeder, who taught Greek and German at the Bryn Mawr School.

[4] Frederic M. Page, Reader in Romance Languages at Bryn Mawr College, 1892-95.

[5] He refers to Martha Carey Thomas and Mary Elizabeth Garrett, who dominated the Board of Managers of the Bryn Mawr School.

[6] Laura Hall Woods, born December 22, 1891.

## From Ellen Axson Wilson

My own darling,          Princeton, N. J.  Sunday [Feb. 17, 1895]
How can I tell you how much I like your beautiful verses! By some special good fortune they reached me last night so that I have had them all day; and each time I read them I like them better. Though to say I *like* them is indeed a colourless word with which to describe the sweet confusion of pleased thought and tender feeling into which the lines throw me. I admire you as the author of them—and oh how I *love* you for writing them to me! There is no use protesting again that I don't deserve to have them written to me. I have done that too often before in vain. It is best to take the good that the gods,—and you,—provide, with silent thankfulness, or rather to thank *them* most fervantly for having given me a poet for a lover. For you see you are a poet after all; you prove it in two ways, first by writing a *poem*, and second by showing yourself such an *idealist* as only a poet could be. I can only hope and trust that like Mr. Perry's hero you are "an incorrigible poet" and so will never find me out. Had you written such things when we were first married I should have been in a fine panic, expecting soon to become "a lost illusion"; feeling sure that "however fain, you could not see me always as befell your dreams to see me." But ten happy years have given me a  still happier confidence in the immortal *strength* as well as immortal *beauty* of love like yours. It is such love as yours—as *ours*, for in this matter of loving I am your equal,—that the poet-painter[1] dreamed of when he painted his "Love and Life"—a love that is lord of life itself. That life may have been but a "poor, pale, miserable, despicable *Actual*," but when she has yielded to his guiding hand she finds him *strong* to make of her what he will,—to transform her into an *Ideal*. For it is not true that "the situation that has not its Ideal was never yet occupied by man. The Ideal is in thyself, the impediment too is in thyself: thy condition is but the stuff thou art to shape that same Ideal out of: what matters whether such stuff be of this sort or that, so the form thou give it be heroic, be poetic. Here or nowhere is thy Ideal: work is out therefrom & working, believe, live, be free."
But I have indeed wandered far afield and must make haste to return,—in time for the mail! I hear the boys "shutting up" and must send this to the corner.
It has been a perfect day—rather warm & very bright. All the children went to church, and all seem very well.
Best love to father, and *love, love, love* beyond all measure for my dear one from                    His little wife,  Eileen.

ALS (WC, NjP).
¹ George Frederic Watts.

## To Ellen Axson Wilson

My own darling,                    Baltimore, 18 February, 1895
Father seemed to enjoy himself very much indeed at Mrs.
Bird's yesterday. We stayed till nearly five o'clock, with very delightful conversation,—as you may imagine: though father is
inclined to object to Mrs. Bird that she "chatters" too much, and
that, though she talks extremely well, it is *about nothing*,—in all
of which there is, of course, a grain of truth. But who could
mistake or resist her appreciation of those who *do* have something
to say! We are invited to dine next Sunday with Mrs. Small,¹ Legh
Reid's aunt, and Mrs. Bird's neighbour.
Before dinner I took father to hear Mr. Babcock,—and he was
*delighted*, pronouncing him a man of genius, and applauding his
mastery of doctrine no less than his mastery of exact and pointed
and eloquent speech. For a little space he was too much affected by
the man and all that he had said, first and last, during the service,
to be able to speak about him with unbroken voice. It was delightful to see him so much gratified. I introduced him to Mr. Babcock
after church and he thanked him for the sermon in tones I had
never heard him use before,—almost humbly,—saying he hoped he
should be the better man for having heard it. The tears, or something very like, came into Mr. Babcock's eyes when he heard it,
and expressed his gratitude.
I have no engagements for this week,—except those for Washington, about which I am growing a trifle nervous. I wonder if
I shall ever get accustomed to my business!
What you say about Perry's lecture on Hawthorne interests me
very much. Your praise is certainly very high, and, knowing you,
I know it must be deserved. I am the more impatient to hear
him,—and the more content that you cannot hear me. How fortunate we are to have once more a colleague who can delight us
in that way. I am more glad than I can say for your sake especially. You have so few pleasures, so little entertainment,—so dull
a round of life, that I cannot sufficiently rejoice at anything that
brings you pleasure or diversion:—and *this* is the sort of enjoyment to which you most respond,—my dear little thoughtful artist,
my sweet little born critic! Dear me, how I fear and stand in awe
of you, Eileen! How abashed I am to do my work under your
constant scrutiny,—to keep my mind constantly under your eye,
with its *in*sight. It is beyond measure healthful and stimulating,

but, ah me, it's embarrassing too! For you are not simply my
critic and mentor: you are also my wife. I am madly in love with
you. I live upon your love,—would die if I could not win and hold
your admiration: the homage of your mind as well as of your
heart! And to think of the critical business! To think how slender
my title is,—and how open to your closest inspection! My defence
is, that you are a woman, and *loyal* beyond all words!

Your own   Woodrow

ALS (WC, NjP).
¹ Mary G. Small, who lived at 16 East Mt. Vernon Place. Mrs. Bird lived at
22 East Mt. Vernon Place.


## From Ellen Axson Wilson

My own darling,        Princeton, N. J.   Monday [Feb. 18, 1895]

First one thing then another has interfered with my writing
all day, until now it is quarter of ten and I must confine myself
to a hasty line if I wish to get it mailed tonight.

I didn't acknowledge the book;¹ many thanks for it. It came
Saturday and I finished it that night, sitting up until midnight;—
don't believe I *could* have stopped until it was finished. It is *delightful,*—absorbingly interesting. What a contrast to a novel I
read last week,—Miss Wilkin's "Pembroke."² I could scarcely go
to sleep after finishing it from sheer indignation with its author.
Such a book is an insult to ones intelligence. She makes of New
England one huge lunatic asylum. If it is like that it certainly
ought to be walled in and keepers appointed!

I was so surprised to learn from todays "Times" that George
Patton was some time ago³ appointed assistant professor,—in
"Biblical Instruction." Did you know it? I didn't even know he
taught. It seems a rapid rise. Truly it is a good and pleasant thing
for a young scholar to have a fond father in the president's chair!
And it seems that Walter Harris⁴ & Mr. Lewis⁵ were also made
assistant professors.

Did you see the double page birds-eye view of Princeton (the
college buildings) in last week's "Harpers Weekly"? It is very
good. And they gave us a big puff too, or rather let Prof. Sloane
do it for them.⁶

Do you mean you have finished *all* the examination papers? I
fear that is too good to be true,—that it is only the black list. If
you *do* mean all, I congratulate you with all my heart,—but am
more than ever convinced that you are having a dull time in Balt.
this year! But I *must* get this mailed. I love you Woodrow darling
with all my soul.                          Your own   Eileen.

ALS (WC, NjP).
¹ Wilson had probably sent her his copy of Stanley Weyman's *Under the Red Robe*.
² Mary E. Wilkins, *Pembroke* (New York, 1894). The author is better known under her later married name of Mary E. Wilkins Freeman.
³ George Stevenson Patton, President Patton's son, became Assistant Professor of Biblical Instruction as of the academic year 1895-96.
⁴ Walter Butler Harris, then Instructor in Civil Engineering.
⁵ Edwin Seelye Lewis, then Instructor in Romance Languages.
⁶ A two-page reproduction of a detailed drawing of the Princeton campus, which appeared in *Harper's Weekly*, XXXIX (Jan. 26, 1895), 84-85. The accompanying article, on pp. 84-86, was anonymous but may well have been written by William Milligan Sloane.

## Edward Southwick Child to Ellen Axson Wilson

Dear Mrs. Wilson:                    New York. Febry 18, 1895.

I send you by this mail the new floor plans. We have altered them in some respects from those sent by you. For instance: We have taken two feet from the butler's pantry and laundry and added it to the kitchen, and have made a lobby between the kitchen and the door leading to the first step of the stairs. Our idea would be to light this lobby from the kitchen and to ventilate it by a small flue into the chimney, otherwise the odors will leak through the door and all up your main stairway. Except in this respect, the first floor is exactly as you figured it.

On the second story we have altered the sizes of some of the rooms slightly in order to get the partitions one over the other. We feel that we have carried out in this however the spirit of your design. We really believe that this arrangement will give you more room and can be built for quite considerably less money than the plans submitted by you first. All of the points on the exterior which you admired can be carried out in this design.

Hoping that you will find these drawings satisfactory¹

We are,   Yours respectfully,   E S Child

TLS (WP, DLC).
¹ The sole surviving floor plan of the Wilson house is the one (in the Wilson Papers, Library of Congress) printed in the photographic section of this volume. This plan not only shows the layout of the first floor but also gives the dimensions of the house. There are now, as there presumably were in the house when it was completed in 1896, six bedrooms, two baths, and a studio on the second floor. The Wilsons had the attic floored and studding and lathing installed for rooms before the house was completed. These rooms were finished at a later date.

## To Ellen Axson Wilson

Baltimore, 19 February, 1895

Ah, my little lady, have I not reason to stand in awe of your critical powers! No, sweet, I am no poet, unless the mere fact of being an idealist of itself constitutes me one,—and those lines written the other day are no poem. The night I wrote them I thought they were. A hot fire was in my brain: my imagination was thronged with every sweet image of love; and, while I wrote I thought it was writing poetry—for I thought I was writing down what was in my head. But reading the lines now I can see no reason for their measure (their occasional rhymes were purely accidental): they are mere metrical prose. That I am an idealist, with the heart of a poet, I do not hesitate to avow: but that fact is not reassuring. On the contrary, it is tragical. My heart fairly breaks to utter itself like a poet,—and cannot. It longs for the metrical form: its air is suffused with colour; prose seems intolerable to it. It will *die* of prose yet, I sometimes think— so galling, so intolerable are the fetters,—the *mean* fetters, so humiliating to an idealist. Ah, how I *hate* prose—that *any*body can write,—because I *must* write it: I *cannot* write anything else! I suppose I shall continue to be fool enough to hate my own limitations, and shall continue at long intervals to attempt poetry, as long as I shall live. If I could only write prose that was delicate, imaginative, full at once of grace, force, and distinction, that would be something: my thoughts would at least go clad like aristocrats. But alas! I shall but wear my soul out trying. Why should a passion such as I feel for you be born dumb, I wonder, and tormented with the dumb devil all its life: quivering with a poetry that it can never utter. Ah, Nellie, there is, I sometimes fear, such a thing as dying from excess of unuttered love! *Why* did you not marry a poet? Certainly you were meant to: you who *provoke* poetry every moment of your life. Oh, *what* poetry a man could write if he were a poet and had you, as I have you, in his heart, *at* his heart. I'm like Svengali! It's all in my head,—at my brain: the exquisite harmonies, the noble images, the unspeakable strains of perfect verse! But nature has given me no voice. And you refuse to be my instrument: I cannot use you. Ah, well, at least I *have* you,—and there are ways of expression by which I can speak to *you*. Never blame me, darling, for being too passionate in my love making,—in my kisses and embraces. The hot fire that is in my heart *must* find *some* passionate expression. Read it for what it truly is: my poetry,—the ecstasy of my heart breaking all bounds to find its satisfaction. Would I not be odiously commonplace were it not for this side of me: would you not yawn if I did not sometimes make you blush? Ah, Nell, if you love me as I love you, you too must be a dumb poet. If so, I pity you, and give you leave to give *me* any passionate evidence you will.

Your own   Woodrow

☞ See two notes round enclosure.

Please have Ed. deposit this tiny thing, dear, in the bank. It's so small it may get lost!

Please look on my calendar and tell me when you write next on what days in June I speak at the University of Va. and at Wellesley.[1]

ALS (WP, DLC). Enc. missing.
  [1] Reports of his addresses at the University of Virginia and Wellesley College are printed at June 12 and 26, 1895.


## From Ellen Axson Wilson

My own darling,          Princeton, N. J.  Tuesday [Feb. 19, 1895]

I was so busy with some sewing today that I put off writing until night and now I can't write because I am asleep! Have just been fast asleep in my chair—though its only half past eight,—and now positively can't see the page on which I am writing. You know fatigue is forever serving me that trick. I suppose tho I *must* wake up enough to write to Mr. Child & acknowledge the new floor plans which came today. They are very nice, just like mine except in a few details. He much prefers this plan to the other and says it can be built for "quite considerably less money"; —but on that point he doesn't go into *details*. This is the night for the big reception at the Brenton Greens, Jr. I sent our cards,— don't like to go out in the evening without you.

We are having perfect weather now, so warm & bright, it is a delight to be out except for the rivers of slush,—a legacy from the blizzard. It is good to be able to send the children out without misgivings,—though Jessie has taken fresh cold, and has head-ache, &c., tonight. Nellie is well & looking splendidly, I never saw such a change as this one bottle of cod-liver oil has apparently wrought. They are now disputing over the *cardinal virtues*, appropriating them,—in *name* only!—and dividing them up. I am called upon to decide which is best, Temperance or Charity, Justice or Hope, &c. It all came from Jessie's reading the "Golden Legend." They have been acting miracle plays ever since.

I was so touched by your account of father at Mr. Babcock's church. I hope he will see something of the man too. They will certainly like each other. By the way, would you have time to go to see Mrs. [Aminta] Green?

I love you, dear, with all my heart, soul, mind and strength. I am in everything          Your own   Eileen.

ALS (WC, NjP).

## To Ellen Axson Wilson

My own darling,                    Baltimore, 20 February, 1895

For once I must confine myself to a little note. I go to Washington at two o'clock, to lecture at 4:15, and I have had so many things to call my attention off during the last day or two that I have not yet conned my lecture at all. I know you will forgive me, therefore, if I send you only these few lines to say that things go with me very much as usual; and that I love you, *love* you, *love* you, with all my heart—all my powers. I am altogether

Your own    Woodrow

Yes, I *did* mean that I have read all the examination papers—not the black list simply.

ALS (WC, NjP).

## From Ellen Axson Wilson

My own darling,      Princeton, N. J.  Wednesday [Feb. 20, 1895]

What do you think I have just been reading? A seventeen page article about *you*—in the "Sewanee Review"![1] The Knoxville professor's paper of course, though it is only signed "X." It is pretty good, on the whole; of course it was beyond hoping for, that it should be entirely satisfactory,—especially to *me*! But I will do him the justice to say that it is most unsatisfactory about comparatively unimportant details; he seems to have a pretty fair grasp of his subject in its larger and more important bearings,—to understand somewhat the true scope and meaning and unique value of your work, and your own extraordinary equipment for doing it. The part about the "Epoch" is quite good, and thoroughly appreciative.

But really almost all our American writers are in a worse case with regard to *style* than that famous Westerner was as to "*the truth*,"—they can't even "tell it when they see it"—much less originate it! In an exhaustive paper like this there is not a word about your style! He is doubtless affected by it unconsciously but he thinks the impressiveness is due entirely to the *matter*,—the thought. It has evidently never occurred to him that there is anything unusual in the *manner* of it. The first part, about your ancestry, is comical in its exhaustiveness. He gives the maiden name of your *great-grandmother*, and every detail of your father's career. Where do you suppose he got his facts? Certainly not from my letter for he mentions any number of things that I never heard of before. He also gives incidentally sketches of the Scotch-

Irish in America, of Hampden-Sidney College, of "the Anaconda Club," of "Dr. Lewis W. Green an eloquent Kentuckian," "best known as the father of the wife of Vice-President Stevenson"! &c. &c. Perhaps you would like me to send the magazine so that Father may see it?

I enclose a letter that came today.² When you answer I would tell him that *when* (!) we build he shall have the chance he wants;—for this reason. Mr. Child said that one reason why it was hard to keep down the estimate was that the style of the house was unusual and builders were a little shy of the novel features. But this man having just finished the Tiger Inn will understand all about "half timbered" houses and over-hanging upper stories.

The Wellesley College date is Tuesday, June 25. the U. of Va. Wed. June 12.

But it is late & I must make haste to get this mailed. Somehow, I don't seem to have strength of mind enough to write *early* in the evening; always think I must 'rest' first. And I havn't yet said a word in answer to that *dear* letter received this morning. I certainly won't try to tuck away an answer in these two lines, but merely say that I love you, dear, as much & in as many ways as you do me & am *altogether*          Your own    Eileen

ALS (WC, NjP).
¹ It is printed at Feb. 1, 1895.
² From Jesse Dall, a New York builder who had just completed the Tiger Inn Club on Prospect Avenue. His letter is missing.

## A Newspaper Report of an Address

[Feb. 21, 1895]

### THE STATE AND SOCIETY

"Society is merely the vehicle of the law, and the law only becomes one of the arms of society after it has been recognized so thoroughly by public opinion as to be practically universal." Such was the succinct statement of statute law's position in national life as given by Prof. Woodrow Wilson, of Princeton, yesterday, in the third lecture of the course on applied ethics under the auspices of the Columbian University. Prof. Wilson's subject yesterday was "The Nature of the State and Its Relation to Society," and the object of the talk was to define clearly the natural place of statute law in the social life of a nation and to explain the ethical relation of law to progress and reform. Prof. Wilson said in the course of his talk:

"We are unconsciously making law all the time by our observance of unwritten customs that have been found by repeated trial to be expedient for the well-being of society. But the custom is not ready to be put into law till its acceptance has been practically universal. The law may be said to be that part of public custom that has been crystalized into definite form such as can be backed by the authority of the government. There is no code outside the Mosaic law that I know of which sums up the requirements of common honesty. But the courts do not hesitate to constantly apply this general estimate of honesty to the adjudication of special cases, as in the case of a milkman, who, when brought into court for watering milk, pleaded that it was the universal practice of his trade, generally recognized and admitted, and that therefore he was not getting money under false pretenses by the adulteration. But the courts held that as a matter of common honesty water at nothing a gallon was not a fair substitute for milk at 8 cents a quart, and made not only that milkman responsible, but made it a generally punishable offense to water milk.

"The law to the great majority means 'I ought.' To the minority it means, 'I must.' As the 'ought' fades out for the majority, the 'must' fades out for the minority, and thus laws become dead on the shelves for lack of public opinion to enforce them. We need not repeal the laws against witchcraft, if any be still in force. Public opinion has failed them as support, and they are henceforth harmless. So much for the law. As to the question of progress, it has been so variously defined in so many ponderous volumes, that I can attempt but a very modest and incomplete answer to the question here. Progress is an intellectual as well as a physical conquest over nature. It comes from understanding nature, living in harmony with her laws, and by accumulated insight molding those laws to suit the requirements of our own complex lives.

"The principle vehicle of progress is the one that we are the most persistently running away from. It is struggle. We are so altruistic in these days that we are constantly endeavoring to get along without struggling. We think the great procession of the world can get on without elbowing and shoving. But it cannot. If it did the progress would not be worth the having. If you have opinions, come down on the sand of the arena and fight for them. We don't want to follow the clean slippered, sweet scented gentleman of ease and leisure. We respect and rally to the brawny victor who smells of the sweat of the battle. When you have put forth your idea, if it is an idea, you will find a host to fight it. You must not flinch from the stroke of the sword; bare your own blade and drive it home. If it is backed by the truth it will stick.

Then when your fight is won you may wipe your sword, sheath it, and write your established custom as a statute on the books.

"Society must be worked for by its members. Even when a man brings the world truth he has to fight for it, and make it prevail. It is not alone necessary to proclaim it. You must make it prevalent. The world does not owe you a living, you owe it a life, and it is in this expending of life from the common advancement of society, that I think you will find the truest answer of the question, the relation of the state to progress."[1]

Printed in the *Washington Post*, Feb. 21, 1895; some editorial headings omitted.
[1] There is another full report of this address in the *Washington Times*, Feb. 21, 1895.

## To Ellen Axson Wilson

My own darling,                    Balto., 21 February, 1895

The first Washington lecture is off my hands, and before many more hours are gone by the other will be also. There was a pretty good audience present,—a hundred and fifty people, say,—I got them thoroughly interested and thoroughly in sympathy with me: and, in the "Conference" which followed the lecture, my answers seemed for the most part to satisfy even those who asked me questions. In the middle of the audience sat Miss Graham.[1] Fortunately I did not have to do more than shake hands with her afterwards. I despise her most heartily. I don't know what she can be doing in Washington. I did not see any of my Washington friends in the audience.

With to-day, dear, goes lecture No. 21 at the Hopkins! Four more next week (for to-morrow, the 22nd, there is none), and then, on Friday, I'm off, to be happy again! I can't start till noon, or thereabouts, because Friday is the first of March and I must get my wages that morning (the first of the month is pay day here) from the Treasurer: but I expect to be home for dinner. How almost painfully the thought excites me! I'm like a child waiting for a holiday—and the little delay chafes me like a prisoner's chain! My heart pants and tugs to be free. And yet I can't for the life of me refrain from looking forward. The slowest part of the journey will be that last part, the ride in the hack from the station to the house. Then I shall have my darling in my arms once more,—and shall not watch how the time passes any more,—except that I shall wish—but, dear me, I'd better change the subject! I don't seem to know any more how to write to you, my sweet one! My wits are scattered. I can form no thought but the wish to be at home,—to be with you:—to *see* you, to *hear* you, to touch you,

—to break down this painful wall of *paper*, that *seems* like ada-
mant between us. I've almost come to the end of my patience:
and without patience one can't write a letter. I can only fill the
paper, in the hope that you may like to see my hand-writing upon
the usual scale!

On the 22nd we are to have the Hon. Seth Low with us, President of Columbia, to deliver the "principal address": who are to
be put upon us to deliver the *minor* addresses we have not been
told.[2] I *hope* great things from brother Low, but *expect* nothing.
I'd much rather lecture myself than hear him,—and come home
on Thursday! The exercises are to be held, this time, in the audience room of McCoy Hall,[3] the new building—capable of seating a
thousand persons. They have obtained this, a library as big as
ours, and what amounts to Dickinson Hall[4] besides for less than
Alexander Hall[5] has cost already! But when I'm with you I wont
carp!                                    Your own   Woodrow

ALS (WC, NjP).
    [1] Mary Graham, identified in EAW to WW, July 26, 1893, n. 1, Vol. 8. At this
time she was completing work for a Ph.D. in economics at Yale that she received in 1895.
    [2] At the Founder's Day exercises of the Johns Hopkins.
    [3] A four-story building with the large auditorium mentioned by Wilson and
offices and meeting rooms on the first floor; lecture rooms and classrooms on
the second floor; offices, departmental libraries, and seminar rooms on the third
floor; and the university library on the fourth floor.
    [4] One of the principal classroom buildings on the Princeton campus, which
stood from 1870 to 1920.
    [5] The gift of Harriet Crocker Alexander, wife of Charles Beatty Alexander,
'70, and named for the Rev. Archibald Alexander and his six sons, who were
Princeton graduates, and their descendants. Begun in 1891, Alexander Hall cost
about $350,000 and was dedicated on June 9, 1894. It is an extraordinary
example of nineteenth-century Romanesque architecture and is still in use as
a lecture and concert hall.

## From Ellen Axson Wilson

My own darling,       Princeton, N. J.  Thursday [Feb. 21, 1895]

I send with this two requests for your services which I fancy
you will find no difficulty in answering in two letters! Who *is*
"Eldredge & Bro." and why should they expect *you* to do hack
work for them?[1]

By the way, one unimportant letter that came for you a few
day[s] ago I in some way misplaced;—have had several vain hunts
for it.[2] It was from Mr Fielder[3] asking to insure the new house!
I can give you the substance, but it is'nt necessary because *I* answered it! He added a postscript to the effect that he expected to
succeed in selling our lot this spring;[4] which so excited my curiosity that I availed myself of the opportunity afforded by his
letter to find out what he meant and what he was really doing.

I told him we had decided not to build until we sold the lot; that we were therefore very anxious to sell and very glad to hear that there was a prospect of it. My note brought a call from him yesterday when I discovered that he meant nothing very definite; he is still talking of that same man who had expressed a desire to build some houses to rent in Princeton but whom he has not succeeded in seeing yet.

I hope you will find the Washington experience pleasant, dear— or at least *have* found it so,—am glad to think that too is over now. Were there to be any social features in connection with the expedition?

This week and last have been quite gay in Princeton though I have shirked it all myself. The Tiger Inn is to give a grand opening reception tomorrow afternoon. I should like to go to it in order to see the building but don't like to go alone, so suppose I will stay away.

Mrs. Hibben says Mr. [Henry B.] Fine at the dance the other night was the most comically tragical figure she ever saw; his face white, set, grim, worn with fatigue, tense with high and righteous indignation. He uttered not a word except once in an hour or so some one oracular sentence, as "this is no place for a rational being"; ["]Hibben, there are times when the best of women lose their heads!!" Speaking of *heads* Mrs. Hibben says Mrs. Fine's, bound about with ivy leaves was most beautiful, most "poetical-looking." Nature must have been in the mood for a comical jest when she made Mrs Fine look *poetical* (as Mrs. Hibben maintains she always does) for if ever there lived an absolute and vulgar materialist it is she.

And to think that at last we have begun on the final week. In *one* week my darling, God willing[,] will be with me! I don't know whether there is most pain or pleasure in the thought, it makes my heart beat with such wild impatience. While a seemingly hopeless weight of long weeks lay upon it that heart lay still in dull despairful resignation. But now it grows mutinous indeed. I can find no spell that will make it tame or reasonable. I think I had better try to forget you altogether! don't you? or must I be, cost what it will, in every thought, in every heart-beat

Your own    Eileen.

ALS (WP, DLC).
1 These two letters, at least one of which was from Eldredge & Brother, a Philadelphia publishing firm specializing in textbooks, are missing.
2 It is still missing.
3 John Wesley Fielder, Jr., Princeton '74, a Princeton insurance and real estate broker.
4 The Wilsons had obviously listed their lot on Washington Street with Fielder.

# A Newspaper Report of an Address

[Feb. 22, 1895]

LIBERTY IS NOT ANARCHY

Prof. Woodrow Wilson, of Princeton, yesterday delivered the fourth of the lectures on social problems of the day, given by the School of Applied Ethics, under the auspices of the Columbian University. His discourse was a discussion of "Liberty, expediency, and morality, in the Democratic State." "The common conception of liberty," said the professor, "held by those who have not been thoughtful upon the subject, is that it is an absence of restraint—that a man is free in proportion as he is not restrained, and I am sorry to say we have a whole party of men asserting that liberty consists of anarchy.

"But we must have a different conception as a working conception. We must speak of it as the best sort of order, by which I mean the best adjustment of restraint. We speak of a ship, of a kite, of a bird being free. They are all images of freedom, I grant you, but are they not all images of adjustment? For their freedom is conditional. I am free to dash my arm against the wall, but in so doing I set at defiance the law of cause and effect, and I would suffer a severe penalty, for my temerity. So men go about the world free on condition of obedience—nothing more or less. If one does not understand and carry out the terms of co-operation, then he is no longer free.

"The social life is a higher form of the individual life—it gives leave and opportunity to the individual life. Let a man try to do without society, and he will be less of a man, because, unless other men will stand shoulder to shoulder with him, it is impossible for him to be otherwise. We give the most distinctive homage to a man who keeps himself in the nicest accommodation to the laws of co-operation. A man must keep his understanding with us, his dignity, or we do not respect him.

"Now, this is all true, as applied to political liberty. It is the best adjustment among men. The restraint that we wish to have absent is the very restraint that has been put on the many by the few. Everything that has native force within it resists subjection. So it is, we conceive, of political liberty being a restraint of government in that it is a distinct understanding between governors and governed, in relation to the terms of government or adjustment; as to what the administration of justice is going to be.

"Consequently we have invented a new thing in the world—a constitution of liberty, which is younger than the constitution of

government. Its terms are such as our bills of right, and the first
eight amendments to our Federal Constitution. We simply mean
by such statements of liberty that government shall not make
arbitrary invasions of our rights. The people upon whom the
government operates have fenced it in. Liberty does not consist
in organization, the constitution of government, but in the constitution of liberty, in the limitations of authority. Every socialistic programme begins with a proposition for a new organization
of society. That reverses the whole process of history. Organization results from motive, not motive from organization. Take care
of the motive and the organization will take care of itself. That
is the law of accommodation to environment.

"What is political expediency? What is it expedient that a man
should do in the body politic? What is the law of progress in
society—modification? Revolution is never expedient, although it
may be necessary, because it may be necessary for the organization to die, being smitten with a hopeless disease. Revolution
always results from a series of acts that have been inexpedient.
The proper law of modification has become disabled, and therefore death follows as a natural consequence for the wages of sin
is death in the natural world as well as in the spiritual. I believe
it is possible for an individual to undergo immediate and permanent change, but society as a whole never. The law of social
change is a mending, a patching, the changing of the pattern
of a nice, intricate weaving of circumstances.

"How can you bring this about? By general opinion, by which
I mean only the best concerted opinion. It des [does] not mean
that you must convert everybody. It means that you must have
the sagacity to perceive the lines of least resistance, then concert
your action along those lines and the Nation will folllow. As to
the matter of political morality, the individual ethic is the proper
ethic. 'Shall I live here on terms of utility?' I ask myself. What
about the other and spiritual world? But society does not know
any other world. It must save itself in this world. Therefore I
believe that the social ethic is a utilitarian ethic, not an absolute
one; that it is what you may accomplish by agreement, not by an
abstract process of right and wrong; that it is so much of the
right as you can get the prevalent majority to observe and
respect.

"Social sin is the transgression of the law of progress; this law
of right modification, of wise adjustment, of improvement. For we
must go to the right meaning of the word morality. It is the science of relationships. My individual morality is my relationship to

God, my social morality my relationship to my fellowmen. The law of modification is the law of discovering and achieving the best relationships. When we have done this we have solved the problem of liberty, expediency, and morality."[1]

Printed in the *Washington Post*, Feb. 22, 1895; some editorial headings omitted.
   [1] There is another full report of this address in the *Washington Times*, Feb. 22, 1895.

## To Ellen Axson Wilson

My own darling,                    Baltimore, 22 February, '95

   I rose earlier than usual this morning so as not to be cheated out of my letter; but I am expected at the University at 10:30, must shave and go an important errand before that time, and so I must after all hurry, write within time, and stop with the stroke of the clock. I *hate* to write hurriedly to *you*: my heart expands so with speaking to you, and I want leisure, for the luxury of it! After the exercises this forenoon, I am to lunch "with the Trustees and a few others" at the President's invitation. It will be a bore, I have no doubt. But the dignified functions of life must be endured. The use of them is hard to see, but the practice of them is obvious enough.

   So "H[enneman]." has published his article about me "sure enough,["] has he? And you are satisfied with it, "on the whole"? Well, in that case, it must be too favourable by half—you would not be satisfied at all under that amount. Bless your heart! How sweet you are to love me so! I can never repay you,—except in kind! No, it is hardly worth while to send the article to me here. Father will, I suppose and hope, come home with me, and we can read it together. It will keep. It's a serious matter to be written about seriously: but I suppose it does not really put a fellow under any additional compulsion to succeed. It's only awkward to have *definite things* confidently expected of you.

   Well, the Washington job is over—twenty-one Hopkins lectures are delivered—and one week from to-day I start for home,—to go to *you*, my haven, my blessing! I believe I can say that I made a hit in Washington. I did not hit very many people,—about a hundred and fifty, I reckoned, but the few who heard me seemed smitten rather hard, and it became, during the course of the performance, a pleasure to speak to them. Being questioned by cranks and dull persons afterwards, which was part of the programme, was a rather painful and stupid experience. But I played the "queer" ones off successfully enough, and seemed to satisfy the serious dull ones reasonably well. I am sure the impression as a whole was good. Hon. W. L. Wilson presided yesterday, but did nothing more,—made no "remarks" of any kind. I wonder what he will do with himself after March 4th?[1]

Renick[2] was at the lecture and I saw him for a little while afterwards, between the lecture and my return train.

I've had a touch of the grippe recently, but Mitchell has a sovereign remedy which has enabled me to master it very promptly.

I love you, my sweet one; I adore you; I long for you unspeakably,—I am altogether          Your own    Woodrow

ALS (WC, NjP).
[1] William Lyne Wilson, chairman of the Ways and Means Committee of the House of Representatives, who had been defeated for re-election in the Republican landslide of 1894. He became Postmaster General in Cleveland's Cabinet on March 3, 1895, serving in that post until March 5, 1897. Soon afterward he became president of Washington and Lee University.
[2] Edward Ireland Renick, Wilson's former law partner and old friend, at this time Chief Clerk of the State Deparment.

## From Ellen Axson Wilson

My own darling                    Princeton, N. J.  Feb. 22/95

I am so glad the Washington lecture passed off so successfully —but of course I knew it *would*. Its easy enough to say why Miss Graham was in Washington. Didnt you know that all the female cranks in the country are there in Congress assembled? Dozens of different associations;—suffrage, dress reform, temperance and what not are represented. Merely to read the list is edifying.[1] And speaking of Miss Graham, I enclose a little billet doux that arrived from her this morning. I heard she had "nervous prostration" but I didn't suppose it was as bad as *this*![2]

I went to the Tiger Inn after all;—was determined to see the house so started out hoping to meet someone on the way that I knew and go in with them; in which I succeeded joining the Hinsdales.[3] The house is certainly beautiful,—splendid; they have some perfectly magnificent medieval carved furniture too. The interior is finished in Geo. pine stained in various ways, some the colour of mahogany[,] some walnut. The effect was very rich. All the walls were brownish yellow or red and all the mantles red brick.

I saw Mr. Bridges at a distance—did not speak to him. He somehow reminds me of Pres. Andrews history.[4] *Have* you seen the reviews of it? Did you ever imagine anything so savage as the "Nation's."[5] And the "Dial's"[6] which I read yesterday is almost as severe.

Aren't you sorry for me? I miscalculated in some way and

fancied you were coming home on Thursday! It is quite heart-breaking to think of that extra day. But I won't talk about—I *will* be a "heroine" as the children say. With dearest love I am always

Your own   Eileen.

ALS (WC, NjP).

¹ Ellen was referring to the second triennial meeting of the National Council of Women of the United States, which met at Metzerott Music Hall in Washington from February 18 through March 2, 1895. The Council was an organization composed of seventeen national women's religious, political, and social organizations whose interests ranged from woman suffrage and social welfare to temperance and dress reform. The president of the Council was the well-known suffragette, May Wright Sewall. Other prominent persons in attendance included Susan B. Anthony, Anna Howard Shaw, and Frances E. Willard. The proceedings were described in considerable detail (without, however, mentioning Miss Graham) in the *New York Times*, February 18-March 3, 1895.

² Her letter is missing. She was committed in 1897 to the Connecticut Hospital for the Insane in Middletown, where she spent the rest of her life.

³ The Rev. Dr. and Mrs. Horace Graham Hinsdale. Dr. Hinsdale was pastor of the First Presbyterian Church of Princeton.

⁴ Because Charles Scribner's Sons had published Andrews' *History of the United States*, cited in F. J. Turner to WW, Dec. 24, 1894, n. 5.

⁵ New York *Nation*, LX (Jan. 24, 1895), 77-78.

⁶ Andrew C. McLaughlin, "An Unsuccessful History," Chicago *Dial*, XVIII (Feb. 16, 1895), 111-13.


## To Ellen Axson Wilson

My own darling,                    Baltimore, 23 February, 1895

The Birthday passed off very well. Mr. Low's address, on "The City and the University," though much too full of references to Columbia, was really very good indeed.¹ There were traces in it of the non-academic hand,—phrases of which literature knows nothing,—but surprisingly few. The ideas were obvious and "credible or incredible by all men equally," but they were well set, impressed the non-literary (which includes nowadays the greater part of the Faculty itself) as quite the thing to say, and have gone on record as constituting "an admirable address." Indeed it was so much better than I expected that I quite admired it myself. After the exercises, lunch was served to "the Trustees and a few others," one of whom I was which. In the evening a big reception was given by Mr. Chas. Morton Stewart, President of the Board of Trustees, which proved an unusually pleasant affair. That little attack of the grippe I had has resulted in my not being quite up to my usual form; but I am taking good care of myself, and, by taking things easily, managed to enjoy myself very much indeed. You need not fear that I will be imprudent. I have too much to live for! I live to love you; and, ah, how the phrases that close this sweet letter I have just received warm my heart and quicken all my pulses. It is the letter of Thursday—for there was only one delivery yesterday, and that brought me nothing. And do you want me so much, my precious Eileen? Oh, how I bless you for it: that you want me, that you *desire* my love and welcome it, as part of your happiness, is to me the very chief wonder and inspiration of my life. This is the love I longed for, from the woman I longed for,—so sweet, so true, so lovely in mind and body,— the woman with whom I can rejoice to live, and for whom I could be glad to die. I was thinking the other day so contentedly, darling, of our growing old together. How sweet it will be to see the same love light in your eyes when your hair is white and our love has the perfect sanction of a rounded life upon it! God grant we shall live and die together, my perfect wife. My wife! How sacred, how lovely a name when you have worn it. You have glorlified [glorified] it for me beyond all I ever hoped for, and your place in my heart can no more be affected by change than these ten years of our delightful life together can be! You have so satisfied me that you have become (it sometimes seems to me literally) a part of me. May God bless you and keep you, my Eileen, my queen!

I feel like chiding you gently for "shirking" the entertainments of which you speak, my sweet one. Why should you act like a widow in mourning while I am away? It makes me fear that you are having a gloomy time, and taking our pain a little morbidly. My darling ought we not to be happy with such love as ours? I am away, but I am none the less

Your own    Woodrow

ALS (WC, NjP).
¹ An account of the Founder's Day celebration and the text of President Low's address appeared in the Baltimore *Sun*, Feb. 23, 1895.

## From Ellen Axson Wilson

My own darling,                         Princeton, N. J.  Feb. 23/95

I am distressed to know that you won't get your letter today because there was no one to mail it last night. Am *so* sorry. I sat up waiting for the boys to come in, so as to ask them to mail it, until I was almost sick with fatigue, then had to give up & go to bed; left it out hoping they would see it & think to mail it, but of course they didn't,—or rather *he* didn't, for I find that Ed was in *bed* all the time!—went to bed at nine. He had been up the *whole* of the night before, didnt get home 'till eight in the morning, was engaged in "keeping the Freshmen straight"! Taking down banners from all sorts of impossible places &c. &c. Doesn't it seem funny to think of staid, sober Ed on such a spree?

I am so sorry to hear of your attack of grippe, darling. Are you *sure* you are really well again? You ought to have told me at the time. I feel very thankful to Dr. Mitchell. If he has discovered such a wonder as a specific for the *grippe* be sure to bring the prescription home with you. By the way, wont you let Dr Smith[1] examine your teeth? You know how much trouble & time it costs to go to Dr. Wilson.[2] And you know he told me to be sure to let him know how many of those tubes of tooth paste were bad (from improper mixing) & he would replace them. So please tell him there were *four*. They are fifty cents each & I don't want to lose it.

I am delighted to hear of your brilliant success in Washington! Am sorry the audience was not larger! Was it "select" as well as small? How did you like Mr. Wilson? Am glad he heard you. What did he say about your lecture?

But I must stop. I am extremely busy trying to get a little sewing done,—a discouragingly slow business with the "school" & everything else. But this is "holiday" and I must make the most of it. But I won't leave my letter for night anymore however hurried I am. Only four more of them to write! how delightful!

I love you, dear, "with my soul and my heart, and my duty, and my life, and my living, and my uttermost power";—I am always and altogether                Your own    Eileen.

ALS (WC, NjP).
  [1] Dr. B. Holly Smith of Baltimore.
  [2] Dr. Penrose J. Wilson of Trenton.


## To Ellen Axson Wilson

My own darling,                Baltimore, Md., 24 Feby, '95

The tone of this little letter written on Friday disturbs me again, as one or two of its predecessors have disturbed me, with the feeling that you were not happy when you wrote it. I may be mistaken this time, the traces of the mood are so slight,—but why else should I get the impression? I opened the letter in *my* usual mood. Ah, my sweet one, what tells upon your spirits? Are you unwell, or does the separation begin to tell upon you, as upon me,— with a certain intolerable addition of impatience? Oh, my little queen, I wish I dared and knew how to write to you in every mood of my love! *Some* moods I can almost translate into words; others I could not, were I to break my heart trying; others I might if I dared. I had hoped you would set me the example: you promised that, if I would destroy the letters, you would: but I have waited in vain. Perhaps, alas! there was no occasion! Perhaps you have thought of me all these weeks as simply as if I were your brother. What ought I to do under such painful circumstances? Ought I to be as demure and as insincere as a priest, or ought I to write colourless letters and say never a word that would betray emotion, or ought I to come out with the passion that is in my thought. 'Mum's the word, lad, till she gives thee leave. Don't make a fool of thyself!' It would not make her blush, I'm sure, could I tell her what I mean. I could not love any other woman so: I could not *imagine* myself loving any other woman so. I never wanted any other woman in this fashion,—and I never shall want any other after that way. It is my passion for my *wife*! 'But, lad, you write in one mood, she reads in another. You would not risk making thy love distasteful to her.' Not for the world! I'll change my tone, if I have to write from *memory* to do it,—and die of the torture of suppression in the doing!

Nell, dids't thou ever hear of a fellow dying of *accepted* love, dying for love of his *wife* while she loved him? I hope I shall not be the first! I hate singular deaths, untimely, unreasonable! It shakes a fellow dreadfully, though, this thing of loving as much as he can, without restraint or measure! Perhaps it were wiser not to love so much,—to study moderation and affect indifference, —approach your lady calmly and without undue or exaggerated show of ardour,—write to her only of affection,—regard her chiefly as the mother and mistress of your little family, and not as the idol of your heart. What do you think of it, love? Which do your [you] prefer? The equable, affectionate husband, or the irregular, passionate lover. I don't know that you have any real choice in the matter; but it would be instructive if you would break your sedate reserve and tell me which you would have,—a model husband and friend, or                Your own   Woodrow

☞ Please have the enclosed deposited.

ALS (WC, NjP).


## From Ellen Axson Wilson, with Enclosure

My own darling,                Princeton, N. J. Feb 24/95

I enclose a photograph to see if you know who it is.[1] None of us did. I tried, rather unsuccessfully to scratch off the name of the town lest it should give you a clue. You must "play fair" and not try to make it out.

Am delighted (for our sakes at least,) that father is coming back with you. Oddly enough a letter from Sister A.[2] of I think the same date as yours, says they expect him there this week! For just one reason I wish he *were* going south now. It is the most *'heartening'* season to go south I think because it cuts the winter off short just at the time when one is getting most tired of it. It is really spring there, and what a delicious sensation it gives one to *suddenly* escape from this fierce struggle with the elements into that balmy air! With eyes shut I could easily dream myself in paradise breathing "an ampler ether, a diviner air." It is bitterly cold here again now, (of course not the former terrible weather,) and my one fear is that father, who dislikes cold almost as much as I, will become immediately disgusted again with Princeton, and country houses in general, and go back to New York and all that old unsatisfactory business.

And to think, darling, that at last I can say 'this week'! Oh I am so miserably happy at the thought that I don't know what to do! How *can* I wait? And it is five whole days yet;—how shall I spend them? Evidently not in writing letters. That is rapidly becoming an impossibility, so violently does it aggravate all the symptoms of my complaint. I think I must betake me either to the study of philosophy or—darning stockings! The case evidently calls for a sedative and not a stimulant.

But though I must not say,—must try not to *think* how much I want you,—how hard it is to wait I can indulge myself by sending you a little poem that I lately found in a *book*. Alas! would that like yours it could have come direct from the heart. But I am in deed and in truth what you only *think* you are, viz., *dumb*!

Yet after all it does come as direct from my *heart* as did yours; it is only my *brain* that it reached by a circuitous route. With all my heart                    Your own    Eileen

ALS (WC, NjP).
1 The photograph is missing.
2 Annie Wilson Howe of Columbia, S. C. Her letter is missing.


ENCLOSURE

E'en like two little bank-dividing brooks,
That wash the pebbles with their wanton streams,
And having ranged and searched a thousand nooks,
Meet both at length in silver-breasted Thames,
Where in a greater current they conjoin:
So I my Best-Beloved's am; so He is mine.

E'en so we met; and after long pursuit,
E'en so we joined; we both became entire;
No need for either to renew a suit.

For I was flax and he was flames of fire:
Our firm-united souls did more than twine;
So I my Best-Beloved's am; so He is mine.

If all those glittering monarchs that command
The servile quarters of this earthly ball,
Should tender, in exchange, their shares of land,
I would not change my fortunes for them all:
Their wealth is but a counter to my coin:
The world's but theirs; but my Beloved's mine.[1]

EAWhw MS. (WC, NjP).
[1] Francis Quarles, "A Divine Rapture."


## To Ellen Axson Wilson

My own darling,                    Baltimore, 25 February, 1895

Two more letters besides this one, and then I come myself, to claim you, to take possession of you,—of all the time and love you can give me: to take you in my arms and hold you till I have made sure, by feeling your heart beat against mine and by seeing once more the very depths of your eyes, that I am really at home once more, with the woman who has made me and kept me what I am. I tremble with a deep excitement when I think of it. I verily believe I never quivered so before with eager impatience and anticipation. I know that I was not half so much excited on the eve of our marriage. Why *should* I be? I knew nothing. How could I know how happy I was to be, what a constant ecstasy it was to be to live with you,—what an inspiration and steady growth of love,—how I was myself to grow under the sweet influence! I am twice as *capable* of enjoyment now as I was then. I am like an instrument till then unplayed upon, but now for ten years strung constantly to sweet music: every fibre more sensitive; my very texture changed. What wonder if I tremble as I never did before at the thought of being once more under the hand of my musician! Ah, little lady, no man can have such tender images of love as a happy husband. A young lover knows nothing of the real, deep ecstasy of tried and accepted and hallowed love. True, there's nobody like you, with such a varied and yet constant sweetness and charm; but then what man would *not* love his *wife* more profoundly, and more eagerly too, than any other woman, if he loved her at all to begin with,—and knew her to begin with? What companionship so mellows and glorifies love as that companionship: what new love could bring such a deep ecstasy?

But, after all, how can *I* generalize? Any woman, young or mature in her charms, would seem stale and slow after you. That I am happier and more eager than a young lover cannot carry any argument with reference to other men. I alone have had the complete satisfactions and education of love: I alone have had you!

Alas, I shall have been at home only four days when I must be off again, to Cleveland![1] But think of those four days, sweetheart, —and think of the zest of my coming home *again*, the end of next week! We shall simply have the wild ecstasy all over again—enough keen joy almost to make us feel that we have been married all over again—with a difference in our favour! I am afraid this is the last love letter I shall dare write this time. As the time for seeing you approaches I can less and less control my words or my hand. The time for *kisses* is too near,—for the unspoken love that makes us man and wife, it becomes a more and more intense matter to be                                    Your own   Woodrow

ALS (WC, NjP).
  [1] Wilson was scheduled to deliver his address, "Democracy," printed at Dec. 5, 1891, Vol. 7, at Western Reserve University on about March 6, 1895. See the announcement in the *Princeton Press*, Jan. 26, 1895.


## From Ellen Axson Wilson

My own darling,                           Princeton, N. J.  Feb. 25/95

A telegram has just come from Mr. Horace Scudder dated Washington,[1] asking if he can see you here at two o'clock tomorrow. I shall answer at once giving him your Balt. address.

And isnt this a singular letter that has just come from Cleveland?[2] A very rude proceeding it seems to me,—or even worse, since the first requisite for a *gentleman* is to abide by your word whether it is convenient or not;—"he that sweareth to his own hurt and changeth not." However I have no doubt I shall soon recover from my vexation with them in my pleasure at the thought that you won't have to leave home again so soon.

I can't remember my Friday letter at all, dear, but I am sure I was not in bad spirits. We are all getting on very nicely indeed. And you know I havn't missed any possible pleasure by staying away from receptions. Tomorrow, alas! I must receive at one. Mrs. Purves is to give a huge one. Mrs. Dewitt has shown herself more cranky than ever by refusing without reason given, to receive with her!

I should be very unwilling to swear, darling, that there has been "no occasion" for the sort of letter you wish. But I havn't the cheek! You will have to spare me. I know you don't want me to force myself to write so against the grain. But I am quite sure that I love you just as much as you wish, and in every way you wish.

> "Thou art my life, my love, my heart,
> The very eyes of me,
> And hast command of every part,
> To live and die for thee."[3]

Your little wife    Eileen.

ALS (WC, NjP).
[1] It is missing.
[2] A letter, which is missing, from Western Reserve University canceling Wilson's address.
[3] Robert Herrick, "To Anthea, Who May Command Him Anything," from *Hesperides*.

## Two Newspaper Reports of a Speech on Municipal Reform

[Feb. 26, 1895]

### FOR GOOD GOVERNMENT.

A meeting in the interest of the movement for good government[1] was held at the Johns Hopkins University yesterday afternoon. The meeting was called to order by Mr. John Haynes,[2] who stated its purpose as being to interest university men in the move-

[1] This movement, sponsored by the Baltimore Reform League, founded in 1885 and led by the prominent attorney, Charles Joseph Bonaparte, and an ephemeral organization called the Union for Public Good in Baltimore, was the most recent revolt against the long-entrenched Democratic city and state machine headed by Senator Arthur Pue Gorman and Isaac Freeman Rasin. The revolt in late 1894 and early 1895 was set off by Senator Gorman's alleged betrayal of Democratic promises of tariff reform by his leadership of the Senate's upward revision of the Wilson Tariff bill of 1894. A bitter and bloody campaign during the summer and autumn of 1895 between independent Democrats and Republicans on the one side and the Gorman-Rasin "ring" on the other ended in the election of a Republican city council and a Republican mayor, Alcaeus Hooper. See James B. Crooks, *Politics & Progress: The Rise of Urban Progressivism in Baltimore, 1895 to 1911* (Baton Rouge, La., 1968), pp. 13-47; John R. Lambert, Jr., *Arthur Pue Gorman* (Baton Rouge, La., 1953), pp. 244-51; and Charles Morris Howard, "The Recent Revolt in Baltimore: Its Results and Its Lessons," *Proceedings of the Fourth National Conference for Good City Government and of the Second Annual Meeting of the National Municipal League Held at Baltimore . . .* (Philadelphia, 1896), pp. 75-87.
    The Baltimore revolt of 1894-95 was also part of a nationwide crusade for municipal reform, which in its most recent manifestation had begun with the organization of the National Municipal League in New York in May 1894 and the proliferation in various cities of Good Government Clubs affiliated with the League. See Herbert Welsh, "Municipal Leagues and Good Government Clubs," *Proceedings of the Second National Conference for Good City Government Held at Minneapolis . . . and of the First Annual Meeting of the National Municipal League . . .* (Philadelphia, 1895), pp. 146-53.
[2] At this time an instructor at the Woman's College of Baltimore (later Goucher College) and a graduate student in economics at the Johns Hopkins, where he took his Ph.D. in 1895.

ment, and to endeavor to induce them to take active part in the various auxiliary clubs which are to be organized in various parts of the city. There is to be no one club organized to consist exclusively of Hopkins men, but the latter are to exercise what influence and knowledge they possess over wider and more general fields outside the university.

The first address was by Prof. Woodrow Wilson, of Princeton, who is an authority upon the subjects of government and administration. His talk was pregnant with thought and a sound common-sense view of the duties of a good government club. . . .

Printed in the *Baltimore American*, Feb. 26, 1895; one editorial heading omitted.

[Feb. 26, 1895]

### "POWER OF REMOVAL."

Prof. Woodrow Wilson, of Princeton, delivered an address yesterday afternoon at the Johns Hopkins University in the interest of the Good Government Club of Baltimore.

Addresses were also delivered by Prof. Herbert B. Adams and Dr. James Carey Thomas.[1]

Professor Wilson pointed out what he conceived to have been errors in the formation of municipal government and errors into which the people are likely to fall in their efforts to correct them. He said in substance:

"It is interesting that, in our efforts to purify our institutions of their later corruptions, we have returned to the school of local government. The great cities which have grown up, created by the social and industrial changes of the last fifty years, having swept away the old arrangements of local government, which used to be our best schools of civic virtue and public spirit, have compelled us to undertake the work of reconstruction in order that we may once more become neighbors and the masters of our own homes.

"We made a radical mistake at the beginning in giving our cities their constitutions. We treated them as if they were small States, with legislative and political, as well as administrative, functions. We tied up and confused their organization by a set of 'checks and balances'; gave them a 'legislature,' an 'executive,' a 'judiciary,' a system of two 'houses' and an executive veto, executive appointments and legislative confirmations. Now we are

[1] James Carey Thomas, M.D., prominent Baltimore physician, member of the Board of Trustees of The Johns Hopkins University, 1870-97, and father of Martha Carey Thomas of Bryn Mawr College.

trying to remedy the mistake by another—by concentrating the whole power of appointment and removal in the hands of a single person, the mayor, as if salvation lay wholly in personnel, and not also in systematic supervision and a careful co-ordination of plans.

"The mayor has only twenty-four hours in his day, like the rest of us. He cannot, in fact, administer the complex and growing affairs of a great city. He cannot even effectually oversee their administration. He can only choose men—choose most of them necessarily in the dark and with only a hearsay knowledge of their antecedents, and then let them go their way to succeed if they can, to blunder if they must. Their departments are left without close co-ordination, to run foul of one another. They must still depend on committees or commissions for the money to defray their expenses, and must still take their instructions from the council, which did not elect them, or from statutes which foresaw very little of what they should actually have to do. Have you really gained in system or fair and reasonable responsibility by such changes?

"Consider what it is that a city corporation is organized to do: To maintain and cleanse the public ways and thoroughfares; to provide for thorough sanitation, with its systems of inspection and its care to prevent epidemics and remove nuisances; to patrol and light all public places; to guard against fires and extinguish them when kindled; to provide and enforce proper sewerage; to regulate, if it does not provide, means of rapid transit from one part of its area to another; to maintain and patrol markets and parks; to relieve the destitute poor; to build, equip and conduct schools of various grades and characters. Extend the list as you will, the character of the work is in all parts the same. It is not political; it is administrative. Not only so: it is also inextricably interrelated and bound together and must be done with a constant view to harmony and system if it is to be done well. The street-cleaning department must co-operate with the police department. Both these departments must take care to understand and help the plans of the sanitary department. All three of these are interested in the systems of poor relief, fire prevention, lighting and paving. As separated departments, prevented from holding constant consultations and making common plans, they must all get on very badly.

"We make them as independent as possible, yet, nevertheless, try to supply them with plans through ordinances passed by a body dissociated from them, or else by statutes passed by a body still further removed, and give them their staff through an officer too busy to consult with them about plans or help them to an agreement, and without any means of bringing them to a common understanding with the isolated yet dictatorial councils. We call it a system of distinct responsibility because we have made it a system without common counsel. Without close integration and matter-of-course common counsel it cannot succeed.

"When we have comprehended this fundamental consideration in all its bearings, it is plain what we must set ourselves to do. We must find out the best way to make city government a coherent, co-operative system, working together by common counsel. Then, when we have not a two-chambered council, plus a row of 'independent' departments, plus an interfering mayor, with absolute powers of appointment and removal, to deal with, but instead a real common council, we can bring opinion to bear.[2] Public opinion can no more effectually deal with a score of dissociated powers than a man can carry an untied bundle of poles. Each single purpose must be worked out through its own confusing round of officials and 'influences.' But with common counsel there can be a concentration of force from without as well as an organization and union of force from within.

"With a real organization to work upon, capable of taking and transmitting suggestions, a proper differentiation ought to be possible. A central body, in which all plans centre, ought to be able to effect the proper sort of division of business, and to obtain the proper sort of assistance. Much of the work of a city is technical. It ought to have, when necessary, technical schools of its own, to supply it with the proper sort of mechanics and overseers. It ought to establish close working connections between its own service and medical schools—schools of civil and electrical engineering—and the colleges and universities in which the proper use and methods of statistics are studied, the right methods of housing and relieving the poor, and the wisest systems of common-school instruction. It might thus avail itself both of expert service and of expert criticism. This is the aid which university men owe their cities in addition to their general duty as citizens.

[2] As will soon become evident, Wilson had in mind what would later be called the commission form of municipal government, with which there had been much experimentation in the United States since the 1870's and about which there was much discussion at this time. See Tso-shuen Chang, *History and Analysis of the Commission and City Manager Plans of Municipal Government in the United States*, University of Iowa Monographs, Studies in the Social Sciences, VI (Iowa City, 1918), pp. 49-54; and, for example, Edmund J. James, "The Elements of a Model Charter for American Cities," *Proceedings of the Second National Conference for Good City Government Held at Minneapolis* . . . (Philadelphia, 1895), pp. 154-73.

"The object of good government clubs is not simply to detect and expose corruption, but also to devise permanent remedies. It is easy to utter criticism, as it is also easy to deserve it, but the real duty of reformers is to urge, step by step and persistently, the necessary practical reconstruction of city government. They owe to the community not so much the agitation of complaint and exposure as the agitation of suggestion and remedy, making it plain to practical men that they really understand what needs to be done and can point out practicable ways of doing it, patiently explaining what they want and why they want it, never wearying in the slow work of creating a true comprehension and a definite purpose on the part of the community. It is not exciting work: it is very hard work and very exacting, but it is the only work that will secure permanent good government."

Professor Adams, in his address, called attention to the good work that can be done by the university man in movements for the bettering of municipal government. "A man," he said, "who is a good scholar and not a good citizen is, to my mind, no true man. It is not merely incumbent upon him to vote and pay his taxes, but to take an active interest in all that pertains to civic government. The result of all these things that have come to pass in New York is the result of the scholar in politics. Charles H. Parkhurst started out as a teacher of Greek verbs in a college in a little country town where it was my fortune to succeed him, and where I remained just one year. Had he been content to remain there he would never have been heard from as the man to whose efforts the overthrow of Tammany and the exposure of the wickedness and corruption of that modern Babylon, New York city, was largely due."[3]

Professor Adams urged his hearers to lend a hand in the support of the good-government movement.

Dr. Thomas explained the objects of the good-government clubs, told how the movement came to be started, and urged the necessity of united action of a large body of citizens in reform movements.

Printed in the Baltimore *Sun*, Feb. 26, 1895; some editorial headings omitted.

[3] Adams was referring to the crusade against Tammany Hall in New York begun and led by the Rev. Dr. Charles Henry Parkhurst from 1892 to 1894. Adams had succeeded Parkhurst as teacher of Latin, Greek, mathematics, and classical history at the Williston Academy in Easthampton, Massachusetts, in 1872.

## From Ellen Axson Wilson

My own darling,          Princeton, N. J. Tuesday [Feb. 26, 1895]

This letter from Florence, full of bad news about the poor girl,[1] came last night. And tonight at the reception I had more bad news and a still greater shock! Dr. Brenton Green told me that Uncle Tom [Hoyt] fell on the ice *three weeks ago* and *broke* his *shoulder*, —that it is said to be a very serious injury. I feel impelled to run over and see him and find out all about it,—just how bad it is, &c., and I feel under some obligation too to make poor Florence a visit.[2] I thought of going tomorrow but then I reflected that I would first have to get Florence's address; and then it suddenly occured to me that it would be a fine idea to go on *Friday*, meet you and come back with you! What do you think of the scheme? If it is impracticable for any reason, write me, or telegraph if necessary. Write me anyhow *when* you reach Phila. and exactly on what spot to meet you. How excited I feel already at the prospect of cutting short this ordeal by several hours! Only it will be very tantalizing to meet you in public! How I wish you could leave Baltimore on the morning train! Is there no chance to get your pay the day before?

This is an interesting letter that I enclose from Mr. Fielder.[3] He really seems to be sure of selling the lot. I can't feel so sure though, and I almost wish he hadn't spoken to the Hibbens until it was absolutely necessary.[4] And yet I suppose it is kinder and fairer and more straightforward to let them know from the first what we are about. I wonder what they think of it. Evidently they do not think badly in any way of us, for they were very cordial to me tonight. Mrs Hibben was even affectionate,—as well as flattering, telling me I looked "perfectly lovely" &c. I rather think Mr. Fielder was anxious to clear up this point *before* he tackled the man;[5] and when you think of it it *is* rather awkward to urge a man to buy a lot and when he says he *will* immediately reply that perhaps *you wont*, and then shilly-shally with him for a month! It *might* cost us the chance to make the trade.

By the way, did you see Mr. Gresham about the Southwestern R. R. and what did you decide to do about the stock?

I am so tired that I *must* bring this very poor apology for a letter to a close, darling. After all perhaps it is well that there was something apart from love that I was *obliged* to write about. How exactly your letter of this morning expresses all that *I* am experiencing at this crisis! Never mind, it will soon be over. I shall soon ah *soon* be in the arms of my love.

                    Your little wife   Eileen.

ALS (WC, NjP).

¹ This letter from Florence Stevens Hoyt is missing. Perhaps it brought news that Miss Hoyt was suffering from tuberculosis of the bone in one of her legs, which was amputated in 1901 after long treatment had failed to produce a cure.

² Miss Hoyt was then an undergraduate at Bryn Mawr College. She received her A.B. in 1898.

³ Fielder's letter is missing, but Wilson's reply is printed at March 4, 1895.

⁴ As the documents will soon reveal, John Grier Hibben purchased the Wilsons' lot adjacent to his wife's on Washington Street.

⁵ An unknown prospective buyer, as J. W. Fielder, Jr., to WW, March 18, 1895, reveals.

## To Ellen Axson Wilson

My own darling,                    Baltimore, 27 Feb'y., 1895

This is actually my last letter! To-morrow (it will be when you get this) I shall, God willing, come myself, to *satisfy* my love with the sight and possession of my little wife! I can think of nothing else. The sweetness and passion of it all has already taken possession of me, and I go about as if in a dream, seeing only my home,—and in it only you! Oh, my sweet one, what a thing it is to be in love with you! How absorbing you are,—what thoughts you compel,—what joys you keep constantly alive! I've been a different man since this week set in that is to take me to you. My friends have noticed the difference, the access of spirits, of vivacity. It comes so much easier to talk, and to talk enthusiastically, imaginatively. To approach you brings out the poet in me,—the idealist. It becomes a pleasure to live, a delight to think: all my faculties seem cheered and excited to a pleasant activity. In short, Eileen, I love you: my life centres in you: to be with you is to be alive, to be separated from you is to stagnate and grow stale, morose,—without originative or active power. I can find no substitute,—no *partial* substitute, even,—for you. There are charming women here, of whom I could, I am sure, make intimate companions if I chose; but they are in no degree *like* you,—they do not *remind* me of your charm,—except by contrast. You seem to appeal to a special set of faculties: the delight you give is so *singular* a delight, so inseparable from yourself. I sometimes have a peculiar feeling that, even if I were to *love* these other women, with *their* own personal attractions, it would not interfere with my love for you: it would be so different in kind and in cause! Other women have delightful minds,—but there is none with the *flavour* of yours: other women are beautiful, but there is no beauty with a spiritual quality like yours:—other women have sweet and deeply affectionate natures, but none shows any trace of the peculiar loyalty and eagerness and *grace* of loving that makes your affection so ravishing. I *delight* to compare you with the most charming women I meet,—the comparison is so much to my advantage. No wonder you are not jealous when I express even an enthusiastic admiration of other women; for you *must* have *some* consciousness of your power,—some knowledge how complete your dominion over me is! Is it not so, my queen? Do you not feel infinitely *safe* in your possession of me? Do you not *know* how you can keep and turn and govern me at your own sweet will? Be generous! Never take advantage of me! Indulge and give me leave! You have only to frown and resist and censure to shrink and dwindle every power there is in me!

Are you ready, darling to be kissed breathless by

Your own    Woodrow

ALS (WC, NjP).


## From Ellen Axson Wilson

My own darling,      Princeton, N. J.  Wednesday [Feb. 27, 1895]

To think that this is the last letter!—that I can really say "the day after tomorrow!" I am filled, as you so well express it, with such "deep excitement" at the thought that writing seems well-nigh impossible. My heart refuses to submit longer to this bondage to pen and ink. How I loathe them! They have been good friends to us too and it seems ungrateful to hurl epithets at them now that our need for their services is almost past, but for the time being the reaction against them is too strong to resist.

> So I shall see him in two days
> And just two nights, but nights are short.
> See how I come, unchanged, unworn!
> Feel, where my life broke off from thine,
> How fresh the splinters keep and fine,—
> Only a touch and we combine!
>
> Too long this time of year the days!
> But nights, at least the nights are short.
> As night shows where her one moon is,
> A hand's-breadth of pure light and bliss,
> So life's night gives my lover birth
> And my eyes hold him! What is worth
> The rest of heaven, the rest of earth?
>
> What great fear, should one say "Three days
> That change the world might change as well
> Your fortune; and if joy delays,

Be happy that no worse befell!"
What small fear, if another says,
"Two days and two short nights beside
May throw no shadow on your ways;
But years must teem with change untried,
With chance not easily defied,
With an end somewhere undescried,"
No fear!—or if a fear be born
This minute,—it dries out in scorn.
Fear? I shall see him in two days
And two nights, now the nights are short.
Then just two hours, and that is morn.[1]

As I sat here musing when I *should* have been writing I suppose it suddenly "came to me" that this poem followed as it were step by step the current of my thoughts. So methough[t] my unwilling pen might at least render me the service of writing *it* down.

And so goodnight darling, God bless and keep you "auf wiedersehen." With all my heart and life

Your little wife—Eileen.

ALS (WP, DLC) with WWhw and WWsh notes concerning quarries and stone prices on env.
[1] Based on Robert Browning's "In Three Days." Ellen altered the words somewhat and omitted the third stanza.

## To John Wesley Fielder, Jr.[1]

My dear Mr. Fielder:                    Princeton, March 4, 1895

I find that I cannot recall anything definite about my conversations with Mr. Hibben and Mr. Davidson[2] about the sum I would be willing to take for the whole of my original piece of land on Washington St. I conversed with several other people about the sale of the lot at nearly the same time, and the several negotiations are now quite indistinguishable in my recollection.

But there is one thing I am quite sure of: and that is, that, even at the sacrifice of much better terms elsewhere, I should be willing to sell what remains to Mr. Davidson at the lowest possible figure. I cannot hope to control, except in a very general way, the use to be made of the land by any purchaser outside the College faculty; neither could I control his subsequent disposition of the property at all; and, for the sake of all the parties concerned, I am anxious that Mr. Davidson should secure it.

Twenty dollars ($20) a front foot is the lowest I have heard asked for such a building site anywhere in town. It is, besides,

$2.50 a foot less than I received for the upper two hundred feet.[3] I should be glad to sell it to Mr. Davidson for $20, though I would not now sell it to anyone else for less than $22.

At the same time, if Mr. Davidson feels that even $20 is more than he can at present afford to pay, I sincerely hope he will very frankly make me an offer, as near to that figure as he feels he can go. I am sorry he should be repeatedly troubled about this matter: but I am very anxious to sell the lot at once, in order to get my plans for building on foot as soon as possible: and I am desirous above all things to dispose of the land in a way I shall like to remember. Hence my strong wish to come to some bargain that will benefit my dear friends Mr. and Mrs. Hibben,—and Mr. Davidson, whom I have had such pleasure in meeting.

Please put the matter before Mr. Davidson in the way and at the time that will best suit his convenience.

I hope your other customer will be willing to leave the matter open for a few days.

Very truly Yours,   Woodrow Wilson

ALS (WC, NjP).
[1] There is a WWsh draft of this letter in WP, DLC.
[2] Mrs. Hibben's father, John Davidson of Elizabeth, N. J., a lawyer and head of the real estate firm of Shearwood Hill Land Company, 90 Nassau St., New York.
[3] That is, when the Wilsons had sold the upper 200 feet of their lot on Washington Street to Mrs. Hibben in 1893 for $4,500.

## From Edward Southwick Child

Dear Sir:                          New York, March, 7, 1895,

I have practically made the changes in your floor plans we talked of yesterday morning. They all work out satisfactorily with one exception. The cellar stairs go down as we figured them to do and leave room for range and boiler in the kitchen and have a good head room. The point we fail (or rather I failed) to realize was that your main staircase did not give as much head-room for the proposed reception space for students as we imagined there would be. Of space 7' high there is now just 3' 6" between the stone wall and the staircase. This is hardly to be called a reception room, even for students. Now it occurred to me that one foot on a small space like this would be a great improvement, and I enclose you a little sketch of a frame effect to take the place of the large cut up stone wall which now holds your side door and the window adjoining it. This should be made of Yellow pine planks 2" thick and with their edges chamfered to give an effect such as I have drawn in this letter.[1] This partition

would be as cheap or cheaper than stone; would be in strict keeping with the English style of architecture and could be made perfectly tight and warm and would have the advantage of giving
your waiting students one foot more of space in which they could
sit. The entire place should be finished, with a seat commencing
at the door and following around the three sides, the same as the
seat which looks into your fire place in the library.

I hope you will consider these things merely as suggestions
and an effort to carry out your wishes, and if they do not meet
the approval of Mrs Wilson and yourself, that you will feel at
liberty to say just what you think. We are going on with the
drawings, leaving this section unfinished. Would be glad to hear
from you as soon as you feel that you can give a decided answer.

Yours truly,   E. S. Child

TLS (WP, DLC) with WWhw notation on env.: "Ans. Mar. 9, 1895."
1 Here Child drew a small cross-section of wall.

## Reading Assignments                    [March 13, 1895]

### COLLATERAL READING IN LAW.

English Common Law: Political Science Quarterly, vol. IV,
pp. 496-518, 628-647; Social England, vol I, portions by F. York

*Begun, 6 March, 1894.*
*4 " 1895.*
*9 " 1897.*
*11 Oct. "*
*18 " 1898*
*23 " 1899.*
*16 " 1900.*
*4 Nov., 1901.*

ENGLISH  COMMON  LAW.

Nature of the Course:  A sketch in broad outline of the main
forces of development and of the leading principles developed.

The Topics of the Course:

    I. Outline of Periods and Forces.

   II. Anglo-Saxon Law: Character and Sources.

  III. Anglo-Frankish Law: Character, Development, and Sources.

   IV. English Law, Common and Statutory.

    V.   The Field of the Common Law (determined by the admin-
         istrative provisions of Henry II.).

   VI.   The Science of Case Law.

  VII. The Law of Real Property: History.

 VIII. The Law of Real Property: Principles.

   IX. The Ecclesiastical Courts: Jurisdiction and Influence.

    X. Contracts.

   XI. Torts.

*The first page of Wilson's notes for his lectures on English Common Law,*
*with his list of the years in which he gave the course.*
*Notes for this opening lecture are printed in Vol. 8, pp. 564-67*

Powell and F. W. Maitland; History of the Law of Real Property, by K. E. Digby; The Common Law, by O. W. Holmes, Jr.; Essays in Anglo-Saxon Law; Essays in Jurisprudence and Ethics, by Sir Frederick Pollock, the essay entitled, "The Science of Case Law"; The Land Laws (in the "English Citizen Series") by Sir Frederick Pollock.

Constitutional Law: The First Century of the Constitution, by Alexander Johnston, in the New Princeton Review, vol. IV, pp. 179-190; Fiske's Critical Period of American History, pp. 211-222; Boutmy's Studies in Constitutional Law; The Law of the Constitution, by E. V. Dicey; Political Science and Constitutional Law, by J. W. Burgess, part II.

The cases referred to in the lectures.

Printed in the *Daily Princetonian*, March 13, 1895.


# From the Minutes of the Princeton Faculty

4 5′ P.M., Wednesday, March 13 [1895].
. . . The President read a letter from the Secretary of the United Chapters of the ΦBK Society which is not now a Secret Society in reference to establishing a Chapter in this College. The matter was referred to a Committee consisting of Professors Murray, Cameron & W. Wilson.[1]

A letter was received from the Harvard Graduate Club in reference to appointing a Committee to consider the subject of Graduate Courses and the publication of the Hand-Book of these Courses.

Professors Magie, W. Wilson & Thompson were appointed the Committee. . . .[2]

College of New Jersey, "Minutes of the Faculty, 1894-1902," bound ledger book (University Archives, NjP).

[1] For the committee's report, see the Princeton Faculty Minutes printed at April 10, 1895.

[2] The committee gathered and sent in the information about Princeton and its graduate program that appeared in C. A. Duniway (ed.), *Graduate Courses. A Handbook for Graduate Students. Lists of Advanced Courses Announced by Twenty-One Colleges or Universities of the United States for the Year 1895-6* (New York, 1895).


# From John Wesley Fielder, Jr.

Dear Prof. Wilson              Princeton, N. J., March 18th 1895

Yours of this date containing check for $100—in settlement of commission on sale of your lot on Washington Street is duly received and allow me to thank you for same. I hope you have

not discommoded yourself in sending it so promptly. I congratulate you on such a pleasant termination of this matter.[1] When I
think of the many letters I have written to different parties in
various parts in order to effect a sale of this lot—it seems so
singular that it should be sold to one I saw almost every day.

I have written to the party I have on hand that his offer cannot
be accepted on account, as stated to him, the priority of another's
privilege. I am in hopes however I can induce him to invest in
another locality, which I think would answer his purpose fully
as well.                    Respy Yours,    J. W. Fielder Jr.

ALS (WP, DLC) with WWhw notation on env.: "J. W. Fielder, jr's Rec'pt for
fee."
    [1] Fielder seems to have been referring to an agreement of sale, which is
missing. The Wilsons gave a warranty deed to John Grier Hibben on June 22,
1895, receiving in return a mortgage to run for five years at 5 per cent for the
entire purchase price of the lot, $3,600. See the deed of Woodrow Wilson and
Ellen A. Wilson to John Grier Hibben dated June 22, 1895, and the mortgage
dated June 22, 1895, both in WC, NjP. On the face of the latter, Wilson wrote:
"This mortgage having been satisfied, I hereby consent that the same be dis-
charged of record.  Woodrow Wilson  Princeton, New Jersey, 1 May, 1901."

# Notes for an Address to the Pittsburgh Alumni[1]

*Pittsburgh*, 21st. March, 1895.
    *Scott's*[2] *"division of topics"*: 'He would take Dr. McCosh and the
Sesqui-Centennial'[3] (the principal theme of memory and the principal
theme of hope). In short, like a geologist, he would take "the earth."
I am left, it would seem, to take the fixed stars.

*Princeton's principal fixed star*
is her character: and I never
feel that character so distinctly as upon an occasion
like this.

*The new constituency of the
college*: not parents, but graduates. To the old commencement came the friends of the
graduating class; to the new
come the sons of the college

"Something that belongs to Cy.
McCormick."

    In our case, this clientage
formed just in time to get a
head of steam for the sesquicentennial.

Having myself been made by
this process, like the rest of you,
I sometimes feel a certain
strangeness at other institutions: like the *old coloured
woman* in the Corcoran Gallery.

    *A clientage*, this, *which the
college has made*, not one
which made the college:
which therefore transmits it
character.

The *Character* of the college *vs.* its *Reputation*. *Princeton's proper character*, a great common school for citizens. *Her Reputation?*
(1) A school for candidates for the ministry.
(2) A training school for athletes.
(3) A group of technical schools.
    *Her real worth* and character *displayed in the "Honour System."* The unquestionable proof of principle.
    *The pledge not of the essence.*

Character is a thing of growth, wh. cannot be borrowed. *"Lamb'd in the Spring."*

*"Fac' is, Morse Zeb.,* didnt know you was a can'date."

*"Blow out a candle."*

*Hand on the tradition*, guard the proper character: keep out the *microbes* of the scientific conception of books and the past.
    *A matter*, this, *fundamental to education.* You cannot hand on what is not an inheritance, what is only temporary and of the present.

Can't make the tonic too stiff[.] Let it, if need be, be as strong as diluted sulphuric acid, and go down the throat like *a torchlight procession.*

WWT and WWhw MS. (WP, DLC).
[1] Wilson used these notes for an address to the Princeton Club of Western Pennsylvania in Pittsburgh on March 22. The only report of this affair was a brief notice which appeared in the *Pittsburg Post*, March 23, 1895.
[2] William Berryman Scott (the other main speaker), born in Cincinnati on Feb. 12, 1858. A.B., College of New Jersey, 1877; Ph.D., Heidelberg University, 1880. Spent his entire academic career at Princeton as Assistant in Geology, 1880-81; Assistant Professor in Natural Science, 1881-83; Professor of Geology, 1883-86; and Blair Professor of Geology, 1886-1930. Author of many works, including an autobiography, *Some Memories of a Palaeontologist* (Princeton, N. J., 1939). Recipient of many honorary degrees. Died March 29, 1947.
[3] That is, the celebration of the sesquicentennial of the College of New Jersey in 1896, plans for which were well under way by this time. See A. F. West to WW, June 19, 1895, n. 1.

## From Child and de Goll, Architects

Dear Professor Wilson:          New York.   March 28, 1895
    Your favor of the 26th of March with enclosure as stated is received.[1] We are very much obliged to you for your promptness. . . . We are . . . preparing another set of white prints for your own use, which we wish you to keep and not give out to the contractors to deface.[2]
    We have not as yet heard from Mr Dall of whom you spoke.
                    Yours truly,   Child & de Goll [per] Holske[3]

TLS (WP, DLC) with WWhw notation on env.: "Rec'pt ($135.00)." Enc.:
Child and de Goll's receipt for payment of $135 for "details & specifications as
per contract."
   [1] Wilson's letter is missing.
   [2] This letter indicates that the Wilsons had now decided to proceed with the
building of their house. As the next letter reveals, Wilson had already discussed with John Davidson the possibility of obtaining a loan from the Mutual
Life Insurance Company of New York.
   [3] L. R. Holske, an assistant in the firm.


## John Davidson to John Grier Hibben

My dear Son Grier                        New York,  Mch 30th 1895

   I enclose application[1] for Prof. Wilson to sign—i.e. the one I
have filled out, the other is a copy for him to keep. I have put
the valuation

   Ground $5,000—because, what with grading, sodding, trees,
plants, gravel walk &c fences—&c. &c. it will run up to that figure!

   Building $9,500.—a $7,000 house will run up to about that,
including architects fees; lots of extras; time of Prof Wilson in
getting out plans &c & overseeing building—& profit of building
to be added to its value. Mark you, it does not say "*cost*" of building but "*Value of Building*" hence we put that valuation on it, we
may be wrong several thousand dollars, nevertheless we "value"
it, at that figure.

   Plans & specifications will have to go in with the application,
& my friend Hon. Amos Clark[2] the Co's representative in N. J.
will visit Princeton to see location &c. I will try as a favor to me
to have him call on Prof. Wilson. If the Co. accept it, only *three*
payts. will be made   say,

   1st when enclosed
   2nd when plastering finished
   3rd when all completed

It will therefore be necessary for Prof Wilson to have arrangements made with some Bank to carry him along until a payt from
the Mutual is reached.

   When the application is signed & plan & specs. are ready, do
*not* send them to the Company—but send them to *me*, & I will
go to the *Co* & as a personal favor to me—I will go to my friend
Clark & lay the whole matter before him. Of course Mr. F[red-
erick]. G[ordon]. Burnham of Morristown will have to read the
title & as each payt. is made from the Co. examine again to see
that no judgts, mtgs or liens are filed. Of course I make no
charge for anything I do. It is a great pleasure to do anything
for such a *man* as Prof. Wilson, & I will give him such an endorsement to the Mutual Co. as few men have.

The only charges will be Burnham's, & these I will work down to the lowest cent. An Insurance policy must go on, as soon as it can be insured, but I had better let the Mutual Co do that, as they have their own agents

Excuse my haste & this horrid writing. My love to Jenny, Beth[3] & yourself                    Ever your devoted Father    J. D.

The sooner it is in, the better it will be, they are flooded with applications

ALI (WP, DLC).

[1] For a mortgage loan from the Mutual Life Insurance Company of New York.

[2] Banker and real estate agent of Elizabeth, N. J., he was a former member of the New Jersey State Senate and of the United States House of Representatives.

[3] The Hibbens' daughter, Elizabeth Grier.


## From Edward Southwick Child

My dear professor Wilson:                    New York. April, 1, 1895.

Yours of 31st of March received. . . .

In relation to the arched entrance you speak of, we can make this 6 ft wide as you request by making the two windows on either side 4 ft wide instead of 4 ft 6 inches. The piers will not permit of any reduction in size—I will await your decision in this matter.

The Robert Mitchell people of Cincinatti are very good people and they do some excellent work.[1] We can just as well buy the mantels now and build the chimneys to fit them, as not.

I send you tonight a set of white prints of the house to permit yourself and friends to examine and criticise it.

Yours truly,    E. S. Child    [per] R Holske

TLS (WP, DLC).

[1] The Robert Mitchell Furniture Company.


## Two Letters from John Davidson

My dear Sir                    New York, Apl 3rd 1895

Yours of 2nd is recd. I will see Mr Clark tomorrow at our Bank meeting,[1]—he is one of our directors—after seeing him, I will write again to you.

You will have to pay interest on the advances from the time of actual payment, only.

The fees of Mr Burnham ought not to exceed $125.—all told. Int. will be payable semi-annually. Have you any abstract of title, searches—old deeds &c: so that they may be put in Mr Burnham's hands to save expense.

With kindest regards

Yours very truly    John Davidson

¹ The First National Bank of Elizabeth, of which Clark was president and Clark and Davidson were both directors.

My dear Sir                    Elizabeth N. J.   April 4th 1895

After our Bank meeting this afternoon I took our Presdt Hon. Amos Clark aside. He has all to do with the Mutual loans in N. J. I laid the whole matter before him, & left the application with him; the plans are to [be] left at his private office in Elizabeth tomorrow, and he will visit Princeton probabily on Saturday—at any rate—in time to have your application, with his report thereon laid before the finance Comte. at their meeting on Tuesday 9th inst. and I will be informed on Wednesday.

I asked for 3 or 4 payments to you &c. &c. He (Clark) said "Mr Davidson, it will be all right, there will be no trouble with it." Between ourselves, I know, Mr. Clark will stretch a point if necessary both on appraisement &c. He will help us

Will your Princeton Bank carry you along? if you want some help, our Bank here, will do what they can for you.

I will keep you fully informed. With kindest regards

Yours very truly    John Davidson

ALS (WP, DLC).

## Notes for a Talk to the Philadelphian Society

[April 4, 1895]
XIX Ps. Text Ps. I., 1-3.

"His delight is in the law of the Lord; and in his law does he *meditate* day and night." (Ps. I., 2.).

"*The law of the Lord*" is here simply the perfect way of life,— *spiritual enlightenment and insight*. A fixed and certain, yet broad and universal standard.

*Meditation not of* the practice of *this Age*,—a thing of old and leisurely times. But *necessary for wisdom, balance, hope*. (Not mere brooding or musing).

(1) *Nourishment, refreshment* ("rivers of water,"—"fruit *in his season*": every man having his season)

(2) *Preservation from* the *drying* process which makes fanatics and cranks ("his leaf shall not wither").

(3) *Assurance in action*,—no fear for him*self*. ("Whatsoever he doeth shall prosper").

(4) *Sane and broadened judgment*.

WWhw MS. (WP, DLC).

# Two News Items

[April 5, 1895]

### PROF. WILSON'S ADDRESS.

Prof. Woodrow Wilson addressed a well attended meeting of the Philadelphian Society in Murray Hall last evening. He chose as his subject "Meditation," basing his remarks on the first Psalm. He said the Bible is like a deep translucent pool, reflecting for a man what he chooses. It is deep enough or shallow enough for any man. Meditation is a thing of stillness. It is letting a thought lie in the mind and do what it will. In this age when so much is made of Christian activity, we are likely to forget meditation. The soul of man is nourished by calm meditation as the tree is nourished by the still waters. As a man advances in years he learns to form less hasty judgments. The meditative man though he reaches his conclusion later will reach a surer conclusion than the man of hasty judgment.

There will be no meeting of the Society next Thursday night on account of the Easter vacation.

Printed in the *Daily Princetonian*, April 5, 1895.


[April 9, 1895]

### MASS MEETING.

There was an attendance of about 200 at the mass meeting of the student voters held in the Old Chapel last evening. Payne '95[1] was elected chairman. He stated that the object of the meeting was that the students might obtain a clearer idea of the issues in to-day's borough election.[2] Professors Woodrow Wilson and West made addresses on the importance of the election to the university.

Printed in the *Daily Princetonian*, April 9, 1895.

[1] Christy Payne, '95.

[2] The only major issue in the Princeton borough election of April 9, 1895, was the question of whether the New York and Philadelphia Traction Company should be permitted to run its projected New York-Philadelphia electric trolley line through Princeton. Indeed, the company hoped to obtain permission to run the line down Nassau Street. The company had been promoting its scheme for some time, and the question had become something of a party issue with the incumbent Republican mayor and council opposed and the Democrats in favor.

The *Daily Princetonian*, April 9, 1895, urged all students eligible to vote to support those candidates (their names were listed) for mayor and council who were "opposed to unwise and hasty legislation on the trolley question, and are in sympathy with the sentiments expressed last night in the mass meeting." These sentiments were presumably the ones expressed by Wilson and West.

The *Daily Princetonian*, April 11, 1895, reported with obvious satisfaction that the Republican "anti-trolley men" had been elected. See also the *Princeton Press*, April 6 and 13, 1895.

## From the Minutes of the Princeton Faculty

4 5′ P.M., Wednesday, April 10, 1895.

. . . Resolved That the Faculty recommend to the Board of Trustees that the necessary steps be taken for securing the establishment of a chapter of the ΦBK Society in the College of New Jersey with the privilege of inducting qualified Seniors at the Commencement at which they are graduated.[1]

[1] The trustees gave their approval on June 10, 1895, and a provisional chapter of Phi Beta Kappa, composed of twenty-seven faculty members, was organized at Princeton in the autumn of 1895. Having been initiated into Phi Beta Kappa at Wesleyan, Wilson was one of the original members at Princeton. The Princeton University Chapter, Beta of New Jersey, received its charter on October 29, 1898. The members held the "Foundation Meeting" on June 7, 1899, and voted to admit twelve members of the senior class to membership. Mrs. Walton B. Butterworth to Elizabeth S. George, May 8, 1959, copy in University Archives, NjP; "Phi Beta Kappa Records," bound book (University Archives, NjP).

## From Josiah Worth Wright[1]

Dear Sir,                              Princeton April 15th 1895

Please pardon me for delaying estimate. In order to be sure I was figuring as low as possible. I have had different estimates for the different parts of the work. And I have taken the lowest responsible bids. The plumbing, and all connected with it in the specification, I have estimated at Eight Hundred Dollars. I have estimated for one cess pool 8 ft diameter 8 feet deep in the clear. I make the cost of house complete except Heating, and mantles, Nine Thousand and Five Hundred Dollars. There is no real personal profit in it at this price. I would like to build for you if I can do it without loss to myself. The above figures will require good financing to get out whole. I thank you for your kindness in asking me to estimate on it. I have done the best I could. Should you desire any explanation I will go to see you any time you may fix, or you can call any evening to see me.

Most truly yours   J. W. Wright

ALS (WP, DLC).

[1] A contractor who lived at 29 Canal (now Alexander) Street, who, as the documents will soon reveal, secured the contract to build the Wilson house. Wright was born in Princeton on February 19, 1829; served as Mayor of Princeton Borough, 1885-87, and as judge of the Court of Common Pleas and Orphans of Mercer County, 1887-96; and died on February 4, 1896.

## From the Minutes of the Princeton Faculty

4 5′ P.M., Wednesday, April 17, 1895.

. . . Professors Perry, Wilson & Daniels were appointed a Com-

mittee to nominate to the Faculty Judges for the Lynde Debate
and to select the Question for debate. . . .[1]

[1] See the Princeton Faculty Minutes printed at May 22, 1895, for the committee's recommendations.

## From Edward Southwick Child

My dear Sir:　　　　　　　　　New York.　April 17th., 1895.
　　Your favor of the 16th. of April is received and in reply would
say I have an idea that the change in the size of the gable will
be an improvement to the front of your house. We do not think
it is business for an owner to have a contract with a builder in
any indefinite shape in regard to the plans, and we would be
glad to alter these plans when the time comes to let this contract without any charge for the drawings, provided we do the
superintendence. If we do not do the superintendence, we would
arrange them with all the changes you wish for a charge of
$10.00.
　　We would advise you not to make any changes at all until
the time arrives when you will decide as to the contractor.
　　　　　　　　　　　　　Yours truly,　E S Child

TLS (WP, DLC).

## From John Davidson

My dear Sir　　　　　　　　　New York, Apl. 19th 1895
　　The Mutual Co. sent you word on Wednesday P.M. [April 17]
that your application was granted[.] If you have any title papers
—if you send them to me, I will write to Mr. F. G. Burnham of
Newark, & ask him to accept the title policy of the N. J. Real
Estate Title & Trust Co. in lieu of search. It is optional with him
to do it, but Mr. Clark will see him & ask him to do it; however
I want to send what papers you have & I want the opportunity
to write to him to make the expense just as *low* as possible.
　　With kindest regards
　　　　　　　　Yours very truly　John Davidson

ALS (WP, DLC) with WWhw notation on env.: "Ans."

## From Josiah Worth Wright

Dear Sir,　　　　　　　　　Princeton April 19th 1895
　　Please pardon me for making a suggestion. I think if the
stone porch is dispensed with, and a small piazza without a

balcony built, it would save enough to furnish the heating &
mantles. A few other changes might be made but I cannot tell
where, that would bring the price down to your limit. I thought
I would write and inform you about the cost of this porch, and
what could be done if you found it necessary.

Most respectfully yours   J. W. Wright

ALS (WP, DLC).


## To Annie Wilson Howe

My precious Sister,                    Princeton, 21 April, 1895
   My heart is so full I do not know either what to say or what
to think. To lose brother George[1] is like losing part of one's own
life: he lived so nobly and seemed so solid a dependence for
one's love, and for all one's expectations of life! I cannot *think*
yet of our lives without his! And oh, my sister, my sweet and
noble sister, how shall I utter my thoughts about you,—the
thoughts that seem likely to break my heart! It is you who are
left desolate,—and our love for you, deep and tender as it is,
beyond all words, can not compensate you. What would we not
do to take some little part of the burden from you. It is a comfort to us, even now, to think what a noble life of effective use-
fulness he lived, and how complete it was, in some senses, in
achievement: what a splendid *man* he was and how noble a
Christian. But for you, as yet, to remember what he was, is only
to know the more keenly what you have lost. The most we can
do is to love you the more tenderly and earnestly—if that be
possible—and to pray with you and for you for grace and comfort
from our God and his. You will have now to learn to lean on
us the more directly, and oh, my sister, God grant we may
know *how* to love you and help you. Our hearts yearn for you,—
and for the boys,—and for darling little Jessie,[2] more than it
would be possible to express,—but not more, I trust, than it will
be possible to show.
   My first impulse, on receiving that dreadful telegram, was to
go at once to Columbia: but it did not come till late this afternoon; I could not get to you till after the funeral: and to go
(unless there were something practical I could *do*) would be to
mar my college work hopelessly—so that it would be left unfinished and broken at the end of the year. It would be but a
poor tribute to brother George to neglect my professional duties
when it was not *necessary* to do so. But if there is anything I
can do, or can help you to do,—if there is any reason I should

be there,—if it would in any way specially comfort and sustain you,—my duty will be plain the other way, and I can follow my heart without scruple or misgiving. I need not explain that to you; and I am sure that you will not hesitate to send for me if you need me.

Oh for some great heart-word that would tell you what we suffer—for our own loss and yours,—and how from the depths of our hearts we love and cling to you!

Your devoted brother,   Woodrow

ALS (WP, DLC).
    [1] For the details of the illness and death of Dr. George Howe, Jr., on April 20, 1895, see the following letter from George Howe III to WW.
    [2] An obvious slip. The Howes' first daughter, Jessie, had died on January 30, 1885. Wilson meant the second daughter, Annie, born in 1891.


## From George Howe III

Dear Uncle,                              Columbia  Apr. 23rd 95
    I am afraid that at present I am not capable of writing to much advantage, but if I can in anyway relieve your anxiety as to how affairs have been conducted I will have accomplished my purpose. I am uncertain whether you have heard *any* of the particulars connected with our sad disaster or not so I shall try to begin at the beginning.

Last Monday night Father played billiards till twelve o'clock, and, except for a little paleness which they attributed to a bilious attack, he seemed to be in his usual good health. On Tuesday Mother was surprised that he made no attempt to get up, because he had an operation to perform that day and it was his custom on such occasions to rise early and prepare for his work. Dr. Taylor[1] was called in. It seems that Father knew that his trouble was appendicitis for he told Dr. T. but no one else. On Wednesday Dr. Price of Phila.,[2] I think, was telegraphed for and on Thursday 12.30 the operation was performed by him. The trouble was not merely appendicitis (which in itself was complicated) but there was also a form of peretinitis connected with it. Besides these Dr. Price said that it was clear that he had had what is known as ambulatory typhoid fever for sometime. He also said that if it had been merely append. he could easily have recovered, but that aside from this disease his death was inevitable. So he it was that told Mother to wire us. We got here 2:00 Friday night and father was not told till Sat. aft. We went in to see him and he greeted me with "Hello, old fellow," trying to be cheerful for my sake though he was so weak I could scarcely hear him. His pain was intense and when they were about to relieve it by a dose of morphine his eyes glistened like a child's in anticipation of some great pleasure. Yet he never once complained[.] On Sat. morning it was only necessary to get his bowels to act, and there was a slight action that morning. Hence my telegram that the symptoms were favorable. But no further action took place, and at 8 P.M. after consultation the doctors agreed that his bowels would have to be opened—second operation[.] This was done as a last chance but an hour later Dr. T. told us he had no hope whatever. He sank slowly till 11.50 when we watched him breathe his last. I can't mention any of the more minute details of his conversation, patience, unselfishness, submission to God's will for I cannot stand it. To show his heroism, however, I will say that in all this intense pain on Thurs. he insisted on getting up and walking from one room to another to the operation table unassisted.

This little town of ours is full of good and truly noble people— a thing the town should be proud of. They did everything that could be done. From morning till night all three of us (the family) received letters of sympathy not only from Col. but from all the state.

The funeral took place 4.30 yesterday. The church was packed and I am told that there was not even standing room from the church door to the gate. This is but poor comfort, but I mention it to show how he was esteemed by all classes. There was no interruption of any kind to the services, except that Dr. Smith[3] was so overcome that when reading the Cor. he could scarcely be heard beyond where we were sitting.

Mother has born like the heroine she is. Today she has a headache and pains in her side and back from trying to lift father to turn him.

I should like to say more but you will pardon me, because I am afraid I cannot attempt to write any more details. I must now speak of my affairs and get your advice. It is of course beyond question that I am to remain here the rest of term. Wilson has to return to his business,[4] Grandfather to the Assembly,[5] and someone must be with Mother. What we wish to know is about my rising to the Junior class next year. Will the faculty make any provision for my case? Would it be possible for me to get through on my grades and with the promise of continuing the work mapped out? If you can explain this to us we will all be grateful to you.[6]

Grandfather wishes me to say that in not coming you did right; that whatever reasons you acted upon we feel sure were just what they ought to have been. We did not answer your telegram because it came after the last train you could have taken had left the Junction.

Tell Ed I shall write soon to him and get him to send my wheel[,] mandolin, etc since it is probable Wilson may take Father's.

If there are any questions to ask I shall be glad to answer them if I can. I have written very hastily because I have some other letters to write this morning. We all send love to your dear household. I feel sure that you unite with us and with *Father* in saying "God's will be done."          Lovingly,   Geo Howe.

This Dr. Price is said to be the greatest authority on appendicitis in the country if not in the world—for fear you should not have heard of him.

ALS (WP, DLC) with WWhw notation on env.: "Geo—Ans. 26 Apr. '95."
  [1] Dr. Benjamin Walter Taylor, an eminent surgeon of Columbia.
  [2] Dr. Joseph Price, a pioneer in modern gynecology and abdominal surgery.
  [3] The Rev. Dr. Samuel Macon Smith, pastor, First Presbyterian Church of Columbia.
  [4] His brother, James Wilson Howe, who was then living in Philadelphia. He was not listed in the Philadelphia directory, and the nature of his business is unknown.
  [5] The General Assembly of the southern Presbyterian Church met in the First Presbyterian Church of Dallas, May 16-25, 1895.
  [6] See WW to George Howe III, April 26, 1895, n. 1.


## From Edward Southwick Child

Dear Professor Wilson          New York. April 26, 95
    Your 15 April just reached me as I have been away. . . .
    What day early next week would it suit you to have me come to Princeton. I think the cut stone could be all left out—and have other suggestions which I think will be satisfactory.
                              Yours Truly   E S Child

ALS (WP, DLC).


## To George Howe III

My dear George,          Princeton, 26 April, 1895
    I thank you from the bottom of my heart for your brave letter. We were longing more than I know how to say for more particular news,—feeling all the more desperately desolate because it did not come. And your letter, for all its burden of news that was fairly heartbreaking, did us some measure of good: it was so brave and so *right* in its telling of the pitiful story. I cannot

tell you how this bereavement has affected us. I feel all the time a sense of loneliness that is an almost intolerable weight on my spirits; and, even when my thoughts are necessarily upon other things, I feel like one who is perplexed by having forgotten or lost something. I shall miss that noble brother of mine till my dying day; and it will be a new bond between us, my dear boy, that we both loved him so well.

As for my precious sister, I know not what to say: my heart cannot frame anything but an inarticulate cry. But this I have settled upon: she—you all—must come and spend the summer here with us,—must come just as soon as your father's business affairs can be settled. I cannot take a refusal, and, more than that, it will be *necessary* that sister should have rest and a change just as soon as possible. She needs *always* a cooler climate in the summer. That she can get here,—and, besides that, such love and companionship as she must surely need just as much. I will not have your wheel sent now, George, because I believe you will come: I could not bear a refusal, I think: we *must* all be together,— all that are left,—and this is the only feasible plan. Sister need not worry about planning it now. Just let her take it for granted for the present, and plan it later.

As for your examinations, I cannot say anything definite yet; but I will bring the matter up in Faculty next Wednesday (May 1st.) I have no doubt some satisfactory arrangement can be made. I will write you about it again next week after Faculty meeting.[1]

Tell dear father I am very anxious to hear from him and learn his plans for the near future. Give him a heartful of love from each one of us. Tell sister Annie that we love her as she would wish to be loved at so terrible a time: that we think and pray for her as only those can who themselves suffer irreparable loss in the death of the one who is gone,—oh that I could say the unspeakable things that are in my heart! And, as for yourself, my dear, dear boy, can you not guess what I would say: how I would almost rejoice at this moment at the splendid memory and example, both as as [a] man and as a Christian, you will have to live up to and take inspiration from in the noble father who is now far happier than we can ever be till we join him in heaven.

Your devoted uncle   Woodrow

ALS (WC, NjP).
  [1] "Mr. Samuel [George] Howe (So. C.) who had been absent from Examination and from College for some time on account of the death of his Father requested to be excused from Examination if possible[.] His request was referred to his Instructors with the recommendation that it be favorably considered and his standing be determined from his work and examinations at the close of

this session." "Minutes of the Faculty, 1894-1902," May 1, 1895, bound ledger book (University Archives, NjP).

## From Edward Southwick Child

Dear Professor—        New York. Apl 30 [1895]
    I will come on train leaving N. Y. at 1 o'clock tomorrow— (Wednesday).       Yours,   E S Child

ALS (WP, DLC) with WWhw address and notes concerning cost of building materials on env.

## From the Minutes of the Princeton Faculty

4 5′ P.M., Wednesday, May 1st, 1895.
    . . . An Invitation was received from the Trustees & Faculty of the University of North Carolina to attend the Celebration of the Centennial Anniversary of the opening of the University, June 5th, 1895.
    The Invitation was accepted and Professors Woodrow Wilson and James M. Baldwin were appointed to represent the Faculty upon the occasion. . . .[1]

    [1] It seems unlikely that either Wilson or Baldwin attended this ceremony, as none of the programs or announcements mention their names, and the North Carolina newspapers did not report their participation.

## From Edward Southwick Child

Dear Sir:        New York. May 7th 1895.
    Your favor of the 6th of May is at hand. . . . It seems to me a very sad thing to leave off the porch in that house, and I would not be afraid that we could not make any of these builders to build the house right from those specifications. I will let you know at once when I hear anything more.
       Yours truly,   E. S. Child

I do not think the house without the porch will add much to our professional repute.[1]

TLS (WP, DLC).
    [1] The porch was retained.

## From John Holladay Latané[1]

My dear Dr. Wilson,     ·     Baltimore, Md. May 8, 1895.
    I thank you very much for the interest you are so kind as to express in my thesis.[2] In regard to the Cavalier immigration, about which you ask, I fear I can give you no definite information.

I do not remember to have come across anything except the statements, which are very meagre, contained in the current histories. There seems to be a general impression that there was a large Cavalier element in Virginia in the latter half of the 17th Century, but its importance, I think, has been greatly overestimated. I must confess that my own statement is probably misleading, although I did not intend it that way.

The only definite statement that I can lay my hands on is contained in the enclosed extract from one of Gov. Nicholson's letters to the Board of Trade in 1701, which my friend, Mr. Ballagh,[3] copied from the Sainsbury Papers in the Va State Library. There are in the State Library 15 or 20 folio vols. of extracts from papers in the British State Paper Office made by Mr. Sainsbury specially for the library, much fuller than the printed calendar. Some of the Governors' reports, of which the enclosed is a sample, are very interesting and instructive. I have myself gone through only the earlier vols.

I think that the Virginia *aristocracy* was based on land and office holding rather than on blood.

I wish very much that I could give you more information on the subject.

With kindest regards, I am

Yours very truly, John H. Latané

ALS (WP, DLC) with WWhw notation on env.: "Latané–Cavalier immigration to Va." Enc.: handwritten extract.
  [1] At this time a candidate for the Ph.D. in history at the Johns Hopkins.
  [2] It was published under the title, *The Early Relations Between Maryland and Virginia*, Johns Hopkins University Studies in Historical and Political Science, 13th Series (Baltimore, 1895).
  [3] James Curtis Ballagh, at this time a candidate for the Ph.D. in history at the Hopkins.

## To Daniel Coit Gilman

My dear Mr. Gilman,        Princeton, New Jersey, 10 May, 1895.

A [An] invitation from you comes almost like a command, so much is my inclination engaged to accept. It goes very hard indeed to decline this one. But unfortunately I have no choice.

I deliver an address at the University of Virginia on the evening of Wednesday, June 12th, and have, in addition, engagements there the next morning which I cannot neglect and which will prevent my getting to Baltimore in time for any exercises on Thursday.

I am sincerely sorry. I appreciate very warmly your kind desire to have me speak at your Commencement. The only thing I do

not regret is, that you will not know how little I should have had
to say!
    Believe me
            Cordially and loyally Yours,    Woodrow Wilson

WWTLS (D. C. Gilman Papers, MdBJ).


## From John Davidson

My dear Sir                              New York, May 10th 1895
    Your letter is just recd. & I have already written to the Mutual
Co. your acceptance of the loan.
    I enclose you a letterpress copy of the letter, which I have just
forwarded to Mr. Burnham.[1]
    As soon as I hear from him, I will let you know. Excuse my
haste                        Yours very truly    John Davidson

ALS (WP, DLC). Enc.: J. Davidson to F. G. Burnham, May 10, 1895, letterpress
copy (WP, DLC).
    [1] In this letter, Davidson asked Burnham if the Mutual Life Insurance Com-
pany would accept a guarantee of title to Wilson's lot on Steadman Street from
the New Jersey Real Estate Title and Trust Company of Trenton.


## A News Item

                                                [May 11, 1895]
    Prof. Woodrow Wilson will deliver a course of lectures this
summer before the American Society for the Extension of University Teaching.[1] He will also give the inaugural lecture on
"Democracy" at the opening of the summer meeting of the society
in Philadelphia on June 29th.[2]

Printed in the *Daily Princetonian*, May 11, 1895.
    [1] About this organization, see G. Henderson to WW, May 18, 1891, n. 1, Vol. 7.
The Philadelphia *Citizen* (published by the American Society for the Extension
of University Teaching), 1 (April 1895), 45-46, announced that during the
week of July 14, 1895, Wilson would give "five lectures on 'Constitutional Gov-
ernment in the United States,' discussing the following subjects: (I) What is
Constitutional Government? (II) Political Liberty; (III) Written Constitutions;
The Nature, Origin, Significance of Our Own; (IV) The Organization and
Powers of Congress; (V) The Function of the Courts Under a Constitutional
Government." The Philadelphia newspapers did not report on Wilson's lectures,
but one of his hearers, Franklin Spencer Edmonds, wrote in the Philadelphia
*Citizen*, 1 (Sept. 1895), 170, "Dr. Woodrow Wilson is a master of English
prose as well as a most profound and scholarly student—the felicity of his
diction would have rendered even a dry and uninteresting subject sprightly and
full of life." In Philadelphia, Wilson substantially repeated the series that he
had first given at the Brooklyn Institute of Arts and Sciences in November
and December 1893. See the Editorial Note, "Wilson's Lectures at the Brooklyn
Institute of Arts and Sciences," Vol. 8, and the notes for these lectures printed
at Nov. 15, 1893, Vol. 8.
    [2] See the news report printed at June 30, 1895.

## From John Davidson

My dear Sir                    Elizabeth N. J.  May 12th 1895
    Mr. Hibben told me yesterday that Mr. Wright had your con-
tract, for the house. I write to congratulate you on that fact. You
have an honest man to deal with, a man who understands his
business, a man who will do honest work in that house, who will
*not* put in inferior work or material, in places where it will not
be seen, and should he find, that it requires stronger timbers,
more expensive work, &c. he will do it—in many instances at his
own cost, rather than have a piece of inferior work. I speak from
experience, he did it in Hibben's house, at an expense of several
hundred dollars to himself. He is a "clean" man to deal with.
You will find in your plans & specifications, many things omitted,
or which you want changed,—(if you don't, you are an exception)
—& he will deal fairly with you about them.
    I have built probably about two hundred houses & have had less
trouble with Mr. Wright than any other builder I ever met. Indeed
I have had no trouble, at all, everything in the most satisfactory,
& just manner. As the contractor is a very important factor, I
write, to give you my estimate of the man, just as I found him.
He deserves all I have said, & I know it will be a comfort to you,
to get this word of endorsement from me.
    With my kindest regards
                            Yours very truly    John Davidson

ALS (WP, DLC).


## To Robert Bridges

My dear Bobby,                    Princeton, 12 May, 1895
    Thank you very heartily. I will come with pleasure. Kindly
leave word of my coming with the Cerberus who sits in the hall-
way and I will leave my bag early in the afternoon.
    Hurrah for the new book![1] You may rest content if it gets as
hearty a reception as the first,—and I confidently expect an even
heartier.
    Princeton 7, Harvard, 2.[2]
    As ever,        Affectionately Yours,    Woodrow Wilson

ALS (WC, NjP).
    [1] Robert Bridges, *Suppressed Chapters and Other Bookishness* (New York,
1895).
    [2] The score of a baseball game played on May 11, 1895.

## Two News Items

[May 15, 1895]

### NEW JERSEY HISTORICAL SOCIETY.

Prof. Woodrow Wilson, is to make the address at the semi-centennial of the New Jersey Historical Society to be held on May 16th, at Newark. Invitations have been sent to all members of the faculty.

The president of the society is Dr. Samuel H. Pennington, '26, senior trustee of the college and a large per cent of its members are Princeton graduates. Determined efforts are being made to raise subscriptions for a new fireproof building to house more properly its many valuable collections, many of which relate to Princeton men. Among them are portraits by Gilbert Stuart, of vice-president Burr 1772, and Senator Bayard [Richard] Stockton 1779, an original edition of the first volume of poems of Philip Freneau 1772, autograph letters of U. S. Supreme Court Justice Brockholst Livingston 1774, and an account of the first commencement of the college which was held in the old Presbyterian church, of Newark, in 1748.

Printed in the *Daily Princetonian*, May 15, 1895.

[May 16, 1895]

### MEDAL FOR GEN. HARRISON
#### Presented at the Historical Society's
#### Semi-centennial Celebration.

In response to the invitation of the New Jersey Historical Society, Benjamin Harrison, Centennial President of the United States in 1889, attended the semi-centennial anniversary of the society, held in Essex Lyceum this afternoon, and was presented with a handsome gold memorial badge. This was the main feature of the celebration and made the affair a pronounced success. . . .

Professor Woodrow Wilson, Ph.D., L.L.D., of Princeton, the orator of the day, delivered the final address. He is an admirable speaker and his address traced the causes which gave pride to the hearts of citizens in their country.

The history of a nation, he said, was merely the history of its village. . . .

Printed in the *Newark Evening News*, May 16, 1895; some editorial headings omitted.

An Address

[*May 16, 1895*]

*The Course of American History.*

*Mr. President, Ladies and Gentlemen*: I feel, perhaps in an unus[u]al degree, the responsibility and the privilege of the honourable function assigned to me this afternoon. The very difficulty and importance of the duty are, however, such as hearten and invigorate. It at least stirs the pulse and cries a sharp summons to the courage to be put at once at the front of endeavour: and there must be occasions when it is easier to go into battle than to face the gaze of a ball room. I believe an occasion like this,—an Association like this,—to be of deep significance.[1] . . .

In the field of history learning should be deemed to stand among the people and in the midst of life. Its function there is not one of pride merely: to make complaisant record of deeds honorably done and plans nobly executed in the past. It has also a function of guidance: to build high places whereon to plant the clear and flaming lights of experience, that they may shine alike upon the roads already traveled and upon the paths not yet attempted. The historian is also a sort of prophet. Our memories direct us. They give us knowledge of our character, alike in its strength and in its weakness: and it is so we get our standards for endeavour,—our warnings and our gleams of hope. It is thus we learn what manner of nation we are of, and divine what manner of people we should be.

And this is not in national records merely. Local history is the ultimate substance of national history. There could be no epics were pastorals not also true,—no patriotism, were there no homes, no neighbours, no quiet round of civic duty; and I, for my part, do not wonder that scholarly men have been found not a few who, though they might have shone upon a larger field, where all eyes would have seen them win their fame, yet chose to pore all their lives long upon the blurred and scattered records of a country-side, where there was nothing but an old church or an ancient village. The history of a nation is only the history of its villages written large. I only marvel that these local historians have not seen more in the stories they have sought to tell. Surely here, in these old hamlets that ante-date the cities, in these little communities that stand apart and yet give their young life to the nation, is to be found the very authentic stuff of romance

---

[1] The text to this point is from a single-page WWT MS. (WP, DLC) and is the only surviving part of Wilson's manuscript of this address. The balance of the text is from the copy published by the New Jersey Historical Society.

for the mere looking. There is love and courtship and eager life and high devotion up and down all the lines of every genealogy. What strength, too, and bold endeavour in the cutting down of forests to make the clearings; what breath of hope and discovery in scaling for the first time the nearest mountains; what longings ended or begun upon the coming in of ships into the harbour; what pride of earth in the rivalries of the village; what thoughts of heaven in the quiet of the rural church! What forces of slow and steadfast endeavour there were in the building of a great city upon the foundations of a hamlet: and how the plot broadens and thickens and grows dramatic as communities widen into States! Here, surely, sunk deep in the very fibre of the stuff, are the colours of the great story of men,—the lively touches of reality and the striking images of life.

It must be admitted, I know, that local history can be made deadly dull in the telling. The men who reconstruct it seem usually to build with kiln-dried stuff,—as if with a purpose it should last! But that is not the fault of the subject. National history may be written almost as ill, if due pains be taken to dry it out. It is a trifle more difficult: because merely to speak of national affairs is to give hint of great forces and of movements blown upon by all the airs of the wide continent. The mere largeness of the scale lends to the narrative a certain dignity and spirit. But some men will manage to be dull though they should speak of creation. In the writing of local history the thing is fatally easy. For there is some neighbourhood history that lacks any large significance, which is without horizon or outlook. There are details in the history of every community which it concerns no man to know again when once they are past and decently buried in the records; and these are the very details, no doubt, which it is easiest to find upon a casual search. It is easier to make out a list of county clerks than to extract the social history of the county from the records they have kept,—though it is not so important: and it is easier to make a catalogue of anything than to say what of life and purpose the catalogue stands for. This is called collecting facts "for the sake of facts themselves"; but if I wish to do aught for the sake of the facts themselves I think I should serve them better by giving their true biographies than by merely displaying their faces.

The right and vital sort of local history is the sort which may be written with lifted eyes,—the sort which has an horizon and an outlook upon the world. Sometimes it may happen, indeed, that the annals of a neighbourhood disclose some singular adven-

ture which had its beginning and its ending there: some un-
wonted bit of fortune which stands unique and lonely amidst the
myriad transactions of the wide world of affairs, and deserves to
be told singly and for its own sake. But usually the significance
of local history is, that it is part of a greater whole. A spot of
local history is like an inn upon a highway: it is a stage upon a
far journey: it is a place the national history has passed through.
There mankind has stopped and lodged by the way. Local history
is thus less than national history only as the part is less than the
whole. The whole could not dispense with the part, would not
exist without it, could not be understood unless the part were
also understood. Local history is subordinate to national only in
the sense in which each leaf of a book is subordinate to the volume itself. Upon no single page will the whole theme of the book
be found; but each page holds a part of the theme. Even were
the history of each locality exactly like the history of every other
(which it cannot be), it would deserve to be written,—if only to
corroborate the history of the rest, and verify it as an authentic
part of the record of the race and nation. The common elements
of a nation's life are the great elements of its life, the warp and
woof of the fabric. They cannot be too much or too substantially
verified and explicated. It is so that our history is made solid and
fit for use and wear.

Our national history has, of course, its own great and spreading
pattern, which can be seen in its full form and completeness only
when the stuff of our national life is laid before us in broad sur-
faces and upon an ample scale. But the detail of the pattern, the
individual threads of the great fabric, are to be found only in local
history. There is all the intricate weaving, all the delicate shading, all the nice refinement of the pattern,—gold thread mixed
with fustian, fine thread laid upon coarse, shade combined with
shade. Assuredly it is this that gives to local history its life and
importance. The idea, moreover, furnishes a nice criterion of interest. The life of some localities is, obviously, more completely
and intimately a part of the national pattern than the life of other
localities, which are more separate and, as it were, put upon the
border of the fabric. To come at once and very candidly to examples, the local history of the Middle States,—New York, New
Jersey, and Pennsylvania,—is much more structurally a part of
the characteristic life of the nation as a whole than is the history
of New England communities or of the several States and regions
of the South. I know that such a heresy will sound very rank in
the ears of some: for I am speaking against accepted doctrine.

But acceptance, be it never so general, does not make a doctrine true.

Our national history has been written for the most part by New England men,—all honor to them! Their scholarship and their characters alike have given them an honorable enrolment amongst the great names of our literary history; and no just man would say aught to detract, were it never so little, from their well-earned fame. They have written our history, nevertheless, from but a single point of view. From where they sit, the whole of the great development looks like an Expansion of New England. Other elements but play along the sides of the great process by which the Puritan has worked out the development of nation and polity. It is he who has gone out and possessed the land; the man of destiny, the type and impersonation of a chosen people. To the Southern writer, too, the story looks much the same, if it be but followed to its culmination,—to its final storm and stress and tragedy in the great war. It is the history of the Suppression of the South. Spite of all her splendid contributions to the steadfast accomplishment of the great task of building the nation; spite of the long leadership of her statesmen in the national counsels; spite of her joint achievements in the conquest and occupation of the West, the South was at last turned upon on every hand, re-buked, proscribed, defeated. The history of the United States, we have learned, was, from the settlement at Jamestown to the surrender at Appomattox, a long-drawn contest for mastery be-tween New England and the South,—and the end of the contest we know. All along the parallels of latitude ran the rivalry, in those heroical days of toil and adventure during which population crossed the continent, like an army advancing its encampments. Up and down the great river of the continent, too, and beyond, up the slow incline of the vast steppes that lift themselves toward the crowning towers of the Rockies,—beyond that, again, in the gold-fields and upon the green plains of California, the race for ascendency struggled on,—till at length there was a final coming face to face, and the masterful folk who had come from the loins of New England won their consummate victory.

It is a very dramatic form for the story. One almost wishes it were true. How fine a unity it would give our epic! But perhaps, after all, the real truth is more interesting. The life of the nation cannot be reduced to these so simple terms. These two great forces, of the North and of the South, unquestionably existed,—were un-questionably projected in their operation out upon the great plane of the continent, there to combine or repel, as circumstances might determine. But the people that went out from the North were not an unmixed people; they came from the great Middle States as well as from New England. Their transplantation into the West was no more a reproduction of New England or New York or Pennsylvania or New Jersey than Massachusetts was a reproduction of old England, or New Netherland a reproduction of Holland. The Southern people, too, whom they met by the Western rivers and upon the open prairies, were transformed, as they themselves were, by the rough fortunes of the frontier. A mixture of peoples, a modification of mind and habit, a new round of experiment and adjustment amidst the novel life of the baked and untilled plain, and the far valleys with the virgin forests still thick upon them: a new temper, a new spirit of adventure, a new impatience of restraint, a new license of life,—these are the characteristic notes and measures of the time when the nation spread itself at large upon the continent, and was transformed from a group of colonies into a family of States.

The passes of these eastern mountains were the arteries of the nation's life. The real breath of our growth and manhood came into our nostrils when first, like Governor Spotswood and that gallant company of Virginian gentlemen that rode with him in the far year 1716, the Knights of the Order of the Golden Horseshoe, our pioneers stood upon the ridges of the eastern hills and looked down upon those reaches of the continent where lay the untrodden paths of the westward migration. There, upon the courses of the distant rivers that gleamed before them in the sun, down the farther slopes of the hills beyond, out upon the broad fields that lay upon the fertile banks of the "Father of Waters," up the long tilt of the continent to the vast hills that looked out upon the Pacific—there were the regions in which, joining with people from every race and clime under the sun, they were to make the great compounded nation whose liberty and mighty works of peace were to cause all the world to stand at gaze. Thither were to come Frenchmen, Scandinavians, Celts, Dutch, Slavs,—men of the Latin races and of the races of the Orient, as well as men, a great host, of the first stock of the settlements: English, Scots, Scots-Irish,—like New England men, but touched with the salt of humor, hard, and yet neighborly too. For this great process of growth by grafting, of modification no less than of expansion,—the colonies,—the original thirteen States, —were only preliminary studies and first experiments. But the experiments that most resembled the great methods by which we peopled the continent from side to side and knit a single polity across all its length and breadth, were surely the experiments made from the very first in the Middle States of our Atlantic seaboard.

Here, from the first, were mixture of population, variety of element, combination of type, as if of the nation itself in small. Here was never a simple body, a people of but a single blood and extraction, a polity and a practice brought straight from one motherland. The life of these States was from the beginning like the life of the country: they have always shown the national pattern. In New England and the South it was very different. There some of the great elements of the national life were long in preparation: but separately and with an individual distinction: without mixture,—for long almost without movement. That the elements thus separately prepared were of the greatest importance, and run everywhere like the chief threads of the pattern through all our subsequent life, who can doubt? They give color and tone to every part of the figure. The very fact that they are so distinct and separately evident throughout, the very emphasis of individuality they carry with them, but proves their distinct origin. The other elements of our life, various though they be, and of the very fibre, giving toughness and consistency to the fabric, are merged in its texture, united, confused, almost indistinguishable, so thoroughly are they mixed, intertwined, interwoven, like the essential strands of the stuff itself: but these of the Puritan and the Southerner, though they run everywhere with the rest and seem upon a superficial view themselves the body of the cloth, in fact modify rather than make it.

What, in fact, has been the course of American history? How is it to be distinguished from European history? What features has it of its own, which give it its distinctive plan and movement? We have suffered, it is to be feared, a very serious limitation of view until recent years by having all our history written in the East. It has smacked strongly of a local flavor. It has concerned itself too exclusively with the origins and Old-World derivations of our story. Our historians have made their march from the sea with their heads over shoulder, their gaze always backward upon the landing places and homes of the first settlers. In spite of the steady immigration, with its persistent tide of foreign blood, they have chosen to speak often and to think always of our people as sprung after all from a common stock, bearing a family likeness in every branch, and following all the while old, familiar, family ways. The view is the more misleading because it is so large a part of the truth without being all of it. The common British stock did first make the country, and has always set the pace. There were common institutions up and down the coast; and these had formed and hardened for a persistent growth before the great westward migration began which was to re-shape and modify every element of our life. The national government itself was set up and made strong by success while yet we lingered for the most part upon the eastern coast and feared a too distant frontier.

But, the beginnings once safely made, change set in apace. Not only so: there had been slow change from the first. We have no frontier now, we are told,—except a broken fragment, it may be, here and there in some barren corner of the western lands, where some inhospitable mountain still shoulders us out, or where men are still lacking to break the baked surface of the plains, and occupy them in the very teeth of hostile nature. But at first it was all frontier,—a mere strip of settlements stretched precariously upon the sea-edge of the wilds: an untouched continent in front of them, and behind them an unfrequented sea that almost never showed so much as the momentary gleam of a sail. Every step in the slow process of settlement was but a step of the same kind as the first, an advance to a new frontier like the old. For long we lacked, it is true, that new breed of frontiersmen born in after years beyond the mountains. Those first frontiersmen had still a touch of the timidity of the Old World in their blood: they lacked the frontier heart. They were "Pilgrims" in very fact,—exiled, not at home. Fine courage they had: and a steadfastness in their bold design which it does a faint-hearted age good to look back upon. There was no thought of drawing back. Steadily, almost calmly, they extended their seats. They built homes, and deemed it certain their children would live there after them. But they did not love the rough, uneasy life for its own sake. How long did they keep, if they could, within sight of the sea! The wilderness was their refuge; but how long before it became their joy and hope! Here was their destiny cast; but their hearts lingered and held back. It was only as generations passed and the work [world] widened about them that their thought also changed, and a new thrill sped along their blood. Their life had been new and strange from their first landing in the wilderness. Their houses, their food, their clothing, their neighborhood dealings were all such as only the frontier brings. Insensibly they were themselves changed. The strange life became familiar; their adjustment to it was at length unconscious and without effort; they had no plans which were not inseparably a part and product of it. But, until they had turned their backs once for all upon the sea; until they saw their western borders cleared of the French; until the mountain passes had grown familiar, and the lands beyond the central and constant theme of their hope, the goal and dream of their young men, they did not become an American people.

When they did, the great determining movement of our history began. The very visages of the people changed. That alert movement of the eye, that openness to every thought of enterprise or adventure, that nomadic habit which knows no fixed home and has plans ready to be carried any whither,—all the marks of the authentic type of the "American" as we know him came into our life. The crack of the whip and the song of the teamster, the heaving chorus of boatmen poling their heavy rafts upon the rivers, the laughter of the camp, the sound of bodies of men in the still forests, became the characteristic notes in our air. Our roughened race, embrowned in the sun, hardened in manner by a coarse life of change and danger, loving the rude woods and the crack of the rifle, living to begin something new every day, striking with the broad and open hand, delicate in nothing but the touch of the trigger, leaving cities in its track as if by accident rather than design, settling again to the steady ways of a fixed life only when it must: such was the American people whose achievement it was to be to take possession of their continent from end to end ere their national government was a single century old. The picture is a very singular one! Settled life and wild side by side: civilization frayed at the edges,—taken forward in rough and ready fashion, with a song and swagger,—not by statesmen, but by woodsmen and drovers, with axes and whips and rifles in their hands, clad in buckskin, like huntsmen.

It has been said that we have here repeated some of the first processes of history: that the life and methods of our frontiersmen take us back to the fortunes and hopes of the men who crossed Europe when her forests, too, were still thick upon her. But the difference is really very fundamental, and much more worthy of remark than the likeness. Those shadowy masses of men whom we see moving upon the face of the earth in the far away, questionable days when states were forming: even those stalwart figures we see so well as they emerge from the deep forests of Germany, to displace the Roman in all his western provinces and set up the states we know and marvel upon at this day, show us men working their new work at their own level. They do not turn back a long cycle of years from the old and

settled states, the ordered cities, the tilled fields, and the elab-
orated governments of an ancient civilization, to begin as it were
once more at the beginning. They carry alike their homes and
their states with them in the camp and upon the ordered march
of the host. They are men of the forest, or else men hardened
always to take the sea in open boats. They live no more roughly
in the new lands than in the old. The world has been frontier for
them from the first. They may go forward with their life in these
new seats from where they left off in the old. How different the
circumstances of our first settlement and the building of new
states on this side the sea! Englishmen, bred in law and ordered
government ever since the Norman lawyers were followed a long
five hundred years ago across the narrow seas by those masterful
administrators of the strong Plantagenet race, leave an ancient
realm and come into a wilderness where states have never been;
leave a land of art and letters, which saw but yesterday "the spacious times of great Elizabeth," where Shakespeare still lives in
the gracious leisure of his closing days at Stratford, where cities
teem with trade and men go bravely dight in cloth of gold, and
turn back six centuries,—nay, a thousand years and more,—to the
first work of building states in a wilderness! They bring the stead-
ied habits and sobered thoughts of an ancient realm into the wild
air of an untouched continent. The weary stretches of a vast sea
lie, like a full thousand years of time, between them and the life
in which till now all their thought was bred. Here they stand,
as it were, with all their tools left behind, centuries struck out of
their reckoning, driven back upon the long dormant instincts and
forgotten craft of their race, not used this long age. Look how
singular a thing: the work of a primitive race, the thought of a
civilized! Hence the strange, almost grotesque groupings of
thought and affairs in that first day of our history. Subtle politicians speak the phrases and practice the arts of intricate diplo-
macy from council chambers placed within log huts within a clear-
ing. Men in ruffs and lace and polished shoe-buckles thread the
lonely glades of primeval forests. The microscopical distinctions
of the schools, the thin notes of a metaphysical theology, are
woven in and out through the labyrinths of grave sermons that
run hours long upon the still air of the wilderness. Belief in dim
refinements of dogma is made the test for man or woman who
seeks admission to a company of pioneers. When went there by
an age since the great flood when so singular a thing was seen
as this: thousands of civilized men suddenly rusticated and bade
do the work of primitive peoples,—Europe *frontiered!*

Of course there was a deep change wrought, if not in these men, at any rate in their children; and every generation saw the change deepen. It must seem to every thoughtful man a notable thing how, while the change was wrought, the simples of things complex were revealed in the clear air of the New World: how all accidentals seemed to fall away from the structure of government, and the simple first principles were laid bare that abide always; how social distinctions were stripped off, shown to be the mere cloaks and masks they were, and every man brought once again to a clear realization of his actual relations to his fellows! It was as if trained and sophisticated men had been rid of a sudden of their sophistication and of all the theory of their life and left with nothing but their discipline of faculty, a schooled and sobered instinct. And the fact that we kept always, for close upon three hundred years, a like element in our life, a frontier people always in our van, is, so far, the central and determining fact of our national history. "East" and "West," an ever-changing line, but an unvarying experience and a constant leaven of change working always within the body of our folk. Our political, our economic, our social life has felt this potent influence from the wild border all our history through. The "West" is the great word of our history. The "Westerner" has been the type and master of our American life. Now at length, as I have said, we have lost our frontier: our front lies almost unbroken along all the great coast line of the western sea. The Westerner, in some day soon to come, will pass out of our life, as he so long ago passed out of the life of the Old World. Then a new epoch will open for us. Perhaps it has opened already. Slowly we shall grow old, compact our people, study the delicate adjustments of an intricate society, and ponder the niceties, as we have hitherto pondered the bulks and structural framework, of government. Have we not, indeed, already come to these things? But the past we know. We can "see it steady and see it whole"; and its central movement and motive are gross and obvious to the eye.

Till the first century of the Constitution is rounded out we stand, all the while, in the presence of that stupendous westward movement which has filled the continent: so vast, so various, at times so tragical, so swept by passion. Through all the long time there has been a line of rude settlements along our front wherein the same tests of power and of institutions were still being made that were made first upon the sloping banks of the rivers of old Virginia and within the long sweep of the Bay of Massachusetts. The new life of the West has reacted all the while,—who shall say

how powerfully,—upon the older life of the East: and yet the
East has moulded the West as if she sent forward to it through
every decade of the long process the chosen impulses and suggestions of history. The West has taken strength, thought, training,
selected aptitudes out of the old treasures of the East,—as if out
of a new Orient; while the East has itself been kept fresh, vital,
alert, originative by the West, her blood quickened all the while,
her youth through every age renewed. Who can say in a word, in
a sentence, in a volume, what destinies have been variously
wrought, with what new examples of growth and energy, while,
upon this unexampled scale, community has passed beyond community across the vast reaches of this great continent!

The great process is the more significant because it has been
distinctively a national process. Until the Union was formed and
we had consciously set out upon a separate national career, we
moved but timidly across the nearer hills. Our most remote settlements lay upon the rivers and in the open glades of Tennessee
and Kentucky. It was in the years that immediately succeeded the
war of 1812 that the movement into the West began to be a
mighty migration. Till then our eyes had been more often in the
East than in the West. Not only were foreign questions to be
settled and our standing among the nations to be made good, but
we still remained acutely conscious and deliberately conservative
of our Old-World connections. For all we were so new a people
and lived so simple and separate a life, we had still the sobriety
and the circumspect fashions of action that belong to an old
society. We were, in government and manners, but a discon-
nected part of the world beyond the seas. Its thought and habit
still set us our standards of speech and action. And this, not because of imitation, but because of actual and long-abiding political and social connection with the mother country. Our statesmen,—strike but the names of Samuel Adams and Patrick Henry
from the list, together with all like untutored spirits, who stood
for the new, unreverencing ardor of a young democracy,—our
statesmen were such men as might have taken their places in the
House of Commons or in the Cabinet at home as naturally and
with as easy an adjustment to their place and task as in the Continental Congress or in the immortal Constitutional Convention.
Think of the stately ways and the grand air and the authoritative
social understandings of the generation that set the new government afoot,—the generation of Washington and John Adams.
Think, too, of the conservative tradition that guided all the early
history of that government: that early line of gentlemen Presi-

dents: that steady "cabinet succession to the Presidency" which came at length to seem almost like an oligarchy to the impatient men who were shut out from it. The line ended, with a sort of chill, in stiff John Quincy Adams, too cold a man to be a people's prince after the older order of Presidents; and the year 1829, which saw Jackson come in, saw the old order go out.

The date is significant. Since the war of 1812, undertaken as if to set us free to move westward, seven States had been admitted to the Union: and the whole number of States was advanced to twenty-four. Eleven new States had come into partnership with the old thirteen. The voice of the West rang through all our counsels; and, in Jackson, the new partners took possession of the Government. It is worth while to remember how men stood amazed at the change: how startled, chagrined, dismayed the conservative States of the East were at the revolution they saw effected, the riot of change they saw set in; and no man who has once read the singular story can forget how the eight years Jackson reigned saw the Government, and politics themselves, transformed. For long,—the story being written in the regions where the shock and surprise of the change was greatest,—the period of this momentous revolution was spoken of amongst us as a period of degeneration, the birth time of a deep and permanent demoralization in our politics. But we see it differently now. Whether we have any taste or stomach for that rough age or not, however much we may wish that the old order might have stood, the generation of Madison and Adams have been prolonged, and the good tradition of the early days handed on unbroken and unsullied, we now know that what the nation underwent in that day of change was not degeneration, great and perilous as were the errors of the time, but regeneration. The old order was changed, once and for all. A new nation stepped, with a touch of swagger, upon the stage,—a nation which had broken alike with the traditions and with the wisely wrought experience of the Old World, and which, with all the haste and rashness of youth, was minded to work out a separate policy and destiny of its own. It was a day of hazards, but there was nothing sinister at the heart of the new plan. It was a wasteful experiment, to fling out, without wise guides, upon untried ways; but an abounding continent afforded enough and to spare even for the wasteful. It was sure to be so with a nation that came out of the secluded vales of a virgin continent. It was the bold frontier voice of the West sounding in affairs. The timid shivered, but the robust waxed strong and rejoiced, in the tonic air of the new day.

It was then we swung out into the main paths of our history. The new voices that called us were first silvery, like the voice of Henry Clay, and spoke old familiar words of eloquence. The first spokesmen of the West even tried to con the classics, and spoke incongruously in the phrases of politics long dead and gone to dust, as Benton did. But presently the tone changed, and it was the truculent and masterful accents of the real frontiersman that rang dominant above the rest, harsh, impatient, and with an evident dash of temper. The East slowly accustomed itself to the change; caught the movement, though it grumbled and even trembled at the pace; and managed most of the time to keep in the running. But it was always henceforth to be the West that set the pace. There is no mistaking the questions that have ruled our spirits as a nation during the present century. The public land question, the tariff question, and the question of slavery,—these dominate from first to last. It was the West that made each one of these the question that it was. Without the free lands to which every man who chose might go, there would not have been that easy prosperity of life and that high standard of abundance which seemed to render it necessary that, if we were to have manufactures and a diversified industry at all, we should foster new undertakings by a system of protection which would make the profits of the factory as certain and as abundant as the profits of the farm. It was the constant movement of the population, the constant march of wagon trains into the West, that made it so cardinal a matter of policy whether the great national domain should *be* free land or not: and that was the land question. It was the settlement of the West that transformed slavery from an accepted institution into passionate matter of controversy.

Slavery within the States of the Union stood sufficiently protected by every solemn sanction the Constitution could afford. No man could touch it there, think, or hope, or purpose what he might. But where new States were to be made it was not so. There at every step choice must be made: slavery or no slavery?—a new choice for every new State: a fresh act of origination to go with every fresh act of organization. Had there been no Territories, there could have been no slavery question, except by revolution and contempt of fundamental law. But with a continent to be peopled, the choice thrust itself insistently forward at every step and upon every hand. This was the slavery question: not what should be done to reverse the past, but what should be done to redeem the future. It was so men of that day saw it,—and so also must historians see it. We must not mistake the programme of the Anti-Slavery Society for the platform of the Republican party, or forget that the very war itself was begun ere any purpose of abolition took shape amongst those who were statesmen and in authority. It was a question, not of freeing men, but of preserving a Free Soil. Kansas showed us what the problem was, not South Carolina: and it was the Supreme Court, not the slave-owners, who formulated the matter for our thought and purpose.

And so, upon every hand and throughout every national question, was the commerce between East and West made up: that commerce and exchange of ideas, inclinations, purposes, and principles which has constituted the moving force of our life as a nation. Men illustrate the operation of these singular forces better than questions can: and no man illustrates it better than Abraham Lincoln.

> "Great captains with their guns and drums
> Disturb our judgment for the hour;
> But at last silence comes:
> These all are gone, and, standing like a tower,
> Our children shall behold his fame,
> The kindly-earnest, brave, foreseeing man,
> Sagacious, patient, dreading praise not blame,
> New birth of our new soil, the first American."[2]

It is a poet's verdict; but it rings in the authentic tone of the seer. It must also be the verdict of history. He would be a rash man who should say he understood Abraham Lincoln. No doubt natures deep as his, and various almost to the point of self-contradiction, can be sounded only by the judgment of men of a like sort,—if any such there be. But some things we all may see and judge concerning him. You have in him the type and flower of our growth. It is as if Nature had made a typical American, and then had added with liberal hand the royal quality of genius, to show us what the type could be. Lincoln owed nothing to his birth, everything to his growth: had no training save what he gave himself; no nurture, but only a wild and native strength. His life was his schooling, and every day of it gave to his character a new touch of development. His manhood not only, but his perception also, expanded with his life. His eyes, as they looked more and more abroad, beheld the national life, and comprehended it: and the lad who had been so rough-cut a provincial became, when grown to manhood, the one leader in all the nation who held the whole people singly in his heart:—held even the

---

[2] From James Russell Lowell, "Ode Recited at the Harvard Commemoration, July 21, 1865." [Eds.' note]

Southern people there, and would have won them back. And so
we have in him what we must call the perfect development of
native strength, the rounding out and nationalization of the provincial. Andrew Jackson was a type, not of the nation, but of the
West. For all the tenderness there was in the stormy heart of the
masterful man, and staunch and simple loyalty to all who loved
him, he learned nothing in the East; kept always the flavor of the
rough school in which he had been bred: was never more than
a frontier soldier and gentleman. Lincoln differed from Jackson
by all the length of his unmatched capacity to learn. Jackson
could understand only men of his own kind; Lincoln could understand men of all sorts and from every region of the land: seemed
himself, indeed, to be all men by turns, as mood succeeded mood
in his strange nature. He never ceased to stand, in his bony
angles, the express image of the ungainly frontiersman. His mind
never lost the vein of coarseness that had marked him grossly
when a youth. And yet how he grew and strengthened in the
real stuff of dignity and greatness: how nobly he could bear
himself without the aid of grace! He kept always the shrewd and
seeing eye of the woodsman and the hunter, and the flavor of
wild life never left him: and yet how easily his view widened to
great affairs: how surely he perceived the value and the significance of whatever touched him and made him neighbor to
itself!

Lincoln's marvellous capacity to extend his comprehension
to the measure of what he had in hand is the one distinguishing
mark of the man: and to study the development of that capacity
in him is little less than to study, where it is as it were perfectly
registered, the national life itself. This boy lived his youth in
Illinois when it was a frontier State. The youth of the State was
coincident with his own: and man and his State kept equal pace
in their striding advance to maturity. The frontier population was
an intensely political population. It felt to the quick the throb of
the nation's life,—for the nation's life ran through it, going its
eager way to the westward. The West was not separate from the
East. Its communities were every day receiving fresh members
from the East, and the fresh impulse of direct suggestion. Their
blood flowed to them straight from the warmest veins of the older
communities. More than that, elements which were separated in
the East were mingled in the West; which displayed to the eye
as it were a sort of epitome of the most active and permanent
forces of the national life. In such communities as these Lincoln
mixed daily from the first with men of every sort and from every

quarter of the country. With them he discussed neighborhood politics, the politics of the State, the politics of the nation,—and his mind became travelled as he talked. How plainly amongst such neighbors, there in Illinois, must it have become evident that national questions were centring more and more in the West as the years went by: coming as it were to meet them. Lincoln went twice down the Mississippi, upon the slow rafts that carried wares to its mouth, and saw with his own eyes, so used to look directly and point-blank upon men and affairs, characteristic regions of the South. He worked his way slowly and sagaciously, with that larger sort of sagacity which so marked him all his life, into the active business of State politics; sat twice in the State legislature, and then for a term in Congress,—his sensitive and seeing mind open all the while to every turn of fortune and every touch of nature in the moving affairs he looked upon. All the while, too, he continued to canvass, piece by piece, every item of politics, as of old, with his neighbors, familiarly around the stove, or upon the corners of the street, or more formally upon the stump; and kept always in direct contact with the ordinary views of ordinary men. Meanwhile he read, as nobody else around him read, and sought to gain a complete mastery over speech, with the conscious purpose to prevail in its use: derived zest from the curious study of mathematical proof, and amusement as well as strength from the practice of clean and naked state-ments of truth. It was all irregularly done, but strenuously, with the same instinct throughout, and with a steady access of facility and power. There was no sudden leap for this man, any more than for other men, from crudeness to finished power, from an understanding of the people of Illinois to an understanding of the people of the United States. And thus he came at last, with in-finite pains and a wonder of endurance to his great national task with a self-trained capacity which no man could match, and made upon a scale as liberal as the life of the people. You could not then set this athlete a pace in learning or in perceiving that was too hard for him. He knew the people and their life as no other man did or could: and now stands in his place singular in all the annals of mankind, the "brave, sagacious, foreseeing, patient man" of the people, "new birth of our new soil, the first American."

We have here a national man presiding over sectional men. Lincoln understood the East better than the East understood him or the people from whom he sprung: and this is every way a very noteworthy circumstance. For my part, I read a lesson in the singular career of this great man. Is it possible the East remains sectional while the West broadens to a wider view?

"Be strong-backed, brown-handed, upright as your pines;
By the scale of a hemisphere shape your designs,"

is an inspiring programme for the woodsman and the pioneer; but how are you to be brown-handed in a city office? What if you never see the upright pines? How are you to have so big a purpose on so small a part of the hemisphere? As it has grown old, unquestionably, the East has grown sectional. There is no suggestion of the prairie, in its city streets, or of the embrowned ranchman and farmer in its well-dressed men. Its ports teem with shipping from Europe and the Indies. Its newspapers run upon the themes of an Old World. It hears of the great plains of the continent as of foreign parts, which it may never think to see except from a car window. Its life is self-centred and selfish. The West, save where special interests centre (as in those pockets of silver where men's eyes catch as it were an eager gleam from the very ore itself): the West is in less danger of sectionalization. Who shall say in that wide country where one region ends and another begins, or, in that free and changing society, where one class ends and another begins?

This, surely, is the moral of our history. The East has spent and been spent for the West: has given forth her energy, her young men and her substance, for the new regions that have been a-making all the century through. But has she learned as much as she has taught, or taken as much as she has given? Look what it is that has now at last taken place. The westward march has stopped, upon the final slopes of the Pacific; and now the plot thickens. Populations turn upon their old paths; fill in the spaces they passed by neglected in their first journey in search of a land of promise; settle to a life such as the East knows as well as the West,—nay, much better. With the change, the pause, the settlement, our people draw into closer groups, stand face to face, to know each other and be known; and the time has come for the East to learn in her turn: to broaden her understanding of political and economic conditions of the scale of a hemisphere, as her own poet bade. Let us be sure that we get the national temperament; send our minds abroad upon the continent, become neighbors to all the people that live upon it, and lovers of them all, as Lincoln was.

Read but your history aright, and you shall not find the task too hard. Your own local history, look but deep enough, tells the tale you must take to heart. Here upon our own seaboard, as truly as ever in the West, was once a national frontier, with an elder East beyond the seas. Here, too, various peoples combined, and elements separated elsewhere effected a tolerant and wholesome mixture. Here, too, the national stream flowed full and strong, bearing a thousand things upon its currents. Let us resume and keep the vision of that time: know ourselves, our neighbors, our destiny, with lifted and open eyes: see our history truly, in its great proportions: be ourselves liberal as the great principles we profess; and so be a people who might have again the heroic adventures and do again the heroic work of the past. 'Tis thus we shall renew our youth and secure our age against decay.[3]

Printed in [New Jersey Historical Society] *Semi-Centennial of the New Jersey Historical Society, at Newark, New Jersey, May 16, 1895* (Newark, 1897), pp. 183-206.

[3] Readers will be struck by the similarity of the theme of this address to that of Frederick Jackson Turner's famous paper, "The Significance of the Frontier in American History." It is impossible to ascribe the authorship of the theme either to Wilson or to Turner. They had known each other intimately since 1889, when Turner was a graduate student at the Johns Hopkins and both men roomed at Miss Ashton's boardinghouse. Wilson and Turner had long talks then and later about the influence of sectionalism and of the West in American history. Turner read a draft of his famous paper to Wilson in Madison in December 1892 (see WW to C. K. Adams, Dec. 23, 1892, n. 1, Vol. 8) and later generously acknowledged Wilson's contribution to his own ideas (see F. J. Turner to W. E. Dodd, Oct. 7, 1919, in Wendell H. Stephenson, "The Influence of Woodrow Wilson on Frederick Jackson Turner," *Agricultural History*, XIX [Oct. 1945], 253).

## From John Davidson

My dear Sir                New York, May 17th 1895

I have just recd. the enclosed from Mr. Burnham's office[1] in reply to my letter of a week ago; they are slow.

Will you please see to getting the survey,[2] a little one will do about twice the size of this piece of paper: & will you please send it to Mr. Burnham.

Will you also see what you can do, with the N. J. Real Estate & Trust Co. re searches.

I go off May 29th to my Adirondack Park, hence, I would like to do whatever I can before that time. On hearing from you, I will take down to Mr Burnham, the original deeds, sent to me by you & leave them with him.

With kindest regards
                Yours very truly   John Davidson

ALS (WP, DLC). Enc.: A. H. Hazeltine to J. Davidson, May 15, 1895, TLS (WP, DLC).

[1] The enclosure stated that the Mutual Life Insurance Company would accept

the guaranteed search of the New Jersey Real Estate Title and Trust Company
of Trenton but would require "in addition an examination of the title and the
preparation of an Abstract by this office."
 2 Mutual's agent had requested a survey of the Wilsons' lot.


## To Walter Hines Page

My dear Mr. Page,            Princeton, New Jersey, 20 May, 1895.
   The kind tone and method of your cordial letter of the fifteenth[1]
would be poorly met by anything less than a full disclosure of
my situation.
   Although the work is still so near its beginning that I do not
wish it generally spoken of yet, I may tell you that I am engaged
in writing a History of the United States, upon the scale, and, as
nearly as I can manage, in the spirit of J. R. Green's incomparable
"Short History of the English People." Its composition will occupy
me, of course, not only until this summer, but through it and
several years more to boot; and it must through all that time be
my one absorbing occupation: for I shall not be content without
examining most of the sources for myself as I go along.
   I cannot turn aside from it to write anything new which does
not lie near it, at least by suggestion. My essays in the meantime, therefore, will concern literary and historical topics of the
broader sort. The only thing I have now to offer you is (the
substance of) an address I delivered last week before the New
Jersey Historical Society on "The Course of American History."
The Society will wish to print it later with its own Proceedings;
but that is only decent burial; and I hope very much that you
will think it suitable for the *Forum*. It is my creed: and the basis
of method for my present work; and I should very much like to
give it a very public utterance. I will send it to you in the course
of a day or two, and you may judge it for yourself.[2] It is somewhat on the lines of my "Calendar of Great Americans."[3]
   My hearty congratulations on your acquisition of a further and
more complete control of the *Forum*.[4] It will always jump with
my desire to contribute to its success anything I can.
   With warmest regards,
                  Very sincerely Yours,   Woodrow Wilson

WWTLS (W. H. Page Papers, MH).
 1 It is missing.
 2 See W. H. Page to WW, May 23, 1895.
 3 Printed at Sept. 15, 1893, Vol. 8.
 4 Actually, Page's attempt to gain control of the Forum Publishing Company
was soon to fail. See WW to W. H. Page, July 4, 1895, n. 1.

## From Child and de Goll, Architects

Dear Sir:                                    New York. May 20th., 1895.

Your favor of the 18th. inst. it [is] at hand. In reply, we are very glad to hear of your decision in the matter of the building.[1] We note the letter from Mr. Davidson and if possible we will see you before Thursday. If not, we will be ready to give you attention on that day. We hope we can carry everything through to your satisfaction.

Yours respectfully,    Child & de Goll

TLS (WP, DLC).

[1] That is, Wilson's decision to award the contract for the construction of his house to Josiah Worth Wright.


## From the Minutes of the Princeton Faculty

4 5′ P.M., Wednesday, May 22, 1895.

. . . Upon the Report of the Committee the following were elected

The Cliosophic Judges of the Lynde Debate.
    Rev. John P. Campbell, Md.
    Sherrerd Depue,          N.J.
The American Whig Judges of the Lynde Debate
    Robert H. McCarter, N.J.
    Edmund Wilson,     N.J.
The Cliosophic Alternates.
    Oscar Keen,                    N.J.
    Rev. Samuel H. Leeper, Jr., N.J.
The American Whig Alternates.
    Rev. Charles H. McClellan, D.D., N.J.
    Monroe Crawford,          N.Y.[1]

Upon recommendation of the Committee on Discipline it was Resolved That it be recommended to the Board of Trustees, That in case the room of any student be entered and he be subjected to indignity or injury to his room or property by any person or persons not undergraduates & consequently not amenable to the College authorities, the Curator of Grounds & Buildings be directed to prosecute the offender or offenders.

[1] The committee's report does not reveal the fact, but the committee also chose as the question for the Lynde Debate, "Resolved, That the higher intellectual interests of our colleges demand a substantial restriction of the privileges now granted to athletics." In the debate, held on June 11, 1895, the first prize went to Benjamin L. Hirshfield, the second to Frederic W. Lewis, and the third to William F. Burns. Hirshfield and Lewis defended the affirmative side, Burns the negative. The other debaters were Alfred Hayes, Jr., Joseph W. Park, and Selden L. Haynes. *Daily Princetonian*, June 11 and 12, 1895.

## From Walter Hines Page

Dear Mr. Wilson:                    New York.  May 23rd, 1895.

I thank you very much for your exceedingly interesting letter that came a day or two ago, and I am delighted at the information it conveys. That is just the kind of thing that you ought to do. I look forward to seeing the results with uncommonly keen pleasure, and I feel greatly complimented that you have told me of the project in its present stage.

Your address which you were kind enough to promise to send has not yet turned up, but I presume will come along in a day or two. (It is just come)

Now there has come into my mind one subject of such a character that I hope you will see your way clear to write about it for the next number of The Forum. It is a subject that falls straight along the line of your work, and I cannot help thinking that in your handling it will yield a very instructive popular essay. I will try to convey my idea, of course only in a vague, general way, for if there be any happy thought in it you will see it at a glance and fill in the details.

Anybody who looks over the country on the morning of the fifth of July nowadays and considers how inanely the preceeding day was observed, if it was observed at all, must be struck with the very remarkable contrast between its observance now and a generation or two ago. There was a definite consciousness of nationality which the two or three generations following the Revolution very naturally felt, and from which we have now drifted very far. I do not know that there is anything discouraging in this, and yet I am old-fashioned enough to feel that the change does in a certain measure indicate a drifting away from a definite and helpful national feeling. If we had or if we showed a consciousness of such a feeling on any other occasion, such as our fathers showed on the fourth of July, of course the decline of the old fourth of July would signify nothing; but I think there is no day in the calendar which now corresponds to the old fourth of July of the fathers. This is one part of my thought and this, of course, comes apropos of the approach of the day and suggests itself to me in connection with the July number of The Forum.

Now a converging idea comes to me, viz., while there has been a sort of general loss on the part of the whole people of national pride and national consciousness—a falling away at least in the habit of holiday expression thereof—there has been within a very recent period, as your own work gives the best evidence of, a most remarkable attention given to the study of American history.

The well-informed school-boy of the age of my own boys knows more American history than men knew when I was a boy.

Along with this have come not only such organizations as the Sons and Daughters of the Revolution and all these things, but also very significant organizations for the preservation of historical buildings, the marking of historic spots, and attention to historical portraits.

Now all these things may seem to you a medley of incongruous ideas; but I believe there is a certain unity in them and that they so group themselves more or less naturally about a Forum article which, without doing great violence to logic, might have a fourth of July head on it—an article which should show that the great mass of people have lost a certain definite consciousness of nationality, but that contemporaneous with this popular loss has been a very extraordinary development of interest in our history and even a popular interest in historical portraits and historical places. Such an article, of course, would give beautiful opportunity for historical reminiscences and incidents of the old-time and of the present time which would afford pleasant and instructive contrasts.

If you would be willing for any reason or for any purpose to turn aside—and I hope it will not seem too far aside—from your main work to give me this by the tenth of June, you will enable me to make a very notable and interesting July Forum.

Very sincerely yours,   Walter H. Page

P. S. I have read "The Course of American History," and it is mine—with very sincere thanks.[1] But I pray you let me have the July paper, too, for use first.[2] Then I'll use the other the next month.                                    *W. H. P.*

TLS (WP, DLC) with WWsh notation on env.
[1] Page published it in a slightly abridged form as "The Proper Perspective of American History" in the New York *Forum*, XIX (July 1895), 544-59. Wilson later published the full text that he had sent to the New Jersey Historical Society in *Mere Literature and Other Essays* (Boston and New York, 1896), pp. 213-47.
[2] Wilson's reply is missing, but in it he obviously declined Page's invitation.


## A News Item

[May 25, 1895]

### SOUTHERN CLUB BANQUET.

The banquet of the Southern Club was held last evening at the Inn. It was the first banquet that the club has held for a number of years and much enthusiasm was manifested. A large number were present and letters of regret from Senator George Gray, '52, of Delaware, Senator Faulkner, of W. Virginia, and Representative John D. Cowan, of Maryland, were read by President John W. Garrett ['95]. The toasts were responded to as follows:

"Princeton and the South in Former Years," Woodrow Wilson, Ph.D., LL.D., '79, of South Carolina.

"The Work ahead of Us," Philip George Walker, '95, of West Virginia.

"The New South," Joseph William Park, '95, of Mississippi.

"Princeton's Southern Hopes," James Johnston Elliott, '96, of Tennessee.

"Pretty Girls, Fast Horses and Good Whisky," David Fentress, '96, of Tennessee. . . .

Printed in the *Daily Princetonian*, May 25, 1895.

## From John Davidson, with Enclosure

My dear Sir                              New York, May 28th 1895

I received your very kind letter, and I thank you for all the good things you say. I assure you it has been a great pleasure to aid you.

As I go away to my Adirondack place tomorrow, & as I have not heard, about the search from Mr. Burnham, I think I had better return to you, your deed & the mtg. so that when he goes on with the search, you may have in your hands, these papers to loan to him, if he desires them—(altho' being now of record, he ought to get along without these originals, & trust to the records) —I therefore enclose them.

Trusting you will get along pleasantly & that in the fall I may see you, in your new home, & with kindest regards

Yours very truly   John Davidson

ALS (WP, DLC).

### ENCLOSURE

## From Samuel Witham Stockton

Princeton, N. J.   April 1, 1895

Received of Prof Woodrow Wilson Two thousand and fifty Dollars and sixty six cents being in full satisfaction of principal and interest of a mortgage dated Oct 29, 1894—for $2000—given by said W. Wilson & ux to S W. Stockton a purchase money mortgage on property in Princeton, N. J.

$2050.66                                    S. W. Stockton

ALS (WP, DLC).


## To Child and de Goll, Architects

Messrs Child & deGoll,        Princeton, N. J.  May 29th, 1895.

You are to superintend the construction of my house, paying your own travelling expenses for the sum of Three Hundred and Twenty Five Dollars, payable, Fifty Dollars this day, One Hundred Dollars when roof of building is on, One Hundred Dollars when lathed and plastered, balance on completion of the house.

Woodrow Wilson

TCL (WP, DLC) enclosed in L. R. Holske to WW, Nov. 16, 1895, TLS (WP, DLC) with WWhw on env.: "Contract w. C. & de G."


## Ellen Axson Wilson to Anna Harris

My dearest Anna,                Princeton, N. J.  June 1/95

I was extremely glad to get your interesting letter.[1] . . .

As for ourselves we are all "well and doing well." It has of course been an extremely busy winter for me with the "school"[2] added to everything else, for I still do all the sewing; the social duties during the winter are heavy, and they have now "roped" me in for a good deal of regular weekly work in connection with benevolent societies. So my days are very full. The "school," which takes the morning until twelve, has gone on finely. I feel quite proud of my youngest pupil. She took her first lesson last Oct. on the day after her fifth birthday, and in four months she could read fluently *anything* she could *understand*. She has now read through a number of books of fairy stories, Bible stories, "nature" stories, poems, myths, &c. It is very funny to hear that little tot talk about her "Plato,"—which she has "read through"!

Thank you very much for your valuable suggestions in this letter; I shall certainly try to carry them out. They are in some respects exactly in line with Prof. Perry's ideas. I must try and get one of his little pamphlets on this general subject to send you;—am sure it will interest you.

You ask about Woodrow's work. He delivered an address lately before the New Jersey Historical Society which is being enormously praised, and which you will soon see in the "Forum": but apart from his college work he has been chiefly absorbed this winter in his magnum opus,—his "short history of the United States"; and which is coming on finely. It is to be of about the character and length of Green's England, and I assure you it is *superb*. It will be strange indeed if it is not recognized as an English prose classic no less than Green's. Of course I am not an impartial judge so I am glad to add that the few men of letters[3] who have seen the completed chapters are as much impressed with it as I am. Of course it will not be out for perhaps five years yet. Isn't it a shame that he must lay it aside for four months next fall and spend all his leisure *lecturing* instead!—thanks to the *house*! We told the architect it must not cost, with the lot, more than $12000.00 *complete*; he assured us that it should not! but of course we could not escape the universal experience of builders;—when the bids came in they were nearer $14000.00.[4] I wanted to pospone building, but he had gotten his heart set on it and has agreed to lecture this fall for the University Extension Society to make up the deficit.[5] He will do it of course quite easily since they pay him more than twice as much as any of the other lecturers except two. They have been making desperate efforts to get him for years and now seem as much overjoyed at their "streak of luck" as I am bored. For it is one of my chief occupations to resist people who want him to write articles, make addresses, &c. &c. and so interrupt his life-work. . . .

Yours most truly and affectionately,    Ellen A. Wilson.

ALS (WC, NjP).
  [1] It is missing.
  [2] That is, the school that she conducted for her daughters.
  [3] Possibly Robert Bridges and Bliss Perry.
  [4] Ellen's figure was not far wrong. Wilson calculated on December 3, 1895, that the total cost of the house, exclusive of the lot (which cost $3,000), would come to $11,571.80. See the WWhw memorandum on the envelope of J. W. Wright to WW, Dec. 3, 1895.
  [5] See the Editorial Note, "Wilson's Lectures on Great Leaders of Political Thought."


## To Albert Shaw

My dear Shaw,            Princeton, New Jersey. 1 June, 1895.

I send you today by express the essays handed in in competition for the prize of which I spoke.[1]

Unfortunately I have been unable to have more than one copy of each supplied. I shall have to ask you, therefore, when you have read the papers, to send them around to Mr. [Theodore] Roosevelt. I am writing to him, to tell him of the arrangement;[2] and I shall ask him to send them on to Mr. Pryor.[3]

I am heartily obliged to you for consenting to undertake this job: I appreciate it more than I can say.

As ever

Faithfully and cordially yrs.   Woodrow Wilson

There are three essays.

TCL (in possession of Virginia Shaw English).

[1] The New York Herald Prize, consisting of the interest on $1,000, presented by James Gordon Bennett and awarded to that Princeton senior or special student of satisfactory standing "who shall have taken the prescribed course in Political Science and English Literature, and who shall have prepared the best essay in English prose upon some subject of contemporaneous interest in the domestic or foreign policy of the United States Government." *Catalogue of the College of New Jersey at Princeton . . . 1894-95* (Princeton, n.d.), pp. 128-29. The subject for the essay in 1895, set presumably by Wilson, was "The Taxation of Incomes by the Federal Government as Provided by the Bill Which Became a Law August 28, 1894." For the outcome, see WW to A. Shaw, June 17, 1895, n. 1.

[2] This letter is missing.

[3] Roger Atkinson Pryor, a former Confederate soldier and politician, at this time a lawyer and judge in New York.

## From Stockton Axson

My dear Brother Woodrow:                    Philadelphia June 3, 1895

Bob Finley[1] passed through here last night, or rather stayed over night with me, on his way from the south. He has asked me to write to you on a matter of great importance to him. He has gone through the ordeal of asking Judge Lurton,[2] of Nashville, for his daughter [Mary], and the Judge has very naturally been distressed at the thought of losing her and is, also quite naturally, anxious to know something more of Bob than he can know from Bob's flying visits to Nashville—in short he has asked for "references." Bob gave him three names, Dr. [Richard T.] Ely's, Bancroft's[3] (a prominent Chicago lawyer whom you may know of) and your own. Judge Lurton was particularly pleased to get your name, not merely because of your reputation but also because of his knowledge of your family. Now, Bob lays more stress on the reply which you will make to Judge Lurton's letter than on any of the others. He said to me last night, "Woodrow Wilson has my fate in his hands. What does he really think of me?"

The object of this note which I am writing is two-fold, first to forewarn you of the fact that you will probably have a letter from Judge Lurton soon,[4] and second to ask you, according to Bob's request, to write quite frankly about him. I suppose it is perfectly reasonable of Judge Lurton to demand some such testimonies, and you will easily understand that what you say will be anxiously considered.

I think you know Bob well enough to be able to do him justice. What you dont know through your personal acquaintance with him, you know through me. He is really one of the noblest fellows that ever lived. We both know his faults, . . .

I write you about these things because in the nature of the case you could know nothing of them, and I want you to be able to write with a clear conscience.

You already know about his positive virtues—his high sense of honor, his magnanimity, his pluck, perseverence, and his unusual ability in his profession. He has made his own way in the world since he left the academy, and the results are something that he deserves to be proud of. Excuse this long letter which may be superfluous; I write it, I suppose, simply because I feel so deeply on the subject. I imagine that a father's disapproval would not dissuade Finley from his quest, but he has already had enough to contend against[5] and I do think that the way ought to be made easy for him now.

I dont remember when your commencement comes. Is it this week? If not, will it be convenient for me to come up to Princeton and stay a few days this week, say from Wednesday or Thursday? I know you are always full of company during commencement week, and so I dont want to happen in on you unprepared.

I have been better for some weeks until within the last few days. I hope that you are all very well. Give Sister and all my best love.　　　　Most affectionately yours　Stockton Axson

ALS (WP, DLC).
　[1] Robert Johnston Finley, an old friend of Axson's and Wilson's and a former student of Wilson's at the Johns Hopkins. At this time Finley was assistant editor of the New York *Review of Reviews*.
　[2] Horace Harmon Lurton, at this time a judge of the United States Circuit Court of Appeals for the Sixth Circuit; he was Associate Justice of the United States Supreme Court, 1909-14.
　[3] Edgar Addison Bancroft.
　[4] Wilson did indeed receive the letter. See H. H. Lurton to WW, June 8, 1895.
　[5] Axson was probably referring to Finley's ill health. Finley died on June 8, 1897, of what the *New York Times*, June 10, 1897, called chronic heart illness.

## From Talcott Williams

My dear Wilson,　　　　　　Philadelphia, Pa.　June 4, 1895.

The [Philadelphia] "Press" printed the article which I wrote this morning, your letter reaching me last night, and I enclose it.[1] I enclose a copy of the letter of which I spoke to you, which I recently received from the Mardin congregation.[2] Aside from the personal interest which makes it most dear to me, you will, I am sure, agree with me that it is a most interesting example of Oriental thought and expression. It is written twenty-four years after my father's death. There are few lives I think which have a response like this after so long a period.

Yours cordially,    Talcott Williams

TLS (WP, DLC) with WWhw notation on env.: "Letter from East." Enc.: clipping of editorial from the Philadelphia *Press*, June 4, 1895.
<sup>1</sup> Wilson's letter is missing. The enclosure was an editorial about the operation of the honor system at the University of Virginia and Princeton and was undoubtedly based on information supplied by Wilson.
<sup>2</sup> This enclosure is missing. Talcott Williams' father, the Rev. William Frederic Williams, was a Congregational missionary at Mardin in Turkey.

## From Child and de Goll, Architects

Dear Sir:                                   New York. June 7, 1895,
    Your favor of the 6th is at hand, and in reply, I will come to Princeton on Monday on the 2.10 train. Endeavor to have everything in shape so we can make a start at once.

Yours truly,    Child & de Goll [per] L. R. Holske

TLS (WP, DLC).

## From Horace Harmon Lurton

Dear Sir:                                   Cincinnati. June 8, 1895
    I have been advised that you have a somewhat intimate acquaintance with Mr Robt Finley of New York, a gentleman in some way connected with the staff of The Review of Reviews. My acquaintance with Mr Finley is somewhat slight. He has applied to me for the hand of my daughter and refers me to you. Under such circumstances it is perhaps not inadmissable that, though a stranger, I ask you in confidence to frankly give me opinion of Mr Finley, especially as to his habits, character, family and prospects in life. By so doing you will greatly [oblige] an interested Father
    With great respect

I am very truly    Horace H Lurton.

P.S. My address is Nashville Tenn though I address you from Cincinnati where much of my time is spent as a member of the United States Court of Appeals for the Sixth Judicial Circuit.[1]

ALS (WP, DLC) with WWhw notation on env.: "Ans. 10 June, 1895."
<sup>1</sup> Wilson's letter to Lurton of June 10, 1895, is missing. It must have helped Finley's cause, for Finley married Miss Lurton in January 1896.

## To Howard Walter Caldwell[1]

My dear Professor Caldwell,

Princeton, New Jersey,
8 June, 1895.

It was not necessary to reintroduce yourself. I remember most agreeably our pleasant meetings in Colorado Springs.[2] I have thought of them often since.

I know that you will pardon me for having taken some days to consider your important letter.[3] It could not be answered without debate. Both my instincts and my training incline me very strongly to executive work, and such a proposition as you so kindly make is hard to put aside.

But I am afraid that in this case I must say that I could not consider a call to the chancellorship of your University. Not because it is in the West; but because I am now in the midst of work which I really could not leave without the most serious loss. I am engaged upon a piece of literary work which will, I anticipate, occupy all my time for some four or five years to come. The work of a college presidency would make its prosecution impossible, as I know only too well; and to break off from it at this stage would really be nothing less than the loss of the two years I have already spent upon it. In short I, am just now too deep in private work to undertake public.

I appreciate none the less your kindness, and the sincere compliment conveyed, in making this suggestion to me. It is hard to decline, but it is easy to appreciate, such a proposal.

With warm regard,

Most sincerely Yours,   Woodrow Wilson

TCL (RSB Coll., DLC).
[1] Professor of American History and Jurisprudence, the University of Nebraska.
[2] That is, when Wilson lectured at the third annual Summer School of Colorado College in 1894.
[3] It is missing.

## From Franklin William Hooper[1]

My dear Professor Wilson:          Brooklyn, June 11th, 1895.

I beg leave to state, on behalf of the Board of Trustees, that the outline of receipts and expenditures for the coming year has been approved, and I am able therefore to fix on the price to be paid to you for your lectures on "Leaders of Political Thought."

The amount appropriated is $250.00 for the six lectures, and a sum not exceeding $50.00 for travelling expenses.

We should be very glad indeed to have your lectures begin on the first Thursday in October and continue on successive Thursday evenings until they are completed.[2]

I should be glad to receive from you a list of the subjects of your lectures in such form that each subject will begin with the name of the "Leader" and will be followed by a clause which will call attention to that particular side of political thought which he emphasized.

An announcement of the subjects in that form will make the lectures more attractive to those who read the announcement of them.

Trusting that the dates proposed will be agreeable to you, I am                Very respectfully yours,    Franklin W. Hooper.

Aristotle, Machiavelli
Montesquieu, Burke, Tocqueville, Bagehot[3]

TLS (WP, DLC). Att.: WWhw and WWsh list of lecture topics.
  [1] Director of the Brooklyn Institute of Arts and Sciences.
  [2] See the Editorial Note, "Wilson's Lectures on Great Leaders of Political Thought."
  [3] Transcript of WWsh.


# A Report of a Meeting of the Alumni of the
# University of Virginia

[*June 12, 1895*]

### ALUMNI GATHERING

Another interesting feature of the day was the regular meeting of the Society of the Alumni.

Captain Micajah Woods[1] gracefully introduced as the alumni orator Professor Woodson Wilson, of Princeton. Professor Wilson, in commencing his address, alluded to the fact that he had come back home, where, fifteen years ago, he had received Alma Mater's benediction and had gone forth to do the work she gave him to do. He came back to report, and, with glad and grateful heart, to greet his old mother and to mingle with his brothers.

The South, he said, held the uncontaminated blood of old England. The South ruled the country for many happy years. We have been called "Rebels" for many years. Would it not be a happy revenge if our section should yet come to the front and save the nation!

Charles Lamb used to say, "Whenever a new book comes out I read an old one." Would it not be well for the South in these times to recall old principles, old times, and old history, and to bring to the solution of the economical and serious problems the grand ideas and deeds of our fathers—bring to the rescue the conservatism and unity of the South? The function of the southern people is to recall the lessons of the past—the ideals of the purer days of the republic.

The speaker made an eloquent and forcible plea for the thorough study of English literature and the culture of our young men. He appealed to the alumni of the University, to the men of the South, to come to the front, and once more lead our country. Professor Wilson was warmly applauded and heartily congratulated. . . .

Printed in the *Richmond Dispatch*, June 13, 1895; some editorial headings omitted.
    [1] University of Virginia Law School, 1868; prominent lawyer and Commonwealth attorney for Albemarle County, 1870-1911.

A Report of an Address at the University of Virginia

[*June 12, 1895*]

ADDRESS BEFORE THE SOCIETY OF ALUMNI.

The annual address before the Society of Alumni was delivered in the Public Hall on the final day, Wednesday, June 12, 1895, by Prof. Woodrow Wilson, ('81) now of Princeton College. Prof. Wilson's address was one of the handsomest of the many orations which have been delivered before the Society. It was well conceived and was delivered with such charm of voice, diction and manner, that we might say of him as Ben Jonson so sententiously said of Lord Bacon, "the fear of every man who heard him was lest he should make an end."

We regret that we are not able to publish the discourse in full. We supposed, until too late, that it had been written out [in full] by the speaker, and no effort was made to take it down as delivered. The following synopsis[1] scarcely conveys an adequate idea of the address:

*Mr. President, Brother Alumni, Ladies and Gentlemen:*
    I should indeed be insensible did I not feel very keenly to find myself again in this place and on this stage. It was from this place I set out, upon such journey as I have made these fifteen years;

    [1] There is a slightly different version of this address in the University of Virginia *College Topics*, June 12, 1895, which seems to have been the text of the address supplied by Wilson. Apparently the editor of the *Alumni Bulletin* sent a copy of the report in *College Topics* to Wilson for editing, and the text printed here includes deletions and additions made by Wilson from his memory of the address. For commentary on the significance of this address, see Arthur S. Link, "Woodrow Wilson: The American as Southerner," *Journal of Southern History*, XXVI (Feb. 1970), 3-17.

and hither I come again, as if to round out a stage of my life, make report of the past, and take orders for the future. It is thus a man assures himself of his identity, and learns his spirit cannot grow old: by returning to the places of his youth and inspiration—and recognizing his home again.

Did I thus come home again to speak with each one of you apart, our talk would be of personal themes of memory; the days of youth and comradeship and hope and first endeavor, spent upon these spreading lawns and in these cloistered walks.

But standing face to face as we do to-day our speech must be of the things we have in common as citizens and neighbors; of our life as a community, our faith taken out of the past and our inspiration prepared against the future.

Those of us whose fortune it is to be much away from home return to it with a fresh zest and appreciation of its charm and power to rule our spirits; and we ask ourselves what it is that makes this home for us, live we never so long away from it?

The answer is not far to seek. It is because of the heart there is in this southern land; the sensibility, loyalty, imagination for a cause, power of steadfast conviction.

It is not so by accident. Long processes of history have worked here, as elsewhere, to mould and train us for our part and fate in the general drama of affairs.

Did you never stop to think what it meant, that through all the formative period of our Government the nation was led by men out of the South, of whom Washington was the consummate type?

> "Virginia gave us this imperial man
>     Cast in the massive mould
>     Of those high-statured ages old
> Which into grander forms our mortal metal ran.
> \*     \*     \*     \*     \*     \*     \*     \*     \*
>
> Mother of States and undiminished men,
> Thou gavest us a country, giving him."[2]

In Washington we may discern the "brief chronicle and abstract" of a time and nation. His courageous calmness in seasons of political crisis; his steady aptitude for affairs; his solemn sense of public duty; his hold upon men of various and diverse natures; his capacity for persuasive counsel; his boldness without dash, and power without display. Do we not see in these qualities

---

[2] From James Russell Lowell, "Under the Old Elm: Poem Read at Cambridge on the Hundredth Anniversary of Washington's Taking Command of the American Army, 3rd July, 1775." [Eds.' note]

the perfect epitome of what the slow processes of English national history had proved themselves capable of producing in the way of manhood and character? Washington was neither an accident nor a miracle. Neither blind chance nor a special Providence need be assumed to account for him. It was God, indeed, who gave him to us; but God had been preparing him ever since English constitutional history began. He was of the same breed with Hampden and John Pym. Burke and Chatham both recognized him as of their own blood and breeding so soon as they saw opened before them the credentials of his deeds. He was of such heroic stuff as God had for centuries been so graciously and lavishly weaving into the character of our race.

Do you recall that striking story of one of the opening incidents of the great constitutional convention, related by Gouverneur Morris, an eye-witness of the scene? "Of the delegates," he says, "some were for halfway measures, for fear of displeasing the people; others were anxious and doubting. Just before there were enough to form a quorum, Washington, standing self-collected in the midst of them, his countenance more than usually solemn, his eyes seeming to look into futurity, said, 'It is too probable no plan we propose will be adopted. Perhaps another dreadful conflict is to be sustained. If, to please the people, we offer what we ourselves disapprove, how can we afterwards defend our work? Let us raise a standard to which the wise and honest can repair; the event is in the hand of God.'" That is an utterance, not of statesmanship merely, but of character as well; and do we not understand that character? Do we not thrill at its expression? It strikes thus to the quick of our sensibilities because we are of the same race and derivation that this man was of.

Washington was of the English, not of the American type, in those qualities which gave him leadership in the Revolution. He had the American vision of empire; but the English quality in government and the close relations of society.

The American type belongs to the middle States and the West. In New England we have one class and element in English society localized and brought to its perfect development. In the South a general English population; not all Cavalier, but mixed of almost all the elements of the home population, not excluding the Puritan. Hence the general English temperament and capacity in affairs which we note in the men of the old Southern training. Out of the South came the general principles of liberty, which gave form and practice to the general government. Out of New England, the special adjustments of local and individual liberty.

The South alone, in the transformations of the century, has been left with her original stock almost intact, unspoiled. She may still make again her original contribution to the strength and self-possession of the nation.

When I see this people, bred thus, and bringing unimpaired out of the past a great tradition of antique faith, I seem to see whence the ideal forces of the nation are to come.

Ours is a region unspoiled as yet by the too rapid and overwhelming set of foreign and material forces. A region still of small towns and local community; of neighborhoods and friendships and admirations. A people preserved apart to recall the nation to its ideals, and to its common purpose for the future. What a sweet and noble revenge it would be could we save the nation we have been thought to hate!

The new evils need none but the old remedies; we alone, perhaps, can supply them, recovered out of the past; make them once more vital and effectual.

> "This tract which the river of Time
> Now flows through with us, is the plain.
> Gone is the calm of its earlier shore.
> Border'd by cities, and hoarse
> With a thousand cries is its stream.
> And we on its breast, our minds
> Are confused as the cries which we hear,
> Changing and shot as the sights which we see.
> And we say that repose has fled
> For ever the course of the river of Time.
> That cities will crowd to its edge
> In a blacker, incessanter line;
> That the din will be more on its banks,
> Denser the trade on its stream,
> Flatter the plain where it flows,
> Fiercer the sun overhead.
> That never will those on its breast
> See an ennobling sight,
> Drink of the feeling of quiet again.
> But what was before us we know not,
> And we know not what shall succeed."[3]

If this be so; if we are to recall a nation to the ideals of its first age, what should we do, alumni of this great University, itself the child of that old generation? Is not this the seminary of

---

[3] Matthew Arnold, "The Future." [Eds.' note]

southern thought and purpose, where her young men come to take their orders for the future? Should we not cherish, repair, magnify, establish, and enable it for this great function till liberty shall once more live and be young as of old?

The means are open to us. Our blood still runs pure, and the great literature of our race still lies open before us. As spirit, it apprises us of the permanent thoughts and fixed aspirations of our race. As politics, it enables us to know ourselves for what we are; to know each other as neighbors and friends, and our rulers as our ministers.

Let us keep the long memory of affairs; know our political life as an experience, and not as a scientific formula—read Montesquieu and Burke more than Kidd, and all the race of those who would give us a new formula.

This the South is fittest for by reason of her tradition, to know the whole life of the race.

The Spirit of the Age? Is it not manifold; complex, compounded of things both new and old? Ours be the function of recollection; to recollect and call to life again the best things of the thought and experience of the great and capable race to which we belong; that we may give to this compound nation of ours a new coherency and self-possession.

The signs of the time change: thus once more shall we lead the nation, and the age.

Printed in the *Alumni Bulletin of the University of Virginia*, II (July 1895), 53-55.


## From Edward Southwick Child

Dear Professor                    New York. June 13 [1895]

All the details necessary for the stone construction will be ready tomorrow and copies be sent Mr Wright. I have sent contract[1] to County Clerk at Trenton. . . . Will you be in Princeton Monday— P.M. so that the plumbing can be fixed up?

Yours,   E S Child

ALS (WP, DLC).
[1] "Articles of Agreement" between Woodrow Wilson and Josiah W. Wright, dated June 10, 1895, unsigned copy (WP, DLC). Accompanying this contract is also a copy of "SPECIFICATIONS OF Workmanship & Materials to be used in Erection of Two Story House for PROF. WOODROW WILSON, Princeton, N. J.," prepared by Child and de Goll, Architects, undated but signed by Wilson and Wright.

## From Addison H. Hazeltine[1]

Dear Sir:                                        Newark, N. J. June 17, 1895

I enclose herewith bond, mortgage, draft and affidavitt in loan of $7000 approved to you by the Mutual Life upon property at Princeton, N. J. Kindly execute and return to me these papers together with policy of insurance, and also notify me when you will be ready for the first payment.

In examining the deeds at Trenton I found that a part of the sixth course in the deed from Richard S. Hunter Tr. to Samuel W. Stockton was omitted from the records. This is probably an error of the recording clerk. The 7th course also appears to be defective. If you will have Mr Stockton mail me the deed I will have the record rectified. I also enclose the survey made by Sandoz.[2] He has not shown the location of the buildings on the property to be mortgaged. Will you kindly have him do so and return survey to me. Also kindly insert the name of your wife in the mortgage.

Very truly yours,    A H Hazeltine

TLS (WP, DLC). Encs. missing.
[1] Of Newark, general counsel of the Mutual Life Insurance Company of New York for New Jersey.
[2] Ernest Sandoz, surveyor, of 12 Steadman St., Princeton.

## To Talcott Williams

My dear Mr. Williams,      Princeton, New Jersey, 17 June, 1895.

The editorial pleases me entirely; and we are sincerely obliged to you for it.

As for the letter from the East, of which you send me a copy, it is most beautiful and touching. I had to read very slowly and carefully, in reading it aloud to Mrs. Wilson, in order to keep my voice. I thank you for it; and shall keep it for its own sake, as well as to remember your kindness.

Remember us most cordially when you write to Mrs. Williams. Your visit cheered and delighted us deeply.

Faithfully Yours,    Woodrow Wilson

WWTLS (in possession of Henry Bartholomew Cox).

## To Albert Shaw

My dear Shaw,              Princeton, New Jersey. 17 June, 1895.

Thank you most heartily for your kind service in the matter of the essays. The finding and the method thereof were in every way most satisfactory.[1]

I was away from home, on an errand to Virginia, when your letter came: else I should have written sooner to make my acknowledgements, and express my warm appreciation of an unselfish service.

As ever, with warmest regards,

Faithfully yours,    Woodrow Wilson

TCL (in possession of Virginia Shaw English).

[1] The "finding," at any rate, was that the New York Herald Prize should go to Arthur Dunn, '95, of Chicago.

## An Historical Essay[1]

[c. June 17, 1895]

### ON THE WRITING OF HISTORY.

#### WITH A GLANCE AT THE METHODS OF MACAULAY, GIBBON, CARLYLE, AND GREEN.

"Give us the facts, and nothing but the facts," is the sharp injunction of our age to its historians. Upon the face of it, an eminently reasonable requirement. To tell the truth simply, openly, without reservation, is the unimpeachable first principle of all right living; and historians have no license to be quit of it. Unquestionably they must tell us the truth, or else get themselves enrolled among a very undesirable class of persons, not often frankly named in polite society. But the thing is by no means so easy as it looks. The truth of history is a very complex and very occult matter. It consists of things which are invisible as well as of things which are visible. It is full of secret motives, and of a chance interplay of trivial and yet determining circumstances; it is shot through with transient passions, and broken athwart here and there by what seem cruel accidents; it cannot all be reduced to statistics or newspaper items or official recorded statements. And so it turns out, when the actual test of experiment is made, that the historian must have something more than a good

[1] The sole manuscript remains of this article is a WWhw MS. with WWsh and WWT additions (WP, DLC). This first draft was entitled "The Truth of the Matter" and dated March 7, 1895. It seems likely that Wilson prepared it for delivery to the New Jersey Historical Society soon after receiving the invitation to deliver the semicentennial address to that body on May 16, 1895. After completing his first draft, Wilson apparently decided that the paper was inappropriate for the occasion, set it aside, and then composed the address, "The Course of American History," printed at May 16, 1895. Soon after the Princeton commencement of 1895, Wilson went back to "The Truth of the Matter," adding a new opening paragraph and renumbering the pages. Soon afterward he sent a typed version to the Century Magazine. Perhaps the title was changed in the Century office—correspondence relating to the publication of the article is missing. In any event, when Wilson reprinted the essay in Mere Literature and Other Essays (Boston and New York, 1896), pp. 161-86, he used his original title, "The Truth of the Matter."

conscience, must be something more than a good man. He must have an eye to see the truth; and nothing but a very catholic imagination will serve to illuminate his matter for him: nothing less than keen and steady insight will make even illumination yield him the truth of what he looks upon. Even when he has seen the truth, only half his work is done, and that not the more difficult half. He must then make others see it just as he does: only when he has done that has he told the truth. What an art of penetrative phrase and just selection must he have to take others into the light in which he stands! Their dullness, their ignorance, their prepossessions, are to be overcome and driven in, like a routed troop, upon the truth. The thing is infinitely difficult. The skill and strategy of it cannot be taught. And so historians take another way, which is easier: they tell part of the truth,—the part most to their taste, or most suitable to their talents,—and obtain readers to their liking among those of like tastes and talents to their own.

We have our individual tastes in history, as in every other sort of literature. And there are histories to every taste: histories full of the piquant details of personal biography, histories that blaze with the splendors of courts and resound with drum and trumpet, and histories that run upon the humbler but greater levels of the life of the people; colorless histories, so passionless and so lacking in distinctive mark or motive that they might have been set up out of a dictionary without the intervention of an author, and partizan histories, so warped and violent in every judgment that no reader not of the historian's own party can stomach them; histories of economic development, and histories that speak only of politics; those that tell nothing but what it is pleasant and interesting to know, and those that tell nothing at all that one cares to remember. One must be of a new and unheard-of taste not to be suited among them all.

The trouble is, after all, that men do not invariably find the truth to their taste, and will often deny it when they hear it; and the historian has to do much more than keep his own eyes clear: he has also to catch and hold the eye of his reader. 'T is a nice art, as much intellectual as moral. How shall he take the palate of his reader at unawares, and get the unpalatable facts down his throat along with the palatable? Is there no way in which all the truth may be made to hold together in a narrative so strongly knit and so harmoniously colored that no reader will have either the wish or the skill to tear its patterns asunder, and men will take it all, unmarred and as it stands, rather than miss the zest of it?

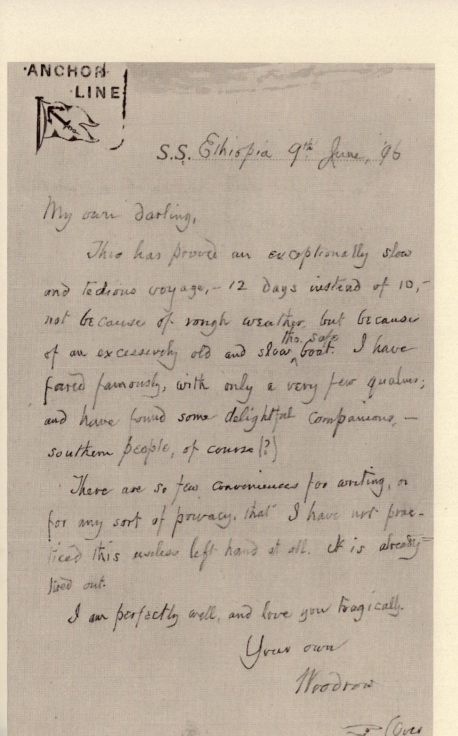

ANCHOR
LINE

S.S. Ethiopia 9th June, '96

My own darling,

This has proved an exceptionally slow and tedious voyage, — 12 days instead of 10, — not because of rough weather but because of an excessively old and slow, tho. safe boat. I have fared famously, with only a very few qualms; and have found some delightful companions, — southern people, of course (?)

There are so few conveniences for writing, or for any sort of privacy, that I have not practiced this useless left hand at all. It is already tired out.

I am perfectly well, and love you tragically.

Yours own
Woodrow

[Over]

A shipboard letter that Wilson wrote to his wife with his left hand
en route to the British Isles

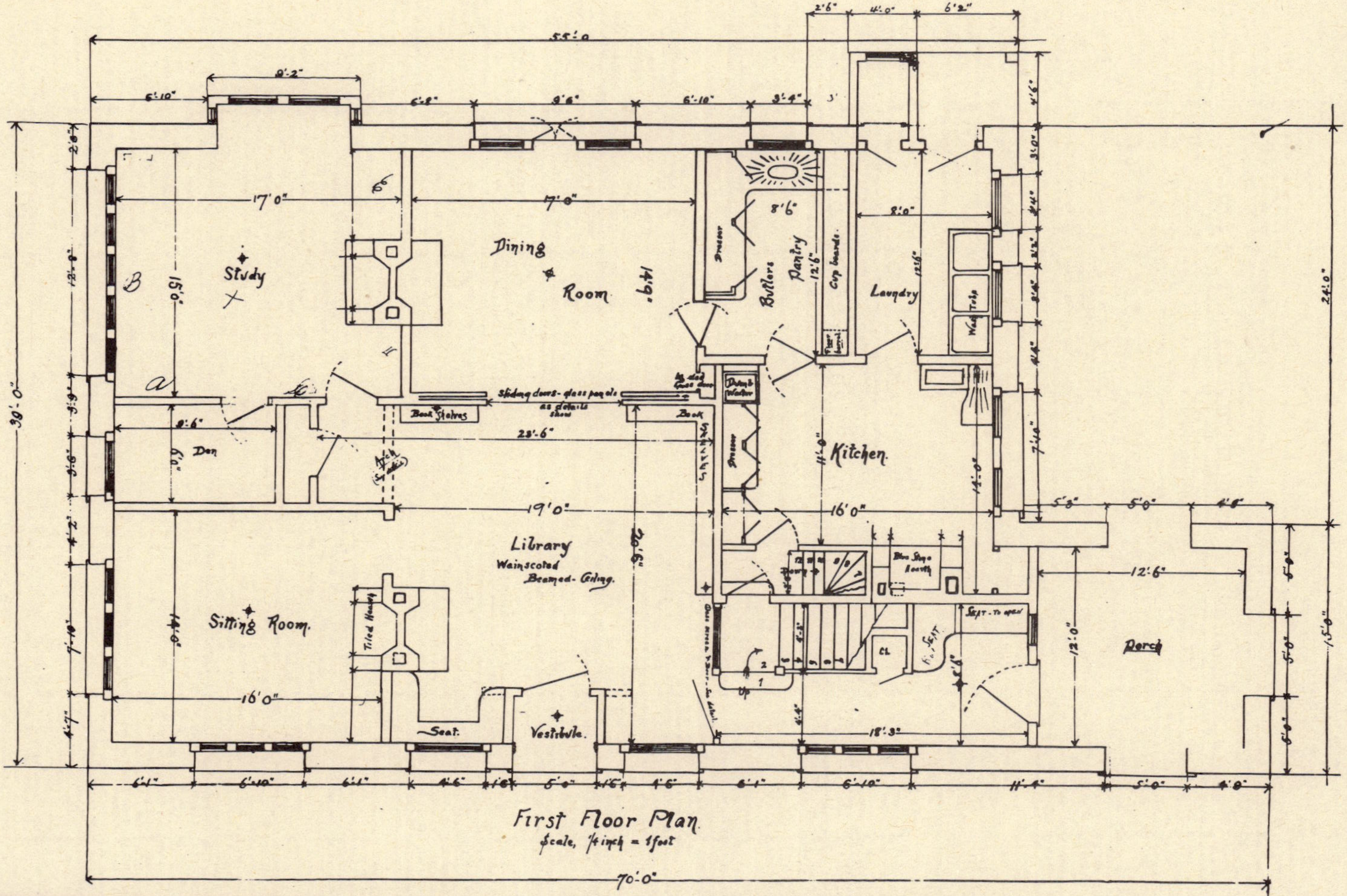

First Floor Plan

Scale, 1/16 inch = 1 foot

Porch

Kitchen

Laundry

Pantry

Butler's

Cup Boards

Dining Room

14'9"

Library

Wainscoted. Beamed Ceiling.

Vestibule

Study

Den

Sitting Room

Tiled Hearth

Seat

The Wilson house on Library Place

Bliss Perry,
Professor of Oratory and Aesthetic
Criticism, 1893-1900

John Grier Hibben,
Assistant Professor of Logic,
in 1896

Howard Pyle, the illustrator of Wilson's
*George Washington*

Marquand Chapel on the Princeton campus

Alexander Hall, soon after its completion in 1894

Tiger Inn, an upperclass eating club on Prospect Avenue,
completed in 1895

University Hall, a student dormitory at Nassau Street and
University Place, formerly a hotel

It is evident the thing cannot be done by the "dispassionate" annalist. The old chroniclers, whom we relish, were not dispassionate. We love some of them for their sweet quaintness, some for their childlike credulity, some for their delicious inconsequentiality. But our modern chroniclers are not so. They are, above all things else, knowing, thoroughly informed, subtly sophisticated. They would not for the world contribute any spice of their own to the narrative; and they are much too watchful, circumspect, and dutiful in their care to keep their method pure and untouched by any thought of theirs to let us catch so much as a glimpse of the chronicler underneath the chronicle. Their purpose is to give simply the facts, eschewing art, and substituting a sort of monumental index and table of the world's events.

The trouble is that men refuse to be made any wiser by such means. Though they will readily enough let their eyes linger upon a monument of art, they will heedlessly pass by a mere monument of industry. It suggests nothing to them. The materials may be suitable enough, but the handling of them leaves them dead and commonplace. An interesting circumstance thus comes to light. It is nothing less than this, that the facts do not of themselves constitute the truth. The truth is abstract not concrete. It is the just idea, the right revelation of what things mean. It is evoked only by such arrangements and orderings of fact as suggest meanings. The chronological arrangement of events, for example, may or may not be the arrangement which most surely brings the truth of the narrative to light; and the best arrangement is always that which displays, not the facts themselves, but the subtle and else invisible forces that lurk in the events and in the minds of men—forces for which events serve only as lasting and dramatic words of utterance. Take an instance. How are you to enable men to know the truth with regard to a period of revolution? Will you give them simply a calm statement of recorded events, simply a quiet, unaccentuated narrative of what actually happened, written in a monotone, and verified by quotations from authentic documents of the time? You may save yourself the trouble. As well make a pencil sketch in outline of a raging conflagration; write upon one portion of it "flame," upon another "smoke"; here "town hall, where the fire started," and there "spot where fireman was killed." It is a chart, not a picture. Even if you made a veritable picture of it, you could give only part of the truth so long as you confined yourself to black and white. Where would be all the wild and terrible colors of the scene: the red and tawny flame; the masses of smoke, carrying the dull glare of the fire to the very skies, like a great signal banner thrown to the winds; the hot and frightened faces of the crowd; the crimsoned gables down the street, with the faint light of a lamp here and there gleaming white from some hastily opened casement? Without the colors your picture is not true. No inventory of items will even represent the truth: the fuller and more minute you make it, the more will the truth be obscured. The little details will take up as much space in the statement as the great totals into which they are summed up; and the proportions being false, the whole is false. Truth, fortunately, takes its own revenge. No one is deceived. The reader of the chronicle lays it aside. It lacks verisimilitude. He cannot realize how any of the things spoken of can have happened. He goes elsewhere to find, if he may, a real picture of the time, and perhaps finds one that is wholly fictitious. No wonder the grave and monk-like chronicler sighs. He of course wrote to be read, and not merely for the manual exercise of it; and when he sees readers turn away, his heart misgives him for his fellow-men. Is it as it always was, that they do not wish to know the truth? Alas! good eremite, men do not seek the truth as they should; but do you know what the truth is? It is a thing ideal, displayed by the just proportion of events, revealed in form and color, dumb till facts be set in syllables, articulated into words, put together into sentences, swung with proper tone and cadence. It is not revolutions only that have color. Nothing in human life is without it. In a monochrome you can depict nothing but a single incident; in a monotone you cannot often carry truth beyond a single sentence. Only by art in all its variety can you depict as it is the various face of life.

Yes; but what sort of art? There is here a wide field of choice. Shall we go back to the art of which Macaulay was so great a master? We could do worse. It must be a great art that can make men lay aside the novel and take up the history, to find there, in very fact, the movement and drama of life. What Macaulay does well he does incomparably. Who else can mass the details as he does, and yet not mar or obscure, but only heighten, the effect of the picture as a whole? Who else can bring so amazing a profusion of knowledge within the strait limits of a simple plan, nowhere encumbered, everywhere free and obvious in its movement? How sure the strokes, and how bold, how vivid the result! Yet when we have laid the book aside, when the charm and the excitement of the telling narrative have worn off, when we have lost step with the swinging gait at which the style goes, when the details have faded from our recollection, and we sit removed and thoughtful, with only the greater outlines of the story sharp upon our minds, a deep misgiving and dissatisfaction take possession of us. We are no longer young, and we are chagrined that we should have been so pleased and taken with the glitter and color and mere life of the picture. Let boys be cajoled by rhetoric, we cry; men must look deeper. What of the judgment of this facile and eloquent man? Can we agree with him when he is not talking and the charm is gone? What shall we say of his assessment of men and measures? Is he just? Is he himself in possession of the whole truth? Does he open the matter to us as it was? Does he not, rather, rule us like an advocate, and make himself master of our judgments?

Then it is that we become aware that there were two Macaulays: Macaulay the artist, with an exquisite gift for telling a story, filling his pages with little vignettes it is impossible to forget, fixing these with an inimitable art upon the surface of a narrative that did not need the ornament they gave it, so strong and large and adequate was it; and Macaulay the Whig, subtly turning narrative into argument, and making history the vindication of a party. The mighty narrative is a great engine of proof. It is not told for its own sake. It is evidence summed up in order to justify a judgment. We detect the tone of the advocate, and though if we were just we must deem him honest, we cannot deem him safe. The great story-teller is discredited; and, willingly or unwillingly, we reject the guide who takes it upon himself to determine for us what we shall see. That, we feel sure, cannot be true which makes of so complex a history so simple a thesis for the judgment. There is art here; but it is the art of special pleading, misleading even to the pleader.

If not Macaulay, what master shall we follow? Shall our historian not have his convictions, and enforce them? Shall he not be our guide, and speak, if he can, to our spirits as well as to our understandings? Readers are a poor jury. They need enlightenment as well as information: the matter must be interpreted to them as well as related. There are moral facts as well as material, and the one sort must be as plainly told as the other. Of what service is it that the historian should have insight if we are not to know how the matter stands in his view? If he refrain from judgment, he may deceive us as much as he would were his judgment wrong; for we must have enlightenment—that is his function. We would not set him up merely to tell us tales, but also to display to us characters, to open to us the moral and intent of the matter. Were the men sincere? Was the policy righteous? We have but just now seen that the "facts" lie deeper than the mere visible things that took place, that they involve the moral and motive of the play. Shall not these, too, be brought to light?

Unquestionably every sentence of true history must hold a judgment in solution. All cannot be told. If it were possible to tell all, it would take as long to write history as to enact it, and we should have to postpone the reading of it to the leisure of the next world. A few facts must be selected for the narrative, the great majority left unnoted. But the selection—for what purpose is it to be made? For the purpose of conveying *an impression* of the truth. Where shall you find a more radical process of judgment? The "essential" facts taken, the "unessential" left out! Why, you may make the picture what you will, and in any case it must be the express image of the historian's fundamental judgments. It is his purpose, or should be, to give a true impression of his theme as a whole—to show it, not lying upon his page in an open and dispersed analysis, but set close in intimate synthesis, every line, every stroke, every bulk even, omitted which does not enter of very necessity into a single and unified image of the truth.

It is in this that the writing of history differs, and differs very radically, from the statement of the results of original research. The writing of history must be based upon original research and authentic record, but it can no more be directly constructed by the piecing together of bits of original research than by the mere reprinting together of state documents. Individual research furnishes us, as it were, with the private documents and intimate records without which the public archives are incomplete and unintelligible. But separately they are wholly out of perspective. It is the consolation of those who produce them to make them so. They would lose heart were they forbidden to regard all facts as of equal importance. It is facts they are after, and only facts— facts for their own sake, and without regard to their several importance. These are their ore,—very precious ore,—which they are concerned to get out, not to refine. They have no direct concern with what may afterward be done at the mint or in the goldsmith's shop. They will even boast that they care not for the beauty of the ore, and are indifferent how, or in what shape, it may become an article of commerce. Much of it is thrown away in the nice processes of manufacture, and you shall not distinguish the product of the several mines in the coin, or the cup, or the salver.

Indeed, the historian must himself be an investigator. He must know good ore from bad; must distinguish fineness, quality, genuineness; must stop to get out of the records for himself what he lacks for the perfection of his work. But for all that, he must know and stand ready to do every part of his task like a master workman, recognizing and testing every bit of stuff he uses. Standing sure, a man of science as well as an artist, he must take and use all of his equipment for the sake of his art—not to display his materials, but to subordinate and transform them in his effort to make, by every touch and cunning of hand and tool, the perfect image of what he sees, the very truth of his seer's vision of the world. The true historian works always for the whole impression, the truth with unmarred proportions, unexaggerated parts, undistorted visage. He has no favorite parts of the story which he boasts are bits of his own, but loves only the whole of it, the full and unspoiled image of the day of which he writes, the crowded and yet consistent details that carry, without obtrusion of themselves, the large features of the time. Any exaggeration of the parts makes all the picture false, and the work is to do over. Test every bit of material, runs the artist's rule, and then forget the material; forget its origin and the dross from which it has been freed, and think only and always of the great thing you would make of it, the pattern and form in which you would lose and merge it. That is its only high use.

'T is a pity to see how even the greatest minds will often lack the broad and catholic vision with which the just historian must look upon men and affairs. There is Carlyle, with his shrewd and seeing eye, his unmatched capacity to assess strong men and set the scenery for tragedy or intrigue, his breathless ardor for great events, his amazing flashes of insight, and his unlooked-for steady light of occasional narrative. The whole matter of what he writes is too dramatic. Surely history was not all enacted so hotly, or with so passionate a rush of men upon the stage. Its quiet scenes must have been longer—not mere pauses and interludes while the tragic parts were being made up. There is not often ordinary sunlight upon the page. The lights burn now wan, now lurid. Men are seen disquieted and turbulent, and may be heard in husky cries or rude, untimely jests. We do not recognize our own world, but seem to see another such as ours might become if peopled by like uneasy Titans. Incomparable to tell of days of storm and revolution, speaking like an oracle and familiar of destiny and fate, searching the hearts of statesmen and conquerors with an easy insight in every day of action, this peasant seer cannot give us the note of piping times of peace, or catch the tone of slow industry; watches ships come and go at the docks, hears freight-vans thunder along the iron highways of the modern world, and loaded trucks lumber heavily through the crowded city streets, with a hot disdain of commerce, prices current, the haggling of the market, and the smug ease of material comfort bred in a trading age. There is here no broad and catholic vision, no wise tolerance, no various power to know, to sympathize, to interpret. The great seeing imagination of the man lacks that pure radiance in which things are seen steadily and seen whole.

It is not easy, to say truth, to find actual examples when you are constructing the ideal historian, the man with the vision and the faculty divine to see affairs justly and tell of them completely. If you are not satisfied with this passionate and intolerant seer of Chelsea, whom will you choose? Shall it be Gibbon, whom all praise but so few read? He, at any rate, is passionless, it would appear. But who could write epochal history with passion? All hot humors of the mind must, assuredly, cool when spread at large upon so vast a surface. One must feel like a sort of minor providence in traversing that great tract of world history, and catch in spite of one's self the gait and manner of a god. This stately procession of generations moves on remote from the ordinary levels of our human sympathy. 'T is a wide view of nations and peoples and dynasties, and a world shaken by the travail of new births. There is here no scale by which to measure the historian of the sort we must look to see handle the ordinary matter of national history. The "Decline and Fall" stands impersonal, like a monument. We shall reverence it, but we shall not imitate it.

If we look away from Gibbon, exclude Carlyle, and question Macaulay; if we put the investigators on one side as not yet historians, and the deliberately picturesque and entertaining *raconteurs* as not yet investigators, we naturally turn, I suppose, to such a man as John Richard Green, at once the patient scholar—who shall adequately say how nobly patient?—and the rare artist, working so like a master in the difficult stuffs of a long national history. The very life of the man is as beautiful as the moving sentences he wrote with so subtle a music in the cadence. We know whence the fine moral elevation of tone came that sounds through all the text of his great narrative. True, not everybody is satisfied with our *doctor angelicus*. Some doubt he is too ornate. Others are troubled that he should sometimes be inaccurate. Some are willing to use his history as a manual; while others cannot deem him satisfactory for didactic uses, hesitate how they shall characterize him, and quit the matter vaguely with saying that what he wrote is "at any rate literature." Can there be something lacking in Green, too, notwithstanding he was impartial, and looked with purged and open eyes upon the whole unbroken life of his people—notwithstanding he saw the truth and had the art and mastery to make others see it as he did, in all its breadth and multiplicity?

Perhaps even this great master of narrative lacks variety—as who does not? His method, whatever the topic, is ever the same. His sentences, his paragraphs, his chapters, are pitched one and all in the same key. It is a very fine and moving key. Many an elevated strain and rich harmony commend it alike to the ear and to the imagination. It is employed with an easy mastery, and is made to serve to admiration a wide range of themes. But it is always the same key, and some themes it will not serve. An infinite variety plays through all history. Every scene has its own air and singularity. Incidents cannot all be rightly set in the narrative if all be set alike. As the scene shifts the tone of the narrative must change: the narrator's choice of incident and his choice of words; the speed and method of his sentence; his own thought, even, and point of view. Surely his battle pages must resound with the tramp of armies and the fearful din and rush of war. In peace he must catch by turns the hum of industry, the bustle of the street, the calm of the country-side, the tone of parliamentary debate, the fancy, the ardor, the argument of poets and seers and quiet students. Snatches of song run along with sober purpose and strenuous endeavor through every nation's story. Coarse men and refined, mobs and ordered assemblies, science and mad impulse, storm and calm, are all alike ingredients of the various life. It is not all epic. There is rough comedy and brutal violence. The drama can scarce be given any strict unbroken harmony of incident, any close logical sequence of act or nice unity of scene. To pitch it all in one key, therefore, is to mistake the significance of the infinite play of varied circumstance that makes up the yearly movement of a people's life.

It would be less than just to say that Green's pages do not reveal the variety of English life the centuries through. It is his glory, indeed, as all the world knows, to have broadened and diversified the whole scale of English history. Nowhere else within the compass of a single book can one find so many sides of the great English story displayed with so deep and just an appreciation of them all, or of the part of each in making up the whole. Green is the one man among English historians who has restored the great fabric of the nation's history where its architecture was obscure, and its details were likely to be lost or forgotten. Once more, because of him, the vast Gothic structure stands complete, its majesty and firm grace enhanced at every point by the fine tracery of its restored details.

Where so much is done, it is no doubt unreasonable to ask for more. But the very architectural symmetry of this great book imposes a limitation upon it. It is full of a certain sort of variety;

but it is only the variety of a great plan's detail, not the variety of English life. The noble structure obeys its own laws rather than the laws of a people's life. It is a monument conceived and reared by a consummate artist, and it wears upon its every line some part of the image it was meant to bear of a great, complex, aspiring national existence. But, though it symbolizes, it does not contain that life. It has none of the irregularity of the actual experiences of men and communities. It explains, but it does not contain, their variety. The history of every nation has certainly a plan which the historian must see and reproduce; but he must reconstruct the people's life, not merely expound it. The scope of his method must be as great as the variety of his subject; it must change with each change of mood, respond to each varying impulse in the great process of events. No rigor of a stately style must be suffered to exclude the lively touches of humor or the rude sallies of strength that mark it everywhere. The plan of the telling must answer to the plan of the fact—must be as elastic as the topics are mobile. The matter should rule the plan, not the plan the matter.

The ideal is infinitely difficult, if, indeed, it be possible to any man not Shaksperian; but the difficulty of attaining it is often unnecessarily enhanced. Ordinarily the historian's preparation for his task is such as to make it unlikely he will perform it naturally. He goes first, with infinite and admirable labor, through all the labyrinth of document and detail that lies up and down his subject; collects masses of matter great and small for substance, verification, illustration; piles his notes volumes high; reads far and wide upon the tracks of his matter, and makes page upon page of references; and then, thoroughly stuffed and sophisticated, turns back and begins his narrative. 'T is impossible, then, that he should begin naturally. He sees the end from the beginning, and all the way from beginning to end; he has made up his mind about too many things; uses his details with a too free and familiar mastery, not like one who tells a story so much as like one who dissects a cadaver. Having swept his details together beforehand, like so much scientific material, he discourses upon them like a demonstrator—thinks too little in subjection to them. They no longer make a fresh impression upon him. They are his tools, not his objects of vision.

It is not by such a process that a narrative is made vital and true.[2] It does not do to lose the point of view of the first listener

[2] From here to the end of the essay Wilson explains and defends the method that he was following in writing his "Short History of the United States" and which he would later follow in writing his biography of George Washington, about which numerous documents will appear later in this volume.

to the tale, or to rearrange the matter too much out of the order
of nature. You must instruct your reader as the events themselves would have instructed him had he been able to note them
as they passed. The historian must not lose his own fresh view
of the scene as it passed and changed more and more from year
to year and from age to age. He must keep with the generation
of which he writes, not be too quick to be wiser than they were,
and look back upon them in his narrative with head over shoulder. He must write of them always in the atmosphere they themselves breathed, not hastening to judge them, but striving only
to realize them at every turn of the story, to make their thoughts
his own, and call their lives back again, rebuilding the very stage
upon which they played their parts. Bring the end of your story
to mind while you set about telling its beginning, and it seems
to have no parts: beginning, middle, end, are all as one—are
merely like parts of a pattern which you see as a single thing
stamped upon the stuff under your hand. It is a dead thing dis-
sected.

Try the method with the history of our own land and people.
How will you begin? Will you start with a modern map and a
careful topographical description of the continent? And then,
having made your nineteenth-century framework for the narrative, will you ask your reader to turn back and see the seventeenth
century, and those lonely ships coming in at the capes of the
Chesapeake? He will never see them so long as you compel him to
stand here at the end of the nineteenth century and look at them
as if through a long retrospect. The attention both of the narrator
and of the reader, if history is to be seen aright, must look forward, not backward. It must see with a contemporaneous eye.
Let the historian, if he be wise, know no more of the history as he
writes than might have been known in the age and day of which
he is writing. A trifle too much knowledge will undo him. It will
break the spell for his imagination. It will spoil the magic by
which he may raise again the image of days that are gone. He
must, of course, know the large lines of his story; it must lie
as a whole in his mind. His very art demands that, in order that he
may know and keep its proportions. But the details, the passing
incidents of day and year, must come fresh into his mind, unreasoned upon as yet, untouched by theory, with their first look
upon them. It is here that original documents and fresh research
will serve him. He must look far and wide upon every detail of
the time, see it at first hand, and paint as he looks; selecting as
the artist must, but selecting while the vision is fresh, and not

from old sketches laid away in his notes—selecting from the life itself.

Let him remember that his task is radically different from the task of the investigator. The investigator must display his materials, but the historian must convey his impressions. He must stand in the presence of life, and reproduce it in his narrative; must recover a past age; make dead generations live again and breathe their own air; show them native and at home upon his page. To do this, his own impressions must be as fresh as those of an unlearned reader, his own curiosity as keen and young at every stage. It may easily be so as his reading thickens, and the atmosphere of the age comes stealthily into his thought, if only he take care to push forward the actual writing of his narrative at an equal pace with his reading, painting thus always direct from the image itself. His knowledge of the great outlines and bulks of the picture will be his sufficient guide and restraint the while, will give proportion to the individual strokes of his work. But it will not check his zest, or sophisticate his fresh recovery of the life that is in the crowding colors of the canvas.

A nineteenth-century plan laid like a standard and measure upon a seventeenth-century narrative will infallibly twist it and make it false. Lay a modern map before the first settlers at Jamestown and Plymouth, and then bid them discover and occupy the continent. With how superior a nineteenth-century wonder and pity will you see them grope, and stumble, and falter! How like children they will seem to you, and how simple their age, and ignorant! As stalwart men as you they were in fact; mayhap wiser and braver too; as fit to occupy a continent as you are to draw it upon paper. If you would know them, go back to their age; breed yourself a pioneer and woodsman; look to find the South Sea up the nearest northwest branch of the spreading river at your feet; discover and occupy the wilderness with them; dream what may be beyond the near hills, and long all day to see a sail upon the silent sea; go back to them and see them in their habit as they lived.

The picturesque writers of history have all along been right in theory: they have been wrong only in practice. It *is* a picture of the past we want—its express image and feature; but we want the true picture and not simply the theatrical matter—the manner of Rembrandt rather than of Rubens. All life may be pictured, but not all of life is picturesque. No great, no true historian would put false or adventitious colors into his narrative, or let a glamour rest where in fact it never was. The writers who select an incident merely because it is striking or dramatic are shallow fellows. They see only with the eye's retina, not with that deep vision whose images lie where thought and reason sit. The real drama of life is disclosed only with the whole picture; and that only the deep and fervid student will see, whose mind goes daily fresh to the details, whose narrative runs always in the authentic colors of nature, whose art it is to see and to paint what he sees.

It is thus, and thus only, we shall have the truth of the matter: by art—by the most difficult of all arts; by fresh study and first-hand vision; at the mouths of men who stand in the midst of old letters and dusty documents and neglected records, not like antiquarians, but like those who see a distant country and a far-away people before their very eyes, as real, as full of life and hope and incident as the day in which they themselves live. Let us have done with humbug and come to plain speech. The historian needs an imagination quite as much as he needs scholarship, and consummate literary art as much as candor and common honesty. Histories are written in order that the bulk of men may read and realize; and it is as bad to bungle the telling of the story as to lie, as fatal to lack a vocabulary as to lack knowledge. In no case can you do more than convey an impression, so various and complex is the matter. If you convey a false impression, what difference does it make how you convey it? In the whole process there is a nice adjustment of means to ends which only the artist can manage. There is an art of lying; there is equally an art—an infinitely more difficult art—of telling the truth.

Woodrow Wilson.

Printed in the *Century Magazine*, L (Sept. 1895), 787-93.

## From Andrew Fleming West

Princeton, New Jersey,

Dear Professor Wilson:                    June 19th, 1895.

As Secretary of the Sesquicentennial Celebration Committee, I have the pleasure of conveying to you the desire and request of the Trustees of the College of New Jersey that you will deliver the Oration (on Princeton's part in the American Revolution and in framing our National Constitution) at the approaching Sesquicentennial Celebration. The time appointed for the Oration is Wednesday morning, October 21st, 1896.[1]

Ever truly yours,    Andrew F. West

TLS (WP, DLC) with WWhw notation on env.: "Ans. 20 July, 1895."

[1] For the earlier planning for the Sesquicentennial of the College of New Jersey, see the Princeton Faculty Minutes, Oct. 26, 1892, n. 1, Vol. 8. Acting under the authority of a resolution approved by the Board of Trustees on February 14, 1895, President Patton, in early March 1895, appointed most of the members of a new and enlarged Committee on the Sesquicentennial Celebration, headed by Charles

E. Green and broadly representative of the trustees, faculty, and alumni. Wilson was a member of this committee. It held its first meeting at Princeton on March 14, 1895, elected West as permanent secretary, and conducted other preliminary business. Following this meeting, the subcommittee on the program, of which West was also the secretary, drew up a program on May 11, 1895, which was adopted by the full Sesquicentennial Committee on June 10, 1895, and approved by the Board of Trustees two days later. Patton later said that he had nominated Wilson as the Sesquicentennial orator. (F. L. Patton to C. H. McCormick, April 4, 1898, Vol. 10.) Wilson's reply of July 20, 1895, to West, accepting the committee's invitation, is missing. Wilson's Sesquicentennial address, "Princeton in the Nation's Service," is printed at Oct. 21, 1896, Vol. 10.

# A News Report of a Commencement Address at Oberlin College

[June 20, 1895]

### COMMENCEMENT DAY.

The old-time commencement day with thirty or forty speeches by the graduates has passed into history, but the attraction still seems to be sufficient to call in a full house and hold the people to the close. Prof. Woodrow Wilson of Princeton College delivered the oration on Wednesday [June 19], taking for his theme "Leaders of Men."[1] A nice distinction was made between the capabilities for leadership of the orator and the writer, the weight of the argument according to the speaker, being on the side of the orator. The address was a fine discussion of the elements which go to make up a leader of men, and incidentally a number of ethical points were discussed. Prof. Wilson is a gentleman of excellent physical proportions and voice, and his language is clear cut and of a high literary style. . . .

Printed in the *Oberlin News*, June 20, 1895.
[1] This address is printed at June 17, 1890, Vol. 6. Wilson had been invited by vote of the senior class, as was the Oberlin custom of that day, to deliver the commencement address.

# From Franklin William Hooper

My dear Professor Wilson:          Brooklyn, June 20th, 1895.

Your very kind letter of June 14 is received, in which you inquire whether we could have your lectures given on Saturday evenings as conveniently as on Thursday evenings.

In reply I beg leave to say that it would not be advantageous to us to have your lectures given on Saturday evenings. We should not secure nearly so large audiences and the quality of the audiences would not be as good on Saturday as on Thursday evenings.

It is possible for us to place your lectures on Saturday evenings and we would prefer to have them on Saturdays rather than to lose them altogether.

I trust that you will be able to so arrange your work that you can conveniently come to Brooklyn on Thursday evenings. If, however, it will inconvenience you over-much we can give way to oblige you.[1]

Very cordially yours,   Franklin W. Hooper.

TLS (WP, DLC).
[1] See the Editorial Note, "Wilson's Lectures on Great Leaders of Political Thought."

## To Ellen Axson Wilson

My darling,                     New York, Monday, 24 June [1895]

Here is the proper power of attorney, filled out, and dated the 25th, to-morrow[.] Sign it, and acknowledge it, before a notary, as before, and then send it with the Certificate of Indebtedness (whose *number* insert in the blank space I have left in the Power of Att'y), by registered mail, to The Mercantile Trust Co., 120 Broadway, New York. That will complete the business for us.[1]

I cannot get an outside stateroom on the boat, and shall therefore take the 3 o'clock train from the Grand Central Station.[2]

Am quite well and love you *painfully*.

Your own   Woodrow

ALS (WP, DLC).
[1] The Wilsons were undoubtedly borrowing on short term from the Mercantile Trust Company of New York, using Ellen's bonds as collateral, until the Mutual Life Insurance Company's payments were to begin.
[2] Wilson was on his way to deliver the commencement address at Wellesley College on June 25.

## From Frederick Gordon Burnham

Dear Sir:                       Newark, N. J.  June 24, 1895

I have your favor of the 24th inst. The rule in regard to the interest upon Mutual Life mortgages is that the borrower pays interest only from the date of the check as signed and not from the date of the bond and mortgage. In your case therefore interest will be charged upon each installment from the day the check is drawn by the Company, and as the payment will be made immediately to you why you will be out of pocket the interest on that amount but a day or so, merely during the transmission of the check to you. If you can wait for the first payment until shortly after the first of July you can then change the date of the bond and mortgage to the first of July instead of some day in

June and the interest days will then be first days of July and January.

I see no other way to accede to your request without violating the rules of the Company.

If you will kindly date the papers and then acknowledge them on or after July 1st and sent ehm [them] back here, the first installment of $2000 will be obtained as soon as can be after receiving yours.

Very truly yours,   F. G. Burnham [per] G.

TLS (WP, DLC).

## A Newspaper Report of Commencement Exercises

[June 26, 1895]

### WELLESLEY GIRLS.

Wellesley, June 25.–The 17th annual commencement at Wellesley College today called out such a grand crush that many had to stand in the corridor outside the hall, disappointed and dejected. For a time the great crowd at the door was composed of many of the Wellesley girls who declared that in the course of their collegiate existence they had never yet attended a commencement, and on this occasion they hoped to "manage it," but as the crowd increased the leader and spokesman finally raised herself on tiptoe and addressed the coterie: "Well, girls, we'd better give it up, and let the fathers and mothers have a chance." So they gracefully slipped away, and the outsiders crowded to the door, guarded by white-robed ushers bearing white wands tied with blue ribbon.

Inside the hall was systematically packed in every square inch. Upon the platform were seated Mrs. Durrant,[1] Dr. Alex. McKenzie, president of the board of trustees, who presided over the exercises; Mrs. Julia Josephine Irvine,[2] who was seated at the centre of the front of the stage; Prof. Margaret Eliza Stratton[3] and the speaker of the day, Woodrow Wilson, Ph.D., LL.D. Others on the platform were the trustees and faculty, while the Beethoven Choral Society occupied the rear of the stage.

Just in front were seated the 127 graduates in dainty white gowns and roses in profusion. After the organ prelude by Prof. J. W. Hill,[4] came the reading of the scriptures and prayer.

The Beethoven Society then rendered with fine expression St Saens "Now Gentle Spring Her Flowers."

The address by Woodrow Wilson of Princeton was listened to with keenest attention, for the subject, "Political Liberty," was treated with a breadth and fineness of feeling which appealed to all. He said in part:—

"Liberty is a word of enthusiasm, hope and heroism, and yet liberty is a principle of license and folly. It is a difficult thing to speculate about, and to enjoy liberty. The nations who have enjoyed liberty have not speculated about it. In France they have said most about liberty and know it the least. Can it be that it destroys liberty to speculate about it? When we wish to be most ourselves, self-consciousness breaks the charm. Liberty is a thing to have, not to speculate upon. We sometimes think that the looser we are from binding ties, the more at liberty one is. It is not so; the freest engine is the best adjusted one. The moment I defy controlling forces the more I am controlled. We master nature by understanding her. Liberty consists in a certain sort of a negation of the general acceptance of the general meaning of the word. It is, in a person, always reserved strength, or restraint, which we admire, and not the absence of restraint. Liberty belongs to mature years and not to youth. That is the one compensation in growing old—that we lose ourselves in doing for others and so come into perefct [perfect] harmony with humanity, and your own soul grows larger and stronger for the reason of the masse with which you move. Political liberty consists in restraint. Our safety depends on our knowledge beforehand; on a general understanding of what we can or cannot do.

"One thing a college should be warned about. A college is not a representative of mankind. Collegians are ready to believe that things are true which have never been heard of. The mass of mankind will not follow the becoming spirit, but must go slow-footed and slow-witted. The socialist proposes that society shall mould the individual—which is the opposite that experience has taught us.

"It is in society that the individual reaches his highest development. Common strength and individual initiative are the two principles of true progress."

When the Beethoven Society had sung "Sing Softly, O Sirens," by Boits, and "The Golden-haired May," by Johns, Dr. McKenzie arose and, after acknowledging the excellent work done by Mrs. Irvine during the past year, announced that she had accepted the presidency of Wellesley College. Mrs. Irvine's popularity was strongly testified to by long continued applause, which compelled her to repeatedly bow acknowledgment.

When quiet again reigned Dr. McKenzie announced that Prof. Margaret Eliza Stratton, professor of English, who had so ably assisted Mrs. Irvine during the past year, had been made dean of the college, an office which, for the first time, has been created. This announcement was also received with great demonstrations of delight. The benediction was followed by the organ postlude, Overture to "Alessandro Stradella," by Flotow, brilliantly played by Prof. J. W. Hills.

The alumnae dinner immediately followed. Mrs. Irvine presided, and cordially welcomed all the guests of her hostess, Mrs. Durrant, who sat at her right. Dr. McKenzie was the first after-dinner speaker. He paid a charming tribute to Mrs. Durrant, then said it was 25 years since the board of trustees were organized, and that he was proud of the fact that the three presidents of Wellesley had all been chosen from their ranks, and that four of the college were on the board of trustees.

Dr. N. G. Clarke, LL.D.,[5] spoke entertainingly. His theme was: "How to get the most out of everything and the best out of everybody." Woodrow Wilson made a bright speech and amusingly introduced himself by saying that he felt not at all strange because he had been connected with institutions for young ladies before. In fact he felt as though an epitaph similar to the one he once read would be apropriate: "This is cacred [sacred] to the memory of Jane Collier, who was a faithful and loving wife to the following persons."

As the day faded the class ode was sung.

At 8 o'clock the reception was held in the Browning room. In the great square near the central square of palms the orchestra was stationed. Mrs. Durrant, Mrs. Irvine, Prof. Stratton and members of the graduating class received.[6]

Printed in the *Boston Daily Advertiser*, June 26, 1895; one editorial heading omitted.

[1] Pauline Adeline (Mrs. Henry Fowle) Durant, widow of the founder of Wellesley College.

[2] Professor of Greek Language and Literature, who had become Acting President on the death of Helen Almira Shafer on January 20, 1894. Mrs. Irvine, widow of Charles James Irvine, became President, as this report indicates, at the end of the academic year 1894-95 and served until 1899.

[3] Margaret Elizabeth Stratton, Professor of the English Language and Rhetoric and Dean of the College.

[4] Junius Welch Hill, Professor of Music and Director of the School of Music.

[5] The Rev. Dr. Nathaniel G. Clark, member of the Board of Trustees and Secretary of the American Board of Commissioners of Foreign Missions.

[6] For another report of Wilson's addresses, see the *Wellesley Magazine*, III (June 29, 1895), 502-503.

# From Frederick Gordon Burnham

Dear Sir:                              Newark, N. J.   June 27th 1895.
Yours of the 26th inst. is received. Besides changing the date of the bond and mortgage, change the date of the payment of interest in them to the First days of January and July, or if you prefer, and will return them to my office, I will have it done here and return them to you.

Very Truly Yours,   Fred G Burnham

TLS (WP, DLC).

# From Henry Mills Alden[1]

Dear Sir                              New York. June 28, 1895
Would it be convenient to you to contribute to our Magazine a few articles on General Washington for publication next year? I know that you are now absorbed by historical studies relating to an earlier period,—otherwise I should have written to you before. There is now a growing popular demand for an adequate view of Washington's place in American history. I know of no one who can do this, for our purpose, as well as you, & at the risk of interrupting your present work, I wish you would meet the present demand.

The articles need not follow each other uninterru[p]tedly. We would like the first one—which would probably be about the state of the country, especially in Virginia, from 1750 to 1775, considered as the matrix of the hero—for publication in our January number, if possible. This would give you two months for its preparation. It should not exceed from 10,000 to 12,000 words in length: & all the papers should be of about this length—each having an independent status; thus, e.g., Washington's relation to our Western Country might be the subject of one paper.

There should not be more than six papers altogether. We would pay you three hundred dollars for each, if furnished at intervals of two months, beginning with Sept. 1, 1895. Kindly let me know at your earliest convenience if our proposition & its terms are acceptable to you.[2]

Yours sincerely   H. M. Alden   Edr Harper's Magazine

ALS (WP, DLC).
  [1] Born at Mt. Tabor, Vt., Nov. 11, 1836. A.B., Williams College, 1857. Was graduated from Andover Theological Seminary in 1860 but was never ordained. Managing editor, *Harper's Weekly*, 1863-69; editor, *Harper's Magazine*, 1869-1919. Author of several books and some poetry. Died Oct. 7, 1919.
  [2] Although Wilson's reply is missing, it is clear that he accepted with alacrity. The six essays were "In Washington's Day," *Harper's Magazine*, XCII (Jan. 1896),

168-89; "Colonel Washington," *ibid.*, March 1896, pp. 549-73; "At Home in Virginia," *ibid.*, May 1896, pp. 931-54; "General Washington," *ibid.*, XCIII (July 1896), 165-90; "First in Peace," *ibid.*, Sept. 1896, pp. 489-512; and "The First President of the United States," *ibid.*, Nov. 1896, pp. 843-67.

The ensuing correspondence in this volume fully illustrates Wilson's research methods and progress in writing these articles. The small groups of notes in the Wilson Papers, Library of Congress, and in the Charles L. Swem Collection of Wilsoniana in the Library of Princeton University seem to be the only ones that Wilson took while writing on George Washington. These notes, written on long cards, consist mainly of chronologies and outlines of events.

## A Report of an Address

[June 30, 1895]

### SUMMER MEETING TO PURSUE STUDIES

The opening session of the University Extension Summer Meeting was held in the library building of the University of Pennsylvania, Thirty-fourth and Walnut streets, last evening. Professor Edmund L. [J.] James, Ph.D., presided. An address of welcome was made by Professor W. A. Lamberton[1] on behalf of the University. The inaugural address was delivered by Dr. Woodrow Wilson, of Princeton University. His subject was "Democracy."[2] This address strikes the keynote of the entire meeting, as one of its most important departments is that of civics and politics. . . .

The school this year bids fair to be a great success. About 170 students have already enrolled, coming from different parts of the country—Pennsylvania, New Jersey, New York, Virginia, Maryland, North Carolina, Arkansas, Iowa and Louisiana. . . .

Printed in the *Philadelphia Inquirer*, June 30, 1895; some editorial headings omitted.

[1] William Alexander Lamberton, Professor of Greek Language and Literature.

[2] For this address, Wilson used the text printed at Dec. 5, 1891, Vol. 7. A long abstract appeared in the Philadelphia *Citizen*, 1 (August 1895), 144-45.

## To Walter Hines Page

My dear Mr. Page,              Princeton, New Jersey, 4 July, 1895.

I was very much startled to get this morning the notice that you had resigned the editorship of the *Forum*.[1] I thought that you had the magazine at last practically in your own control, and I had expected to see you make a very notable success in running it altogether in accordance with your own ideas. I am sincerely sorry to see you give it up. All thoughtful men must have admired the way in which you conducted it, and elevated it to a place of authority; and I know that I shall not be alone in deploring your loss from the editorial chair.

With warm regard,

Sincerely Yours,   Woodrow Wilson

WWTLS (W. H. Page Papers, MH).

1 Page had just resigned the editorship of the New York *Forum* following the failure of his attempt to gain financial control of the Forum Publishing Company. See Burton J. Hendrick, *The Training of an American: The Earlier Life and Letters of Walter H. Page, 1855-1913* (Boston and New York, 1928), pp. 227-32.

## From Frederick Gordon Burnham

Dear Sir:                    Newark, N. J.  July 5, 1895

I enclose check of The Mutual Life Ins. Co. of New York to your order for $2000. being on account of your loan of $7000. from the Mutual Life. This check is sent to you with the understanding that you are to send me within a day or two a certificate from the architect showing the cost of the building in process of erection and also that you send me a release of mechanics liens for all labor performed and material furnished up to the present time. No insurance is required by the company at this time but when another payment is made the company will require a policy of insurance. Kindly acknowledge receipt of check and oblige

Very truly yours,   F G Burnham

TLS (WP, DLC).

## From Child and de Goll, Architects

Dear Sir:                    New York. July 8, 1895,

I enclose you a certificate as requested in your favor of the 6th of July. You will have to have Mr Wright get you a release of liens from the people who have dug the cellar, which I understand is all the work which has been done at present.

I think it is distinctly understood about the height of the first story joists, but I will write again to Mr Wright so that it will be on record.

The clause in regard to plaster showing in first story to have champfered edge and head should read: "Plaster *arches* showing in the first story to have champfered edge and head." I was quite puzzled by this clause myself until I read the original specifications. In the typewriting work the word "arch" was omitted. I will also call the contractor's attention in writing to this.

Yours truly,   Child & de Goll

TLS (WP, DLC).

## From Josiah Worth Wright

Dear Sir,                               Princeton July 9th 1895
I enclose you a bill receipted for change in beams of second floor in your house, as now a part of the specifications, viz from 2 x 10 to 2 x 12. I find the difference to be about 1650 feet. The addition[al] cost of timber alone will make the amount charged. The work & freight &c will be a little more. But I have made it even twenty five dollars. You may either send me a check for this, or something that will show that you owe the amount.
                    Most Resp. yours   J. W. Wright

P.S. Would it not be best to defer the release until the 1st floor of beams are on? As this will be a fair release for the interested parties, against liens at the time the first payment is made, this will be in about ten days or two weeks. I will do as you think best. The parties might be informed that there is really nothing at present on the premises to release.
    And at the time I have 1st tier of beams on, I can release everything up to that time.            Yours truly   J. W. W.

ALS (WP, DLC). Enc.: J. W. Wright to WW, July 9, 1895, ALS (WP, DLC).


## To Henry Mills Alden

My dear Mr. Alden,        Princeton, New Jersey, 12 July, 1895.
    Thank you very much for your cordial letter,[1] and for its encouraging words, which have heartened me not a little. I can work all the better for your appreciation.
    I think that illustrations would be very helpful to the series, if they were made truly illustrative. The first article, for example, will treat of the general situation of things in the colonies during Washington's boyhood and youth: the state of the colonies; the circumstances of French exploration and settlement which were slowly bringing the rivalry of the two nations to a critical stage; British colonial and commercial policy; colonial politics; the contrasts between the northern, the southern, and the middle colonies; etc., etc. I do not suppose that there is much, if indeed there be any, new material for illustrations in connection with such topics; but it would be greatly helpful to the reader's imagination if we could have a sketch map of half a page, say, showing French exploration and the French posts about 1750; views of Boston, Quebec, Williamsburg, and New Orleans some time between 1732 and 1750; portraits of one or two contemporary French and English colonial governors; pictures of contemporary

English sea craft, etc. These are hasty suggestions, of course; but I could develop them carefully if you wished. Much of the sort of thing we should want we have a guide to in Winsor's Narrative and Critical History.[2] Mr. Phair[3] would no doubt know just where to lay his hand on such things. Of course the making of a book out of these papers is a matter for subsequent negotiation;[4] but, in case such a book should be decided on, such illustrations would add immensely, I should suppose, to its popular sale.

My ideas are forming slowly, but I hope surely, for the work; and I hope soon to "have way on," as the sailors say. The importance of such a task, undertaken thus after so many capable men have gone over the ground so carefully, gives me pause: but it is a tonic rather than a deterrent.

With much regard,

Most sincerely Yours, Woodrow Wilson

WWTLS (Berg Coll., NN).
[1] It is missing.
[2] Justin Winsor (ed.), *Narrative and Critical History of America* (8 vols., Boston and New York, 1884-89).
[3] John F. Phayre, a long-time employee of Harper and Brothers.
[4] Wilson's articles were published as *George Washington* (New York, 1896).

## A News Item

[July 13, 1895]

Professor Woodrow Wilson's new residence in Library Place is making good progress.[1] The foundation is finished and shows the ground plan of a spacious dwelling.

Printed in the *Princeton Press*, July 13, 1895.
[1] Ground had been broken on about June 10. See EAW to WW, June 4, 1896.

## From Henry Mills Alden

Isles of Shoals

My dear Mr. Wilson, Off Portsmouth N. H. Aug. 10. 1895

Your letter[1] was sent to me here where I am having my vacation. I have asked my assistant Mr Adams[2] to make a thorough search for the book you wish. He will find much difficulty because the Lenox & other large libraries are closed, but he will do the best he can & report to you. He will also consult you more fully as to illustrations for your first paper—beyond the indications given in your letter relating to that matter: i.e. as to subjects for some really effective pictures. Or an engraving [of] one of Peale's portraits for frontispiece to the January No.

Yours sincerely H. M. Alden

ALS (WP, DLC).
  [1] Wilson's letter is missing.
  [2] John Davis Adams, assistant editor of *Harper's Magazine*, 1891-96.

## From John Davis Adams

My dear Sir:                              New York. August 19, 1895
  Thank you for your suggestions regarding the illustration of your first article on Washington.[1] Mr. Alden has already seen some of them and directed that they be carried out. I will show him the others on his return this week.

  A copy of *Harpers Magazine* for May 1891[2] will be mailed to your address to-day.     Yours very truly    John D. Adams.

ALS (WP, DLC).
  [1] Wilson's letter is missing.
  [2] Wilson had asked for a copy of this issue because it contained an article by Moncure D. Conway on the English ancestry of Washington.


## Two Letters from Henry Mills Alden

Dear Mr. Wilson:                          New York. August 21, 1895.
  I have secured from Mr. Pyle[1] the promise to undertake illustrations for your papers on Washington. We must move rapidly with those for your first paper. I infer from a telegram just received from Mr. Pyle that he can meet you next Sunday and get from you *motifs* for three or four effective drawings for that paper. Will it be convenient for you to see him on that day?

  Please telegraph *Yes* or *No* (in the latter case appointing earliest day you can meet him).

                              Yours sincerely,    H. M. Alden

  [1] Howard Pyle, born in Wilmington, Del., March 5, 1853. Attended Quaker schools in Wilmington and studied for three years with a Flemish art teacher, Van der Weilen, in Philadelphia. Pyle went to New York in 1876, where he taught himself the art of illustration and gradually worked his way into the growing field of illustrating popular magazines. His first successful picture appeared in *Harper's Weekly*, March 9, 1878. He returned to Wilmington in 1880, where he lived and maintained his studio for the rest of his life. From 1894 to 1900 he conducted a class in illustration at the Drexel Institute in Philadelphia; in 1900 he established his own art school in Wilmington. Pyle specialized in delineating the characters and events of early American history in pen and ink drawings, the accuracy of which was established by much background reading. His illustrations for Wilson's Washington essays and book and Wilson's *A History of the American People* (5 vols., New York and London, 1902) are considered classics of their kind. Died Nov. 9, 1911.


Dear Sir:                                 New York. August 23rd., 1895.
  We are sending you to-day, by Adams Express, the edition of 1840 of the papers of Colonel Bird.[1]

We have promised the librarian of Columbia College to return the volume in two weeks.

Sincerely yours, H. M. Alden

TLS (WP, DLC).

[1] Presumably this was Edmund Ruffin (ed.), *The Westover Manuscripts* (Petersburg, Va., 1841).

QUOTATION. (Byrd).

Washington.

(fr. Fredericksburg)

(fr. Petersburg) King

On the other side of the river, in ~~Stg~~ George County, not far from a "spring of strong steel water, as good as any at Tunbridge Wells" "are England's Iron Mines, called so from the chief manager of them, though the land belongs to Mr. Washington. [1652, Augustine.] These mines are two miles from the furnace, and Mr. Washington raises the ore, and carts it hither for 20 s. the tun of iron that it yields. The furnace is built on a run, which discharges its waters into Potomac. And when the iron is cast, they cart it about six miles to a landing on that river. Besides Mr. Washington and Mr. England, there are several other persons, in England, concerned in these works. Matters are very well managed there, and no expense is spared to make them profitable." (Byrd MSS., II, 72, 73).

*One of Wilson's research note cards for his first article on George Washington, "In Washington's Day"*

# From Lyon Gardiner Tyler[1]

My dear Mr. Wilson, Williamsburg, Va., Sept 2 1895

I take pleasure in replying to your enquiries of Aug 28.,[2] though I fear I can add very little to your stock of knowledge.

In relation to the first question I think that the evidence referred to in the last Quarterly[3] established beyond cavil the fact that Col. John Washington did have 3 wives and that he reached Virginia in 1656. This agrees very nearly with George Washington's own account, who puts it "in 1657 or thereabouts"

Why Dindwiddie picked Washington out in the first instance was due, I think, to his being already the Major of that District in which he lived. This position was obtained for him, I suppose[,] by his brother Lawrence and Col. Fairfax, who knew his ability. Then besides being adjutant general and Major he was known to Dinwiddie as a surveyor best acquainted with the region of country towards the Ohio. He had been over every inch of the ground in the employment of Lord Fairfax

*The Ball letter.* I refer you to Hayden's Genealogies,[4] under

"Ball Family," where the letter is given much fuller than in Meade.[5] It is taken from the Letter Book of Joseph Ball. I do not think there is any *tradition* about George proposing to go to sea. Sea-faring stood in high repute, and all the early settlers were more or less seamen. Sparks[6] (vol I, p. II) has an extract from a letter of a Mr. Jackson, a friend of the family on the same subject. The journals (published by Dr. Toner)[7] in 1747-48, 1751, 1754 are probably the best sources for an insight into Washington's character. Then Moncure Conway's "Barons of the Potomac and Rappahannock"[8] might be read to advantage for the early boyhood of the General.

As to the Byrd MSS. I can only refer you to J. H. Whitty[9] of Richmond, Va, who is very much interested in the collection of Virginia books.

I wish you much success in presenting Washington's character to the public

With kind regards I am

Lyon G. Tyler.

ALS (WP, DLC) with WWhw notes on env.
[1] President of the College of William and Mary, proprietor and editor of the *William and Mary College Quarterly Historical Magazine*, and son of President John Tyler.
[2] This letter is missing.
[3] Lyon G. Tyler, "Washington and His Neighbors," *William and Mary College Quarterly Historical Magazine*, IV (July 1895), 28-43.
[4] Horace Edwin Hayden, *Virginia Genealogies* (Wilkes-Barre, Pa., 1891).
[5] William Meade, *Old Churches, Ministers and Families of Virginia* (2 vols., Philadelphia, 1857).
[6] Jared Sparks (ed.), *The Writings of George Washington . . . with a Life of the Author* (12 vols., Boston, 1834-37).
[7] Joseph M. Toner (ed.), *Journal of My Journey Over the Mountains* (Albany, N. Y., 1892), *The Daily Journal of Major George Washington, in 1751-2 . . .* (Albany, N. Y., 1892), and *Journal of Colonel George Washington . . . in 1754 . . .* (Albany, N. Y., 1893).
[8] Moncure D. Conway, *Barons of the Potomack and the Rappahannock* (New York, 1892).
[9] James Howard Whitty, assistant to Joseph Bryan, president of the Richmond *Times*.

## From James Howard Whitty

Dear Professor—                    Richmond, Va. Sept 6, 1895.

Mr. Bruce[1] of the Historical Society mentioned that you were anxious to secure a copy of Wm Byrds "Dividing Line" or as we call it down here the "Westover Papers" 1866[2]

I have a duplicate number but fear it may be more expensive than what you are looking for.

It is one of 200 & uncut & handsomely bound. It stood me about $25 and I had intended holding at $40. at which price similar copies have been sold here. If you care for it at $25 I will be pleased to send you or if price is high I will keep on the lookout for a cheaper copy for you. It is in 2 vols & they are very rare now

If you have any duplicate books touching Virginia I would be glad to exchange with you. I prefer to exchange when possible

Yrs truly   J. H. Whitty

ALS (WP, DLC) with WWhw notation on env.: "Ans 7 Sept., 1895."
  [1] Philip Alexander Bruce, historian of Virginia and corresponding secretary and librarian of the Virginia Historical Society in Richmond.
  [2] William Byrd, *History of the Dividing Line, and Other Tracts*, Thomas H. Wynne, ed. (2 vols., Richmond, 1866).

## To Henry Mills Alden

My dear Mr. Alden,     Princeton, New Jersey, 6 September, 1895.

I have not heard from Mr. Pyle since he was here, but take it for granted he has sent you the first of the Washington papers.

You will be glad to know that I hope to send you the second paper by the first of October, so that the matter of illustration may not be quite so straitened for time in it and the papers to follow.

May I trouble you to obtain another book for me? It is Moncure Conway's "Barons of the Potomac and Rappahannock." It was published in 1892 by the Grolier Club. It is quite out of my reach; but I hope you can induce some library to lend it to me.

With much regard,

Most sincerely Yours,   Woodrow Wilson

WWTLS (NBuU).

## To James Howard Whitty

My dear Sir,          Princeton, New Jersey, 7 September, 1895

Your kind letter of Sept. 6 reached me this morning, and I hasten to reply.

I must thank you very heartily for your offer of the "Westover Papers" to me at $25.00 The sum is large for my purse; but it is small, even generously small, on your part, and I make a special effort to pay it,—in part to show my appreciation of your liberality, as well as because I need the book in my historical work.

You will find enclosed my check for twenty-five dollars ($25.00). I should be obliged if you would send the volumes by express.

I am sorry to say I have no duplicates that would be worth your while. My little collection of books is of a very irregular kind: for I buy as I write, and only such books as our college library cannot supply me with.

With renewed expressions of my appreciation of your generous courtesy,

Most sincerely Yours,   Woodrow Wilson

ALS (in possession of Gilbert J. Tilbury).

## From James Howard Whitty

Dear Professor—                Richmond, Va. Sept 9th 1895

Yours 7th to hand, enclosing check $25.00 for the 2 vols of "Westover Papers[.]" I send them to your address by Adams Express this day prepaid. They are in most excellent condition and bound by the best binder in the South.

What is the work you have in preparation & when will it be ready.

I will want to see it & if possible to help you with anything I have. Will be glad to do so. I have perhaps one of the most complete libraries on Virginia in the state. Altho a Marylander by birth my specialty takes a turn for Virginia.

Yrs truly   J. H. Whitty

The Va Historical Society has Wm Byrds *Letter book* containing much interesting matter. I have his *stock book* & perhaps they may have something of interest to you. *"His Great Self"* by Marian Harlan[1] is a history of Byrd & his times (Romantic)

ALS (WP, DLC) with WWhw notation on env.: "Ans. 18 Sept. 1895."
  [1] Marion Harland [Mary Virginia Hawes Terhune], *His Great Self* (Philadelphia, 1892).

## From Josiah Worth Wright

Dear Sir,                Princeton  Sept 10th 1895

I have figured over the work we were considering yesterday and find the following:

New stair case from 2d floor to attic. Floor in attic 14 feet wide the whole length, and 14 feet wide in front gable to center floor.

Two partitions of studding along the entire length of attic, raising main roof 2 ft higher at peak.        $154.00

I find we can easily get two rooms in each large gable if needed. We can get one in each with level ceiling of 7 ft 8 each.

Very truly   J. W. Wright

ALS (WP, DLC).

## To Howard Pyle

My dear Mr. Pyle,      Princeton, New Jersey, 11 September, 1895.

Two frigates were sent out to reduce Virginia to the Commonwealth, under the command of Capt. Robert Dennis; and Thomas Steg, Wm. Clayborne, and Richard Bennet were named as commissioners to act with Capt. Dennis. But Dennis and his ship, with Steg aboard, were lost on the voyage. Only *three* commissioners acted in Virginia: Captain Edmond Curtis of the remaining frigate (as substitute for Capt. Dennis), Clayborne, and Bennet.

I have never seen a portrait of any one of these three, I am sorry to say: and I think if portraits existed they would have been reproduced in some one of the books I have.

In haste,          Sincerely Yours,   Woodrow Wilson

P.S. Since writing the above, I find a cut of Clayborne in Appleton's Cyclop. of American Biography, vol. I, p. 620.

WWTLS (deCoppet Coll., NjP).

## From the Minutes of the Princeton Faculty

3 P.M., Wednesday, Sep. 18, 1895.

The College was opened in the Chapel with with [sic] the reading of the Scriptures, an address and prayer by the President after which the Faculty met.

The Remit from the Board of Trustees was read. The portion of it referring to the appointment of the Proctor as a State Constable by the Governor was referred to the Faculty Committee on Discipline.

Upon the report of the Dean and the recommendation of the Committee on Discipline, ——, a member of the Freshman Class in the School of Science, who near the end of the last term entered the room of a servant for illicit purposes, was finally dismissed from College. . . .

## From James Howard Whitty

Dear Professor—          Richmond, Va. Sept 19, 1895.

I have read yours 18th[1] & am pleased to know that the books reached you safely. I have given but little attention to Washingtonia, but have two books you should read. Most likely you have them or have read. McGuires "Religious Opinions & Character of Washington,"[2] & Phillip Slaughters "Christianity the key to character & career of Washington."[3] I would take pleasure in sending them to you for as long a period as you desire[.] The "Fairfax Family" by Neill[4] has some material in it, but I imagine matter on order of "Slaughters" would be of much interest & what you want. As I go along & find anything it will be a pleasure to advise with you.

I am a large collector of Virginia Americana & am constantly hearing of works I knew nothing about previously—only showing that we can & do learn something every day.

When you get into your history of the United States I may be of more assistance.                Yrs truly   J. H. Whitty

ALS (WP, DLC).
[1] Wilson's letter is missing.
[2] Edward Charles M'Guire, *The Religious Opinions and Character of Washington* (New York, 1836).
[3] Philip Slaughter, *Christianity the Key to the Character and Career of Washington* (New York, 1886).
[4] Edward Duffield Neill, *The Fairfaxes of England and America in the Seventeenth and Eighteenth Centuries* (Albany, N. Y., 1868).

## From Henry Mills Alden

Dear Mr. Wilson:                New York. Sept. 20, 1895.
    Your manuscript of "In Washington's Day" was received in good time from Mr. Pyle. Proofs will be sent to you in a day or two.

Mr. Bangs[1] wishes me to assure you that his copy of the "Barons of the Potomac and Rappahannock" may be returned at your convenience.

I am desirous of obtaining a map showing the condition of colonial America at the period best suited to the illustration of your first paper; you are the best judge of what that time is. Do you know any one who could prepare under your direction a page map for the MAGAZINE, showing the English colonies, Canada, Florida and Louisiana? If you think best Louisiana might be given in a separate map. Of course this work would be done at our expense. We could wait until November first for the drawing.
                Very truly yours,   H. M. Alden

TLS (WP, DLC).
[1] Probably John Kendrick Bangs, who at this time was on the staff of *Harper's Magazine*.

## From the Minutes of the Princeton Faculty

                12 5′ P.M., Saturday, Sep. 21st, 1895
    . . . On recommendation of Dis. Com. Resolved, That for intoxication on the Campus on the Monday of Commencement

Week Mr. —— (S. Sci. '98) be not allowed to return to College at present. Resolved, That for participation in the practice of procuring kegs of beer and drinking in the outskirts of the town Mr. —— (Sc. Sci. '98) be suspended from College for four weeks, Sep. 28th to Oct. 26th.

## From Annie Wilson Howe

My darling brother,     Philadelphia Oct. 5th 1895

I have waited until you were better, before troubling you with my affairs. I do hope you are feeling much better by this time. I cannot tell you how distressed I was to hear of your illness.

I return the letter from Mr. Dickinson and think that, if you approve, I will take the first one mentioned, for $1300—and will send you the check on the Carolina National Bank. If you do not think it best to send the money, or that it is too late, please let me know.

Silas Duffie wrote me a long letter, as satisfactory as I could wish. I send it to you to read.[1] Do you think I better take the stock?

We are very nearly fixed in our new home.[2] I will take my time about the rest of the work.

I will not worry you with a long letter. Give a great deal of love to dear Ellie—love to the children, and a heart full for your dear self.    Your devoted sister, Annie.

I sent the sofa and organ off, yesterday. I am afraid you will find both sadly damaged.

ALS (WP, DLC). Enc.: J. Dickinson & Co., per Samuel Dickinson, to WW, Sept. 28, 1895, TLS (WP, DLC).

[1] This enclosure is missing.

[2] She had moved to 424 North 33rd Street, Philadelphia, to be with her son, James Wilson Howe.

## From Howard Pyle

Dear Professor Wilson:  Wilmington, Del., October 5th., 1895.

I have put off answering your letter thinking to reply to you in a more personal manner. But I know such a busy man as yourself will excuse the necessity that compels another busy man to write in this way.

I was extremely sorry to hear of your illness and hope it may not be anything serious. As for your article, I dare say we can manage to make the illustrations for it even without having the text fairly in hand. If you will let me know what point you intend to treat in this second article, I will look up authorities and make a sketch or two which I will send you so that you may see that they will agree with the text.

I would suggest some such plan as this:—That you tell me the different points you have in mind to touch upon, making a list as you did in the other article. Then I can choose from them three subjects to be illustrated. Of course if you have your article so far arranged that you can make quotations from it, it would be better to give a more particularized idea, but if not I think we can manage quite well if you will give me some general idea of the different subjects.

I would run on to Princeton to see you if it were possible for me to do so just now, and indeed my very delightful, though so short visit, makes me feel very strongly that I would like to renew our brief acquaintance.

I did feel very much the impertinence of criticising your article, and I only came to the conclusion that the two commissioners, representing the Provinces, were not aboard the Parlimentary frigate when I came to study into the matter more closely with the idea of illustration in my mind.

With kindest regards to Mrs Wilson, I am

Very truly yours   Howard Pyle

TLS (WP, DLC).


## To Howard Pyle, with Enclosure

My dear Mr. Pyle,          Princeton, New Jersey, 7 October, 1895.

I have just received your kind letter of Saturday. My illness went deeper than I supposed and has held me in its grip until now. I am still weak; but expect to get to work on the second paper again almost immediately. I am exceedingly sorry for the delay on every account.

Rather than keep you waiting any longer, I enclose my first draft of what I have written. It is unrevised and incomplete, lacking some eight or ten pages, say; but I can send you the rest when it is written, I hope very shortly.

I don't know whether the list of phrases I made last time was of any assistance to you or not, but I venture to send another with this. Pray pardon the rough appearance and execution of the whole thing. If I had a secretary, I would not send it in such shape.

I shall be extremely interested to see your sketches. I expect to like them a great deal better than I like the text.

Hoping that you can make something out of my MSS.,
With much regard,

Most sincerely Yours,    Woodrow Wilson

WWTLS (photostat in RSB Coll., DLC).

List of Phrases.

"In that hospitable country," p. 5.
"Consorting with huntsmen and Indians and traders," p. 10
"Took a turn at the broadsword," p. 11.
"Where lonely boats floated slowly down," p. 14.
"An English lieutenant at Oswego descried the fleet," p. 16.
"It was their absolute design to take possession of the Ohio,"
p. 19.
"Standing there in the drenching downpour," p. 26.

WWT MS. (photostat in RSB Coll., DLC).


## To M. P. Grant[1]

Everett House, Union Square, New York.
My dear Miss Grant,              7 Oct., 1895
I was obliged to bring your letter here to get its answer.

No, there is no mistake about the 20th,—though I don't wonder
you feel nervous about it; and I accept your invitation to stay with
you in Tarrytown with grateful appreciation.

My lectures are still in course of preparation, and there is, as
yet, no printed syllabus; but there soon will be.

The only books (in English) one can recommend with a clear
conscience on Aristotle are Grote's Life of A. and Welldon's translation of the *Politics*.[2]

In haste        Sincerely Yours,    Woodrow Wilson

ALS (deCoppet Coll., NjP).
  [1] Of Tarrytown, N. Y., who presumably had charge of the arrangements for
Wilson's University Extension lectures in that town. About these lectures, see
the Editorial Note which follows.
  [2] George Grote, *Aristotle* (2 vols., London, 1872), and James Edward Cowell
Welldon, trans., *The Politics of Aristotle*, 2nd edn. (London, 1888).

## EDITORIAL NOTE
## WILSON'S LECTURES ON GREAT LEADERS OF
## POLITICAL THOUGHT

Ellen Wilson's letter to Anna Harris of June 1, 1895, reveals that Wilson had just accepted an invitation from the American Society for the Extension of University Teaching to lecture under its auspices during the coming academic year. Wilson's letter to J. Franklin Jameson of November 11, 1895, discloses very candidly the motive behind this decision. Wilson was building a house and needed the $250 that the Extension Society had offered for each series of lectures.[1] At about the same time, Franklin W. Hooper, Director of the Brooklyn Institute of Arts and Sciences, invited him to lecture for a second time at the Institute.[2] Thereupon Wilson decided to give his Extension lectures in Brooklyn on great leaders of political thought and chose Aristotle, Machiavelli, Montesquieu, Burke, de Tocqueville, and Bagehot as his subjects.[3]

At some time during the coming autumn—most probably in early October—Wilson began work on the series, making two preliminary outlines of his lectures on Aristotle.[4] He then drafted detailed outlines of the six lectures very near the date on which he was scheduled to speak at the Brooklyn Institute. His list of subjects, with composition dates when given, follows:

"Aristotle, the Father of Political Science."
"Machiavelli, the Politician of the Renaissance." (Oct. 15, 1895)
"Montesquieu, the French Political Seer." (Oct. 23, 1895)
"Burke, the Interpreter of English Liberty." (Oct. 30, 1895)
"De Tocqueville, the Student of Democracy." (Nov. 5, 1895)
"Bagehot, the Literary Politician." (Nov. 15, 1895)[5]

Soon afterward, Wilson prepared a syllabus (with lecture outlines and recommended reading) for his course, which the Extension Society in Philadelphia printed and distributed to its subscribers.[6]

In preparing notes for his lectures on great leaders of political thought, Wilson of course did not begin *de novo*. For Machiavelli, he had the rather long shorthand outline of a lecture that he had given at Bryn Mawr in 1887.[7] His lecture on Burke was a slightly embellished version of the lecture on the same subject printed at August 31, 1893, Volume 8. And for his lecture on Bagehot, Wilson did not have to go much beyond the text of his essay, "A Literary Politician," printed at July 20, 1889, Volume 6.

Delayed a week on account of illness in early October, Wilson delivered his lectures at the Brooklyn Institute on October 10, 17,

---

[1] WWhw figures on the recto of the envelope of J. W. Wright to WW, Dec. 3, 1895, disclose that Wilson planned to use his earnings of $500 from the Extension Society to help pay for the house.

[2] About Wilson's first lectures at the Brooklyn Institute, in 1893, see the Editorial Note, "Wilson's Lectures at the Brooklyn Institute of Arts and Sciences," Vol. 8, and the notes for these lectures printed at Nov. 15, 1893, Vol. 8.

[3] See F. W. Hooper to WW, June 11, 1895, and its attachment.

[4] Outline of Aristotle's life and quotations, on cards in WP, DLC; outline entitled "I. Aristotle," in *ibid*.

[5] Lecture notes in *ibid*.

[6] Woodrow Wilson, *Syllabus of a Course of Six Lectures on Great Leaders of Political Thought* (Philadelphia, 1895).

[7] A transcript is printed in Vol. 5, pp. 459-61.

24, and 31, and November 7 and 22, 1895.[8] He gave the same lectures under the auspices of the Extension Society at Tarrytown, New York, on November 20, December 6, 13, and 20, 1895, and on January 3 and 10, 1896;[9] and at Lancaster, Pennsylvania, on November 21 and December 5 and 12, 1895, and on January 2, 9, and 15, 1896. No newspapers seem to have reported on the lectures in Brooklyn and Tarrytown. However, the Lancaster newspapers ran extensive reports of the series in that city. Printed at November 22, December 6 and 13, 1895, and January 3, 10, and 16, 1896, these reports give a good view of the level and contents of Wilson's lectures, as well as of his methods as a speaker.

[8] *The Eighth Year Book of the Brooklyn Institute of Arts and Sciences,* . . . *1895-6* (Brooklyn, 1896), p. 208.
[9] See the announcement in the *Princeton Press,* Nov. 23, 1895.


## From Guyon de Goll

Dear Sir: New York. October, 16, 1895.

Your letter of the 15th inst, enclosing check for $50, under our agreement received, for which please accept our thanks.

While at your house on Saturday Mr Wright asked my advice in regard to the covering of the rear porch and suggested a straight roof extending over the stone steps to cellar instead of the gable as drawn on plans. He was to talk the matter over with you and have you decide. We think it would protect the cellar stairs from storms, and also prevent breaking in to the upper part of the house and make a tighter and more water-proof job to have the roof as suggested by Mr Wright.

Another point arose about the hand rail for the front stairs. It is difficult to make a twisted Yellow pine rail that will be free from splinters, and it would be our suggestion—as I stated to Mr Wright—to have red oak. This can be colored to look very similar to the Yellow pine and would certainly be safer. Mr Wright also suggested having newels instead of the continuous rail, but we advise to follow the detail as we understand it would be more in keeping with Mrs Wilson's ideas to copy really the old style staircase,—and aside from this, the continuous rail is much more comfortable. We think Mr Wright can brace it in a proper way to make it just as strong as with the newels. I have in my own house the same style of stair rail and find after two years that it is apparently as strong as though I had newel posts.

Mr Child is out of town and will return the latter part of the week, but should you need my presence at Princeton please communicate.

Enclosed you will find receipt.

Yours truly,—Guyon de Goll, Child & de Goll.

TLS (WP, DLC). Enc.: typed receipt by Child & de Goll dated Oct. 16, 1895 (WP, DLC).

## To Howard Pyle

My dear Mr. Pyle,          Princeton, New Jersey, 17 October, 1895.

Here is the rest of the second article,—a little more legible, I believe, than the first part. Again I must apologise for sending it in this shape, and for asking that it be returned as soon as convenient. If I were to hold it for the revision which must precede copying (when a fellow does the copying himself), it would delay its reaching you too long.

I hope the reference to Miss Philipse[1] will be to your mind,— and that my telegram was long enough to be intelligible.

Cordially Yours,   Woodrow Wilson

WWTLS (deCoppet Coll., NjP).

[1] See Wilson's "Colonel Washington," *Harper's Magazine*, xcII (March 1896), 572-73, for the reference and Pyle's picture.

## A News Item

[Oct. 23, 1895]

### MONITORS FOR THE ELECTIVE CLASSES.

The Faculty has appointed four monitors, one from each of the four largest elective classes, to take cuts in their respective classes. This move was deemed necessary on account of the difficulty and waste of time experienced by the Professors in spotting so many men. The four courses are: Dr. Patton's class in Ethics numbering 235; Prof. Ormond's History of Philosophy, 235; Prof. Wilson's Jurisprudence, 190; and Prof. Sloane's History course, 68.

Printed in the *Daily Princetonian*, Oct. 23, 1895.

## From the Minutes of the Princeton Faculty

4 5' P.M., Wednesday, Oct. 23rd, 1895.

. . . A communication was received from the Treasurer in reference to the indebtedness of Mr. —— of the Senior Class to the College and for his room in town was referred to his Class Officer, Prof. Wilson. . . .[1]

[1] For Wilson's report and the faculty's action on this case, see the Princeton Faculty Minutes printed at Oct. 30, 1895.

## From Franklin William Hooper

My dear Prof. Wilson:    Brooklyn, October 23rd, 1895.

I write to ask on what date you will be able to give the sixth lecture in your course before our Department of Political Science. The course was to have ended on Thursday, November 7th.[1]

It will be possible to have the sixth lecture in the course given on Friday evening, November 29th, but we should prefer to have the lecture come earlier. Mr. Edwin D. Mead[2] is to lecture on Thursday evening, November 14th, but it is possible that he will be willing to change his date, and in case he will do so, we could have your sixth lecture on the 14th.

The Rev. Dr. Gunsaulus[3] is expected to lecture on Thursday evening, November 21st, but he may be prevented from coming east for that date. In case he should not come, it would be possible to have your lecture on the 21st.

To sum up the situation,—the 29th is now clear; the 14th and 21st may possibly be clear.

      Very cordially yours, Franklin W. Hooper.

Mem. Hold the 14th and 22nd[4]

TLS (WP, DLC) with WWhw and WWsh research notes on verso.
 [1] That is, since Wilson had originally been scheduled to begin his series at the Brooklyn Institute on October 3. He had actually begun the series on October 10 on account of illness.
 [2] Edwin Doak Mead, author, lecturer, and editor of the *New England Magazine*.
 [3] Frank Wakeley Gunsaulus, Congregational clergyman, at this time pastor of the Plymouth Church in Chicago.
 [4] WWhw. Wilson gave his last lecture on November 22.

## To Samuel Sidney McClure[1]

          Princeton, New Jersey,
My Dear Mr. McClure:    October 23, 1895.

I thank you very much for the portrait of Lincoln you were kind enough to send me,[2] reproduced from an early daguerreotype. It seems to me both striking and singular. The fine brows and forehead, and the pensive sweetness of the clear eyes, give to the noble face a peculiar charm. There is in the expression the dreaminess of the familiar face without its later sadness. I shall treasure it as a notable picture.

      Very sincerely yours, Woodrow Wilson

PCL (WP, DLC).
 [1] Editor and publisher of *McClure's Magazine* of New York.
 [2] *McClure's Magazine* was about to begin publication of Ida Tarbell's famous series of articles on Lincoln. The "portrait" which McClure sent to Wilson was probably a copy of an illustration for Miss Tarbell's series.

## To Walter Hines Page

Everett House, Union Square, New York.

My dear Mr. Page,                                24 October, 1895

I had not forgotten your letter,[1] neither had I neglected it,— I had simply been obliged to postpone my answer. When it came I was ill in bed; and when that was over with, I was driven by conscience to attack a formidable bulk of work that had been piling itself up while I lay abed. I'm all right now, and almost abreast of my work; but I am still gadding about filling lecture engagements, in Brooklyn (where I hope I shall meet the Clark's[2]) and other places.

I am sincerely glad to know that you are with the *Atlantic*,[3]— and gratified to be allowed to believe that I had some sort of small part in the choice.[4] I don't wonder that you enjoy the change; and I wish with all my heart that the truly *literary* and non-journalistic magazines might by some means gain a greater prominence and power.

As for my *History*, I am not likely to forget Houghton, Mifflin, & Co. I agree with you as to their dignity and standing. But the completion of the work is yet a long way off—four or five years, at a guess,—particularly interrupted, though also in a way aided, by the articles on George Washington I have undertaken for *Harper's*; and I want to indulge myself with the luxury of writing quite without promises made to anybody about the work, as slowly, as fast, as voluminously, as briefly, as I please,—as if there were no publishers, and I were writing the thing for myself alone. I don't want even to promise to show it to any firm in particular. I know that you will understand this and indulge it. You may rest assured the great Boston firm is not excluded.

Cordially Yours,   Woodrow Wilson[5]

ALS (W. H. Page Papers, MH).
[1] Page's letter is missing.
[2] A mysterious allusion.
[3] Actually, Page had just gone to the Boston firm of Houghton, Mifflin, and Company as "literary adviser." He became assistant editor of the *Atlantic Monthly* in 1896 and editor in 1898 upon the retirement of Horace Elisha Scudder.
[4] Wilson's "small part" in Page's move to Houghton Mifflin is unknown to the Editors.
[5] Page wrote across the top of this letter: "If we are smart enough, we will get this 'History' in due time, I think—W.H.P."

## From the Minutes of the Princeton Faculty

4 5′ P.M., Wednesday, Oct. 30th, 1895.

. . . The case of —— (Spec. Stud.), reported as failing to pass in the work of the Second Term, was referred to the Committee of Special Students to consider. . . .

Prof. Wilson reported on the case of the member of the Senior Class heavily indebted to the College and also for his room in town. In view of the peculiar circumstances the case was left in the hands of Prof. Wilson with power.[1] . . .

[1] Wilson must have helped the student to make arrangements to meet his obligations, for he was graduated with his class in June 1896.

## A News Report

[Oct. 30, 1895]

### DEMOCRATIC MEETING.

The meeting held last night in University Hall to ratify the nomination of Alexander T. McGill, '64, for Governor,[1] was presided over by ex-Mayor Anderson[2] of Princeton. . . . Mr. R. S. Green, '86, was the first speaker and said he thought the meeting superfl[u]ous as he could imagine no reason why Princetonians should not support McGill. He stated the reason why the townspeople should vote for McGill, and concluded by expressing his expectation that McGill would be elected. Mr. A. C. Wall, '86, spoke of the importance of the Court of Chancery and of Chancellor McGill's faithful attention to his duties. Prof. Daniels '88 said that he should vote for McGill on account of his character and record, as an encouragement to the administration, and as a true Princeton man.

Mr. E. A. S. Lewis, '91, dwelt on the independence of the Chancellor under trying circumstances. Prof Wilson closed the meeting confirming the points previously made.[3] During the meeting, Farr's Princeton Band furnished music.

Printed in the *Daily Princetonian*, Oct. 30, 1895.

[1] Alexander Taggart McGill, Jersey City jurist and Chancellor of the State of New Jersey, who was opposed by the Republican nominee, former State Senator John William Griggs. The Democrats, who had controlled the State House for thirty years, were under attack for widespread corruption and waste, and the election resulted in a resounding victory for Griggs.

[2] Leroy Hammond Anderson, '61, Mayor of Princeton Borough, 1888-89.

[3] Insofar as is known, this was the first time Wilson spoke in a political campaign in behalf of a particular candidate.

## To Howard Pyle

My dear Mr. Pyle,                                              30 Oct., 1895

You may have seen a portrait of Mary Philipse, but, in case you have not, there is one within, page 91.[1]

The magazine is borrowed from our library, and I shall have to ask you to return it.

> With very cordial regards,   Woodrow Wilson

ALS (deCoppet Coll., NjP).
[1] This enclosure was the New York *Colonial Magazine*, 1 (Oct. 1895).

## To Henry Mills Alden

My dear Mr. Alden,     Princeton, New Jersey, 30 October, 1895.

I am sorry to have used up *all* the time allowed me for the preparation of the second article on Washington, which I send you along with this, but under another cover. My illness delayed me beyond all expectation. As it has turned out, however, the delay has not been without its advantages. I have happened upon several scraps of material lately which might have come to me too late had the printers already gotten hold of my copy.

I have the following illustrations to suggest:

*Portrait of Lawrence Washington.* (One given in Lossing's "Mt. Vernon and Its Associaciations"[1] (Lenox Library), p. 25.; but *a much better one*, i.e. more like G. W., in Conway's "Barons of the Potomac" opp. p. 255.)

*Portrait of Lord Fairfax.* (See frontispiece of Conway's *Barons*, which is much the most striking) ☞ *N.b.* There is a copy of Conway in the Lenox; but I will return the one I have from Mr. Bangs if necessary. Otherwise I should like to keep it a little longer.

*Greenway Court.* (Ld. Fairfax's forest seat. See Howe's "Historical Collections of Virginia,"[2] p. 255.

*Portrait of Governor Robert Dinwiddie.* (See Dinwiddie Papers, Virginia Historical Society,[3] frontispiece to second volume.)

*Fort Duquesne* (if any good cut can be found)

*The signature of Duquesne.* (Winsor's Narrative and Critical History, V., p. 492.)

*Mount Vernon.* (As early a picture as possible, and I suppose all extant are to [be] found reproduced in Lossing's "Mount Vernon and Its Associations," mentioned above.)

*Portrait of General Braddock.*

*Braddock's Field.* (See references in note to p. 500 of Winsor, vol. V.). Sparks's Washington vol II. p 90.

*Braddock's grave.* (See Winthrop Sargent's "Braddock's Expedition," Phila., 1855,[4] p. 280.)

I was in the Lennox Library the other day, and Mr. Eames[5] showed me your note about maps. Winsor's references are misleading. The map which he reproduces on page 274 of volume V. is a section of the map the whole of which is to be found in Sir William Keith's "History of the British Plantations in America,"[6] which is in the Lenox.

Will you pardon me if I ask when the pay for these articles is due? I am neither impatient nor impertinent; but I am building a house, and, under such circumstances, one always wants to know, I take it, just when he may expect what is owing him to come in. I know that, in view of this fact, you will indulge the question without deeming me uneasy.

With warm regard,

Most sincerely Yours,   Woodrow Wilson

WWTLS (L. W. Smith Coll., Morristown, N. J., National Historical Park).
[1] Benson John Lossing, *Mount Vernon and Its Associations, Historical, Biographical, and Pictorial* (New York, 1859).
[2] Henry Howe, *Historical Collections of Virginia* (Charleston, S. C., 1852).
[3] R. A. Brock (ed.), *The Official Records of Robert Dinwiddie . . .* (2 vols., Richmond, Va., 1883-84).
[4] Winthrop Sargent (ed.), *The History of an Expedition Against Fort Du Quesne, in 1755 . . .* (Philadelphia, 1855).
[5] Wilberforce Eames, librarian of the Lenox Library on Fifth Avenue. Earlier in the year (on May 23, 1895), the Lenox had been consolidated with the Astor Library and the Tilden Trust to form the New York Public Library.
[6] William Keith, *History of the British Plantations in America* (London, 1738).

## From Henry Mills Alden

Dear Mr. Wilson:                    New York. October 31, 1895.
Please find herewith Messrs. Harper & Brothers' cheque for Six Hundred Dollars ($600.00), in payment for the first and second papers in your series on Washington.[1]

Sincerely yours,   H. M. Alden

TLS (WP, DLC).
[1] For other such letters, see H. M. Alden to WW, March 21, 1896, April 9, 1896, and May 14, 1896, all TLS (WP, DLC).

## From Howard Pyle

Dear Professor Wilson:       Wilmington, Del., Nov. 1st, 1895.
I have just received the copy of the Colonial Magazine and am extremely obliged to you for sending me the portrait of Miss Phillipse. I wish I knew something as to the original—color of the hair, etc.

I shall probably start upon the drawing on Monday or Tuesday next and shall make it the first to be done of the three illustrations for your second paper. The subjects I have chosen are as follows;—

I. Washington's Retreat from Great Meadows.
II. Burial of Braddock.
III. Washington and Miss Phillipse.

For the headband I thought of making a suggestion of either the battle at Great Meadows or more probably the battle in which Braddock was defeated, the tailpiece possibly a view of Mount Vernon.

I wish you would let me know if you approve of this.

The manuscript and notes you have sent me are all that is necessary for these subjects, only I wish I knew something of the appearance of Great Meadows. I suppose, however, I can get some ideas of it from the picture of Braddock's grave in Winthrop Sargent's "Expedition."

Shall I send your manuscript back to you, or shall I keep it till I have made the drawings and then return it?

Please remember me most kindly to Mrs Wilson and, awaiting your reply, I am            Faithfully yours   Howard Pyle

TLS (WP, DLC).


## From Franklin William Hooper

My dear Professor Wilson:            Brooklyn, Nov. 4th 1895

You did not understand me on Thursday evening.[1] I did not express any disappointment in the result of your lectures for I do not know what the result is, nor did I say that the lectures were not in my judgement equivalent to those that I had expected that you would give. What I did say was that the lectures were different from what I expected they would be. They are in my judgement addressed to a more popular audience than I had hoped they would be. We desire particularly to emphasize the instructive element in our work rather than the attractive or popular or entertaining element. Your course of lectures given two years ago was one of the strongest courses, if not the strongest course we have ever had given before the Institute from the point of view of instruction.[2] And of course you will allow that I must in judging of lectures think not only of the subject-matter presented from the point of view of an interested student of Politics, but also of the manner in which the subject-matter is presented.

I have not in my own mind considered as yet sufficiently to give a pronounced opinion whether more good may not be done by your present course of lectures presented in a most interesting and attractive form than would be done by presenting more in detail the work of the several men whose work you are describing. Indeed I stated to you that possibly more good might be done by the method which you are pursuing than by the one which I had in mind on Thursday evening last but which I did not attempt to describe.

The question often arises with those who lecture before the Institute as to the nature of our audiences;—"are they popular? are they serious? are they thoughtful? how much will your audiences take of good solid instruction?["] It is a legitimate question for you and I to discuss, namely the quality of the audiences that assemble to hear you at our Institute lectures with a view of adapting the method of the lecture to the audience.

In speaking to you on Thursday evening I only had in mind the question of the best method of instructing our Institute audiences, —a question which lies on the surface of things and is in no sense fundamental or serious. Indeed the misunderstanding lies in the fact that I was speaking not at all seriously, while what I said has been, on reflection and through no fault of yours, taken as a serious and fundamental criticism of your lectures from the point of view of the officers and members of the Institute.

I wish now to ask your pardon for not speaking more explicitly on Thursday night (since I spoke at all) concerning the kind of lectures that we had anticipated that you would give. It would have been better as the matter now stands if I had said nothing. I was extremely tired or I would have made myself clearly understood at that time and what I would have said would have in no way been an attempt to detract from the ideal which you hold up as an object to be accomplished by the lectures.

It is, however, the policy of the Institute to give the platform of the Institute to the lecturer in an absolutely free and unhampered manner. The last thing we would do would be to place any restrictions of any sort on anyone who is invited to lecture or instruct under the name of the Institute. As an artist who is to paint a great picture must be free, so must we insure freedom to him who addresses an audience on a great theme.

Personally I would not speak except as one who heard two of your lectures, two years ago, that were capital from the point of view of instruction, and as one who believes that our members desire instruction in such form as you gave it two years ago. But in saying this much I do not wish to place my judgement over against yours. It is for you to determine what your lectures shall be both in form and matter.

Pardon my long letter, but my position is an awkward one,

but I do not believe I should take the time of yourself or my own time to explain the matter by writing further. A brief conference should make you feel entire freedom in continuing your course to the end.[3]

Very cordially yours    Franklin W. Hooper.

ALS (WP, DLC) with WWhw notation on env.: "Ans. 5 Nov., '95."

[1] October 31, 1895, when Wilson delivered his fourth lecture, on Burke, at the Brooklyn Institute of Arts and Sciences.

[2] See the Editorial Note, "Wilson's Lectures on Great Leaders of Political Thought," n. 2.

[3] Hooper warmly invited Wilson to lecture again at the Brooklyn Institute in 1896. See EAW to WW, June 15 and 22 and July 8, 1896.

## To Howard Pyle

My dear Mr. Pyle,      Princeton, New Jersey, 4 November, 1895.

I was out of town when your letter came.

I like your choice of subjects very much indeed. I should say that, since the retreat from Great Meadows is to form the subject of one of the full-page illustrations, it would be best to make the headband a suggestion of the Braddock affair. For the tailpiece nothing could be better than a view of Mount Vernon.

I wish very much I could help you with some suggestion of Miss Philipse's colour; but I have searched in vain for any indications of it. The picture I sent you, indeed, is the only one I have ever seen of her.

As for Great Meadows, it has disappear[ed] from modern maps, but the place cannot be far away from Uniontown, Fayette County, Pennsylvania. Is it not possible that, through the postmaster of Uniontown, you (or the Harpers for you) could get at some photographer of the place who would make you a view of the Meadows which would at least show how the mountains lay disposed, and so suggest what the place may have been when the forests were still thick upon it. I have never seen any sort of sketch of the locality.

You need not return the manuscript until you are done with it. I have revised without it, and Mr. Alden now has the revised version.

I am about to begin on the third article. I shall have your convenience in mind in hurrying it forward.

Mrs. Wilson sends her kind regards.

Cordially Yours,    Woodrow Wilson

WWTLS (deCoppet Coll., NjP).

## From Howard Pyle

Dear Professor Wilson:          Wilmington, Del., Nov. 5th., 1895.

I have just received your very satisfactory letter in answer to my several inquiries concerning the Washington pictures.

In regard to Great Meadows (which you speak of as having disappeared from the map) am I not right in my surmise that the place of Braddock's burial is identical with Great Meadows? Both from Washington's own written account and from the several histories of the affair I read that the final encampment of Braddock's retreating army was at Great Meadows; that it was there Braddock died at night, and that early the following morning he was secretly buried on a spot, (Washington says,) over which the wagon trains and guns were driven so as to hide all sign of the place of his sepulchre.

If I am right in this supposition, I suppose the picture of Braddock's burial place would be all that is necessary. Or maybe it would be better for me to run out and see the ground.

I am sorry to trouble you further in this matter, but awaiting your reply, I am          Faithfully yours   Howard Pyle

TLS (WP, DLC).

## To John Davis Adams

My dear Sir,          Princeton, New Jersey, 6 November, 1895.

I send you Mr. Bangs' copy of Conway's "Barons" to-day by Express.

I should like to have it again for some details in connection with the third article in my series. After that I shall be through with it. And of course there is no hurry about its being sent back to me. Any time within three weeks will do.

Sincerely Yours,   Woodrow Wilson

WWTLS (Berg Coll., NN).

## To Howard Pyle

Everett House, Union Square, New York.

My dear Mr. Pyle,                              8 Nov., 1895

Your last letter came just as I was leaving home, and I had to bring it off with me to find time for an answer.

You will notice that Washington in his account of Braddock's death says *"near* the Great Meadows,"[1] careful Mr. Parkman says exactly the same,[2] writing before the publication of W's account.

It would not be safe, I think, to take the picture of Braddock's grave as a picture of Great Meadows. Dunbar's camp at the time of B's death was, I should judge, between Gist's and Great Meadows, nearer the latter than the former. See map opposite page 438 of Winsor's "Mississippi Basin,"[3] on which Gist's is called "Guests."

In haste,          Cordially Yours,   Woodrow Wilson

ALS (photostat in RSB Coll., DLC).
[1] Wilson was referring to Henry G. Pickering (ed.), "The Braddock Campaign: An Unpublished Autograph Narrative by Washington," *Scribner's Magazine*, XIII (May 1893), 535.
[2] Francis Parkman, *Montcalm and Wolfe* (2 vols., Boston, 1884), I, 226.
[3] Justin Winsor, *The Mississippi Basin . . . The Struggle in America Between England and France, 1697-1763* (Boston and New York, 1895).

# A Literary Essay[1]

[*Nov. 10, 1895*][2]

## ON AN AUTHOR'S CHOICE OF COMPANY.

Once and again, it would seem, a man is born into the world belated. Strayed out of a past age, he comes among us like an alien, lives removed and singular, and dies a stranger. There was a touch of this strangeness in Charles Lamb. Much as he was loved and befriended, he was not much understood; for he drew aloof in his studies, affected a "self-pleasing quaintness" in his style, took no pains to hit the taste of his day, wandered at sweet liberty in an age which could scarcely have bred such another. "Hang the age!" he cried. "I will write for antiquity." And he did. He wrote as if it were still Shakspere's day; made the authors of that spacious time his constant companions and study; and deliberately became himself "the last of the Elizabethans." When a new book came out, he said, he always read an old one.

The case ought, surely, to put us occasionally upon reflecting.[3] May an author not, in some degree, by choosing his literary company, choose also his literary character, and so, when he comes to write, write himself back to his masters? May he not, by examining his own tastes and yielding himself obedient to his natural affinities, join what congenial group of writers he will? The question can be argued very strongly in the affirmative, and that not alone because of Charles Lamb's case. It might be said that Lamb was antique only in the forms of his speech, that he managed very cleverly to hit the taste of his age in the substance of

[1] For the suggestion which led to the composition of this essay, see WW to R. U. Johnson, Nov. 19, 1895.
[2] Wilson's composition date on the WWT and WWhw text (WP, DLC).
[3] Here Wilson begins to explain his own method in writing his "Short History of the United States" and his articles on George Washington.

what he wrote, for all the phraseology had so strong a flavor of quaintness and was not at all in the mode of the day. It would not be easy to prove that; but it really does not matter whether it is true or not. In his tastes, certainly, Lamb was an old author, not a new one; a "modern antique," as Hood called him. He wrote for his own age, of course, because there was no other age at hand to write for, and the age he liked best was past and gone; but he wrote what he fancied the great generations gone by would have liked, and what, as it has turned out in the generosity of fortune, subsequent ages have warmly loved and reverently canonized him for writing, as if there were a casual taste that belongs to a day and generation, and also a permanent taste which is without date, and he had hit the latter.

Great authors are not often men of fashion. Fashion is always a harness and restraint, whether it be fashion in dress or fashion in vice or fashion in literary art, in thought and expression; and a man who is bound by it is caught and formed in a fleeting mode. The great writers are always innovators; for they are always frank, natural, and downright, and frankness and naturalness always disturb, when they do not wholly break down, the fixed and complacent order of fashion. No genuine man can be deliberately in the fashion, indeed, in what he says, if he have any movement of thought or individuality in him. He remembers what Aristotle says, or if he does not, his own pride and manliness fill him with the thought instead. The very same action that is noble if done for the satisfaction of one's own sense of right or purpose of self-development, said the Stagirite, may, if done to satisfy others, become menial and slavish. "It is the object of any action or study that is all-important," and if the author's chief object be to please he is condemned already. The true spirit of authorship is a spirit of liberty which scorns the slave's trick of imitation. It is a masterful spirit of conquest within the sphere of ideas and of artistic form—an impulse of empire and origination.

Of course a man may choose, if he will, to be less than a free author. He may become a reporter; for there is such a thing as reporting for books as well as reporting for newspapers, and there have been reporters so amazingly clever that their very aptness and wit constitute them a sort of immortals. You have proof of this in Horace Walpole, at whose hands gossip and compliment receive a sort of apotheosis. Such men hold the secret of a kind of alchemy by which things trivial and temporary may be transmuted into literature. But they are only inspired reporters, after all; and while a man was wishing, he might wish to be more, and climb to better company.

Every man must of course, whether he will or no, feel the spirit of the age in which he lives and thinks and does his work; and the mere contact will direct and form him more or less. But to wish to serve the spirit of the age at any sacrifice of individual naturalness or conviction, however small, is to harbor the germ of a destroying disease. Every man who writes ought to write for immortality, even though he be of the multitude that die at their graves; and the standards of immortality are of no single age. There are many qualities and causes that give permanency to a book, but universal vogue during the author's lifetime is not one of them. Many authors now immortal have enjoyed the applause of their own generations; many authors now universally admired will, let us hope, pass on to an easy immortality. The praise of your own day is no absolute disqualification; but it may be if it be given for qualities which your friends are the first to admire, for 't is likely they will also be the last to admire them. There is a greater thing than the spirit of the age, and that is the spirit of the ages. It is present in your own day; it is even dominant then, with a sort of accumulated power and mastery. If you can strike it, you will strike, as it were, into the upper air of your own time, where the forces are which run from age to age. Lower down, where you breathe, is the more inconstant air of opinion, inhaled, exhaled, from day to day—the variant currents, the forces that will carry you, not forward, but hither and thither.

We write nowadays a great deal with our eyes circumspectly upon the tastes of our neighbors, but very little with our attention bent upon our own natural, self-speaking thoughts and the very truth of the matter whereof we are discoursing. Now and again, it is true, we are startled to find how the age relishes still an old-fashioned romance, if written with a new-fashioned vigor and directness; how quaint and simple and lovely things, as well as what is altogether modern and analytic and painful, bring our most judicious friends crowding, purses in hand, to the book-stalls; and for a while we are puzzled to see worn-out styles and past modes revived. But we do not let these things seriously disturb our study of prevailing fashions. These books of adventure are not at all, we assure ourselves, in the true spirit of the age, with its realistic knowledge of what men really do and think and purpose, and the taste for them must be only for the moment or in jest. We need not let our surprise at occasional flurries and variations in the literary market cloud or discredit our analysis of the real taste of the day, or suffer ourselves to be betrayed into writing romances, however much we might rejoice to be delivered from the drudgery of sociological study, and made free to go afield with our imaginations upon a joyous search for hidden treasure or knightly adventure.

And yet it is quite likely, after all, that the present age is transient. Past ages have been. It is probable that the objects and interests now so near us, looming so dominant in all the foreground of our day, will sometime be shifted and lose their place in the perspective. That has happened with the near objects and exaggerated interests of other days, so violently sometimes as to submerge and thrust out of sight whole libraries of books. It will not do to reckon upon the persistence of new things. 'T were best to give them time to make trial of the seasons. The old things of art and taste and thought are the permanent things. We know that they are because they have lasted long enough to grow old; and we deem it safe to assess the spirit of the age by the same test. No age adds a great deal to what it received from the age that went before it, no time gets an air all its own. The same atmosphere holds from age to age; it is only the little movements of the air that are new. Fleeting cross-winds venture abroad in the intervals when the trades do not blow, the which if a man wait for he may lose his voyage.

No man who has anything to say need stop and bethink himself whom he may please or displease in the saying of it. He has but one day to write in, and that is his own. He need not fear that he will too much ignore it. He will address the men he knows when he writes, whether he be conscious of it or not; he may dismiss all fear on that score, and use his liberty to the utmost. There are some things that can have no antiquity and must ever be without date, and genuineness and spirit are of their number. A man who has these must ever be "timely," and at the same time fit to last, if he can get his qualities into what he writes. He may freely read, too, what he will that is congenial, and form himself by companionships that are chosen simply because they are to his taste; that is, if he be genuine and in very truth a man of independent spirit. Lamb would have written "for antiquity" with a vengeance had his taste for the quaint writers of an elder day been an affectation, or the authors he liked men themselves affected and ephemeral. No age this side antiquity would ever have vouchsafed him a glance or a thought. But it was not an affectation, and the men he preferred were as genuine and as spirited as he was. He was simply obeying an affinity and taking cheer after his own kind. A man born into the real patriciate of letters may take his pleasure in what company he will without taint or loss of caste; may go confidently abroad in the free world of books and choose his comradeships without fear of offense.

More than that, there is no other way in which he can form himself, if he would have his power transcend a single age. He belittles himself who takes from the world no more than he can get from the speech of his own generation. The only advantage of books over speech is that they may hold from generation to generation, and reach, not a small group merely, but a multitude of men; and a man who writes without being a man of letters is curtailed of his heritage. It is in this world of old and new that he must form himself if he would in the end belong to it and increase its bulk of treasure. If he has conned the new theories of society, but knows nothing of Burke; the new notions about fiction, and has not read his Scott and his Richardson; the new criminology, and wots nothing of the old human nature; the new religions, and has never felt the power and sanctity of the old, it is much the same as if he had read Ibsen and Maeterlinck, and had never opened Shakspere. How is he to know wholesome air from foul, good company from bad, visions from nightmares? He has framed himself for the great art and handicraft of letters only when he has taken all the human parts of literature as if they were without date, and schooled himself in a catholic sanity of taste and judgment.

Then he may very safely choose what company his own work shall be done in—in what manner, and under what masters. He cannot choose amiss for himself or for his generation if he choose like a man, without light whim or weak affectation; not like one who chooses a costume, but like one who chooses a soul. What is it, let him ask himself, that renders a bit of writing a "piece of literature"? It is reality. A "wood-note wild," sung unpremeditated and out of the heart; a description written as if with an undimmed and seeing eye upon the very object described; an exposition that lays bare the very soul of the matter; a motive truly revealed; anger that is righteous and justly spoken; mirth that has its sources pure; phrases to find the heart of a thing, and a heart seen in things for the phrases to find; an unaffected meaning set out in language that is its own—such are the realities of literature. Nothing else is of the kin. Phrases used for their own sake; borrowed meanings which the borrower does not truly care for; an affected manner; an acquired style; a hollow reason; words that are not fit; things which do not live when spoken—these are its falsities, which die in the handling.

The very top breed of what is unreal is begotten by imitation. Imitators succeed sometimes, and flourish, even while a breath may last; but "imitate and be damned" is the inexorable threat and prophecy of fate with regard to the permanent fortunes of literature. That has been notorious this long time past. It is more worth noting, lest some should not have observed it, that there are other and subtler ways of producing what is unreal. There are the mixed kinds of writing, for example. Argument is real if it come vital from the mind; narrative is real if the thing told have life and the narrator unaffectedly see it while he speaks; but to narrate and argue in the same breath is naught. Take, for instance, the familiar example of the early history of Rome. Make up your mind what was the truth of the matter, and then, out of the facts as you have disentangled them, construct a firmly touched narrative, and the thing you create is real, has the confidence and consistency of life. But mix the narrative with critical comment upon other writers and their variant versions of the tale, show by a nice elaboration of argument the whole conjectural basis of the story, set your reader the double task of doubting and accepting, rejecting and constructing, and at once you have touched the whole matter with unreality. The narrative by itself might have had an objective validity; the argument by itself an intellectual firmness, sagacity, vigor, that would have sufficed to make and keep it potent; but together they confound each other, destroy each other's atmosphere, make a double miscarriage. The story is rendered unlikely, and the argument obscure. This is the taint which has touched all our recent historical writing. The critical discussion and assessment of the sources of information, which used to be a thing for the private mind of the writer, now so encroach upon the open text that the story, for the sake of which we would believe the whole thing was undertaken, is oftentimes fain to sink away into the foot-notes. The process has ceased to be either pure exegesis or straightforward narrative, and history has ceased to be literature.

Nor is this our only sort of mixed writing. Our novels have become sociological studies, our poems vehicles of criticism, our sermons political manifestos. We have confounded all processes in a common use, and do not know what we would be at. We can find no better use for Pegasus than to carry our vulgar burdens, no higher key for song than questionings and complainings.

Fancy pulls in harness with intellectual doubt; enthusiasm walks apologetically alongside science. We try to make our very dreams engines of social reform. It is a parlous state of things for literature, and it is high time authors should take heed what company they keep. The trouble is, they all want to be "in society," overwhelmed with invitations from the publishers, well known and talked about at the clubs, named every day in the newspapers, photographed for the news-stalls; and it is so hard to distinguish between fashion and form, costume and substance, convention and truth, the things that show well and the things that last well, so hard to draw away from the writers that are new and talked about and note those who are old and walk apart, to distinguish the tones which are merely loud from the tones that are genuine, to get far enough away from the press and the hubbub to see and judge the movements of the crowd.

Some will do it. Choice spirits will arise and make conquest of us, not "in society," but with what will seem a sort of outlawry. The great growths of literature spring up in the open, where the air is free and they can be a law unto themselves. The law of life, here as elsewhere, is the law of nourishment: with what was the earth laden, and the atmosphere? Literatures are renewed, as they are originated, by uncontrived impulses of nature, as if the sap moved unbidden in the mind. Once conceive the matter so, and Lamb's quaint saying assumes a sort of gentle majesty. A man should "write for antiquity" as a tree grows into the ancient air—this old air that has moved upon the face of the world ever since the day of creation, which has set the law of life to all things, which has nurtured the forests and won the flowers to their perfection, which has fed men's lungs with life, sped their craft, borne abroad their songs and their cries, blown their forges to flame, and buoyed up whatever they have contrived. 'T is a common medium, though a various life; and the figure may serve the author for instruction.

The breeding of authors is no doubt a very occult thing, and no man can set the rules of it; but at least the sort of "ampler ether" in which they are best brought to maturity is known. Writers have liked to speak of the Republic of Letters, as if to mark their freedom and equality; but there is a better phrase, namely, the Community of Letters; for that means intercourse and comradeship and a life in common. Some take up their abode in it as if they had made no search for a place to dwell in, but had come into the freedom of it by blood and birthright. Others buy the freedom with a great price, and seek out all the sights and privileges of the place with an eager thoroughness and curiosity. Still others win their way into it with a certain grace and aptitude, next best to the ease and dignity of being born to the right. But for all it is a bonny place to be. Its comradeships are a liberal education. Some, indeed, even there, live apart; but most run always in the marketplace to know what all the rest have said. Some keep special company, while others keep none at all. But all feel the atmosphere and life of the place in their several degrees.

No doubt there are national groups, and Shakspere is king among the English, as Homer is among the Greeks, and sober Dante among his gay countrymen. But their thoughts all have in common, though speech divide them; and sovereignty does not exclude comradeship or embarrass freedom. No doubt there is many a wilful, ungoverned fellow endured there without question, and many a churlish cynic, because he possesses that patent of genuineness and of a wit which strikes for the heart of things, which, without further test, secures citizenship in that free company. What a gift of tongues is there, and of prophecy! What strains of good talk, what counsel of good judgment, what cheer of good tales, what sanctity of silent thought! The sight-seers who pass through from day to day, the press of voluble men at the gates, the affectation of citizenship by mere sojourners, the folly of those who bring new styles or affect old ones, the procession of the generations, disturb the calm of that serene community not a whit. They will entertain a man a whole decade, if he happen to stay so long, though they know all the while he can have no permanent place among them.

'T would be a vast gain to have the laws of that community better known than they are. Even the first principles of its constitution are singularly unfamiliar. It is not a community of writers, but a community of letters. One gets admission, not because he writes,—write he never so cleverly, like a gentleman and a man of wit,—but because he is literate, a true initiate into the secret craft and mystery of letters. What that secret is a man may know, even though he cannot practise or appropriate it. If a man can see the permanent element in things,—the true sources of laughter, the real fountains of tears, the motives that strike along the main lines of conduct, the acts which display the veritable characters of men, the trifles that are significant, the details that make the mass,—if he know these things, and can also choose words with a like knowledge of their power to illuminate and reveal, give color to the eye and passion to the thought, the secret is his, and an entrance to that immortal communion.

It may be that some learn the mystery of that insight without tutors; but most must put themselves under governors and earn their initiation. While a man lives, at any rate, he can keep the company of the masters whose words contain the mystery and open it to those who can see almost with every accent; and in such company it may at last be revealed to him—so plainly that he may, if he will, still linger in such comradeship when he is dead.

It would seem that there are two tests which admit to that company, and that they are conclusive. The one is, Are you individual? the other, Are you conversable? "I beg pardon," said a grave wag, coming face to face with a small person of most consequential air, and putting glass to eye in calm scrutiny—"I beg pardon; but are you anybody in particular?" Such is very much the form of initiation into the permanent communion of the realm of letters. Tell them, No, but that you have done much better—you have caught the tone of a great age, studied taste, divined opportunity, courted and won a vast public, been most timely and most famous, and you shall be pained to find them laughing in your face. Tell them you are earnest, sincere, consecrate to a cause, an apostle and reformer, and they will still ask you, "But are you anybody in particular?" They will mean, "Were you your own man in what you thought, and not a puppet? Did you speak with an individual note and distinction that marked you able to think as well as to speak—to be yourself in thoughts and in words also?" "Very well, then; you are welcome enough."

"That is, if you be also conversable." It is plain enough what they mean by that, too. They mean, if you have spoken in such speech and spirit as can be understood from age to age, and not in the pet terms and separate spirit of a single day and generation. Can the old authors understand you, that you would associate with them? Will men be able to take your meaning in the differing days to come? Or is it perishable matter of the day that you deal in—little controversies that carry no lasting principle at their heart; experimental theories of life and science, put forth for their novelty and with no test of their worth; pictures in which fashion looms very large, but human nature shows very small; things that please everybody, but instruct no one; mere fancies that are an end in themselves? Be you never so clever an artist in words and in ideas, if they be not the words that wear and mean the same thing, and that a thing intelligible, from age to age, and ideas that shall hold valid and luminous in whatever day or company, you may clamor at the gate till your lungs fail and get never an answer.

For that to which you seek admission is a veritable "community." In it you must be able to be, and to remain, conversable. How are you to test your preparation meanwhile, unless you look to your comradeships now while yet it is time to learn? Frequent the company in which you may learn the speech and the manner which are fit to last. Take to heart the admirable example you shall see set you there of using speech and manner to speak your real thought and be genuinely and simply yourself.

*Woodrow Wilson.*

Printed in the *Century Magazine*, LI (March 1896), 775-79.

## To Talcott Williams

Princeton, New Jersey,
My dear Mr. Williams, 10 November, 1895.

Your letter[1] would have had an immediate answer, had I been at home; but it had the ill luck to arrive the very day I went away and I did not get back till last night, after our last Saturday mail had gone out. On Sundays, you know, we are hermetically sealed.

I am not in the least surprised that you should like the election to "Whig Hall,"[2] as we call it here: for the truth is, those boys choose with discrimination, and only when they wish to honour. There is no fee or diploma; but a speech is exactly what they would most like; and I am sure they will be delighted to have you offer it. I will be equally delighted to see that it is put upon some day or evening when I shall be at home, so that my share of the pleasure, in addition to the speech itself, m[a]y be a little visit from you. And why could not Mrs. Williams make that the time to give us the visit she could not give before? The good prospect widens delightfully as I think of it.

I will myself see the Whig men, and you shall hear from me again. We can, I have no doubt, hit upon a time, and then the pleasure will be ours.[3]

With cordial regards from us both, and the pleasantest anticipations, Most sincerely Yours, Woodrow Wilson

WWTLS (WP, DLC).
[1] It is missing.
[2] Williams had been elected an honorary member of the American Whig Society on November 6, 1895.
[3] Williams was initiated at a special meeting of the Whig Society on February 14, 1896, at which he addressed the Hall on the subject of "Speaking."

## From Midori Komatz[1]

Dear Sir:                    Yokosuka, Japan, Nov. 10, 1895.

It gives me a great pleasure to introduce to you, although through communication only, Prof. Sanaye Takata, who has just translated your world-renowned work "The State."[2] I hope you remember that while at Brooklyn I sent you a part of a pamphlet, containing his translation of the book. As I then wrote you,[3] Prof. Takata graduated from our Imperial University with the title of Bungakushi which, I presume, corresponds to the degree of M.A. in America. He is now a professor of Sen-Mon Gokko, a College much renowned for the excellence of the departments of Jurisprudence and Political Science. Besides, he is one of the leading members of the House of Representatives, very eloquent and active.

I cannot help thinking it extremely fortunate that your invaluable work has been turned into Japanese by such a competent scholar as he. I am sure that the first edition will soon be devoured by the hungry public. Prof. Takata desires to insert in the second edition a sketch of your life, together with your picture. I think the idea is excellent, and I join with him in requesting you to send your photograph and a sketch of your life. The rest Prof. Takata will write himself.[4]

Hoping that you will consider his communication[5] with your habitual kindness and generosity,

I remain        Yours very respectfully    Midori Komatz

ALS (WP, DLC).

[1] Or Komatsu (1862-1942), a Japanese writer and statesman, who had anglicized his name to aid in pronunciation.

[2] Japanese political scientist, educator, and statesman (1860-1938). His translation of *The State* appeared in the Waseda University Series under the title, *Seiji hanron* (Tokyo, 1895).

[3] Komatsu's earlier letter is missing.

[4] The second edition did not appear until 1916.

[5] S. Takata to WW, Dec. 5, 1895.

## To John Franklin Jameson

My dear Jameson,    Princeton, New Jersey, 11 November, 1895.

You may depend upon it that it would not have occurred to my home-keeping mind to write a series for one of the vulgar-rich magazines, had it not been pressed upon me by the editor. It being proposed to me, however, "on terms honourable to them and grateful to me," I could not be unmindful of the fact that I was building a house, which would certainly have to be paid for some time, and the sooner the better. And so I did.

Meanwhile, ere that offer came, I had, under the pressure of the same considerations, put myself at the disposal of the University Extension people in Philadelphia as a lecturer. The result is, that I am loaded with lecture engagements to such an extent that the question arises, when am I to write the Washington articles for Harpers? There are to be six of the latter, and only two of them are finished. And so "you see how it is"; and why I must still only look on at the distinguished company who frequent the pages of the American Historical Review.[1]

With warmest regards from both Mrs. Wilson and myself to Mrs. Jameson and her worthy husband,

Yours in Bonds,   Woodrow Wilson

WWTLS (J. F. Jameson Papers, DLC).
[1] In a missing letter Jameson, managing editor of the newly founded *American Historical Review*, had obviously asked Wilson for an article.

## To William Burhans Isham, Jr.

Princeton, N. J.   13 Nov., 1895

Alas, my dear Billy, I am booked for a lecture in the quiet town of Brooklyn on the evening of the 22nd,—I need not say what a sore disappointment it is to be to be [*sic*] obliged to say so. I shall be with you in thought,[1]—and the best thing I can hope for *you*, my dear fellow, is that you may get as much pleasure as you give.

Affectionately Yours,   Woodrow Wilson

ALS (WC, NjP).
[1] At one of the annual Isham dinners, about which see WW to R. Bridges, Nov. 16, 1894, n. 1.

## To Robert Underwood Johnson[1]

My dear Mr. Johnson,        Princeton, N. J.   19 Nov., 1895

I send you, under another cover, a little essay[2] the thoughts of which were suggested by that interesting conversation of ours on the train. This is my excuse for directing it to you in person. I hope it may seem to you a suitable thing for the *Magazine*;[3] and that, whether it does or not, you will believe me

Very cordially Yours,   Woodrow Wilson

ALS (deCoppet Coll., NjP).
[1] Associate Editor of the *Century Magazine* of New York.
[2] "On an Author's Choice of Company," printed at Nov. 10, 1895.
[3] It was published in the *Century Magazine* in the issue of March 1896.

## A News Item About Wilson in Lancaster, Pennsylvania
[Nov. 21, 1895]

WOODROW WILSON'S OPENING LECTURE TONIGHT.

When Mr. Woodrow Wilson alighted from the train this afternoon it was the occasion of his first visit to Lancaster. The acquaintance cannot fail to be mutually agreeable. He will be sure to like the University Extension work in this city, as have all his predecessors without exception, and the attendants of the course will enjoy him immensely. Both in matter and manner his six lectures, on the men who have shaped the world's science of government, will be masterly in the highest degree. By securing a course ticket for a dollar the entire six lectures will cost less than three of them by paying single admissions at thirty-five cents, though this of itself is an exceedingly reasonable price. This evening he will treat of "Aristotle," at eight o'clock in Maennerchor Hall.

Printed in the Lancaster, Pa., *New Era*, Nov. 21, 1895.

## A Newspaper Report of a Lecture on Aristotle in Lancaster
[Nov. 22, 1895]

THE UNIVERSITY EXTENSION.

The Admirable Selection of the New Lecturer, Prof. Woodrow Wilson, and His First Talk.

That the Committee of the local University Extension Course have been eminently successful in the selection of a lecturer for this year in the person of Prof. Woodrow Wilson, of Princeton College, was made evident in the most pronounced manner, by the universally and unreservedly favorable impression he made on the large audience which gathered at Maennerchor Hall on Thursday evening [November 21] to hear his first lecture, on "Aristotle, the Father of Political Science," in a series which he will deliver on the topic of "Leaders of Political Thought." As was said by Rev. Chas. L. Fry, who introduced Prof. Wilson in the most glowing but all deserving terms, the Extension movement has reached the top notch of success in securing such an able instructor and he declared that no man in the country to-day was better fitted to present the subject which will engage the attention of the class this winter than he.

To attempt an abstract of the lecture would be futile, as the line of thought which pervaded the whole talk was so skillfully connected, the syllogisms were so pertinently inserted, the logic so smooth, and the conclusions so convincingly drawn that each division bore an intimate relation to the ones immediately preceding and succeeding, and in turn to the whole, that nothing but a full publication would do it justice. Prof. Wilson makes every point particularly clear, and is specially apt in the choice of his illustrations. He talks in a didactic manner, acquired, doubtless, through class-room influence, and this style is very appropriate for a University Extension lecture. He makes no attempt at oratory, is modest and unpretentious in all respects, and yet what he says is oratory of the most polished type in that it unconsciously appeals to the mind and heart. In the course of his talk he delved in the most profound and abstruse thought, but he was never ambiguous nor obscure and he made the subject which (in the hands of a less skillful person) might have been unentertaining, so intensely interesting, that he held the undiverted attention of his auditors from the time he uttered the first word till his lips closed on the last syllable. His manner, also, in speaking is pleasant. His gestures, which are few, are graceful but emphatic; he possesses a strong voice, and is very distinct in utterance. In fact, he combines all the qualities essential in a highly successful lecturer.

In prefacing his excellent talk, he referred to the immensity of the subject and said it would be impossible in the limited time to treat it in all its bearings. He spoke at length of the relations existing for twenty years between Plato and Aristotle, the master and the "disturbing" pupil. He analyzed the minds of each, the former being characterized as a visionary and the latter a lover of the practical and concrete. He pointed out, distinctly, the singular characteristics of Aristotle's mind, which had the rare faculty of analyzing and studying a subject, philosophizing and drawing conclusions upon it, as a result of the study and analysis, without considering the relationship of Aristotle himself to that subject. As this theme exhausted itself, a glimpse of his philosophy naturally followed, and it was in the explanation of its almost intangible theories and principles that Professor Wilson showed his genius. The main topics dwelt on were his ideas of political government; his seemingly paradoxical opinions in regard to the public good and private viciousness of great men; his principles of altruism, which, if in vogue in this day, would materially aid in the solution of the labor and social problems that vex our legislators, and his views on the communistic and individualistic tenure of land.

Professor Wilson left the stage amidst rapturous applause, and then engaged on the floor in a general discussion of the subject.

Printed in the Lancaster, Pa., *New Era*, Nov. 22, 1895.

## Two Letters from Henry Mills Alden

Dear Mr. Wilson:                    New York. November 23, 1895.

If you have in hand all the material for the map (showing the General Situation as to the English and French occupation of this country when Washington came on the military field) which you are preparing for your second paper perhaps we can assist you in its preparation. If this material is in condition to satisfy you and you could give us a rough sketch of the proposed map, we could give it to our own map drawer who could prepare it for the MAGAZINE, submitting a proof to you before its acceptance by us. In any event, I shall be glad to give you any help in my power.

We have been unable to obtain the engravings for Mr. Pyle's illustrations on scheduled time. The result has been unsatisfactory from the standpoint of the mechanical departments and if you could give Mr. Pyle enough of your third paper to furnish him suggestions, on or before December 15, both he and we would have greater freedom in the illustration with, we believe, better results than our engraving and printing departments have been able to achieve so far.

Sincerely yours,   H. M. Alden


Dear Mr. Wilson:                    New York. November 26, 1895.

As soon as you are prepared to give them, we shall be glad to have from you suggestions regarding portraits and any other illustrations you wish to have made for your third paper on Washington. We are desirous of giving to the artists and engravers as much time for the preparation of these illustrations as possible in order to obtain the best results.

Very truly yours,   H. M. Alden

TLS (WP, DLC).

## To Henry Mills Alden

Princeton, New Jersey,

My dear Mr. Alden, 30 November, 1895.

I am having very ill luck. I have been on my back again, with a sharp attack of indigestion, which has delayed the map, and everything else.

The map, however, is in large part sketched, and I think I am perfectly safe, if I take good care of myself, in promising it and the list of portraits, etc., for which you ask, early next week.

Neither will I forget the fifteenth of December,

Sincerely Yours, Woodrow Wilson

WWTLS (WC, NjP).

## From Josiah Worth Wright

Dear Sir, Princeton Dec 3d 1895

Some time ago you requested my bills for extras. I have neglected sending them, not having had really time to do all that I should have done. And as I would like to have some funds if convenient, I now send them to you. Please look over them, and if I have ommitted anything you will remind me of it. Or if anything is not satisfactory please tell me. I have really charged you no profit on anything, and perhaps hardly cost for some of it. The gas pipe you will pay Princeton gas light company for. I have charged you with the digging & filling. The cess pool cost rather more than I told you on account of rock, which I told you if we found rock the cost would be more.

I have given you the cost of all attic work, no charge for the bath room work, as the partitions in lower story I thought would pay it. The white coating will cost one hundred and eight dollars. It is really worth more.

The extra in dining room quartered oak will be twenty five dollars.

If the mountain stones are used for steps at front door the two steps would cost set about eighteen dollars. I think I have stated all to this time. You are not charged with soil pipe to cess pool.

Most Respectfully yours J W. Wright

P.S. The white coating will be done next week.

J. W. W.

ALS (WP, DLC) with WWhw figures on env. showing cost of house and sources of funds.

## From Eliphalet Nott Potter[1]

Dear Prof. Wilson                    Geneva, N. Y., Dec. 3d 1895

It will be a privilege to aid somewhat your excellent work of which I know favorably from the printed page as well as from your reputation. My matter was put together in enforced haste, the proofreading entrusted to others, & the list of erata at the end of the book[2] I discovered too late to correct the plates. I packed my material away intending deliberate rewriting; & it will require a hunt to find what you want, & delay as I am just preparing to leave on College business; but return next week. Kindly drop me a line of reminder then *if it will still be of use to you*; & tell me somewhat of the impression of my Washington &c you speak of having read.

In haste              Very sincerely yours   E N. Potter

ALS (WP, DLC).
[1] President of Hobart College.
[2] Eliphalet Nott Potter, *Washington a Model in His Library and Life* (New York, 1895).

## From Josiah Worth Wright

Dear Sir                        Princeton Dec 4th 1895

Your favor of this date received containing check for five hundred dollars for which I thank you very much.

I have receipted two bills and credited on the other, so as to make the amounts all right. The door that would be left by the change in second story, I thought would match the one under attic staircase. This stairs I estimated would cost $70.00. The stair builder charges me for his work $58. leaving me $12. I did not estimate the closet under it. So you will see by the time I have the partition put up and plastered to make the closet under and the wash boards down and shelves and hooks, or what you desire in closet, and the stair rails & balisters stained & varnished, and all wood work completed, I will not have much. So in order to keep this within the price, I would take this door, and make no other charge. The closet in lower hall leading to your study will balance what wainscotting it will take around this place. If the closet is not put up elsewhere.

We can arrange all this satisfactory. I have laid down boards in cellar for heater men to work on, so they will not injure cellar floor.

The[y] say it will take them two weeks to get through. We will be ready to white coat and trim as soon as they are done. And will push it to completion as fast as possible.

Most Respectfully yours   J. W. Wright

ALS (WP, DLC) with WWhw notation on env.: "Receipt for Extras." Encs.: two receipted bills dated Nov. 28, 1895.

## From Sanae Takata[1]

My dear Sir;                         December 5th 1895. Tokio, Japan.

Though I have never had the honor of meeting you, still your name is quite familiar to me for I have derived much pleasure and profit from the study of your books. About five years ago one of them, "The State," was brought to me by a friend on his return from America. Many English and American works on Political science have from time to time been brought to Japan, but few books exist in which the subject is similarly treated, and certainly not one covering the same ground has yeat [yet] appeared in the Japanese Language.

Accordingly it was my earnest desire that I might be permitted to translate it for the use of my students in Tokio Senmon Gakko, the college in which I occupy the chair of Political science. So I undertook the task, but as I have since been engaged in addition to my college duties, being responsible for much political and journalistic works, the translation has occupied me quite four years.

Having now at last completed it I take great pleasure in sending to you a copy of your work as it appears in Japanese with the hope that you will do me the great honor to accept it. I can not of course expect that the translation will bear comparison with the original and yet believe me it contains but few errors. Since its publication the Japanese version has received very favorable criticism from our press, and I assure you that your teachings have made you many earnest followers amongst my countrymen

For my own part I wish to thank you also for your other work entitled "The Congressional Government" which I read with interest

It is my earnest desire that I may sometime have the privilage of seeing you, but in the mean time believe me with science [sincere] wishes for your good health.

I remain yours very truly   Sanae Takata

ALS (WP, DLC) with WWhw notation on env.: "Ans. 6 Apr/96."
[1] Identified in M. Kamatz to WW, Nov. 10, 1895, n. 2.

A Newspaper Report of a Lecture in Lancaster

[Dec. 6, 1895]

MACHIAVELLI

At Maennerchor hall last evening a cultured and appreciative audience of fair numbers assembled to hear the second in the present series of University Extension lectures by Prof. Woodrow Wilson, on "Machiavelli, the Politician of the Renaissance." It was a lecture of more than usual merit, both in the subject matter which it contained and in the manner it was presented. Following is an abstract:

Machiavelli is not a man to be held up as a model of political doctrine. His name has been a synonym for subtlety and intrigue. But he is not as bad a man as he has been painted. His own age did not condemn him. We should not take a man out of his own times and judge him by subsequent times. He was not a rogue; he was a man of science, of profound philosophy—not a monster, but a type of his age.

He came of age before the world began, as Americans say— just one year before the discovery of America. It was an age of transition. It was not singular that Machiavelli's political bias should be what it was, coming into the maturity of his powers in the full flood of the renaissance, in an age which has been defined as a revival of the world, the flesh and the devil. Men had heretofore looked upon the world as exterior to themselves. The lesson of the middle ages was, keep your eye upon your heart; live a life of discipline; the exterior world is not to be enjoyed. The renaissance was an awakening; men enjoyed their sensations again; life became a fete-day. No wonder men went too far in this new and ample ether; and the natural consequence was a revival of the devil, for there was no moral restraint. Men in these times wrote for beauty of language and rhythm, without regard for morals.

It was at this period that Machiavelli came into public notice, being the age of tyrants in Italy, but tyrants in a technical sense only. Men made themselves tyrants by their wits rather than by blood. Conditions were such as to stimulate men to be singular. There was a bidding for wits—a universal stimulant for originality. There were two lines along which genius expressed itself— the military and the intellectual. Machiavelli was a composite photograph of his contemporaries, plus extraordinary genius.

He was born in 1469, of a noble family which had contributed thirteen gonfalonieri and fifty-three priors to the public service of Florence. He entered the service of the city during the brief period of the freedom from the Medicean tyranny, 1494-1512. Florence was then under the influence of the genius of that remarkable religious leader, Savonarola, who for four years, with the whips of God in his hand, had held the licentious city in restraint. It was within a few months of Savonarola's death that Machiavelli came into the public service. His office was second chancellor and secretary of the city. His duties were to conduct the correspondence, both foreign and domestic, of the government. He was twenty-three times sent upon embassies. No man knew as much about the courts of Europe as Machiavelli. Some of his best writings are descriptions of his foreign visits, and form the most acute analysis of national life in political literature. He was absolutely devoted to Florence during this time. He studied the politics of other governments so as to derive the best political results for Florence.

When the Medici came into power again he was expelled from office. During his retirement he led an aimless and frivolous life, and longing once more for political power, he, to his eternal dishonor, became fawning and servile, and begged to be restored to power, not so much for the welfare of Florence, as simply to have a hand in the game of power. He died in 1527.

The writings that immortalized Machiavelli as a leader of political thought are "The Prince," and his "Discourse on the First Book of Livy." He went back for inspiration to the pure, pristine thoughts of Livy, and yet in his "Prince," which was a book of doctrine for the Medici, he advocates the doctrine of craft. Machiavelli studied politics as a means to an end. His political doctrines were dynamic rather than moral. He said the best form of government is republican, but this is not the age for that sort of a government. The prince must reign by craft, because morals are out of fashion. His whole aim was the unification of Italy. He conceived what Victor Emmanuel has only accomplished several hundred years afterwards.

His service to political thought was "that he thoroughly, if cynically and even brutally, separated politics and morals, and created statecraft into a distinct science." His error was "in leaving morality, good habit and righteous principle out of his calculation of forces, and regarding only craft and courage."

The lecturer, in concluding, remarked that it was a good thing for sentimental men to read Machiavelli, as he would cause the scales to fall from their eyes, in their view of the world of politics.

Printed in the Lancaster, Pa., *Daily Intelligencer*, Dec. 6, 1895; one editorial heading omitted.

## Notes for Remarks to the Philadelphia Alumni

Reception to Dr. Patton,      Philadelphia, 10 December, 1895.

In approaching the Sesqui-Centennial we are approaching a day of Reckoning, as well as a day of gratulation and hope.

We have an ideal and a responsibility which are set us by our past and by the nature of the society which we serve.

The object of all education in such a polity as ours should be the creation of thoughtful observation and a wide-eyed sagacity in action.

Not the elaboration of a university where anybody can come to learn anything (as Ezra Cornell wished), but a place where, if a man come, he shall be subjected to the wisdom of the world.

Change is not necessarily improvement; addition is not always development. Development and improvement are, in such a case, organic processes, not arithmetical.

Addition, however, is much cheaper than development, which means an enrichment and rounded completion of the whole organism. It needs more money to develop than to add.

Surely money may be asked for such purposes with confidence, for to effect such a development is to serve the nation in the most opportune fashion.

It is exactly our danger as a nation that we are, though much informed, too little enlightened. We have too little subjected ourselves to the wisdom of the world; have gone too little abroad in our instruction in the free air of un-localized thought, valid without regard to latitude or longitude.[1]

WWT MS. (WP, DLC).
[1] It is interesting that these notes constitute a partial outline of Wilson's Sesquicentennial address, "Princeton in the Nation's Service," printed at Oct. 21, 1896, Vol. 10.


## A Newspaper Report of a Meeting of the Philadelphia Alumni

[Dec. 11, 1895]

### PRESIDENT PATTON GIVEN A RECEPTION

A reception was given to Dr. Francis Landey Patton, president of Princeton University, by the alumni of this city, at the Philadelphia Bourse last night. Next October the celebration of the one-hundred-and-fiftieth anniversary of the founding of the institution will take place, and the reception had more than the usual interest attached to it. The friends and the alumni of

Princeton are anxious to signalize the anniversary celebration by the creation of a large fund to enable President Patton to carry out his plans.

President Patton was accompanied by Professor Woodrow Wilson and Professor Andrew F. West, and when he faced the happy throng of alumni at the Bourse building he was greeted with loud applause. Perhaps Dr. Patton looks better to-day than he has for many years. His cheeks are filled out and had considerable color last night. Heretofore Dr. Patton's face has been pale and showed the effects of a severe scholastic life. So with the return of almost youthful vigor he is ready to usher in a new era for Princeton when the se[s]quicentennial occurs. . . .

President Patton . . . gave a brief sketch of what the new era of Princeton would be. He said that the institution had been conducted on lines that have stood the test of time. In the old days Princeton rested on the classics, mathematics, natural sciences and mental and moral philosophy. On these broad grounds there had been developments. So in the future Princeton would continue her expansion in the same logical manner. He was opposed to individualism, but was in favor of a policy of free exchange of sound learning among the classes.

Dr. Patton referred to the university spirit of Princeton. He said that the true university spirit exists in the institution. Specialization is offered to the students, but it is related in a logical manner to the fundamental branches of learning. He said that he was ready for a stern struggle in order to carry out the liberal policy on which the institution was founded. . . .

Professor Woodrow Wilson in a speech said that in the new era of Princeton it was her duty to follow the same organic method of expansion. He deplored from an educational standpoint any indiscriminate mixture of special courses. The point with a university is to enlighten and to bring wisdom to the students. There must be a synthesis of branches so that the liberal education will be thoroughly rounded. After Professor West had spoken the alumnae sat down to a lunch. . . .

Printed in the *Philadelphia Press*, Dec. 11, 1895; some editorial headings omitted.

## To John Davis Adams

Princeton, New Jersey,

My dear Mr. Adams,                    11 December, 1895.

I write to make one more suggestion with regard to the illustration of the third paper on Washington.

At page 69 of volume six of Winsor's Narrative and Critical History of America there is a very striking picture of a statue of James Otis, at least the upper part of which, I think, ought to be reproduced for the article (which will have a passage about Otis)[1] and placed just before the portrait of Henry.[2]

Thank you for the corrected proofs.

Very truly Yours, Woodrow Wilson

WWTLS (NNPM).
[1] The passage on Otis appeared in Woodrow Wilson, "At Home in Virginia," *Harper's Magazine*, xcii (May 1896), 939-40.
[2] Neither the picture of the Otis statue nor the portrait of Patrick Henry appeared in the article just cited.

## To Howard Pyle

My dear Mr. Pyle,     Princeton, New Jersey, 11 December, 1895.

Only about one half of my third paper on Washington is written. That half I will send you a copy of early next week. Meanwhile, the whole of the paper being pretty thoroughly in my mind in detail, let me tell you what it is to contain and put you in the way of planning your illustrations.

The article will have three parts, if you will let me analyze it. The first part will deal with Washington's early domestic life: his marriage and settling down at Mt. Vernon, his farming, his hunting, his social diversions, his standing candidate for the Burgesses, etc., etc. This part seems to me to need, as illustration, a picture of some part of the marriage ceremonial (the scene in the church, the procession home from the church, or etc.,—all described in detail in G.W.P. Custis's Memoirs;[1] or a picture of a fox-hunting meet with Lord Fairfax (best pictured in the frontispiece to Conway's "Barons of the Rappahannock and Potomac"), Colonel Fairfax (whose portrait I have not seen), Bryan Fairfax, George Mason (frontispiece to Kate Mason Rowland's Life of Mason),[2] "Jacky" Custis, and one or two others in the group; or Washington standing for the deer in the woods about George Mason's place, Gunston Hall.

The second part of the article will be full of a mixture of politics and social life, in Williamsburg and elsewhere, in which politics will predominate. Here, I can't help thinking, the very best illustration for my purpose would be the following group in deep private consultation (the thing is historical) in a small room of the Raleigh tavern: Patrick Henry, Richard Henry Lee, Dabney Carr, Thos. Jefferson (age 23 or 24), and F. L. Lee. They were often in counsel how to bring the Burgesses to the proper radical measures towards England after the Stamp Act. There could be nothing more really illustrative of this part.

The article culminates in the sending of delegates from Virginia to the first Continental Congress: and the illustration which most "sticks in my head" is one which would represent the three delegates, Washington, Patrick Henry, and Peyton Randolph, getting to their horses in front of the door at Mt. Vernon, to set out for Philadelphia.

These illustrations, with a head-piece of Williamsburg and a tail-piece containing Carpenters' Hall in Philadelphia, seem to me to constitute an ideal illumination of the article.

I need not say in what way I mean these suggestions: not as limiting you, but as interpreting the paper. It is to run through the scenes, both social and political, at Williamsburg during the years 1764-1774, including the "reigns" of the ineffective Botetourt and the pretentious Dunmore: balls, debates, horse-races. The scenes I have imagined are most central and typical.

Please ask me what you like, if this is not clear or sufficient; and expect the paper itself, in installments, as fast as it can be gotten ready.

With warm regard,

                    Cordially Yours,   Woodrow Wilson

WWTLS (photostat in RSB Coll., DLC).
  [1] George Washington Parke Custis, *Memoirs of Washington . . .* , ed. by Benson John Lossing (New York, 1859).
  [2] *The Life of George Mason,* 1725-1792 (2 vols., New York and London, 1892).


## A Newspaper Report of a Lecture in Lancaster

[Dec. 13, 1895]

### MONTESQUIEU.

Lancastrians who lay claim to any degree of culture and erudition, and who are neglecting to attend the present University Extension lectures by Prof. Woodrow Wilson, are simply missing a grand intellectual treat, such as they may not have opportunity to enjoy soon again. Prof. Wilson is a lecturer who has now a foremost place among the most polished scholars of the day. One is hardly able to determine whether one is more struck with wonder at the inexhaustible knowledge he has at ready command, or charmed with the 'well of English undefiled' from which he draws so copiously and pleasantly in clothing his thoughts and presenting his subject to his hearers.

The subject of last evening's lecture was "Montesquieu, the French Political Seer." Prof. Wilson said in substance:

It is a little difficult for people of other nations to appreciate a Frenchman; they are too expressively humorous. French literature seems flippant; the French writer has a way of playing with his subjects which does not meet with general approval from foreigners.

Montesquieu was a typical Frenchman. He came from the south of France and was touched, as it were, by the soil of that country. In coming from Machiavelli to Montesquieu we come from the politician to the observer. Montesquieu was a man who wrote to please the world. He wrote as if for people reading in the evening after business was over. He recognized the fact that one must please a French audience to instruct them.

Montesquieu belonged to the same age as Voltaire, 1685-1755— just after the age of Corneille, Racine, Moliere and others of that galaxy of illustrious men. It was the golden age of French literature—the time of Louis XIV, when under the smile of the king all France seemed to find its tongue; a grand time in which to live— just after the great Elizabethan age of English literature. He was born at the chateau La Brede, ten miles from Bordeaux, and was, therefore, a fellow countryman of Montaigne's. There was a great deal of similarity between these two illustrious Frenchmen, and they both show the qualities of that sunny country, the south of France. It is said that a beggar came to the door when Montesquieu was an infant, and was made to stand as godfather to the child, in order that he would realize that he was a kinsman to the common people. He was put to school at a monastery, subsequently receiving a legal training. In 1714 he was admitted a counsellor in the parliament of Bordeaux. He inherited the office of president of parliament from his uncle, and the office fell to his heritage most appropriately. He was extremely near sighted, and would never assist his eyesight by wearing glasses; that was the reason, it is said, why he put his nose so deep into things and looked at things so near at hand and understood them so thoroughly.

Machiavelli's study was how states are made by statecraft. Montesquieu's study was how states are made by nature. He traveled extensively, and while Machiavelli studied the politics of other governments in order to derive the best advantages for his own country, Montesquieu, on the other hand, studied politics in order to get at the best results for mankind in general. He sympathized with other countries because he felt he belonged to them. He said "the best government is that which attains its object at the least expense, and which, therefore, governs men in the way best suited to their disposition, and to their inclination." His purpose was the doctrine of circumstances. "Laws must have regard to the historical, physical, intellectual, and even accidental conditions of each nation, and must, besides, have definite relations to one another. These various circumstantial relations of the law to national conditions and to one another constitute, when taken together and analyzed, what I have called ' The Spirit of the Laws.' "

He said: "Each government has its distinctive and characteristic principle, resulting from the nature of its political constitution. In democracy the principle is virtue—a regard for the public good; in monarchy it is honor,—a love of the monarch and of privilege.

"The corruption of governments generally results in each case from the degeneration of its characteristic principle. The vital principle of democracy becomes corrupt when equality is either lost or carried to extremes. The vital principle of monarchy becomes corrupt when the love of honor degenerates into pride and selfish aggrandizement."

"Political liberty exists only where government is moderate, where the powers of government are exercised impartially and in the careful observance of law, and where a just balance of social forces makes no part of the government supreme. Hence a division and constitutional balance of the executive, legislative and judicial powers of government necessary to liberty. Reform, like nature works well only when it works slowly and equably."

His style and method were the rich and pointed observations of a man of insight and a master of style, rather than a systematic treatment by a master of science.

His influence was such as made Voltaire say: "Humanity had lost its title deeds, and Montesquieu found them."

The political philosophy of Montesquieu stands test to this day. We, as Americans, especially owe him a debt such as we do not owe to any other political philosopher.

Printed in the Lancaster, Pa., *Daily Intelligencer*, Dec. 13, 1895; one editorial heading omitted.


## From John Davis Adams

Dear Mr. Wilson:                    New York. December 14th 1895

Mr. Alden wishes me to say that the *Magazine* has already published a portrait of James Otis, which will be available for your book. The same thing is true of several other portraits omitted from the *Magazine* papers: but all of them will be at your service if you wish to use them later.

Permit me to say, for my own part, that your Washington is a very real person to me and that I have had a keen pleasure in reading the two papers you have already sent us.

Yours sincerely,   John D Adams

ALS (WP, DLC).


## To Howard Pyle

My dear Mr. Pyle,     Princeton, New Jersey, 17 December, 1895.

I send you what is, perhaps, half my third article, including the whole of the transition from the first to the second part, as I analyzed it in my recent letter to you. I shall hope to get the rest into your hands within ten days or two weeks.

In great haste,

Cordially Yours,   Woodrow Wilson

WWTLS (deCoppet Coll., NjP).


## From Howard Pyle

Dear Professor Wilson:       Wilmington, Del., Dec. 18th., 1895.

I have received your note speaking of the subjects you would suggest for the third Washington article. They are exactly such as I myself would have chosen, and it seems to me that their selection by you shows a singular similarity in our views.

I think that Washington's marriage is essentially one to be taken rather than the other one of the hunting party, but it seems to me that the home-coming of the newly married couple at Mt Vernon (probably in the state coach—I have not yet read up the details) would make a most interesting point—representing the house servants standing around, grinning a welcome, and the major domo opening the door of the coach.

To represent this correctly I shall probably have to have a view of Mt Vernon and shall, if possible, run down to Washington and take a photograph. Can you tell me how near the Mt Vernon of the present is like the Mt Vernon of that time? I do not know of any picture of it at the time of Washington's marriage.

The other subjects, it seems to me, are also very well chosen, especially the meeting of the patriots at the Raleigh tavern. I remember a picture of the room in the Raleigh tavern in Lossing's Field Book of the Revolution.[1] Do you know whether there is any better picture than that?

I shall probably begin work upon the third article in the course of two or three weeks.

Please remember me most kindly to Mrs Wilson and, thanking you for your very satisfactory letter, I am

Faithfully yours    Howard Pyle

TLS (WP, DLC).
[1] Benson John Lossing, *The Pictorial Field-Book of the Revolution* (2 vols., New York, 1851-52).

## Memorandum for an Interview[1]

[c. Dec. 18, 1895]

Whether the policy now being pursued by the President be, or be not, a just and logical inference from the doctrine wh. Monroe uttered to check the aggressions of the Holy Alliance, it should be discussed and assessed upon its own merits. The general question wh. it raises is this: Do we wish to assume such a protectorate and dictatorship over South America as always to let the internal rivalries and disorders of that Continent run what course they will, provided no European power have any interest in them, and yet always to interfere, with menace of war if we be snubbed, in every matter, tho. it be only a boundary dispute, in wh. any European power has part or lot, even when our interference is in breach alike of international law and courtesy? To that question I sh. answer, most assuredly not, if we are to keep our immemorial dignity and self-respect.

But there is a special question, besides, involved in this particular case; for the difficulty is with Eng. Do we wish—ought we to dare, unless driven by imperative justice and necessity—to bring about a deadly war between the two branches of the Eng. race, in whose hands lie, if they be united, the future destinies of the world; whose literature but just now begins to rise to a common voice in a common cause of enlightenment and progress; who, if divided, may be ousted of their supremacy? I sh. recoil fr. such a war as I sh. from laying violent hands on civilization itself. The disaster of it, in any case, no man can adequately imagine; the disgrace of it, if provoked upon a slight cause, no man could speak.

WWhw MS. (WP, DLC).
[1] Wilson probably drafted this memorandum after a reporter from the *New York Times* asked him for an interview about President Cleveland's message to Congress of December 17, 1895. In this message, Cleveland recommended that an American special commission be established to settle a long-standing boundary dispute between Venezuela and British Guiana because British retention of the disputed territory might constitute a violation of the Monroe Doctrine. The British government had earlier refused American offers of mediation and had re-

pudiated the right of the United States to intervene. Cleveland concluded his
message with the ominous statement that he was fully aware of the consequences
which might ensue from unilateral action by the United States Government.

## To Howard Pyle

My dear Mr. Pyle,

Princeton, New Jersey,
20 December, 1895.

Your letter of the eighteenth gratified me very much. It is delightful to find that we jump so together in the matter of the illustrations, and have such a natural community of taste.

The only trouble about selecting the home coming of the bridal
party is that, as you will see from my narrative sent you the
other day, they did not go at once to Mount Vernon. For the first
three months they lived at the "White House," Mrs. Custis's own
residence (I do not know whether it is still standing or not, or
whether there is a picture of it),[1] then they attended the session
of the House of Burgesses at Williamsburg, and *then* went to
Mount Vernon. But this final home coming may well have been
as picturesque, children and all in the group, as the other would
have been.

There are various views of Mount Vernon in Lossing's "Home
of Washington: Mount Vernon and Its Associations." I presume
that he also gives an account of such changes in its appearance
as had taken place when he wrote. Unfortunately, I have not a
copy at hand.

The group of radicals who met from time to time for conference in a private room in the Raleigh did not meet in the "Appolo
room" shown in page 484 of Lossing's *Handbook of the Revolution*, Vol. II. That was the assembly or ball room, in which the
convention did meet. They met "in a private room": possibly (it
would at any rate be picturesque) in one of the up-stairs rooms
with a dormer window (see Lossing's *Handbook*, page 486, Vol.
II., for the exterior of the Tavern as a whole.)

With warm regards from both Mrs. Wilson and myself,

Faithfully Yours,   Woodrow Wilson

WWTLS (deCoppet Coll., NjP).
  [1] A picture of the "White House" did appear in Wilson's "At Home in Virginia,"
*loc. cit.*, p. 933.

## To John Davis Adams

My dear Mr. Adams,

Princeton, New Jersey,
20 December, 1895.

I enclose memoranda for the correction of the map. I return
the map itself, with copy, under another cover.

I want to thank you very warmly for your kind words about my papers. To make Washington real and thoroughly human to the imagination is just what I am trying to do: in a certain sense, it is *all* I am trying to do; and your opinion that I have so far succeeded heartens me not a little. It was generous of you to volunteer the praise; and I appreciate it most warmly. I cannot myself judge in what degree I am succeeding.

I note what you say, for Mr. Alden, about portraits which have already appeared in the Magazine. I had hoped that it would not be thought amiss to repeat such illustrations when they came so naturally, and almost necessarily in in [sic] another connection; but I can see that it might be tiresome, and I am much obliged for Mr. Alden's kind suggestion about the use of illustrations for the book, should we subsequently arrange to have these articles take that shape.

Very cordially Yours,   Woodrow Wilson

WWTLS (Berg Coll., NN).


## From Eliphalet Nott Potter's Personal Secretary

My dear Sir,                        Geneva, N. Y. Dec. 20th, '95.
President Potter has been engaged in duties away from the college; we do not find the letter of which the extract referred to in your favor forms part. But President Potter requests us to call your attention to Payton's Reminiscences of "Gen. Braddock's stay (1755) at Williamsburg,"[1] or Rev. Dr. Edward Neill's "Washington adapted for an emergency";[2]—one or both for the letter referred to.

Respectfully yours   President Potter<br>per Pres' Personal Sect'ry.

ALS (WP, DLC).
[1] Probably John Lewis Peyton, *The Adventures of My Grandfather* (London, 1867), pp. 225-49.
[2] Edward Duffield Neill, *Washington Adapted for a Crisis* (St. Paul, Minn., 1889).


## To Howard Pyle

My dear Mr. Pyle,     Princeton, New Jersey, 23 December, 1895.
I must write at once to express my admiration for the illustrations you have made for my first article.[1] They seem to me in every way admirable. They heighten the significance of the text, not only, being entirely in its spirit, but are themselves, besides, perfect in their kind. The last of the three seems to me especially

delightful for its humour and truth. I have just written to beg the publishers to let me have proof copies of them, and of the rest as they follow: for I shall certainly want to frame some: all, indeed, that I can find room for.

You have my sincerest thanks.

Cordially Yours,   Woodrow Wilson

WWTLS (deCoppet Coll., NjP).
    [1] The first article had just appeared in *Harper's Magazine*.

## To Winthrop More Daniels

My dear Daniels,       Princeton, New Jersey, 25 December, 1895.

I used a pen all this morning, and I know that you will pardon my falling back on this[1] for a rest.

I am sincerely obliged to you for your letter.[2] I sympathise most heartily with every word in it; and have taken a day or two to think over its advice. Almost immediately after the publication of the message a correspondent of the New York *Times* came down to see me; and I expressed myself to him very freely. What he published I do not know. Somehow I missed it. But I know that he published my opposition because several people I met in Tarrytown and New York soon afterwards spoke of it and expressed their hearty concurrence with my views.[3]

A letter, therefore, would only be more to the same effect, and would almost necessarily be argumentative. If I sent it to the *Post*, it would be coals sent to Newcastle; if to the *Times*, it would either be thrust in a corner or editorially belittled or distorted:[4] whereupon other letters from W. W., etc.

I have come to the conclusion that the present is not the time to do more, therefore. I have expressed my opinion: people's minds are at present too biassed and excited one way or the other to hear more. The sober second thought is coming. If it does not come in satisfactory shape, there will at least be a season for rational argument.

I cannot write more now, being pressed for time with my Washington matter; but I thank you again and most heartily for having such confidence in me as to know me on the right side.

Mrs. Wilson joins me in warmest regards,

Faithfully Yours,   Woodrow Wilson

P.S. What a talent the University of Chicago is developing for family quarrels![5]

WWTLS (W. M. Daniels Coll., CtY).
    [1] His typewriter.
    [2] This letter is missing.

³ The Editors have been unable to find Wilson's interview in the extant editions of the *New York Times*.

⁴ The New York *Evening Post* was in the vanguard of the opposition to the growing anti-British sentiment, while the *New York Times* was leading the jingoists.

⁵ Wilson presumably was referring to the public controversy over the dismissal of Edward Webster Bemis from his position as lecturer in the University Extension Department of the University of Chicago. Bemis stated publicly in October 1895 that he was being dropped because of his pro-labor opinions, especially the sentiments that he had voiced at the time of the Pullman strike of 1894. William Rainey Harper, President of the University, insisted that the sole reason for Bemis' dismissal was his incompetence as a teacher. See Richard J. Storr, *Harper's University: The Beginnings* (Chicago, 1966), pp. 83-85, and Richard Hofstadter and Walter P. Metzger, *The Development of Academic Freedom in the United States* (New York, 1955), pp. 427-36.

## From James Howard Whitty

Dear Professor—                    Richmond, Va., Dec. 26, 1895.

Yours 23d to hand. The little book you ask me about is quite rare and should be for it is full of interest.¹

I knew of a copy for sale and have written my New York buyer to try to get it and forward to your address. If he succeeds you can remit me $3.75 at your convenience—the cost. If he fails, I will send you my own copy by express to be loaned until you finish whatever task you have on hand. I know a Virginia collector who has been looking for this book fifteen years. I rarely meet with it but recently had an intimation of a copy for sale. Hoping that the copy will reach you as it is worth a place in your library & that I may be of further service to you I am

                         Yours truly   J. H. Whitty

I have your article in Harpers before me to read.

ALS (WP, DLC) with WWhw notation on env.: "Ans. 29 Dec. '95."
¹ Since Wilson's letter of December 23 is missing, the name of the little book is unknown.

## From Edward Ireland Renick

My dear Wilson:                   Washington December 29, 1895.

You are always giving me surprises. For several years I have been going inch by inch over the ground that I now see in your Harpers serials you have been traversing with much more observant eyes, and all the time I was reproaching myself for not paying attention to what I supposed you considered alone worthy of study—great political movements. Yet here you now appear cheek by jowl with my old friend Colonel Byrd, whose good company, unbeknown to me, you have been keeping all these years, pointing out to me the various classes of people who were his contemporaries and entertaining me with their modes of life & habits of thought. I have run across you, as it were, in an out-of-the-way place, visited only by a few folks of quiet tastes and ample leisure, and learn to my great joy that you have an intimate acquaintance with all of its inhabitants.

When you next visit this city I hope you will go with me to see Dr Toner, whose Diaries of Washington, I hope you have consulted, and Dr George Byrd Harrison whose walls are adorned with portraits of Colonel William Byrd & his descendants. I hope that the visit will be made this winter. My object now is to tell you how much I have enjoyed your first chapter and how eager I am to see what is to come. You have done it all well & have most admirably and truthfully set before us the various classes of people living in Virginia in the 17th and first half of the 18th century, something only half done by others. Only one word of caution. Are you sure of the English ancestry of Washington? I have never looked into this, but I have reason to think that much has been written on the subject that is not trustworthy. As to the way folks along the rivers lived, have you seen Mrs. Rowland's Life of George Mason? I read it at a country place adjoining Gunston Hall & then visited the old place. I wish you had been with me. Then I went to Pohick church. With kindest regards to Mrs. Wilson & the family & wishing for all of you a happy new year,          I am, as ever yours,    E. I. Renick

ALS (WP, DLC) with WWhw notation on env.: "Ans. 8 Jan'y '96."


## To Howard Pyle

My dear Mr. Pyle,      Princeton, New Jersey, 30 December, 1895.

I take pleasure in sending you the rest of No. III., whose title I wish to change to "At Home *in Virginia.*"

You will notice that the meetings of the young leaders of the assembly at the Raleigh tavern were held in the evening.

As to the three men starting for the congress of 1774 (Washington, Henry, and Pendleton), at the end of this narrative, you will not need to be told anything about two of them. I add this, however, to what I say of Edmund Pendleton at pp. 36, 37 of my MS. He was fifty-five in 1774 (Washington, forty-two, Henry, thirty-eight), but described as in the full vigour of an unusually fine physique (he was to live twenty-seven years longer). He was fully six feet, of noble form, lithe and graceful; and had the reputation of being the handsomest man in the colony. The only picture I have found of him is a little cut in Appleton's Cyclopaedia of American Biography.

I have already expressed my delight with the illustrations of the first article; but I cannot help adding Mrs. Wilson's comment on the third one,[1] that it reminds one, in its subtle touches of character, of Gérôme.[2]

With much regard,

        Cordially Yours, Woodrow Wilson

WWTLS (deCoppet Coll., NjP).

[1] It was a full-page illustration depicting Governor William Berkeley standing at a large table opposite three commissioners from the Puritan Commonwealth. Berkeley is in the act of signing the terms of submission on March 12, 1652.

[2] Jean Léon Gérôme (1824-1904), French painter, sculptor, and teacher, known chiefly for his genre and figure studies and illustrations.

*Howard Pyle's tailpiece for Wilson's article,*
*"In Washington's Day"*

## To Henry Mills Alden

            Princeton, New Jersey,
My dear Mr. Alden,        1 January, 1895 [1896]

The proof copies of the engravings for Nos. I. and II. of my Washington papers came to-day; and I wish to thank you for them most cordially. I will of course regard those for the March number as confidential till Feb'y 22; and greatly appreciate your kindness in letting me have them thus beforehand.

With much regard,

      Most Cordially Yours, Woodrow Wilson

ALS (NNPM).

# A Newspaper Report of a Lecture in Lancaster

EDMUND BURKE.                [Jan. 3, 1896]

The subject of last evening's lecture of the University Extension course was "Burke, the Interpreter of English Liberty." It is simply impossible for a mere report to do anything like justice to this superb lecture by Professor Woodrow Wilson. Nothing like it has probably ever been heard in this city. A very meagre abstract follows:

In the middle of the last century two Irishmen, Edmund Burke and Oliver Goldsmith, crossed the Irish sea to cast their wits upon the English market. The gifts of these two rare men were certainly diverse, though they resembled each other in their innocency and readiness "to be taken in." We could not have forgiven Ireland if she had not given us these two great men. We could not have spared either of them. Though a true Irishman no man more distinctly uttered the English voice in politics than Edmund Burke.

The function of the lecturer on Burke is clear; it is to stand between the audience and the man as little as possible. Burke can speak for himself. The singular quality of Burke's writings is their beauty of phrase combined with their soundness of sense.

Of Burke's private life we know very little. He took advantage of the privacy of a great city, where every man is conveniently near to his burrow. For years, for decades, we know only his public acts. He was born January 12, 1729. From 12 to 14 he went to school at Shackelton's (a Quaker), at Ballytop, County Kildare. He was singularly subject to the influence of this cool, suave man. From 14 to 18 he went to Trinity college, Dublin. Tradition says that he never read the talks [tasks] assigned to him, but read other things that helped him better for his purpose in life. He had a singular taste for Cicero, which developed into the deepest companionship of his days of early reading. He graduated at Trinity college in 1748. He undertook the study of law, but did not look forward with pleasure to spending his life as a lawyer.

The four great questions of his political life were the American war, the reform of the English administration, the French revolution, and the administration of India's affairs.

He did not aim to immortalize himself by means of his utterances, but rather to serve the purposes of the hour. He combined common sense politics with the imagination of the poet. His philosophy was expediency—to do the things that are best to do under the circumstances. "If you wish to better your government and yet keep it from revolution, keep it from corruption, and by making it wise and pure render it permanent." This is unquestionably the message of England to the world in politics. Burke's method was "to take the questions of the moment to the light, and hold them up to be seen where great principles of conduct may shine upon them from out the general experience of the race."

Printed in the Lancaster, Pa., *Daily Intelligencer*, Jan. 3, 1896; one editorial heading omitted.

## From Margaret Randolph Axson

My dear Brother Woodrow,　　　　　　　Athens Ga. Jan. 3, 1896.

I am afraid you will think that I do not appreciate the lovely books you sent, as I have not written to thank you but I went to Gainesville two days before Xmas and stayed much longer than I intended and as Mama[1] did not send the books I have just seen them. I am so glad that you sent me your own books instead of any other, but it will be sometime before I get an opportunity to read the smaller, for Aunt Mayme[2] claimed it immediately and I will have to wait.

Leila Axson[3] is visiting some friends in town. It seems that we are not to meet often for her friends keep her busy and as she is staying on the campus the girls all refuse to go with me, and there are too many boys to face alone. She has been here twice however.

Give much love to Sister and the children with a great deal for your dear self from

your devoted sister　Madge

ALS (WP, DLC).
　[1] Her Aunt Louisa, Mrs. Warren A. Brown, who was rearing her.
　[2] Her cousin-in-law, Mrs. Edward T. Brown.
　[3] Daughter of Randolph Axson of Savannah.

## To Albert Shaw

My dear Shaw,　　　　　　　[Princeton, N. J., c. Jan. 4, 1896]

Your letter[1] a propos Henry Randall Waite conveys an unintentional rebuke. I do "pose as a member of the Advisory Faculty of the Institute of Civics"[2]; and yet I have absolutely nothing to do with its actual administration, and I know no more of Mr. Waite himself than you do. This has long lain heavy on my conscience; and yet, rather than seem to declare my lack of sympathy with what the Institute is trying to do, I have done nothing to get out of so false a position. If I knew a single item about the man, I would give you the benefit of it; but I know nothing.

You can't really believe that I am in the least danger of "blotting you out of the book of my remembrance." I am as little likely to as any fellow you know, valuing our friendship just, I think, as you would most like me to. But in my efforts to pay for a house I am building I have made engagements so many and so exacting that I am afraid all my friends will cool towards me, on the ground of gross neglect, before the winter's over.

I am sincerely distressed to hear of Mrs. Shaw's illness, and heartily hope she may soon come out of it.

I received today a copy of your "Municipal Government in Europe,"[3] marked "with the compliments of the Century Company," which I interpreted to mean the compliments of the author. I am delighted to get the book, and shall read it, engagements or no engagements, with the assurance of being as much instructed, and as well, as by the volume on England.[4] You certainly have the method of this thing to perfection, and lay all the studious world under obligations to you which grow with the addition of each volume.

With affectionate regard,

Faithfully yours,    Woodrow Wilson

TCL (in possession of Virginia Shaw English).
    [1] Shaw's letter is missing.
    [2] The Institute was founded by H. R. Waite in 1885, and from the outset Wilson was listed as a member of the faculty and lecture corps.
    [3] Albert Shaw, *Municipal Government in Continental Europe* (New York, 1895).
    [4] *Municipal Government in Great Britain* (New York, 1895), which Shaw had sent to Wilson on January 5, 1895.

## A Newspaper Report of a Lecture in Lancaster

[Jan. 10, 1896]

### DE TOCQUEVILLE.

A very highly entertained and delighted audience it was that heard Prof. Woodrow Wilson's lecture at Maennerchor hall last evening, on "De Tocqueville, the Student of Democracy." Owing to a deficiency of something over $100 for this present course of University Extension lectures, it had been proposed by the executive committee to combine the two last lectures on Tocqueville and Bagehot into one, which would have reduced the expenses to a point where they could have been met with the funds now in hand. But a strong sentiment against this move was held by the patrons of the course; and as there were enough pledges received last evening to cover the deficiency, the full course of six lectures will be given; the last lecture on "Walter Bagehot," the literary politician will be delivered on next Wednesday (instead of Thursday) evening at half past 8 o'clock. The day has been changed in order not to conflict with the Y.M.C.A. Star course.

Prof. Wilson last evening said, in substance: Tocqueville, like Burke, had no "system" of politics. He was not what we would call a systematic thinker. We Americans owe him a debt of gratitude such as we owe to no other man for his exposition and defense of American democratic institutions; and yet it was because he wanted to help France and not America that he wrote his "Democracy in America."

Tocqueville belonged to the nobility of mankind. There is a great deal that is pathetic about this man. He lived in a period when France went breathlessly from change to change. His recollections went back to the time when men suffered as men never had suffered before; and he himself was not the least of these sufferers during the French reign of terror. Kinsmen of his had been hauled through the streets of Paris to the guillotine; and ties of friendship and consanguinity had been cut asunder during that awful bloody period. Yet withal he seemed driven by a sense of duty to do inestimable service for the country that had served him so cruelly. He was in every sense a man of marked and most attractive character.

Alexis Clerel de Tocqueville was born July 29, 1805, of an ancient Norman family. There was a great deal of Norman capacity lingering in this man's blood. He received an academic and legal training. After the restoration he entered the public service as judge auditeur at Versailles. He served also in the Assembly and on several constitutional committees. He visited America with Beaumont in 1831. Retired from active participation in affairs in 1851, after a brief imprisonment by Louis Napoleon. Died April 16, 1859.

The works that have given Tocqueville high standing as a leader of political thought are "Report on the Penitentiary System of the United States," 1832. "Democracy in America," 1835-40. "Histoire Philosophique du Regne de Louis XV.," 1846. "L'Ancien Regime," 1856.

His principal work is "Democracy in America." His object in writing it was "to show what a democratic people is in our days, and by this delineation, executed with rigorous accuracy," to accomplish a twofold object: (a) dispel the illusions of fanatical advocates of democracy by showing the solid qualities prerequis[i]te to its successful establishment; and (b) quiet the fears of those who feared democracy, by showing how firm and just and orderly a form of government it could be under the right conditions. He thoorughly [thoroughly] understood the character of the French people and did not mince matters in describing it. His eye, throughout the whole study, was upon France, whose unstable temper and political inexperience he keenly felt, and whom he ardently wished to instruct in the sane practice of politics.

Sir Henry Maine deemed democracy a mere form of government; but Tocqueville deemed it a form which expressed a very definite substance of character, being based upon particular social, economic and political conditions which were susceptible of clear analysis.

Sovereignty of the people, he saw "recognized in the customs and proclaimed by the laws" of the United States; and its consequences he clearly perceived. He saw that just because it was habitual it was exercised temperately and with self-possession; and that it engendered a universal habit of association among people of all grades which made effectual action possible in all things.

He believed, on the other hand, however, that it too much chilled and rebuked individual independence of opinion; that it introduced the principle of averages into the public service; and that it made possible a corruption more demoralizing than the corruption of an aristocracy.

He showed his real understanding of our system of government by beginning his study, not with the federal, but with the state governments. "The federal government is the exception; the government of the states is the rule," and he saw this to be the strength of the system. Within the state governments, too, he saw that the root of efficiency lay in local government. "Town-meetings are to liberty what primary schools are to science."

He expected our government to be able because he noted with how great deliberation and self-possession we had established it; because the constitution took for granted, with evident confidence, "variety of information and excellence of discretion" on the part of the people; because he observed a certain uniformity of civilization to obtain throughout the country; because of our fortunate separation from European politics; because of the steady religious habit of our people and their clear sense of right.

It was said of Tocqueville that unfortunately he had begun to think before he began to learn; and the criticism is in part just. But it is his thinking that keeps his matter fresh and vital, quite independently, often, of the accuracy of his observation, and adds him to the small number of political philosophers.

Printed in the Lancaster, Pa., *Daily Intelligencer*, Jan. 10, 1896; one editorial
heading omitted.

## From Howard Pyle

Dear Professor Wilson:          Wilmington, Del., Jan. 11th., 1896.

I have just returned from Washington where I have been making some inquiries and trying to collect material for our pictures for the third Washington article.

I think now I shall be able to illustrate it with three drawings instead of two, as I was afraid I would have to do.

I am getting a photograph of a certain view of Mount Vernon to depict the departure of the three delegates for Philadelphia. I thought it would be better than to have them riding along a road devoid of especial surroundings.

I have just sent on to Harpers a drawing of the meeting of the five men in the upper room of the Raleigh Tavern. As to the third drawing representing the wedding of Washington, I find myself becoming involved in a quandary, so much so that I am going to venture, with great hesitation, to ask you if you are quite sure as to the little insignificant facts? If I understand you[r] article corrcetly [correctly] you say:—

    I.   That they were married at the St Peter's Church.

    II.  That Mrs Washington rode home thence in the coach, General Washington riding beside the coach on horseback.

I find that the family tradition has it that they were married at the bride's residence and that on the following day "Colonel Washington and Mrs Washington attended morning service at the St Peter's Church. They came in the bridal state coach and four of the train of wedding guests, among whom were Speaker John Robinson, etc."

The tradition that they were married at White House and not at the church, may of course be incorrect, but do you think it is rather risky to place Washington upon horse-back riding beside the coach on their return from church? I think he would be riding within the coach, for I find his dress described as follows:—

"A citizen's dress of blue cloth, a coat lined with red silk and orn[a]mented with silver trimmings and a waistcoat of embroidered white satin. The shoes and knee buckles were of gold. His hair was powdered and at his side hung a dress sword."

It seems to me hardly probable that the gallent young Colonel, trigged out in such fine style, would have risked his fine clothes and gold buckles on horse-back. What am I to do about this? I would suggest that if you are sure they were married in the church, that I represent the coach standing in front of the church and the groom leading the bride out by the hand; or else that it be represented by the bridal party riding homeward with an escort surrounding the coach; or else I would represent the imaginary arrival at White House, of which, by the by, I believe there is no picture.

If you bid me represent the St Peter's incident, I will try to obtain a photograph of the church, which, however, I am afraid will be a matter of some difficulty.

Please do not think I am impertinent in questioning what you write, and will you not kindly let me hear from you at the very earliest moment possible, so that I can obtain a photograph if you decide upon that subject

Remember me most kindly to Mrs Wilson, and believe me to be
Faithfully yours    Howard Pyle

TLS (WP, DLC).

## To Howard Pyle

My dear Mr. Pyle,        Princeton, New Jersey, 12 January, 1896.

I take pleasure in answering your letter of yesterday. I can say with all sincerity that the more you test my details the more I shall like it. I am not in the least sensitive on that point.

I think that I can reasonably say that I am sure of the facts. As for the marriage having taken place at St. Peter's Church, you will find it so stated both in Lodge's Life,[1] the latest authoritative biography of Washington, and in the notes to Ford's edition of W's. Works, the latest and most authoritative edition.[2] And Lodge gives all the details as I do, even the the [sic] ride home with the groom on horseback.

But of course I did not rest content with these secondary authorities. I spent a morning in the Lenox browsing over the details, and there satisfied myself on these points; though I did not, on these minor matters, bring away specific references; and can, therefore, not satisfy you, but only say that I convinced myself.[3] My record of his costume corresponds with yours; but I do not see anything intrinsically improbable in a short horseback ride under the circumstances. Only the "citizen's dress of blue cloth" would come into contact with the saddle, in such a rig.

My preference, among the situations you suggest for your picture, would be for the scene at the church, rather than on the road: the young soldier leading his bride forth, and the gallant company of officers and ladies grouped about. No doubt the group was larger and more various in its picturesque quality at the church than at the White House upon the arrival there of the bridal party. But I have unlimited confidence in your artistic knowledge and instinct in such a choice, and express this preference merely because you give me leave, and seem to invite an opinion.

I am delighted to learn that you are to give the article three and not two illustrations. It seems to me to give opportunity for illustration rather better than any of the rest.

With much regard, in which Mrs. Wilson cordially joins,

Faithfully Yours,    Woodrow Wilson

WWTLS (deCoppet Coll., NjP).
1 Henry Cabot Lodge, *George Washington* (2 vols., Boston and New York, 1889).
2 Worthington C. Ford (ed.), *The Writings of George Washington* (14 vols., New York and London, 1889-93).
3 Pyle, however, was apparently right. See Douglas Southall Freeman, *George Washington, A Biography* (7 vols., New York, 1948-57), III, 1-2, which contends that the wedding took place at the White House, not at St. Peter's Church.


## From Edward Ireland Renick

Department of State, Washington.
My dear Wilson:                        January 13, 1896.

I am delighted to hear that you will come to Washington next month, and I will take pleasure in showing you the letters to Washington in this Department. We have Sparks's manuscript index of these letters arranged under the names of the writers, the letters following each other in chronological order.

I saw Dr. Byrd Harrison yesterday. He pronounced your article one of the most interesting he had ever read, and your description of his ancestor, Colonel William Byrd, by far the most appreciative and discriminating that has appeared. He lends you the photograph of the Colonel, which I now enclose,[1] the original of which is at Brandon,—not at his house, as I believe I said in my former letter. The portrait in his possession is one of Colonel Byrd's ancestors. It is by Van Dyke.

I am charmed with your idea of writing Washington's life in the way in which it might have been written by one who did not know what he was going to amount to. In this connection you will use (if you have not already used) W. S. Baker's "Character Portraits of Washington,"[2] published at Philadelphia in 1887, containing descriptions of Washington by his contemporaries and others. Consult also "Journal of Colonel George Washington, 1754," edited by Dr. J. M. Toner, published by Joel Munsell's Sons,

Albany 1893, page 78. From this you will see that Colonel George Mercer, an intimate friend of Washington, gave a very particular and minute pen picture of the personal appearance and prominent characteristics of Colonel George Washington as he appeared when he took his seat in the House of Burgesses in 1759. Dr. Toner has a copy of this letter which was written in 1760, and when you come here I will see that you have an opportunity to look at it.                Very truly yours,   E. I. Renick

P.S. Senator Gray,[3] at the Japanese Minister's dinner the other night, highly eulogized your book "The State," which he had procured for his boy, now I believe at Princeton,[4] but which he himself devoured, though he intended merely to glance through it. He heartily recommended it to those present.

TLS (WP, DLC).
    [1] The enclosure is missing.
    [2] William Spohn Baker, *Character Portraits of Washington* . . . (Philadelphia, 1887).
    [3] George Gray, United States Senator from Delaware, 1885-99.
    [4] Charles Black Gray, a student in the John C. Green School of Science, 1895-98.

## To Herbert Baxter Adams

My dear Dr. Adams,     Princeton, New Jersey, 13 January, 1896.
    I am not only willing, but shall be glad to lecture in the Donovan Room;[1] and I am quite willing to take the most convenient afternoon hour for all concerned. But the idea of outsiders as well as students attending startles me a little. I hope it is understood that the lectures are class lectures, not at all popular in theme or style. I can imagine some outsiders being wofully disappointed!
    If those who attend are satisfied, however, I shall certainly be glad to give them my best within the theme and method of my course.[2] There is some likelihood of my giving one or two University Extension lectures while I am in Baltimore; and I have told the managers that my course at the Hopkins is a class course exclusively, and not a popular or public course; and I should not like to ever seem to have deceived them.
    I presume, though, that the only persons not graduate students whom Mr. Gilman had in mind were his daughter and a few other ladies who wish to join the class, and who will most certainly be welcome and more than welcome.[3]
    With warm regard,
                        Faithfully Yours,   Woodrow Wilson

WWTLS (H. B. Adams Papers, MdBJ).
    [1] The Donovan Room, named in memory of Caroline Donovan, a benefactress

of the Johns Hopkins, was the smaller of two lecture and meeting rooms on the first floor of McCoy Hall.

2 In 1896 Wilson gave the third series of lectures—on local government—in his three-year cycle, using the notes printed at February 3, 1890, Vol. 6, and at January 26, 1893, Vol. 8.

3 As letters, newspaper reports, and other documents will soon reveal, Wilson's lectures were highly publicized and attended by many non-students.

## From Howard Pyle

Dear Professor Wilson:           Wilmington, Del., Jan. 13. 1896.

Since writing to you I have eaten a little private piece of humble-pie in finding that it seems to have been needless for me to have questioned the fact of Washington's marriage having taken place at church. The only point to the contrary is a statement of the family tradition that it occurred at the house of Mrs Custis. That, however, has been tacitly withdrawn by a letter lately received from Washington.

I am still, perhaps, a little disposed to question the fact of the groom having ridden on horseback from the church, but am altogether ready to bow to your superior knowledge as to such details.

At any rate, we can be perfectly safe in representing the groom, with his hat tucked under his arm, leading the bride by the hand out from the church.

I am in communication now with a photographer in Washington, looking to obtaining a good picture of St. Peter's church; I would go thither and sketch it, only that the pressing nature of my engagements prevents me doing so.

Should I now and then appear to question your details, I hope you will consider that I do so with all deference, and only with a desire to obtain the uttermost accuracy possible.

                    Very sincerely yours   Howard Pyle

HwLS (WP, DLC).

## A Newspaper Report of a Lecture in Lancaster on Bagehot

[Jan. 16, 1896]

### THE CLOSING LECTURE.

The second course of university extension lectures by Prof. Woodrow Wilson ended last evening. The attendance was greater than upon the previous occasions, Maennerchor hall being fairly filled. The subject of the lecture was Bagehot, the literary politician, and it was treated in a manner highly pleasing to all. Prof. Wilson said in part:

In studying Walter Bagehot, the literary politician, we come to a man of our own country and nationality,[1] yet he is singularly obscure especially to people of the United States. Whoever misses reading Bagehot loses great fun of the most invigorating and re- freshing kind. Bagehot is a mixture of a man of letters and a man of affairs. No man ever less commonplace and yet with more sympathy for commonplace people than he. A man hard to de- scribe. He was born February 3, 1826, in Somersetshire, that land of golden light, with sea on either side, and the sunlight remained in his soul during his whole life. His father was a banker of keen mind and accurate statements. His mother a woman of brilliant intellect who stimulated without irritating.

Walter Bagehot inherited his tongue of eloquence from his mother. He was a great clarifier of thoughts. When asked about unfamiliar subjects, he would say, "I don't know, my mind is to let on that subject," but his cross-questionings always brought new light. Bagehot graduated from University college, London, 1846; called to the bar, 1852; succeeded his father as vice presi- dent of Stuckey's Banking company. He thoroughly enjoyed his business—his keen insight into human nature made him master of every situation. He was editor of the London *Economist* from 1860-77, the year of his death, and became a great authority on finance. By profession he was a man of business, but a man of letters for pastime and the satisfaction of a mind of extraordinary activity. He is most charming when he writes about things that were not any of his business. Knowing human nature so well, his criticisms are far from conventional. He always saw with his own eyes, never with another's. He even gave new ideas to the Shakespearian critics. When he approached politics he spoke as no other man spoke. He knew politics because he knew so much besides. He looked at politics through medium of men and stripped it of its "literary theory." In "The English Constitution," his greatest book, written just as essays, he shows the constitu- tion of England to all men for what it is, a government by a com- mittee of the House of Commons; the crown serving only to steady the administration of the government and to give warning without taking any responsibilities; the House of Lords, only at most as a revising chamber.

In his "Physics and Politics" he applies the reasoning of the principles of heredity and national selection to the development of society. In his "Lombard Street" (English Wall street) he exhibited the whole machinery and the whole psychology of the subtle game and business of finance. He said that currency that can depreciate will depreciate no matter what value is set on it by the government. Only such currency should be used as will always have the same value.

Burke is the politician who inspires—Bagehot the one who illuminates. He had an eye for the details that constitute the realities of business and politics such as no man before him had had and his contribution to political thought is at once distinctive and invaluable.

Printed in the Lancaster, Pa., *Daily Intelligencer*, Jan. 16, 1896; one editorial heading omitted.
    [1] That is, he was a member of the Anglo-American community.

## Two Letters to Howard Pyle

My dear Mr. Pyle,          Princeton, New Jersey, 18 January, 1896.

I was so keenly disappointed at the news that the third article (which seems to me to lend itself to illustration much better than the next is likely to) was to have but two of your drawings, that I telegraphed you this afternoon to ask if you could not substitute for the wedding a picture of a hunting dinner or breakfast (a meal before or after the hunt) at Mount Vernon. I hope very heartily you will give the matter a favourable consideration.

The personnel would be the same as that indicated in my first letter about this article: Washington; George Mason (whose portrait is in Kate Mason Rowland's Life of him recently published by the Putnam's, which I could send you, if you have not access to it), Lord Fairfax, whose portrait I send now under another cover; Bryan Fairfax, say, whose portrait you will find in Lossing, unless I am mistaken; and two or three others whose appearance you could make to your mind. A dinner scene, after the ladies had retired, would suit my fancy immensely; and I hope you will indulge me, if I may make free to urge you.

Forgive me if I am taking too great a liberty, and believe me, in much haste,

Faithfully Yours,   Woodrow Wilson


My dear Mr. Pyle,     Princeton, New Jersey, 21 January, 1896.

My fourth paper still lies inchoate in my head; but I think that I can suggest at least one exceedingly effective picture, which I feel somewhat confident you will like.

The paper is to cover the period 1774-1781; and I wish very

much the three stages of it could each have its illustration: first the interval of peace (for Washington) between the meetings of the first and second Continental Congresses, the year of home life which was the last he was to see for six years (and here, no doubt, we can manage a quiet interior scene at Mount Vernon, as you suggest,—but I am not yet clear just what). Second, the mid-revolution: and here I have a picture to suggest. Arnold's treason marked the darkest hour of the Revolution, and there is a most dramatic scene in which to give hint of it: the moment when, while he sat at breakfast with his wife, Hamilton, Lafayette, etc., a courier entered and handed Arnold the letter which apprised him of the capture of André and his own imminent danger of discovery. The whole thing is most adequately given in the second volume of John Fiske's "American Revolution,"[1] in the Chapter headed 'Benedict Arnold.' Third, the close of the Revolution. But here I am still much too uncertain of my treatment to suggest anything yet. I am only clear that the peace before war, the darkest hour of the war, and the bright close of it are the three things to illustrate, to give the article adequate finish.

To-morrow I start for Baltimore, for my annual course of lectures (five weeks) at the Johns Hopkins. So soon as I am settled there, and have put my mind in shape,—say by the beginning of next week,—I shall be able to see a little more clearly and concretely what is ahead of me; and will write you again, as fully as possible.

I am desperately sorry it was too late for another illustration for No. Three.

Mrs. Wilson joins me in warmest regards,

Faithfully Yours,   Woodrow Wilson

WWTLS (deCoppet Coll., NjP).
[1] John Fiske, *The American Revolution* (2 vols., Boston and New York, 1891).


## A Notice

[Jan. 22, 1896]

NOTICES.

All those who elect International Law for the second term will be examined, in written recitation, on T. J. Lawrence's Principles of International Law (D. C. Heath & Co.) on Monday, March 2, 1895. This is not the text-book mentioned in the catalogue.[1]

All those who elect English Common Law will be examined

on Boutmy's English Constitution (Macmillan) on Tuesday, March 3, 1896.                                    Woodrow Wilson.

Printed in *Daily Princetonian*, Jan. 22, 1896.
    [1] It was William Edward Hall, *A Treatise on International Law*, 3rd edn. (Oxford, 1890).

## To Ellen Axson Wilson

906 McCulloh St.,[1]
My own darling,                    Balto., Md., 23 January, 1896
    I arrived last night, according to schedule (leaving all in Phila.[2] in good spirits; and Wilson within sight of a very considerable electrical job), and found everything here just as of old,—except that there is, of course, the usual proportion of new faces. Cousin Mary[3] was waiting for me in the parlour of 906; and, after I had had my dinner, I went up to her little room (third story front hall room, tiny, heated by gas stove, but tidy and comfortable enough, and looking intelligently enough inhabited) and chatted with her fifteen or twenty minutes before going to my own little room to unpack. She looks very well, seems quite content, though working very hard at routine tasks;[4] expects to be re-employed without trouble "when the new contracts are signed," March 15, because she understands that the girls young and old approve of her(!); does not boast more than usual, or talk in deliberate literary phrase more than is bearable and becoming;—altogether seems in very good form.
    My own quarters are not half bad. The room measures ten, six by eleven, six, has everything in it that is necessary for my convenience, and admits of my being very neatly and comfortably bestowed. The stove is small and, apparently, most amenable to man[a]gement. I spent last night in perfect comfort, neither too hot nor too cold; and confidently expect things to turn out quite well enough for anybody. You need give yourself no anxiety.
    The books came all right; but I discovered, to my great chagrin, upon opening them, that I had left out two wh. I shall need,—and need at once: Vol. II. of the Washington, and the Roget's Thesaurus. The former should be on top of my desk, the latter within it, in a pigeonhole to the extreme right. Please get Ed. to send them to me, separately, by mail, protecting the Washington most carefully. He will find book corners in the long drawer of my small desk, which the key of the glass book-case in the hallway, or any ordinary key, will fit.
    Well, I've very literally obeyed your injunction so far: I have written a whole letter about what I am doing, and said not a

word about the love and longing of which my heart is so full,—the deep anxiety to know how my love is, and how all the dear ones fare! Ah, my darling, every year *adds* a pang, it seems to me, to the pain of this tedious separation. I don't know that I could find it in my heart to wish it to grow less: but I do very deeply wish that I might be spared it,—that I could have you always!

With love unspeakable,          Your own   Woodrow
Love to one and all.

ALS (WP, DLC).
[1] The address of Mary Jane Ashton's boardinghouse.
[2] His sister, Annie Wilson Howe, and her son, Wilson, and daughter, Annie.
[3] Mary Eloise Hoyt.
[4] She was teaching English at the Bryn Mawr School in Baltimore.


## From Ellen Axson Wilson

My own darling,                    Princeton, N. J. Jan. 23/96
I hope you had a pleasant journey and are finding things there— your room &c. "reasonable pleasant," too;—that you are in short as comfortable as we are. We are all getting on very well. I was out a good deal of the morning yesterday, went to see Mrs. Brown & Miss Ricketts and it did me good. Thought I would try Mrs. Perry's this morning, but it is a raw unpleasant day so will put it off.

I enclose all the letters. What *can* Corbin[1] mean by the "hands" of the door? What shall I tell him? I suppose the vestibule doors are not made yet. By the way, dear, did you write to Brown[2] about the shades, or shall I?

The lessons of course prevented my writing until after lunch and I am hurrying to get this off by the two thirty,—know that for today at least you would rather have a short note & get it promptly. Love to Minnie and kind regards to the ladies.[3] The children all seem well. Jessie has not been coughing anymore.

I love you, oh, *how* I love you, my darling. I am almost afraid to let myself think how much,—or how desperately I *want* you! With all my soul—                    Your little wife   Eileen

Find there isn't an envelope in the house that will hold your letters. Must keep them till tomorrow. They are not important.

ALS (WC, NjP).
[1] Of the P. & F. Corbin Company of New Britain, Conn., which supplied the hardware for the Wilson house.
[2] C. E. & J. W. Brown of New York, dealers in wall paper, window shades, etc.
[3] Mary Jane Ashton and her sister, Hannah.

## To Ellen Axson Wilson

My own darling,                    Baltimore, 24 January, 1896

The regular round is begun. I paid my respects to Mr. Gilman and Professor Adams yesterday morning, delivered my first lecture yesterday afternoon, began work on "General Washington" this morning; am to go to Mr. Gilman's Saturday evening to a sort of reception, and to Mrs. Bird's on Sunday for dinner. It's the same old thing! Last night, though it was very stormy, I went to call at Mrs. Bird's, to answer in person her note of invitation received in the afternoon; but found no one at home, and so crossed the street to the Peabody [Library] and sat there till ten examining Washington material. They haven't very much, I am sorry to say; but they have some things I have not found elsewhere.

The first lecture has left a rather bad taste in my mouth. They've put me at 5 o'clock (the customary hour, as you know, for public lectures) in the "Donovan room," where outsiders lecture on English literature on the "Donovan foundation,"[1] and have made arrangements which really amount to making the lectures semi-public, if not semi-*demi*-public. There were in attendance graduate students, women grave and gay (maybe a dozen) and one or two old gentlemen,—in all perhaps forty persons. How was I to know how to address such a company, mingled of all elements? I *didn't* know how—and came off with the impression that I had said nothing in particular, after no method in particular. No doubt I shall get used to it (I get used to almost any sort of speaking, if I am forced to); no doubt I shall hit upon a method; but at present I feel very much at sea and a whit distressed at the look of the weather.

Your first note has come to comfort me, and the comfort of it is great; but it would be more if you had said explicitly that you were *well*,—rid of the nausea and all that went with it. Please, ma'am, say that next time, if you can: for my anxiety about you is by no means dispelled by hearing that you are "comfortable."

I continue to find my room most agreeable,—and its isolation, here in the extreme rear of 909,[2] is delightful. There is nothing over me, and nothing (inhabited) under me, and a hallway separates me from my neighbours. I can study and be my own man to my heart's content.

If only I could *get* heart's content away from you, I should be all right: but oh, my love, my passionate longing for you is beyond all words,—almost beyond endurance when we are separated! I am altogether and in all things

                                        Your own    Woodrow

I am quite well. Love to all.

☞ Please send me my visiting cards. They are in my small desk. I wrote to Brown about the shades. Did you answer Norris's?

ALS (WP, DLC).
[1] Caroline Donovan had given $100,000 to the Hopkins in 1889 for the endowment of a chair of English Literature, but no permanent incumbent was named until 1905.
[2] This was the old number of the Ashton boardinghouse.


## Two Letters from Ellen Axson Wilson

My own darling,          Princeton, N. J. Friday [Jan. 24, 1896]

I cannot tell you how it vexes me to have to write to you from bed!–not that there is much the matter but because I foresee how worried you will be,–& will insist upon remaining I fear, you dear unreasonable fellow, in spite of all my reassurances.

The fact is I didn't get over that little attack of indigestion as easily as I expected, but now that the doctor[1] has me in hand I am sure he will straighten me out in short order. He it is who has sent me back to bed.

I felt much better Wed. morning but towards night the severe pain in my bowels began again, together with a little feverishness. Yesterday morning it had passed off again & the only symptom was a little nausea; but at five again the pain & slight fever promptly returned. So remembering your final injunction, I thought it time to see the doctor about it. I am *quite* comfortable this morning–it really seems absurd to be in bed. *Please* dearest, don't worry at all about it. I am not at all weak,–would "put in the time" writing a long letter to you but for the fact that the room is persistently cold & I am afraid to sit up. Excuse this scrawl[.] I write leaning on my elbow, quite cosily covered. Your dear letter has come. I love you, my darling, deeply, tenderly, devotedly. I am always and altogether

Your little wife    Eileen

[1] James H. Wikoff, M.D., of 22 Nassau St.


My own darling          Princeton, N. J. Sat. [Jan. 25, 1896]

I still write from bed where the doctor insists upon my remaining until he breaks up this low, only 100% fever, but if you could see how bright and well I feel and look I am sure that even you would admit there is no cause for worry. The pain in my bowels was much less yesterday & this morning I am quite free from it again. In fact I never felt more comfortable in my life than I do just now,—so my love must follow my example & be comfortable too!

Your second sweet letter came duly to hand today. Am so sorry they have made unsatisfactory arrangements about the lectures. Can't you have it all changed to suit yourself?

I am having Ed see about the books and cards today.

Yes, I wrote to the Norrises.

I am *so* glad that you find the room comfortable and that you are "well,"—are you *sure* of that? As you love me, dear, tell the truth, the *whole truth* and nothing but the truth about your health. Of all the hard things involved in your absence, the hardest *this* year is that I am not able to watch you & see for myself how you are. Take care of yourself my love, my treasure. Remember "thou are the very life of me"—in simple truth all the world to                    Your little wife   Eileen

ALS (WP, DLC).

## To Ellen Axson Wilson

My own darling,                    Baltimore, 26 January, 1896

I did not write yesterday: partly because it was Saturday and you would not get the letter any sooner than you would get one written to-day, and partly because I was "laid up." Your letter of Friday, written in bed, found me in bed with a colic! It woke me at about four o'clock in the morning, and "went for" me (with steadily decreasing force) till about noon, when it passed off. I took a short walk in the afternoon, and went to Mr. Gilman's reception in the evening, feeling quite weak and not enjoying myself a bit; but, rather, I think, because of the small amount of food I had eaten during the day than because of the severity of the attack. For it was not very severe, and went off very gently. It returned about the same hour this morning, and was very sharp for, it may be, an hour or two; but then it took itself off almost as quickly as it had come; I went to sleep again comfortably enough; and got up to breakfast feeling about as usual. I went to the post office to fetch your letter—without suffering inconvenience—and am now, instead of going to church, telling my darling "the truth, the whole truth, and nothing but the truth" about my health. Can it be that we both ate something or inhaled something, that we should be so similarly affected? I am taking the utmost care of myself. I did not go to church this morning, not because I do not feel equal to going, but because I have to go to

Mrs. Bird's to dinner, and am taking care not to accumulate fatigues.

I will not deny that I have been in a state of mind about you, my precious, precious darling, and that my heart is torn, more, almost, than I can bear, by the thought of your slow and mysterious illness. Does the doctor say anything intelligible about it? What is it,—and what is his explanation? It is not its degree, but its kind that works upon my apprehension. This dear letter written yesterday, so cheerily,—so like you in its reassuring tones, —gives me a great deal of comfort; still the fact remains, that the doctor keeps you in bed (for which I thank him heartily) and fights a slow fever. Oh, what would I not give to be beside you, nursing you, my treasure, my darling!

I really feel *very much* steadier and stronger to-day—and I've come out of these little attacks with no dosing but a single dram of whiskey—but if the improvement halts or lingers at all I will call [Charles W.] Mitchell in and get all the doctoring and attention you could wish. You don't know, either, how handsomely I am taken care of here. Both Miss Hannah and Miss Jane are as kind and attentive as possible, and Cousin Mary devoted herself to me almost all day yesterday. You may be sure I shall lack for nothing.

As I lay here on the bed yesterday morning, who should come in but *Stock!*[1] He had been lecturing at Catonsville (which is near here) the night before, and was on his way to do an Extension errand in Washington. He sat with me about an hour; and the sight of him helped me immensely toward getting  well. He *looks* well, as usual, but says he has lost his mending pace the last month or so. I hope it's a mere temporary set-back; and he keeps to his work and to his good spirits in a way which certainly argues physical improvement.

I love you, my darling, my precious little wife,—with a devotion, a longing, a loyalty, a passion which sometimes seems to me not only to fill but to *be* my life. I would write you a love letter if I dared.                    Your own   Woodrow

ALS (WP, DLC).
1 Stockton Axson.


## From Ellen Axson Wilson

My own darling,          Princeton, N. J. Sunday [Jan. 26, 1896]

You see I am still in bed, and I have been struggling all the morning to decide whether or not to tell you "the whole truth about" it—that is to report all the doctor says. It seems such a shame to worry you for nothing now that the danger is practically over. Yet on the other hand how would you ever place implicit faith in my reports again if I kept things from you now. Best not take the risk I suppose, and so,—in brief—he says I have been quite seriously threatened with either peritonitis or typhoid fever; that I am undoubtedly better and in all probability will escape either, but that a very little thing might yet turn the scale and so I must be excessively careful and stay in bed as long as there is *any* fever. For as long as there is fever there is still something wrong at the seat of the trouble. I have had no pain there, which was at first quite severe, since day before yesterday but there is some soreness.

I rather suspected that he feared typhoid fever the first night when he asked so particularly about the drainage; but when I asked he evaded,—said "plenty of things could come from bad drainage." Now that is the whole story, darling, except that I have but one degree of fever, no pain or weakness, & a good appetite. I have a little food every two hours & am always impatient for the time to come.

The servants are as good as possible, and you can't imagine what care I am taking of myself! So now be a dear, good boy and *don't worry*. I don't need you in the least except for company.

I don't deny its lonely, notwithstanding I am keeping very bright and cheerful. You see I have many pleasant things to think about, especially my darling,—his goodness and sweetness and manifold gifts and graces; my pride and delight in him, and my love for him and his love for me. Are not these things enough to keep me happy even in his absence? The children are all well & as good as gold. Not one of them has opened her lips in the night since you left, isnt that fortunate? With a heart always & altogether yours          Your little wife,   Eileen.

ALS (WP, DLC).

## To Ellen Axson Wilson

My own darling,          Monday  Baltimore, 27 January, 1896.

That pain *did* return again last night, just after I went to bed, and gave me about two hours of acute discomfort. But then it took itself off and I slept very comfortably till breakfast time. After breakfast I went around to see Charlie Mitchell: he was not in, but has just now been to see me. He went over me *very* thoroughly and has gone off saying that I may expect a great deal of discomfort and a good deal of pain for a little while; but can go about my business without apprehension of anything at all serious. He has told me to stop the [stomach] pump for a while, and take the medicine he has given me till he gets me well in hand. He went off very cheerful and reassuring,—and he is no humbug. Now, my sweet one, isn't that enough of the truth about my health to satisfy even you? It is all, and it seems to me more than enough to quiet apprehension. You knew I was not *well* in the matter of my digestion already; and now I am to get from Mitchell just the needed supplement to Delafield,[1]—which we so much desired. Charlie believes in the syphon, but says that sometimes its constant use may grow hurtful; and so advises an intermission, with change of treatment. Need you ask if I am taking care of myself?

I can't tell you how I *hate* to have to lay all this before you: but you may be sure I will withhold nothing, and minimize nothing.

And now, sweetheart, for a little matter of business. Mrs. Bird tells me that the Southwestern[2] is now paying arrears (at 7%), and is to pay hereafter at 5%. With my fatal facility for forgetting, I do not remember whether we deposited the S. W. as well as the Central [of Georgia], in N. Y. in view of a reorganization. If we did, we have only a registered letter receipt to show for it: for the change of securities was never effected. If we did not, the S. W. stock is in the little drawer within my safe, in some one of the envelopes there. This is the way to open the safe,—and if you do not remember distinctly, you had better,—Oh, I remember—we sold the S. W.,—alas.

Well the books and visiting cards have come in perfect condition, thanks to Ed's careful wrapping, and I am so much obliged. They are in plenty of time, for I have not worked much at the General yet.

I found a noble portrait of Washington, by the way, in a book in the Peabody, reproduced from Rembrandt Peale, and I am going to urge its reproduction for No. IV.

I enjoyed my afternoon at Mrs. Bird's, of course, to the full,—as did cousin Mary, who went with me. I was as subtly and elaborately flattered as any fool could wish to be,—and would give every word of praise or appreciation ever spoken to me for one sound, one single tone, of your voice,—one moment's look into your eyes, one sight of you,—of any part of you! Ah, how I wonder what my darling is doing, how she looks, how she feels, what her thoughts are,—how she *fares* in all things. My queen! My yearning for you would become intolerable were I to indulge it for so much as a moment! I am diligently practicing a Spartan courage and self-forgetful steadfastness; but I am not built on the Spartan plan, and the discipline sits uneasy upon me! Imagine yourself kissed and embraced till forced to fight for breath by

Your own

*That's Franklin's flourish.*

ALS (WP, DLC).
¹ Francis Delafield, M.D., of New York, whom Wilson had consulted in the autumn of 1895.
² The South Western Railroad Co.

## From Ellen Axson Wilson

My own darling          Princeton, N. J. Monday [Jan. 27, 1896]

Oh, how distressed I am to hear of my darling's sickness! Truly misfortunes never come singly. This separation has always been bad enough, but it seems we are only now to learn how hard it *can* be. Perhaps we have repined more than we should when it was mere separation without added anxieties and now are being punished.

That your trouble should come back the second morning is *so* distressing, also that you are not taking care of yourself but going about as if you wer'nt sick. How I wish you had sent Mrs. Bird word and stayed in bed all Sunday! But what a shame for me to write so! I am afraid I can't deny that the news of your illness has unstrung me somewhat and made me very blue.

As to myself I am just the same. "Peritofletis," if I caught the word aright, is what the doctor says I have. I suppose that is to peritonitis what scarletina is to scarlet fever. Certain "glands" I believe,—the same that are affected in typhoid fever—are inflamed but not acutely. The place is quite sore but there has been no return of the pain. Everything it seems depends on my staying in bed and being phenomenally "careful,"—about food, exposure—everything. And as I *am* careful you really have no just cause for anxiety my darling.

The children are quite well & good and the weather is lovely.

God bless you my darling and make and keep you well and safe. Oh how I love you—*love* you!

Your little wife    Eileen.

ALS (WP, DLC).

## To Ellen Axson Wilson

My own darling,                                    Balto., 28 Jan'y, 1896.

Charlie has made *me* stay at home to-day, and lie down most of the time. I must therefore write you only a little note. But all of that may be full of reassurance. Charlie declares himself sure of having me all right again within a couple of days; and there is no *disease* as in my poor, poor darling's case, but only a derangement of the bowels, giving pain without bringing *any* danger at all. I don't understand his explanation.

And so my darling *must* not be alarmed, for there is absolutely nothing to be alarmed at,—but *must* get a competent nurse for herself, and so help to cure *me*. That's my *command*, darling, for your safety and mine, till I can come to you.

I do not *dare* to think of your illness, with no one in the house to nurse you; but I keep myself in spirits by the resolution to come to be your nurse just so soon as Mitchell gets me well on my feet once more.

Let's keep each other in heart, my queen, by the care we take of ourselves, by thought of the deep access of love that will come out of this even for us, by knowledge of the love and goodness of God. *I* am in no danger and I am, oh, how passionately,

                                              Your own   Woodrow

Please let Ed. deposit the enclosed.

ALS (WP, DLC).

## From Ellen Axson Wilson

My own darling          Princeton, N. J. Tuesday [Jan. 28, 1896]

Perhaps I am very hard to satisfy but I am afraid this isn't "enough" about your health. What has caused the trouble to become acute again? *Why* must you expect "a good deal of pain"? You have had next to no pain for a long time. What does Dr. Mitchell think is the matter? Please tell me all he says. I am very wretched about you—so wretched that I am afraid it is impossible today for me even to pretend that I am not. As for my malady it is "just the same," but when I grumbled about that to the doctor he said "but think how much better that is than being 'a great deal worse'—which you might easily have been"; and to be sure that is both the philosophical and Christian way to look at it!

All the rest are quite well,—which certainly is another very great blessing.

I love you, darling, more than I dare try to tell you,—almost more than I dare let myself realize—it *hurts* so—sometimes.

Always and altogether,            Your own    Eileen.

ALS (WP, DLC).

## A News Item

[Jan. 29, 1896]

### LECTURES AT THE HOPKINS.

. . . Prof. Woodrow Wilson was prevented by indisposition from giving his regular lecture yesterday in the course on "The Theory and Organization of Local Government."

The lectures of Prof. Dewey[1] and Prof. Wilson are given daily in the Donovan-room of McCoy Hall at 4 P.M. and 5 P.M., respectively, and are open to the public. No tickets are required. Without ostentatiously announcing the fact, the University is really furnishing free an excellent course of University extension lectures, and not a few Baltimoreans interested in the study of sociological and political problems are availing themselves of the opportunity. . . .

Printed in the *Baltimore News*, Jan. 29, 1896; one editorial heading omitted.

[1] Wilson's old friend from graduate student days at the Hopkins, Davis Rich Dewey, at this time Professor of Economics at the Massachusetts Institute of Technology.

## To Ellen Axson Wilson

My own darling,                    Balto., 29 January, 1896

I have good news for you to-day: I am *much* better, and what little worry there was in Charlie's face is quite gone off. He is surely the most sensible, helpful, and satisfactory of doctors! He keeps me lying down most of the time still; but that's only for precaution. He says the difficulty was *mechanical*. The "dilitation" (enlargement) of the stomach had (very likely) bent a little passage of the small bowel at a sharp angle, like a rubber tube hung over a rail, and irritation had ensued. He was only afraid it would *spread*; but, instead of that, it's gone, and I may expect to be my own master again just as soon as I am reasonably quieted within, rested without, and recuperated.

And so, darling, *I* am all right. These days of missed lectures will not involve a prolonged stay, either. I can arrange to make them up without difficulty.

It is *you* now, my pet; that is the only serious trouble I have. I know of no tonic I could have equal to being with you, nursing you, making my great love manifest as best I might. If *you* will only get well, I can get on famously and without another twinge, I am sure. Oh, that *I* could take care of my love, guard my treasure, make sure of her comfort and welfare! Of course you arrange to have one of the servants at call, if the children should need anything at night. You must, sweetheart. It might be fatal for you to get up and expose yourself. She could sleep on the sofa in the dining room.

God bless you and keep you, my queen, for

Your own     Woodrow

ALS (WP, DLC).


## From Ellen Axson Wilson

My own darling,          Princeton, N. J. Wednesday [Jan. 29, 1896]

Everything is going quite well here, better I am afraid than with *you*. How my heart sinks with each letter that tells me of your pain and suffering! To think that you too are confined to bed now! I am glad at any rate that the doctor is keeping you there, for as Dr. Wykoff says it is the best place for sick people. I think I am making some progress.

I had already so little fever that it would be hard to have less and have any at all; yet I think there *is* a little less, and the soreness is certainly diminishing. I don't think the doctor has any apprehensions now—so long as I "stay in bed,"—and you know he isn't one to minimize troubles.

And now, dearest, please believe me when I say in [it] would be ridiculous to have a nurse. There is absolutely *nothing* in the shape of *nursing* to be done. The servants are as kind as possible in *waiting* upon me, and there is very little even of *that* needed. The *doctor* says I *don't need* a *nurse*! Isn't that enough. If she were here I am sure she would make me very ill—forever sitting around doing nothing and talking me to death. She would make me so bored and nervous that I really couldn't stand it. Won't you trust my judgment, dear? I will swear to you if necessary to take as good care of myself as if I were taking care of you. If in spite of all this you still feel anxious, how would it do for you to ask Sister Annie to come over for two or three days with little Annie?

I sent for Margerum[1] when I was first taken sick—the doctor, as I told you, having enquired about the plumbing. He has this morning finished a most thorough examination & reports everything in perfect order. The doctor says "taking things" depends chiefly on the state of a person's system after all;—that I have probably been getting ready to be sick for a long time,—my total want of appetite &c.

But I am about to miss my mail[.] With love inexpressible

Your own   Eileen

ALS (WP, DLC).
  1 John H. Margerum, plumber, of 32 Mercer St.

## To Ellen Axson Wilson

Balto., 30 January, 1896

I am steadily improving, my sweet darling, and the doctor sees no reason to doubt that he will have me out and in shape by Saturday, so that next week shall see me at work, not only, but ought to see me in better form than ever: for that, he says, is what is to be expected after one of these "gastric crises"—a very marked recuperation. In short, I may be all the better for this compulsory putting to rights, unpleasant, and, domestically speaking, ill timed, as it has been! My darling *must* not worry: there is absolutely *no* ground for that: and *my* spirits are steadily rising with the good reports from you.

*Of course,* my sweet one, if you feel as you say about a nurse, and there is *really* nothing for her to do, I withdraw my urgent request. It *would* worry you indeed, if she were fool enough to act as you fear; and I don't want to risk that.

Let us comfort ourselves, sweet love, by thinking of what all this will mean to us hereafter,—how much deeper our knowledge of ourselves, and of our love for each other. A sort of solemn intensity has crept into my love for you during these past days,— which seem so many,—and has acted both to deepen and illuminate it. I *know* how purely I love you,—how all the *best* parts of my nature are engaged and ennobled by this sweet love for my precious little mate. After all, love, it is not youth, with its elation, its *variable* elation, that is best, but maturity with its profound devotion, its forces of majesty and conquering power, that can give calm and self-control, and at the same time an even deeper happiness than the other. How I glory in my love for you! How our lives are rounded, perfected, completed by this mighty passion that dwells in our love! Why should *we ever* be anything but happy, is what I ask myself when I realize how entirely I am permitted to be

Your own   Woodrow

Great love to the precious chickens, and to dear Ed. and George. Thank Maggie and Annie[1] for *me*!

ALS (WP, DLC).
  [1] The servants. "Maggie" was Maggie Foley.


## From Ellen Axson Wilson

My own darling,        Princeton, N. J. Thursday [Jan. 30, 1896]

Your letter this morning has at once relieved and frightened me in about equal proportions. The trouble *sounds* very serious. Does the doctor think the twist in the bowel is straightened out again? Is it a thing that that [*sic*] can and will remedy itself? Oh dear! how much I still want to know about it and can't!

You ought to see this room! It is a bower of flowers, chiefly exquisite roses,—contributions from half a dozen friends, Mrs Perry, Mrs [Ernest Cushing] Richardson, Mrs. Purves, Mrs Hibben &c. Everybody is *so* kind, if I had any need of a nurse at all it would be simply to answer the bell, for there have been incessant enquiries for the last few days,—since it became generally known that I was ill. I have seen three or four,—Mrs. Perry, Mrs. McCosh, Mrs. Hibben and the Millers[1] and found it very cheering. Mrs Hibben is perfectly lovely; she has been here *every day* since she heard I was sick and she couldn't show more genuine interest or solicitude if I were her sister. Perhaps it is a good thing you can't *see* how lovely she is in manner—you know you have already confessed that I have a rival in her! Miss Ricketts, rather oddly, has not been over to enquire.

The fever yesterday was only 99% & so far,—half past one,—I have had *none* today. Of course I need not telegraph after tonight. It seems I need "a great patience" though, for he says I must stay in bed for "several days" after the fever has *all* gone! But if my darling will only be well anything else would be easy to bear. God bless and keep you, dear, for

Your devoted little wife,    Eileen.

ALS (WP, DLC).
  [1] Margaret ("Maggie"), Susan, and Elizabeth Miller, daughters of the Rev. and Mrs. John Miller, who had both died the previous year.


## To Ellen Axson Wilson

My own darling,                Balto., Md., 31 January, 1896

What would you say to a visit from your husband? Charlie approves,—thinks it will do us both good to have me spend Sunday at home, has been getting me ready for it, indeed, for three days, at my earnest suggestion. And so, my pet, I hope, God willing to reach Princeton on Saturday (the same day this letter reaches you) at one o'clock. Don't be alarmed, however, if I do not come till an hour and a half later.

With such love and excitement as you may imagine,

Your own    Woodrow

ALS (WP, DLC).

## From Ellen Axson Wilson

My own darling,            Princeton, N. J. Friday [Jan. 31, 1896]

I am so happy, so very happy, dear, by reason of the good news in today's letter! That prediction that you may even be the better for it has had quite a magical effect on my spirits. I am sure now I shall get well too.

I thought I was going to miss the fever altogether yesterday, it was so slow in beginning, but it came on a little towards evening. I feel quite well, only of course very tired and "achey" from lying in bed. Though it goes against the grain I suppose I must quote Miss Miller's[1] crazy remark for the comfort it will give you as proof that I don't *look* as if I had been at the door of death. She says someone ought to come and take my picture in bed for I look "more beautiful" (!) than she ever saw me!

Mrs. Hibben came again yesterday. I am sorry to say she left town today for a week. Dear old Mrs. McCosh also came again yesterday, wasn't that kind? Mrs. Hibben was a great help about the house, she & Mr. H. going over to see if the staining was turning out right. The man had sent me over a sample colour for the hall that I liked, but I was regretting that I could not see how it looked in mass. She says it is a *beautiful* colour & tones in *perfectly* with the paper. She says the dining room oak is *so beautiful* in colour & grain, & begged me to have it simply oiled, not stained. So he sent me over a specimen bit, and I decided on that.

Stockton dropped in on us last night, to my very great pleasure, —is gone again now. Of course you know how he fares &c, having seen him so lately. Sister Annie has just sent word through George to ask if I would like her to come up. I asked Stockton to see her & explain that I didn't need nursing, but that if she could without inconvenience come for a few days it would be a very great pleasure of course to me & comfort to *you*. I have been wishing very much for your sake that she could come. I love you, dear, deeply, tenderly passionately—in every way more than words can say.

Your own    Eileen

ALS (WC, NjP).
¹ Probably Maggie Miller of 38 Washington St.

## A Final Examination

February 1, 1896.

### EXAMINATION IN THE HISTORY OF LAW.

1. How must Law be defined, if it is to be made possible to trace its history? Explain.

2. Why must Roman Law occupy the chief place in such a study?

3. What are our materials for the study of primitive law, and what is their relative importance? Trace, through the Greek terms for Law, the development of the Greek conception of Law.

4. By what several stages did the original system of Self-help give way to the sovereign jurisdiction of courts of law?

5. What circumstances gave richness and variety to the Roman law? Through what instrumentalities did it become rich and various? In what particular field is it most rich, and why?

6. Trace the development of the consensual contract in Roman law.

7. Upon the basis of what codes, Roman and barbarian, was the Roman law of the Middle Ages built up? What was the character, and what were the sources of the barbarian codes?

8. *What* Roman law was "received" in Germany and France, —the law of the *Corpus Juris Civilis*? Explain.

9. What special circumstances brought about the reception of the Roman law in Germany; and what parts of German law became Roman?

10. Reproduce Sir Henry Maine's discussion¹ of the origin and uses of Legal Fictions.

"I pledge my honor as a gentleman that, during this examination, I have neither given nor received assistance."

Printed examination (WP, DLC).
¹ In *Ancient Law*, 14th edn. (London, 1891), the textbook for the course.

## A News Item

[Feb. 3, 1896]

. . . This afternoon Professor Dewey of Boston lectured at 4 o'clock on "Insurance Against Non-Employment." Prof. Woodrow Wilson of Princeton has telegraphed that his health will not permit him to resume his lectures this afternoon.

Printed in the *Baltimore News*, Feb. 3, 1896.

## To John Davis Adams

My dear Mr. Adams,                          Baltimore, 4 February, 1896.

Your letter followed me here (the above will be my address until February 25), but found me ill in bed, and I have not been able
to attend to my correspondence until now.

The picture of Gunston Hall I want for the Third article; but
the picture of Carpenter's Hall ought to be kept for the fourth,
which will open with the first continental congress. There is some
mistake about the legend on the picture of Gunston Hall. The first
draft of the Virginia Declaration of *Rights* (which was written
by George Mason, the owner of Gunston Hall) may have been
written in that House; the Declaration of Independence was certainly not drafted there.

                          Sincerely Yours,    Woodrow Wilson

WWTLS (Berg Coll., NN).


## To Howard Pyle

My dear Mr. Pyle,                          Baltimore, 4 February, 1896.

Of course you have been wondering what has become of my
promised letter of the first part of last week. The fact is,—a very
humiliating fact, for a man accustomed to the best health,—that
I no sooner reached Baltimore than I fell ill. I am only just now
able to attend to my correspondence again.

I have been thinking over subjects for illustrations even while
I lay on my back in bed, and have some suggestions to make,
which I hope and believe will meet with your approval and
acceptance.

Subject no. 1. Washington and Richard Henry Lee, soon after
the opening of the first continental congress (1774), seek a conference with the Massachusetts delegates (Sam'l and John
Adams, Robert Treat Paine, and Thomas Cushing) at their lodg-
ings, in order to "size them up," see whether they are justly or
unjustly reckoned extremists and demagogues; and are satisfied,
in the course of it, of their uprightness and sincerity. It could be
made a scene of at almost any stage of the interview (beginning
very formally, we may suppose, ending in good fellowship, the
glass no doubt passed around[)]. It would afford contrasts in costume and manner between New England and Virginia, particularly at the close of the interview, and so would not be like any
previous conference in the story. I could furnish you with a brief

character sketch of each of the Massachusetts men, which I have just written.

Subject No. 2. On the eleventh day of December, 1775, Mrs. Washington, with escort of horsemen, arrived at her husband's headquarters in Cambridge in a coach and four, the horses ridden by black postilions in scarlet and white liveries. What a scene, of Virginian display and ceremony, for the somewhat bucolic and very democratic volunteers from the farms of New England, no doubt standing by with open, and leering, mouths, the stately commander-in-chief receiving the little lady, etc. What could you *not* make of it! It has taken great hold upon my fancy.

Subject No. 3. Washington and Charles Lee. Washington riding up at the battle of monmouth to find Lee retreating, almost caught in a narrow way near a morass, when he ought to have been strongly attacking an army that was at first almost at his mercy:—coming up with that haste and black wrath of which he was capable on occasion, to order Lee to the rear, when the first explanations were over, and himself rally the willing men to regain their ground.

These, with the Arnold breakfast which has taken such a seat in my preference, are all the subjects that have yet formed themselves in my head. If you cannot find three out of the four to jump with your own taste and judgment, I have no doubt others will occur to me fast enough as I read and construct the narrative.

With much regard,

Faithfully Yours,    Woodrow Wilson

WWTLS (deCoppet Coll., NjP).


## To Ellen Axson Wilson

My own darling,                    Baltimore, 4 Feby, 1896

I am very well and very much in my right mind, all things considered,—considering that you and Jessie are in bed, and sister Annie not come. The journey did not fatigue me too much,—though my thoughts did,—I loafed the evening through with some success, and went to bed in calm spirits, and rose this morning with a clear head after a *very* good night's rest. This morning I put in a fair stint of work, *almost* two pages of character sketching (Sam. and John Adams)—the sort of work which least easily runs,—is most intensive. I can easily fill out the limit this evening, if I feel like it! It is now three o'clock; and I am about to write a couple of business letters and settle down to my lecture. I have already had my outing,—in the cars, the weather being so inclem-

ent,—I went down town and bought some "light reading" to un-
bend on. I find I don't know so clearly what I've written, when
I can't read my daily stint to you: but then there are several
things that are different away from home, and I shall have to
get used to that! Ah, my darling, my darling, how I *love* you and
yearn for you. But I am as brave as you can wish, and try
to prove myself in *that* way          Your own    Woodrow

ALS (WP, DLC).


## From Ellen Axson Wilson

My own darling          Princeton, N. J. Tuesday [Feb. 4, 1896]

You see I am up at last—up and *well*;— and *how* good it feels!
We had quite a good night except that for a couple of hours or so
Margaret developed a croupy cough. It has entirely past now and
they both seem as bright as pins this morning. They are not
coughing at all, have no fever and are sitting wrapped up in bed
as lively as crickets making doll-clothes. Nellie is still all right.
Not the most anxious husband or father could find save what is
cheerful in the appearance of things. When I hear again from my
darling and am assured that his journey in the storm did him
no harm & that he is doing well in all respects & is *happy* I shall
have perfect hearts-ease.

How sorry I am, just when we are leaving our domestic crisis
so successfully behind us, to have to distress you in another way
with a very sad and startling piece of news! Mr. Wright was at our
house this morning at half past seven, went from there to the
station, and just as he was about to board the train suddenly
dropped *dead*! Isn't it awful? I feel as if it were a personal loss,
I had gotten so fond of the old man. And what a loss to Princeton!
one of our best citizens! one of the most interesting figures of the
old Princeton life.

I have been sorely tempted all the morning to decide to keep
it from you for a few days so as to save you worry. But I could
hardly feel myself justified in treating the head of the house like
a child!

Dr. Wykoff says that as regards the house we need apprehend
*no trouble at all*,—and you know he is not naturally optimistic. He
is a good business man too. Miss Ricketts has been in; says the
Frothingham contractor died while their house was being built &
all went quite smoothly. That man had no partner either. The
head carpenter & Mr. Titus[1] have been over & say everything will
be all right. The carpenter says the house will certainly be finished

"at the time fixed"—whenever that is. Mr. Titus has present charge of the house, the heating &c. They say the executors will simply assume the responsibilities of the contract, pay his bills, &c. How fortunate it is that the house is so nearly finished! There doesn't seem the least thing for you to worry about,—or to *do* indeed. Except *one*,—if I were you I should write to Mr. Child & insist that he personally should give it the closest supervision for the remaining few *weeks*,—come over twice a week.

They have all stopped work until after the funeral which will be Friday.

Sister Annie came while I was writing, so must close now in haste to catch the mail. She was afraid to bring Annie out in the storm yesterday. I love you darling—ah *how* I love you. Always and altogether,                    Your devoted wife,    Eileen.

I have just found Henderson's bill![2] It was in a cuddy hole of my desk! the first thing my hand touched when I sat down here! The laugh is on you, sir! I am quite relieved.

ALS (WC, NjP).
   [1] Neilson Woodhull Titus, 26 Canal St., a dealer in carpets.
   [2] It was probably from the firm of Robert Henderson of Philadelphia, coal dealers.

## A Final Examination

February 5, 1896.

### EXAMINATION IN JURISPRUDENCE.

1. How does the associated life of men in society produce Law? What do Ethics, Political Economy, and Politics contribute to Law?

2. Discuss Law as a body of principles (as contradistinguished from an active force), showing what elements it must have, and what relationship Expediency bears to Justice in its make-up.

3. Illustrate the difference between Public and Private Law by discussing the question, why Crime falls under the one and Tort under the other.

4. What is a Right? What are the characteristic incidents of a Right? What, for a lawyer, is the difference between a legal right and a moral right?

5. What are the several kinds of "legal transactions"? What limits does the law place upon their consequences; and in what typical instances does it extend those consequences? What features have "legal transactions" and "illegal acts" in common?

6. Criticise the following definition of Ownership: "Property includes, within determinate statutory limitations, in case of doubt and according to its tendency, a universal, exclusive, and unrestricted legal power over a thing."

7. What is involved in the idea of Security; and through what several steps, as illustrated by Roman law, have the actual means of Security been developed?

8. What does Holland[1] conceive to be the object of Law?

9. What does Holland mean by "abnormal rights"?

10. What analysis does Holland make of the questions (a) as to what the Forum is to be, and (b) as to what Law is to be applied, in his discussion of the Application of Private Law?

"I pledge my honor as a gentleman that, during this examination, I have neither given nor received assistance."

Printed examination (WP, DLC).
[1] Thomas Erskine Holland, *The Elements of Jurisprudence*, 7th edn. (Oxford, 1895), the textbook for the course.

## A News Item

[Feb. 5, 1896]
. . . Prof. Woodrow Wilson of Princeton, who has been ill for nearly a week, resumed his lectures on "Local Government" yesterday afternoon. Professor Wilson is one of the most popular of the regular non-resident lecturers at the Hopkins. He speaks with great fluency, and has an original way of putting things, and a very keen sense of humor. His theme yesterday was the "Development of Local Government in England." He spoke chiefly from the historical standpoint. He said that the difference in the past between local self-government in England and America was that in the former country the governing officers were largely appointed by the central authority from among the governed, while in this country the governed themselves chose their officers from among their own number. . . .

Printed in the *Baltimore News*, Feb. 5, 1896.

## To William Rainey Harper

My dear Sir,                    Baltimore, 5 February, 1896.
I trust that you will pardon my delay in answering your letter of January twenty-second. It found me ill in bed here, where there was no one to whom I could delegate the task of attending to my

correspondence; and I am only just now able to attend to it myself.

I am sorry to say that it will not be possible for me to meet your wishes about giving a course of lectures at Chicago next summer. My winter has been full of engagements of all kinds, and I find that I shall be obliged to take a vacation abroad when the summer's pause comes.[1]

With much regard,

Most sincerely Yours,   Woodrow Wilson

WWTLS (W. R. Harper Papers, University Archives, ICU).

[1] Obviously Wilson and Ellen had discussed a trip abroad for Wilson when he was in Princeton over the weekend. As will soon become evident, the suggestion had first come from Dr. Charles W. Mitchell.

## From Howard Pyle

Dear Professor Wilson:          Wilmington, Del., Feb. 5th., 1896.

I am sorry indeed to hear of your sickness in Baltimore. I suppose you have very close, warm friends there, else I should be still more sorry that, if you had to be sick, you could not have managed it here in Wilmington so that we might have had the priviledge of looking after you.

I hope very much that you will be able after your lectures are ended in Baltimore to pay us a visit, stopping at least over night so that I may have the pleasure of renewing my acquaintance with you and that my wife m[a]y have the pleasure of knowing you. I will not take a refusal unless something very, very positive should prevent. Just drop me a line or a telegram when you are to come, and I will meet you at the station.

Concerning the matter of illustration for the Fourth Washington Article, I am going to venture some queries before I finally begin upon the work.

In your letter from Princeton, dated 21st. January you fixed as the three divisions for your fourth paper:—

I.   The home life at Mount Vernon before the opening of the War.
II.  The dark period of the struggle.
III. The bright close of the War.

In your last letter just received you make some other suggestions as to subject differing from these. I wish very much for the first subject we could have some Mount Vernon interior, though perhaps something relating to the political formative period preceding the Revolution might be even better. No doubt the interview between Washington, Richard Henry Lee and the three

Massachusetts delegates would be a very good subject. I think, also, your subject of Arnold's receiving the letter while at breakfast apprising him of the discovery of his treason is very dramatic.

But I find myself wishing that the supreme and crucial test of that terrible winter at Valley Forge might not be passed by. Not only is it a very sublime subject, but there are no doubt instances of individuality displayed by Washington at that time that would be very dramatic.

I wish you would consider that and see what you think of it, for I feel very sure that it is a point we should not miss.

In regard to the arrival of Mrs Washington at the headquarters at Cambridge, I see you are in love with the idea, but do you not think we might reserve some such picture for a later period of the history—a period, say, about the time of the presidency when, no doubt, there would be many such semi-royal progressions that would, perhaps, more aptly illustrate the history of that time than the grim and bitter period of the mid-struggle.

In short, how would such three selections as these fit with your ideas?

I. Washington and Lee meeting the Massachusetts delegates; or else some other and more pictorial scene of the time of the immediate ante-bellum period.

II. Valley Forge.

III. The breakfast scene when Arnold receives the letter; or else some scene concerning the evacuation of New York by the British.

I shall probably begin upon one of these subjects the latter part of this week, and I would suggest Valley Forge to commence with, the others to be built up as we may afterwards determine.

Some scene of the Battle of Monmouth—perhaps the meeting between Washington and Lee—is a very fine subject. Indeed, there are so many of them one does not know where to choose.

Faithfully yours   Howard Pyle

TLS (WP, DLC).


## To Ellen Axson Wilson

My own darling,           Baltimore, 5 Feb'y, 1896

This is indeed startling and distressing news about Mr. Wright. It has filled me with sad thoughts, and a very real sorrow for our loss; for he was of a very noble sort, and worthy to be regretted by any community. For the present at any rate my thoughts of him swallow up my thoughts of the quandary into which his death puts us. Strangely enough, I have several times of late,—since a visit I paid him when he was confined to the house with the grippe,—thought that he looked like a failing man who could not live long; and more than once the question came into my head, What if he should die before the house is completed? I did not utter the thought simply because it seemed too idle and too selfish, though I had it on the point of my tongue more than once; but the minute I read the words "Mr. Wright" after your preface about bad news I knew the rest. Of course you will keep me posted as to any developments that affect us.

I am *so* delighted to know that dear sister came after all. Give her my dearest love and thanks.

I am getting along very comfortably indeed, gathering strength and steadiness in spite of the depressing weather we are having. I did a satisfactory morning's work without any trouble again to-day, and had time to lie down before lunch, besides. The lecture went off without distress yesterday afternoon; I spent most of the evening reading Ian Maclaren's latest book, "In Days of Auld Lang Syne," and went to bed betimes in a most excellent state of mind. So, you see, I am prospering. I must do a little "looking up" now for my lecture this afternoon, to bring it "up to date."

I love you darling, oh so passionately and so tenderly, and am *so* happy to think of you up and about again,—if I were in better fettle I would write you a love letter pure and simple.

Your own   Woodrow

ALS (WP, DLC).


## Two Letters from Ellen Axson Wilson

My own darling,        Princeton, N. J. Wednesday [Feb. 5, 1896]

Your reassuring note has come to hand and I feel a great deal better about you. Am glad too that the work is going on so well. Are you sure that you enjoy it and that it doesn't fatigue you overmuch?

Things are going on beautifully here. Dear Sister Annie is *such* a comfort. Jessie and Margaret seem almost well,—cough scarcely at all, are up of course and as gay as possible. Nellie coughed a good deal in the night but had no fever and seems as well as the others today. It looks as though they were all going to get well without further trouble. I was upstairs and of course had a fine nights sleep. Maggie volunteered to stay in the nursery anyhow so that Sister Annie should not be overburdened. I am making fine progress in regaining strength, feel a good deal less shaky than I did yesterday. As soon as I can stop the quinine am sure I shall feel *quite* like myself. Of course it affects my head more disagreeably now I am up than it did when I was lying down.

I enclose a letter from Stock which explains itself.[1] I shall write, or have Ed write, him today to relieve his mind. Miss Mills (?) would make her fortune as a reporter I am sure!

Sister Annie and all send love. As for what *I* send you would be ruined indeed if there were express charges on it! Always and altogether                                  Your own    Eileen.

[1] This enclosure is missing.


My darling,                    Princeton, N. J. Wed. [Feb. 5, 1896]
Mr. Titus has just been in from Dr. Wright,[1] Mr. Wright's son and administrator, (he left no will nor executors, by the way.) He seems to think it absolutely necessary to see you before he resumes work. I asked him if writing wouldn't do; "no" he insisted not. So I told him I would see if you could come Saturday, though I warned him it was very doubtful if you could come at all. I told him I thought the architect as your representative would do. But I promised to write you & told him that if you came you would be here at one o'clock Saturday. He says he must see you and "the boys," meaning the carpenters, together,—why I can't imagine! If he had not said that, I should suggest that you insist on Dr. Wright going down to see *you*.

Whether you come or not will you write to Mr. Child & make a *special point* of *his* being here at the same time, one o'clock Saturday? I have told you what he said but *I* can't see any necessity for your having the fatigue of a journey & losing two of your precious mornings. I believe correspondence *would* do, and I wouldn't come,—unless it seems to your judgment best.

In great haste and with *dearest* love
                                  Your own    Eileen.

ALS (WC, NjP).
[1] Howard Edwin Wright, M.D., of 14 University Place.


## To Ellen Axson Wilson

My own darling,                    Baltimore, 6 February, 1896
It's rather an expensive luxury coming to Princeton *every* Saturday,—expensive both of time (which is very precious just now) and of money (which is very scarce); but a thorough understanding all around about the house is extremely important just at this crisis, and I will come, Providence permitting, on Saturday, ar-

riving at one, as you told Mr. Titus. I will write to Mr. Child at once, as you suggest, and urge him to be there too, in order that the arrangements made may be complete.

If I am feeling as well and strong on Saturday as I am feeling to-day, I think I shall return the same evening,—for, though I am well up with my work, it is really out of the question for me to lose *two* mornings just now. I dare not run so close to the schedule.

I am feeling better to-day, much better, than for some time past. I worked this morning not only with ease but also with pleasure and a novel touch of elation. But I do not mean to be deceived. I shall take as painful care of myself as before.

Oh, how I rejoice in dear sister's presence with you, and in the rapid improvement of my dear ones. I love her and I love them only less than I love you, my queen, my perfect and precious little wife.                    Your own   Woodrow

ALS (WP, DLC).

## From Ellen Axson Wilson

My own darling,          Princeton, N. J. Thursday [Feb. 6, 1896]
I have just had to write several letters to other people and now my head is beginning to buzz so that I fear I must put my darling off with a little note.

I answered the accompanying letter of Mr. Fry's[1] begging him to stop over with *us* on Monday. Am also sending a telegram to Mrs. [Talcott] Williams (whose letter came by special delivery) to say you cannot speak.[2]

I wrote to Mr. Child yesterday and received enclosed telegram. Have just written to say that six thirty would do. There was also confusion about the china-closet door & I had to write to Mr. Holsky [Holske] about it. He was here Monday afternoon, and I tried to send him messages through Annie!

We are all doing nicely. The children had a perfectly quiet night and all seem bright and well. My progress is *perfectly* satisfactory.

Dear Sister Annie is *so* sweet and kind. We are both so happy at the good reports from you. You are sure you tell me *everything* about your health? You don't know how I *weigh* your every word on that subject.

The more I think of it the less reason I see why you should be forced to return on account of the house,—why Mr. Child cannot be your representative. Though I made every effort I could not find out from Mr. Titus *why* Dr. Wright thought it so essential to see you.

With love unspeakable.

Your devoted little wife    Eileen.

ALS (WC, NjP). Encs. missing.
  [1] He is unknown to the Editors.
  [2] That is, upon the occasion of Talcott Williams' induction into the American Whig Society on February 14, 1896. See WW to T. Williams, Nov. 10, 1895, ns. 2 and 3.

A Newspaper Report of a Lecture on Local Government in England and the United States

[Feb. 7, 1896]

GOVERNMENT CONCENTRATION.

Professor Wilson Contrasts English
and American Local Government.

On account of the storm yesterday afternoon the audience at Professor Wilson's 5 o'clock lecture was comparatively small. The lecturer explained the difference between local government in England and America and the advantages of the former over the latter. He said that English local government was at present in a transitional stage. Formerly, local officials were appointed largely by the central administration, to which they were responsible. This was centralization. Now, they were mostly elected by the locality itself, but were still supervised by the central administration. This was concentration. The local Government Board exercised this general supervision.

For example, if a town wished to contract a loan, this Board investigated the conditions before granting permission. It was the same in matters of sanitation. Not all country physicians were competent to take charge of the sanitation of a town. Expert central inspection obviated danger. The Local Government Board also inspected schools. Whether such a system would be oppressive depends upon the action of the Government, which in turn depended upon the spirit of the people as a whole. This last was such in England that the supervision described was not felt to be centralization, but a means of giving the whole country the benefits of larger wisdom and experience in a helpful and advisory way.

Turning to local government in the United States the lecturer said there was no single uniform system. In New England the system of town-meetings prevailed; in the South the system of counties. The system of the Middle States was a mixture. The striking fact about the development of local government in the United States was that it had been deliberate and self-conscious. It would have been better had it been less so. It was the same with the Constitution of the United States. After it was framed, it began to be worshiped. It neede[d] improvement, but it had not been improved because it had not been criticised. The lecturer said he knew whereof he affirmed because he had criticised it and had been called unpatriotic and un-American in consequence.

As to the contention whether American institutions were of native growth or imported from England or Holland, Professor Wilson said that both views were correct. The elements and many of the forms of the institutions were of European origin; the adaptations American.

The lecturer explained that one reason why there were many incongruous things about local government was that its development had largely been controlled by statutes, and statutes in this country were not framed to carry out any wide-reaching policy, because those who passed them did not have to carry them out. In England it was far different. On only one day in the week could bills drawn by members be introduced into Parliament. All other days are reserved for bills introduced by the administration. Hence, at the beginning of the session, members drew numbers to determine the order in which they could present bills, and only those who drew the higher numbers ever reached their turn. Thus it practically came to this, that those who must administer the laws had the preliminary drafting of them. The lecturer said that there was no cold bath quite so cold as the carrying out of a system of your own planning. Hence, the most extreme Radicals in England become thoroughgoing Conservatives as soon as they entered the Cabinet. John Bright and Joseph Chamberlain furnish examples. The lecturer said that drafting of bills was as easy as lying; that it was often a form of lying, because it declared things possible to be done, which were impossible. In conclusion the lecturer said that the English system of questioning the [g]overnment in Parliament compelled a strict and detailed accounting for the way in which the administration was carried out. Although the lecturer did not say so in as many words, he evidently strongly approves of Cabinet representation in Congress.

Printed in the *Baltimore News*, Feb. 7, 1896.

## To Howard Pyle

My dear Mr. Pyle,                    Baltimore, 7 February, 1896.

Let me thank you most heartily for your warm expressions of sympathy for me in my illness away from home, and for your cordial and thoughtful invitation to come to your home in Wilmington to be taken care of. It makes one's heart warm to receive such messages, and I could almost wish that enough of my ailment remained to keep me in countenance in accepting the invitation. But my lectures here must be finished; I am really very well again; and I must content myself with having won kind friends without making use of them.

As for the illustrations, the fact of the matter is, that when I wrote you my first letter about No. IV. I had not yet put pen to paper in the actual preparation of it, and did not know how it was going to develop under treatment. Now that I have fairly set out upon it, I see very much more clearly what there is going to be to illustrate.

I shall tell as little of the general history of the Revolution as possible, and continue to make it my chief and almost only object to exhibit Washington's character and environment. Campaigning incidents are in the usual line of everybody's treatment; but what I want to make real to the reader is, the other things besides the fighting that gave colour to W's life and to the life of the times.

The reason I chose the arrival of Mrs. W. at headquarters was, not that it would afford us a pageant or "function," but because it would afford a fine contrast between New England plainness and Virginian pomp: a chance to witness the arrival as a Maine militiamen or a Massachusetts farmer lad might have witnessed it. Similarly, my only objection to an incident taken from Valley Forge is, that it would almost necessarily be an incident of the war rather than of Washington or of America in the revolutionary time.

I find that the quiet life of 1774-1775 at Mount Vernon must be made so little of in proportion that I think we had better postpone our Mount Vernon interior until No. V. Then we shall have the best possible opportunity for illustrations of that sort. There were all sorts of gatherings at Mount Vernon during the period 1781-1789 which tempt to illustration. That was the period during which W. guided from Mount Vernon the events which led to the constitutional convention and the establishment of the present government, over which he was to preside; and I have already several taking situations at Mount Vernon in my mind's eye.

So much for my own ideas and plans. Now for our joint purpose. I have stated my own view only to show how gracefully I can yield! I can give up the arrival at Cambridge with a very slight effort; and I can agree very heartily to an incident taken from Valley Forge, if only you hit upon something that took place there which dramatically reveals the man, and not merely the now conventional subject of the sufferings of the troops from cold and privation. Washington's greatness at Valley Forge was moral: can you get at that in a picture of any veritable incident? I will do my best to find one such for you; but I do not now recall any.

This seems to be really our only point of difficulty. I hope you will make your own decision, and then let me help you out with such details and suggestions as I can.

Shall I send you at once my account of the consultations between Washington and the Massachusetts men? Dr. Shippen, of Philadelphia, by the way, was present too.

With warm regards, in which I hope you will let me include Mrs. Pyle, whom I very much wish to meet,

Faithfully Yours,   Woodrow Wilson

WWTLS (deCoppet Coll., NjP).

## A Newspaper Report of a Lecture on Local Government in the United States

[Feb. 8, 1896]

LOCAL GOVERNMENT IN AMERICA.

Professor Woodrow Wilson Explains<br>Why It Is Inefficient.

The subject of Professor Woodrow Wilson's 5 o'clock lecture at the Hopkins yesterday afternoon was the development of local government in the United States. At the beginning of the lecture he said that local government in this country, instead of being allowed to develop naturally, had developed largely according to statute. By this process the State is disintegrated in an administrative sense. The localities have been segregated from the central administration instead of being closely united to it.

Law-making in the Western States, the lecturer said, was frequently a wholesale process. When they changed from Territories to States they often adopted the constitution of some State farther East almost without change. Local government has sprung up by settlement and expansion in two ways. The New England way was to go out to found a town and take along a complete ready-made organization. The Kentucky way was to let a form of government spring up in a hap-hazard way according to instinct for organization and as the needs of the time directed.

The last stage in the development of local government is marked by the growth of large industrial cities. The population of this country a century ago was chiefly rural. In a modern State legislature the bucolic element still predominates. Hence the ideas of local government held by our Revolutionary forefathers still hold sway. These were that the State should be divided into distinct political bodies or corporations. The city, like the State, must be equipped with three separate branches of government, executive, legislative and judicial. If damnation means "loss," according to its Latin derivation, the lecturer said that state of things was sheer damnation—sheer loss of efficiency.

Printed in the *Baltimore News*, Feb. 8, 1896.


## To Ellen Axson Wilson

My own darling,                    Baltimore, 10 February, 1896

I made the journey in perfect comfort,—coming out of the storm I left in Princeton to bright skies and perfect weather here; —ate *all* my chicken on the way, with keen relish; found my fire burning and my room ready for me; had a shave and a good nap before supper; and felt spry enough after supper to make a (refreshing) call on Mrs. Bird and Mrs. Smith, who (metaphorically) petted and consoled me. I was tired, of course, when I went to bed, but not unhealthily so.

This morning (it is now just noon) I have written three pages on the General without distress and am still in excellent form. Usually I make my revised copy of the morning's work between 12 and 1, as you know; but there is something to be put into what I have already written and copied; and what I am writing now may have to be changed and amplified after I've seen the papers in the Department of State: so I've stopped copying for the present, lest it should all have to be done over again. I am not hankering just now after double work!

Ah, love, it was cheering, so cheering to see you again, see you getting well, and coming back to your bloom. It was sad, too, to leave,—more sad than I dare to think: but how much we have to be thankful for, that we should both be well again—and more than ever bound together by a single great love.

                         Your own   Woodrow

ALS (WP, DLC).

## From Ellen Axson Wilson

My own darling,        Princeton, N. J. Monday [Feb. 10, 1896]

I have been so interrupted by one thing—or person—and another that now it is 10 m. after two o'clock & I have only time for a *very* hasty note.

I was kept in bed half the morning waiting for the doctor, you know. He made me submit to the examination. I knew he would think me weak and childish if I refused absolutely,—but it turned out as unnecessary as I expected. He says I am "in a really *wonderfully* good condition"! So after all it is some compensation to have had such a clean bill of health made out for me.

I feel *quite* strong again today—he won't let me go out yet though,—doesn't like the melting snow. The children are about well—didn't cough at all last night.

George returned at one,—says he is well and the others are better,—though Sister A. had some fever yesterday.

I expected Mr. Fry to lunch today, but he writes that he was obliged to go directly home to a funeral.

I love you, dear, with all my heart, soul, strength, and mind and I am in every thought,        Your own,    Eileen.

ALS (WC, NjP).

## To Ellen Axson Wilson, with Enclosure

My own darling,        Baltimore, 11 February, 1896

So you had to submit to the examination, did you? I am *so* sorry my pet,—though the "clean bill of health" *is* an immense compensation. I hope the doctor acted with all consideration and in every way as you would have had him. Anything that causes you mental distress, my darling, acts upon me almost like a corrosive, and I believe I suffer quite as acutely as you do. Ah, how I love you, and what would I not do to shield you!

I know that the enclosed letter will make you like Prof. Hunt better than ever. It really touched me.

Fortunately I can reassure him very fully. The stint was run off as smoothly and readily this morning as yesterday,—three pages, not two; and I still have time before lunch to answer two or three business letters, the copying being out of the way.

Did the carpenters and painters go to work again on Monday and do things seem to be fully under way again at the house? For precaution's sake, I wrote to Mr. Bayard Stockton,[1] Dr.

Wright, and the paint supply men yesterday, making a clear statement of the present arrangement as *I* understand it.

I am feeling perfectly well except for a neuralgic headache fr. that bad tooth,—wh. I will have attended to as soon as possible. Oh, how I love you, my sweet one; my Eileen, my queen. You are all the world to me, and I am        Your own    Woodrow

ALS (WP, DLC).
1 Probably because he was the attorney for the Estate of Josiah Worth Wright.


ENCLOSURE

## From Theodore Whitefield Hunt

My dear Professor,                 Princeton College. 2  6, 1896.

I am very sorry to hear that you are not well, especially as you have in hand so much extra work. Can we not persuade you to lessen your work and conserve your health! It is clear, Professor, that you are unduly taxing your strength, when your system can bear no special strain.

I write as a colleague, a neighbor, and a personal friend. Cut short your course at Baltimore and cancel some of those numerous engagements. I rejoice to hear that Mrs Wilson is rapidly recovering.                 Anxiously Yrs   T. W. Hunt.

ALS (WP, DLC).


## From Ellen Axson Wilson

My own darling,          Princeton, N. J. Tuesday [Feb. 11, 1896]

Your note with its fine report as to your journey &c. came this morning and brought me good cheer.

All is going equally well here. The children did not stir all night and I feel about as well as ever. We have had the lessons this morning and it is a pleasure to be busy again. I derived *great* pleasure yesterday from darning and sponging the children's old red dresses!

Everybody seems to be busy at the house,—carpenters, painters, plumbers & heater men. Also they have just finished unloading the stairs so I suppose the "stair-builders" will be busy too.

I have just finished lunch and a delicious one it was,—wish you could have shared it. Mrs. Brown sent me this morning three quail and some *delicious* butter. Mrs. [W.H.] Green sent me Sunday a bowl of delightful soup. Quite like the South—isnt it? I thought I would venture out today & perhaps see Mrs. Brown, but there is a regular wind-storm blowing though the sun shines.

I wonder if that is a bad omen for Miss Paxton's wedding, which comes off at six in the chapel.[1]

I held an impromptu reception yesterday afternoon. One of my guests was Mrs. Humphreys[2] who tells me they are not going to build this spring. They spoke vaguely of "another year" but I think it is all in the air.

Mr. Holsky has interrupted me & I am *afraid* I've lost this mail!

With *dearest* love    Eileen.

ALS (WC, NjP).
[1] Caroline Denny Paxton was married to the Rev. Lewis Seymour Mudge in Marquand Chapel on February 11, 1896.
[2] Mary C. Humphreys of 10 Bayard Ave., mother of Willard Humphreys, Assistant Professor of German.


## From Howard Pyle

Dear Professor Wilson:        Wilmington, Del., Feb. 11th., 1896.

I am now ready to begin upon your Fourth Washington Article and have given a great deal of thought to it.

I would represent as an opening the arrival of Mrs Washington at the headquarters at Cambridge in her state coach, with attendants, out-riders, etc. I think it will make a very charming illustration, indicating the opening of the grim struggle that was to follow and in strong contrast to its dreadfulness.

The second picture, by your leave, shall be concerning Valley Forge.

The more I consider your intent as to this fourth article, the more sure I am that this would embody a very radical idea of the mid-struggle.

To illustrate this I would choose one of three subjects, the picture of Washington paying a visit to one of the huts—a sick man huddled in his cot, another lean man near, and a cadaverous soldier standing near him, or else I would represent a picture of Washington in his own hut—the log shanty into which he moved after living in the stone house called his headquarters—either reading his Bible or else receiving one of his many worrying letters, the messenger standing warming his hands by the firelight, or else a picture of Washington and Baron Stuben passing down the street of huts with a foreground group of soldiers standing at the door saluting as the two officers pass.

In my opinion the last of the three subjects will make the best illustration.

I think I understand why you do not enforce the military side of Washington's history, but it seems to me (unless I altogether misunderstand your motives) that a picturial suggestion relating to the war might enforce in the minds of your readers the very fact that you [are] refraining from speaking of it. I find very often that the writer's periods are enforced by my not illustrating them too directly—and I think the subject, particularly the third, is a very fine one.

The third picture of the set should, in my mind, embody the final effort to overcome resistance of the colonies, and in that connection I should certainly do the subject of the discovery of Andre's[1] treason. The point you suggest—the receipt of the letter at the breakfast table—is not exactly susceptible to illustration. It is distinctly a literary subject and it would be be [sic] almost impossible to make the point intelligible as a picture which gives none of the context, either of that which precedes or that which follows. The very coolness and self-suppression of Andre which is so strong when written about, would, if illustrated, represent only the picture of a military gentleman receiving a letter while his friends sat about the table, laughing and talking. As such it would fall altogether flat as a picture.

So, by your leave, I will choose in connection with this subject either the point of Andre rowing down the river with his pocket handkerchief, as a flag of truce, tied to the end of his cane, or else (and I think far better) the reception of the baffled and heartbroken traitor aboard the Vulture, Man-of-War.

My voice then stands as follows:—

I.  The arrival of Mrs Washington at headquarters, Valley Forge [Cambridge].

II.  The picture of Washington and Baron Stuben at Valley Forge.

III.  Andre about to board the Vulture, Man-of-War.

I shall begin to-day upon the picture of Washington and Stuben, meantime collecting material for the other two subjects. If you approve of them you had better drop me a telegram simply saying, "Go ahead." I hope you will approve.

                    Faithfully yours   Howard Pyle

This is very hastily written to catch the mail.
I *hope* you will let us see you in Wilmington before you return to Princeton.                                        H. P.

TLS (WP, DLC).
[1] Here and below, he meant Benedict Arnold.

## To Ellen Axson Wilson

My own Eileen,                    Baltimore, 12 Feb'y, 1896.

My morning's work is over: three pages, and over, reeled off with perilous ease,—full of peril for the reader,—in a little over two hours (I begin nowadays at nine o'clock); and nothing between me and lunch except a letter to Mr. Pyle and "emptying."[1] I rise now at half past seven, having no little wife to tempt me to stay longer (I can afford to when I spend quiet evenings in my room and go to bed sleepy at ten o'clock!) and get through my work the easier. A reckoning will come, no doubt, when I have to settle down to catch up my arrears of copying—but *one* copy I am going to *have* made for me, as you said I must.

Mr. Pyle and I are about to agree on these three as the illustrations for No. IV.: (1) The arrival of Mrs. Washington at headquarters, Cambridge (after all); (2) Washington and Baron Steuben "passing down the street of huts (at Valley Forge) with a foreground group of soldiers standing at the door saluting as the two officers pass"; (3) Arnold about to board the "Vulture," man-of-war, after his discovery and escape. I am perfectly satisfied.

I am so glad to hear that all work is proceeding at the house, my darling; but nothing is so good as your returning strength. What would I not give for just one look at my bonnie sweetheart, for whom I live!                    Your own   Woodrow

ALS (WP, DLC).
[1] That is, his stomach.

## From Ellen Axson Wilson

My own darling,     Princeton, N. J. Wednesday [Feb. 12, 1896]

I do like Mr. Hunt better than ever for his nice *human* friendly letter. How thankful I am that you can truthfully reassure *him*,—not to mention myself! Am *so* glad darling that the work is going so smoothly. I presume you mean to go to Washington on Sat.?

Yes, the work is going well at the house. I have just been over myself. *Isn't* everything lovely! They got stuck about the vestibule —the tiles,—and sent for the architect. So Mr. Holsky came over yesterday and is going to send out samples at once. I told him I thought we could get them cheaper in Trenton. But he said they would have to make a trip to Trenton for them and they were in a great hurry for them; besides there were so few of them they wouldn't cost much anyhow. James Wright[1] says the architect is coming again tomorrow—also the mill man. The post of the staircase was made after Mr. Holsky's design after all & its rather ugly

and queer looking I think. Wish I had had sense enough to enquire in time about the details. However it will do well enough.

An odd thing happened today. A letter came directed to you
from University Extension, and inside there was nothing but a
long letter from Mr. Devine[2] to Prof. Woolsey of Yale![3] I am sending it on to him.

The children are still doing well—almost free of cold. It is a
glorious day; I enjoyed so getting out. I feel as well as ever. The
going out, the lessons, &c. have crowded my morning so that I
write in great haste. Love to Minnie, Mrs. Bird, &c. I hope you
will go to the dentist at once, darling. And are you taking care of
your hair again now that you are better?

With love unspeakable

Your devoted little wife    Eileen.

The doctor was *very* nice indeed.

The butcher is hard up and begs for his Jan. money. Can you
send a check? It is $15.23—payable—is it not?—just to Sullivan
Bros.

ALS (WC, NjP).
  [1] Another son of Josiah W. Wright.
  [2] Edward Thomas Devine, staff lecturer on economics for the American Society
for the Extension of University Teaching.
  [3] Theodore Salisbury Woolsey, Professor of International Law at Yale University.

## To Howard Pyle

My dear Mr. Pyle,                    Baltimore, 12 February, 1896.

Your letter of yesterday came while I was away from my rooms,
and I did not have an opportunity to answer it until this morning.

My telegram really embodied all the answer that it is necessary
to make. I am unaffectedly delighted with your choice of subjects
for illustration:

  I.   Mrs. Washington arriving at headquarters at Cambridge.
  II.  Washington and Steuben passing among the huts at Val-
       ley Forge.
  III. Arnold about to board the Vulture after his discovery and
       flight.

It is a much better choice than mine. I am particularly attracted
by the last; and imagine I can already see the purturbed and dejected traitor sitting in the boat. Your letter interests me very
much; and more than ever convinces me that you understand the
objects I have in view quite as sympathetically as I do myself.

I shall certainly try to arrange for a brief stop at Wilmington on my way back, if it is at all possible, if only to show my appreciation of your kindness; but it is some way ahead yet, for I shall be three weeks longer here; and it may not be possible, for I make close connections with my college work on my return. In any case, you have made me most grateful.

With much regard,

Sincerely Yours,    Woodrow Wilson

WWTLS (deCoppet Coll., NjP).

## To Ellen Axson Wilson

My own darling,                              Baltimore, 13 February, 1896

There were so many points to look up and consider for my narrative this morning that I am an hour late in finishing my stint,—as compared with the last few mornings. But it went well enough after I got started. But one thing is troubling me seriously: I have written twenty-four pages (out of the forty-five set as my limit) and am still not out of the year 1775. Twenty-five pp. for two years; twenty-one left for seven years! There's a lack of proportion for you! But, as usual, I have said a score of things in the 24 pp. already written which need not be said again, and which will speed the narrative and save space throughout all the twenty-one that remain. I'm still hopeful of coming out within my reckoning; for I've been in the same hole before, and managed to crawl out in time. But it makes one's head swim to think of compressing the years 1776-'81 within twenty-one *ms.* pages, none the less!

Yes, I shall go over to Washington on Saturday, if the weather permits. There's a steady rain falling now; but it is not likely to last so long.

I rejoice so, darling, that you are out again, and feeling so strong and well,—that you have seen the house and enjoy it, and that my little ones are coming on so well. But don't *overdo* anything, darling, or take the least risk, I beseech you. I *need* you so much,—shall, I trust, need you so long, as

Your own    Woodrow

ALS (WP, DLC).

## From Ellen Axson Wilson

My own darling,      Princeton, N. J. Thursday [Feb. 13, 1896].

Your quite satisfactory report came duly to hand and has brought its usual cheer. I *can't tell* you how glad, dear, I am that the work is going so well. I feel personally obliged to you for not making the second copy; but can't you avoid having the second made at all, now that Mr. Pyle has decided on the illustrations. Or let Mr. Pyle have it made if he wants it? It will cost him nothing, you know, as he has a secretary.

I think the choice of pictures very good; am sorry to give up the dramatic breakfast table at Arnold's though. Still there is much compensation in the fact that Mr. Pyle is especially fine at shipping and water scenes generally.

I have been over at the house for some time this morning. The radiators are all in place and the men are gilding them. The heat is on again and the house very comfortable. The mill-man has been there all the morning. He has an appointment with the architect (I saw Mr. Holsky pass five minutes ago) to see about the storm doors. They havn't been made and the man doesn't understand about them. I regret to say that your window-seat is not made either. He says it was not ordered and is not on his plans. The *latter* at least is true!—but, as I told you, he and I were *both* in the house with Mr. Wright when he measured for it. However that may be, it is now an "extra" and will cost us eight dollars. I am glad to add though that the stained glass is going to be a great deal less than we feared. Mr. Holsky told me the other day that it was 80 cts a square foot. So I had them measure the spaces carefully this morning and it comes to $36.00. That is better than the $75.00,—or was it $100.00?—that you calculated on last.

I send with this Corbins bill[1] because I didn't know what else to do with it;—though of course I know you don't pay it.

Mr. James Wright must have a touch of the old man in him after all; he was *so* disgusted at the idea of putting simply raw oil on those floors. He said "you would better just put water; oil would do no good and turn them *black* in no time." I told him the architect said it would do and we simply couldn't afford the other. So he said rather than put the oil he would do the laundry and pantry both for $3.00 and the nursery and halls for $6.00! And he had already said it would cost five dollars extra for the halls alone! Wasn't that nice in him? Of course I told him to go ahead. But it is quarter past two & I must close before Mr. Holsky comes in and interrupts again.

With a heart brim full and overflowing with love for my darling I am as always,                    His devoted little   Eileen.

ALS (WC, NjP).
[1] This enclosure is missing.

## To Ellen Axson Wilson

My own darling,                    Baltimore, 14 February, 1896

This, you observe, is St. Valentine's Day, and it may be that you are expecting some token from your lover; but what would you have me say? For eleven Februarys I have belonged to you; each recurrence of the day has found me more in love with you, more consciously and more deeply in love with you, than the year before; it has grown to be almost the only dominant, constant force of my life. You are my wife, darling,—and what more could I say,—for that sweet word, when it means anything true, means everything: love, intimacy, a companionship that embraces hours of thought and of care,—hours of anguish even,—as well as moments of leisure and of lightness of heart, till no other companionship suffices or can make compensation. All my ambition seems now to express itself, whenever I am conscious of it, in times of your happiness and pride. All my pleasure waits to be complete till you have shared it. All my sorrow seems intolerable until your sympathy has lightened me of it. *That* is what it means to me that you are my wife; but even that has not enough of *tenderness* in it. It's the lover that predominates in me, after all, not the husband: it's my yearning, more than my satisfaction, that I am conscious of; and when I speak of my love my inclination is to *urge* it, as if I were your suitor instead of

                              Your own accepted   Woodrow.

ALS (WP, DLC).

## From Ellen Axson Wilson

My own darling          Princeton, N. J. Friday [Feb. 14, 1896].

Am sorry to lose the regular mail today but it was unavoidable. Mrs. Hunt came in and made a very long visit—then wanted to see the house,[1] so lunch was delayed a good deal.

Most of the upstairs except the halls will be ready for the paperer on Monday, and he will begin then.

By the way Mr. Wright says his father said the side walls of the third floor ought to be lathed because children playing up there would certainly run or fall over the edges of the floor now and then and if they did they would certainly break the ceilings below and perhaps break clear through themselves! He says the lathing is all on the ground,—(he supposes his father ordered it with the rest thinking he would induce us to take his advice in the matter!)—and on that account we could have it done cheaper now than later. The whole thing he says would cost us less than ten dollars. So I told him I would write to you about it; what do you think?

Mr. Brown's estimate on the shades has just come. It is shocking to see how we have multiplied windows by reason of those mullions! Think of 55* windows not counting your high ones or the third story. I am afraid shades would not look very well on your little ones; so suppose we leave them off for the present, and find out by experience whether we need them or not. The whole thing is $74.61 without those 5;—which is *dreadful*. We estimated $100.00 for shades and window cushions; this makes them nearly $109.00. We could bring it down to about a dollar a window if we get a little inferior quality & have them with raw edges at the sides—such as we have now. Mrs. Ricketts paid $100 for such at Carrolls. Her windows are quite small though. Of course when the edges are raw they ravel and look shabby in a few years; whereas I don't know why these others shouldn't last a life-time. Yet $74.00 is a shocking sum just for shades. I don't know what to think. I will enclose Brown's letter & let you do as you think best.[2] Suppose you see how they run in price at some good Balt. house so that we will have some basis of comparison. Am sorry to fill my letter with this but of course it *must* be decided soon.

I am so sorry you are having trouble about "getting in" your matter. I was afraid of that. Of course you will come out all right; you always do, though *how* you do is and will always remain a mystery to me! It is sheer genius. But the wear and tear, and I fear the worry, involved in the doing is what I dread for you.

You will find in the other envelope your letter that went to Prof. Woolsey.[3] His very polite card makes me feel cheap for I sent nothing of the sort to him, & now I am *so* afraid he will think *you* rude! Can't you send him a little note of acknowledgment in which it will appear incidentally that you were not at home when his letter was received & remailed. I *wanted* to send a note with it but I didn't know how to explain *my* part in the matter, & I couldn't, like Mrs. Rice,[4] imitate my husband's writing! We are all well, and I love you, dear, more than words can tell.

Your own    Eileen.

\* Have just found that I overlooked the first item on the bill. There are 59 windows.

ALS (WC, NjP).
 [1] Professor and Mrs. Theodore Whitefield Hunt had rented the McGill house and planned to move into it as soon as the Wilsons had vacated it.
 [2] This enclosure is missing.
 [3] That is, a letter from Devine to Wilson that had been missent to Professor Woolsey. This letter is missing.
 [4] An obscure allusion.

## From Ellen Axson Wilson, with Enclosure

My own darling,        Princeton, N. J. Saturday [Feb. 15, 1896]

I have again failed to get my letter written in the morning. I had to go down town to get shoes for Nellie, then the heater man came to say he had finished, was about to leave, and wanted me to go over and be shown about everything. Then I had to come home and write down all he said, for I knew I would forget it in ten minutes. The stair-builders have disappointed us. They were to have come the first of the week but they are not here yet; they say now they will come Monday. It has delayed the carpenters who today have had to quit work until the stair builders are through.

By the way, I can cut down the shade bill $12.00 by using the old ones in the kitchen &c. &c. To cut them down will cost only two; making the sum total for shades $68 instead of $78.00. It looks ugly from the outside, of course, to have shades of different colours but it will show very little at the back. If you write to Mr. Brown please mention that I want to leave out 9 windows.

I had a lovely time last night. Mr. and Mrs. Perry came in, by appointment, for Mr. Perry to read to me. He read a lot of Browning *beautifully*. I was invited to dine at the [J.O.] Murrays to meet the [J.H.] Westcotts, [G.M.] Harpers & Mr. Talcott Williams who addressed Whig Hall in the afternoon & spent the night at the Murrays. But of course I am too much of a home body to resign so quickly and easily as all that my invalid's privilege of taking mine ease at my own fireside. I really am as well as ever though, and the children too are almost entirely free of cough. Night before last one of them coughed rather violently & I *could* not tell which; she would *never* cough when I was in the room. I couldn't spring out of bed quick enough to surprise them at it. So after three times waiting about their beds for what seemed an age I grew disgusted, gave them cough medicine *all around* and heard no more from anybody that night!

Isn't Col. Irwin (of course he's a Col.) whose letter I enclose an absurd old Bourbon? What a *tr-r-raitor* he will think you!

Another interruption about the house!—and now I must close in haste to catch even the late mail.

        Your devoted little wife and sweetheart,    Eileen

ALS (WC, NjP).

## From Harriet Morrison Irwin

Dear Sir:                              Charlotte, N. C. [c. Feb. 13, 1896]

I am delighted with your "In Washingtons Day" in Harper's Magazine. As you are a Southerner, I am looking to you to do justice to the most maligned of human beings;—the slaveholders of the South. The Yankees still speak of Slavery as the sum of all villanies; & still show their fanaticism by exalting the negro of the South, & defaming the whites. They wish to justify the sacrifice of 900 000 lives, & the destruction of $5000,000,000. worth of Southern property by proving that the results of the Civil War has been good for the whole Nation. I think the slaveholders of the South were the blessed result of wise statesmanship & consistent Christianity. And the negro slaves were the most comfortable, contented, & law-abiding laboring class in the world. Dr. Curry's defence of the South,[1] published by G. P. Putnam's sons 1895, ought to open people's eyes somewhat;—& Miss Letitia M. Burwell's charming little history "Life of a Girl on a Virginia plantation"[2] gives added light to a very much darkened subject:—it is so true to southern life as I myself know it, that I felt as if I had written it myself. But neither Curry nor Miss Burwell wield as strong a pen as yours—& we are looking to you for a more forcible expression of the truth on our side. The English freed their slaves in Jamaica because *it did not pay*, & for no other reason. You will find this fact so clearly stated in one of the British Quarterlies "West Indies as they were & are," that there is no question on the subject. The owners were absentees & the slaves were treated so cruelly by their agents that they were dying out. In the Southern states, the case was entirely different. Most planters lived at home, & it was to their own interest to keep their negroes healthy, happy & comfortably. The owners were the busiest of men, because nothing but constant supervision could make slave labor pay. They were patient because they *had to be*. They were provident because it was positively necessary. They were kind, because no human being can fail to have some attachment for creatures whom they have known & loved from infancy. Our Bible sa[n]ctions Slavery & hence Stonewall Jackson said, "We will conquer, as sure as the Bible is true!" Alas, the whole civilized world was against us, as it was against Protestantism in 15th century. But both are founded on God's truth, "Deo vindice," dear Brother;—stand up to your country's motto.

Respectfully,   H. M. Irwin

ALS (WP, DLC).

¹ Jabez Lamar Monroe Curry, *The Southern States of the American Union Considered in Their Relations to the Constitution of the United States and to the Resulting Union* (New York, 1895).
² Letitia M. Burwell, *A Girl's Life in Virginia Before the War* (New York, 1895).

## To Ellen Axson Wilson

My own darling,                                    Baltimore, 16 Feby., 1896

My little trip to Washington was very enjoyable and very successful. I went through Washington's diaries and the letters to him for the winter 1774-'5; found what I wanted, and expected to find; got some vivid impressions,—and was satisfied. I met Dr. Toner, the extraordinarily erudite editor of Washington's diaries, and Dr. Harrison (Col. Byrd's lineal descendent); and I saw, in the Vice President's room at the Capitol, the original of Rembrandt Peale's portrait of W. That made a pretty full day, you will admit. I went over the night before, and got an early start. Dr. Toner is a charming old gentleman,—a physician too well-off to care for practice, who has devoted his life and his fortune to the elucidation of Washington's life and the collection of materials relating to him,—for the benefit of the nation: for he has put his collection into the Congressional Library for the use of students. Dr. Harrison, I am sorry to say, made no objection to receiving back again that photograph of Col. Byrd's portrait; but he proved himself a very affable and agreeable gentleman.

The Vice President's room at the Capitol is "within the enclosure"—within the bar of the Senate—and it was a somewhat formal business getting access to it at all; but, with [Edward I.] Renick at my elbow, it was managed,—and the picture rewarded us, and more than rewarded us, for the trouble. It is splendid, impressive, *almost* entirely satisfying. I don't know why I should qualify the praise at all,—except that it would appear that no portrait can come quite up to one's own conception of Washington. It is far and away the best, and deserves to be called great.

I differ with you, dear, about the shades. I am going to order them *all*, except for the small windows in the study, which it will be *much* better to fix with sufficiently thick sash curtains. You must remember that the house can be, and will be, more critically examined as a whole from the kitchen side than from any other. There is one point I want to make sure of, though, before sending the order off. The estimate says "green" Holland. Is that all right. If it is, return it to me, and I will write the order at once. I think the estimate reasonable and the expense necessary.

*What* a Bourbon letter this is about "Washington's Day." I shall be put to it to frame a proper answer!

I will write a little note to Prof. Woolsey.

Ah, my sweet one, how I love you,—my sweetheart, my Eileen. I've just dined with the Babcock's; they warmed my heart, as they always do,—and the warmth, as usual, spends itself upon *you* who make life *constantly* a joy for me, who are my inspiration at home and everywhere, healing and vitalizing by sheer sweetness, sense, and loveliness          Your own   Woodrow

ALS (WP, DLC).

## From Ellen Axson Wilson

Princeton, N. J. Sunday [Feb. 16, 1896]

How I wish my darling were here "just for tonight" again! *Wouldn't* it be fine if those long weeks in Balt. could be broken by Sundays at home! My annual widowhood would be robbed of half its terrors. Or would you think it too much trouble? I think you would like to be here tonight at any rate if you saw how cosy this little room looks with its dear little fire in a merry blaze. The wind is howling outside and it is turning very cold; but it is deliciously warm in here. It is curious,—I *always want* a fire, but when you are gone I often feel as though I *must* have it, for company and cheer.

How I wonder what my darling is doing? Perhaps "being petted" at Mrs. Birds,—perhaps,—but how idle this is! I wish mental telepathy (?) could be reduced to a system so that one could *work* it "ez a constantcy," and not merely experience it perhaps once in a life-time. It really seems hard,—almost unnatural that two people who are almost as one,—so near and dear are we to each other, should be as completely separated by space as the veriest strangers. Not even when, as tonight, I feel the closest to my darling in spirit can I lift the veil one inch. I must e'en take refuge in dreams. Do you remember Coleridge's charming little lines,—"Something childish, but very natural"?

I really think I must get the book and quote it, because, as Bagehot's worthy citizen says, "It's just my idea,—couldn't have been better if I'd written it myself!" The last two lines, of late, are especially true

If I had but two little wings
And were a little feathery bird,
    To you I'd fly, my dear!
But thoughts like these are idle things
    And I stay here.

But in my sleep to you I fly:
I'm always with you in my sleep!
    The world is all one's own.
But then one wakes, and where am I?
    All, all alone.

Sleep stays not, though a monarch bids
So I love to wake ere break of day:
    For though my sleep be gone,
Yet while 'tis dark, one shuts one's lids,
    And still dreams on.

Yet after all, and in the midst of my unsatisfied longing for the sight of your dear face, what happiness it is to feel that this is but an incident of our life; as it were a passing twinge of pain. The life itself in all its essential meanings and values is untouched even for the moment. I can love you as profoundly and as proudly,—can take the same deep joy in *you* and your love as if you were here. That love is indeed my life, and I breathe as freely and as strongly in its atmosphere,—am as fully conscious that all is well with me as if I were in my darling's arms. And so after all love *does* conquer space and time.

We are all well and all love you.

Love to Minnie, &c.

Always and altogether,                    Your own    Eileen.

ALS (WC, NjP).


## To Ellen Axson Wilson

My own darling,                    Baltimore, 17 Feby, 1896

I am writing in the afternoon this time, for I began copying again this morning after my stint was written. I am in the thick of 1776,—and it's *very* thick, crowded with a dense underbrush of details which both obstruct and wound me. I made my way through some months of the way this morning; but am none too cheerful as to the result as I look back upon the track I have made. I feel as Robert Louis Stevenson described himself as feeling when fighting the weeds and breaking roads at Vailima. The exercise stirs the blood; but the results are less than encouraging.

What *am* I to do without you to read this stuff to! How am I to know what I have done, or how I've done it without your comment (whether of words, tone, manner, or look) to enlighten me. It will actually have to be *sent off* without being read to you; and the thought disconcerts me.

Ah, my precious one, I'm full of needs for you,—every moment seems to disclose fresh ones. Whether I am at work or at ease, busy or loafing, happy or anxious, I need you—and *know* that I do, with a keen, almost intolerable longing!

I am none the worse for work or for travel (to Washington); but feel quite well, and am always sustained by the consciousness of being                    Your own   Woodrow

The enclosed are called houses "in the *French* style."

ALS (WP, DLC). Encs.: three pictures of houses "in the French style," clipped from newspapers.

## From Ellen Axson Wilson

My own darling,          Princeton, N. J. Monday [Feb. 17, 1896]

I am afraid my penmanship, always on the ragged edge of illegibility, will go quite over to the other side today so stiff are my hands with cold. It is 4° below zero today. Still with the help of our wood fire we are doing very well, my chief grievance being the cold hands which won't let me sew to advantage. I havn't had the courage even to go over to the house today though I am anxious to know if the stair builders are there.

I selected for the shades a *very* dark green almost like that on our sashes—so dark that I did not think it would jar with the colours in any of the rooms; and of course it will serve better as a substitute for blinds than a lighter shade. I saw them at Mrs. Richardsons & they looked very well. But if you don't like the idea please don't hesitate to suggest a change. When you write ask them if they are sure they know which *shade* of green we want.

I have been hearing what the several houses cost complete; grading and all. Mrs. Ricketts was $3500;—contract including plumbing and mantles $2400. The Perry's $9900 almost;—contract without "p. & m." 6500. The Magies is a trifle under $10000;—contract with mantles $8500. So they have somehow gotten off very much better than the rest of us. Therefore the Westcotts, who have been collecting these data, are going to have Mr. Stone.[1]

The Magies had to put in a second furnace last week the house was so bitterly cold.

I am delighted, dear, that you had such a satisfactory trip to Washington. And how goes the work?—especially as regards "getting it in"? What year have you reached now.

I am perfectly well. M. & N. seem a little "stuffed up" thanks to the violent change—42° in one day. I love you, *love* you, dear, more than life itself and am in every heart-throb

Your own　Eileen.

ALS (WC, NjP).
　[1] William E. Stone, a New York architect whose work was popular in Princeton at this time. His Dutch colonial building originally built for the Princeton Bank (now the Princeton Bank and Trust Co.) at 12 Nassau Street was then under construction.

## To Charles Scribner's Sons

My dear Sirs,　　　　　　　　　　　Baltimore, 17 February, 1896.

Your letter of February thirteenth has been forwarded to me here.[1] I wish very much that I could serve you in the examination of Mr. Thorpe's work;[2] but I am just now so pressed with work that it is out of the question. A recent touch of illness has sharply bidden me take care not to multiply tasks; and I must regard its warning whether I will or no.

Thanking you for the compliment of the request, I am, with much regard,　Very sincerely Yours,　Woodrow Wilson

WWTLS (Charles Scribner's Sons Archives, NjP).
　[1] This letter is missing.
　[2] This was probably a manuscript submitted to Scribner's by Francis Newton Thorpe. The work referred to here may have been a draft of Thorpe's *A Constitutional History of the American People, 1776-1850*, published in two volumes by Harper & Brothers in 1898.

## To Ellen Axson Wilson

My own darling,　　　　　　　　　　Baltimore, 18 Feb'y, 1896

How can I thank you sufficiently for the sweet, sweet love letter you wrote on Sunday! I can't describe the grateful thrill with which I read it, my heart growing warmer and happier with every sentence; but that's the least part of the pleasure of such a letter. It has *kept* my heart warm and glad all day, and things have gone with the snap and bouyancy it gave them all the morning. It's an incomparable tonic, such a letter, to a jaded fellow like me,—jaded with longing and loneliness, pining for one sight or tone or touch of the woman who is all in all to him! It's a deep mystery to me, sweetheart, how I can work (creatively, constructively) away from you. What I reel off each morning seems of much the same quality as what went into Nos. I., II., and III., but I cannot believe that it is—without you. Certain I am that work has a touch of dreariness in it for me away from you, requires a steadier and more resolute exercise of the will, sentence by sentence. And yet, with letters like this, warm with my darling's love, seeming almost like a kiss and caress, I can count myself happy and deem myself strong even in separation[.] What could *not* a man do, knowing that such a woman loved him and yearned for him in such sweet fashion! My queen! I am

Your own   Woodrow

ALS (WP, DLC). Enc.: advertisement for "Minnie's Seaside Rest" at Old Orchard Beach, Maine.

## From Ellen Axson Wilson

My own darling,          Princeton, N. J. Tuesday [Feb. 18, 1896]

Your letter failed to go on the right mail yesterday for a provoking reason. Mr. Marchand[1] was measuring for carpets for Mrs. Hunt & I asked him to take it to the corner for me;—and at six o'clock I found it just where I had left it beside him!

He and the plumber are both disgusted and amazed at the coldness of this house. Mr. M. thinks the Hunts will rue their change. The plumber is spending the day here; most of the pipes are frozen and some of them burst. Yet we had the little stove in the bath-room & I thought it quite decently warmed. The worst is due to the fact that he hadn't time to attend to things yesterday, having half the rest of the town on his hands.

I am thankful to say that it is much milder now,—23° above.

I enclose what little mail there is; nothing seems to come now but invitations to speak. I see they have actually gotten Dr. Patton in harness,—making a grand tour.[2] What a martyr he must feel himself. Perhaps he will expire from "overwork" and so settle a number of problems.

How thankful I am, darling, for the continued good report as to health,—and how sorry for the difficulties in handling your subject. But I remember your chapter on the "Civil War"[3] & know it will all end well. You can't possibly be as sorry as I am that I am not to see it before it goes off. But I must close in haste as I have to dress for the Employment Society. I am perfectly well. Nellie coughs a little; the others are quite well. With love inexpressible.          Your own   Eileen.

ALS (WC, NjP). Encs. missing.

1 William W. Mershon, 13 John St.
2 That is, of alumni association banquets.
3 Chapter IX of *Division and Reunion*.

## To Ellen Axson Wilson

My own darling,                                        Baltimore, 19 Feb'y, 1896
I am so glad to hear that the cold has moderated with you: this savage weather makes me desperately anxious about you all when it comes. How thankful I shall be to get you out of that house! Have you learned, by the way, how the heat behaved in the new house while the thermometer was 4° below zero? My little stove keeps me very cozy here; but Monday I too was almost too stiff-fingered to write.

I fought the battle of Princeton (3 January, 1777) this morning on page 34. It's to be a desperate business finishing within limits; but I still have hopes. I *can't* stop short of Yorktown (which is still almost five years off); and I have now made up my mind, rather than compact the narrative to the point of spoiling it, to run over the limit as much as may prove absolutely necessary upon my present scale. Still I have hopes yet. I comfort myself in the present distress with the reflection that this is by far the hardest number of the series to write, and that No. V. will give me scope in the field I most love—the formation of the new government. I shall have passed all dangers when No. IV. is done—as it will be next week! Two weeks from to-day, Eileen, I give the last lecture of the course—and then what delight there will be for           Your own   Woodrow!

ALS (WP, DLC).

## From Ellen Axson Wilson

My own darling,      Princeton, N. J. Wednesday [Feb. 19, 1896]
The lessons, a visit from Mrs. Harper, and the paper-hanger have taken all my time this morning and I write in great haste to catch the mail.

The paperer has begun today, on the day nursery and very sweet and pretty it looks. The stair-builders came Monday & will soon be through; it is going to look very nice,—post and all. In fact the whole house is getting to look so elegant that it is hard to believe it is really ours! The wood-work of the dining-room is perfectly beautiful and your room and the library are almost as pretty.

There is one thing I am a little worried about. Mr. Marjoram,

Sen.[1] said to Maggie that he had been examining the house and he "didn't like the plumbing." She didn't know *why.*

There is probably nothing in it, but Mr. M. is considered an especially honest and thorough workman, and it weighs on my mind a little. I am inclined to be nervous about plumbing anyhow from a sense of our own ignorance and helplessness. I suppose the only way to be perfectly safe would be to have a sanitary expert. I wonder if that is frightfully expensive. We might write to one & just find out what his fee would be.

By the way, Mr. Wright spoke to me again about the lathing,— you forgot to answer.

I find we can't very well have that "settle" by the library window; it would be too much in the way. That will save some $14.00 on our estimates & perhaps it would be well to devote $10.00 of it to the lathing.

We are all well; weather mild & pleasant again. With love *unbounded,*                    Your own    Eileen.

ALS (WC, NjP).
[1] John H. Margerum, the plumber.


## To Ellen Axson Wilson

My own darling,                    Baltimore, 20 Feb'y, 1896

Alas that this cold should continue,—and even grow more intense! It makes me wretchedly anxious about my dear ones at home. How do you fare, Eileen, my darling? Please tell me frankly. I am afraid you don't *say* how you are suffering. Do you know how the heating arrangements have been working in the new house?

As for the lathing in the third storey, by all means have it done, sweetheart. I so take it for granted that you will order whatever you judge necessary that I had forgotten that I ought to say Yes.

You did not send back Brown's memorandum about the shades, and I do not know his new address. Wont you—to save time— write the order yourself?

Next time any one comes down from the architects suppose you ask about a plumbing (or, rather, sanitary) expert,—cost of examination, &c.—and direct them to send down an impartial and capable person whom they can be sure of.

I've made, and am executing a plan by which I hope to finish No. IV. within the 45 pp. after all. Whether the change of pace will be noticeable or not I dont know; but it's necessary, and I may be able to disguise it. At any rate, I'm more hopeful than I was yesterday,—and I love you as I love nothing else in the world!                                        Your own   Woodrow

ALS (WP, DLC).


## From Ellen Axson Wilson

My own darling,        Princeton, N. J. Thursday [Feb. 20, 1896]

I am afraid I shall have to give up trying to write you in the day-time. I am *always* so rushed that I hardly know what I am about. Yet if I waited 'till night my letter would be stale before it reached you for Ed comes in so late that I could not get it mailed 'till the next day.

The papers are turning out *beautifully*. Mine is lovely, and you never saw anything more charming than the way it tones in with those straw-coloured tiles.

The plumber finishes tomorrow. I am thinking of writing to Mr. Marjoram and asking him what he found amiss in the plumbing. I wonder if the architects don't know enough to *judge*, if they examined thoroughly. I have an idea Mr. DeGoll is rather sharp and knowing about such matters. Of course it is every architect's *duty* to be a sanitary expert, but whether they are or not is another thing.

Isn't this a queer new departure of Mr. Brower's?[1] A very dubious one, it seems to me.

The weather has turned cold again, but it is beautiful to *look* at; the snow is so white & the sky so blue. I didn't go to the house while it was below zero but whenever I have been I have found it *delightful*,—that same peculiar soft *balmy* air. If I shut my eyes I could fancy myself in Sav. on a day in early spring. We are doing very well here thanks to the little wood fire—and the hot water bottle at night! After one utterly wretched night I bethought me of it, and have been happy ever since.

I am *so* glad, dear, that you have decided to enlarge the limits of your space to suit your matter. That is eminently the wise thing to do. And your articles could really be a good deal longer without seeming excessive. Think how long Mr. Sloane's are.[2]

We are all well—quite well. With a heart full, *very full* of love,
                              Your devoted little wife,   Eileen.

ALS (WP, DLC) with WWhw notation on env.: "Marchand! Marjoram!"

[1] She probably refers to a missing letter from Wilson's first cousin, Jessie Bones Brower, reporting that her husband, Abraham Thew H. Brower, had just become editor of *The International,* an illustrated monthly magazine of Chicago, which printed "tales and timely articles from foreign tongues."

² She refers to Professor William Milligan Sloane's "Life of Napoleon," which ran in the *Century Magazine* in regular installments from November 1894 to October 1896.

## A Newspaper Report on a Lecture on City Government

[Feb. 21, 1896]

GOOD GOVERNMENT IN CITIES.

Professor Wilson's Lecture at the
Johns Hopkins University.

Prof. Woodrow Wilson lectured on city government at Johns Hopkins University yesterday afternoon. The reform of city government, he said, was the greatest problem before the American people today.

"The helplessness of the situation," said the lecturer, "is greater because we have no long line of historic precedents to guide us. The modern city is an industrial city. The ancient city was like a political state.

"The modern industrial city has arisen in three ways—by the superimposition of modern industries upon a city already organized, by the opening of canals and railroads, and by the development of a town around some great manufacturing establishment.

"The elements of a modern city are twofold. The first is the commercial class. They have more of the community feeling. Their motive is self-interest, but self-interest, if it be broad enough, is the best force for the proper organization and government of cities. The second element is the manufacturing class. The manufacturer is not so much for his city as for his market.

"Connection between the commercial element and the city is, therefore, essential. That between the manufacturing element and the city is incidental."

Professor Wilson will lecture on the same subject this afternoon.

Printed in the *Baltimore News*, Feb. 21, 1896.

## To Ellen Axson Wilson

My own darling,                              Baltimore, 21 Feb'y, 1896

I have been highly edified and amused by your spelling of the names of two of our useful friends, Mr. Mershon ("Marchand") and Mr. Margerum. I wish you *would* ask the latter for explanations about his comment upon our plumbing; but, if you write to him, do not spell him "Marjoram." I did not recognize these well known characters at first, in your version; but I see now why Mershon has been confused in your mind with Marquand![1]

It is delightful to hear such good reports of the successful finishing touches on the house. I should judge from what you say that the whole thing ought to be finished by the time I reach home, on the 7th of March (I get through here on the 4th, lecture in Sewickley on the 6th,[2] and can't get home before the 7th, alas!). Perhaps, when the weather moderates, and you feel equal to it, you had better go into town and buy the matting &c. you need; so that we can have the floors made ready for the furniture at once, and begin moving over, room by room, the minute I get home,—say on Monday, the 8th. What do you think?

What sweetness and good cheer there is in all your letters, Eileen, my darling,—what an unmixed, incalculable blessing it is to have you to love me, and accept me as

Your own   Woodrow

1777 finished, p. 38; all goes well; and I feel in very good form.

ALS (WP, DLC).
[1] Because Allan Marquand was a professor of art at Princeton, and Mershon was a kind of interior decorator who specialized, among other things, in pictures and picture framing.
[2] All extant Pittsburgh newspapers are silent about this address.


## From Ellen Axson Wilson

My own darling,          Princeton, N. J. Friday [Feb. 21, 1896]

*I* don't think it at all "necessary" for you to limit yourself so rigorously to 45 pages. *I* approved much more of your yesterday's plan of taking whatever space you needed. Please don't worry yourself and perhaps mar your article for the sake of keeping with[in] those arbitrary limits.

The stair-builders have finished & the carpenters are back. The last things have just come from the mill too, so they have a clear field before them.

Mr. Holsky was out yesterday and I told of Mr. Marjoram's criticism. I was a good deal comforted in talking to him for I gained the impression that he himself really *understood* the matter. There was nothing in the least pretentious in his manner. He said that he considered it a very good job, with two exceptions; —and *one* of those two was a matter on which experts themselves differ. That is the location of the "vent," which you know is just outside the front wall of the house. He himself prefers them *within* the building; in New York it is required that they be so placed, but in most small towns they are outside. In some other places again they are forbidden altogether. Of course there is no danger to health or anything else unless it freezes, but the pipe (or whatever it is) is so far under ground that there is very little risk of that.

The other is a matter which can & indeed must be remedied. It was, he supposes, a necessity, but an unfortunate one that the pipes are in the cold north corner of the building. They have already frozen and burst. There is a tub of water there full of ice,—with that big furnace burning so near! Therefore the pipes must be wrapped and boxed, and that he thinks will remove *all* danger. To wrap them in mineral wool would give us the greatest security but would be rather expensive; the material alone would cost perhaps fifteen dollars. So don't you think we had better try the other? This matter must be settled now, of course, so that the carpenters can do the boxing. It was very probably this that Mr. M. "didn't like." Mr. Holsky went to see Mr. Marjoram "to get the benefit of his criticism";—it was his own idea. I fear he had small chance of finding him at home though.

I am sorry, darling, to fill my letter with this stuff, but it seemed necessary; the matter is so important. We are all well and comfortable. You don't say in this letter how *you* are feeling. Remember I take alarm whenever that omission occurs. With a heart brimming over with love          Your own   Eileen.

Did you remember, dear, to take my waist & the little rug to be cleaned?

ALS (WC, NjP).

## From Edward Southwick Child

Dear Sir:                         New York. Feb. 21, 1896.
We have to report as follows in regard to the progress of your building at Princeton:

The heater-men are finished and have left.

The stairs were to be finished last night.

The carpenters are daily expecting the receipt of the seats, and the last of the mill-work, and will then lay the finished floors.

We have a bill from J. W. Fiske, for Mr Wright's Estate, of $24.50. This is practically a notice to us to deduct it from the settlement, but presume from our conversation with Dr Wright that this will not be necessary.

Our Mr Holske saw Dr Wright and he expressed himself as satisfied with the progress of matters, and as far as we could ascertain none of the creditors had served any notice, or were in anywise disturbed about the prospect of their being paid in full. We see no reason now to doubt that the house will be entirely finished in a week from date.

Please let us know when you expect to return from Baltimore and the writer will then meet you at Princeton and see Dr Wright and finally inspect the house.     Yours truly,   E. S. Child

TLS (WP, DLC) with WWhw notation on env.: "Ans. Feby 22/95 [96]."

## From Edith Gittings Reid

My dear Mr. Wilson,                    [Baltimore] Feb. 21, 1896
    I cannot refrain from sending you the enclosed—it delights me so to know that I am your "intimate friend[.]"[1] When so great a creature as the President of the "Arundell Club" says so, why that settles it! I have, however, advised Miss Brown that she must communicate with you herself.
    But what concerns me most is: When can you spare me an evening? Any day you name we will dine at seven.
    I sign myself with full authority your friend
                                    Edith Gittings Reid

Please note the deliciously humble tone of Miss Brown's note. What a very great man you must be to whom the lofty Arundell lowers its crest!

ALS (WP, DLC).
    [1] The enclosure was Mary Willcox Brown to Edith G. Reid, Feb. 19, 1896, ALS (WP, DLC). Miss Brown said that she had been told that Mrs. Reid was an intimate friend of Wilson's and was therefore writing her to ask whether Mrs. Reid thought it would be possible to persuade him to speak to the economics section of the Arundell Club on some economic subject. "I think the section would be interested in hearing Mr. Wilson speak on any subject at all," Miss Brown concluded, "and I should not presume to suggest a topic." The Arundell Club, organized in 1894, was a woman's club devoted to the discussion of civic problems.

## To Edith Gittings Reid

My dear Mrs. Reid:                    [Baltimore, c. Feb. 22, 1896]
    I am delighted it's settled! I knew, so far as I was concerned, that it needed only some sanction to make us intimate friends: and now the finishing touch has been given!
    You give me delightful confirmation of the fact by asking me to choose my own day for dining with you. Monday and Wednesday of next week are the only days now left me. I hope you will make choice between them,—no, may I not save you trouble by

saying Wednesday, unless I hear that Monday would be more convenient?

I am indeed overwhelmed by the tone of Miss Brown's note. I shall have at once to set about a careful study of the rôle of great man!

With gratitude and warm regard,

Your sincere friend,    Woodrow Wilson

ALS (WC, NjP).


## From Ellen Axson Wilson

My own darling,          Princeton, N. J. Saturday [Feb. 22, 1896]

The "Harpers" came this morning by way of celebrating "the day." I think, coming out when it did, it ought by all means to have opened the number this month. But I suppose it is against their principles to have the same man lead two months in succession. The pictures are very pretty—are they not?—though not equal to last months.

You seem to be getting on finely with No. 4;—so glad to hear you are in "good form."

The weather is growing somewhat milder—indeed it is what is known as a "fine day" in this frozen zone. The town is full of visitors. It is to be hoped no one will come here for I am in a regular "mess" stuffing feather pillows.

I am planning to go to Phila. the first mild day in March for curtains, your rug, &c. We don't need matting. Have you looked for old andirons? And by the way, you know I was to send for my year's supply of soap and that desk for the children. If you can spare a check for $10.00 now, please send it, made out to "the Larkin Soap Mfg. Co." Buffalo, N. Y. We are all well—Nellie coughs a *very* little,—I am surprised to see how perfectly free from cold I keep through all this cold.

I love you darling deeply, tenderly, passionately—I am altogether,                    Your own    Eileen.

ALS (WP, DLC).


## From Joseph Ruggles Wilson, with Enclosure

My precious son—                    [Philadelphia, Feb. 23, 1896]

I enclose a note from our dear Dode which tells its own story. Please steal time enough to write him encouragingly and to warn him against giving up his present position, although at reduced salary, until he gets something else. Something *must* be done for the dear boy for whose future I am extremely anxious. Never was I more depressed than I am now—from several causes, yet the chief is our dear Tenn. boy.

I have just come from hearing your Sparhawk Jones.[1] He has no pulpit merit whatsoever in my judgment: smart without being talented: eccentric with no genius: talks in abstractions and has no road to the heart.

But I'll not trouble you with a *letter*. We are all pretty well bodily. Annie got an attack of grip by going over to Princeton, but she is a good deal better. God bless you my loved one.

Yours affc    Father

ALS (WP, DLC).
   [1] The Rev. Dr. John Sparhawk Jones, pastor of Calvary Presbyterian Church of Philadelphia, 1894-1910. Jones had been pastor of the Brown Memorial Church in Baltimore when Woodrow Wilson was a graduate student at the Johns Hopkins.

E N C L O S U R E

## Joseph R. Wilson, Jr., to Joseph Ruggles Wilson

My dearest Father:                    Clarksville, Tenn. Feb. 20 1896.

I am sorry to say that business must take precedence of other subjects in this letter.

The crowd of men[1] who compose the publishing company that owns this paper, The Times,[2] are narrow minded, close fisted and, to me, underhanded. They threaten a reduction of my salary to the tune of about $10.00 per month, and pretend to reduce the salary of the business manager when in reality they give him privately to understand that his pay will not be touched. They find no fault with my work and can make no "pick," but evidently do not like it because I do not submit to their petty prejudices and narrow desire to conduct a personal organ, for it amounts to this. In brief, their treatment is, according to my notion, an effort to replace me by degrees with one of their own number who has had but little experience in the work. My work has, I am gratified to know, built up the paper and made it very popular as a medium of live, local news. I cannot stand the low way they are acting, so must, in self respect, make an immediate change for I will not be the tool of any man or set of men and act contrary to principle.

Now can you possibly help me with any of the papers in Philadelphia. Brother has wide acquaintance and influence with newspaper men, but I do not want to write him for he evidently considers my ability as of very little consequent. Perhaps it is in editorial work, for I have never had the occasion to study it, but in reportorial, telegraph, exchange and other such work, I know I can hold my own for I have received many letters of commendation from newspaper acquaintances who know. Possibly if you confer with brother, some opening might be secured. I must act at once, and if I cannot get a position, start out for myself.

Kate[3] is well, I am in statu quo., but baby[4] has not been well for a week past. Nothing alarming so far, the doctor says. We both send unbounded love to you, sister Annie & the rest. Please let me hear from you as soon as possible.

Your aff son   Joseph.

ALS (WP, DLC).

[1] Among them were H. P. Gholson, president, and M. G. Lyle, secretary and treasurer.

[2] The Clarksville *Daily Times*, successor to the Clarksville *Progress-Democrat*.

[3] His wife.

[4] Alice Wilson, born May 7, 1895.

## To Ellen Axson Wilson

My own darling,                       Baltimore, 23 Feb'y, 1896

I am distressed to hear of the bursting of the pipes in the new house. By all means have them wrapped and boxed in any way that will *certainly* be sufficient. It will obviously save money in the long run, and should be done at once. Mr. Child wrote me a letter, which I received yesterday, saying that he saw no reason to doubt that the house would be entirely completed by next Friday, the 28th. Do *you* think it will?

No. IV. goes slowly but surely forward. I passed the winter of Valley Forge yesterday (1777-'78); but it cost me three pp. to do it. I am now on 41. Fortunately Washington himself did very little fighting between Monmouth (June, '78) and Yorktown (Oct., '81); the fighting of those two years was almost entirely confined to the Carolinas, and can be passed over very lightly "by the present writer,"—so that I *still* have hopes,—though some very inviting detail awaits me and may "draw me out." I am going to make a dash to finish by Wednesday,—but not if the pace hurts. I am feeling very well and the spurt would be a very mild one.

I wish, my love, that I could write you such a letter as you wrote me last Sunday. It has put a sort of song in my heart,— and I would give a great deal to be able to make you as happy. Your love for me is such a well-spring of surprise to me, as well as of joy, that I have, as it were, a double reason for dwelling on it. These warm expressions of it always come to me like something new,—with a sweet freshness, as if I had not been prepared for them,—and are an incomparable tonic in my blood. Ah, my darling, I shall never be able to say anything half so sweet in return, though I were able to coin my heart into words: for surely, *surely* you have always been jesting when you pretended surprise at my love for you! I wish (provided it would not spoil you) that you could be somebody else for a little while and know my Eileen, the sweetest woman in the world, with deeper sympathies of head and heart, truer divinations of whatsoever is pure and noble and of life's essence, than any other sweet helpmate and companion that ever lived. And, after all, I've not the slightest fear it would spoil you: for your qualities are just those that make a woman unspoilable,—and would make a man so, if he could have them. Don't you see that it is always the sweetest characters, like Mrs. Hibben and Mrs. Perry, who love you most? Why, darling, it is my deliberate judgment that such qualities of mind as you have (brilliant, with a soft, not a hard, glitter—like some sweet, soft radiance) were never in any one else combined with such *graces* of heart,—such loving, clinging tenderness and self-abnegation. I never deem myself great except when I am conscious that you love me, and have actually *chosen* me to be

Your own    Woodrow

ALS (WP, DLC).

## From Ellen Axson Wilson

My own darling,        Princeton, N. J. Sunday [Feb. 23, 1896]
    I have been having a delightful time this afternoon reading a certain article on "Col. Washington"! I didn't really *mean* to read it,—at least not then,—was only going to "look at it" a bit; but at once became so absorbed that I simply couldn't put it down;—even shamelessly postponed the "Sunday School"[1] until a late hour in order to finish. I was surprised to find with what absorbing, thrilling interest it seized hold upon me,—exactly as if I had never seen it before. Like a fine poem it made me "feel queer down my backbone," and even moved me to tears—such happy tears! Oh, it is a masterpiece!—and you are indeed a genius,—and my pride and delight in you is *far* past all telling. And then your work is not only fine, but fine in such a large, noble way! The qualities of your thought and style and method are so far beyond *merely* clever, brilliant work,—even the best of *its* kind,—Lowell's, for instance, that I really believe that is the reason the average new[s]paper man so often overlooks the fact that you have a style at all. There is something so *inevitable* about a perfect thing after it is done,—one feels that it *must* have been just so; moreover it

so completely *possesses* one, that one doesn't consider *how* it was done, or even think much of the doer; that is no one does who is still a naive reader and not a conscious and determined "literary critic." I am really afraid, my dear, that if you should happen to care for the the applause of the gallery-gods—or even of the dress circle,—you will be found to have over-reached yourself. I believe people do not generally remark how brilliant Shakspere is when they have just witnessed "Othello," or comment upon Raphael's technique when they first stand before the "Sistine Madonna."

I have been interrupted by a long visit from Mr. Daniels and now must go to bed, I fear, as the fire is almost out. He tells me that George Patton is said to be engaged to that handsome, dark-haired girl who has been there all winter.[2] She is from Bermuda. That was I believe his only news, except that there seems a little feeling about Dr. Patton in his addresses insisting especially on a new chair of Philosophy, as if that were *the* crying need of Princeton. It is supposed he wants it for Wister Hodge![3]

Wisner[4] says he saw you in Balt. and you were looking "badly"; which of course makes me *feel* badly. So please, darling, let your next letter be a detailed account of how you are in *every* respect, and how other people think you look,—whether better or worse than when you first went there. You have been slighting this matter of health in your last few letters and I had already been anxiously pondering whether it were done of malice aforethought, because you were not very well, or whether perhaps you were feeling so much better that the subject was not so immediately on your mind. Please, darling, tell me the whole truth whether bad or good. You do not know, dear, how unspeakably precious you are to me, how my life in its every fibre is wrapped about yours, so that separation from you, always so hard, becomes indeed terrible when any element of suspense as to your welfare enters into it. With love untold,     Your own    Eileen.

ALS (WC, NjP).
[1] That is, the Sunday School that she conducted for her daughters at home.
[2] Winifred Outerbridge. She married Patton in Bermuda on June 23, 1897.
[3] Caspar Wistar Hodge, Jr., at this time Instructor in Philosophy at Princeton.
[4] Charles Wesley Wisner, Jr., '96, of Baltimore.


## To Ellen Axson Wilson

My own darling,                              Baltimore, 24 Feby, 1896

I had an interesting piece of good fortune the other day. There was a book entitled "George Washington and Mount Vernon"[1] which I could not find, nor even get track of: and a few days ago I hit upon it among a "job lot" of books on a table in the back part of the principal book store here, obtainable (and obtained) for the sum of $1.20.

I passed the battle of Monmouth (1778) this morning; ought to dispose of 1779 and 1780 to-morrow; and, on Wednesday hope to see the glories of Yorktown.

I am getting tired of the work on No. IV. and shall be glad to change to house moving for pastime. I am beginning to realize that it is next week that I am to go home. It would seem very near if it were not for that trip to Pittsburgh. A week from next Saturday (this being Monday) can be called "next week" only by courtesy. But I am thankful enough as it is. This will be for me the gladdest home coming I have ever known, I think. Not that I have not held my own in my progress away from that attack: for I am getting steadily better; but that combination of illness and anxiety that has filled so much of my time here has demoralized me and made me infinitely homesick,—has made me long for you unspeakably—and my patience could not hold out much longer. With love unutterable                    Your own    Woodrow

ALS (WP, DLC).
    1 Moncure Daniel Conway (ed.), *George Washington and Mount Vernon: A Collection of Washington's Unpublished Agricultural and Personal Letters*, Long Island Historical Society, *Memoirs*, Vol. IV (Brooklyn, 1889).

## From Ellen Axson Wilson

My own darling,                              Princeton, N. J. Feb. 24/96
    I am surprised indeed that Mr. Child thinks the house will be finished this week; that is quite impossible. The carpenters will be out this week and I think the rest ought certainly to be finished next week. Some things are not here yet—the stained glass[,] the tiles, the hardware for the front doors and some of the paper.

The weather has turned *beautiful*—just like spring. I wish I could do my shopping at once, but I havn't any money. My idea was to wait till the 1st of March & try and get most things at Wanamakers so that you would not have to pay 'till the first of the quarter. Of course if you could send me money to pay cash now,—say $100.00—it would be better to go to N. Y. and buy wherever I can to most advantage. There are curtains for various rooms, your carpet, bed & springs, small rugs, pedestal, lantern, chair, kitchen oil-cloth, stuff for your window-seat, & picture frames.

You would think we had begun to move already if you saw this room. Mr. *Mershon* has the table & small desk to mend, Mr. Titus the stool, Mr. Wright a chair,—to stain where Mr. T. mended it;—Mr. Krespach[1] has the lounge to cover, and I have made cushions of the little table cover & the yellow silk screen!

I am *so* glad, darling, that the work is going on so finely and that you are "feeling very well"—that is a word of comfort indeed.

I love you, darling, with all my heart,—that love alone must explain the opinion you persist in holding of me. Now *that* opinion *deserves* to be, what it must ever remain, "a well-spring of surprise"!          Your devoted little wife    Eileen.

ALS (WC, NjP).
[1] John R. Krespach and Son, general upholsterers, 38 University Place.


## To Ellen Axson Wilson

My own darling,                    Baltimore, 25 Feb'y, 1896

You must not allow yourself to be affected by what is said of my appearance by Wisner and others who happen to have seen me. Everybody (very considerately) tells me that I am "looking thin," and of course I am—my present diet is not likely to fatten me, either—but my colour is much better and all who saw me when I first came remark upon the improvement in my looks. I am keeping *nothing* from you. When I do not speak of my health it is because it is just the same as when I last mentioned it. I have ups and downs, of course. Last evening, for example, my bowels were abominably uncomfortable till I went to bed; but not at all in the same way as at the beginning of my recent attack —just in a way to be expected after eating apple sauce (which Mitchell had told me to experiment with, and which on a previous day had done me no harm at all). To-day I feel quite bright and well again. Now, that's the whole case, darling; and you may be sure you'll hear everything from headquarters.

I finished page 45 (which is itself 3pp. beyond my usual limit, you must remember) this morning at almost the end of 1780. Three pp. more, I am hoping, will bring me to the end—to-morrow: and if ever a man needed encouragement and could not get it from such an intoxicating letter of appreciation as you wrote on Sunday, he must indeed be beyond encouraging. The idea, you dear little lover, of your reading "Colonel Washington" again, and enjoying it! Bless your heart! is all I can say. I am mad with love for you. If I have literary power, it is because you have bewitched me and given me what you wont use yourself.

Your own    Woodrow

ALS (WP, DLC).

## From Ellen Axson Wilson

My own darling,          Princeton, N. J. Tuesday [Feb. 25, 1896]

That was a great piece of luck in the way of book buying. I wonder if you need now some books that came for you from the college a few days ago. "Diary of Christopher Marshall" 1774-1781,[1] and three little vols. of Washingtons Journals. The dates are 1751-2, 1747-8, & 1754.[2]

I am truly glad that the moving is coming at just the right time,—in what ought to be a breathing space between Nos. Living next door, as we do, it ought not, if we have decent weather, to be much harder than spring house-cleaning,—and much more interesting of course. I feel as if I were moving now—am in such a rush of business with so many calls upon me from various people. Am writing in mad haste now because lessons are just done, it is nearly lunch-time, then comes the architect, & then the Employment Soc. Mr. Margerum it seemed had not been in the house but had seen something that he considered seriously wrong from the *outside*,—some bent tube in the roof or upper wall is only two *ins*[.] in diameter whereas it ought to be four. So I had him examine the house yesterday inside & he is too [to] meet the architect here today & give him the benefit of his criticism. Holsky missed him the other day. We are all very well; the weather, alas! is turning quite cold again. With love unspeakable.

Your own,    Eileen.

Of course you ar'nt looking for dining-room furniture? I fancy we both tacitly dropped that plan. It will be much better to wait at least until we actually sell what we have.

ALS (WC, NjP).
  [1] William Duane (ed.), *Extracts from the Diary of Christopher Marshall* . . . *1774-1781* (Albany, N. Y., 1877).
  [2] For bibliographical references to these journals, see L. G. Tyler to WW, Sept. 2, 1895, n. 7.


## To Robert Underwood Johnson

My dear Mr. Johnson,          Baltimore, 25 February, 1896.

I hope that you will pardon my delay in answering your note of the nineteenth.[1] It had to follow me here (where I am lecturing), and it found me both busy and unwell.

And now that I can answer it, I do not know what to say. I am opposed to woman suffrage: but my exact attitude would be a rather long story, which would have to be carefully put to contain my real thought; and which I have just now neither the time nor the stomach for.

I have no doubt, from what I see in "The Princetonian," that Magie has something worth speaking of in the line of Roentgen rays;[2] and as for literary editorials, I am as dry just now as a squeezed sponge. I may get a literary mood on me some day, though, for there's no telling; and, if I do, you shall know.

With much regard,

Sincerely Yours,    Woodrow Wilson

WWTLS (L. W. Smith Coll., Morristown, N. J., National Historical Park).
  [1] It is missing.
  [2] An article on Professor Magie's experiments with cathode rays had appeared in the *Daily Princetonian*, Feb. 8, 1896.

## A Newspaper Report of Two Lectures on the Modern City and Its Problems

[Feb. 26, 1896]

### GOVERNMENT OF THE CITY
PROF. WILSON'S LECTURES AT THE
JOHNS HOPKINS UNIVERSITY.

The subject of Prof. Woodrow Wilson's 5 o'clock lectures at the Hopkins this week has been the "Modern City and the Organization of Its Government." Many of his views are interesting in connection with the recent and present political situation in Baltimore. While Professor Wilson, who is recognized as one of the most eminent lecturers on municipal government in this country, mentions no names, his statements have often so much point and directness that the hearer unconsciously substitutes "this city" for "the city in general." Professor Wilson, for instance, advocates the municipal ownership of gas works, a plan which an editorial in The News on Monday proposed as the future solution for the gas problem in this city.

In his Monday's [February 24] lecture Professor Wilson said in substance:

"We cannot look to the selfish interest of the well-to-do or leading classes alone to advance the interests of the city in the way they should be advanced. They will insist upon a good police system, perhaps, but they will not be inclined to insist upon thoroughness of sanitation in those parts of the city which they do not occupy, nor will they urge the city to provide in general that higher education which they can provide for themselves. The upper classes often, likewise, make their wealth tell corruptly on the way in which the city makes its expenditures, so as to secure more than their share of advantages from the outlay for paving, lighting, locomotion, preparing of districts for occupation, etc. The wealthy classes cannot, therefore, be relied upon to promote the delicate and difficult tasks which arise from the masses of men being economically dependent upon the city. Their interest, in short, is a special interest. The only wholesome power can come from a general interest.

### Tow [How] to Interest the People.

"The problem at once arises, how to get and hold the attention of all classes of citizens. The easy method and the common method to get it is by a long course of outrageous corruption and ring domination. Unfortunately, this way is terribly expensive. But if the interest of citizens has been aroused this way, for want of wisdom in hitting upon a better, how shall this interest be maintained?

"I answer by giving the city more important, wide-reaching and conspicuous functions. People are always interested in what they feel immediately concerns them. If, therefore, the convenience of the citizen is touched constantly by the action of the city administration, he will be much more apt to take care that the administration be pure. Hence, I believe in the municipal ownership of the gas system and the street railways, both because the way in which they are managed affects the whole community, and likewise because municipal ownership would lead citizens to take a greater interest in municipal affairs.

"In our attempt to secure an organization of city government that is at once open, accessible and respected it is well to inquire what the modern industrial city really is. One view is that it is an economic corporation. If this is so, the chief stockholders, property-owners, ought to control the expenditures. The other view is that it is a political unit, or society, a State on a small scale—or, better, a delegate plenipotentiary of the State in all local matters. Sometimes there is a temptation to regard it as both. In reality it is neither. For want of another term we may call it a humane economic society.

### A City's Functions.

"We next ask, what are the organs of this modern city by means of which its functions are exercised? They are the ordinance-making body and the executive. The analogy usually observed both in theory and in practice between the City and the State in organization is the most conspicuous and practically important in this country of any place in the world. Yet it is the least justified here, and, perhaps, the most mischievous. The City is looked upon as a subordinate organ of the State, but the confusion arises because its chief duties concern not the State, but itself.

"The long argument historically enforced and illustrated about the division of power has given us the idea of the necessity of the separation of the executive function from the originative function. All our thinking about executive action and law-making has been of one piece. But, in fact, the common council is not a legislative body. In dealing with the different classes of the city, its business is to keep order, preserve health, furnish education, facilitate locomotion, and care for those in distress. This is not law-making, but administration. Stated another way, the common council is an ordinance-making body, and an ordinance-making body is an administrative body; for an ordinance lies closer to facts, to practical conditions and details than does a law. Its test is its feasibility as shown by direct experiment. Hence the council should not be separated from, but closely associated with, the administration. Such under most systems is the arrangement in Germany, France and England. It is noteworthy that no foreign city has a bicameral council.

### Too Many Checks.

"In view of all these facts, the system of checks and balances becomes ridiculous. They cause lack of efficiency and prevent locating responsibility. A single body should originate and apply the measure. The persons who pass the ordinances should have the duty of carrying them out either directly or through their agents for whom they are responsible.

"For instance, the London citizen votes only for the member of the council. He does not delude himself by saying that if ward politicians are elected to the council he will elect 'a mayor with a backbone' to checkmate them; for the mayor's power is not constructive, but obstructive. He can stop things, but he cannot push them forword [forward]. He can send in the same nominations again and again, but the only way he can win is by tiring the council out, like the woman and the unjust judge in the Scripture.

"In short, what we have at present in this country is a mayor to nominate and control all administrative machinery; a finance board, to spend the money; a council, checked within by the bicameral system and without by the mayor's veto to 'ordain' the administration of which it knows nothing, and to vote the moneys which it is not suffered to specifically apportion; and, finally, sometimes a State-made and State-controlled police force. The complexity is added to by many boards appointed in every way conceivable.

### The System Futile.

"The system of checks and balances is futile. The only check that is or can be effective is public opinion, the check of the master over the servant. Checks and balances are desirable only for the politician who wants to get in a corner where he can shirk responsibility. One reason why we have so many more politicians than statesmen to the square mile in this country is because public servants are so many removes away from direct responsibility to the people.

"Finally, how ought the common council to be elected? What is the system and principle of representation to be? The method of election by wards should be abolished. The common voice should tell in the common choice. Common interests should be determined by a common vote. A city is not a group of localities, nor an aggregation of interests nor a public works corporation, but an organism, whole and vital only when conscious of its wholeness and identity."

### POWERS AND DUTIES OF A MAYOR.

### Tendency to Magnify the Executive— The Remedy.

In his lecture yesterday afternoon, Professor Wilson continued the subject of city government by discussion of the powers and duties of the municipal executive, or the mayor. He said that in our city government we had reversed the method of history in which the representative body was given its powers in order to act as a check upon the sovereign, or executive. Now we put in an executive to check the representative body. In foreign countries the mayor is part of the administrative power of the city, and is either elected from and by the council or acts conjointly with it. The English mayor, for example, is only the presiding officer of the board of aldermen and councillors, excepting that he is also a justice of the peace. This board taken together constitutes at once the executive and ordinance-making power.

"In our country the mayor is a creation developed indeed, but developed according to a theory. There was an effort to reproduce the national executive on a small scale. This process is best illustrated by the history of Boston, New Haven and Philadelphia. At present everywhere in the United States the mayor is separate, president-like, a sort of shadow-king, making appointments, checked by the council, and in his turn checking it. Co-ordinated with him are various independently-elected officers and commissioners. We have much less faith in the democratic system and less trust in representative principles as far as city government is concerned than any civilized country in the world. There may or may not be any connection between these facts, but they are worth considering.

["]The tendencies of present-day reform in our cities are well known. They are to magnify the office of Mayor, to make of the mayor a dictator. It is noteworthy that in no other country in the world is the mayor thus made boss without being subordinated to the central government. These tendencies are based upon a radically false theory—false in three respects. In the first place, it is held that there will be a concentration of the public gaze and editorials upon him, and, therefore, a concentration of administrative responsibility. In this there is the danger of public inattention to the ordinary course of administration which it is vain to hope to compensate for by a spasmodic arousal to occasional official misbehavior.

## Present-Day Reform.

["]After the reform mayor has been elected he is handicapped. For instance, the mayor cannot determine how the streets shall be cleaned. He can appoint responsible persons to do this work, but such persons must do it, not as the mayor directs, but in accordance with ordinances passed by the common council. The same is true of other city departments. They must be administered according to city ordinance, or State statute. Suppose the mayor thinks the heads of these departments inefficient. They can commonly cite such ordinance or statute in their defense, and though the mayor has power to remove them and substitute others he seldom feels it quite expedient to do it.

["]The only thing a mayor can do is to appoint honest persons. But an honest person is not necessarily an efficient person. I have known honest fools. It is not enough to secure a good personnel. The administration should be conducted by good methods also.

## Danger From Change of Officials.

["]The second fallacy of the theory of attempting to remedy evils by trusting to the power of the mayor is that it entails the danger of a complete upheaval of the administration by official removals, etc., upon the change of mayors. This is why our political system has been called an astronomical system. I do not care how honest a new man may be, a new man is a bad man for a certain time in difficult administrative positions. It often does no more good to change the municipal official body for the sake of purifying it than to try to keep certain kinds of dogs clean by washing them. You must get another breed of dog.

["]The third fallacy in the theory is the expectation that the mayor can do everything. Bagshot [Bagehot] has said that a good despot is a failure because he has only 24 hours in his day. We demand that a mayor hampered in many ways shall do more than a king. He is expected to scrutinize everything, to see that the street-cleaning department is doing its work, that the public schools are properly managed, that the public health is not being endangered through official carelessness and a thousand and one other things.

["]We desire[,] to use a current phrase, a good business administration, and divide the control of the business so that no one is responsible. Analyzing the phrase, a good business administration means to most people simply a clean administration. Now cleanliness is commonly said to be next to godliness. But I would rather have some dirty men do things for me if they know how to do them than clean men who don't know how. I do not believe any more that there can come out of the present system a reform of affairs by a good mayor than I believe that here on earth there is going to be an anticipation of those changes which belong to the future existence.

["]To sum up, then, I believe that the government of a city should be in the hands of one body. I contend that the way in which a thing should be done should be determined by those who appoint the persons to do it. Public administration should be conducted by 'common counsel,' not by a system of a divided common council, checking and checked by a mayor. The government should be arranged so simply that there is only one set of men to be voted for. It is folly to watch one man who is watching another, and leave both without any direct and undivided responsibility to the people.["]

Printed in the *Baltimore News*, Feb. 26, 1896; some editorial headings omitted.

## To Ellen Axson Wilson

My own darling,                    Baltimore, 26 Feb'y, 1896

I have this moment finished No. IV., copying and all,—*how*, I hardly dare ask myself. There will be a great many threads to pick up at the beginning of No. V., and the bulk of this No. is enormous, 48 pp. of my closely written manuscript—6 pp. more than the longest of the preceding three. There will very likely be a "kick" in Franklin Square;[1] but it's the best I can do,—that I'm sure of,—and the relief of getting it done is immense,—to say nothing of the excitement at this present moment! To-morrow I shall have the luxury of the relief without the strain of the excitement, and shall be happy and at ease,—as happy and as much at ease, at any rate, as I can be away from you.

If it were not that I feel obliged to send the thing at once to Mr. Pyle, so that he may at least read it before the first of Mar., and have it copied if he will, I would send it to you to read—for it is not *due* till the end of the week. The manuscript[2] is unrevised and, in part, in short-hand. In brief, you can't read it until it comes back in proof. But, if you are going to read all the numbers in the Magazine itself, you wont want so many rehearsals! Ah, my Eileen, I know you will rejoice with me,—and that increases my own happiness ten-fold. I love you passionately, every moment, and altogether.                    Your own    Woodrow

ALS (WP, DLC).
  [1] At the editorial offices of *Harper's Magazine*.
  [2] That is, the copy that Wilson kept.


## To Howard Pyle

My dear Mr. Pyle,                    Baltimore, 26 February, 1896.

I have not had the energy to make two copies of No. IV. I send you, therefore, by express, the only copy I have; and take the liberty to beg that, when you have read it, you will forward it to Mr. Alden. It is due at Franklin Square on the first of March; but I have just written to Mr. Alden to say that it has gone to you, and that you will forward it as soon as possible. I trust the arrangement will cause you no inconvenience.

   With warmest regards, in haste,
                    Sincerely Yours,    Woodrow Wilson

WWTLS (deCoppet Coll., NjP).

## From Ellen Axson Wilson

My own darling,      Princeton, N. J.  Wednesday [Feb. 26, 1896]

I have the hard luck to be obliged to fill another letter with that wretched plumbing business. Mr. Margerum did the inspecting and came here to report but Holsky did not come. Mr. M. found all that was in sight right with that one, as he think[s], very big exception before mentioned; viz that the air tubes going to the roof are only 2 in. ones whereas he thinks they ought to be *four* inch. They begin as four inch, and when they get to the partition wall the two inch are pointed into them. Mr. M. says they will "choke up" and foul stuff will be "forced back" and some other things will be "sucked out" and—oh dear! I can't explain it at all, for I don't understand it, but according to him we are all as good as dead if we don't have them changed. There are two of these tubes, one for each bath-room, pipes from the several sources running into it (Wasn't *that* what Dr. Wykoff said was wrong anyhow? Didn't he say one would "suck out" the others?) The one in the third story is exposed and could be changed without any trouble. The other is a different matter, it runs up in the partition; the other would be too large for that and would have to run up in the corner of the servant's room and be boxed. I am so oppressed by uncertainty due to my own ignorance that I don't know what to do. These 2 in[.] pipes are in the specifications so there is no use going to the architect about it as of course they are what *his* judgment approves. By the same sign, to have it changed would be an extra. (I omitted to say that all these dreadful things will happen, according to Mr. M. only in *cold* weather; so perhaps if we do have to change, we can postpone it until next fall.) What I propose is for you to go and get the opinion of an expert there in Balt.—he would not have to see the house in this case.

I shall send the plumber's specifications on to you today as you ought to take them with you when you go to his office.

The plumber[1] was in such haste to get through Sat. and go home that he did his work in the bath-room in a really disgraceful manner. He did it *all* in part of a day and it is utterly slip-shod. Several of the joints are leaking, the pipes are slanting instead of verticle, the marbles are put in crooked with bits of wood smeared with cement stuck in to fill out, &c. The architect has written to have him come and do it all over. I am not a little reassured by your letter this morning, darling, but oh how glad I will be to have you at home, so that I can watch and see for myself how you are! We are all perfectly well. With love unutterable.

                                        Your own   Eileen.

I feel better!—I was just finishing this, when Mr. Margerum came in again. He said he was so intent on having those pipes changed yesterday that he didn't think of a substitute that would serve every purpose without tearing up the house. They are "McClellan Anti-Siphon Trap Vents" & cost only a few dollars. He has given me a pamphlet about them which I should like to send you but must save to show the architect tomorrow. You had better not go to the expert until I send it. I have engaged Mr. M. to wrap the pipes with mineral wool. He says the material will cost only 3 or 2 dollars, and it is entirely unnecessary to both *wrap* and *box* them.

ALS (WC, NjP).

1 An employee of C. C. Hoffmeier of Cranford, N. J., who had the plumbing contract for the Wilson house.

## To Ellen Axson Wilson

My own darling,                                   Baltimore, 27 Feb'y, 1896

It is too bad the most essential work in the house,—the plumbing,—should have been done in the least workmanlike manner; but of course I will not pay the man's bill until he has made everything shipshape: and where the specifications fall short we will put in any number of extras that may be necessary to make the whole a perfect job: for this is not a matter of choice. When you send the specifications I will of course see an expert,—if I can find a genuine one,—and get his opinion. I wish I knew better how to judge what it may be worth.

Did you read that invitation to deliver a course of lectures before the Yale Law School in the autumn of 1897, which you sent me the other day, my darling? What do you think of it? I have declined all other invitations as a matter of course,—almost as a matter of routine,—but this is really no common honour, and I shall not reply till I hear from you about it.[1] The course would not be "popular," but "scholarly" about law or its practice. (5 lectures in all).

You may imagine what a relief it is to me to be rid of "General Washington" when I tell you that it rests me to turn to my pile of examination papers![2]

I am feeling well and bright today—and I love you with an accumulated fervour which will fairly overwhelm you when I come.                                   Your own   Woodrow

ALS (WP, DLC).

1 Wilson declined the invitation.

2 For the final examinations in his courses in the history of law and of jurisprudence printed at Feb. 1 and 5, 1896.

## From Ellen Axson Wilson

My own darling        Princeton, N. J.  Thursday [Feb. 27, 1896]

I congratulate you again and again—and once again! I am sure you can't draw a longer, deeper breath of relief than I. It is so good too that you have gotten it done so soon,—long enough to have a good week of rest there. I hope you will sleep all the mornings and go and be petted by Mrs. Bird, &c. in the evenings. That reminds me that Mrs. [Legh Wilber] Reid has just been here, and she was telling me how savage and unreasonable Mrs. Bird is at *whist*! I had a quiet laugh all to myself.

She has been making my mouth water telling me about the most *beautiful* old English carved sideboard and table (dining-room) now to [be] had at that place in Alexandria. She says the side-board is the lovliest thing she ever saw. The side-board is $45.00 and the tables $30.00 for the two. They are in the old style, you know, two very wide square ones; for your family you use one, & the other with leaves turned down for a sidetable. For a big dining you put the two together. They have just been done up and polished in fine style. She wants you to go down there and see them. But it is a shame for me to tempt you telling about them for of course we *must* not think of them.

The storm doors are up and are *lovely*. The carpenters have finished & gone. The hall paper is going on upstairs and looks beautiful!—in fact the whole house is [a] "dream"!

I don't see how I *am* to bear not seeing No. 4 now!—but what must be—must be! When do you suppose it will be in proof? Oh how I love you & how proud of you I am!

Your own   Eileen.

ALS (WC, NjP).

## From Ellen Axson Wilson, with Enclosure

Princeton, N. J.

My own darling,              Thursday eve. [Feb. 27, 1896]

I send with this the plumber's specifications[1] for I think you had better see an expert as soon as possible. Mr. Holsky came out today, was told about the trouble by Mr. Wright before he came here. He admitted that the vents were not quite up to the mark, "didn't know why Mr. Child had ordered them so"; the usual rule was that the vent pipe should be the same size as the waste pipe. The idea is that the vapours in it condense into hoar frost and if it is too narrow choke it up. He said he thought there was "not much danger" in this case, it was very probably large enough.

Also that the danger would be chiefly at the top and he thought it might do very well to change it from the third story floor up. That of course would be easy enough. He seemed perfectly disgusted with the idea of using the "Anti-Siphon Trap Vents." He said the present arrangement *might* be bad and that would *certainly* be. It seems this is a sort of make-shift to be used in situations otherwise impossible,—as where there is a trap fifty feet away from all vent pipes. When you use them you sever connection with the vent pipe,—so that if we put them in it would be as it were admitting that our plumbing as it stands is a hopeless failure. No wonder our architect should object to their use! He granted however that the things were said to work very well. So now I am again quite at sea; the only alternatives seem to be to go to an expert or, saving that fee at least, to go ahead ourselves and order the big pipes in. But that can wait 'till your return.

Poor little Denny Paxton[2] died last night of some heart trouble; it seems he has always had a difficulty in breathing, the direct result of his malformation. It is better for him, poor fellow, but how sad for the family,—coming just after the wedding too!

Isn't this a charming letter that I enclose from Martha Williams?[3] Now thats the way to talk! I feel as though I *must* meet her—am sure she is worth knowing. Did you ever hear of her before? It is to be hoped so; 'twill be rather embarrassing if you don't at least know whether she is "Mrs." or "Miss." Her letter was sent to "Harpers."

We are all well,—as I remarked this morning—for you see I am writing tomorrow's letter! It has been a lovely, bright mild day.

I love you, dear,—I have no words to say how deeply, how *passionately*.                    Your own    Eileen.

I promised Mr. Margerum that I would be sure to return this pamphlet *soon*.[4]

And please, dear, be sure to get from Minnie my "Classic Myths."[5] I need it.

If you go to an expert ask him to [too] about that other vent outside the house—the thing Mr. Holsky doesn't like. He thinks that "about as bad as the too small pipe." Mr. Margerum didn't mention it.

ALS (WC, NjP).

[1] This enclosure is missing.

[2] Harmar Denny Paxton, '91, son of the Rev. Dr. William Miller Paxton of 20 Library Place.

[3] Martha McCulloch Williams of New York, prolific author of short stories and other fiction.

[4] This enclosure is missing.

[5] Charles Mills Gayley (ed.), *The Classic Myths in English Literature* (Boston, 1893).

## From Martha McCulloch Williams

My Dear Professor Wilson:        New York City. Feb 26th 1896.

You will not I hope be angry if another of the writing guild ventures to tell you that you have achieved the im[pos]sible—at least so far as she is concerned. You have made "Colonel Washington" human and delightful to her—even at the thrice-wearisome epoch of Braddock's defeat. Through much reading of many histories, she had come heartily to endorse E E Hale's suggestion of writing Washington's life without reference to the House of Burgesses, Braddock, or the Revolution. Unrelieved panegyric palls— becomes so cloying, that the unregenerate mind longs naturally for a glimpse which shall show the great person a man of like passions unto itself.

Indeed I must confess that my very first thrill of admiration for Washington arose when a very old man told me a legend of how he had outsworn the army in Flanders because the hoofs of his white coach horses, were not properly black and shining for some occasion of state. It was such a relief, after the tons of history I had dutifully absorbed, wherein he was not man but a very great God, with no suspicion of tim [tin] about him, upon wheels that were the chariot of the universe. I am so glad to have finally got rid of that impression. Of course you were not the first to dissipate it—my head is pretty gray—but you are helping me to a delightful realization of my country's father, in his habit as he lived. And I make no doubt you are doing much more and much better for the new generation. Wherefore I take off my hat to you, and beg you to keep writing until we have a gallery of ancient worthies, as human and likable, as they unquestionably were in life.

Jesting aside, I do wish to thank you honestly and earnestly for the pleasure I have derived from your Washington papers—not alone for their matter, but for their manner—which is entirely after my own heart. It has a tang and savor truly Elizabethan— the tang and savor I most truly love. I think one can not cultivate it—that it is som[e]thing to be got wholly by absorption, th[r]ough early and intimate contact with the masters of English. Best thing of all, it so beseems the subject, time, and place. I pray you sir, make me and the reading world still further your debtors by a happy continuance in your present vein.

For the rest I beg to sign myself.

Very Sincerely.   Martha McCulloch Williams.

TLS (WP, DLC).

# A Newspaper Report of a Lecture on the Defects of American City Government

[Feb. 28, 1896]

## GOVERNMENT BY BOARDS.
### PROF. WILSON ON "CITY DEPARTMENTS AND COMMISSIONS."

Professor Woodrow Wilson of Princeton, whose 5 o'clock lectures at the Hopkins on local government have been attracting much public attention, chose for his special subject Wednesday "City Departments and Commissions."

The lecturer is a specialist on municipal government, and his lectures are of great importance, coming as they do at this time of peculiar crisis in the affairs of the city government of Baltimore. While the Mayor has been in a struggle with the City Council for good government against the spoils system, Professor Wilson has been pointing out the dangers of just such a situation.[1]

Professor Wilson unites to a thorough mastery of his subject a remarkable command of language—he never reads a lecture—and the interest of the audience does not flag for a moment. His subject is a very timely and practical one, and some of his statements are very pertinent to the condition of affairs in this city.

In his lecture yesterday Professor Wilson said in substance:

"We shall consider this afternoon that part of the administrative business of a city which is concerned with boards and commissions. In our city government we have followed a long-standing English custom. When the English people become dissatisfied with the management of an office by one man they put it in commission. The result is many boards. The growth of such instrumentalities in this country is aptly illustrated by the history of Philadelphia. It has four phases: First—The municipal administrative body was a close corporation, with judicial and governing power, but without taxing power. The right to determine the amount of taxes and the way in which they were to be raised was reserved to the State Legislature. The second stage was govern-

---

[1] The City Council, dominated by partisan Republicans, was at this time engaged in a bitter controversy with Mayor Alcaeus Hooper over the appointment of city officials. Mayor Hooper, an independent Republican, was sympathetic to the ideals of the municipal reformers who had helped to elect him in 1895 and sought to make appointments on merit alone, even retaining some Democrats in office. The Council, eager for the spoils after the first city and state-wide Republican victory since the Civil War, had refused to approve the Mayor's appointments and, on February 27, 1896, adopted ordinances taking the power of appointment of any salaried city officials from the Mayor and vesting it in the Council.

ment by a close corporation supplemented by commissions. These commissions—e.g., the street commission—were erected by the Legislature and were authorized to levy taxes.

## Government by Boards.

"With the use [rise] of more modern conditions there sprang up government by boards under the direction of council committees. The fourth and present stage was reached in 1887, when government by committees was abolished and much of the executive work was put under the charge of single officers, who were appointed by the Mayor, with the advice and consent of the Council, or elected by the people. In this arrangement we see the idea developed that one person can be better watched than a number. We have the complete severance of the administrative and legislative bodies. In this country, indeed, no attempt has been made to unite them. I believe, as is probably well known to you by this time, in the close union of the two, if not in their complete identity. But because of no such attempt to unite them we cannot pick out particular illustrations of failure and cite them as arguments against the theory. Perhaps this strengthens my position.

"Instead of taking cities, however, as examples, we may find an illustration of the way in which the theory might work by turning our attention to the National Government. Did you ever notice the debates in Congress on the letters of the Secretary of the Treasury? The Congressmen discuss what this passage may mean, and what the Secretary had in mind in that, as if they had discovered a medieval manuscript in some old monastery, of which the key had been lost. All this time the writer is at the other end of the avenue. Yet it would be considered revolutionary to invite the Secretary of the Treasury to come into the House and explain and defend his letter. We are so much afraid of the shadow of a king that we shrink from the slightest union of the legislative and executive powers. Sometimes the Secretary may be consulted in a committee meeting, but the sessions are private and the public does not know what is said or done. This secrecy is secured purposely, in order that the Secretary or other administrative officer who may chance to be interviewed may not have this means of championing his views before the public, and that the information obtained may not be brought up against the committee in the debates in the House. These are not conjectures, but facts. Everyone who has been within hailing distance of Washington knows them, and Representatives themselves—in their lucid intervals—have acknowledged to me that they were true. Accordingly, from our fear of bringing together the administrative and legislative functions, we call such a plan an interference of the executive with the freedom of legislation, and thus damn a good thing with a bad name.

### Division of Responsibility.

"But in our city government let us consider what we have done. For we have done it, and must stand by it. From a comparison of half-a-dozen typical cities I find that the usual commissions are as follows: A Board of Public Improvements, a Board of Police Commissioners, a Board of Fire Commissioners, a Board of Assessors and a Board of Commissioners of Finance. These boards are elected sometimes by the council, sometimes by the people; sometimes in any way Divine Providence or the ideas of reformers may suggest.

"In any case there is no direct responsibility, and the result is a process of disintegration, and consequently a process of corruption. The corruption does not arise from the way in which appointments are made, but because of the disintegration of the administration. Hence the abolition of boards and the appointment of single officers by the mayor is no remedy. For there is still disintegration, still inter-communication and investigation where there ought to be consultation and co-operation. Moreover, as was pointed out yesterday, the mayor cannot possibly, for want of time, control and oversee all departments. The departments are none the less separate because they are presided over by a single 'responsible' head. As far as personal incorruptibility is concerned, the system may work well as long as we can watch the appointer and know the appointee. But in nine cases out of ten the persons appointed are unknown to most of the citizens. If you want to find out anything about them you have to ask their friends, for their friends are the only persons who know them. Of course, therefore, you get a good report of them. Well-known men are apt to be too busy to accept such appointments, and those who are not too busy are likely to be of no capacity. In the long run, it does not make a pepper-corn of difference how the appointments are made. The Hon. L. Q. C. Lamar almost lost his will-power while Secretary of the Interior because of the results of his own appointments. So many turned out badly that he became almost afraid to sign a commission, and he escaped with alacrity to the Supreme Court Bench when an opportunity offered.

## Departments Overlap.

"The trouble with our city government lies not in the way appointments are made, but in the general disintegration of the system. This is seen likewise in the multiplicity of departments, in the attempt to divide what should be indivisible. The different departments also often overlap—for instance, the Police Department and the Health Department. In New York City the regular police and the sanitary police have come into face-to-face controversy. One arrests persons for doing what the other advises. If they take the matter to their chiefs, statutes or ordinances will likely be produced upholding the action of each, and the only way to get the matter straightened out for the future is to go to the Legislature or the Common Council and secure a repeal of the measures. Likewise the Health Department and the Street-Cleaning Department overlap—e.g., when the former forbids the latter to disturb certain refuse for fear of spreading infection. There has been actual conflict between the representatives of the two departments with clubs and brooms. The Fire Department and the Department of the Inspection of Buildings also overlap. The two should be consolidated, the latter being subordinated to the former. As things are now, the inspection of buildings is confined largely to an examination of the strength of the materials and the thickness of the foundation walls. But the heating apparatus, too, should be made the subject of careful examination, as well as the general architectural plans of the building.

"The idea of checks and balances is wholly out of place in administration, but its most extreme and most absurd application is found in the non-partisan or 'bi-partisan' boards. Not only must we have many boards, but we must divide each into two parts, for that is what bi-partisan practically means. The two-party system is good, and I believe in it. But the bi-partisan system is an invention of the devil. Its practical design and real method of operation is the trading off of patronage between the managers of the two parties. We have, in effect, balanced boards, so that they cannot co-operate for good, and balanced parties, so that they can co-operate for evil. It is absurd to think that a Democrat because he is a Democrat has one idea of efficiency in city administration, and a Republican because he is a Republican has another.

## The Lobby a Good Thing.

"Minute legislative prescription as to the composition and detailed duties of boards, as to salaries, funds and every point of action, carries the disintegration still farther. It leads to the most unfortunate policy of legislative interference. If you want to get a thing changed in the administration of Baltimore, you often have to go to Annapolis to do it. There you have to join the lobby. Now, the lobby is not in itself a bad thing; indeed, if it were rightly constituted it would be a good thing. But the lobby that influences the making of regulations for city administration should be nearer home and handier, and should be subject to the same body of public opinion that you are. But if you go to the Legislature you will find it largely made up [of] country members. They are jealous of the city's influence, and think to become popular with their constituencies by ranging themselves in opposition to it. So suspicious are they that their first question when they are asked to consider a measure relating to the city is 'What are you scheming for now?' In brief, the upshot of the whole system of checks and balances may be expressed in the theory that the more ways in which it is possible to get a thing done, the better it will be done. And this is radically wrong."

Printed in the Baltimore *News*, Feb. 28, 1896; some editorial headings omitted.

## A Call for a Mass Protest Meeting

[Feb. 28, 1896]

### "A TREMENDOUS PROTEST."
#### PROF. WOODROW WILSON SUGGESTS CALLING
#### AN INDIGNATION MEETING—LET
#### THE PEOPLE BE HEARD FROM.

Prof. Woodrow Wilson of Princeton University, who is delivering a course of lectures on municipal problems at the Johns Hopkins University, has decided views as to the action of the Council last night. He said this morning:

"The people of Baltimore ought to hold a mass-meeting and utter a tremendous protest against this action on the part of the Council. It ought to be a meeting for the purpose of indorsing the course of Mayor Hooper. Let the general question of municipal government alone. That is too big a subject for a mass-meeting to handle, but the simple question as to whether Mayor Hooper's course is the proper one could be easily settled and vigorous expression could be made.

"Really, this is not a question of municipal government. It is a matter of rascally bad faith. These Councilmen are repudiating the issue on which they were elected. The whole matter is still in the realm of politics. As I understand it, the issue at last fall's election was reform and a non-partisan administration of municipal affairs. If these Councilmen, elected on such a platform, now turn around and demand partisan appointments, they should hear from the citizens of Baltimore on their course.

"In my study of municipal affairs, I do not remember ever to have come across a similar situation in connection with any city. The charter given to the city by the State usually settles such a problem and defines how far the Council may go in making radical changes with regard to the other departments of city government. I am anxious to know about the charter of Baltimore in this regard. Does it give the Council power to pass ordinances of this sort?

"If a mass-meeting should be arranged it should have a varied list of speakers from all elements of politics. For instance, it would not do to confine the list of speakers to recognized reformers, for it is well known that this element is already opposed to the spoilsmen, and it would be too much like getting Spain to declare that it opposes the Cuban insurrection. Prominent Republicans should be among the speakers, so as to show this Republican majority that even the members of its own party do not approve its course."

Printed in the *Baltimore News*, Feb. 28, 1896.

## To Ellen Axson Wilson

My own darling,                               Baltimore, 28 Feb'y, 1896

Do you know, my heart is failing me about going to England this summer! I wonder if it would not do me just as much good to go to that countryside in Virginia and be *with you*? I think I will ask Mitchell. You see the point is this, I must engage my passage immediately, if I am going,—or else stay at home whether I will or no. The question is getting exigent and must be decided at once,—hence my failing resolution.

I've just come from the dentist's (our friend B. Holly Smith). He has been pulling a nerve out almost by main force; and I am not in an angelic frame of mind; but there is no pain worth mentioning now; and otherwise I am quite well. The examination papers are not hurting me at all. I am taking them very calmly and easily.

How many times am I to be asked to speak, I wonder, before I go out of this "decline"? It's getting monotonous.

I am going to run down to Washington again to-morrow, to

see about getting a photograph of Rembrandt Peale's portrait of Washington for the Harpers, and I shall certainly try to get over to Alexandria to see that side-board and table,—running directly into temptation!

I love you, darling, with every thought, and my heart is now growing lighter with every day—for next week!

Your own    Woodrow

ALS (WP, DLC).


## From Ellen Axson Wilson

My own darling,    Princeton, N. J.   Friday night [Feb. 28, 1896]

I have just come in from hearing "Mrs. Sara Tawney Robsen,"[1] —Mr. Tawney's[2] stunning cousin, you remember—read Browning. She has been giving a course of three evenings, one Victor Hugo & two Browning. Mrs. [Legh W.] Reid asked me to go with them tonight. It was a disappointment because for "Pippa Passes" as advertised, she had, "by request," substituted "Saul," which of course you know is not nearly so suitable for such a purpose. Thereby hangs a funny tale. The reading was in the Millers' church for its benefit and the first one was "A Blot on the Scutcheon"! The dear innocent Millers, who had never read it, naturally got a terrible shock; with the result that they investigated "Pippa Passes," condemned it too, and begged for something religious. The result was a rather a failure. But she is worth looking at, at least.

I am afraid I can't form any judgment, darling, about the Yale lectures because I have *no idea* how much they would cost you of time and effort. I know of course that *personally* I should be glad to hear that you had declined *anything* that involved the preparation of new lectures and interruption of your plans for writing. Think how much you have been interrupted already! You will probably be in the thick of your history again then, and think how you will hate to break off to prepare *five* lectures,—enough to fill a book! Though of *course* you wouldn't for a moment think of *writing* them in any event! If that were necessary there could hardly be a moment's question as to the proper decision.

Miss Ricketts has heard Miss Garland[3] speak of Martha Williams and remembers that she is *un*married and a southerner, but knows nothing else about her. But that at least gives you the essential fact!

I am so glad you are feeling bright, darling, and oh *so* relieved at your relief from intense work!

We are all well. Ah, how I *love* you, darling, & how I am wearying for a sight of your dear face! With all my heart—

Your own    Eileen.

ALS (WC, NjP).

[1] An announcement of her lectures appeared in the *Daily Princetonian*, Feb.
11, 1896.

[2] Probably Guy Allen Tawney, Princeton, 1893.

[3] Probably a daughter of Mrs. M. J. G. Garland of 86 Stockton St.

# A Newspaper Report on Two Lectures on Problems
# of City Government

[Feb. 29, 1896]

## HEAVEN FORBID IT!
### Prof. Wilson's Fervent Utterance
### Regarding the City Council.

#### MAY NO MORE POWER BE GRANTED IT
### The Municipal Economist Speaks
### Strongly in His Lecture.

"Heaven forbid that under present conditions greater administrative powers should be granted to the city's Common Council."

This devout wish, which finds an echo in the hearts of thousands of the best citizens of Baltimore, was uttered yesterday by
Prof. Woodrow Wilson in his lecture at the Johns Hopkins University. He talked in general about the city's expenditures, but
made an explanation also as to his position on the question of
municipal ownership of gasworks and street railways. He said he
wished it understood that he did not believe in the city assuming
such ownership under the existing organization, and then came
the fervent utterance quoted.

Coming at this time, such a statement is particularly apropos
to the Baltimore situation and is entirely in line with Professor
Wilson's interview in The News yesterday. It will a[l]so have
special weight on account of Prof. Wilson's eminent position in
the world of municipal economics. His well-known abilities in
that line led to his engagement by the Johns Hopkins University
to deliver a series of lectures on municipal problems, and the
lectures have proved to be exceedingly practical and up-to-date.
Much interest has been taken by the public in this course by a
specialist on the subject, and it has seemed that the engagement
of Professor Wilson was peculiarly timely in view of the present
crisis in Baltimore's municipal affairs.

### The City Budget.

Professor Wilson took up the specific topic of his lecture, "The City Budget," and said in substance:

"A particularly bad feature of legislative control of municipal taxation is that it entails the making of certain inflexible rules for all the cities in the State. For instance, it is determined by statute that the tax-rate in any city shall not exceed a certain per cent. Now, some cities may need to go above this rate, on account of the exigencies of their growth. Hence, to make such a regulation is simply to put a strain upon official honesty in that city. For the statute will surely be evaded generally by raising the valuation of property.

"There is another reason why the city's expenditures, and especially the amounts of salaries, should not be determined by the Legislature. The most vital thing about the patriotism of public servants is the way in which their salaries are paid. This is well illustrated in the history of the Revolutionary War, by the fluctuations in the success of our arms, which accompanied fluctuations in the financial policy toward the troops. For whatever we say of other motives, we must not forget that in the main the ordinary conduct of men is determined by economic motives. Hence salaries of a department should not be fixed by a body unless it is in close touch and sympathy with the department.

### Control of Expenditures.

"We now come to the fundamental question, Who shall control taxation and expenditure in the city? A New York commission, appointed in 1876, proposed for New York city a Board of Finance to be elected by 'payers of upward of $250 rent a year, or owners of $500 worth of property on which taxes were paid,' to have a veto on proposed expenditure and power of confirming the appointment of Corporation Counsel and Comptroller.

"How far is the principle proposed in this suggestion wise? Only so far as the theory of co-operative real estate administration is admitted as the basis of municipal action. But the modern industrial city, with its wide social functions, must act in many things involving the heaviest expenditures, not for property owners, but for the working and economically dependent classes. It is, therefore, impossible to justify the theory in principle or in practice.

"For my part, I do not believe that the persons who pay the largest taxes are the best judges of the needs of a city. This class is able to secure for itself by expenditure of its own means those advantages of street-cleaning and street-lighting and personal protection by private detectives which the poorer parts of the city are able to secure only by municipal outlay. The selfish interest of this upper class is not impelled to make adequate expenditures for the needs of the slums; it is not a co-operative interest, but a disintegrating interest.

"The question of municipal expenditure furthermore involves two subsidiary questions—how to determine the objects of the expenditure and how to secure the most in return for the expenditure through administrative efficiency?

"What is it that makes Washington known far and wide as a handsome city? Because it has been administered from the beginning by one body (Congress), and not by a joint stock company of property owners. Hence we have a Capital which is a place for delectation—so attractive that Congressmen are anxious to go there and do nothing after they get there but enjoy it. Even if they have ideas of doing something when they start for the city, they lose all trace of them by the end of the first session. There is no overcrowding of houses in tenement districts, but, instead, magnificent open spaces which correspond to analogous open spaces in the minds of the national legislators.

### For the Benefit of All.

["]This illustrates the principle that the city should be administered for the benefit of all. The question is made even more complex by the migration of so many people from the rural districts into the city. They must have healthful homes and surroundings or there will soon be marked moral and physical degeneration of the population. Cities should be administered as a trust from Providence.

"The general policy of expenditure should be determined by the representative general voice, endowed with full choice, and, therefore, with full responsibility. Even an honest business Mayor is apt, in his attempt to administer the city's government on business principles to do it in accordance with the advice of business men. The result is a disproportionate representation of one class in the city.

"In Princeton, which is only a borough town, without a mayor, we have an illustration of the control of public improvements in accordance with the desire of the poorer classes. Streets in the poorer districts of the town were improved first. Now this is not what a body of wealthy property-owners would arrange to do.

Yet—unpalatable as the truth may be—the management of affairs by these poorer classes—mostly Irish and negroes—has resulted in a better condition of things than if it had been left to the educated classes. Those poorer districts threatened the health of the town, and the improvement of the streets effected improvement also in the conditions of sanitation and drainage.

"To sum up the whole matter in a word, we must revert to the proposition laid down in a preceding lecture, that the city is not an economic corporation, but a humane economic society."

The subject of Professor Wilson's next lecture, on Monday afternoon, will be, "The General Reorganization of City Government."

## POLICE AND PUBLIC WORKS
### Prof. Woodrow Wilson's Thursday
### Afternoon Lecture.

Professor Wilson discussed "Police" in his Thursday [February 27] afternoon lecture. He said:

"The police duties of the city are two-fold—for the State and for itself. The former are the less numerous. In enforcing the criminal statutes, in protecting the lives and property of citizens, the police act as agents of the State. In the making of such laws the city, as such, has no part. Hence there should be a certain general supervision of the police by the State. Just as the State inspects its National Guards, so it should inspect the police throughout its borders. In this way only can it secure a uniformly efficient instrument for the suppression of crime. Such State inspection of both the rural and urban police would weed out many incompetent members from the force.

"But the main duties of the police relate to the city itself. Their first duty is to carry out the city ordinances and arrest those who violate them. They should break up all disorderly houses of whatever sort. They should furthermore aid the Street-Cleaning Department by preventing the obstruction of the streets, and should aid the Health Department in securing the abatement of nuisances.

"The police are thus manifestly agents, directly or indirectly, of almost every branch of the city government. No department, therefore, is less suited than the police to be separately administered. Yet the police are not at all responsible to those other departments. They serve one set of persons while they are responsible to another set of persons, partly the head of the department and partly the courts. In other words, the police have a moral responsibility to one body, an official responsibility to another and a legal responsibility to a third.

"Thus, if you want to reform a police force, you often have to change three sets of persons. This can be done only once in a long time, when a political cyclone strikes.

"The question of public works is evidently an important part of the subject of city government. The functions of the Department of Public Works are important and varied. They include the grading, paving and widening of streets, for these things benefit not merely the adjacent property-holders, but facilitate the passage of persons and the free distribution of goods throughout the city.

"The object of a street is primarily public and only secondarily private. The supplying of light and water also belongs, or should belong, to the Department of Public Works. To give one set of persons the right to tear up the streets and another set of persons the duty of putting them in shape again is entirely wrong. If we are to have water-works run by a private company—which I believe to be a pernicious principle—the Department of Public Works should put down the mains and charge the companies cost price. For water-works and gasworks are not something devised for the benefit of private companies, but for the whole city.

"Trade facilities, such as docks and water approaches, should be constructed by the Department of Public Works and paid for by all taxpayers, whether they have anything to do with the water front or not.

"To provide transit, whether slow or rapid, falls also within the duties of this department.

"If we had our present government to make all over again no innocent would so arrange matters that the Legislature at Annapolis should have it to say whether the Baltimore City Passenger Company should erect trolley poles on Charles street. Such an arrangement is absurd. Charles street is one of the finest residence streets in the whole city, and its beauty is the common possession of the city. The form of city government should be such, therefore, that a question like this could be settled by the people of Baltimore themselves.

"The Department of Public Works should also be intrusted with the extension of streets and the annexation of new districts.

"This enumeration of functions emphasizes how wide is the scope of city administration and how communal is the character of such administration. The city is no longer a charter of liberties, but a constitution of duties. If you don't like the way things are being administered, make your opposition felt. But stay in and do your fighting. Don't fling out of the attempt to secure good administration. It is your duty to help secure it, not to leave the matter to someone else.["]

Printed in the *Baltimore News*, Feb. 29, 1896; some editorial headings omitted.


## To Ellen Axson Wilson

My own darling,                            Baltimore, 1 March, 1896
I went over to Alexandria: the man had taken his prettiest things over to Washington to be sold. I followed them thither, to find that the side-board, a veritable beauty, had been sold (for $50.00); the tables I could not find. I found two sideboards, however, of which I enclose drawings (made just now, from memory). No suggestion of *detail* is reliable in either of these drawings. No. I. I would have bought on the spot, had I not wanted your sanction. It is, I think, about six or seven feet long, and could not get between the chimney and the wall. It is perfectly plain,—not a carved spot on it,—but is in fine condition and a beautiful piece of mahogany. Twenty-five dollars is certainly cheap for it. If you are willing to forego looking for a handsomer, will you not go down and send a telegram, "Go ahead," as soon as you get this? For it is to be disposed of at auction on Tuesday or Wednesday. The columns at the sides are not fluted but round and smooth. But the whole thing is in perfect taste. No. II. I do not care for except that it too is tasteful and it is cheap.

I secured a photograph of the Rembrandt Peale and had some very interesting experiences in doing it. Indeed I enjoyed the whole day. But I am so near you now that I can't stop to *tell* things! I can't do anything now but think of being in your arms! Ah, how I long for it—how my pulses quicken at the thought of it! My darling, I am not worthy of the sweet love you lavish upon me; but it makes me infinitely more worthy than I should be without it. It puts me in such humour with goodness and purity and everything that is lovely and *like you*; and I feel so great an exaltation,—so great an exhileration in it all. I seem to need such a motive, and such an authentication; and I really look upon all that makes me love what is honourable and beautiful as coming to me from you. There is so much of the idealist in me now that was not in me when I married you,—or that was merely latent, if it was there at all. All that you praise (and that Miss, or Mrs., Martha Williams praises) in my writings,—the glow as of large feeling, the colour of words rightly chosen,—all that makes me more than a capable, clear, and clever writer, comes from my life with you. And I realize it best when we are in each other's arms. I seem to take inspiration from physical contact with my darling, —as if we were then veritably one spirit, and I could *feel* your sweetness passing direct into my thoughts and my heart. I could not write on in the same vein if I could not go again and again to the source of my inspiration; and now I am about to come to get ready for No. V. I can't do anything till you have kissed me!

Your own    Woodrow

ALS (WP, DLC). Encs: two sketches of sideboards.


## From Ellen Axson Wilson

My own darling          Princeton, N. J. Sunday [March 1, 1896]

And so you, with the aid of the "Century Co." have kindly provided me with another Sunday treat! I have just finished "An Author's Choice of Company,"[1]—and *how* I have enjoyed it! I could almost hear your dear voice as I read, it made me feel so close to you. It has given me a brilliant idea too,—the accident of these articles coming just in time for these successive Sundays,—which is to read something of yours *every* Sunday when you are away. What else in your absence could give me so true a sense of communion with you? What else could so nearly satisfy my longing for *you*, or give me so happy a day? Don't you think it a fine scheme?

Mr. Sloane stopped me after church to ask after you and to express his delight with this essay; he thinks it one of the best things you ever wrote; and so do I. It is an *exquisite gem*, so profoundly true in thought, so subtly beautiful in expression that it is almost a poem. One has a vision of it in future collections of "English Classics"—"Hearts of Oak," &c. If you had never written another thing it would firmly establish your permanent place in that "Community" you describe.

It is rather unfortunate, darling, that you must engage your "passage" just now, for of course there couldn't be a harder time to finally decide upon *one* long separation than in the midst of *another*,—and a peculiarly trying one. I'll not deny that when I read your letter yesterday the first involuntary movement of my own heart was a great leap of relief at the bare thought of escaping it. I am not so foolish as to try and tell you how hard I find it to have you away when you are unwell,—not to be able to watch you and see for myself, hour by hour, how you are,—and to have you *so far* away!

But this is only a temporary weakness; my permanent feeling will be one of deep disappointment if you give it up. For of course, *if you will only go in the proper frame of mind*, it will do you infinitely more good than to bury yourself in the country here. I am counting so much on the sea voyage and after on the mental refreshment, the *rest* without ennui, the complete change from all the trains of thought that have been making such exhausting demands upon you for so long. I simply *can't* have you give it up, darling. Let us be very brave about it, dear, and remember, what *I* am to apt to forget, that bravery implies something more than *merely* bearing things in any sort of dismal fashion because we *must.* The best courage shows always an undaunted front, and a calm cheerfulness or a gay smile,—according to temperament,—in the face of the danger or the pain.

But as I said this is an ill time to let our thoughts dwell overmuch on *that* separation. *This* one at least is drawing to an end and we shall have time to gather strength for the next.

Oh how good,—*how* good it is to be able to say, "He is coming this week"! I feel as if my heart must fairly break with longing and impatience as the time drawers [draws] near. Ah but I *love* you, dear,—with all I am—

"Feeling, thinking, seeing,—
Love you in the lightest part,
Love you in full being.

Through all hopes that keep us brave,
Further off or nigher,
Love you for the house and grave,—
And for something higher."

Your little wife    Eileen.

ALS (WC, NjP).
[1] Printed at Nov. 10, 1895.

## To Ellen Axson Wilson

My own darling,                    Baltimore, 2 March, 1896

Pardon me for not having sent you a check before. I ought to have thought of it myself: for it is incredible you should have got on so long with the small sum I left you, you dear little manager!

I return the circular my Margerum lent you.[1] There will be no such weather as will bring danger from the too small vent pipe till next winter: and I think, in the mean time, we had better have the whole of the one vent (the one that can be got at) and the accessible part of the other changed. I hope the plumber has returned to fix the bath room. A letter from Mr. Child which I received this morning[2] says that the leaded glass and the tiles for the vestibule have been shipped. Very likely they will be there by the time this reaches you.

Dear me, how my impatience increases, my sweet one, as I see the last lecture approaching: my longing for you—repressed all these weeks with the strong hand—steadily gains in ascendency and makes my thoughts quite unmanageable. And yet they are comforting thoughts, too,—very sweet thoughts—full of you— of your sweet face and of the tones of your voice,—full of the *satisfaction* as well as of the yearning of love. You are so *good to love*: I am so happy in the mere thought of you and so carried away to be          Your own   Woodrow

ALS (WP, DLC).
  [1] This enclosure is missing.
  [2] Child's letter is missing.

## From Ellen Axson Wilson

My own darling,          Princeton, N. J. Monday [March 2, 1896]
    I have had quite a struggle over the side-board question but finally decided not to send the telegram. Of course it is "good enough" and I have many misgivings at letting such a bargain escape us. But it is beginning at the wrong end. Table & chairs without sideboard would do well, but a sideboard without table and chairs is another thing, and we *can't* buy the latter now, unless we happened to find them too at a great bargain. I hope these bargains in sideboards are not so very uncommon after all, and that another will turn up when we are in better condition to take advantage of it. Miss Conover[1] got a good one in Phila. for $25.00.

    There have been nothing but interruptions today. I began this at my first opportunity, that is just after lunch, was sent for to the house, then had to go to the Kneisal[2] concert, and so have lost *all* the mails. Oh! how I wish you could have heard the concert! We had two of the most *delicious* cello solos! It is something to remember all one's life. And you *would* have heard it if you could have come home at the regular time, for the concert was postponed a week.

    I think *you* had better write to the plumber and see if you can make him come and finish his work. *Everything* is waiting on him; I am afraid it is going to keep us from getting in next week.

He promised the architect to be here last Thursday & there has not been a word from him. The water can't be turned on until he repairs his leaks, &c. The paperer is waiting for more paper;— it ran short in several rooms—the painter is waiting on the paperer & plumber and the house cleaners are waiting on the weather;—it has turned too cold for window-washing—so a halt has been called all around. But such things were of course to be expected. With dearest, truest love          Your own    Eileen.

Can't you tell, dearest, at what hour you will reach here on Sat.?

ALS (WC, NjP).
[1] Juliana, daughter of Helen Field and Francis Stevens Conover, of 59 Bayard Ave.
[2] About the Kneisel String Quartet, see EAW to WW, Feb. 4, 1895, n. 1.


## A Newspaper Report of a Lecture on the Reorganization of City Government

[March 3, 1896]

### ORGANIZATION OF CITIES.

#### PROF. WOODROW WILSON ADVOCATES
#### A NEW PLAN.

Prof. Woodrow Wilson took for the subject of his lecture at the Hopkins yesterday afternoon "The Reorganization of City Government." The lecture was intended to sum up the main points of preceding lectures on city government and to show how the different abuses treated of might ultimately be abolished. In his introductory remarks Professor Wilson said it was no part of his function to prescribe individual remedies for individual cases. He said that in his capacity as an academic lecturer it was not his intention to indicate a course of action for any particular city, but to lay down certain propositions that should be applicable to all. Granting the need of municipal reorganization, he said the question was, On what principles is it to be conducted? In answering this question, he spoke as follows:[1]

"The plans of which I speak to you this afternoon are not brought forward with the belief that they can be put into execution all at once. The process will be a slow one, but the city government when reorganized should be possessed of the following seven features:

[1] Compare Wilson's earlier speech on municipal reform, two newspaper reports of which are printed at Feb. 26, 1895.

### Administration by One Body

"First—The administration should be by one body—the ordinance-making power. At least this body should be one in all counsel and origination. Furthermore, administration and executive action are not one and the same thing. Administration means the determination of what the executive officers shall do, and how they shall do it. The methods and purposes, everything except the performance of the actual work with the hands, should fall within the duties of the administrative body. Everything cannot be done by a single individual or a single class. There must be, so to speak, a compound of opinions. I do not believe in the government of a city by a single individual or a single class. But that is quite another thing from a single administrative body, which I do believe in.

"Second—There should be a minority of experienced or trained officials in this governing board. By trained I do not mean merely educated persons, but men trained for specific duties, as trained inspectors of schools and public works. This matter of training shows that such a system could not be inaugurated in a day, but must be a patient process. Notice I say minority, for I do not wish that the city government should fall into the hands of a body of technically trained officials, for such persons are apt to become narrow in their views and be too much given to the use of red tape. On the contrary, the policy should be determined by a majority freshly elected from time to time, who shall take a broader outlook. The minority should be chosen by competitive examinations, so that efficiency as well as purity of government would be secured. We have limited our notion of civil service reform too much. I should desire a civil service reform in accordance with which men would work as well as not steal; would be capable as well as honest.

### Only One Councilman to Vote For.

"Third—The majority of the Council above referred to should be chosen by only one act of election on the part of the voters. So little of a pessimist am I with regard to democratic government that I fully believe we could trust to popular vote to elect good men. But this can be secured only by seeing to it that the office is of enough importance to make it worth while for the voters to exercise care in their choice. The voters should have only one member of the Council to vote for. This single act of election would simplify and point responsibility. There would be a concentration of public gaze upon one man, and hence a better chance to ascertain the fitness or unfitness of the candidate for office. Moreover, abler men would be willing to take office. As it it now, there are so many offices in this country that really able men do not care to fill positions to which such a small amount of power attaches. In England better men are elected because there are fewer offices. It may sound radical to say it, but I believe that from the City Council thus chosen should be chosen, directly or indirectly, the Mayor and all the other city officers. The system has been tried in England, where they have much better municipal government, partly because of this system. There the "minority" part of the council is chosen by the council and called aldermen. If for aldermen you substitute a minority of trained officials, not elected but appointed, as on the Continent, the system would be even more effective.

"Fourth—There should be a widening of city functions, but not without a better organization of city government. Then, and not till then, should the city undertake the ownership of the gas system and the street railways. Under such conditions also rapid transit should be operated by the city, and so managed that lines should be provided to relieve conjested parts of the city, whether those lines paid financially or not. Charity should likewise become a municipal function, although not to the exclusion of public [private] charity. Yet public charity should be so thorough as to be independent of private charity, and should be made the imperative legal duty of the whole. The same arguments as are valid for the need of public sanitation are valid also for the need of public charity and public education, and for the former even more than the latter. For public charity and public education are a sort of moral sanitation.

### Compulsory Citizenship Duties.

"Fifth—Before we wake up to this we are likely to be compelled to resort to an enforcement of wide compulsory citizenship duties, as in the Prussian system. Such duties would include poor relief, tax assessment, mercantile arbitration, education, etc., by a system of committees. Such services are generally without pay and the penalty in Prussia for their non-performance is an increase of the individual's taxes and loss of the franchise. In the city of Berlin over 10,000 persons thus have a part in the municipal government. In other words, self-government must not remain a privilege alone, but become a duty. For voting, which is merely electing someone to govern, is not all of self-government. There must be active co-operation in addition.

"Sixth—There should be a separation of the judicial from the administrative function of city government—except, perhaps, in the case of police courts for passing upon offenses against city ordinances. Popular election of judges should some day be done away with, although it is likely that the day is still far distant when this can be accomplished. But all things come to those who wait—and know what they are waiting for.

"Seventh—There should be a certain amount of wise central control in the interests of administrative integration. This will be the concluding subject of the course, and I will take it up for discussion tomorrow."

Printed in the *Baltimore News*, March 3, 1896; some editorial headings omitted.

## To Ellen Axson Wilson

My own darling,                              Baltimore, 3 March, 1896

You will spoil me, if you don't take care, with these Sunday letters in praise of my writing. They are so subtly mixed of love and criticism that in appropriating the love, as I do, eagerly and without question as to whether it is deserved or not, I am in danger of accepting the criticism along with it! In that case, I sh. be as vain as I am happy. But *this* letter, of last Sunday, contains, after all, more love than praise,—and love of a kind that must assuredly make a man rich beyond measure. I mean in what it says about my going abroad. Was ever there any courage like that of my darling, so sweetly spoken, and so nobly! It *would* be *best* for me to go across the water, no doubt. No doubt, too, it would enrich as well as relieve my thoughts by way of holiday,—enrich them by a sight of the old land I love. Maybe I could be still more truly than before a literary man,—my imagination enlarged and instructed; my intellectual pulses quickened,—all my mental processes stretched to a new scale. But, ah me! what do I want and need so much as I want and need *you*, my Eileen. *You* will have courage enough for the separation, my little heroine,— but will                              Your own   Woodrow

ALS (WP, DLC).

## From Ellen Axson Wilson

My own darling,       Princeton, N. J. Tuesday [March 3, 1896]

Your notice in the "Princetonian"[1] has caused much excitement, everybody thinks you are ill again & I am besieged by enquirers. And now comes a telegram from Pittsburg about it!—

asking if you will be able to lecture on Friday. How I wish it were Thursday instead so that you could save a day! Oh how good it is to think that this is the last letter,—that I can almost count the hours! Indeed I could if I knew when you were coming on Sat.

I am happy to report that the plumber is here today. The glass has also come and is *lovely*; it is all more or less opalescent, but distinctly golden too in tone. I am wild to see it up.

I write in desperate haste, the "Employment Soc.," & several other things at once demanding my attention, so must say good-bye, my darling, 'till the happy day now so near at hand. I hardly dare give myself full leave to think of that day yet lest my impatience fairly overpower me. I must keep my head as long as possible at least, what will become of it when you are really here is more than I can say. God bless and keep you, dear, and bring you safe home to

Your own,   Eileen

ALS (WC, NjP).
   [1] A notice in the *Daily Princetonian*, February 27, 1896, saying that Wilson had been detained in Baltimore on account of illness and certain written recitations would therefore be postponed.


## Edward Southwick Child to Ellen Axson Wilson

My dear Mrs Wilson:                    New York. March, 3, 1896.
   Mr Hoffheimer [Hoffmeier] was in to see us and promised to leave Cranford for Princeton yesterday. We explained to him pretty forcibly that he would have to fix this work right if he wanted his money, which he said he did, and he also stated that it was a mistake of his employe to leave the work in the shape it was. He promised to go at once and put it in shape. I presume that the storm of yesterday may have deterred him from starting, but if he is not at the job when you receive this letter, will you please telegraph to us and we will do all in our power to hurry him there.

   We are very sorry, indeed, that you should have an annoyance of this kind just at the last of the work and feel confident that Mr Hoffheimer will eventually make things correct and satisfactory.
Yours truly,   E. S. Child
I will endeavor to see you and the Professor on Monday next.

TLS (WP, DLC).

A Newspaper Report on a Lecture on Relations
Between the City and State

[March 4, 1896]

THE CITY AND THE STATE.
Professor Wilson's Final Lecture at
the Johns Hopkins.

Prof. Woodrow Wilson concluded his interesting course of lectures on local government yesterday afternoon, taking for his final subject the relations of central and local government. He said in part:

"An American city is the creation of the legislature, to be made, altered and unmade at pleasure. The central control which we have adopted is legislative control, and we have adopted it without limitation or reservation. The objections to such control are obvious. In the first place, it does not represent real control, which should be systematic, pliable, selective and discretionary, but simply outside interference, occasional, arbitrary and haphazard. In the second place, no one is really responsible for it. This want of responsibility arises not only because the legislature is numerous and the origin of measures hard to trace and their passage hard to follow, but because there is no plan of interference. One city at a time is tinkered with, and a single city cannot resist or fix responsibility through the franchise even if it were of a mind to do so. For if all the representatives from the city should agree they would still be in a hopeless minority. The representatives from different cities also are jealous of each other, and this prevents concerted action in securing good municipal legislation.

"The general lines alone of a city government can be advantageously determined by statute. The rest should be left to local administration. You cannot have excellent administration without variety. But under general statutes there can be no variety—unless you give much discretionary power to individual officials.

"In this country the limit of a municipal loan is fixed absolutely for all cities at a certain percentage of their valuation, although often this needs to be exceeded in particular instances. Yet it is almost impossible to get the law changed.

"Now, I must say what always sounds like a hopeless thing—we have not the central government in this country to undertake such supervision. The Secretary of State, for example, in the various States, is merely a clerk. If we are going to organize local government so that central government will have control over it, we will be obliged to reorganize central government. This may mean a long process. But it is worth while to have a political programme looking forward many years into the future, if you really know what you want.

"By way of summary, note the three points which have been emphasized in these lectures:

"First—That the city has a characteristic life of its own, but that its functions are nevertheless chiefly, if not exclusively, administrative in character.

"Second—The integration of that government.

"Third—The integration also of the State government and the exercise of a central administrative control, to get rid of the present pernicious system of legislative interference."

Printed in the *Baltimore News*, March 4, 1896.

## A Newspaper Report of a Reform Rally in Baltimore

[March 4, 1896]

### A PUBLIC WARNING

#### TO COUNCIL SPOILSMEN TO CHANGE THEIR COURSE BEFORE IT BECOMES TOO LATE.

#### Throng at the Music Hall.

A rousing protest of the people against the attempted assumption by the City Council of the authority to appoint all persons holding municipal offices was made last night at Music Hall, where a mass-meeting was held that filled the building.

Not only was every seat in the vast auditorium taken, but many were standing. About four thousand persons were present.

The meeting was called by the Reform League, both to protest against the action of the Council majority and to uphold Mayor Hooper in the policy he has pursued since he entered upon the duties of his office. Every mention of the Mayor's name was enthusiastically applauded.

Emerich's Orchestra occupied the band gallery and entertained the assembly during the wait preceding the arrival of the speakers. The orchestra also played selections between the addresses.

Mr. Joseph Packard called the meeting to order and Mr. Eugene Levering presided.

The speakers were Police Commissioner Theodore Roosevelt, of New York; Messrs. Joseph Packard, Eugene Levering, Prof. Woodrow Wilson, of Princeton University; George Whitelock, George R. Gaither, Jr., and Charles J. Bonaparte.

Mr. Roosevelt's appearance on the stage was the occasion of a great demonstration. All the other speakers were also applauded and cheered as they walked from the door to their seats in the centre of the large platform. Behind them were seated two hundred citizens who served as vice-presidents of the meeting and whose names are given elsewhere in this report.

The following resolutions, introduced by Mr. William Reynolds, were adopted by a unanimous "aye":

"The City Council has passed ordinances taking from the Mayor and vesting in themselves the powers of appointment and removal of city officers, which powers have heretofore, under our form of government, been uninterruptedly exercised by the Mayor as executive.

"It is generally recognized that such a mode of appointment and removal would be subversive of good government and would lead to intolerable abuses.

"This action of the Council constitutes a violation of their plain duty and a usurpation of powers, executive in their nature, which the Mayor was elected to exercise.

"This attempt of the Council to seize the public offices of this city, if carried into effect over the veto of the Mayor, will throw the municipal government into confusion, will of necessity lead to inefficiency and waste and will bring disrepute upon the city.

"All members of the Council who shall participate in this breach of trust, either by voting or by purposely abstaining from voting, will deserve and will receive individually and personally the condemnation and scorn of their fellow-citizens.

"In this grave crisis in public affairs the citizens of Baltimore, in this mass-meeting assembled, invoke the aid of the General Assembly to prevent by appropriate legislation the consummation of this scheme of spoliation with which our city is now threatened."[1] . . .

### PROF. WOODROW WILSON.

Prof. Woodrow Wilson said: "I know that this meeting has been called to protest against an action of the City Council, but I wish to express my obligations to that Council for giving me the opportunity of appearing on this stand as a citizen of Baltimore. I can speak of myself as a Baltimorean, I think, for I spent several years in this city and have been a regular visitor here since I left.

"For the last two or three weeks I have been lecturing at the Johns Hopkins University, and the subjects of my lectures have

*Cartoons from the* Baltimore News *report of the rally*

been so timely that I have had the best advertising I ever had. I suddenly found that I had become an authority upon municipal government, simply because I got in the position of agreeing with the best people in town.

"A scene like this tonight ought to suggest to the members of the City Council that they should have themselves nominated for re-election. [Laughter.] No Council for years has stirred up so much feeling, and, by offering themselves for re-election, the Councilmen can readily ascertain what that feeling is.

"What I want to know is whether you who are here tonight have come to this meeting 'to stay'? By that I mean whether you will leave with an abiding inspiration or whether you will forget all about it as soon as you go out; whether this will be a display of spasmodic strength on your part, or whether you will go forth and put your shoulder to the wheel of good government. All I will say is if you have come 'to stay' the City Council has not. [Cheers.] Take up the sword before you take up the horn.

"The motive of this meeting is to show that the last election meant something[2] and that the next election will mean something. [Applause.] The next is more important from the politicians' standpoint than the last. [Laughter.] Before the last election there was a tacit understanding that the city government, as it stood, should be reformed as you intended it should be. The questions of machineries and arrangements are not questions of this moment. If any of these spoilsmen says he did not comprehend that understanding he may not be a knave but he is surely a fool. [Applause.]

"I am a believer in the long processes of refrom. Everything will come as you mean it if you only continue to mean it. The old saw says that everything comes to him that waits—if he knows what he is waiting for. By knowing what you propose and maintaining a strict abiding by that purpose you must necessarily finally attain the ends which you have been and are even now striving for."

Printed in the Baltimore *Sun*, March 4, 1896; some editorial headings omitted.
¹ Mayor Hooper refused to recognize the legality of the appointments which the Council had made and took the issue to the courts. A lower court upheld the Council. Hooper at once appealed the case to the Maryland Court of Appeals. This court sustained Hooper, who eventually proceeded to make his own appointments.
² That is, that the Republican victory of November 1895 (see n. 1 to the first news report printed at Feb. 26, 1895) had come about because reformers of every political hue, including a large number of Democrats, had banded together behind Hooper and the Republican slate in order to defeat bossism and eradicate corruption. The "motive of the meeting," Wilson was saying, was to force the Council to recognize the meaning of the election of 1895 and cease its partisan attempts to thwart the mayor.


## From Henry Mills Alden

Dear Mr. Wilson:                          New York. March 4, 1896.

We have received your letter of March 1.¹ Mr. Pyle has also forwarded to us the manuscript of your paper on General Washington and has written that the pictures will be in our hands within a few days.

We are anxious to give you all the time possible and if you can let Mr. Pyle have the material for his illustrations for your fifth paper on April 1 and for your sixth paper by May 15, we shall be glad to wait a little longer for the manuscript. We should be glad to have also by the same dates your suggestions for further illustrations, since the Art department needs considerable time for obtaining photographs from a distance and prints in rare books.                          Sincerely yours,   H. M. Alden

TLS (WP, DLC).
¹ It is missing.

## Edward Southwick Child to Ellen Axson Wilson

Dear Mrs Wilson: New York. March. 7, 1896.

Your favor of the 5th, inst, is received and in reply I hand you the statement as requested.[1]

I find it will be impossible for me to come to Princeton on Monday or Tuesday. Trust it will be convenient for the Professor to see me and go over matters on Wednesday of next week. I could send Mr Holske down on Monday, but prefer to make the final settlement myself. Yours truly, E S Child

TLS (WP, DLC).
[1] This enclosure is missing.


## From Burton Norvell Harrison[1]

My dear Sir: New York March 8. 96

I have read with much pleasure your very engaging "Colonel George Washington" in *Harper's* for this month; it has an atmosphere and tone quite delightful, and is written in a literary style so charming as to make it an altogether admirable magazine article.

The old story cannot be told too often, if told as you tell it.

In finishing, at the very end, you mention an occurrence I do not remember to have seen before alluded to in print—the encounter between two parties of Washington's advance in the campaign to Du Quesne in 1758, when, each mistaking the other for the enemy, there was an exchange of a deadly fire.

Won't you be so good as to furnish me a reference to any published or accessible account of the particulars?

A kinsman of mine was killed, in the campaign, under precisely those circumstances and I fancy it was on the occasion you mention.

I shall be grateful for information which may enable me to get at the fullest report of what then occurred.

Thanking you for the pleasure you have afforded me and thanking you in advance for kind attention to this request

With great respect Burton N. Harrison

ALS (WP, DLC).
[1] Private secretary to Jefferson Davis during the Civil War; New York lawyer in 1896; husband of Constance Cary Harrison, the writer; and father of the future New York congressman and Governor-General of the Philippines during the Wilson administration, Francis Burton Harrison.

## From Edward Ireland Renick

Department of State,
My dear Wilson:                          Washington. Mar 10/96
    I have found my notes & transcribe for you those bearing upon
the subject of our discussion during the drive from the Capitol.
I am seriously thinking of offering my Christopher Gadsden to
a publisher.[1]                    Yours as always   E. I. Renick

ALS (WP, DLC) with WWhw notation on env.: "Liberal Education Southern
young men."
    [1] Renick never published a full biography of Christopher Gadsden, but "Chris-
topher Gadsden" appeared under his name in the *Publications of the Southern
History Association*, II (1898), 242-55.

## To Burton Norvell Harrison

My dear Sir,         Princeton, New Jersey, [c. March 16] 1896
    I take great pleasure in answering your kind letter of the eighth
of March, if for no other reason, because it affords me an opportunity to thank you most warmly for the kind terms of appreciation in which you speak of my article on "Colonel Washington"
in *Harpers*.
    The account of the skirmish on the last expedition to Du-
quesne, of which you speak, I took from a narrative of Washington's own, written many years after the event, and published for
the first time in the number of *Scribner's Magazine* for May,
1893.[1] An account of the origin and character of the paper itself
is there prefixed. No names occur in that portion of the narrative
except that of Col. Mercer, who commanded the scouting party
with which Washington's relief by mistake became engaged.
    Again thanking you for your very kind letter,
                    Most sincerely Yours,   Woodrow Wilson

ALS (B. N. Harrison Papers, DLC).
    [1] Henry G. Pickering (ed.), "The Braddock Campaign: An Unpublished Auto-
graphed Narrative by Washington," *Scribner's Magazine*, XIII (May 1893), 529-
37.

## From Howard Pyle

Dear Professor Wilson:    Wilmington, Dec., March 16th., 1896.
    I suppose you are back in Princeton now, at any rate I will ad-
dress my letter to that place.
    I looked forward with much pleasure to the thought of your
paying us a visit on your way through Wilmington, and even until the last moment hoped against hope to receive a telegram saying you would be here.

I am going to ask you now if you can give me an outline of your Fifth Washington Article. I must push forward this work to make way for other that is following fast upon it; and if we are only as successful in arranging the Fifth set of drawings as we have been in arranging for the Fourth, I shall feel myself very fortunate.

I hope it will not crowd you too much, or cripple too much your intention, for I do not want to do that, and if there is any danger of it we will put off the illustrations until a later date. Still, I would like to go on with them, for I want to so arrange my engagements that I may get away from home the last of May.

The last set of illustrations are, I think, by far the most successful that I have made, and I am almost sure you will like them —especially the one of Washington and Stuben at Valley Forge.

Please remember me most kindly to Mrs Wilson and believe me to be as always,      Faithfully yours    Howard Pyle

TLS (WP, DLC).

## From Lawrence Fraser Abbott[1]

My Dear Professor Wilson:          New York March 19, 1896.

The weather prevents my making my proposed visit to Princeton to-day, but may I not by letter lay before you the plan which I wished to talk with you about, and if you are willing to consider it I can have a conference with you later.

It has occurred to me that while the Declaration of Independence has been treated historically and politically, its story has never yet been told from the personal and human point of view, so to speak. We should like to have that story told to our readers. I, for example, should like to know what the effect of the Declaration was on Hancock's business and social affairs in Boston, and such anecdotes about Sherman and Livingston, and the rest, as would put me in flesh and blood contact with their everyday lives. Would it be possible to discover in old archives, or old letters, or old reminiscences, what Burke and Lord North said at their clubs about the rebellious colonies? Probably they said there things very different from those uttered officially by them— things much more vivid and entertaining. No one knows better than you whether it is possible to treat the Declaration of Independence in this way. If you decide that it is possible we know of no one whom we would rather have do it for The Outlook and its readers than yourself. The length of the work and the elaborateness of it are somewhat hazy in my own mind. Perhaps it could be done in the form of half a dozen or more personal and anecdotal biographical sketches of some of the prominent signers. At all events, my main object in writing this letter is to find out whether this rough idea interests you and whether you are willing to consider it still further. If so, I will make another attempt to call on you at Princeton. The approaching centennial of Washington's farewell address makes perhaps an appropriate time for the announcement of such a series of articles, even if the series could not be prepared for publication next autumn and winter. Awaiting with interest your reply,[2] I am,

Yours very truly,   Lawrence F. Abbott.

TLS (WP, DLC).
[1] President of the Outlook Company, publisher of the New York *Outlook*.
[2] Wilson's reply is missing, but it is a safe assumption that he declined, because no such articles ever appeared in the New York *Outlook* under his name.

## To Howard Pyle, with Enclosure

My dear Mr. Pyle,        Princeton, New Jersey, 24 March, 1896.

I am afraid it must have seemed to you something less than kind that I should pass you without stopping on my way home from Baltimore, after the kind invitation you had pressed upon me. The fact is, I was both hurried and unwell,—as I have been ever since I got home, almost, for that matter; and the hurry and bad health together must be my excuse for not writing long before this. There were alarming arrears of college work awaiting me here, and I have not had more than strength enough for them.

Now, at last, I am feeling almost like myself again. I shall take it as easy as possible from this till the thirtieth of May, when I mean to sail for a vacation in the rural parts of England. It is the best possible proof of your indulgent kindness that you should add an invitation to the Mahogony Tree Club[1] to your invitation to your home in Wilmington;[2] and I thank you for it most heartily. If I were not under bonds to my doctor, I would accept with pleasure; but, well as I am now, I am still under promise to him to avoid every sort of engagement to which I am not already committed; and I must decline with genuine regret.

I have written, perhaps, about a half of No. V. of the Washington articles ("Making A Government"). As the name shows, it is to cover the period between Yorktown and the inauguration of the new government in 1789. It lies, at any rate for the present, in three parts in my mind. First there is the trying three years (1781-1783) of waiting for peace and keeping the army from mutiny. For this period, I had thought of two subjects for illustration between which a choice might be made. (1) The farewell scene with his officers at Fraunces' Tavern in N. Y. (See Lodge, I., 337). (2) Washington entering the ball room at Fredericksburg with his aged mother on his arm. A ball was given at Fredericksburg to Washington and the French officers just after Yorktown, and Washington entered the room with his mother, aged seventy-four, but straight and strong, on his arm.

The second period would be that (1783-'86) which he spent at home concerting new plans for union with the leading men of the country (by correspondence and conference). This would be our best chance for a Mount Vernon interior. I enclose the account of one scene which was a little out of the usual run. Others could easily be imagined: e.g., out of Mrs. Burton Harrison's "Washington at Mount Vernon after the Revolution" in the *Century* for April, 1889, or out of Conway's "Washington and Mount Vernon" Long Island Hist. Soc'y, 1889.

For the third period (The Constitutional convention) my head is as yet so empty of details as to be empty of ideas for illustration. I will write again about that, a week or so hence. In the meantime, what are your own ideas about periods one and two?

I am delighted that the illustrations for No. IV. turned out so much to your mind. Let us now manage the same for No. V.

With sincerest regard,

Most cordially Yours,    Woodrow Wilson

WWTLS (deCoppet Coll., NjP).
1 The Mahogany Tree Club, 1811 Walnut Street, Philadelphia. This invitation was given in a letter which is missing.
2 Extended in H. Pyle to WW, Feb. 5, 1896, and renewed in H. Pyle to WW, Feb. 11, 1896.

### ENCLOSURE

In 1785, John Hunter, an Englishman, visited Mt. Vernon in company with R. H. Lee, "his sons and servants." About nine in the evening, "we had a very elegant supper." "The General with a few glasses of champagne got quite merry, and being with his intimate friends, laughed and talked a good deal. Before strangers he is generally very reserved, and seldom says a word. I was fortunate in being in his company with his particular acquaintances."

WWT MS. (deCoppet Coll., NjP).

## From Amy O. Wright

Dear Sir and kind friend:        March the twenty sixth [1896]

I enclose you a receipt in full for all demands[.] I asked my brother (Howard) to write you concerning the extra work which he did, so now you will understand without my giving you particulars.

I thank you for the payment[,] also for your kind words for us as well as to my fathers memory. Thanking you for all past kindnesses to us all. Hoping the house will always be as satisfactory as it is now        Very truly   Amy O. Wright.

ALS (WP, DLC). Enc.: hw receipt by Amy O. Wright dated March 14, 1896.

## From Howard Pyle

Dear Professor Wilson:   Wilmington, Del., March. 27th., 1896.

I received your letter the other day and am very sorry that your doctor had forbidden you even the mild dissipation you would have in a visit to me and a dinner at the Mahogany Tree Club.

I am very anxious for you to meet my wife, and I would like you to become acquainted with her in our home as I have had the pleasure of meeting Mrs Wilson. Some time I hope this desire may be realized.

In regard to the other part of your letter speaking of the Fifth Washington Article, I would say that the following subjects have suggested themselves to me from the outline of your proposed treatment. It seems to me that we should have first of all something to do with the evacuation of New York. To this end I would propose either a meeting of Washington with Sir Guy Carleton in which the evacuation of New York was arranged for; or else I would suggest the entrance of the American troops into New York city.

I have already painted that subject (rather insufficiently, to be sure, for Harper's Weekly), but I do not know that that would at all interfere if you preferred it to the meeting of Washington and Sir Guy.

I rather apprehend it would be difficult to get historical accuracy in the meeting of Washington and Sir Guy Carleton, but suppose you may have some detailed information as to it. Either of these subjects would relate to the termination of the war.

As a second phase of the article I would suggest the arrival of Washington at Mount Vernon after his resignation of the command of the army. He returned home, I believe, on Christmas eve of a very rigorous winter; and I think the contrast of that to the departure of Washington and his friends from Mount Vernon (such as I have already depicted in the Third paper) might make a pleasing diversity.

If you prefer the subject better, I would represent him, as you suggest, leading his mother into the ball-room at Fredericksburg.

For the third subject, I would represent Washington in his rural life at Mount Vernon. I am informed that the box-walk at Mount Vernon is now very much as it was in Washington's day. It is very picturesque, and it would be interesting to place Washington in it as a setting.

Perhaps a good arrangement of this idea would be in the visit of Lafayette to Mount Vernon. I would represent Washington as directing the old negro gardner in the setting out of some shrub or small tree, and Lafayette standing at a little distance looking on with a certain remote dignity, Mrs. Washington, perhaps, standing with him. In this way we might not only represent the way Washington was sought after in his retirement by great folk, such as Lafayette, but also indicate the idea of his Cincinnatus character.

I shall await with much interest to hear your opinion of these suggestions.

Please remember me most kindly to Mrs Wilson, and believe me to be                    Faithfully yours   Howard Pyle

TLS (WP, DLC).


## To Frederick M. Hopkins[1]

My dear Sir,          Princeton, New Jersey, 30 March, 1896.

It certainly behooves us to do this tardy honour to Poe's memory. We talk as if we could live better than he could, though with his temperament; but we know that we cannot write with any touch of the genius he had; and we ought to do what lies in our way to show ourselves liberal in appreciation, generous in reverence for a well earned fame.

Very sincerely Yours,   Woodrow Wilson

ALS (Presidential Series, PHi).
[1] About Hopkins, it is known only that he was associated with the movement to preserve the Poe Cottage at Fordham, N. Y.


## To Howard Pyle

My dear Mr. Pyle,          Princeton, New Jersey, 31 March, 1896.

I thank you heartily for your friendly letter. I need not say that I appreciate your wish to have me meet Mrs. Pyle, and meet her in her own home; and I by no means feel that I have been cheated of that pleasure yet. I shall hope for some very early opportunity of doing so delightful [a] thing as I am sure visiting your home would be; and I hope that Mrs. Pyle will regard me as a friend in the meantime. For the present, everything must wait until my doctor declares me well. I *feel* well now, except for strength.

I like your suggestions for illustrations for No. V. extremely well. I had a great fancy for Washington entering the ball room at Fredericksburg, with his mother, as showing his character, and being besides a most picturesque subject, with the gay French officers and a bevy of young women for setting; but, upon second thought, I like your pictures better, for we shall probably have to have some 'function' like a ball in No. VI.

I do not know of any authentic details of the meeting between Washington and Carleton: I should think the entry into New York a more satisfactory subject. Had you thought at all of Washington's parting with his officers at the dock, after the scene at the Tavern? They followed him to Whitehall Ferry; he entered his barge; and in silence they stood uncovered (as he was, standing in the boat), as he was pulled away. It's a most impressive scene, and your water scenes are stunning.

With the return to Mt. Vernon on Christmas eve, 1783, and the scene, Washington, Mrs. W. and Lafayette in the box walk, I am more than satisfied. They are capital. Coupled with either the entry into New York or the farewell at Whitehall Ferry, they would content me altogether.

With cordial regard, in which I beg leave to include Mrs. Pyle,
Most sincerely Yours,   Woodrow Wilson

P.S. I am to call No. V. "First in Peace": does that suggest a head-piece?

WWTLS (deCoppet Coll., NjP).


## From Howard Pyle, with Enclosure

Dear Professor Wilson:       Wilmington, Del., March 31st., 1896.
I have received the enclosed letter from Mr Alden which will explain itself.

I suppose it would be rather risky to go on with the illustrations for the Fifth Washington Article until the paper is finished. But I am very sorry, for I foresee a great deal of inconvenience unless the articles are pushed through with a rush.

I have so much work lying before me that almost an[y] delay

will make it impossible for me to get away from home in June as I have planned to do.

Of course it is altogether out of the custom for Harpers to purchase illustrations before the articles are written, although in this instance they seem to be willing to accept any reasonable arrangement.

Awaiting your reply, I am

Faithfully yours   Howard Pyle

TLS (WP, DLC).

ENCLOSURE

## Henry Mills Alden to Howard Pyle

Dear Mr. Pyle:                    New York. March 30th, 1896.

Your letter of March 27th. is just received.

The engravings for your illustrations of Professor Wilson's fifth paper on Washington will be needed on May 20th, and we shall be glad to have you make the drawings from Professor Wilson's notes, with the understanding that he has the general scheme well in hand and that he is to inform you of any minor modifications that will affect the illustrations. We suggest that it would be well to confer with Professor Wilson after your pictures are planned.

From our correspondence with Professor Wilson, we suppose him to have his fifth paper so well under way that the illustrations may be safely made.

Very truly yours   H. M. Alden

TCL (WP, DLC).

## Two Letters to Howard Pyle

My dear Mr. Pyle,                    Princeton, 31 March, 1896

I wrote to you this afternoon, but must add a line by way of answer to your letter just received, inclosing a copy of Mr. Alden's letter to you.

It seems to me perfectly safe for you to go ahead with the illustrations. I have written all of the article which they affect: for they don't concern the concluding one-fourth of it at all: and I know that the illustrations I sanctioned in my letter of this afternoon will go perfectly with what I have written. I expect to send you the whole article by the end of this week—would send what I have were it in shape to be read. Of none of the scenes you expect to draw does my narrative contain any detail: text and drawings cannot clash.

In haste,            Sincerely Yours,    Woodrow Wilson

ALS (deCoppet Coll., NjP).


My dear Mr. Pyle,                         Princeton, 4 April, 1896.

No. V. is finished; but I must keep it a few hours for a last looking over. It shall go to you on Monday, by express.

As ever,            Cordially Yours,    Woodrow Wilson

WWTLS (deCoppet Coll., NjP).

## From Henry Mills Alden

Dear Mr. Wilson:                    New York. April 6, 1896.

Thank you for your note of Saturday just received. I am glad that your manuscript will be forwarded to Mr. Pyle to-day, as he seems to have misunderstood my letter and has not begun the illustrations. The manuscript, however, must clear up all doubts.

Sincerely yours,    H. M. Alden

TLS (WP, DLC).

## To Howard Pyle

My dear Mr. Pyle                    Princeton, 6 Apr., 1896

I send the fifth Washington article this morning, by express. Will you not be kind enough to forward it to Mr. Alden so soon as you shall have read and extracted such parts as you wish?

You will find on page 31 a hint as to the character of the gardener at Mt. Vernon, and on p. 30 an intimation of Lafayette's relation to the children—in case you should care to add children to the box walk scene.

With warm regards,

Cordially Yours,    Woodrow Wilson

ALS (deCoppet Coll., NjP).

## From the Minutes of the Princeton Faculty

5 5′ P.M., Wednesday, April 8, 1896.

... An Invitation was received from the University of Glasgow to appoint two persons to represent the College at the Celebration by the University and the Municipality of Glasgow of the Semi-

Centennial Anniversary of the appointment of Lord Kelvin as Professor of Natural Philosophy in the University to be held June 15th and 16th, 1896. It was referred to the President and Professors West and Fine to prepare a reply and to nominate representatives of the College. . . .[1]

[1] For their report, see the Princeton Faculty Minutes printed at April 15, 1896.

## Notes for a Talk

Laymen's Conference[1]          12 Apr/96[2]

A layman = one who does not make the service of Christ his profession.

Approach of laymen and clergymen, of conscience and Scripture.

An uninstructed conscience = a bad conscience: laymen have undertaken the duty of knowing what they are about.

Instructed by what—new ideas or old facts, old human nature? Experience.

No man's information can be complete, but his insight may be: he must use every means to *see*.

WWhw MS. (WP, DLC).

[1] About this organization, see n. 1 to the news item printed at April 6, 1894, Vol. 8.

[2] The *Daily Princetonian*, April 11, 1896, announced that Wilson would address the Laymen's Conference on April 12 but did not subsequently report on the address.

## From the Minutes of the Princeton Faculty

5 5′ P.M., Wednesday, April 15th, 1896.

The Faculty met. The Minutes of the last meeting were read and approved.

The President reported that the Committee on the subject had prepared the letter in response to the Invitation of the University of Glasgow to appoint persons as representatives of the College at the Semi-Centennial Celebration of the appointment of Lord Kelvin as Professor of Natural Philosophy to be held in Glasgow, June 15th & 16th, 1896.

Upon the nomination of the Committee Professor Cyrus Fogg Brackett, M.D., LL.D., or Professor William F. Magie, Ph.D., as alternate, & Professor Woodrow Wilson, Ph.D., LL.D., were appointed to represent the College at the Celebration. . . .[1]

[1] As future correspondence (particularly WW to EAW, June 17, 1896, n. 1) will reveal, Wilson did represent Princeton at the celebration. Neither Brackett nor Magie attended.

## From Joseph Ruggles Wilson

My precious son—                    [Philadelphia, Pa.] April 16/96
    Yours of 14th inst got to me by a miracle, being misdirected
324 N. 33rd instead of 424!
    Of course appropriate the $300 you need for your extravagant
mansion. I return the notes (B) for you to destroy.[1] By the way
I can't find your two notes for $2000.00.[2]
    After writing these words I found your two notes—all right.
    In haste and great love                    Your affc    Father

ALS (WP, DLC).
    [1] The nature of this obligation, which Wilson had apparently just discharged,
remains mysterious to the Editors.
    [2] About this loan, see WW to EAW, Jan. 25, 1895.


## From Horace Elisha Scudder

Dear Mr. Wilson                            Boston, 25 April 1896
    It is a pleasure to welcome you again to our list,[1] and though
we suppose your own expectations are not very high, as our sober
judgment compels us also to have moderate hopes with a volume
of essays, we shall be pleased to publish the book you send us
"Mere Literature" and other Essays.[2] We should like to ask you
however if it is not possible to increase the volume a little without
including anything of slighter or more ephemeral character?
The book will be rather undersized as it stands.[3]
                    Yours very truly    Houghton, Mifflin & Co.    S.

ALS (WP, DLC).
    [1] Wilson's letter to which this letter was a reply is missing. However, he had
no doubt just sent to Houghton Mifflin tear sheets of the following essays:
" 'Mere Literature,' " Atlantic Monthly, LXXII (Dec. 1893), 820-28; "The Author
Himself," ibid., LXVIII (Sept. 1891), 406-13; "On an Author's Choice of Company," Century Magazine, LI (March 1896), 775-79; "A Literary Politician," At-
lantic Monthly, LXXVI (Nov. 1895), 668-80; "On the Writing of History," Century
Magazine, L (Sept. 1895), 787-93; "A Calendar of Great Americans," New York
Forum, XVI (Feb. 1894), 715-27; and "The Proper Perspective of American His-
tory," ibid., XIX (July 1895), 544-59. Wilson made a few stylistic changes in
these essays and changed the titles of "On the Writing of History" and "The
Proper Perspective of American History" to "The Truth of the Matter" and "The
Course of American History," respectively. The above essays are published in
this series, in their first forms whenever possible, respectively at June 17, 1893,
Vol. 8; Dec. 7, 1887, Vol. 5; Nov. 10, 1895, Vol. 9; July 20, 1889, Vol. 6; June 17,
1895, Vol. 9; Sept. 15, 1893, Vol. 8; and May 16, 1895, Vol. 9.
    [2] A copy of the contract, entitled "Agreement between Woodrow Wilson and
Houghton, Mifflin & Co. for the Publication of Mere Literature & Other Essays
13 May, 1896," is in WP, DLC.
    [3] Wilson apparently responded by sending a slightly embellished version of
his lecture, "Edmund Burke: The Man and His Times," printed at Aug. 31, 1893,
Vol. 8, with the new title, "The Interpreter of English Liberty." See H. E. Scudder
to WW, May 18, 1896.

## To John Franklin Jameson

My dear Jameson,            Princeton, New Jersey, 27 April, 1896.

Again, alas, I must beg off.[1] Washington will not be off my hands before May twelve; our examinations bring in hundreds of papers on the thirteenth (to me); and on the thirtieth I sail for foreign parts. You see how impossible it is.

Please believe me when I say that it is no small point of pride with me that you should so much wish me to write for you. I have stopped reviewing; but almost thou persuadest me to begin again.

Mrs. Wilson joins me in the most cordial messages; and, in spite of appearances, I am

Faithfully Yours,   Woodrow Wilson

WWTLS (J. F. Jameson Papers, DLC).
[1] Jameson's letter to which this was a reply is missing.


## From Frank Walker Ball

Ball & Tempel, Attorneys & Counselors at Law.
Dear Sir:                    Fort Worth, Texas April 29 1896.

Having no personal acquaintance with you, but knowing you by reputation and especially admiring your work on 'Congressional Government,' I feel warranted in addressing you this letter.

I am a member of the Board of Regents of the University of Texas, being Chairman of its Committee on Instruction; which Committee has lately been charged with the duty of recommending to the Board a suitable person for the position of President of the University. The Chief Executive officer of the University has hitherto been the Chairman of the Faculty, but the last legislature abolished that office and provided for the election of a President instead. I have good reason to believe that if it were known to the Board that you would seriously consider the acceptance of the position in question if tendered to you, they would agree with my views concerning you and the desirableness of procuring your services as the head of our University.

The salary of the office is $5000 per annum. I have directed the Proctor to send you a catalogue which will, possibly, give you all the information you may desire. I should be pleased to hear from you on the subject, and if you so desire, all communications from you will be treated as strictly confidential by me and the Board

Hoping to hear from you at your earliest convenience,[1] I am,
Dear Sir,                              Yours Truly    F. W. Ball

I direct care Harper Bros not knowing your address

ALS (WP, DLC) with WWhw notation on env.: "Ans. 11 May/96."
   [1] Wilson's reply of May 11, undoubtedly declining to be a candidate, is
missing.

## To Howard Pyle

My dear Mr. Pyle,           Princeton, New Jersey, 2 May, 1896.
   I hasten to reply to your letter.[1]
   I very readily assent to your purpose to depict some feature
of the disbanding of the army rather than the meeting between
Washington and Carleton. You will remember that I feared from
the first it would not be possible to obtain definite enough details about the latter incident.
   I think I can promise to send you No. VI. one week from to-
day; and I sincerely hope the work on the drawings will not
interfere with your plans for the summer.
   In haste,           Cordially Yours,    Woodrow Wilson

WWTLS (deCoppet Coll., NjP).
   [1] It is missing.

## From Harper and Brothers

Dear Sir:                        New York City May 5, 1896.
   Referring to our correspondence regarding your articles on
Washington & his Time, which are now appearing in *Harper's
Magazine*, we beg leave to say that we should like to publish them
in book-form after their serial completion, and we would be
pleased to pay you a royalty of fifteen (15) per cent. on the retail
price of all copies sold, subject to the terms & conditions of our
usual contracts with authors. With a view to saving time, & so as
to put our proposal clearly before you, we enclose herewith a
memorandum of agreement for the publication of the work,
which if it meet your views, please to sign and return to us, and
we will send you a duplicate with our signature.[1]
   We are, dear sir,
                         Very truly yours,    Harper & Brothers.

ALS (WP, DLC).
   [1] As WW to Harper and Brothers, May 16, 1896, reveals, Wilson returned the
contract with his signature on that date. The duplicate contract, entitled "Agreement between Woodrow Wilson and Harper & Brothers, for the Publication of
'George Washington' 5th May, 1896," which Harper's sent to Wilson, is in WP,
DLC.

## To Howard Pyle

My dear Mr. Pyle,              Princeton, New Jersey, 7 May, 1896.

On the whole, I think I prefer the picture you are drawing in any case; and I would not now return to the meeting of Washington and Carleton. The subject you outline is most engaging.[1]

I finished No. VI. this morning; shall copy it to-morrow; and get it off to you, if nothing goes wrong, by Saturday,—with such suggestions as I have to make about subjects for illustrations.

With much regard,

Cordially Yours,   Woodrow Wilson

WWTLS (deCoppet Coll., NjP).

[1] This letter is missing. The subject Pyle selected was "Mustered out—a Rest on the Way Home."

## From French Ensor Chadwick

Dear Sir,                    12 May 1896 Washington D. C.

I beg that you will allow me to express the pleasure with which I have read your book "Congressional Government."

Being in administration myself, as Chief of the Bureau of Equipment in the Navy Department, I have been able to see somewhat of the startling disabilities under which we labor. I am convinced that a change of some sort, a fixing of responsibility somewhere, is a necessity.

Our Constitution was debated and formed at a most unfortunate epoch from one point of view: its framers had in mind the early parliaments of George III, and with their corruption and with the interference of the Crown in legislation in view, they had but one idea: to dig an impassible gulf between the executive and the legislature and they dug it. Had our Constitution been framed 50 years later, after English parliamentary reforms, I am sure it would have been very different.

No thoughtful man can study our present conditions without serious apprehension: our machinery is framed, so far as I can see it, to work from bad to worse: it is a badly designed engine which can never be made to work without radical changes.

The great misfortune of such books as yours is that they reach comparatively so very few, and that few composed as a rule of those who do not need conversion. The demagogue, the ordinary member of Congress, the great electorate as a whole do not touch it. If these subjects could be made a study of every school as they should be there might be hope.

I am dear Sir

Yours very truly,   F. E. Chadwick Commander USN

ALS (WP, DLC) with WWhw notation on env.: "Ans. 15 May/96."

## An Announcement

[May 14, 1896]

### PHILADELPHIAN SOCIETY.

Professor Woodrow Wilson will speak in Murray Hall this evening at 6:40. Prof. Wilson is so well known and his talks are always so interesting that further introduction is unnecessary.

Printed in the *Daily Princetonian*, May 14, 1896.

## From Henry Mills Alden

Dear Mr Wilson,                                New York. May 14. 1896

Now that we have your sixth & last paper of the Washington series, I would like to arrange with you for other papers on American History for 1897. There are two papers I have now in mind as desirable on account of their timeliness in view of the interest felt in Venezuelan & Cuban affairs. The general subject would be *Spain vs America*: one paper treating the subject as relating to North America (Mexico, old Louisiana, etc), & the other dealing with the more permanent Spanish dominion in South America. Would it be convenient to you to undertake these, so as to have them in our hands by August 1 & September 1 (1896) respectively?

Having indicated my predilection, from a journalistic point of view, I still would like, if possible, to defer to yours, if you will kindly indicate what you would most like to do in this field. As I am now making arrangements for next year's work in the Magazine I hope to hear from you soon.

Yours sincerely   H. M. Alden

ALS (WP, DLC).

## Report of a Religious Talk

[May 15, 1896]

### PROF. WILSON.

Prof. Woodrow Wilson addressed the Philadelphian meeting in Murray Hall last evening. Prof. Wilson took as his subject "The Expulsive Power of a New Affection." If we wish to get a bad thing out of our souls we must get a good thing in. True virtue consists in having a purpose which will dislodge the inclination and tendencies to vice. Such a virtue must be aggressive in its nature. There is also great danger in the inoccupancy of the soul, danger that in such a condition small evils may creep in and displace the good. So then, even if a man be not distinctly given up to any form of soul, yet this very negative position renders him liable to attacks from insidious vices. On the other hand, love is the one thing which can displace, by the expulsiveness of its nature, the very evils of the soul. And inasmuch as the love of God is the greatest and most perfect form of love it is not only our duty but our privilege to allow this affection to fill our whole life and soul.[1]

During the course of the exercises a selection was rendered by a quartette.

Printed in the *Daily Princetonian*, May 15, 1896.
    [1] There is a brief WWhw outline of this talk, entitled "Philadelphian Soc'y, 14 May, 1896," in WP, DLC.

## To Henry Mills Alden

My dear Mr. Alden,            Princeton, New Jersey, 15 May, 1896.
    I sent No. VI. of the Washington articles ("The First President of the United States") to Mr. Pyle last Saturday, the ninth, with the request that he forward it to you this week; and I have no doubt he will do so. I enclose, with this (on another sheet) my list of suggestions for illustrations,[1] in addition to Mr. Pyle's.

Since sitting down to write this, your kind letter of yesterday has been handed to me. I am sincerely gratified to know that you like what I have done well enough to want more; and I wish I could accept the new job without more ado. But I am going abroad on the thirtieth of this month, for an imperatively needed rest, and shall not be back before the tenth of September. So soon as I return I must settle down to the serious business of composing an "oration" to be delivered at the "Sesquicentennial Celebration" which we are planning here for October twenty-second. I shall not be free to write anything, therefore, till after that date.

If you care to consider engaging articles from me to be delivered (say) January first and February first respectively, I will take a few days to consider what I could make out of the Spanish-American subject you suggest; or else submit a choice of subjects of my own; but I fear there will be no timeliness in them by that time.[2]

Thanking you very much for your kindness, and with cordial regards,         Most sincerely Yours,    Woodrow Wilson

N.B. Might I have all proofs before May 30?

WWTLS (Berg Coll., NN).
    [1] This enclosure is missing.
    [2] Alden seems to have agreed with Wilson. In any event, Wilson did not write the articles.

## To James Fairbanks Colby[1]

My dear Sir,                    Princeton, New Jersey, 15 May, 1896.

I take pleasure in answering, as best I can, the questions put in your letter of the eighth of May.

Unfortunately the only source of information I can hit upon is the file of our catalogues. In the announcements there, Political Science is added to the title of the professor of Mental and Moral Philosophy (Dr. Lyman H. Atwater) in 1868, on the coming in of Dr. McCosh; but it does not appear as a distinct title among the subjects of study until 1871; though Political Economy had been one of the studies of the course since 1850.

In 1883, upon the death of Dr. Atwater, Professor W. M. Sloane was made Professor of History and Political Science, and under him the department of Political Science has been developed.

At the same time (1883) Professor Alexander Johnston was appointed Professor of Jurisprudence and Political Economy, and law courses for undergraduates were for the first time offered. It was not until my own appointment, however, in 1890, that the teaching of that department on the legal side was much developed, Professor Johnston putting his strength, rather, into other branches assigned him.

Hoping that this sufficiently answers your questions, I am, with much regard,

Most sincerely Yours,   Woodrow Wilson

WWTLS (deCoppet Coll., NjP).
    [1] Parker Professor of Law and Political Science at Dartmouth College.

## To Harper and Brothers

My dear Sirs,                    Princeton, New Jersey, 16 May, 1896.

I take pleasure in returning, with my signature, the contract for the publication in book form of my articles on Washington.

I take it for granted that the book will be illustrated, as the articles have been; and I should think that a book so illustrated would sell best by subscription, for it might be made both very handsome and, I should think, very reasonable in price.

There are a number of illustrations suitable for the book which did not appear in the Magazine because they had more than once

appreared [appeared] in it already; but Mr. Alden was kind
enough to say that I would be at liberty to use them in the book,
should the articles finally reach that form. I wish also to re-
divide the matter of the articles, and to make some slight additions, for which there did not seem to be room within the limits
of a magazine article. The six articles would be too long for six
chapters as they are. I shall arrange them, with the additions,
in (say) twice the number of chapters.

I go abroad, for a much needed rest, on the thirtieth of this
month, to be back in this country again by the tenth of September; but I suppose, since the book cannot in any case appear
much before the holidays without being ahead of the last article
in the Magazine, all the work of preparing the book for the press
and getting it into print can very easily be done after my return.
My own part of the preparation ought not, in any event, to con-
sume more than two or three weeks, if so much.

Trusting that these suggestions and explanations will prove
acceptable, I am

Very sincerely Yours,   Woodrow Wilson

N.B. I am not yet clear what the title should be; but will consider
the matter as carefully as it deserves. It ought to be as attractive
as possible.                                    W.W.

WWTLS (Berg Coll., NN).


# From Horace Elisha Scudder

Dear Mr. Wilson                [Cambridge, Mass.] 18 May [189]6
We have to-day your favor of the 16th and are returning your
MSS for revision as you desire. With it we are sending the Burke
paper which we hope you will include in the volume, though with
our provision for *The Atlantic* we do not think it expedient to
use it there first.[1] Were you not going away so soon we might
arrange with you for certain reconstruction of the article for the
Atlantic use, but under the circumstances it seems to us wisest
not to trouble you in the matter.

Very truly yours   Houghton, Mifflin & Co.   S.

ALS (Houghton Mifflin Letterpress Books, MH).
[1] It was included in *Mere Literature and Other Essays* (Boston and New York,
1896), and not printed separately in the *Atlantic Monthly*.

## From Howard Pyle

Dear Professor Wilson:          Wilmington, Del., May 19th., 1896.

In thinking over the subject for this Sixth Washington Article, I would suggest, by your leave, the following:

1 Thomson, the clerk of Congress, bringing to Washington the official papers notifying him of his election. It seems to me that this is a very good point and I am going on with it now.

Two gentlemen came down from Alexandria along with Thomson and were present during the interview, Thomson addressing the General in a formal speech, to which he replied in as formal a fashion, accepting the honor done him.

2 The other subject I chose was the meeting between Washington and Genet. So far as I can learn Genet was introduced to Washington (by Jefferson (?)), on the 22nd. of May. The meeting took place in the parlor of the house Washington was then occupying and there was no one present at the interview excepting Jefferson. Am I right in these historical points? If not, I hope you will correct me vigorously.

3 The third subject I should have either Washington and Nellie Custis upon the eve of their wedding, or, (preferably to me,) the death of Washington. I think this, to my mind, might be made very effective with the lamp-light and its element of tragedy. I should prefer it as being historical, the other being in a certain sense only legendary, as I understand it.

However, in this as in all things, I hold myself at your disposal.

I had thought instead of a picture of the meeting between Washington and Genet, one of Washington's cabinet, but I do not know just where the cabinet met. Can you tell me? Was it in the old State House at Philadelphia or did they meet at Washington's private residence? I suppose the latter. If you prefer that subject I will gladly make it.

Faithfully yours   Howard Pyle

P.S. Will you at your early convenience let me know which of the last named pictures you desire me to make, and if you approve of the former subject?

TLS (WP, DLC).


## To Harper and Brothers

My dear Sirs,                    Princeton, May 27, 1896.

I have been looking over the Washington articles again, and think that the first three may go to press for the book before my return from Eng. in Sept., as you desire,[1]—with a slight addition which I hope to send you tomorrow. I have no suitable "copy" for these three articles, but presume that you will print from the Magazine.

I shall ask you to print the first paper entire as Chapter I., under the title "In Washington's Day." Chapter II., I should like to have entitled, "A Virginian Breeding," and to include the first half of the second article down to the end of the paragraph which ends on the first column of 561 of the March number of the Magazine.

Chapter III., "Col. Washington,"—the rest of the second article.

Chapter IV., "Mount Vernon Days," comprising the first part of the third article through the paragraph which ends on the second column of page 937 of the May number of the Magazine.

Chapter V., "The Heat of Politics,"—the rest of the third article.

For the rest of the book I will send you "copy" as soon as possible after my return. I have decided to make no material division in any but the fourth article, which I think needs a little expansion in the part which deals with the Revolution. I ought, therefore, to be able to send the whole to you within a couple of weeks after my return.

I think it would be both most natural and least pretentious to call the book simply "George Washington." I have racked my brain in vain for a better title.

I have written to Mr. Adams about the illustrations.

Letters addressed here during my absence will be forwarded to me.

Very sincerely yours, Woodrow Wilson[2]

EAWhwL, WWS (Berg Coll., NN).

[1] The letter from Harper & Brothers to which this is a reply is missing.

[2] At some time near the date of this letter, Wilson seems to have suffered a small stroke, most probably from an occlusion of a branch of the left internal carotid artery, causing pain in his right arm and numbness in the fingers of his right hand. His letters during the coming months will chart the course of his recovery, which was fairly complete by March 1897.

## To Robert Bridges

My dear Bobby,                              Princeton N. J., May 27, 1896.

I am ever so sorry I shan't see you before sailing, but thank you for your note and the card of introduction.

Won't you be in your rooms between five and six on Friday [May 29]? I may come down Friday afternoon. In case I should'nt turn up, could you leave me a memorandum of that Scotch trip you spoke of, at the Grand Union Hotel by bed-time Friday night?

If I should have the hard luck not to see you, here's the heartiest kind of farewell.[1]

                    Affectionately yours,   Woodrow Wilson

EAWhwL, WWS (WC, NjP).
   [1] Wilson sailed from New York for Glasgow on May 30 on *S.S. Ethiopia* of the Anchor Line.


## Francis Landey Patton to William Thomson, Baron Kelvin

My Lord:                              [Princeton, N. J.] May 29 1896

   Allow me to introduce to you my friend & colleague Dr. Woodrow Wilson, Professor of Jurisprudence in Princeton University, who goes to Glasgow as the representative of Princeton on the occasion of the celebration in honour of your distinguished services in the cause of Science as Professor of Glasgow University.

   Professor Wilson bears with him the very cordial congratulations of Princeton University to the University of Glasgow & to yourself.

   I thank you for your exceedingly kind letter of April 6th. It was of course a disappointment to us to learn that we could not expect to have your Lordship with us in October;[1] but we realise very fully & appreciate the reasons which hinder you; & are greatly pleased to learn that our invitation was so favorably received.

   With best wishes for your health & praying that you may be long spared to the University which has been honoured so many years by your services & scientific discoveries I remain my Lord

                    Very faithfully yrs   Francis L. Patton[2]

ALS (Patton Letterpress Books, University Archives, NjP).
   [1] For Princeton's Sesquicentennial celebration.
   [2] For similar letters of introduction, see F. L. Patton to John Caird, May 29, 1896, and F. L. Patton to William Stewart, May 29, 1896, both in the Patton Letterpress Books, University Archives, NjP.


## Three Letters from Ellen Axson Wilson

My own darling,                         Princeton June 1/96

   Margaret today insisted upon being told *just* where you were—in what *part* of the ocean, &c., and though we all laughed at her, as usual for asking impossible questions, I for my part was quite on her side. What wouldn't I give to be able to watch that ship on all its way, to see at every moment just where it is and how it fares! And oh, if some bird could only assure me *just now* that my darling was well and enjoying himself! My greatest comfort is the glorious weather; you are at least safe so far, and oh, I *hope* you are well enough to enjoy it!

I am thankful for the superb weather on my own account too, being as you know, too well, I fear, very susceptible to the influences of sunshine & balmy air—or the reverse! I have been keeping up nobly so far; tonight I admit, I feel more like creeping into bed & and hiding my head than doing anything else,—even writing to you. I miss Sister Annie terribly,—they left today at 2.15.[1] You can imagine how lonely the house is with no one in it but me and the sleeping children. But enough of this.

I had a very good day Sat. at the Museum,[2] was simply astonished at the treasures they have accumulated since I saw it last; I was especially overwhelmed by one large room full of old masters, Rembrandts, Vandycks, &c. all given by Mr. Marquand, Sen.[3] They have all arrived since my day.[4] There is one portrait of a gentleman by Franz Hals that I am sure you would be carried away with. I have seldom seen a more delightfully interesting face. And the execution is *superb*. What wouldn't I give for a try at it! Then there was another new room full that I particularly enjoyed,—a splendid collection in full size casts of the Rennaisance period. *All* the Michel Angelos, Donatellos, Della Robbias, &c. I enjoyed it all extremely—in spite of—things. I don't believe I can ever see them again though without having vividly recalled the peculiar, mixed feelings—the intense, "Il penseroso" mood in which I saw them then.

Speaking of pictures, I found the proof plates for the 5th Article,[5] and also the missing ones, here on my return. The new ones are *very* pretty. They are, 1st, Washington entering the ballroom with his mother, 2nd Old soldiers at an inn door, & third, Washington alone in his garden directing his men. To my surprise I found the Lafayette & Washington scene in the grounds only the head-piece. There are several *beautiful* pictures of Va. homes too. There is no other mail of the least consequence. We are all *quite* well.

I *love* you,—I *dare* not try to tell you—I hardly dare think just now how much I love you, dear. God bless & keep you safe and well for                              Your own    Eileen.

[1] Annie Wilson Howe and her daughter, Annie.

[2] The Metropolitan Museum of Art in New York.

[3] Henry Gurdon Marquand, a wealthy New York businessman and philanthropist, at this time president of the Metropolitan Museum and one of its principal benefactors during a period of much growth. He was directly responsible for the Metropolitan's acquisition of all the art works and reproductions mentioned by Ellen in this paragraph. Henry Gurdon Marquand was the father of Professor Allan Marquand of Princeton.

[4] That is, since she was in New York studying art, 1884-85.

[5] "First in Peace," which appeared in *Harper's Magazine*, XCIII (Sept. 1896), 489-512.

My own darling, Princeton, June 4/96

Now you really are in the very middle of the ocean,—half seas over so to speak. I hope so at any rate; in such glorious weather even the Ethiopia ought to make fairly good time. How I have rejoiced in each one of these fine days for your sake! Surely I will hear on Tuesday, or at latest Wednesday!—that, by the way, will be the anniversary of the day on which the house was begun—a day not altogether of good omen.[1] I hope *this* time it may bring me an unmixed good. I was wishing you could have started a little earlier, but I am glad you didn't go when the Baldwins[2] did, for they had a very stormy voyage and were wretchedly crowded besides. They couldn't have a stateroom together;—he was with two other men and she with two other women!

Everyone seems so interested in you and your trip; I have been making calls the last day or two and have seen a good many. I took Nellie to a large party at the Waterman's[3] today, & while she was there called at the Hibben's, Fines, &c.

You know Mr. Marquand marries on the 17th[4] and goes away for the *year*,—to take Mr. Frothingham's place at Rome.[5] Too bad that he shouldn't be here to entertain at the Sesqui-Centennial! George Patton has gone to Bermuda, & his engagement to that handsome girl is now definitely announced.[6] Miss Kingsbury[7] told me herself. Prof. Smith[8] of the Seminary is also engaged and has gotten his salary *doubled* in consequence, I am informed. That I believe exhausts my budget of Princeton news.

There are no letters of consequence except one that pleased me very much from the University Extension. That Phila. centre can arrange for lectures *only* on Monday or Tuesday night;—so you are free of them! The letter came today; of course I shall write & tell them to make no further effort to secure you another engagement in its stead. *How* glad I am it has turned out so!

We are all perfectly "well and doing well." The children are still wild over base-ball. I have had to "call time" on them (is that the proper phrase) for fear they will over-exert themselves. The lessons are going on much more steadily and satisfactorily than they have recently. They have quite electrified me the last two days by their sudden brilliance in arithmetic; I hope it will last.

What a stupid letter I am writing! To tell the truth I don't know what to say! Until I hear from you I simply *dare* not indulge myself in love-letters. No,—I have nothing to say as to "the state of my affections";—I almost wish I *hadn't any*. Mrs. Purves, I gather, thinks me a very hard-hearted creature because I went quietly to an Art Gallery and looked at pictures after you left. She told me yesterday with much pride that when Mr. Purves started for Europe she was "so overcome that she couldn't leave the station for two hours." She was "really in a dreadful state!"

Good-night, my darling, God be with you, and keep you;—and grant to me all the desire of my heart.

Your little wife,    Eileen.

[1] A mysterious statement.

[2] Professor and Mrs. James Mark Baldwin. Baldwin was Stuart Professor of Experimental Psychology at Princeton.

[3] Mr. and Mrs. Frank Allan Waterman. He was an Instructor in Physics.

[4] Allan Marquand, Professor of Archaeology and the History of Art at Princeton, married Eleanor Cross of New York City on June 18, 1896.

[5] Arthur Lincoln Frothingham, Jr., Professor of Archaeology and the History of Art at Princeton, was associate director of the American School of Classical Studies in Rome, 1895-96. Marquand was a visiting professor at the school in 1896-97.

[6] See EAW to WW, Feb. 23, 1896, n. 2.

[7] She is unknown to the Editors.

[8] Henry Wilson Smith, J. C. Green Instructor in Elocution at the Princeton Theological Seminary, 1878-1926.


My own darling                         Princeton, June 8/96

To think that tomorrow at noon it will be ten days! I am trying very hard not to expect news until the next day, at the earliest, so as to avoid, if possible, disappointment. I suppose you are too far off now to be much affected by our weather; it has been quite uncertain for the last two days, ending in a violent thunderstorm this evening. I was glad you were not near our coast; there was not much wind however, so I suppose there was little danger for those at sea.

It is the first stormy commencement we have had since we came to Princeton. The boys[1] begged *very hard* to have May[2] and Minnie[3] invited, leaving out the dance. I told them frankly that you and I had both felt we could not afford the expense this year, and I couldn't disregard an opinion of yours, when you were away, especially. Then they insisted upon footing the bills; said it was all for their pleasure anyhow & it was only proper when they were to be the escorts to the games, &c. You will understand that I simply found it impossible to say to *them*, the boys, that I didn't want the expense of feeding them for five days! So they are here after all; and May is so wild with delight to *be* here that I can not but be glad to have her; and her mother seems almost as much pleased. I thought I *hated* to have them in the mood I was in, but now I am glad of the distraction. It has at least put an end to those lonely evenings all by myself in the house, and they were pretty bad. I never really knew what lonliness was before. In very truth I am just as lonely when they are all about me, I must always be lonely when you are absent; but there is too much noise and confusion for me to brood over it.

We are telling May that she is a little mascotte,—think of keeping Yale from scoring *again*! I will send you an account of the game. The boys say it was a splendidly played game on both sides.[4]

The girls are to go to the dance after all. When I wrote for them I told them I couldn't arrange it; but a friend of Minnie's has invited them; and unless I find tomorrow that Mrs. Reid[5] is going I must chaperone them. I am also to pour tea at the President's reception tomorrow.

It was a mistake about Mr. Marquand shirking the Sesqui-Centennial. He is to be in Rome for the winter, but will not start until after all is over,—will spend the summer here and at Newport. Prof. Minturn Warren[6] will be at the head of the Latin school there[7] this year. They have already sailed,—nice for her, isn't it?

We are all quite well and comfortable. And however lonely I am I am also very, very happy, dear heart, at the thought of all the good this *must* be doing you. Oh how I am hoping & praying now for news—*good* news. I hope it will be a *long* cablegram, there is so much I want to know. With a heart full—full & running over with love          Your little wife     Eileen.

ALS (WC, NjP). Enc.: report of the Princeton Yale baseball game clipped from the *Daily Princetonian*, June 8, 1896.

[1] Edward William Axson and George Howe III, both members of the Class of 1897 at Princeton. They lived in Dod Hall, a college dormitory, during the school year and with the Wilsons during vacations.

[2] A daughter of Ellen's first cousin, Harriet Hoyt Ewing, of Nashville.

[3] Mary Eloise Hoyt.

[4] Princeton defeated Yale 5 to o in baseball on June 6.

[5] Mrs. Legh Wilber Reid.

[6] Minton Warren, Professor of Latin at the Johns Hopkins.

[7] Warren was to be the director of the American School of Classical Studies in Rome during the academic year 1896-97.

## Three Letters to Ellen Axson Wilson

My own darling,                          S. S. Ethiopia 9th June, '96

This has proved an exceptionally slow and tedious voyage,—12 days instead of 10,—not because of rough weather, but because of an excessively old and slow tho. safe boat. I have fared famously, with only a very few qualms; and have found some delightful companions[1]—southern people, of course(?)

There are so few conveniences for writing, or for any sort of privacy, that I have not practiced this useless left hand at all. It is already tired out.[2]

I am perfectly well, and love you tragically.

Your own   Woodrow

I have enjoyed myself, despite the monotony, and feel really very much invigorated. Ah, with what a pang I love you, my little wife!

We are to have an entertainment on board to-night, and I am to be chairman.                              Your   W.

[1] Mr. and Mrs. Charles Albert Woods of Marion, S. C., and John McSween of Timmonsville, S. C.

[2] Wilson wrote this letter (and most of his others during the following year) with his left hand.

The Grand Hotel, Glasgow,

My own sweetheart                              [June 11, 1896]

Here I am in Glasgow. We got in at about two this morning, had breakfast at six on the boat, and got up to the hotel about 8:30.

I am *very* well. The voyage did me good for all it was so tedious. We did not learn of the savage gale that caught the "Umbria" (Cunarder)[1] in the n. Atlantic till we reached Londonderry yesterday, tho. we had very rough weather on the same days, catching, no doubt, the outer edge of the storm. The U. left the same day but went further north.

When I say "we" reached the hotel I mean my delightful southern friends of the voyage and I.

I called on the Sec'y of the University faculty[2] this afternoon, but he was out. To-morrow I call again; and *rest*.

Your sweet 1st. letter came to-day, and fills my heart with a love and tenderness unspeakable. Ah, my love, my Eileen, how *can* I *stay* away from you!

I must not drive this hand further. Love to Mrs. Brown.[3] Ask Hibben to make out the check for interest *in your name*.[4] Write to father.

I would give my trip and everything else to be in your arms!

Your own   Woodrow

[1] *Umbria* could not have been severely damaged by the storm. The "Mail and Shipping Intelligence" column of the London *Times*, June 8, 1896, noted her arrival without comment. The *New York Times*, June 28, 1896, reported the vessel as having sailed from New York on June 27 on her next regularly scheduled voyage to London.

[2] Regarding his participation as Princeton's representative in the Kelvin Jubilee at the University of Glasgow, about which see WW to EAW, June 17, 1896, n. 1.

3 Who, according to Eleanor Wilson McAdoo, *The Priceless Gift* (New York, 1962), p. 201, was financing Wilson's trip.
4 That is, interest on the mortgage which the Wilsons held on the Hibbens' property on Washington Street.

The Clarendon Hotel, Edinburgh,
My own Eileen,                              June, 13, 1896

What infinite pleasure your sweet letters give me! God bless you for them and for all the sweet things of my life that have come from you!

We came over to Edinburgh this morning, and have been doing the castle and Holyrood palace to-day. My friends are Mr. and Mrs. C. A. Woods of Marion, S. C., people whose kindliness, simplicity, and quiet way of being cultured would delight you (he is a lawyer of local eminence), and Mr. Jno. McSween, a merchant of Timmonsville, S. C., who is of their party,—a sturdy Scotsman who went to Am. 28 years ago in the steerage, has prospered, and makes up in Presbyterian character what he lacks in culture. They are to do England on their bicycles, and I am hoping to be a good deal with them. They mean to go slowly, as I do.

I found it impracticable to make the highland trip before the affair at the Univ. of Glasgow, our boat arriving so tardily and a day of rest being necessary after landing; and I am spending Sat., Sunday, and Monday here. Monday evening and Tuesday morning and evening I am due at 'functions' at the celebration in Glasgow; but Edinburg and Glasgow are as near one another as Baltimore and Washington, and I can get back in an hour and five minutes.

I was obliged to neglect my arm on the boat because of the absence of all conveniences; but it has grown steadily better, all the same, and now gives me scarcely any trouble at all.[1] I am feeling *very* well; get tired (with these wretched piles) going about sight-seeing, but rest easily and quickly. The voyage certainly invigorated me.

Sunday, the 14th

This morning we went to St. Giles's for the 9:30 service, saw the Highland regiment march down from the castle and file in, and heard a most interesting sermon in the noble pile. After that, Mr. Woods and I made a pious pilgrimage to the tomb of Adam Smith in the yard of the Canongate church and to the churchyard of the Gray friars,—altogether the most interesting morning I have had yet. This afternoon I rest, and to-night we go to church and to tea with some people we met on the boat.

To-morrow, my business calls at the University of Edinburgh,[2] and then back to Glasgow.

Ah, how I do wish, my darling that this left hand were not so slow and so quickly fatigued: I have such a heartful of love to pour out as surely no other man was ever obliged to contain in silence! Oh, why was I ever so selfish as to come without you,— how shall I endure to see all these things with your absence all the while at my heart? I am fairly *possessed* with love of my darling!                    Your own   Woodrow.

Kisses for the chicks, love to Ed. and Mrs. Brown.

ALS (WC, NjP).
    [1] Even so, he wrote this letter with his left hand.
    [2] Probably concerning the participation of certain members of the faculty in the Sesquicentennial of the College of New Jersey.


## From Ellen Axson Wilson

My own darling,                    Princeton, June 15/96

All our commencement crowd is scattered; Ed has moved from the college today and we are getting nicely settled down to our delightful summer calm. I have been at the college today "tar-balling"[1] all the boys things for them. This afternoon I took advantage of the glorious day to make some long deferred country calls on the Howes[2] &c. Margaret and Nellie went with me to their great delight; Jessie was driving with the Armour's.[3] I am just now making a business—after my fashion!—of wiping off old scores in the way of calls and letters; was of course belated in doing both this spring, but am almost through now; have only five more of each! I attend with the utmost promptness to all of your mail, but fortunately for me there has been none worth mentioning so far. Besides that from the Brooklyn Inst.[4] there has been only one of the least consequence. Since it is *very* short I will copy it to avoid sending a huge thick sheet of paper. It is dated from the President's Office—J. H. U.—"I am requested to say that the trustees will esteem it a favour if you will continue your services[5] here another year at the compensation hitherto offered you." "Yours respectfully,—T. R. Ball—Registrar." That is all.

I was certainly embarrassed as to what I should do with such a letter as that, but finally decided it would be best to write to Dr. Gilman explaining that you were abroad, could write no letters so did not wish them forwarded and had left me to attend to your affairs. I told him that I did not understand the letter; that yours was a three years course; that I noted the trustees "would esteem it a favour if you would continue your services for *another* year" at the old rate, that if they meant by that to imply that at the end of the one year they hoped to offer you compensation more fairly proportioned to the length of the course and your own reputation I could answer for you that you would gladly accede to their request; for the Hopkins had no more loyal son nor one more willing to make sacrifices to help her in an hour of need.* For it went without the saying that you would not wish to give the first year of such a course without some definite understanding as to the other two; and it was your misfortune that you simply could not afford—having builded an house—to lecture indefinitely at so low a rate. And I reminded him delicately of how much more you could make by giving up those five weeks to popular lecturing—a fact which your necessities and not your will made a temptation. Of course I am not giving my exact words;—wish I had kept a copy. I put it all very circumspectly and unobjectionably, I think. Hope he will answer soon.

How I hate to force your mind back to business of any kind! But let me finish while I am about it, for there is one very small matter I want to ask about. In looking for the M. & F. bill[6] I found in the pile you said were receipts a number of small unpaid bills chiefly for publications, & dues to various societies. There is one of $5.00 to the "Academy"[7] for which you seem to have been dunned four times(!) Unless I hear from you to the contrary I shall take for granted that I am to pay all these the first of the quarter, but I thought I had better ask, since it was barely possible to wish to drop the Academy for instance.

We are all well—perfectly well, and getting on nicely; the weather is superb. Yesterday we had a cold wind and rain storm & spent the day actually shivering, and today the earth looks "as if our Lord but yesterday had finished it." I enjoyed my little drive to the Howes *so* much. I had a rare treat last week too. Ed took May and me boating on the "Millstone"[8] for two hours. It was simply perfect. I was lost in wonder and delight to think we had such an exquisite bit of nature near us. I havn't seen anything so lovely or had such a good time,—of that sort—since the summer we were married. The water was *so* clear, and the lilies and other water-plants in it and the tangle on the banks of flowers and vines with here and there a noble tree *so* beautiful. I am sure the Yarrow when you see it will not be more charming—though of course it will be more thrilling, for *we* saw no haunted spot where "the Flower of Millstone dale lay dying"(!)[9]

I can't tell you, darling, what an intense satisfaction it is to me to think you are actually *there*—seeing all those charméd spots, getting all that delicious refreshment of mind. Surely to a sensitive nature nothing could so renew one's youth. Be sure to enjoy it with all your might for my sake. I love you my own Woodrow devotedly, tenderly, passionately, beyond all power of words to express. Oh for "the great heart word" that would tell you all!

Your little wife    Eileen.

\* (On that understanding I could speak as with authority from you in saying they might consider you engaged for next year; otherwise the matter could of course not be settled without further consultation with you.)

ALS (WC, NjP).

1 That is, moth-proofing.

2 Either Mr. and Mrs. Edward Howe or Mr. and Mrs. Leavitt Howe. Both families lived in the country outside Princeton.

3 George Allison and Harriette Foote Armour, who lived in what was then called Allison House (now the Walter Lowrie House), at 83 Stockton St. Armour, a member of the Class of 1877, had recently moved to Princeton from Chicago.

4 Inviting Wilson to deliver a series of lectures at the Brooklyn Institute of Arts and Sciences in the autumn. See EAW to WW, June 22 and July 8, 1896. Ellen had forwarded the letter from the Brooklyn Institute in a letter of hers which was lost. See WW to EAW, June 28, 1896.

5 As "Reader upon Administration."

6 Probably from Mitchell, Fletcher and Company, grocers of Philadelphia.

7 The American Academy of Political and Social Science.

8 The Millstone River, which flows near Princeton.

9 She is paraphrasing, rather inaccurately, two lines of Wordsworth's "Yarrow Visited": "Where was it that the famous Flower/ Of Yarrow vale lay bleeding?"

## Daniel Coit Gilman to Ellen Axson Wilson

Dear Mrs. Wilson,                               Baltimore. June 15. 96

I am sorry to have made any commotion by my recent note. Prof. [Herbert Baxter] Adams has always carried on the correspondence with your husband, & he has now left the country. That there might be no question of our desire to have Dr. Wilson continue his most valuable lectures, I sent the formal "intimation" that you have received in his absence.

As the two "principals," Dr. Adams & Dr. Wilson, are both beyond reach I suggest that we defer for the present all questions of re-adjustment,—with the simple understanding that we shall want Dr Wilson next year, & shall renew our request in the autumn.

I am very sorry that he is so 'under the weather[.]' Please give him my kindest regards when you write & believe me

Sincerely Yours    D. C. Gilman

ALS (WP, DLC).

## From Ellen Axson Wilson, with Enclosure

My darling,                                    Princeton June 16/96

I have just received this from the U. Ex. with one to me in which they make a special point of having it forwarded *immediately*. So of course I send it; though I shall write to them too and explain once again that you can't lecture on Monday nights. I suppose you *could* give a course of six U. Ex. lectures at Phila. while in in [*sic*] Balt. by taking your whole six weeks away from home, giving five a week at the J. H. U., and leaving one day and night free for Phila. But I hope you won't think of it. What do you think of the plan of giving those six weeks altogether to the U. Ex. instead of the J. H. U., giving them three courses running? It would clear you $750.00 instead of $400.00 and you would be at home every Sat. and Sunday at least. We would be spared that long *solid* five weeks separation. And you would only have to give eighteen lectures, instead of twenty-five. I should think it would be much easier for you and oh! so much easier for me![1]

Dr. Gilman's answer has just come, perfectly non-committal as was to be expected from him.

In extreme haste to catch the 10:30 mail.

Your own Eileen.

ALS (WC, NjP).
[1] Wilson did give his lectures on administration at the Johns Hopkins and did not give the series for the American Society for the Extension of University Teaching in Philadelphia in 1897.

E N C L O S U R E

## From John Nolen[1]

My dear Professor Wilson:        Philadelphia, June 15, 1896.

Will you please let me know if you can accept an engagement to give a course of six lectures on Monday evenings, at fortnightly intervals, beginning January 4th, at the West Philadelphia Centre. The lectures will probably be given in the Chapel of the University.

This Centre intends to make next winter an American year, having a course in American Literature in the fall, and a course from you on Constitutional Government in the United States, or some other phase of American History, after the first of the year. They want to do real study work for your course, and from my conversation with the Secretary, Miss Stockton, I think they would prefer a general American History course. They have fixed the lectures at fortnightly intervals and intend to have study meetings on the alternate Mondays, for which they would have a class leader. Last winter they did splendid student work, as you can see from the copy of Mr. Shaw's report, which I am forwarding under separate cover. I hope that you will be able to accept this engagement, as we should like to have you lecture for us in Philadelphia.

Mr. Graham Wallas[2] is to lecture for us on The English Towns and the English Institutions after the first of the year. I had the pleasure of seeing him in London, and I hope that if you are there you will give him an opportunity to call on you. His address is 32 Great Ormond Street, W. C. He told us that he would like to meet you while you are in England.

We had a very pleasant trip abroad,[3] returning to Philadelphia about a week ago.          Cordially yours,   John Nolen

TLS (WP, DLC).
  [1] Later a prominent city planner and landscape architect, Nolen was associated with the American Society for the Extension of University Teaching from 1893 to 1903.
  [2] At this time a Lecturer in the London School of Economics and Political Science.
  [3] Nolen married Barbara Schatte of Philadelphia on April 22, 1896; they probably went to Europe on their honeymoon.


## To Ellen Axson Wilson

My own darling,          The Grand Hotel, Glasgow. 17 June, 1896
    Here I am in Glasgow again. The Kelvin Jubilee is over, as hard a thirty-six hours' work as a able-bodied man would want; and I have been able-bodied enough to come through it without unreasonable fatigue,—feel quite spry indeed this morning. The affair quite beggars description,—at any rate with one's left hand. I am delighted to have witnessed so unique a Scots function.[1]

A telegram just received from [Andrew F.] West commands me to see Prof Maitland[2] at once. I must drop everything, therefore, leave my wheel here, and join my friends here again the first of the week for a run through the lochs and the Trossachs. That trip will not take more than a day and a half, and after it is made we shall start southward on our wheels,—say on Wednesday. Our route will be: Ayr,—the Burns country;—Carlisle; the lake district; Durham, York, etc.

I have not had a moment for writing since the Kelvin affair began,—it is such a painfully slow process with me as yet,—and I must break off now to catch my train for Cambridge.

I love, ah *how* I love and long for you!
                              Your own   Woodrow

ALS (WC, NjP).

¹ The Jubilee to celebrate the fiftieth anniversary of the tenure of the Chair of Natural Philosophy in the University of Glasgow by William Thomson, Lord Kelvin, was held June 15-17, 1896, at the university. The first event—a "conversazione" in the halls of the university—took place on the evening of June 15. It was followed by a "Gaudeamus" by the students and a reception for the delegates. On the morning of June 16, congratulatory addresses were presented to Lord Kelvin in Bute Hall by representatives of universities, colleges, scientific societies, and other institutions from all over the world. Wilson presented the address from the College of New Jersey, but the accounts do not indicate whether he made any remarks. Lord Kelvin, as the senior representative of the University of Glasgow present, then conferred a number of honorary degrees (Wilson was not among those so honored) and made a brief speech in reply to the addresses. There was a banquet for Lord Kelvin in St. Andrews Hall on the evening of June 16, and the celebration ended on the following day with a "sail through some of the more picturesque parts of the Clyde" on board the steamer *Glen Sannox*. See Silvanus P. Thompson, *The Life of William Thomson, Baron Kelvin of Largs* (2 vols., London, 1910), II, 964-91, and *Lord Kelvin, Professor of Natural Philosophy in the University of Glasgow, 1846-1899, with . . . an Account of the Celebrations on the Occasion of Lord Kelvin's Jubilee as a Professor* (Glasgow, 1899).

² West's telegram, asking Wilson to talk to Frederic William Maitland, Downing Professor of the Laws of England at Cambridge University, about participating in Princeton's Sesquicentennial, is missing.

## From Ellen Axson Wilson

My own darling,                          Princeton June 18/96

Your second cable—or rather *third*¹—came this morning and has of course made me sick with disappointment and apprehension all day. What *can* it mean that there is no allusion to your health? I have tried all day to persuade myself that it means nothing much; but in vain, for I know perfectly well that at the *least* it must mean you are no better, for if you were *improving* you would not have had the heart not to add that one word;— especially since the only object in having cablegrams at all is to keep us informed of your health. I went with it to Mrs. Brown secretly hoping to get some comfort by finding that it struck her differently, but she was as much dismayed as I was.

Please, dear love, don't try to spare me again this summer by keeping silent about anything; tell *me* the *truth*,—the whole truth, whatever it is; anything is better than this awful suspense. It seems tonight almost more than I can bear. In the next cable after you get this please tell me particularly about your arm— won't you, dear?

We are all well. The weather is still lovely, all is going nicely with us and until today I have felt very cheerful and happy. Maggie² came Tuesday and is as sweet as ever. She is also as *beautiful* as ever, though not as *pretty*. That is she is pale and thin and unformed looking, but her eyes and mouth, her smile, her whole expression have still their rare beauty,—an exquisite beauty I think. She is entirely unchanged in manner,—is perfectly simple and child-like: plays "queen" with the children, &c., is evidently quite untouched by the danger we feared for her in a Southern college town,—that of considering herself "grown up" as soon as she reached her teens. She took first honour in *everything* the only girl in her class.[3] I have the printed "honour list" and it is exactly like Ed's at Bingham,[4]—Maggie's name appearing in solitary glory,—the only one in the Sophomore class.

There is no other news,—except that this is Mr. Marquand's wedding day,—and no letters except one from Florence Hoyt asking if she can come here, and one from Father giving his address, "524 West Grace St., Richmond Va."[5] He reached there Saturday the 13th and expects to be there "many weeks." Says he is in a very pleasant house. He wrote to beg for news of you & I meant to write him tonight, but think I will wait now till tomorrow and see if things strike me anymore cheerfully then! I don't want to frighten him too. Oh but it is a tragedy to love anyone as much as I do you. My Woodrow, my *love* "Thou art the very life of me." Oh may God in His mercy bless and keep you, and bring you back to me safe and *well*.          Your own,    Eileen.

ALS (WC, NjP).
[1] Wilson sent frequent cablegrams to Ellen during his travels through Scotland and England in order to keep her abreast of his whereabouts. Only two of these cablegrams have survived.
[2] Her sister, Margaret Axson, who lived with Mrs. Warren A. Brown in Athens, Ga.
[3] At the Lucy Cobb School in Athens, Ga.
[4] The Bingham School in North Carolina, which Edward Axson had attended.
[5] Dr. Wilson's letter is missing.

## To Ellen Axson Wilson

My dearest          Royal Station Hotel, York, 19 June, 1896

I am stopping off here on my way back from Cambridge, by necessity of schedule rather than as a tourist. It proved most convenient to spend a night here each way. I shall taste it again on my way south on my wheel, but I have delighted myself this time with a look at the outside of the great minster and a long walk on the city walls and thr. the quaint streets of the singular old town.

I saw a good deal of Cambridge yesterday, being there from noon till nearly six. The town seemed to me rather mean, but the colleges most of them beyond measure attractive,—some of them exceedingly beautiful.

I found Prof. Maitland most natural and agreeable, but our interview was very short because he had to hasten away to meet an engagement. I think the invitation made a considerable impression upon him (he is to take a few days to decide), but he urged weak health, with only too evident good reason, as an argument for declining, and I can only *hope* he will accept.[1] I of course invited him to stay with us, and to bring Mrs. M.

The grass is from Adam Smith's grave in Edinb., the daisies from Holyrood abbey.

This journey has proved rather fatiguing, but I am taking good care of myself am [and] feel very well. My chief enjoyment I find in the (now) fearful joy of loving and thinking about you, my far-away treasure.          Your own,   Woodrow

Love to Mrs. B.

How will this do for the dedication of the Essays, sweetheart?
To Stockton Axson,
By every gift of mind a critic
and lover of letters,
By every gift of heart a friend,
This little volume
Is
Affectionately Inscribed[2]

P.S. Don't forget the interest due June 30, my love.

ALS (WC, NjP).
[1] For Maitland's answer, see F. W. Maitland to WW, June 26, 1896, printed as an Enclosure with WW to EAW, July 5, 1896.
[2] Wilson used this dedication verbatim (except for changing "Inscribed" to "Dedicated") in his *Mere Literature and Other Essays* (Boston and New York, 1896). There is an earlier draft of this dedication on a loose page in WP, DLC.


# A Memorandum

[c. June 19, 1896]

P[hilosophy]. o[f]. P[olitics]. Topics:

The functions of the state should not be regarded (even in the field of taxes) as the administration of property. They are functions of organic life. What then of the representation of the classes and balance of forces in a state upon which Burke laid so much stress and in which I so thoroughly believe? How is this theory to be read into his theory of organic life? Double processes in modern nations: the disintegration of politics and the interruption of the standards of life and opinion, the growing (?) action and power of the idea of nationality.

Transcript of WWsh on loose page (WP, DLC).

## To Ellen Axson Wilson

My own Eileen,          The Grand Hotel, Glasgow. 21 June, 1896

There is no news with me. I reached here Friday night, but my friends have not yet returned from a trip to the islands which they were to take while I ran down to Cambridge; yesterday it rained; and to-day is Sunday (observed with Scots, almost with Princetonian, rigour.) I have busied myself with making small purchases for the tour, and with doing as little as possible, as the best preparation. I suppose we shall make the run through the lochs and Trossachs on Tuesday, and mount our wheels for the ride into Ayrshire on Wednesday. I have given up the longer trip through the Highlands which Bridges suggested. It wd. take both too much time and too much money.

I enjoyed the flying trip to Cambridge very much, all except the 18 or 19 hours on the cars, and even they brought not a few glimpses of the country that were rewarding. I am feeling and, I believe, looking very well. My arm suffers scarcely a twinge, and is a most promising patient. But there is danger in thus sitting still, with nothing to do,—the danger of thinking too much about you (as you are thinking too much about me),—the danger of heartsickness. How cheerfully would I give all I have seen and enjoyed in this charming, lovable country, and all I am likely to see and enjoy, to hold my darling for one moment in my arms! You must not brood, my pet. I like to think that dear Maggie will be with you before this reaches you, and with her you will have real companionship, such as you could not have with May and Genevra.[1] Yours is the *strain* of this separation, my brave darling (mine the sharp pang at sight of every new thing I know you would delight in seeing), and I rejoice so to know how sound and sane you are, with more gifts, and finer, for putting high sense into life and for getting good sense out of it than any one else that ever I knew. How did it happen that nature was so lavish, and gave you who was to have so much mind such unspeakable charm too, both of mind and of person? Ah me! I wish I could think of you less,—or else write of you more! It takes me half an hour to one of these pages. But that's not quite as bad as before,—and the writing looks a trifle better,—don't it? If I did not have the distraction of making plans from day to day, I feel sure I should incontinently take ship and come back to you as fast as I could. Three thousand miles does not seem to make the least difference in your power to attract, my queen: it is just as hard not to think of you, just as hard not to come to you, as if you were in the next room, and I am all the while and altogether

Your own    Woodrow

Kisses for our darlings and love for Ed. and Mrs. Brown.

ALS (WC, NjP).
<sup></sup>¹ Genevra is unknown to the Editors.


## From Ellen Axson Wilson

My own darling,                                    Princeton June 22/96

I wish I could tell you with what a thrill of delight I saw your dear handwriting last Friday night! and then again today when the second note came. They have reassured me in large measure about your health, in spite of the fact that they are so far in the past tense as compared with the cablegram. I am *so* pleased that you wern't much sea-sick, and that you found people worth making friends of on board.

You were a naughty fellow not to tell me how your *arm* is; you can't imagine how hungry I am for details about that, and your general health. Alas, these little notes are certainly tantalizing in that respect. Suppose you write in short-hand full bulletins of "news" each time and let Ed read them to me,—answers to such questions as these, for instance. Did you have the state-room to yourself? If not what sort of companion had you? Were you really comfortable on the steamer? Was the fare good and suitable for you? Could you get the conveniences to apply thoroughly the treatment to your arm? What in *detail* is the present condition of your arm? (Remember if you *do* try the short-hand that Ed doesn't use the "reporters style.")¹

Speaking of that, Ed is in luck. Mr. Magie² has asked him to help him this summer rewrite Prof. Brackett's physics.³ The publishers for whom he does it, have allowed him money to pay a stenographer and he prefers Ed to a professional, because he will be more intelligent in the subject. He is to dictate to Ed two or three hours every morning & then he wants Ed to copy it on a typewriter. I take for granted you won't mind his using yours. Ed was apparently shy about asking me for it so Mr. Magie came to see me on the subject. Ed has written to the Hammond people for a ribbon for himself, & a book of instructions, since I did not know where yours was. He began work with Mr. Magie today.

Prof. Young⁴ has given Ed too the use of the telescope and he has been spending a good deal of time up there studying. He is as intelligent about it all as Russell.⁵ We have been there tonight with Miss Ricketts—didn't get back until ten. I didn't want to go on my letter night but it was the last chance to see Jupiter & Miss R. was eager for it. The result is a stupid letter, for I am quite tired, having been working hard all day. It is very hot at last, but still cool in the evenings,—and *such* moonlit nights, and such sunsets,—I never knew them finer.

There is *one* bit of news; they have begun work today on the street in front of the house and have cut down the *cherry-tree*. Such murder! I am watching like a dragon over the pine-tree. Good-night, my love, *my life*. I love you with my heart and my soul and my strength and my mind and my innermost being. "I am in every thought, in every heart-beat, always and altogether["]

Your own    Eileen.

We are all perfectly well.

Don't forget to write *somehow* to the Brooklyn Institute. They have written again urging a definite answer from you as soon as possible.[6] Don't know why,—they couldn't expect one yet. I told them before I had sent the other to you at once. This is the *only* letter you have had since I last wrote.

ALS (WC, NjP).

  [1] Edward Axson used the Corresponding Style of Graham shorthand, while Wilson used the abbreviated form known as the Reporting Style.

  [2] William Francis Magie, Professor of Physics.

  [3] William Arnold Anthony and Cyrus Fogg Brackett, *Elementary Text-book in Physics* (New York, 1884). The revision by Magie was the eighth edition (New York, 1897).

  [4] Charles Augustus Young, Professor of Astronomy.

  [5] Henry Norris Russell, '97, later a noted Professor of Astronomy at Princeton.

  [6] Ellen forwarded this letter. See EAW to WW, July 8, 1896.

## From Walter Hines Page

My dear Mr. Wilson,          [Charlemont, Mass.] 22 June 1896.

Wicked as you may be, I am sure that you are not wicked enough to deserve bombardment by work when you have gone away on purpose to escape just such things. Take assurance, for I do not come, as I have often done, seeking an article at once. I wish only to make a request that I meant to make before you went away ———ing.

It will be greatly to your advantage, and to ours if we have an *Atlantic* paper by you about the time that your book of essays is published. There is one subject that I tried to formulate in the old *Forum* days[1] which has come to me more clearly since I have had the laboring oar on the *Atlantic*, to get at, from different points of view, just what constitutes American nationality: what is a present-day justification of our national existence. This is

large and vague; but the particular approach to it that I wish to
call your attention to while you are abroad is this:

There is a passage in Jefferson's Letters (indeed I think that
he frequently wrote about the subject) wherein he draws a strong
contrast between the advantages of European residence and
American citizenship. With the fervid patriotism of his time and
especially of his nature, he makes the advantages and duties of
citizenship in the Republic stand out in very noble lines. I recall
(my Jefferson is not in my summer quarters where I write) one
passage that seemed to me years ago particularly stirring. That
for—a starting point, or something like that.

Now, your own observations as the basis of a corresponding
statement for the present. Since Jefferson's time life in the United
States has become very much fuller and richer in many ways.
Per contra the disadvantages (as he reckoned them) of European
residence have become less: government has become more liberal
almost everywhere and the individual (unless he be very low-
born or very poor-born) has chances such as only noblemen had
in Jefferson's day. But these changes on either side only add to
the fascination of the study. Have we kept the promise of the
early time to make an incomparable home for men?

Do not interpret what I write as asking for a paper during
your holiday or even as a request that you consciously think of
it while you are abroad, and this does not call for any reply till
you return. I mean merely to say that the *Atlantic* must have a
characteristic and significant paper by you in the early Autumn
when your book appears, and I submit this only as a suggestion.
And you will, perhaps, tell me, what you think of it when you
come home.[2]

A pleasant holiday!   Sincerely yours,   Walter H. Page

ALS (Houghton Mifflin Letterpress Books, MH).
  [1] In W. H. Page to WW, May 23, 1895.
  [2] See W. H. Page to WW, Nov. 21, 1896, Vol. 10.

## Four Letters to Ellen Axson Wilson

My own darling,        The Grand Hotel, Glasgow. 23 June, 1896

We have made the delightful run through the lochs and the
Trossachs, and start out in fine spirits on our wheels at last, to-
morrow morning (Wednesday) Mr. and Mrs. Woods wear extremely well, and are ideal companions under the circumstances.
He is, if anything, less strong than I am, and wants to travel by
as easy stages as I do; they have practically let me determine the
line of travel; and they are gentle and accommodating. What

more could I say? They are to sail for home again on the fifth of August and we must part before my outing is over; probably our paths will diverge in about three weeks, and I expect to miss them sadly. Mr. McSween has gone to visit his old home in the Hebrides, and it is hardly likely he will join Mr. and Mrs. Woods again while I am with them,—a fine man, but not so indispensable as the others.

'Twill be two weeks, almost, when we start to-morrow, since we landed. I had no idea the 'preliminaries' would detain us so long a time. And, dear me, how long it has *seemed*, not only by mind measure, because of novelty and variety, but also by heart measure, because of—something I can't safely write about. When I think about my darling this poor old left hand becomes more clumsy and uncertain than ever,—no doubt because it is on the heart's side. I can only say that this separation makes me more deeply and passionately than ever   Your own   Woodrow

Love to Mrs. B.


My own darling,     King's Arms Hotel, Dumfries. 26 June, 1896
    Here we are at the end of the third day of our bicycle tour. The first day we went from Glasgow to Ayr (33 miles), over excellent roads; the second day we started late and made only seventeen miles, partly because we turned aside to see the cottage in which Burns was born, "auld Alloway Kirk," and "auld Alloway brig" over which Tam O'Shanter rode; partly because the way was very stony and hilly—the only bad roads we have had; to-day we have ridden 35 miles with delight over splendid roads amidst the most engaging scenery, and are here in excellent spirits, very well, and not at all too tired. Another day's ride (of 34 miles) will bring us to Carlisle, dear mother's birth place, where we shall get our Sabbath rest, and where hope I shall find grandfather's church[1] and worship in it. I am enjoying the riding even more than I expected. We have been favored with extraordinarily fine weather, and the riding has been exhilarating beyond expression. My spirits rise with the work, and my companions are most agreeable. They send you their warm regards. Ah, my darling, how all this pleasure makes me pine for you; how everything beautiful reminds me of you, so beautiful yourself and such a lover of what is beautiful. I could almost cry sometimes for very longing, and for very pleasure, too, at my sweet visions of you, which these things bring. I am altogether and in everything your lover.

My appetite, digestion, and arm are in equally good frame.

Love to Mrs. B. and to Ed., kisses for the lassies, and for your-self the whole heart and life of       Your own   Woodrow

1 The Annetwell Street Congregational Church, of which the Rev. Thomas Woodrow was pastor from 1820 to 1835.

Great Central Hotel.

My own darling,                    Carlisle.  28 June, 1896

The 4th day's ride is over. We have made one hundred and twenty miles, and are taking our Sunday rest. It is astonishing with how little fatigue the thing can be done on these roads; and it is quite as exhilarating and entertaining as I expected. The sweet, quiet country, the hawthorn hedge-rows, the quaint road-side villages, the great gates of estates with their pretty lodges, the good natured, friendly people,—in Scotland (we have had only 8 miles of England as yet) the green slopes of the great hills,—all combine to make a great overmastering charm which itself makes the wheel run easily and with zest, as if to hurry from beauty to beauty.

I have had a considerable disappointment here. I cannot, after the most diligent enquiry, find out anything about grandfather's residence here, not even which church he was pastor of. I planned to spend Sunday here for the express purpose of attend-ing the church he had, and of seeing, if possible, the house in which dear mother was born,—but I have seen and learned nothing.

One of your precious letters,—the one written at the time of the arrival of my first cable message,—seems to have miscarried, love, and with it a letter from the Brooklyn Institute, I infer from a reference in your letters of the 15th. Of course Mr. Nolen will have to be told again that I cannot lecture on Monday or Tuesday evenings. How well you are attending to my letters, sweetheart. In all things it is the same: I don't know whether to love or to admire you the more. Your letters, Nell, are a tonic, a delight to me, as your sweet nature is. I am in a sense that at once comforts and exalts me       Your own   Woodrow

Love to Mrs. B. and all.

My own Eileen,                    [Rydal] 29 June, 1896

I must write you a little letter from this Wordsworth country (the tiny flower enclosed I plucked from a wall near Words-worth's cottage at Rydal Mount). Mr. Woods' wheel broke down last week, and he could not get refitted and ready for a new start from Carlisle till to-morrow. I came on alone, therefore, this morning to Keswick by train, and from K. rode on my wheel the 16 enchanting miles to this place, by Thirlmere, Grasmere, and Rydal Water. Mr. and Mrs. W. will rejoin me here to-morrow about noon, and while I am waiting for them I shall go back a few miles on the road I came to-day, to identify some places I missed,—Hartley Coleridge's "Nab Cottage," Dr. Arnold's "Foxe How,"[1] and Grasmere village, with its church and Wordsworth's grave, lying aside from the road. I declare I hardly have the heart to tell you of being in these places, knowing how you will yearn when you read of them, and how better *right* you have to see them than I have. I don't know how I shall ever describe what I am seeing, when I hold you in my arms again. One who knew nothing of the memories and the poems associated with these places might well bless the fortune that brought him to a region so complete, so various, so romantic, so irresistable in its beauty, —where the very houses seem suggested by Nature and built to add to her charm. I shall be haunted, and perpetually *hurt* by it all till I get *you* here,—and shall we ever get away again when I do?

I am perfectly well, and would be perfectly happy if only you were here!                    Your own   Woodrow

The usual messages and kisses uncounted for our precious ones.

ALS (WC, NjP).
[1] The summer home of Thomas Arnold and his son, Matthew Arnold.


## Two Letters from Ellen Axson Wilson

My own darling,                    Princeton June 29/93 [1896]
I have just sent the check to the Mutual down to the corner so that it will be sure to go tomorrow morning. I have got to take the eight o'clock train to Trenton with all the children bound for the dentist, so wouldn't wait till tomorrow to get it off. By the way the borough tax bill came today[1] and was an agreeable surprise, being only $39.00 for "real," "personal" and poll tax. The place is assessed at $7000, and the tax is only one half of one per cent. I feel quite relieved, because the man came soon after you left to ask what the house cost, and I was well scolded by Mrs. Ricketts afterwards for telling him the truth! She said I might have refused to answer at all; but I don't see what I should have gained by that since I am sure no one would suppose the

house cost *less* than it did. She also said the rate was nearly 2 per cent; so I have been trembling in my boots.

Your cable from Carlisle came yesterday and pleased me greatly. It sounded as if you were in fine spirits. Your letter from York reached me *Sat.*, only 7 days after it was mailed. Wasn't that quick work? I am *perfectly delighted* with the inscription.[2] It is the most charming thing of the sort I ever saw. It has given *me* already an *exquisite* pleasure, dear, and will give him the same. I was in a sort of flutter of delight over it all day Saturday.

By the way, the Adelphi Academy has just been turned into a *college*: connected with the University of New York. There was a long article about it in the "Tribune" the other day, which Mr. Hunt gave me. It had a nice notice of Stockton who it seems is one of the eight "full professors" of the *College*;—they are to keep an academic department.[3] I meant to send you the paper, but Mrs. Perry borrowed it to show her husband, they having some interest in the school. Carroll Perry[4] taught there this winter, filling temporarily the very vacancy for which Stockton is wanted.

We are all perfectly well still and prospering. We have had cold rains for several days but it was glorious again today,—cool and bright. We have had a great deal of rain this month and it has been fine for our grass. That at the back was planted just four weeks ago and the ground is already green with it; in two more weeks it will be as fine as the front. Are the Eng. lawns as superior to ours as we are led to suppose? And have you had a revelation as to the true meaning of the word "green"!

Was prevented writing till almost bedtime tonight, so am scribbling in great haste; must close now as I have an early start to make tomorrow. All send love, Mrs. Brown particularly. And I love you 'till it seems as though my heart must break with loving,—with the mere joy of it, and hurt of it combined.

Your little wife,    Eileen.

---

[1] The bill, dated June 20, 1896, and endorsed July 1, 1896, is in WP, DLC.

[2] That is, the dedication of *Mere Literature* to Stockton Axson, in WW to EAW, June 19, 1896.

[3] The article appeared in the *New York Tribune*, June 26, 1896. The "notice" of Stockton Axson was contained in a statement by Adelphi's president, Charles H. Levermore. As for the University of New York, Ellen was referring to the Board of Regents of the University of the State of New York, which had general supervision of the educational institutions of the state, including the power to grant charters of incorporation.

[4] A younger brother of Bliss Perry who was entering the Episcopalian ministry.

My own darling,                    Princeton, July 2/96

I fear my letter to you tonight is going to suffer because of Mrs. Purves! I had the temerity to run over after supper to see how she was, and simply *could* not get away, without absolute brutality, before 9 o'clock. And I have come back so sleepy I can scarcely see straight. She *is* the greatest curiosity; the children were telling me today, very innocently, how Mrs. Purves kept calling them to "come there a minute" and then would keep them such a long time talking that they were "afraid Mamma wouldn't like it." I asked what she talked about, and they said she asked them what they had for breakfast, and dinner, and supper, and told them what they had (!)

I have absolutely no news; there are not even any letters for you I am glad to say. Things are going quite smoothly and comfortably with us, and we are all *perfectly* well; the children seem to be becoming sturdy little romps, even Jessie. We hear of nothing but base-ball and tennis with the boys. The weather is still splendid, though a little warm in the heat of the day. The street is finished in front of the house and past Mr. Magie's,[1] and looks fine,—is very hard and good. It leaves our edge[,] beyond the boardwalk, looking sadly disreputable though.

Oh there *is* one bit of news, the second [Presbyterian] church had a meeting last night and elected Maitland Alexander, pastor.[2] It is however very doubtful if he will accept; but they are "not unhopeful."

I have had no further news from my darling since I last wrote, but am still enjoying the former letters. You don't know what a *great* comfort I take in those friends,—in feeling that you are not alone. How I *hope* you will be with them all the time. When do they return? You must be sure to make them promise to look in on us here before they go South, so that I may meet them. Ah me! It is hard not to envy Mrs. Wood the daily sight of you, dear! What wouldn't I give for a magic mirror in which I could follow you in every detail of your journey! I take great pleasure in *imagining* it all even. Oh it is so delightful to think of my dear hard-working darling having a perfect holiday at last! I like to think of you as getting light-hearted and "carrying on,"—the way you did in the Carolina Mts.![3] I love you dear,—ah *how* I love you! I believe I think of you literally *every* moment of the day.

Your little wife,   Eileen.

ALS (WC, NjP).

[1] At 58 Library Place.

[2] Pastor of the Presbyterian Church of Long Branch, N. J. He did not accept the Second Church's call.

[3] On their honeymoon in Arden, N. C., in 1885.

## To Ellen Axson Wilson

My own darling,                              York, 3 July, 1896

What an inexcusably careless, thoughtless brute I have been! I have just received the sweet, pathetic, heart-breaking letter in which you declare your unhappiness because my cablegram did not say I was well. I have no excuse, and don't know that I should be less unhappy and ashamed if I had. You will just have to esteem me less, as a fool. The truth is, I supposed I *had* said that I was well, simply because I was so well it seemed already a matter of course. I was withholding nothing: I should certainly have said so had I *not* been feeling well. Ever since the last four or five days of the voyage I have been feeling better and stronger every day, and my arm has been getting well as calmly and steadily as you please. I use it freely for everything but writing, and it gives me scarcely a twinge. I can do anything I like except lie on my right side.

I am not getting fat, because riding keeps the flesh down; and one or two days when the roads have proved rough or hilly I have over-exerted myself. But I am learning by experience, and shall not allow myself to be deceived again by the delightful sense of vigour that has come with this out-door life. To-day I am resting, and shall take the next stage of the journey by rail. I am feeling very well indeed, and recover from fatique very quickly and prosperously but I shall not again suffer myself to get excessively tired.

Really this out-of-door life is a delicious tonic, and I feel confident of getting strong by means of it. It enables me to do everything with facility except write with my left hand: that continues as tedious and labourous a task as ever, almost.

Ah, my Eileen, how I love you, for all I show it so ill. I do not deserve your love, but you must love me out of mere pity,—for I am irrevocably                    Your own    Woodrow

Love to Mrs. B. Of course Ed. may use the Hammond[.] The ivy leaves are from Dove Cottage.[1] The Brooklyn letter has not turned up.

ALS (WC, NjP).
[1] At Grasmere, where Wordsworth had lived.

## From Ellen Axson Wilson

My darling,                         [Princeton, N. J., July 3, 1896]

I wrote this person[1] that you could not possibly do anything about a syllabus,—at least until you get back to your books & MSS.

Also that you had some understanding with Miss Underhill[2] on the subject. But you see she insists on my forwarding the letter!

ALS written on Myrtilla Avery to EAW, July 2, 1896, TLS (WP, DLC). Enc.: Myrtilla Avery to WW, June 27, 1896, TLS (WP, DLC).
[1] Myrtilla Avery, "Director's Assistant" of the Extension Department, State Library, University of the State of New York in Albany, who had corresponded with Wilson (in letters that are missing) about giving a series of lectures at the Regents' Center in Sing Sing (now Ossining) in the autumn of 1896. About these lectures, see Anna Underhill to WW, Dec. 19, 1896, Vol. 10.
[2] Anna Underhill, secretary of the Regents' Center in Sing Sing.

## To Ellen Axson Wilson, with Enclosure

My own darling,          Woolpack Hotel, Warwick. 5 July, 1896

Here I am writing to my queen by candle light in a quaint inn at the heart of the Shakspere country. My heart burns with a keen remorse that I should be here without you,—in this inexpressibly beautiful region, where England is to be seen looking as I had dreamed it would look, and where memories crowd and haunt so as to fill the mind and heart to overflowing. My constant thought and longing for you do not spoil the pleasure for me exactly; they do not quite make me sad; they only seem to transmute all impressions into a tenderer and tenderer love for you, and my enjoyment is elevated into a sort of worship of you. What a setting for *you* this country would make, my sweet one, and how it would enrich one's imagination and give him individuality as a writer to live in this sweet Warwickshire! We have just come. We have seen nothing *but* the country, a glimpse of the ruins of Kenilworth, and one tower of the castle here; but the impression made by this exquisite land, after the comparatively bleak and arid north, is itself reward and joy enough, were there nothing else. Ah, how I wish I could write! Until now I have been homesick for *America*; here I am homesick (oh, how homesick!) only for you. Part of my desire for you is purely selfish. I enjoy things so much more *through* you than directly and of myself. I need you for completeness; seem to be short of faculties without you.

I am *very* well, sweetheart. My stomach and my arm give me next to no trouble at all. Sometimes when I forget and subject my arm to some muscular strain it resents it for the moment, but the rest of the time I am reminded of its disability only by the slight numbness of the ends of the first and second fingers. I feel more vigourous than I have felt for a very long while, and ride the greater part of the day with less fatigue than I have often felt at home after a ride of one third the length. In short, I feel that I am getting well. I am careful now not to overexert myself, and I can rest almost as rapidly as you can. Is not that a good report? I am getting so that I am scarcely conscious of my stomach once a week!

Since writing the above I have been to Stratford and to Anne Hathaway's cottage, and have had sensations which I cannot describe with this hand.

Will you not show the enclosed letter to West, dear, *and make him give it back to you*?

Please ask the Brooklyn people to write me again or to cable to the Bank address.[1] Your letter enclosing theirs seems hopelessly to have miscarried.

I love you with a supreme devotion, and am every day more than ever                              Your own    Woodrow

Love to dear Maggie, to Mrs. B., and Ed.—kisses innumerable to the chicks.

ALS (WC, NjP).
[1] The Cheque Bank, Ltd., 4 Waterloo Place, Pall Mall, London, S. W.

E N C L O S U R E

## From Frederic William Maitland

Dear Professor Wilson,    Stroud, Gloucestershire, 26 June 1896.

I fear that I must not allow this very pleasant dream to continue. I have been thinking long of the proposal that has come to me from Princeton through you. It is extremely attractive. I feel the honour keenly. I want to see America, but more especially an American university and law school. I owe much to what has been done in your schools and would gladly do what I could—it's little enough—towards repaying the debt. Then I can not but admit that your terms are magnificent. Add to all this that your own very great kindness[1] has made the project far pleasanter than it would otherwise have been. To decline so much hospitality goes (you will believe this) against the grain. And yet, when I reckon up the powers that I have at my command, decline I must. I will not trouble you with my woes, but to get through a term at Cambridge without neglecting the most obvious duties is just all that I can do, and I dare not undertake the voyage and the lectures at the very beginning of an academic year. Also I have been compelled so often to ask the indulgence of the Cambridge authorities that if I can help it I must not be absent during the week when all our courses begin.

I am sad as I write this letter. It is a confession of feebleness; but must be written. I trust that you will convey to Princeton

my warm thanks for the great honour[,] also that you will believe me to be in very truth

Yours gratefully   F. W. Maitland

ALS (WP, DLC).
    1 That is, Wilson's invitation to Professor and Mrs. Maitland to stay at his
home while in Princeton.

## Two Letters from Ellen Axson Wilson

My own darling                          Princeton July 7 [1896]
    I shall have to confine myself to a hasty note this morning, so
as not to miss the usual mail,—the half past ten. I was quite sick
yesterday and the night before with a sharp stomach attack,—
extreme nausea, &c., and so was too exhausted to write last night
as usual. But I am *all right* this morning except of course for a
little weakness. I think the heat and humidity caused it rather
than anything I ate. There is a decided change in the weather
now; cool and threatening rain. The rest are quite well.
    Your letter from Dumfries came yesterday and gave me more
than usual pleasure because of the keen enjoyment of your trip
it expresses. I can't tell you, darling, how *delightful* it is to me to
think of you as having such good times. I fairly gloat over every
word that expresses pleasure and satisfaction on your part. Am
so glad that your friends are such good companions. You can't
imagine what a comfort it has been to me to think that you were
with friends. So I am proportionally disappointed to learn that
you part from them so soon. What is their plan for their last three
weeks? Something I suppose that does not appeal to you. But
how I wish you *could* be with them as long as they *are* over there.
Give them my regards and *beg* them for my sake to run down to
Princeton before they go south. *How* good it would be to get such
a direct and full report from you!
    By the way, while I think of it, don't forget to be on the look-out
for a suitable and charming name for our house. There is no
news—and no letters. All goes smooth[l]y and well with us.
    I love you, dear, with every fibre of my being,—deeply, tenderly,
passionately, devotedly,—I am altogether

Your own   Eileen.

ALS (WP, DLC).

My own darling,                          Princeton, July 8/96
    The two *dear* little letters from Carlisle and Ambleside came
today, and my heart has been dancing with delight ever since.

That it should all be so lovely, even beyond your expectation, and that you should be evidently enjoying it so enthusiastically,—so deeply, gives me the most perfect and intense satisfaction conceivable. You dear, dear thing! I wish you could stay a year. The cable came yesterday with its splendid report of your health, so I am beyond measure happy about you today.

I am *perfectly* well,—have had no return whatever of my little attack of Monday. All the rest entirely well too. The children are excessively happy because of the whirl of gaiety in which they find themselves—a big party at the Raymonds day before yesterday, one at the Sloanes today, and one at the Paxtons, for the little Roberts girl,[1] tomorrow. Margaret took a prize at the Raymonds in some guessing match—a *beautiful* Watteau fan;—and it was pretty to see her delight. The other children too, I am glad to say, rose to the occasion, and made it a family triumph.

Speaking of "families" Mrs. Purves has a fine 12 pound boy,—born yesterday.[2] In spite of her tearful leave-takings of most of her friends, she got through in a very short time and without any trouble, and is doing nicely now. Another item of news is that Maitland Alexander has refused the call to the second church. Dr. Duffield[3] is entirely crushed and the rest of the people knocked all of a heap, for it seems he had led them all on to be pretty confidant; and they are wild to get him because he is rich and can support himself! It seems they are not going to offer anyone more than a thousand. In that case, say I, they don't need us to help pay it.[4] I shouldn't like to commit myself to listening "es a constantcy" to a thousand dollar man,—at least not until we found a Presbyterian order of begging friars to serve our churches.

Another bit of news very satisfactory to me is that Ed's report is in today and he not only made *first* group for the *year*, but also first group in every separate subject,—Eng., Philosophy,—all! He really must have done splendidly this half, to so make up lost ground in the first half of the year.

I told you, did I not? that Madge also took first honour in every subject in her school, leading her class. So I am a very proud sister. I am so sorry you won't see her at all;—for her school opens the 8 of Sept. She is really *charming*, has the dearest little "ways." Mrs. Hibben says she is perfectly fascinating and is destined to make the most tremendous "tear" as a young lady. But such ideas are as far as possible from her head at present. She is wild to go to college when she finishes in Athens.

I am sorry the Brooklyn Inst. letter was lost. Mr. Hooper is probably tearing his hair with impatience. I wrote to him at once this morning & gave him your Bank address so you will doubtless hear from him. He wanted you to deliver another course of six lectures for $300.00. I told him you couldn't, as you would have no time to prepare new ones and had given there the only *long* courses you had. But he refused to take *my* word for it! Also he wanted you to deliver one of their "special addresses," fee $100.00, to be prepared especially for them, though it might afterwards be delivered elsewhere. I told him I could not answer so positively as to it, but did not think you would have time. I told him you had one—"Democracy,"[5] that was just the thing. Perhaps if he found he couldn't get a new one he might take it. I wish you would deliver "Democracy" at the summer meeting of the University Ex. Soc. in Cambridge in Aug. Then perhaps you *could* stay forever in the country with which you have fallen so in love(!) The meeting is from July 30 to Aug. 24.

But it is quite late,—I *must* stop. It was so hot that I was tempted to stay in the piazza too long before beginning.

With a heart brim full & running over with a perfect ecstasy of love for my darling I am as ever

His own   Eileen.

ALS (WP, DLC) with WWhw notations, addresses, and figures on env.

[1] Professor and Mrs. George Lansing Raymond, Professor and Mrs. William Milligan Sloane, and the Rev. Dr. and Mrs. William Miller Paxton. The "little Roberts girl" is unknown to the Editors.

[2] George Tybout Purves, Jr.

[3] John Thomas Duffield, D.D., Dod Professor of Mathematics at Princeton.

[4] The Wilsons, who still retained membership in the First Congregational Church of Middletown, Conn., had obviously discussed formally uniting with the Second Presbyterian Church of Princeton. They took this step on May 5, 1897.

[5] It is printed at Dec. 5, 1891, Vol. 7.


## Two Letters to Ellen Axson Wilson

My own darling,        Wilberforce Hotel, Oxford. 9 July, 1896.

We 'lay' last night in Woodstock, partly for the name of it, partly because we wanted to sleep at a quiet country inn, partly because it was on our road and we were too tired to go the remaining 8 miles to Oxford. We reached here about lunch time to-day, and have had only the afternoon to look about us, but, dear me, a mere glance at Oxford is enough to take one's heart by storm. It's true we went at once to Magdalen, the most beautiful of the colleges, but we saw within the quads of others too, and it is what nature as well as art has done for the incomparable place that has taken us captive. I have seen as much that made me feel alien as that made me feel at home since I came to England, and have been made on the whole to love Am. more rather than less,—for all Eng. is so bonny and so full of treasure for the mind and fancy,—but Oxford! Well, I am afraid that if there were a place for me here Am. would see me again only to sell the house and fetch you and the children,—and yet I have not seen a prettier dwelling than ours in Eng!

I am still in excellent shape, darling, stomach, arm, and all. My friends say they never saw anyone improve more in appearance within the same space of time than I have improved since they first met me on the steamer. It may be partly the colour the sun has given me but it's not all that.

I love you with all my nature, and am getting well to be more than ever                     Your own   Woodrow.

Love to Mrs. B. and all.

ALS (WC, NjP).


My own darling,      The Market Hotel, Winchester. 13 July, '96
The weather is very hot and a short ride in the heat has made me feel a little badly in my midst: it is the more extraordinary, therefore, that I have an *excellent* report to make about my stomach. The funnel of my syphon was broken just after I reached this side, and until to-day I had not been able to use it since about 2 weeks ago. I have taken two or three glasses of hot water every day instead,—morning and evening and just after riding—and when I emptied my stomach just now there was nothing at all in it but a very little mucous. It was clearer than I've ever seen it. Isn't that jolly? The disturbance in my midst is a trifle, and my arm is perfectly comfortable. Doesn't that report satisfy you?

Oxford is so compact that it proved possible to see what we chiefly wanted to see much more quickly than we had supposed, and so we came on here, by easy stages over the chalk downs. It was hard to leave Oxford: its fascination is extraordinary; but I can go back if I wish, after I have looked up Mr. Bryce in London and plied him again with the invitation to lecture for us next October. My friends must leave me presently, for their time is nearly up. They sail Aug. 5th and must see both London and Paris first. After they leave me I shall move about much more slowly, and probably stay a good while in some one place. I shall mind being left alone the less because I may now be much surer of keeping well and able to take care of myself; and I could not be more homesick than I am,—more hopelessly

Your own    Woodrow.

Love to Mrs. Brown and all, kisses for the bairns.

ALS (WP, DLC).


## Two Letters from Ellen Axson Wilson

My own darling,                                    Princeton, July 13/96

Your cable from Winchester came duly to hand this afternoon and was right welcome. The last word in it miscarried in some way; nobody knows what it is. I went down and asked the agent what he meant by it, for it was no word at all. He said he had supposed it was a cypher, but it *might* be "prosperous." Of course I had feared it was the name of some place to which I was to send my letters, that he had gotten wrong. But he assures me, it *couldn't* be a place; so I shall send this to the bank again.

You seem to be making great progress in your journeyings. I wonder what your route was from York to Warwick. I hope by Lincoln and Peterborough Cathedrals. And of course you go to Canterbury from London. Do you go back to Cambridge? If you do you will see Ely won't you? I suppose from your turning back from Salisbury to London that you mean to go to Somerset and Devon after your friends leave you? Have you been through any "great house" yet? Pray do;—don't be too proud! It must be great fun.

Stockton came over for Sunday—left last night, being very busy with the summer meeting. He is going to Clifton[1] the first of Aug. for six weeks, "if he can stand it." He seems to be in a very good humour with his new place now. He is left so absolutely free to do what he chooses in his department. You know both Academy and the new College are co-educational; and Stock is wild to have Madge there with him. So we have settled it between us that she is to go a year from this fall. Won't it be *splendid* for her?—to be with Stock and have all the advantages of the city and the college both. It seems to me almost as fortunate for her that Stockton is going there, as it was for Ed that you came here.

By the way, I meant but hadn't time when writing then two weeks ago—when I first read it over, to tell you how *delighted* I was with "Article No. 4."[2] It was the first time I had read it to myself, you know, and it seemed to me really *perfect*; to need no expansion, or *anything*;—so clear, so strong, so *adequate*;—

and in just and harmonious arrangement and proportion of parts, superb,—a perfect whole. What reminded me of it now is that Stockton liked it so much and that Mr. Perry is so enthusiastic over it. I told him you feared it needed expansion. He said the trouble with all the other accounts of it he had ever read was that there were too many details; "you couldn't see the forest for the trees." Yours had given him the clearest and the most impressive idea of it as a mighty whole, that he had ever had. Indeed, dear, there is something really epic in your treatment of it.

But there is another letter that must be written tonight so I must close. We are all perfectly well. Your letter from York came Sat., only eight days after it was written. I have been vexed with myself, dear, ever since I got over my panic at that time for writing the letter of which you speak. I wish *it* had been the one to get lost. It seems peculiarly atrocious somehow to indulge ones "feelings" or anxieties so in a letter that is to cross the ocean,—to prepare worries for another person *weeks ahead*!

Everybody sends love and shows genuine delight at the good reports from you. And as for me I am as happy as the day is long thinking of them. Oh how I *do love* you darling!—and *admire* you! I am sure you can have no idea how proud and happy you make me, and in how many ways. Scarce a day passes that does not bring me some pure and fresh and perfect pleasure derived directly from the fact that you are mine and I am

Your own    Eileen.

ALS (WC, NjP).
¹ Clifton Springs in the Finger Lakes area of New York.
² "General Washington," *Harper's Magazine*, xciii (July 1896), 165-90.

My own darling,                              Princeton, July 16/96
I suppose you are now in London. I wonder how you are enjoying it, and how long you will stay. I rather fancy you will miss the bicycling through the beautiful country lanes and will be eager to get back to it again. Alas! you will now be parting from your friends, unless either your plans or theirs have changed. How I hate to think of you as all alone. Would you like me to furnish you with a companion for your last two weeks? Rose's husband, Mac Dubose,¹ sails for Eng. with *his* wheel the first of Aug. They have all been sick this summer, and his church is now sending him for rest and change. Rose has written me questioning me about your plans, as Mac is "longing for a congenial companion." I wish I knew whether or not you feel a corresponding longing rising in your breast! In the old days I not only liked

but loved "Mac"—he was such a perfect gentleman; and extremely sensible too, and manly. How far ecclesiasticism has in the meantime set its mark upon his spirit I have no means of knowing. How would you like to make your Devon tour with him? I sent Rose your London address last night and asked him to write to you there upon his arrival, so that you could if convenient meet at least. Of course Rose and I would like our husbands to be friends,—and we would also be more comfortable, decidedly, to know that those precious posessions were not knocking about the world "all by their lane."

Florence [Hoyt] left on Monday for Rome [Ga.], and I miss her a great deal. She is the sort of person no one could help liking who took the trouble to know her. Sweet, sensible and sympathetic,—and quiet without being dull,—a thoroughly *restful* person to have about. She left before she was really well enough for the journey; but they are so anxious about their mother that she was ready to take almost any risk to get there.[2]

We are all perfectly well and enjoying ourselves. The weather has been rather warm, but is delicious now. I have been going to the college to draw for the last three days; but won't go tomorrow, as the children and I are to take dinner at the [John Howell] Westcotts at one o'clock.

Good-night, my precious one. It is high time I stopped talking to you, and began *dreaming* about you. I have had the luck to do that often of late, to my great delight. I would I could offer some oblation on the altar of the dream-god that would enable me to do it *every* night and all night long; there is nothing like dreaming for cheating time and space. With love unspeakable, believe me, darling, as ever          Your little wife,   Eileen.

ALS (WC, NjP).
[1] The Rev. McNeely Dubose, rector of Trinity Church, Asheville, N. C.
[2] Her mother, Florence Stevens (Mrs. William Dearing Hoyt), who died on October 2, 1896.


## Two Letters to Ellen Axson Wilson

My own darling,
                                        The Covent Garden Hotel,
                                        London, W. C. 16 July, '96

Here I am in London, and I'm not a bit glad to get here, *so thoroughly do I hate* a big city. But of course I felt that I must see the place, and I came with my friends (who must see it now or not at all) in order to avoid the intolerable loneliness of being here alone. We have only just arrived, so that I have no impressions, beyond a more intense desire than ever to be at my own sweet home. I shall ride about the city on the tops of 'buses, to get the 'look' of the huge thing, but shall see as few specific objects as possible, besides the abbey, the Museum, the National Gallery, and the House of Commons. After London is safely done with, and my friends off for Paris, I shall make my way up to Cambridge again, to see if the summer school is in progress. Thence I shall go (by rail, no doubt) to Chester, to ride thence along the borders of Wales down into Somerset and Devon. And then, I fervently hope, it will be time to start for home. That seems more and more every day the goal I am yearning and straining towards! Not because I am not enjoying myself,—for I am, intensely; but because I seem every day to realize more acutely my separation from you,—and your love and companionship constitute my happiness,—you are, in some literal sense, the light of my life. Ah, what unutterable thoughts I do have of you, my Eileen,—with how intolerable a longing am I

Your own   Woodrow

I am quite well, but very tired to-night. Love to Mrs. B. and all.

The Covent Garden Hotel,

My own darling,                     London, W. C. 20 July, 1896

Now I feel guilty indeed: I have been long in the National Gallery, and all the while with the feeling strong upon me to sadness that the Rembrandts, Rubenses, Reynoldses, Gainsboroughs, Turners, Titians, and the rest that I was seeing *belonged to you*, and that I was a selfish thief to take sight of them without you. The feeling isn't temporary with me; it is all the while in my heart. I do not know that I try to throw it off, tho. it saddens me. It is just the uppermost part of the love upon which I live, that supreme love for you which has brought everything that [is] bright and ennobling into my life. I can't afford to be selfish thus alone any more: it's too uncomfortable.

I have not looked up many specific things in London yet. You know how poor a hand I am at systematic sight seeing,—how I hate it, and how it tires me. But I have gotten a very vivid impression of London externally, have realized it, and felt its singular charm

I am to breakfast with Mr. Bryce on Wednesday, to urge the Princeton lectureship upon him again. He is so busy just now that I have not seen him yet, and a breakfast hour, it seems, is the only time he could name for an interview. I must take what I can get, I suppose.[1]

Life in a city hotel is making me feel a little stale again, tho. I am still uncommonly well and strong, and I shall be delighted to get afield and on my wheel once more—and I hope to do so by Thursday next, at latest.

I have urged Mr. and Mrs. Woods to stop over at Princeton, but I am afraid they are not likely to do so. Tho. they are together, they seem almost as eager to get home as I am; and if the steamer arrives conveniently for the train they want to take they will certainly take it at once. Otherwise they may visit you between trains, for they evidently like the idea very much.

The letter which brought the news of your sharp trouble with your stomach filled me with a sadness I could not shake of[f], my precious one; but this sweet, gay one that has followed it has fairly set my heart singing again, and I have gone about my sight seeing with as light spirits as I have had yet. The breadth of the Atlantic does not seem to diminish a whit the direct force with which you act upon me, my queen,—I am *altogether*

Your own   Woodrow

Love to dear Maggie and Ed., to the chics, and to Mrs. B.

ALS (WC, NjP).
[1] Bryce did not accept Wilson's invitation to be a Sesquicentennial lecturer.

## From Ellen Axson Wilson

My own darling,                         Princeton, July 21/96

I am obliged to write in a very great hurry this morning to catch the early mail because Uncle Tom[1] was here and I could not without rudeness leave him to write last night. He has just left on the 9.38. He appeared quite unexpectedly on Sat. evening, and we have had a very pleasant little visit from him. He was in an extremely genial mood; indeed it was really funny, the effervescence of enthusiasm into which he worked himself over all of us. I think it was finding Madge, whom he had never seen before, so unusually charming and pretty, that started him off. His heart seemed to melt within him at sight of her:—"the little gazelle"! And indeed there is some thing about the young thing to move the heart and the imagination, something of poetry and ideality. And then Ed is a "perfect wonder," so strong and complete in mind, body and character; and "there never was such a young man as Stockton";—and as for me he almost equalled *you* in the nonsense he managed to talk on that subject! It will be surprising if he hasn't left a very conceited family behind him!

Your dear letter from Oxford came yesterday, the one from Warwick Sat. and both were read with *delight*. It is *so* good to see the charm and the pleasure in it all constantly growing with you. How glad I am that you began in the north, so that the effect will be cumulative. And you must not vex your heart, my darling, because *I* can't see it too; you really don't know what an intense pleasure I am taking in your pleasure. I don't see how I *could* be happier if I were there than I am when I read these expressions of delight in your letters. And for *me* ever to take such a trip is so absolutely out of the question that I am not even conscious of an active wish to do so.

> "We will not see it, will not go
> Today nor yet tomorrow.
> Enough if in our *hearts* we know
> There's such a place as Yarrow."[2]

We are all perfectly well and getting on beautifully,—With a heart brimming over with love

Your little wife,    Eileen.

ALS (WC, NjP).
[1] The Rev. Dr. Thomas Alexander Hoyt of Philadelphia, maternal uncle of Ellen.
[2] William Wordsworth, "Yarrow Unvisited."

## Ellen Axson Wilson to Albert Shaw

My dear Mr. Shaw,          Princeton, New Jersey. 22 July, 1896.
    Mr. Wilson is at present on a bicycle tour in England, leaving me in charge of his correspondence.

He does not return until the 10th of Sept., and would not therefore be able to prepare the article[1] in time. I am sure he will be extremely sorry, for it is manifestly of the greatest importance to the college that articles such as you describe should appear in the leading magazine this fall. But of course you can get someone else to do it. Either Prof. Sloane or Prof. West would do it finely, but I believe the former is also on his travels. Prof. West (A. F. West) is still in Princeton. So too is Prof. Bliss Perry, one of our best writers, though as a newcomer he is not as familiar with the subject as some others. George Wallace, one of our graduates who has written a book on Princeton,[2] would do it extremely well. He lives in either Pittsburg or Alleghany. Then there is Jesse Williams, a clever writer whose "Princeton Stories"[3] have been so successful. I do not know his address; it could be gotten through the Scribners. I trust that my great interest in the subject will excuse my venturing upon these suggestions. It occurred to me that they might possibly be of service to you, your time for making arrangements being so short.

With sincere regards in which I should like to include Mrs. Shaw, I am                    Yours very truly,    Ellen A. Wilson

TCL (in possession of Virginia Shaw English).
  [1] For the New York *Review of Reviews*, of which Shaw was the editor.
  [2] George Riddle Wallace, *Princeton Sketches. The Story of Nassau Hall* (New York, 1893). Wallace was a member of the Class of 1891.
  [3] Jesse Lynch Williams, *Princeton Stories* (New York, 1895). Williams was a member of the Class of 1892.


## From Ellen Axson Wilson

My own darling,                                        July 23/96
    I am having hard luck, it seems, in getting my letters written at the proper time. Prof. Smith[1] came in just as I had finished with the children and spent the evening! It is now half past ten; and I fear the result will be a hurried and unsatisfactory letter.
    Speaking of letters here is one from Mr. Shaw wanting an article by you on Princeton for the Sept. number; to be fully illustrated.[2] I hope he will get some one else; as of course it is important to the college that such articles should appear this fall. Of course I wrote and told him you could not do it. Wrote the same also to "The Journal," who wants an article from you for a series entitled, "The Battle of the Standards."[3] I wonder if you are fortunate enough to escape temporarily from all knowledge or thought of American politics. I have purposely refrained from all mention of them, hoping that such might be the case. But this last blow to the good cause,—the death of Ex-Governor Russell,[4] is enough to force a cry of dismay from anyone under any circumstances. The one to whom everyone's thoughts seemed to turn as the natural leader in such a crisis as the present! Mr. Whitney speaks[5] with wonder of his wisdom and courage, his firmness, his perfect temper and cheerfulness[,] his clear-sightedness and quickness of mind[,] his eloquence, not of the impassioned but of the persuasive and illuminating sort, and above all of his elevation of character and perfect disinterestedness. What a combination of qualities for the leader of an almost desperate cause like that of the "true Democracy,"—one that offers absolutely no prizes at present to self-seekers! What a mystery that he should be *dead*—at thirty-nine! Milton's lines come into mind instinctively—
                "For Lycidas is dead,—dead ere his prime
                Young Lycidas, and hath not left his peer.["][6]
    We are all perfectly well, as usual, and are having glorious weather. We are getting on nicely in every respect and are very happy. Mrs. Sloane called this afternoon; and you ought to have

heard us rejoicing together over the absence of our husbands!
It seems she has been frightened about him too, as he seemed
about to break down from overwork. He sailed only last week
with his girl and boy for company,—returns the last of Sept.

The lost letter from Carlisle came from the Dead letter office
Tuesday. It contained also Mr. Hinton's letter of introduction
to his brother-in-law.[7] It's too late now to make it worth-while
re-enclosing.

No other letter of importance unless Lottie Woodrow's wedding
invitation can be so described. She marries next Thursday at
"high noon."[8]

By the way I didn't have time to tell you before how intensely
enthusiastic Uncle Tom was over Washington No. 4.

But I must close. Good-night my dear, dear love;—somehow
it makes you seem a bit closer to simply say "good-night." Ah
how I *love* you, *love* you *love* you!     Your own     Eileen.

The letter from the Dead letter office was directed to Mrs. Eileen
Wilson!

ALS (WC, NjP).
  [1] See EAW to WW, June 4, 1896, n. 8.
  [2] This enclosure is missing.
  [3] This letter is missing.
  [4] William Eustis Russell, Governor of Massachusetts, 1891-94, and a leading
gold Democrat and supporter of President Cleveland, died on July 16, 1896.
  [5] She is paraphrasing William Collins Whitney's statement made to the New
York newspapers upon hearing the news of Russell's death. See the *New York
Times*, July 17, 1896.
  [6] These lines from Milton's "Lycidas" were quoted in an editorial on the
death of Russell in *ibid*.
  [7] Charles Howard Hinton, Instructor in Mathematics.
  [8] Mary Charlotte Woodrow, daughter of the Rev. Dr. James Woodrow, was
married to Melton Clark, a student at the Columbia Theological Seminary, on
July 30, 1896.


## Two Letters to Ellen Axson Wilson

My own darling,          Royal Hotel, Slough [c. July 23, 1896]
   You must know that this is not Bunyan's Slough of Despond,
but a neat and cheerful village near Windsor. I left London this
afternoon, having had quite enough of it for the present. I did
not take my wheel into the huge place, but left it at Windsor.
I reclaimed it there this afternoon, and rode over here to make
a small beginning on my circuitous ride to Cambridge, which
will take me, no doubt, till Wednesday next, the 29th. My plan
is, to be in Beaconsfield on Sunday, and attend service in the
church in which Burke is buried, taking the high-road to Cambridge from the neighbouring High Wycombe on Monday. The

somewhat roundabout route I have chosen will take me through Tring and Luton, two places connected with the history of Washington's family, just before the emigration to America.

I have not yet made up my mind what I shall do when I get to Cambridge. I shall get there two or three days before the Summer School opens, and shall be able to look the ground over,— see what sort of men are to be engaged, what the plans are, of how much consequence the thing is to be, etc.,—and be governed by what I find out. I *may* want to remain *incog.*

I feel very lonely, of course, without Mr. and Mrs. Woods, and shall no doubt be haunted by recollections of their good qualities and kind companionship for some time to come; but there is a sense of freedom, too. All the timidity which I felt about this sort of travelling at first has worn off. I can set my own pace, and follow my own daily whim more completely. I can do more resting and less touring—and that is much. I am quite well, and in every pulse                    Your own   Woodrow

My own darling,                              [Tring] 26 July, 1896
I begin this letter on a Sunday afternoon at the "Rose and Crown" inn, Tring, county Herts, having ridden further than I expected yesterday. I reached Beaconsfield yesterday forenoon, and was not long in finding what I was in search of. Burke is buried in the church, and with him not only his son and his wife (who survived him more than twenty years) but also his brother Richard. There is a simple, a very simple, tablet in the wall of the plain church, recording the fact of burial without comment or sentiment,—that is all. In the churchyard stands a somewhat elaborate monument to the poet Waller. The local policeman of the quaint village pointed that out readily enough but did not know where Burke was buried.

Tring is "the usual thing" in the way of an English village, but has a rather unusual church, worth seeing, and is proving, with its sufficiently comfortable inn, a restful Sabbath-day haven. I do not find any distinct traces of the Washingtons; but I did not expect to. I only wanted to get the look of the country into my mind's eye; and certainly it was worth seeing. It ought surely to have bred a poet. Just here it is as beautiful as Warwickshire.

The day before I left London, darling, I ordered an engraving sent to you, by mail, which was absolutely the only copy I could find in all that great city of Leonardo's cartoon of St. Anne and the Virgin which you love so much. I spent an entire day (or, rather, two half days) in the search,—and never did I enjoy anything more, for all I failed to find just what I wanted. The whole business seemed to connect me so directly with you, that I was happier than I've been since I broke my life off leaving you! The engraving does not satisfy me: no line engraving could reproduce the soft beauty of the original; but I hope you will not be wholly disappointed. The cartoon is very large,—about four feet by three, I should say,—and is altogether the most beautiful thing I saw in London. I could hardly stand looking at it without you! It's a comfort to get away from the London galleries because of such feelings.

Now that I am alone I find that my life seems wholly to consist of thoughts of you, my Eileen; and I don't know just how long I can bear that. One month from to-morrow,—it will be only three weeks, about, when you read this,—I shall sail for home: ah, how I wish the Anchor Line boats were faster,—and the days, too, that separate us. All the time from now till I have you safe in my arms again will be a time of conscious waiting.

I finish, darling, on Tuesday, the 28th, in Cambridge, whither good roads have brought me more than twenty-four hours sooner than I expected. I arrived this morning, and have already looked over the programme of the summer meeting of the University Extension Society. The university really has no official connexion with it at all, and its list of lecturers has hardly a name upon it of more than local repute. They are 'staff' lecturers and young men 'on the make,' for the most part, apparently. Mr. Churton Collins[1] is the greatest light amongst them; and most of them I never heard of before. The subjects, besides, hardly come within hailing distance of me. It would really be too bad to miss the sweet country, and my good steed, which I love more and more the more I ride, for such an affair, and I think I shall be off to-morrow or next day.

I shall be very glad indeed to arrange a meeting with Mr. DuBose, but whether we can make our plans chime or not remains to be seen.

I am very well; and love you and yearn for you as

Your own   Woodrow

Love to Mrs. B. and all the dear ones

ALS (WC, NjP).
[1] John Churton Collins, English author and literary critic; a famous lecturer on literary subjects for the London University Extension Society and the Oxford Extension Society.

## From Ellen Axson Wilson

My own darling,                    Princeton, N. J., July 27/96

To think it is just a month today before you sail for home! After all time does pass, even when we are separated! I am even sorry to think that the return is so soon; how I wish you could stay until Oct., at least! though to be sure, judging from your last letter, you do not second the wish. I was sorry to find such a strong note of home-sickness in that letter, dear love; you did not seem nearly so happy as in those that have gone before. But doubtless it was a passing mood, the effects of fatigue,—and *London.* One always feels lonely and sad on one's first arrival in a great, strange, city. Am *so* glad your friends were still with you there. And I am sure you will have a charming time in Devon and Somerset. Arn't you going to Canterbury and some other cathedrals before starting west? That reminds me of Mr. Dubose. I am expecting him here on Wednesday or Thursday for a few hours on his way to N. Y. to take the steamer. He is going to write to you at your Bank address when he reaches London and see if he can manage to meet you.

Ed goes to N. Y. tomorrow to try and find a bargain in bicycles for Madge. She is wild for one, and it seems he wrote to Uncle R.[1] asking for one for her; so today a letter came saying that if he could get one for $50.00 or $55.00 she could have it. So they are all excitement over it. Stockton comes the latter part of the week to spend a few days before going to Clifton,—where he has really decided to remain for six weeks. IIe is going to to [*sic*] leave his wheel here for Ed to use.

A letter came today to me from *your* Uncle too (Dr. Woodrow)[2] apologizing for not answering your letter. He has been ill for a month, he says, but is getting well now. He sent no addresses of the Scotch kin, evidently thinking it too late now.

Another letter received last week is one of twelve pages from Mrs. Frémont,[3] daughter, you know, of Thos. H. Benton, and now an old lady of seventy-two. The letter consists mainly of an interesting though irrelevant history of her *grandmother,*—who was a Gooch, niece of the Va. governor.[4] She doesn't herself know much about "the Goochs" and her object in writing is to find out what *you* know and where you learned it! She is much fascinated by your phrase "gentlest of Marlborough's generals";[5]—and no wonder; it is one of those touches of yours, inimitable, though suggesting Macaulay, which makes your narrative, however short, seem so full of detail, so rich in colour, so crowded with varied and vivid sources of interest, so stimulating to the imagination. I myself felt a keen curiosity about Sir William Gooch whenever I read that chapter and meant to ask you about him, but never had time, being always hurried breathlessly on to a hundred other interesting points.

Prof. Smith lent me the new "Life of Dr. McCosh"[6] and I am reading it now with extreme interest. It seems quite well done,— as a life of "the Doctor";—there is not much of "Jimmie" in it,—nothing about his eccentricities; no good stories. But perhaps the gleaners will come after and give us another, less stately volume, of "McCoshiana"! There are some funny things in it though. Here are two good things in one sentence, the first part of it being something of a joke on *you*, sir, in your former editorial capacity.[7] "The 'Princetonian' some years ago was in the way of attacking the faculty. Now it is conducted in the most admirable spirit, ( ! )—only it gives more space to gymnastics than to literature. 'Pray,' said an Oxford Don to me, after reading several numbers, 'are you the president of a gymnastic institution?' "

I have just now been reading an interesting chapter about his foreign travels, with a really charming account of his intercourse with Humboldt and Bunsen. Humboldt at eighty-nine was learning his thirtieth language, "to keep his mind from failing."

We are all *perfectly* well; are still having really glorious weather. There has been a heavy thunder-storm this afternoon, but that too was agreeable.

I wish I knew more certainly where to send this! That last cable gave no instructions.

Goodnight, dear, dear love, "Thou art the very life of me." I am in every thought,—in every heart-throb,

Your own    Eileen.

ALS (WC, NjP).
    [1] Her uncle, Randolph Axson, of Savannah.
    [2] This letter is missing.
    [3] Jessie Benton Frémont to WW, c. July 15, 1896, ALS (WP, DLC) with WWhw on env.: "Ans. Mrs. Frémont."
    [4] Anne Gooch Benton, daughter of James Gooch, the younger brother of Sir William Gooch.
    [5] "In Washington's Day," *Harper's Magazine*, xcii (Jan. 1896), 189.
    [6] William Milligan Sloane (ed.), *The Life of James McCosh: A Record Chiefly Autobiographical* (New York, 1896).
    [7] That is, when Wilson was managing editor of *The Princetonian*, 1878-79.

## To Ellen Axson Wilson

Suffolk Hotel,
My own darling,          Bury St. Edmund's, 29th July, 1896
    I begin this epistle as above, in the ancient and celebrated town

of St. Edmund's Bury, in the county of Suffolk. The place does not, I admit, lie on the road from Cambridge to Ely, for which latter place I this afternoon set out, according to my cablegram; but they charge double for a word or name of more than ten letters, and St. E. B. had to be left out of the telegram from motives of economy. I meant all the while to come here; and, from the hasty glance around which I took this afternoon, I fancy it is as well worth seeing as any place I have been yet, except, no doubt London and Oxford and Cambridge. They are more various; but I doubt if any place has a character or flavour more thoroughly its own than this has.

The 30th: I am kept at 'Bury' this morning by rain and cannot even get out to see again the splendid ruins I saw for a little last evening in the twilight. But I am not impatient. The place somehow contents me. I shall doubtless see what I most wish to see again this afternoon, and get some part of my way to Ely. It does not rain very hard or very persistently here. I can understand why Shakspere said "*the* gentle rain from heaven" and not *a* gentle rain.

I have got to loving the open country amazingly and hating towns very heartily, so wholesomely does this life on the wheel work upon me; but Bury somehow does not seem like other towns. No doubt, too, an improved digestion and a general access of vigour has bettered my disposition and cleared my temper. Inaction at least gives opportunity for quiet thoughts of you, and there's solace in that, now sailing day is no longer so very far off!

It stopped raining about noon; I saw what I wanted to see; and an afternoon's ride of twenty-nine miles over the level 'fens' has brought me to Ely. The roads were wet and a bit trying, but the look of the country after the rain,—and in the rain,—repaid me. Once and again as I rode there came a little shower, from which a wayside tree would entirely shelter me, and I would see the fields smile brightly through it. It was charming. This flat country is tame in many respects, but not in the colour of its fields or in the splendid trees that adorn it everywhere.

I saw the cathedral loom up when I was six miles away, and a most gracious and al[l]uring landmark it made. Now I sit in a room from the window of which one can, when it is light, look straight up at the noble pile over the roofs of a few low houses.

Friday evening, the 31st., at the Angel Inn, corner Narrow and priestgate sts., Peterborough. I attended service in the cathedral at Ely this morning, and then a ride of twelve miles before lunch and 17 after lunch brought me to Peterborough, my way lying much of the distance across the great "Bedford Level" of which I never heard before. The country looked for all the world like pictures of Holland. For some miles the road ran upon the top of an embankment which kept a "river" on its side, as another embankment did on the other, from overflowing the flats about it. The river was really a great drain or canal, embanked to reclaim the fens on either side. It ran in straight lines like a canal. The rich fields of grain beyond its dykes looked like those within the dunes at Sagg;[1] and great windmills like those on Long Island stood in a row along the sides of the sluggish stream.

I shall take the train for Chester after seeing the cathedral here in the morning. I want to set out from there early on Monday to make my way down the borders of Wales to Bristol, and so into Somerset and Devon.

To-morrow August begins, and I shall feel as if I were nearing the end of my exile from you: I may then venture to think deliberately a little how passionately I am

Your own   Woodrow.

Love to Mrs. B. and to all. Best wishes always to the servants. I am feeling quite well and jolly.

ALS (WC, NjP).
  [1] Sagaponack, Long Island, where the Wilsons had gone for summer vacations.


## From Ellen Axson Wilson

My own darling,                              Princeton, July 30/96

For the first time this summer it is rather unpleasantly hot, though now, with the evening, has come a cool breeze. I have been tempted to stay in the hammock on the upstairs piazza, getting cool and "rested," much too late I fear; have left little time for writing tonight; must try and do it early in the morning instead, for I have made myself tired with painting, &c. and can't sit up late.

I did finally, when I had almost despaired of such a consummation, get through with my sewing some three weeks ago; and since then I have been painting and drawing more or less. Did one charcoal at the college,—which I gave to Mrs. Perry,—shall do that large Eng. landscape by Brunet-Debaines[1] that you liked so much as soon as the weather permits. In the meantime I am trying my hand at water colours. Have done four landscapes,—copies,—for practice, and one for "keeps";—to be framed for the little parlour. I find I am getting the knack of it much faster than I hoped. There are three more that I want to do for the parlour.

Then I want to try it instead of pastel for sketching from nature. This, the children's lessons, and *weeding* are my main occupations and keep my days as full as usual.

I am sure that I have pulled up a million weeds this summer,— and you would scarcely miss them, there are so many left. I go every day from tea-time until dark, and after a rain when the softened ground makes it pay best I spend the afternoon at it. But they are a perfect plague, and almost choke the grass to death in spite of all I can do. I was told that the cause of the trouble is that we did not plant enough seed; if we had, the *grass* would have choked the weeds;—now it is the other way about. Sure enough I looked in Henderson's catalogue and found that the proper amount for our land was two bushels and a half instead of *one* bushel!

Madge's wheel came this afternoon and she is very happy over it. It is a "Monarch" I believe,—a $75.00 one,—Ed got it for $49.00. They sell for that price at several of the great variety shops like Hilton's.[2]

We are all perfectly well still. No letters come for you these days, and there is no news of any sort. Mrs. Brown has been quite sick but is getting about again. She always sends her love to you of course. The town is getting completely deserted;—there have been a great many left here so far, but all will be gone by the first of Aug. The Perry's left today. She has been in very often and sociably this summer, and I shall miss her not a little.

Mr. West stopped me on the street the other day to ask what guests we want now that the Maitlands arn't to come. I wanted him to wait until your return of course, so that you could choose those you want, but he says that is impossible. Am so sorry. He asked if we would like the Dowdens,—the Prof. his wife and daughter.[3] I told him I would be charmed;—but promptly took it back when I found it was for *two weeks*!—most of it *before* the great time. For of course you would not be master of yours [your] own time while he was here; and that is exactly what you *must* be (your own master, I mean) with that [Sesquicentennial] address impending. He said he would call sometime this week to settle with me who it should be. I understand—not from himself! —that Mr. West is horribly bored at the "prospects" at the Westcotts and Armours;[4] two good houses being thus closed to guests.

Am so glad you are going to Peterborough and Ely. And there are some more fine cathedrals "down Somerset way," arn't there? I can't remember which;—"Wells," perhaps. Did you see Lincoln; it must be *lovely*,—from the pictures. How I should like to see that country for Tennyson's sake! His earlier poems are an endless series of exquisite and delicate pictures of it.

By the way, I had yesterday an agreeable experience in the reading line. I had just finished Mallock's little volume on Lucretius[5] and found it *very* interesting. You see, I had known nothing definitely before about him or his philosophy. Then I turned to Tennyson's "Lucretius," a poem the reading of which has heretofore given me but a very "languid pleasure." But this time lo! I was thrilled to my very soul; and began to understand,—though not to agree with,—Dr. Shorey[6] when he calls it the greatest poem of the century. So is one rewarded for a very little learning.

Have you a copy of "Lorna Doone" to take into Devon? By the way, Madge has read that through five times, and Ed Brown's wife *seven* times! I wonder why he could never write another as good. When Florence was here she read one of Blackmores aloud to us the scene of which was also in Devon.[7] And it was wretched, dull stuff. The style was shocking.

You have stopped giving me any addresses for my letters, I fear they are all going astray. My darling will have to take my love somewhat for granted; I find it impossible to be very expansive on that subject,—to write out and out love letters—under the circumstances. It is really too uncomfortable to think of them wandering about the world, being opened at Dead Letters offices, &c. But you *know* how I love you, dear;—how my love and my thoughts attend you *every* step of your way,—how I am always and in *every* way,          Your own    Eileen.

Friday morning.—Your sweet letter from London—of the 20th is just at hand, dear, and *so* welcome. A glorious change in the weather came on in the night too. It is like a breezy fall day. So for both these reasons I am in high spirits this morning.
         With infinite love    Eileen.

ALS (WC, NjP).

1 Alfred-Louis Brunet-Debaines, French etcher noted for his technical skill.

2 Hilton, Hughes and Co.

3 Edward and Elizabeth Dickinson Dowden and either Hilda or Hester Dowden, Dowden's daughters by an earlier marriage. He was Professor of English Literature and Rhetoric at Trinity College, Dublin, and a noted literary critic.

4 Mrs. Westcott and Mrs. Armour were both expecting. John Howell Westcott III was born on October 9, 1896; Allison Armour, on August 27, 1896.

5 William Hurrell Mallock, *Lucretius* (London, 1878).

6 Professor of Greek and newly appointed head of the Department of Greek Language and Literature at the University of Chicago; an old friend of the Wilsons from Bryn Mawr days.

7 Either Richard Doddridge Blackmore's *Christowell. A Dartmoor Tale* (3 vols., London, 1882) or his *Perlycross. A Tale of the Western Hills* (3 vols., London, 1894), both of which were set in Devonshire.

## To Ellen Axson Wilson

My own darling      Westminster Hotel, Chester. 3 August, 1896

I have quite a joke on you this morning. You directed one of your letters[1] to the Cheque Bank without my name on it at all; they opened it, discovered it was not for them (!), sent it to me here because of the Princeton post-mark, and ask me in a courteous note to return it to them if it is not for me! It is quite unusual, my dear, to address a corporation as "My own darling," and quite inexplicable when you are not even a stockholder!

I am stranded here in Chester. My luggage, which I had forwarded from Cambridge last Wednesday has not come (tho. I have news of it), and to-morrow is a special 'bank holiday' on which the "goods" offices of the R. R. will not be open. The banks being closed, moreover, I can't get any money, and I have not enough to pay my hotel bill. I shall evidently have to stay here till Tuesday. The situation is highly amusing. It's well Chester is so interesting a place!

It will not be worth while, I am afraid, my darling, for you to write after the 18th; but it would be a great comfort to me if you would *cable* me a word or two on the 26th, addressing it, Anchor Line, Glasgow.

It relieved me very much to get your good report of the favourable impression No IV. of the Washington articles had made upon you, on your own reading of it, and upon Stockton and Perry; for I bought the number over here and tried to read it, but could not. It seemed to me dull, very dull indeed. New impressions have so crowded upon me during the last eight weeks that it seems to me quite two years since I wrote about Washington. I have, besides, the feeling I have often had before when I had not written or systematically applied my mind to anything for a long time: I feel as if I never *had* written anything, and never could write anything again,—am entirely unconscious of any literary gift or any literary impulse,—am simply one of the crowd on the road. It is no doubt a very fortunate and restful state of mind; but it's just a bit startling to perceive how readily and almost naturally I can exchange one set of habits for another!

I have just learned from two cyclists,—one an elderly gentleman who lives there, the other a young fellow who has ridden the district through,—that the roads, though fairly good in Somerset, are simply wretched in Devon, and they *can* be bad in England, I can tell you. They say the Devon roads would wear any rider out; and I must take the warning. I can see little chosen bits by rail, but the most of my tour in that direction I must give up.

It's rather a sharp disappointment, of course, but it's the first, and I can find some excellent substitute, no doubt. There are lots of fair counties I have not seen yet. When we come cycling together the roads in Devon may be better, and we can discover the county together! That's my dream all the days through now: "when we come cycling together"! Ah, my darling, how I want you! Nothing can for so much as a moment at a time make up to me for that lack. How I envy Mr. and Mrs. Woods who are to sail for home on Wednesday, on a fast White Star liner, the *Britannic*! By-the-way, I have not seen a house or cottage yet prettier than ours.

Really, you know, you are having a most extraordinary presidential campaign in that odd country of yours! I shall have to be told where I am when I get back. It looks as if *I* would have to vote for *McKinley*![2] Oh Lord, how long!

I have begun, continued, and am about to end this letter all on one day, my greatest feat of left-handed penmanship; but I shall not seal or send it till it is time for it to go, so that its news of my health (viz. that I am quite well) may be the latest when it goes.

I have not gone to church to-day, because I was ashamed to go in my bicycle clothes and had no others. But I have explored the quaint town somewhat thoroughly since I began writing this morning and am thoroughly charmed with all but the odour of it, which in parts seems as old as the houses, though, unlike them, unrenovated. Much of the elaborate wood-work of these old houses is beautifully and richly carved: and one good sign I noticed,—a house as beautiful as any of the old ones, even in respect of the carving, though more simple, and built in 1892, in the old style. The modern buildings here are most of them, however, as commonplace and ugly as anything in America.

I love you darling, oh how passionately, and am altogether
                                                Your own   Woodrow
Love to Mrs. B. and all the dear ones.

ALS (WC, NjP).
    [1] He refers to EAW to WW, July 13, 1896.
    [2] In fact, as he later wrote to Edward Mandell House on October 18, 1911 (House Papers, CtY), Wilson voted for John McAuley Palmer, the candidate of the gold Democrats or the National Democratic party.


## From Ellen Axson Wilson

My own darling,                                Princeton, Aug 3, 1896
    Your letter from Slough came today and is *especially* satisfactory to me as showing that the loss of your friends has not resulted in any depression of spirits, or spoiled in the least your

pleasure in your journeyings. I have been really dreading for you the separation and am truly relieved to find that you have become so independant and at home over there as not to mind it. Your letter tells me exactly what I most wanted to know and so is a real comfort. The last sweet one from London also came since I wrote last,—on Sat.

I have just had a letter from your father;[1] he arrived in New York Sat., from Wilmington[2] and is going on to Saratoga. He wrote to ask when you were expected; seemed to think it was almost time and that perhaps he could see you *before* he went to Saratoga! How glad I am that he is mistaken and that you have still more than a month of holiday! I begged him to come and see *us*,—but don't expect him!

Stock spent one night last Friday and then went on to Clifton Springs. He is going first to Niagara with a friend. He is perfectly *wild* about having Madge with him in Brooklyn,—says he can scarcely think of anything else! Poor fellow; it is the sudden vision of creating something like a little home of his own that has so dazzled him. For as he never can marry,—he thinks,—he never expected to have such a thing. His idea now is to have a little flat, and some good old darkey to take care of them. I wonder how Nannie and Minnie would like it!

Stock brought his wheel, & Ed and Madge could scarcely wait until they had their tea to take their first ride together. They rode only half an hour and came back with three punctures in Madge's and *seven* in Ed's! How they came was a complete mystery, until Maggie told them she had seen in the "Press,"[3] that some miscreant had sprinkled tacks along the Stony Brook road between Stockton and Mercer Sts. And the man who mended Ed's told the same tale.

We are still perfectly well and the weather is cool and delightful. Indeed it has been a wonderful summer so far as regards the weather; there have been but two days when I have suffered in the least. True I have heard grumbling from other people about the heat, so perhaps our comfort is partly due to our cool house and our delightful situation. The house is certainly as charming to *live* in as it is to look at. And you will be glad to know that next to the library the study is the coolest room in it, getting as it does the prevailing breeze. The colours in both those rooms are even more successful than I hoped, looking warm and comfortable in winter, yet cool and shadowy in summer,—and *restful* always, whereas the libraries finished in white paint manage to look cold in winter and dazzlingly, glaringly hot in summer.

There are no letters for you and no news of any sort. Everything is going smoothly and pleasantly with us but there is nothing to tell. I have been taking a little plunge into novel-reading, by way of emphasizing the fact that it was my holiday time, but owing to ill fortune in my selections was so bored that I have instead taken up the study of "modern philosophy" as a diversion!

The "new women" ought certainly to take heart; their cause— the equality of the sexes,—is rapidly gaining ground, among writers of books at least. They are now heartily according her many new and *valuable* rights, privileges and immunities. Du Maurier, their great leader, is getting a brave following in his noble battle for an equal code of morals. Not that they maintain that men should be virtuous; Heaven forbid! Such a thing is not even dreamed of. But generously, unselfishly, chivalrously do they contend for the woman's right to be just as bad as the man!

But Meredith, rather than Du Maurier, seems entitled to the leadership now, because of the courage and skill with which he has "carried the war into Africa" by making a pure soul in a woman synomymous with a shallow heart and an empty head; and sneering at all three together. With him unchastity becomes, under some circumstances, not so much a womans right as her *duty*—her crowning glory. It is a *height* to which as soon as she rises she becomes "a grand creature."

But I wrote a long letter to Father this evening, telling him all about you; so now it is time to say good-night. It is a comfort, dear, to think that the time of your absence now is no longer than when you go to Baltimore, just five weeks! Where do you want me to meet you when you come? Or shall I sit quietly here and await you?—that would be more satisfactory in the *end*,—if I can stand it! With a very passion of love and devotion, believe me darling always & altogether        Your own    Eileen.

ALS (WC, NjP).
    1 Dr. Wilson's letter is missing.
    2 He was temporarily supplying at the First Presbyterian Church of Wilmington, N. C.
    3 *Princeton Press*, July 25, 1896.

## To Ellen Axson Wilson

Shrewsbury. Aug. 6 1896
Crossed north Wales bangor to Shrewsbury now follow Severn to Gloucester Well

Hw cablegram (WP, DLC).

## From Ellen Axson Wilson

My own darling,          Princeton, N. J., Thursday, Aug 6/96
   This with its nice long letter and nice long cablegram, has been a red letter day indeed. I am charmed that you have seen so much of Wales; am sure the scenery must be beautiful. What is your plan, by the way, for your return trip to Glasgow? Are you going to work your way back partly on your wheel, or take the whole journey by rail? Since finding you so independant and happy alone, I have ceased to feel any interest in Mr. Dubose's* plans. You will probably prefer *not* to have him. However I need not concern myself; as he has but two months in all, incompatability of plan will almost certainly develop naturally;—and if it doesn't, it will be easy for you to quietly assist nature in the matter.
   How very, very kind in you, darling, to give so much time to searching for that picture! I thank you with all my heart; and am awaiting its coming with the greatest eagerness. How strange that it should be so hard to find a copy! It seems most extraordinary that there should not be photographs of it. The one in the book is evidently a photograph. You are literally *too* good and unselfish, my own darling; those constantly haunting regrets for my absence when you see all these beautiful things proves it only too conclusively. I wish you could be rid of them, for I fear they will mar the completeness of your pleasure,—and yet I *do love* you for them, you dear thing!
   I am very glad that *weather* is not international always, so that I can at least hope you are not sweltering. It is summer at last with a vengeance. There have been, so far, but two days of it however and we are not at all exhausted. Are all quite well. I have in spite of the heat been painting vigourously and with enjoyment today. Have almost finished the last of my water-colours for the parlour. It is a very pretty one of apple trees, in bloom that came after you left;—just the subject I wanted most for that room. It is by Bruce Crane.[1]
   We had a veritable tragi-comedy here last night. At about one o'clock Margaret slipped in and told me quietly, like a brave & self-posessed little woman, that there was a bat in the nursery. I hastily lit my lamp—hoping to rescue the others before they discovered their danger; but just as I did it, piercing shrieks arose in the nursery & the others tumbled pell-mell into my room. We slammed the door after them only to discover that the bat, like the ghost in the old story, had "flitted" too. So then everybody rushed howling into the dark hall, I having all I could do to save

Nell from absolute convulsions of terror. We made for Ed's room and dashed in (the pitch-darkness alone saving the situation in the the [*sic*] matter of propriety.) He speedily killed it with a tennis racket and we all started back;—but horrors!—when we opened my door, behold *another*! and the whole play was done over again. By that time the poor children were so demoralized and nervous that it was I think hours before they slept. Nellie, shaking like an aspen leaf, staid in my bed of course, and the others had me up several times to fight a large *moth*! For my part I was vexing my brain over the problem "whence came they," had a horrid impression that they "*must* have come down the chimney & we would never be secure against them;—(for we have had one before this summer.) But this morning I found to my relief that some one had left *open two* of the screens on the single windows.

I have just had another note from Father[2] who has gone to Saratoga. No other letters or news. Of public "news" the enclosed item[3] in today's paper struck me somehow as very funny, just because of the solemnity with which it is set forth as a "statement" by Mr. Carlisle and the deep seriousness with which it is commented upon.

But I shall have to stop! The thermometer stands at 99° and I am threatened with prostration from *lamp-stroke*.

Good-night, dear love,—ah how my heart beats to think that day after tomorrow it will perhaps be only a month before I am in your arms! It is well that my heart is sound, else it might then break with joy.           Your little wife   Eileen.

* He did not get here as he expected

ALS (WC, NjP).
    [1] An American artist. Ellen's painting hangs in the Woodrow Wilson Room of Firestone Library, Princeton University.
    [2] Dr. Wilson's letter is missing.
    [3] The enclosed item is missing. However, it probably referred to a statement alleged to have been made by Logan Carlisle, Chief Clerk of the United States Treasury Department and son of Secretary of the Treasury John Griffin Carlisle. The younger Carlisle was said to have asserted that thousands of Democrats in his home state of Kentucky would go to the polls "with clothespins on their noses" to vote for William McKinley. *New York Times*, Aug. 6, 1896.

## Two Letters to Ellen Axson Wilson

My own darling,           Bell Hotel, Worcester. 6 August, 1896
    By means of one of those little railway rides I take every now and then, to save time or skip an uninteresting piece of country, I came here from Shrewsbury this afternoon, having ridden the beautiful 17 miles from Oswestry to Shrewsbury this morning.

It was midday on Tuesday before I got away from Chester; but I had reached Bangor (by rail) and was away for my mountain ride through North Wales by three o'clock, and, thanks to the magnificent engineering of the road (it is the highway from Holyhead to London), I slept 22 miles from Bangor, at an exquisite spot called Bettwys-y-Coed, after an exhilarating run through an extraordinary, beautiful, and varied scenery as ever a man did *not* dream poetry about. Wednesday I rode the 46 miles that brought me out of Wales to the rather Welsh town of Oswestry in Shropshire. Quite 30 of the 46 miles were *down hill*, I should say—else I should not have made so very long a run (my longest by some 10 miles). The scenery continued singularly beautiful and inspiriting; but all its features were large and obvious, and it increased my enjoyment of them to swing along at such a pace from opening to opening. An occasional brief dismount and pause by the way-side sufficed to fix the more delightful spots in my mind's eye,—for you know I see fast. I wish I could sketch, or even describe, with my left hand!

Continued on the 7th at Malvern, an interesting resort clinging, with its three or four tiers of streets, to the side of a high hill somewhere between Worcester and Tewkesbury, with a beautiful 'abbey' all its own, and, I trust, a good lunch a-cooking for me. There is a delightful sense of discovery in coming upon natural beauties and the fine grace and dignity of ancient architecture in places one never heard of before. Here, perched before this fine far view, with the square tower of Worcester cathedral standing below in the misty distance, is an abbey gate as beautiful, I should say, as anything in stone in England,—and this only a summer resort!

Finished in Tewkesbury. I am anxious, very anxious, to press on to Gloucester and get my mail and baggage; but this sleepy old place is too fascinating and soothing to be denied some hours for its noble abbey church and the tribute of a night's sleep. I must stay and experience it.

I am very well indeed, my stomach behaving heroically and my arm not hurting at all. The only thing that disturbs me is the passionate intensity and the intolerable longing of my love for you!                                    Your own   Woodrow

Love to Mrs. B., sweet Maggie, the precious bairns, and dear Ed. Regards—or something—for the servants.

My own darling,      Fowler's Hotel  Gloucester   8 Aug., 1896

It makes me feel nearer home to get here and secure two sweet letters. These letters of yours are more precious than gold to me, and do more to keep me in spirits than all the noble sights of this goodly land. They enable me, I fancy, to see your dear, so lovely face upon the very page as I read, and on it the play of those smiles I love so

> "that with motion of their own
> Do spread, and sink, and rise;
> That come and go with endless play,
> And ever, as they pass away,
> Are hidden in your eyes."[1]

That's not from memory, I need not tell you. I've been wishing ever since I landed on this side that I had brought that tiny volume of Wordsworth with me; and the other day,—yesterday, in fact, at Tewkesbury,—I saw almost exactly the same collection for sale for a shilling, bought it, and have had a perfect feast out of it. I seemed never to have read any of it before, so keenly did it strike upon my palate. It's possession has been a real boon to me, and I shall carry it in my jacket the rest of the journey as I did to-day. Gloucester is not more than twenty miles away from Tinturn Abbey, I think, and I have quite made up my mind to make a pilgrimage to the region where the "Lines" were written.

Prof. Maitland's summer home lies in my way towards Wells,— is only some six or seven miles from here, indeed,—and I think I shall look in upon him for an hour or so,—simply to know him better, not with any hope of changing his decision about accepting our invitation.

9th I find myself a bit restless and uneasy here in the south. It seems so far away from Glasgow and the ship that is to carry me home. You must not forbid me a little homesickness: it is not unwholesome. There is even something sweet in homesickness for a fellow who has such a home as I have. At any rate, whether I ought to or not, I find that the diminishing number of the days between me and the 27th gives me more delight and is a pleasanter thing for me to think about than anything I have seen or done in England.

11th. Here I am in Wells, and this mail must close to-day. Yesterday I rode for nearly twenty miles beside the Wye, and of all the parts of England I have seen it has most won my heart. It is so glad a stream and has so exquisite a secluded path amongst the hills that seem made for its setting

how oft—
In darkness, and amid the many shapes
Of joyless daylight; when the fretful stir
Unprofitable, and the fever of the world,
Shall hang upon the beatings of my heart,
How oft, in spirit, shall I turn to thee,
O sylvan Wye![2]

I read the whole poem sitting on the bank of the stream and was filled with an exalted emotion I don't think I can ever forget. The poem contains, in a degree I had never dreamed of, the very spirit of the place!

This morning I rode over the Mendip Hills to this heart of Somerset, coming down into it from a height whence I could see it in all its beauty, lying in a sort of golden mist with its exquisite cathedral, like a jewel, in the midst. So you see I am very happy, and well,—and everything, by some subtle process, makes me with an intenser love and longing

Your own    Woodrow

The usual messages of love. So sorry to hear of Mrs. B's illness.

ALS (WC, NjP).
[1] From Wordsworth's "Louisa. After Accompanying Her on a Mountain Excursion."
[2] From Wordsworth's "Lines Composed a Few Miles Above Tintern Abbey. . . ."

## From Ellen Axson Wilson

My own darling,                          Princeton Aug 10/96

Your cable from Gloucester came today. And as I have just been reading about its cathedral and looking at the pictures of it I have a very pleasingly vivid impression of where you were this morning! I am sorry that the chapter on "Wells" is not in our collection,[1] so that I cannot follow you there. (Perhaps I can find it at the college.) Let me think!—you have seen eight cathedrals now, have you not?—not counting Canterbury. Did you go there? You have not mentioned it, yet it seems as though you must have gone when you were so near as London. Mrs. Van Rensselaer says that if she could see but one English view it should be Canterbury from St. Martin's church of a summer afternoon; its lovely setting "the whole beautiful green valley of the Stour to the far-off western hills."[2]—And the man who writes of Gothic architecture in the Britannica speaks of it as "culminating in Canterbury and Lincoln."

But judging from these articles I should, next to Canterbury, choose to see Durham, it is so surpassingly *grand* both in itself and in its situation. And then its history is so *wonderfully* interesting. Can't you see it when you turn your face northward again? Mrs. Van R. speaking of its situation "magnificent past rivalry";—says that Ely & Durham "stand well" in exactly opposite senses. "At Ely nature seems to have suppressed herself that there might be no scale by which the immeasurable dignity of man's work could be computed. At Durham she seems to have built a great work of her own just that man's work might complete— and crown it—a lordly pedestal, . . . as kings sit upon thrones, the sole end of whose splendour is to enhance their own."[3]

I am tempted to give you another passage that pleased me from the same article. She says,—"Not in some new Birmingham, not in some old deserted Kenilworth do we find the real England,— but here in this Durham, which was once military and monastic and feudal, and is now commercial, collegiate, domestic, and in politics boldly liberal; yet where there has been neither sudden change nor any forgetting, and very little abandonment or loss— only slow natural growth and development and the wear and tear and partial retrogressions which all growth, all development must involve. Modern life standing upon ancient life as on a worn but puissant and respected pedestal, learning alive despite the hurry of trade; religion alive despite the widening of the moral horizon."[4] And by the way if you go there you are to ask for the head-verger Mr. Wetherell, who is "the best guide in Europe." I am decidedly amused to find that before I knew it I have filled a sheet telling *you* about England! So now I will come home again,—though really—there is nothing to tell about it. We are all perfectly well in spite of the great heat. It is decidedly cooler to-day because of a good *breeze*. Yesterday was terrible. There were forty deaths from it in and about New York. The children are all broken out with prickly heat but are astonishingly good in spite of it. Nell had one great cry yesterday due really to the heat I think, though the immediate cause was a funny one. We were all reading the Bible and she gave as her rendering of the verse: "keep me as the apple of thine eye";—"keep me in the apple tree"! We were all so cruel as to laugh consumedly, whereupon she was broken hearted, poor little darling.

The picture came safely, darling, and I can't thank you enough for it. It is *perfect* in some parts, especially the lovely soft lines of the shoulders, throat, &c. And the face, as you say, is as near it as one could hope to come in an engraving. The mouth is the least perfect feature. It was *so* kind in you to find and get it for me, & you don't know how I appreciate it.

But Ed has just come with a big piece of mending which he wants done tonight, so I must stop abruptly. Ed leaves tomorrow morning for a week at Henry Russell's sea-shore home.[5] He has finished his work with Mr. Magie and made $63.00. The Magie's left today for Maine.

I love you, dear, with *all* my heart, and soul and mind,—with all my might too. I might say, as I have before, that I love you as much as you want me to; but I really don't see what use you can have for *all* the love with which I love you. But of course you would be too polite to admit that I love you *more* than you like! Your little wife, Eileen.

ALS (WC, NjP).
[1] Ellen was referring to a series of thirteen articles on English cathedrals by Mariana Griswold (Mrs. Schuyler) van Rensselaer, which appeared in the *Century Magazine* of New York from March 1887 to March 1892.
[2] Mariana G. van Rensselaer, "Canterbury Cathedral," *Century Magazine*, XXXIII (April 1887), 821-22.
[3] M. G. van Rensselaer, "Durham Cathedral," *Century Magazine*, XXXV (Dec. 1887), 226.
[4] *Ibid.*, p. 243.
[5] Henry Norris Russell's home, at Oyster Bay, Long Island.


## To Ellen Axson Wilson

My own darling, Langport, Somerset, 12 August, 1896
Langport is the place where Bagehot was born and lived; his grave is in the churchyard here, and in the church there is a beautiful memorial window to him, put in by his wife, who still lives at the family place (Herds Hill) here when she is not in London. Almost the first sign that caught my eye when I rode into Wells was "Stuckey's Banking Co.,"[1] and it at once occurred to me to ask how far off Langport was. I found it was only some 18 miles away, and Glastonbury on the same road. I saw Glastonbury this morning, and came on here this afternoon. It is a quaint, interesting little place. The churchyard lies upon a hill from which, standing at Bagehot's grave, one looks out upon just such a view as that from Prospect Ave [in Princeton],—only more beautiful, with a sweet river running through it, and a wonderful golden light lying on it, as, it would seem, on the whole of Somerset. The leaf enclosed is from Bagehot's grave, darling; please press it and keep it for me.

This is the letter, love, which I began, and then packed off in my trunk.[2] I take it up again now, at Lincoln, on the 17th, just ten days before the date for which my heart waits. I have just come from afternoon service in the great minster here, and a tour of inspection around it afterwards; and it is very beautiful,—

in some respects surpassingly fine; but Wells won my heart above all the rest, and keeps it still,—not because it is a more perfect jewel than the others, but because its perfect setting (almost all the ancient ecclesiastical buildings grouped about it unruined, and the quiet town keeping silence about it) make it seem greater and more admirable. Glastonbury too, King Arthur's Isle of Avalon,

"Where falls not hail, nor rain, nor any snow,
Nor ever wind blows loudly, but it lies
Deep meadowed, happy, fair with orchard lawns,
And bowery meadows, crowned with summer sun,"[3]

took my fancy greatly; but its glories are gone to decay and melancholy ruin, while Wells seems to retain her antiquity *alive*. Canterbury disappointed me. Its associations, of course, give it a greatness and majesty which move the imagination very deeply; but it has not now either the beauty or the charm of half a dozen others.

Ah, how my heart beats to be so far north again, and actually on my way home. You will never know, my sweet Eileen, how much I love you. I *cannot* tell you in words, and I *do* not tell you in actions! If you could only know some part of the thoughts and emotions that have clustered about you in my heart this summer (a very eventful summer for my heart) you would know all, and surely your heart would leap within you. It gave me very sweet thoughts to read the enclosed about Lady Tennyson,[4] every word of it (except about the frail health, thank God, and the music) applies so perfectly to you, giving up your exquisite gifts to the service of others,—of *another*. With how full a heart can he adopt the fine lines,—how fervently does he make to you the prayer of the portion underscored,—how worthily *would* he be

Your own    Woodrow

I am feeling very well, darling. I think there is excellent proof of it in the fact that very small things move me easily to keen pleasure.

Much love to dear Madge (*how* I wish I could see her!), my precious chicks, Ed., and Mrs. Brown.

ALS (WC, NjP).
  [1] The largest private bank in western England during the latter half of the nineteenth century, it was controlled by Bagehot's father. Bagehot was first associated with the bank as manager of the Bristol branch and, after 1860, as manager of the London offices.
  [2] See WW to EAW, Aug. 14, 1896.
  [3] From Tennyson's "Morte d'Arthur."
  [4] The enclosure is missing. Emily Lady Tennyson died on August 10, 1896, hence the enclosure was undoubtedly an obituary notice, which the Editors have been unable to find.

## From Ellen Axson Wilson

My own darling,               Princeton, Aug 13/96

Only to think that two weeks from today you start for *home*!—
oh how my heart leaps within me at the thought! To think too
that after this I write but one more letter;—indeed I am not sure
that even that one,—next Monday's—will reach you, but I will
try it. Your charming letter from Bury St. Edmonds came since
I last wrote, with its pleasant description of the fen country. But
didn't you get it backwards about the "river" which you say is
"really a canal"! Though it *looks* like a canal isn't it "really a
river," the famous river Ouse? I have wondered how much the
rains have interfered with your pleasure,—have hoped not much,
as you said so little about it. I trust they have all merely added a
fresh charm to the landscape like the one you describe in this.
I hope your not mentioning it is also proof that it has not been
hot.

*Heat* is almost the only subject discussed in America these
days. All records have been broken the last week everywhere.
There have been several hundred deaths from it in New York
alone. In one 24 hours there were 123 registered from that cause.
A cool wave was predicted for last night, and it really was pleasant this morning, but this afternoon the breeze died down and
it is about as hot as ever. We are all *perfectly* well in spite of it;
and the children don't seem to mind it at all. Indeed they say
they *arn't* hot. It is really surprising. I left them in bed just now
very comfortable and happy, getting ready they said for a "real
good talk about Robert Bruce, and the earl of Buchan, and Isa-
bella Buchan." Madge with the two older Purves girls[1] read together every day; so in imitation our young ones with Mildred
[Purves] have started a "reading circle" as they call it. They sit
around with their "embroidery," and evidently feel very grown
up and important. I am glad they are able to amuse themselves
so for of course in this weather I can't let them romp much.

It was so cool this morning that I went to the college and began my big English landscape. I hope it will look like the genuine
thing to you!

It gave me quite a shock to see the old chapel in ruins,[2] though
of course I knew it was being done. Where *will* you have your
classes? Just at this stage it looks like a legitimate ruin, for part
of the walls are still standing and still vine-covered; though the
cellar of the new building is being dug out all around it. It seems
a pity to tear up the campus so, just before the Sesqui-centennial.
Indeed the whole town looks torn up, so much building is going

on. The first [Presbyterian] church, you know, is being completely "done over," and so is the station, and the "old bank," that large yellow house[3] near the Garretts,[4]—it is being made into stores and a printing-house. Then of course there is the new bank[5] and the Pyne building.[6] The latter is going to be charming I think.

Mrs. Brown says Dr. Patton told her nearly all the Pyne gift of $600,000 was to be put in the *building*,[7]—which seems dreadful. But she says he was sure they would make it all right by a second gift for the endowment. He was sure they would give to the library a million at least before they stopped. It is still said on all sides that East college as well as the old chapel is to be pulled down for it. But I won't believe it until I see it. It would be *such* a same to destroy the old quadrangle. Such a break with the past,—with all the old college life and traditions, it seems to me would strike anyone as shocking; and I can imagine how the Alumni would feel about it. They made the most vigourous protest on the subject at the Alumni dinner.[8] Did it formally and systematically by classes, so as to give their words all the weight possible.

By the way, Mr. West did not come to talk about whom we should entertain as he said he would.

Mr. Brower's magazine[9] arrived today. It makes an excellent appearance; has quite and [an] aesthetic cover, is well printed and seems as far as I have had time to judge quite entertaining. It is chiefly stories; most of them not from magazines but from books; like certain of Zola's published long ago. I hope it will succeed; and really don't see why it shouldn't if they can afford to advertise it sufficiently. It is called "the International." But I think I had best stop this stupid scrawl; the heat of the lamp and the air together makes me almost feel as if I were driving on in my sleep.

Goodnight, dear heart. Only think that in *less* than a month now! Oh how wildly my heart leaps up at every thought of your return. I have tried all this time not to let my mind dwell too much on that for fear of a sort of reaction of sick longing for you *now* that was apt to follow. But my thoughts are beginning to be very unruly now, and perhaps it is safe to let them have their way, so short grows the time. Indeed I am sure the pleasure *far* outweighs the pain; so far indeed that I wonder any one can be pessimist enough to doubt whether life is a good thing when *anticipation* alone can give such exquisite happiness. And then how often, in spite of all they say, it is *far* exceeded by the reality.

Ah, my darling, what a wealth of delights you shower upon me daily, hourly,—a very infinitude of happiness! And how unutterably, overwhelmingly, passionately I *love you*. May God bless & keep you, dear love, and make my best dreams come true.

Your little wife,    Eileen.

ALS (WC, NjP).

[1] Elinor and Rebekah Purves.

[2] The "Old Chapel" had been erected on the east side of Nassau Hall in 1847. Although it was replaced for religious services by Marquand Chapel in 1882, it survived as a lecture hall until 1896, when it was demolished to make way for the new Pyne Library, about which see n. 7 below.

[3] Mrs. Wilson was referring to the building at 4 Nassau Street built in 1836 to house the Princeton Bank (now the Princeton Bank and Trust Company). The Princeton Bank had vacated it some years earlier to occupy quarters in University Hall. In 1896, the new owner of 4 Nassau Street made extensive alterations to the building.

[4] The widowed Alice Whitridge (Mrs. Thomas Harrison) Garrett of Baltimore lived at 3 Stockton Street while her three sons, Horatio Whitridge Garrett, '95, John Work Garrett, '95, and Robert Garrett, '97, were in college.

[5] The Dutch colonial-style building erected in 1896 at 12 Nassau Street to be the new home of the Princeton Bank.

[6] Lower Pyne Building, a half-timbered structure at the northeastern corner of Nassau and Witherspoon Streets, built by Moses Taylor Pyne, '77, in 1896 and presented to Princeton University for use as a dormitory.

[7] The Pyne Library (now known as East Pyne Building) was the Sesquicentennial gift of Albertina Taylor (Mrs. Percy Rivington) Pyne, mother of Moses Taylor Pyne. Moses Taylor Pyne handled the details of planning and financing the building. The gift was announced on April 10, 1896; ground was broken later that spring; and the building was nearly completed and the books transferred to it by November 1897. The old Chancellor Green Library was retained as a reading room, while the new building, which was connected to the old, contained the book stacks, seminar rooms, and storage areas. The cost of the new building was approximately $650,000. The book capacity of the two buildings was estimated at 1,250,000 volumes.

[8] Their protest was in vain. East College was demolished to make place for the Pyne Library.

[9] The Chicago *International*. See EAW to WW, Feb. 20, 1896, n. 1.


## To Ellen Axson Wilson

My own darling,        Shakespeare Hotel, Dover. 14 Aug., 1896

The record for the time since my last letter must begin now, on Friday and here in Dover, for what I was writing you of the time intervening down in Somerset was absent-mindedly put into my trunk and dispatched to Lincoln this morning, and must wait to get finished till I catch up with it next week.

I am not on my way to France, as you might suppose, but to Canterbury! I wanted to see what this famous coast looked like, so I overshot Canterbury this afternoon (in the train, of course) and came on to Dover. I have come all the way from Gloucester by rail to-day, leaving my wheel in London, to be picked up there on Monday when I start for Lincoln and the north. I shall spend Saturday and Sunday in Canterbury, with Westcott's friends, the Headleys.[1] Young Headley not only wrote to me in the most cordial manner, but looked me up in London, and urged me to "give them several days."

For fear the letter went astray, love, I am going to repeat the request that you cable me a few words (Wilson, Anchor Line, Glasgow) early on the morning of the 26th—early because the time on this side is so much ahead of yours. If you send it about 9 or ten, I shall get it early in the afternoon.

I don't know what to say about your meeting me in New York. Perhaps you had better not; but write to the Anchor Line people in N. Y. and ask them to telegraph you the moment they get word of the *Anchoria*, so that if it seems likely that she will get to the wharf too late for me to get through the custom house and catch a train for Princeton that night you may, if possible, run up and spend the night with me. I could not stay a whole—No, no! it can't be managed: stay in Princeton, and I will get there as soon as it can be managed at any cost! Ah, how my heart beats at the thought! How happy I shall be,—happier I believe than ever in my life before. With what an overwhelming passion I am

Your own   Woodrow

The usual messages. I scrawl in great haste. I am very well indeed.

ALS (WC, NjP).
  1 Perhaps Will C. and Rosetta Ayres Headley of East Orange, N. J., parents of Elroy Headley, '01.


## From Ellen Axson Wilson

My own darling,                              Princeton, Aug. 17, 1896

That certainly is a good joke on me about the letter;—or rather a very *bad* one, for it is extremely provoking that I should have been so stupid. I was already bored enough that *one* letter had been opened at the Dead letter office. I was not in the least surprised though when I read your letter, for I caught myself directing *two* letters in that way, and I had an uneasy feeling that I might once have made the mistake without detecting it. One would think I had lost my senses.

But I have something of a joke on you too—viz., the misdirecting your letters to Miss Avery & Prof. Hooper! He sent Miss A's letter to *me*; and, sad to relate, I had not kept her address, not expecting of course to have any use for it. I ransacked your papers in vain for the office of the Extension Society; and finally had to send the poor letter to Miss Underhill at Sing Sing and beg *her* to forward it to Miss Avery. Was there ever such a comedy of errors. Prof. Hooper must have fallen into despair about ever getting into communication with you.

But it's an ill wind that blows no good; I see from his letter to you that only these delays have prevented your binding yourself for a *new* course of lectures at the Institute this winter![1] I was shocked. You *naughty* boy! I am thankful for anything that prevents that. I am *very* glad though that you are to give the "Democracy" there.[2]

I had a queer experience this afternoon, a visit from an English water-colour artist, who I suppose is down on his luck, for he was peddling his pictures about; poor fellow. Indeed he was here twice, I being absent, at the gallery, in the morning. He was sent here by Mrs. Hageman[3] as to one who knew something about art; and was quite determined to "get my influence." He wanted to do my portrait and *make me* a *present* of it in order to get other orders through it. I was "such a very good subject that even if he didn't get the orders he would have nothing to regret"! Indeed it was only with the greatest difficulty that I was able to put him off, and decline his gift! Not that he was rude though. He had quite the manner of a gentleman; and was very fine-looking. I thought it was Mr. Armour as I saw him come up the path. His work was lovely in colour, but terribly over-worked; almost microscopic in finish—all the freshness taken out. He had one quite pretty one—by the way—of "Twickenham Ferry." He thought *I* was English because my "voice and manner of speech was English—and not at all like that of any other Americans he had met." I had to explain the differences between north and south to him. I remember that when Grandfather[4] was in England the people declined to believe that he was an "American" for the same reason.

We are having *glorious* weather again, the air is like new wine today, so fresh and exhilerating. We are all quite well, as usual. Did I tell you that Stockton stayed only a week at Clifton,—didn't like it;—said it bored and depressed him, and that the crowd was so enormous that he could get very little medical attention. I was of course bitterly disappointed at the result. He is now on the Jersey coast, and wants Madge there for a week as soon as he finds a place to suit him. Mr. Daniels,[5] who is wretchedly unwell, is thinking of joining him there too.

Dear little Mrs. Westcott,—the mother,[6]—died on Friday very suddenly of paralysis. She was in Montrose at her brother's. Mr. Westcott, who was in Maine with his wife reached her before she died; but the Harpers are of course still in France. It is all *so* sad; I am glad Mr. Westcott was married before, but it is a terrible blow to him as it is. *What* a sweet little woman she was! —and much more than merely sweet too, not clever but very *wise*, —a singularly clear-eyed little person. She didn't shine at a dinner-party, as you know;—but for all that she seemed to me one of the rare people who "have an atmosphere" and one that it was a good and pleasant thing to breathe. When I dined there a few weeks ago I happened to say of Florence Hoyt that she was such a *restful* person to live with—quiet without being dull; and Mr. Westcott looked over to his mother with a pretty, affectionate look and said "that just describes *her*." And I think it did.

I have had a letter from Cousin Hattie[7] the other day;—she wants May—who is still in the Adirondacks,—to wait here after she leaves there until they find her an *escort*! I found only one answer possible to *her*; so May will be here in about a week I suppose*—unless the "escort" materializes in the meantime.

And to think that this is actually the *last* letter! to put it that way makes it seem sooner than it is, alas!—I mean of course your home-coming. Yet after all, it is only about three weeks, God willing, before I shall be actually in your arms! As I think of that home-coming a great wave of excitement comes surging up into my throat, as it were, from somewhere deep down and almost suffocates me. Do you remember the pretty old English song, "To Lucasta"?[8] I *have* found it very sweet and comforting in this long absence; yet after all I feel too much alive, especially in such weather as this, to find it altogether satisfactory, or to wish myself, as you remember I used to do, a disembodied spirit. I shall be very glad to "greet as"—mortals—"greet." But here is a bit of the poem,—familiar to you of course yet beautiful enough to bear repeating—by *heart*.

> Though seas and lands be twixt us both,
>     Our faith and troth,
>     Like separated souls,
>     All time and space controls;
> Above the highest sphere we meet,
> Unseen, unknown; and greet as angels greet.
>
> So then we do anticipate
>     Our after-fate,
>     And are alive i' th' skies,
>     If thus our lips and eyes
> Can speak like spirits unconfined
> In heaven,—their earthly bodies left behind.

So now goodnight,—"auf wiedersehen,"—somehow I don't like to say "good-by," & yet in its literal meaning how exactly it says what I wish—"God be with you"; & oh may He be very merciful to us & full of *loving kindness*! With a heart full—full to overflowing of love I am, Woodrow my darling, always and altogether,

Your own,    Eileen.

*18th. Have just had a letter: the escort is found, so she will not come.

ALS (WC, NjP).
1 Franklin W. Hooper's letter is missing. Wilson did not give a course of lectures at the Brooklyn Institute in 1896.
2 Wilson gave a very modified version of "Democracy" at the Brooklyn Institute on October 14, 1896. See the news report printed at Oct. 15, 1896, Vol. 10.
3 Probably Mary D. (Mrs. John F.) Hageman, of 83 Mercer St.
4 Isaac Stockton Keith Axson.
5 Winthrop More Daniels.
6 Mary Dunton (Mrs. John Howell) Westcott, mother of Professor Westcott.
7 Harriet Hoyt Ewing of Nashville.
8 Richard Lovelace, "To Lucasta, Going Beyond the Seas."


## To Ellen Axson Wilson

My own darling,          Angel Hotel, Chesterfield, 18 Aug., 1896

This letter might as well be my last before sailing, but I will send a little note off early next week to catch a fast mail boat and beat me home by a day or two as a sort of harbinger. My left hand seems slower and more awkward than ever now that my thoughts are running quick with keen excitement at nearing the 27th. At any rate, I can't write about what is so near my heart "at this poor dying rate," but must give you a notion of my holiday business. I left Lincoln this morning and rode out of the flat country into hilly Derbyshire. Everybody goes into such ecstacies about the romantic and various beauty of Derbyshire that I felt I must see some part of it, and I have chosen to see Haddon Hall and its neighbourhood, which I hope to reach by a couple of hours' ride to-morrow. Chesterfield is nothing but a commonplace and ugly little market town at which I have found it convenient to bait and lodge for the night. It is famous for nothing except a crooked church spire.

19th—I am in York to-night. This is the fourth time I have been here this summer, but each of the other times I have been prevented by one circumstance or another from making a thorough examination of the interior of the great minster,—so I thought I would try it once more—tomorrow morning,—before going on to Durham, of which I have only had sight from the train, on my first trip to Cambridge. After Durham, I mean to find the Yarrow on my wheel, though I am not yet clear how to get to it, or just where it runs.

The only notable thing in to-day's ride from Chesterfield to Rowsley, the little station where I 'booked' for York this afternoon,—at least the only notable thing besides a great deal of exceedingly lovely scenery,—was my visit to Haddon Hall a beautiful and wonderfully preserved old medieval seat of the Earls of Rutland, now unoccupied, but, happily on exhibition for 3d. It was as well worth visiting, in its kind, as anything I've seen, and the country in its neighbourhood was charming enough to kindle anybody's spirits.

20th—To-night, darling, I am in Durham, at the Three Tuns Inn, where it is the custom of the house to offer every guest a glass of cherry brandy on his arrival. I've had only a glance at the interior of the cathedral, but that has made almost as much of an impression on me as my walk around the exterior, seeing how the magnificent pile towers upon its cliff above the river. I am only afraid I shall not give myself time enough to see it properly in all its fine settings and detail, such an impatience to be on has got hold of me now I am on my homeward way! I can hardly get myself to stop; shall probably get to Glasgow much sooner than necessary (there's nothing to do by way of preparation except to get my wheel crated) and sit there cooling my heels for a day or two in a great state of mind!

I was sorry to leave York. Quite aside from the great minster, it is, on the whole, I think, the most interesting *place* I have been, —and I've seen it both before and after the others. It is quainter a great deal than Chester. Chester feels the touch of Liverpool and Manchester.

21st—You must not expect to see me fat, my love, though you may expect to see me looking very like a well and happy man. Bicycling over all sorts of country day after day and week after week and subsisting upon a most restricted and monotonous bill of fare is not calculated to put flesh on the bones, and I weigh just about what I weighed when I left home. What little I have gained has gone to my face; my cheeks are fairly plump.

Durham has put the final touch to my cathedral seeing. I have seen the finest Norman church in Europe and have stood at the tomb of the Venerable Bede. I can now stop, with a full memory and a full imagination. When I shall have seen St Mary's lake and the braes of Yarrow I shall be more than ready to go home.

And now, sweet love, a few lines to go before me next week, and then, God willing, your lover, your husband,

Your own   Woodrow

Love to Mrs. Brown and dear Madge and Ed., deep love to our own sweet chicks.

ALS (WC, NjP).

## To Ellen Axson Wilson

Chesterfield   Aug 19, 1896
Wheeling from Lincoln through derbyshire then rail York and Durham quite well

Hw cablegram (WP, DLC).

## To Ellen Axson Wilson

Clydesdale Hotel   Lanark   24 Aug, 1896
This is the little note that is to go to-morrow, my sweet, sweet love, as the harbinger of my home-coming. You will have news of my sailing, by cable, long before this reaches you;—I rode the whole length of the Yarrow yesterday morning, with the poets at my heart, and spent the afternoon and night beside St Mary's lake,—but that experience may wait for a better telling than I could give it here. This is only to tell you that my heart has travelled not a step from your side all summer,—has drawn closer, rather: that I am coming to you like a lover to whom has been revealed the full beauty and sanctity of love,—with new devotion, new joy, new passion,                Your own   Woodrow.

I know now, too, how much I love our precious chicks, God bless them! Love to Mrs. B. and all.

ALS (WC, NjP).

A Poem

[Sept. 5, 1896]

### ON BOARD STEAMSHIP ANCHORIA

From Glasgow to New York, August 27 to September 7, 1896

*Lines by Prof. Woodrow Wilson, of Princeton College, on reverse
side of Souvenir presented to A. F. Nightingale,
Saturday Evening, Sept. 5, 1896*

> The man who was never daunted
>   By summons to regale,
> Nor yielded up nor fainted,
>   Our lusty Nightingale.
>
> What though the good ship was pitching
>   And straining at every sail,
> He held his own unshaken,
>   Our doughty Nightingale.
>
> All praise to the stout retainer,
>   So self-contained and hale,
> Who kept his faith with nature,
>   Our wholesome Nightingale.

Printed sheet (WP, DLC).

# ADDENDA

## To Hiram Woods, Jr.

My dear Hiram,                    Clarksville, Tenn., 16 Sept., 1886

Your letter of the 13th reached me here this morning,—and its terrible news has fairly overwhelmed me. You never said a truer thing than that the news of dear Allan's death[1] would come as a personal grief to me. I loved Allan as I never loved any man not of my own blood; and I admired him as I never admired any other man I ever knew. His death has brought a pain and a dismay into my heart such as were never there before. Oh, Hiram, Hiram, my dear, dear friend, how can I tell you of my sympathy for you all in the face of this appalling sorrow! If it is any comfort to you to know that someone else loved him, if possible, as much as you did, you may have the fulness of that comfort, for I loved him so.

I had talked to Mrs. Wilson again and again of Allan till she had caught my enthusiasm for the splendid boy, and the single glimpse she caught of him had tended only to strengthen the impression. When I told her the news of his death this morning, her eyes filled with the tears I could not shed, and she sobbed in my arms as if she and I, as well as you, had lost a brother. These are sacred confidences my dear fellow, but I feel that I owe it to you and to myself to open my heart at this moment of solemn grief, too deep and real for conventional reserve.

Hiram, I have—as I hope you have not discovered, but as you doubtless have—an intellectual self-confidence, possibly out of all due proportion to my intellectual strength, which has made me feel that in matters in which I had qualified myself to speak I could never be any man's follower. You will understand, therefore, how great must have been my admiration for Allan when I tell you that he formed in my thought the only possible exception. I have sometimes thought that when Allan came to the maturity of his powers I could, if not follow him, at least heed him as I would no other. If this reveals my overweening confidence in myself, it at least redeems that by showing how I could love and admire Allan.

God's will be done! If we could understand Him He would not be God. I bow to His Providence, and I pray Him in His mercy to soften this blow to you and yours to whom this bereavement comes most terribly—as well as to me, who ask the privilege of mourning with you—as for a personal loss that cannot be repaired! But oh, it is heartbreaking! Love to all—a double portion for yourself.

Most affectionately,   Woodrow Wilson

ALS (WC, NjP).

[1] Allan Chase Woods, younger brother of Hiram Woods, Jr., who had received his A.B. from the Johns Hopkins in June 1886 and had just died from typhoid fever.

## A News Report of an Affair at Wesleyan University

[June 22, 1889]

DOCTORS DISAGREE

Senator Hawley's Address on
American Government.

The excellent lecture which Gen. Hawley[1] delivered before the college some time since[2] was undoubtedly the best that has been delivered in the course.[3] If the other lectures had been on kindred subjects, that is of a nature more pertinent to the popular agitations of the day, they would have received more attention and would have been attended by larger audiences. For the most part the other speakers have been rather unfortunate in their choice of subjects, and so have not won that interest on the part of the students that could be desired. But the subject of the last lecture aside from the popularity of the speaker was one in which every one was interested, not only from his connection with the American government but also because the matter has been much discussed by the members of Prof. Wilson's classes. The Professor's book on Congressional Government has been very extensively read throughout the college, by faculty and students alike, and the author's antipathy to the committee form of government as is exemplified by our National House of Representatives is very well understood. And so when Gen. Hawley announced his subject to be of a kindred nature to Prof. Wilson's treatise all were eager to attend. As was expected, Gen. Hawley as a typical representative of our form of government, strongly opposed Prof. Wilson's criticism and forthwith proceeded to show where the Professor was in error in his judgment. The members of the Wesleyan House of Commons, an organization originated by the well-known Congressional critic, were all present and listened with trembling hearts and blanched faces to the notable Senator's criticism of their fundamental principles of establishment. They sat in submissive patience as the orator pointed out the errors of the book and showed clearly the supremacy of our form of government that has survived for more than a century in the face of the determined opposition of English Parliamentary rule. Their resentment knew no bounds when the speaker personally referred to the author and claimed that ignorance and English affectation alone formed the basis of his work. Yet they were forced to grin and bear it as the saying is, and when the lecturer had finished they breathed a big sigh of relief as though glad to escape from the evils of convincing argumentative torture. On the other hand there were many patriotic admirers of our constitutional methods who rejoiced at each new thought which the speaker brought forth in opposition and applauded loudly each vindication of our national legislative modes of procedure. There was an intense feeling of satisfaction that a man who had the experience of years in both Houses of our Congress could address a body of American students in behalf of an American form of government. In fact the general impression of the entire audience was that the speaker very successfully overcame the tendency toward English affectation which had been previously inculcated among the students. Of Prof. Wilson's ability in his department there can be no doubt, but since Senator Hawley's severe arraignment of his pet theme of American legislative criticism his approbative admiration by his students and Commoners has been chilled to a certain degree. During all the lecture he occupied one of the foremost positions in the audience and endured with calmness all the satirical criticisms of his productions. The next day he attempted a reply in his classes and claimed that the Senator had attacked him at an unfair advantage. But when an author has promulgated his doctrines in a bound volume all over the country and by a pedagogical asceticism has engrafted in the minds of the rising generation an opposition to our fundamental principles of government, it seems one of the strongest indications of fairness for an adversary to logically reply in the presence of a constituency that has only received the affected and hastily formed arguments of a pessimistic critic.

Printed in the Middletown, Conn., *Constitution*, June 22, 1889; one editorial heading omitted.

[1] Joseph Roswell Hawley, brevet major general of volunteers in the Union Army, former Governor of Connecticut and member of the United States House of Representatives, and United States Senator from Connecticut, 1881-1905.

[2] On June 6, 1889.

[3] That is, the course of public lectures at Wesleyan during the academic year 1888-89.

## To Daniel Coit Gilman[1]

My dear Mr. Gilman,          Princeton, New Jersey, 1 April, 1891

I have by no means forgotten your request that I should write out for you my impressions of Mr. Winchester; but this is the first time since my return to my work here that I have had the leisure for a *deliberate* letter.

I knew Prof. Winchester rather more intimately than I knew any other colleague at Wesleyan, and my brother-in-law, Mr. Stockton Axson, was a pupil in all his classes. I had, therefore, the best means of knowing both the personality of the man and his methods as a teacher. I shall speak of the latter first,—not because I esteem personality a secondary matter in the case of a teacher, but for convenience.

The essence of Mr. Winchester's method as a teacher may be said to be, not instruction, in any narrow sense of the word, but work by the pupil under the direct guidance and stimulation of the instructor. He deals with his older classes quite after the 'Seminary method,' though his Seminar resembles that of a German university rather than our own in this, that its members are selected by special tests, not admitted because of mere stage of academic progress. He gets as much work out of his students, and as much intelligent work, as any man I have known, both sending them to exploit for themselves the best sources of literary criticism and subjecting their reports of results to a keen critical examination which at once corrects mistakes and furnishes the incomparable stimulation of points of view to be found only by the mature critic,—and discovered to the pupil in his case in a manner which is itself a model of literary form and matter. The results he accomplishes with the rather crude materials furnished him in the Wesleyan classes seem to me nothing short of extraordinary.

Mr. Winchester's scholarship in the subjects proper to his chair I believe it would be hard to parallel among university professors in this country: it seems more like English literary scholarship than American. I mean his acquaintance with our literature, old and new, big and little, his familiarity with the best criticism, his feeling for form and his insight into substance, his perception of relative values both in our own literature and as between our own and other literatures. He is what a professor of English literature ought to be, both a *born* critic and a *made* critic. He not only has keen powers of appreciating literature of the most varied and even opposite types, but also that salt of sanity—a sense of humor,—which could be proved to be derived from a sense of proportion.

His personality you hardly had a good opportunity to judge: it comes out only upon intimate association such as is open to pupils and colleagues. I know from personal experience how much, and how subtly, he can stimulate,—how subtly one, so to say, *experiences* his knowledge by association with him,—with what pleasure one takes his points, put with such finesse, humour, and suggestiveness. You yourself felt the charm of his public address. He is much the same in familiar conversation, and in his class-room.

I ought to add, however, that, while in his public lectures you get the charm of manner which he carries into all his utterances, you do not get the strength, the thoroughness, or the depth of his class-room method with advanced students. Admirable as his public lectures are, they are designedly 'popular,' designedly devoted to the more obvious aspects of his subjects. His class-room discussions, on the contrary, have a scope and exhaustiveness of method which his popular discourses hardly suggest. Some of the best historical criticism I have ever heard I have heard from him.

I have spoken enthusiastically because I did not in this case know any other way to speak that would convey my sober sentiments or express what I believe to be the truth. When one knows a genuine man, with the equipment he should have for his calling and station, it is right for one to say so,—as I have now done.

Mrs. Wilson joins me in messages of very cordial regard to you, Mrs. Gilman, and your daughters.

Very sincerely Yours,   Woodrow Wilson

P.S. I have just heard from Middletown that there is a rumor afloat there that Prof. Harper is trying to get Mr. Winchester for Chicago.                     Yours,   W. W.

ALS (D. C. Gilman Papers, MdBJ).

¹ A first draft of this recently discovered letter is printed in Vol. 7, pp. 182-83.

# INDEX

## NOTE ON THE INDEX

THE alphabetically arranged analytical table of contents at the front of the volume eliminates duplication, in both contents and index, of references to certain documents, such as letters. Letters are listed in the contents alphabetically by name, and chronologically within each name by page. The subject matter of all letters is, of course, indexed. The Editorial Notes and Wilson's writings are listed in the contents chronologically by page. In addition, the subject matter of both categories is indexed. The index covers all references to books and articles mentioned in text or notes. Footnotes are indexed. Page references to footnotes which place a comma between the page number and "n" cite both text and footnote, thus: "624,n3." On the other hand, absence of the comma indicates reference to the footnote only, thus: "55n2"—the page number denoting where the footnote appears. The letter "n" without a following digit signifies an unnumbered descriptive-location note.

An asterisk before an index reference designates identification or other particular information. Re-identification and repetitive annotation have been minimized to encourage use of these starred references. Where the identification appears in an earlier volume, it is indicated thus: "*1:212,n3." Therefore a page reference standing without a preceding volume number is invariably a reference to the present volume. The index supplies the fullest known forms of names, and, for the Wilson and Axson families, relationships as far down as cousins. Persons referred to in the text by nicknames or shortened forms of names can be identified by reference to entries for these forms of the names.

A sampling of the opinions and comments of Wilson and Ellen Axson Wilson covers their more personal views, while broad, general headings in the main body of the index cover impersonal subjects. Occasionally opinions expressed by a correspondent are indexed where these appear to supplement or to reflect views expressed by Wilson or by Ellen Axson Wilson in documents which are missing.

# INDEX

AND WOODROW WILSON

heart yearns constantly and intensely over him, 125; Were there ever such letters as *yours* and did ever *woman* before have such a lover as has Your own Eileen, 145; I know, I *do* know how you love me, dear, and to know it is a joy so deep and perfect that my heart can hardly bear it, 190; I still must insist, dear, that I can't express my love! I feel the love and I see the words—and they don't *match*, 197; ten happy years have given me a still happier confidence in the immortal *strength* as well as immortal *beauty* of love like yours, 204; In *one* week my darling, God willing, will be with me! I don't know whether there is most pain or pleasure in the thought, it makes my heart beat with such wild impatience, 215; *Wouldn't* it be fine if those long weeks in Baltimore

## WOODROW WILSON

### AND ELLEN AXSON WILSON

should we grow very old together, I am sure that to the last I shall desire you as a young man desires his bride, 142; I am simply *absorbed*—absorbed in you. Any excellence you may think you see in me is simply a reflection of you, 145; If there is one thing more characteristic of you than another, it is, that you respond only to what is best—most refined and most artistic, whether in one art or another. You are tuned only to the fine harmonies, 174; Nothing so fills me with exalted sensations as the thought—so wonderful, and yet so assured—that you love me, 180; When I look into your dear face or hold you in my arms, or have any sort of close and intimate speech with you, my love overmasters my power of expression, 195; You seem made, not only to be an intellectual man's close confidante, companion, counsellor, but also *Love's Playmate*, 195; letter in verse, 199-201;